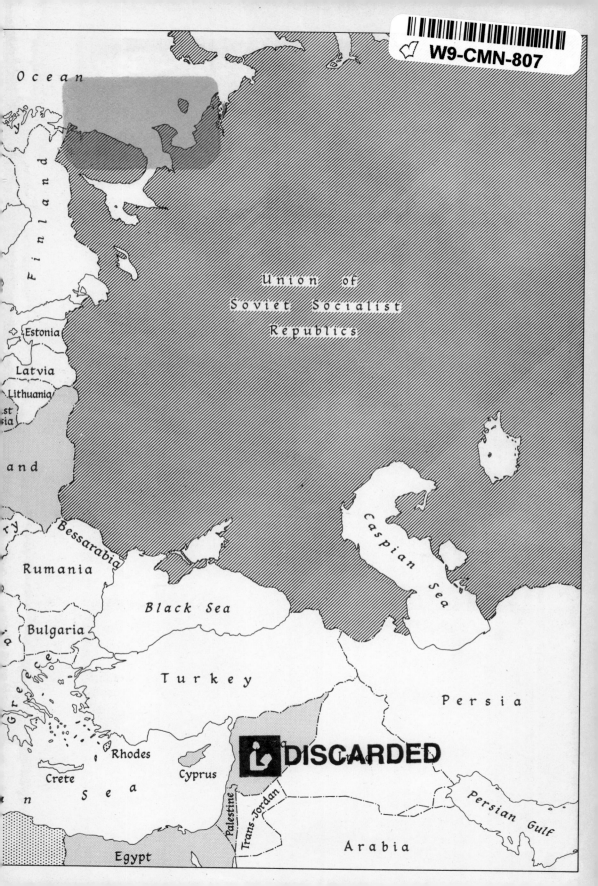

Ocean

Finland

Estonia

Latvia

Lithuania

st
sia

and

Union of
Soviet Socialist
Republics

Bessarabia

Rumania

Bulgaria

Greece

Rhodes

Crete

Cyprus

Palestine

Trans-Jordan

Black Sea

Caspian Sea

Turkey

Persia

n   Sea

Egypt

Arabia

Persian Gulf

HISTORY OF
THE SECOND WORLD WAR
UNITED KINGDOM MILITARY SERIES

Edited by J. R. M. BUTLER

Errata

Page 453, line 4: *for* April 3 *read* April 4

Page 512, line 6 from bottom: *for* 25th *read* 24th

The authors of the Military Histories have been
given full access to official documents. They and the
editor are alone responsible for the statements
made and the views expressed.

GRAND
STRATEGY

VOLUME II

September 1939 – June 1941

by

J. R. M. BUTLER

Vice-Master of Trinity College and
Emeritus Professor of Modern History
in the University of Cambridge

LONDON: 1957

HER MAJESTY'S STATIONERY OFFICE

First published 1957

Crown copyright reserved

Published by
HER MAJESTY'S STATIONERY OFFICE

To be purchased from
York House, Kingsway, London w.c.2
423 Oxford Street, London w.1
P.O. Box 569, London s.e.1
13A Castle Street, Edinburgh 2
109 St. Mary Street, Cardiff
39 King Street, Manchester 2
Tower Lane, Bristol 1
2 Edmund Street, Birmingham 3
80 Chichester Street, Belfast
or through any bookseller

Price £2 2s. 0d. net

Printed in Great Britain under the authority of HER MAJESTY'S STATIONERY OFFICE
by Butler & Tanner Ltd., Frome and London

CONTENTS

CONTENTS

APPENDICES

MAPS

Maps 2, 11, 16, 18 and 19 were prepared for General Playfair's *The Mediterranean and Middle East*; map 3 for Captain Roskill's *The War at Sea*; maps 5 and 7 for Major Ellis' *The War in France and Flanders*; maps 9 and 17 for Mr. Collier's *The Defence of the United Kingdom*; and maps 13 and 15 for General Kirby's *The War against Japan*.

Opposite page

End papers: Europe showing territories controlled by the Allies and Axis respectively in September 1939, September 1940 and June 1941

PHOTOGRAPHS

(These photographs are reproduced by permission of Messrs. Navana Vandyk Ltd.)

PREFACE

IT HAS BEEN explained in the preface to other volumes of this history that the work has been planned in accordance with a Government directive 'to provide a broad survey of events from an inter-Service point of view'. Throughout this book the word 'military' is used to cover the activities of all three fighting Services.

This volume is the second of a series of six on Grand Strategy, or the central direction of the war. The series is intended to supplement and provide the background for the volumes devoted to the several campaigns and special aspects of the war, such as the War at Sea, the Defence of the United Kingdom and the Strategic Air Offensive, just as from another viewpoint those volumes supply the background for the present series. As Field-Marshal Sir William Robertson once wrote, 'the real head-quarters of armies in these days are to be found not in the field abroad, but at the seat of Government at home, and plans of campaign are, and must be, analysed and criticised by civilian Ministers at the Council tables in a way quite unknown a few decades ago'.

Grand Strategy is concerned both with purely military strategy and with politics; some overlapping into both these fields has been unavoidable, but the intention has been to leave the story of operations and local strategy to the volumes assigned to them and not to trespass further either in this direction or in that of political and diplomatic history than is necessary to explain how the war was conducted from the centre at the highest level.

The present volume opens with the outbreak of war in September 1939. The preceding volume, now in preparation, treats of the process of rearmament and pre-war policy as it affected our strategy and readiness for war; since Volume II will appear before Volume I, rather more has been said of the pre-war plans of the Allies than would otherwise have been necessary. The third volume will begin where the present one ends, with the German invasion of Russia on 22 June 1941, but here again there has been some overlapping: the German planning and preparation for war with Russia have been left in the main to Volume III, whereas the present volume has followed the campaign in Syria to its conclusion in July.

Apologies have been offered, in the Editor's Preface to Volume V, the first of the series to appear, for the failure to observe the natural order of publication. They are again due for the appearance of the second volume before the first, but again it may be pleaded that the present volume begins at a recognisable starting-point. Apologies may also be expected for the fact that the volumes have been written by several different hands. The excuse must be that any other plan would have entailed still longer delay. The consequent lack of uniformity is regrettable but inevitable; if the lack is greater than was necessary, the blame must be the editor's. It may perhaps be claimed that some differences of treatment are justified by the changing character of the war itself.

Our narrative is based mainly on official sources, to which we have been allowed full access; particularly the voluminous telegrams, memoranda and minutes preserved in the Cabinet Office and other Departments. Among these Sir Winston Churchill's papers are of outstanding importance.

We have also had at our disposal the great mass of enemy documents, principally German, captured by the Allied armies and now under joint Anglo-American control. For their presentation and interpretation we are greatly indebted to Mr. B. M. Melland and Colonel G. T. Wards; of Mr. Melland's staff I would particularly thank Dr. G. W. S. Friedrichsen, who handles for us the German material in the United States, and Mrs. J. M. Hamilton and Messrs. E. M. Robertson and R. R. A. Wheatley who have compiled important monographs. We have also received valuable help from Commander M. G. Saunders, R.N., of the Admiralty, and Squadron Leader L. A. Jackets of the Air Ministry.

Apart from these primary sources and such diaries and other private papers as have been made available to me by the courtesy of their owners, I have drawn largely on the work, published and as yet unpublished, of my colleagues of both the military and civil histories and, not least, on a study by Sir Llewellyn Woodward of British foreign policy during the war; also on the narratives, monographs and summaries prepared by the Service historical sections. I gratefully acknowledge my debt to the heads of these sections—Rear-Admiral R. M. Bellairs, Brigadier H. B. Latham and Mr. J. C. Nerney—and to the members of their staffs.

The maps have been prepared under the experienced direction of Colonel T. M. M. Penney.

In the period of which this volume treats neither the United States nor the Soviet Union was a belligerent; but relations with America were close and becoming ever closer, and her influence and her help were of immense and growing importance. We have benefited much by arrangements made with the official historians of the United States as well as of Canada, Australia, New Zealand, the Union of South Africa, India and Pakistan for an exchange of information and of draft histories. If these exchanges cannot eliminate differences of interpretation they have, we hope, reduced the amount of disagreement due to ignorance of facts and of points of view.

As has been explained in prefaces to earlier volumes, we have not normally included references to documents not open to public inspection; since our references could not be checked, one of the main reasons for doing so was absent; full references are however printed in a confidential edition which should be available to students whenever the archives are opened. This policy has raised the question whether we should include references to published sources. To do so is open to the objection that, where both unpublished and published sources have been used, the reader may be misled into thinking that the text relies solely on the published authorities. Nevertheless, we have thought it better to depart as little as possible from the usual practice, and have accordingly included references to important published sources; the reader should understand however that the sources mentioned are not necessarily the only ones we have used. Further, while not specifically referring to sources not open to the public, we have indicated the nature of the authority for statements of fact and opinion when there seemed special reason for doing so.

In accordance with the recognised British constitutional principle we have not held ourselves free to reveal individual differences of opinion within the War Cabinet nor to lift the veil of Civil Service anonymity. We have felt bound also to respect the requirements of military 'security'.

I am grateful for such criticisms as my drafts have received from official quarters and I have been glad to make corrections which seemed to me improvements; but I have not made, nor been asked to make, any change of substance which was contrary to my better judgement.

It has been a great privilege to be enabled to attempt the history, on the military side, of twenty-two months so momentous in British annals. Lord Tedder has remarked that as a nation 'we have a tendency to concentrate too much on our successes and our enemies' failures and consequently to draw our lessons too much from the final stages of the war', when 'after some years of lavish expenditure' the Commander knows that he can more or less 'count on a blank cheque'. 'Surely', he says, 'it is the problems of the early stages of the war which we should study. Those are the difficult problems; those are the practical problems which we and every democratic nation have to solve. There are no big battalions or blank cheques then. Here is the real and vital test of our defence policies.'[1] Nothing could be more pertinent to the history of these early months. At every point our efforts were limited by the smallness of our resources in men and munitions. Our commitments had outrun our capacity. It was frequently a choice between action with inadequate means and no

---

[1] *Air Power in War* (Cambridge 1948) p. 25.

B

action at all; too often the action taken was recognised as 'a gamble'; it was obvious that we could not be strong everywhere, and only by the narrowest margins did we succeed in being strong enough at the decisive points. On the personal side, many of our commanders were as yet untested, and the Services had not learnt to work together as effectively as they did later.

Our predicament showed itself also in the nature of our planning. So long as the enemy held the initiative, and especially after the collapse of France and while American opinion was resolute not to enter the war, there was bound to be something unrealistic about many appreciations and proposals. The writers of course assumed their country's survival, and there were few, if any, we may suppose, who did not believe in her eventual victory. But how that victory was to be won could not be foreseen. What was required was not detailed forecasts of the future but practical recommendations as to how to keep our heads above water through the critical months immediately ahead and how to preserve a correct balance in our plans for expansion. This should be remembered if some of the appreciations of the early phases of the war seem unduly optimistic. Appreciations had to be written, but the writers must have realised that in their forecasts they were sometimes out of their depth, and that wisdom must often lie

in masterful administration of the unforeseen.

I am aware of my own disqualifications as a civilian and a contemporary for pronouncing on technical and controversial matters, and I have tried as far as possible to let the facts tell their own story; to say how and why things happened, leaving judgement to the strategists; but a historian shirks his duty if he does not indicate to what conclusions the evidence to which he has had access seems to him to point.

My errors would have been far more numerous if I had not enjoyed the counsel and criticisms of an Advisory Panel consisting of Vice-Admiral Sir Geoffrey Blake, Lieutenant-General Sir Henry Pownall, Air Chief Marshal Sir Guy Garrod and Lieutenant-General Sir Ian Jacob, as well as of the heads of the Service historical sections whom I have already mentioned. To Sir Ian Jacob I owe an especial debt. I must also acknowledge the help I have received from those of my colleagues who have added to their own labours by reading and correcting my drafts and in some cases have generously allowed me to include maps drawn on their instructions. I take this opportunity to express my thanks to all these experts and to the many others who have allowed me to consult them or have read and commented on my chapters.

I am deeply indebted to Miss Y. M. Streatfield's accuracy and skill for the papers she has prepared for me on special topics and for general assistance in the preparation of the book, and to Mrs. F. A. Hort for her patience in typing it and for efficient secretarial help.

Finally I must thank Mr. A. B. Acheson of the Cabinet Office for all that the editing of these volumes owes to his knowledge and care.

J. R. M. B.

December 1955

CHAPTER I

THE OUTBREAK OF WAR: ALLIED PLANS AND ORGANISATION

THE GERMAN armed forces crossed the frontiers of Poland in the early morning of Friday, 1 September, 1939. In the previous March the British and French Governments had given the Polish Government an assurance that, 'in the event of any action which clearly threatened Polish independence and which the Polish Government accordingly considered vital to resist with their national forces', Poland could count on their immediate and full support. Accordingly the British Government, after some delay due to the desire to concert arrangements with the French, presented an ultimatum to Germany demanding that the invading armies should be withdrawn. The ultimatum expired at 11 o'clock on the morning of Sunday, 3 September. When no reply was received the Prime Minister, Mr. Neville Chamberlain, announced to the House of Commons a few minutes after noon that we were at war with Germany. The House, which on the previous day, misinterpreting the delay, had been restive and impatient, now showed a general sense of relief.

When Britain went to war in August 1914 the event had come as a shock and a surprise to most of the country, though the German danger had long been talked of and men in touch with affairs had foreseen and prepared for the catastrophe. To civilians a Continental war was then something remote and hardly imaginable; there was little understanding of what it might mean. When Sir Edward Grey opened his mind and heart to the House of Commons on August 3, he was not certain how it would respond, and the final decision of Mr. Asquith's Government led to a split in the Cabinet. So again in the thirties discord and doubt prevailed until the eve of the final rupture. Even after the long series of National-Socialist perfidies and aggressions the country was confused and divided at the time of the Sudeten crisis in September 1938. But now, a year later, the issue was clear. The rape of Czechoslovakia in March 1939 had convinced Mr. Chamberlain that it was impossible to do business with Hitler; the process of rearmament was accelerated, and the whole people with insignificant exceptions were agreed that war might be unavoidable.

There could be no doubt as to the cause or as to the purpose of our warmaking. The cause was aggression by Nazi Germany against the independence and freedom of other peoples—aggression in some cases already perpetrated, in others clearly threatened; the purpose was to call a halt to this aggression and to extirpate the forces in Germany responsible for it.

'We shall enter the struggle', said the Prime Minister on September 1, 'with a clear conscience. We have no quarrel with the German people, except that they allow themselves to be governed by a Nazi Government. As long as that Government exists and pursues the methods it has so consistently followed during the last two years, there will be no peace in Europe. We shall merely pass from one crisis to another, and see one country after another attacked by methods which have now become familiar to us in their sickening technique. We are resolved that these methods must come to an end.'

Mr. Arthur Greenwood, speaking for the Labour Opposition, used much the same language: 'We have no quarrel with the German people; but while we have no passion against people we shall enter this struggle with a grim determination to overthrow and destroy that system of government which has . . . brought the world back to the jackboot of the old Prussianism.'

Sir Archibald Sinclair, the Liberal leader, agreed: the war, he said, had begun three years before with the occupation of the Rhineland. The goal of our endeavour was not the aggrandisement of our country and Empire, not merely the defeat of Nazi tyranny. 'Let us keep before us the necessity for constructive effort, for the creation in Europe of that new order which, before the emergence of National Socialism in Germany, we were beginning slowly . . . to build, an order based not on the sanctions of power politics but on the moral law, in which freedom, justice, and equality of economic opportunity will be guaranteed to nations great and small alike.'

'This is not a question of fighting for Danzig or fighting for Poland', said Mr. Winston Churchill on September 3. 'We are fighting to save the whole world from the pestilence of Nazi tyranny and in defence of all that is most sacred to man.'[1]

This time there was no division on the crucial issue in the Cabinet, in Parliament or in the country. Once again, as so often in the past, the nation ranged itself in support of the constant policy of the British State: not to allow the domination of Europe by a single aggressive Power. In the present case the traditional adherence to this policy was reinforced by a peculiar detestation of the cruelty, falsehood and meanness of the Nazi system.

In 1914 a declaration of war by the Government of the United

---

[1] *House of Commons Debates*, 5th series, vol. 351, cols. 132 ff., 295. (All references to parliamentary debates are to the 5th series.)

Kingdom bound the whole Empire. In 1939 it was not so, except in the sense that an enemy might find in the common link of the Crown a legal justification for refusing to regard any part of the King's dominions as neutral. But even this exception was now meaningless, since Germany's record showed that in her selection of countries to treat as enemies she would consult nothing but her own interests. In fact Canada, Australia, New Zealand, the Union of South Africa and Eire were now sovereign States; the Locarno treaties of 1925 had made it clear that the Dominions were not pledged to support the European policy of the United Kingdom. They were in 1939 completely free to determine their own course of action. The British ultimatum to Germany of September 3 was launched on the responsibility of the United Kingdom alone, but the Dominion Governments had of course been kept apprised of the movement of events, and some provisional agreements for Service co-operation had been reached, subject to the Governments' final decisions.

These decisions were much as had been anticipated in London in the summer. The Governments of Australia and New Zealand declared their countries at war without awaiting parliamentary approval; the Government of Canada waited for Parliament to assemble before announcing its belligerency on September 10. For the Union of South Africa, General Smuts had given an undertaking in 1921 that the base at Simonstown would always be maintained for the use of the Royal Navy, but otherwise the attitude of the Union was unpredictable: Deneys Reitz has told how General Hertzog, the Prime Minister, had apparently intended to proclaim neutrality without convoking Parliament, and how he was foiled by its unforeseen meeting and by the opposition in his own Cabinet of General Smuts with a majority of his colleagues; in the House of Assembly the decisions against neutrality and in favour of breaking off relations with Germany were carried by 80 votes to 67.[1] Eire alone proclaimed neutrality.

India's belligerency was declared on 3 September by the Government of India without consulting either the legislature or the leaders of the principal parties. It was not at first clear what line would be taken by the Congress party, representatives of which were in power in all but three of the eleven Provinces; shortly before the outbreak of war the Working Committee of Congress had proclaimed their intention to resist all attempts to 'impose a war on India', but they were expected by the Government to take their cue from Mahatma Gandhi, whose attitude to Great Britain was not unfriendly. Moslem opinion, on the other hand, seemed likely to

---

[1] *No Outspan* (1943) pp. 237–243.

support the Government's war effort. Later, however, on September 25, the Secretary of State had to report that his forecast had been too optimistic.

The traditional policy of opposing only an aggressive power implied that Britain could count on the help or at least the sympathy of European countries. It had been the intention of the founders of the League of Nations to substitute for the occasional and laboriously achieved coalitions of the past a permanent and universal alliance of all peace-loving nations. But hopes of such security for peace, scotched from the outset by the abstention of the United States, had been killed in the nineteen-thirties, and it would have been unrealistic to count on any aid from the League of Nations in September 1939. The British Government had given guarantees of assistance to Greece and Roumania in April, but no help was to be expected from them in present circumstances. Russia, from whom hopes of support had been cherished until a few days previously, had now made terms with the aggressor, and outside Poland, the immediate victim, and the nations of the Commonwealth, Britain's only belligerent ally was France.

For the conduct of the wars of the nineteenth century it was not found necessary to recast the supreme organ of peacetime government, the Cabinet of from twelve to twenty members. Nor had any such preparations been made before the outbreak of war in 1914. But the traditional system was then found inadequate, and after a series of experiments Mr. Lloyd George set up at the end of 1916 a War Cabinet of five members of whom only one, the Chancellor of the Exchequer, had serious departmental responsibilities. Despite differences of temperament which led to friction between political and military chiefs, the War Cabinet of 1916–18 proved itself a powerful instrument of war. In the years of peace the machinery was yet further improved by the development of the Chiefs of Staff Committee, and once again, thanks largely to Sir Maurice Hankey and later to General Ismay, effective arrangements were made for the smooth switch-over of the nation to a war organisation.[1]

On the most important point of all, the nature of the supreme direction, the Committee of Imperial Defence had decided that it was impossible to prescribe its form in advance; the War Book merely laid down that it was the responsibility of the Secretary to the Cabinet to submit the matter at the proper time to the Prime Minister. Accordingly on August 31 Sir Edward Bridges and General Ismay placed the papers on the subject before Mr. Chamberlain, and next

---

[1] See Lord Hankey, *Government Control in War* (Cambridge 1945).

day he informed his twenty-two colleagues that he would set up a
War Cabinet at once on the model of that established in the last war.
He secured Mr. Churchill's acceptance of a place that day, and he
wished also to include representatives of the Labour and Liberal
parties. This was found to be impossible, and the War Cabinet which
met for the first time on Sunday September 3 consisted of eight members besides the Prime Minister: Sir John Simon, Chancellor of the
Exchequer; Viscount Halifax, Foreign Secretary; Sir Samuel Hoare,
Lord Privy Seal—these four had since September 1938 formed an
inner group concerned with foreign policy; Lord Hankey, Minister
without Portfolio; Admiral of the Fleet Lord Chatfield, Minister for
the Co-ordination of Defence; and the three Service Ministers, Mr.
Churchill (Admiralty), Mr. Hore-Belisha (War Office) and Sir
Kingsley Wood (Air).[1] Thus five of the nine members were responsible for important Departments of State, though Mr. Chamberlain
had not originally intended so large a proportion. He has left it on
record that he constructed his War Cabinet 'on no theory or rule
governing its size, or the nature of its composition, whether departmental or otherwise. My sole purpose was to find a Cabinet that
would work, which means that personalities must be taken into
account.' Mr. Chamberlain may have been thinking in particular
of Mr. Churchill, whose wish to return to the Admiralty seems to
have carried the Secretaries for Air and War also into the Cabinet.
Mr. Churchill's past tenure of so many great offices, his long study of
war in all its aspects, his prescient warnings during the years just
passed, his independence of mind, his driving power and his eloquence, all set him in a class apart, and until he succeeded to the
highest post his proper place in the team was not obvious. It soon
became clear that he was not content with the prevailing tempo in
the conduct of the war, and he plied the Prime Minister with letters,
some of which to Mr. Chamberlain seemed unnecessary, on many
subjects.[2] Mr. Churchill was loyal to his chief, but the combination
in one Cabinet of two natural leaders, each holding strong opinions
and unwilling to abandon them, called for tact on both sides. We
shall see later how Mr. Churchill's position at the Admiralty involved
certain inconveniences. Other Ministers, officials and experts were
invited to attend the War Cabinet for the discussion of matters specially concerning them; in particular Sir John Anderson, Home Secretary and Minister for Home Security, and Mr. Anthony Eden,

---

[1] See K. Feiling, *Life of Neville Chamberlain* (1946) p. 240; W. S. Churchill, *The Second World War* (henceforward referred to as Churchill); Vol. I, *The Gathering Storm* (2nd ed. 1949) pp. 361, 373; Viscount Templewood, *Nine Troubled Years* (1954) pp. 291, 301. (All references to Mr. Churchill's first volume are to the 2nd edition.)

[2] See Feiling, *op. cit.* p. 421; I have been allowed to see Mr. Chamberlain's papers by the kindness of Mrs. Chamberlain and Miss Hilda Chamberlain.

Secretary of State for the Dominions, were usually present, and the three Chiefs of Staff attended regularly for military business.

The Chiefs of Staff were also present at the meetings of the Standing Ministerial Committee on Military Co-ordination; this body was appointed at the end of October 'to keep under constant review on behalf of the War Cabinet the main factors in the strategical situation and the progress of operations, and to make recommendations from time to time to the War Cabinet as to the general conduct of the war'. Its chairman was Lord Chatfield, and the other members were the three Service Ministers.[1] The formal appointment of this body gave a permanent basis to the meetings of these Ministers, of which several, attended also by Lord Hankey, had been convened during October to consider specific points.

Seeing that it was on the War Cabinet and Chiefs of Staff that the higher conduct of the war on the British side chiefly depended, it is necessary to say something of their organisation and method of work.

The War Cabinet superseded not only the peacetime Cabinet but the Committee of Imperial Defence, and took over the single secretariat, under Sir Edward Bridges, which had served both these bodies. There was no change in the functions of the Chiefs of Staff Committee (originally a sub-committee of the Committee of Imperial Defence) which had been envisaged in 1923 as 'a Super-Chief of a War Staff in Commission'.[2] Henceforward it consisted of Air Chief Marshal Sir Cyril Newall, Admiral of the Fleet Sir Dudley Pound and General Sir Edmund Ironside; their secretary was Major-General Hastings Ismay, hitherto Secretary of the Committee of Imperial Defence and now Deputy Secretary, on the military side, of the War Cabinet; their custom was to meet every morning at 10, preceding the daily meeting of the War Cabinet at 11.30.

Each of the Chiefs of Staff filled a dual role: Sir Dudley Pound, for instance, as First Sea Lord was, in the Admiralty, Chief of Naval Staff with special responsibility for naval operations, senior Service member of the Board of Admiralty and chief Service adviser to the First Lord, Mr. Churchill; he was also responsible for expressing the naval point of view at the Chiefs of Staff Committee and to the War Cabinet and for helping to form common inter-Service decisions and recommendations to Ministers. The official business of the Chiefs of Staff in their corporate capacity was 'to hear reports and consider the situation, to decide day-to-day problems concerning operations' and to consider any matters specially remitted to them by the War Cabinet; they were in fact the joint advisers of the Cabinet on military policy. Moreover, by virtue of their frequent meetings and efficient

---

[1] See Lord Chatfield, *It might happen again* (1947) p. 182.
[2] The phrase occurs in the Report of the Salisbury Committee, Cmd. 2029, 1924.

organisation they became in time an executive body and were in the habit of sending instructions in their corporate capacity to commanders in the field. There was no wartime precedent for this—no Chiefs of Staff Committee existed in 1914–18—but the practice had started several years before 1939, and it was now regularly adopted.

Besides the resources of their respective Departments, the Chiefs of Staff were served by the two inter-Service bodies whose formation is described in Volume I, the Joint Planning and the Joint Intelligence Sub-Committees. Each of these comprised one or more officers from each of the three Services, all holding executive posts in their own Service Departments and working together as a team. The Joint Intelligence Sub-Committee had a representative of the Foreign Office as its chairman.[1] All these bodies, and many others, were served by the single secretariat referred to above, with the result that duplication and misunderstanding were as far as possible avoided and the utmost flexibility in organisation secured.

The Chiefs of Staff worked harmoniously together in Committee, their collective opinion being usually stated to the War Cabinet by the Chairman, but they were not as strong a combination as existed later in the war. Admiral Pound could count on the loyalty of the Navy, and Mr. Churchill has testified to his 'great professional and personal qualities', but he consistently overworked and he was apt not to take much part in discussion except on naval matters.[2] General Ironside had been brought back from Gibraltar in July to be Inspector-General of Overseas Forces; he had met the French General Noguès in June at Rabat to discuss Allied plans in North Africa and more recently had paid an official visit to the Polish army; but he had never in the course of his long career served in the War Office and he had not attended meetings of the Committee of Imperial Defence since his return to England. Moreover the Director of Military Operations, who would naturally have been his right-hand man, sailed as Chief of the General Staff with the Expeditionary Force to France. General Ironside did not find his new post congenial, and the appointment failed to prove a satisfactory one. The chairmanship of the Committee went by rotation, and was at this time held by Air Chief Marshal Newall, the member of longest standing, who had recently commanded in the Middle East.

Procedure in the War Cabinet has not passed uncriticised. Lord Chatfield has reported that 'time invariably pressed, and only the skilled debater, the most powerful talker, usually got in his views'.[3] One of the Chiefs of Staff, regularly present for military business,

---

[1] See Appendix V.
[2] Churchill I 366.
[3] Chatfield, op. cit. p. 180.

noted a desire on Ministers' part to direct strategy without the necessary knowledge, and complained that he and his colleagues had to spend so many hours on committees that they had 'no time to consider the big things—the running of the war'; Mr. Churchill suggested to the Prime Minister that much was being thrown upon the Chiefs of Staff which fell outside their professional sphere, and that it would be helpful for the Ministers sometimes to talk over 'the large issues' among themselves without either secretaries or military experts.[1]

Only a few words need be said about the other important bodies which helped to shape policy.

Lord Chatfield presided over the Ministerial Priority Committee, set up on August 3; the newly created Minister of Supply informed the House of Commons on 18 October that this Committee worked through a number of sub-committees, on Labour, Materials, Production Capacity, Transport, Works and Building, on which all interested Departments were represented. The Civil Defence Committee had been reconstituted on the outbreak of war with the Minister of Home Security (Sir John Anderson) as chairman. The Chancellor of the Exchequer was chairman of a Committee on Economic Policy, advised by Lord Stamp, who was himself chairman of a committee consisting of permanent heads of Departments. A further standing committee of Ministers, the Home Policy Committee, had been set up under the chairmanship of the Lord Privy Seal (Sir Samuel Hoare) to cover all domestic questions other than those specifically referred to other committees. The Prime Minister explained to the House of Commons that the practice was to solve particular problems by means of consultation between the Ministers concerned and to make some member of the War Cabinet responsible for the general direction of these consultations and for reporting their results to it.[2]

The enormous importance of the part played by scientific research and its practical application will become evident throughout this history. The close and successful co-operation between the producers and the consumers of scientific inventions is one of the main features of the British effort in the Second World War. The fact must be emphasised at the outset but in a non-technical history it must of necessity remain in the background, mention being made merely of such central organisation as was created and, on occasion, of the results achieved.

Doubts were raised in the War Cabinet soon after the outbreak of war whether, although the Secretary of State for the Dominions had

---

[1] Churchill I 412.
[2] *House of Commons Debates* vol. 352, cols. 28 ff.

access to its sessions and gave information to the High Commissioners at daily meetings, the arrangements for liaison with their Governments were adequate. It was agreed that the time was not propitious for inviting Dominion Ministers to serve as members of the Supreme War Council, nor for a meeting of Commonwealth Prime Ministers in an Imperial War Cabinet, after the model of 1917. But it was thought desirable to invite the High Commissioners to occasional meetings with members of the War Cabinet and to encourage visits from Dominion Ministers and their technical advisers for the purpose of explaining to them the real nature of the struggle and the magnitude of the war effort of the United Kingdom. Dominion delegations eventually arrived at the end of October and the opportunity was taken to present them with a general strategic appreciation by the Chiefs of Staff—the first since the outbreak of war.[1]

In the former war it had taken three years and a crushing defeat to achieve the requisite unity between the major Allies in the higher direction of the war. In 1939 much thought was given to the problem of securing effective co-operation between the United Kingdom and France. On the French side, the control of the war rested in the hands of the Council of Ministers and of the individual Ministers concerned.[2] In September 1939 M. Edouard Daladier was at once President of the Council (or Prime Minister), Minister of National Defence and Minister for War; in both the latter capacities he had as his chief technical adviser General Gamelin, Chief of Staff for National Defence, charged with the duty of 'co-ordinating', but not issuing orders to, all three Services. The two Prime Ministers had agreed during the summer on a scheme based on the experience of 1917–18 but modified to meet altered conditions. There was to be a Supreme War Council on which France and the United Kingdom should each be represented by the Prime Minister and one other Minister, and other Allied Powers, perhaps, by their ambassadors. The Council was to have no executive authority, final decisions being reserved to the Governments. Each of the two Powers would appoint Permanent Military Representatives to advise on technical matters, working as a joint staff but subordinate to their own Service chiefs; the British Representatives would also be collectively subordinate to the Chiefs of Staff Committee. A French and British secretariat was set up, and branches of the new organisation functioned on both sides of the Channel. The discussions in London were in fact a continuation

---

[1] See below, p. 71.

[2] See J. Vial in *Revue d'Histoire de la Deuxième Guerre Mondiale* No. 18, April 1955; also Gamelin, *Servir* (Paris, 1946) I 53 ff.; P. Reynaud, *La France a sauvé l'Europe* (Paris, 1947) I 462 ff.—henceforward cited as 'Gamelin' and 'Reynaud'.

of the staff talks which had been renewed in August, and took place daily until the collapse of France in June 1940. In France the secretariat of the British War Cabinet was represented by a small section in Paris under Lieutenant-Colonel H. Redman; liaison missions were also established at the headquarters of the three French Commanders-in-Chief. The Chief of the French Naval Staff was Admiral of the Fleet François Darlan; the French air forces were under the command of General Vuillemin.

In order to understand the military situation facing the British Government in September 1939 it is necessary to refer briefly to discussions and decisions of an earlier date. Our policy for the conduct of the war then seen to be impending had been concerted with the French in the spring, when it was assumed that the British Empire and France would be ranged against a coalition of Germany and Italy. The common policy applied in the first place to Europe, taking account of the obligations incurred to Poland, Roumania, Greece and Turkey and of the effect of possible Japanese intervention. Agreement was also reached on naval strategy and the broad lines upon which operations should be conducted in the Mediterranean, North Africa, the Middle East, the Red Sea, West and East Africa and the Far East. The British and French staff delegations had thus summed up their conclusions on 'the broad strategic policy for the conduct of the war'.

'We should be faced by enemies who would be more fully prepared than ourselves for war on a national scale, would have superiority in air and land forces, but would be inferior at sea and in general economic strength. In these circumstances, we must be prepared to face a major offensive directed against either France or Great Britain or against both. To defeat such an offensive we should have to concentrate all our initial efforts, and during this time our major strategy would be defensive.

Nevertheless, Italian action in North Africa may give the opportunity for counter-offensive operations early in the war, without prejudice to the success of the defence of Europe.

Our control of Italian communications to East Africa and adequate measures to raise the tribes in Ethiopia might achieve early results in that area.

In general therefore, we should be ready to seize any opportunity of obtaining, without undue cost, successes against Italy which might reduce her will to fight.

Our subsequent policy should be directed to holding Germany and to dealing decisively with Italy, while at the same time building up our military strength to a point at which we shall be in a position to undertake the offensive against Germany.

During these stages the steady and rigorous application of economic pressure would be reducing the powers of resistance of our enemies.

Meanwhile, in peace, as later in war, all the resources of diplomacy should be directed to securing the benevolent neutrality or active assistance of other powers, particularly the United States of America.'

When allowance is made for the initial non-belligerency of Italy, for the collapse of France, and for the extension of the struggle in 1941, it is remarkable how faithfully the main lines of this strategy of 1939 were followed: the early defensive phase, the elimination of Italy after the conquest of Italian East and North Africa, and the final defeat of Germany, with the active assistance of the United States.

In a later paper, of May 4, the British and French staffs examined the situation which would result from the intervention of other Powers; among these Poland might now be counted on, and the intervention of Poland might bring about that of Roumania and possibly other Balkan states. Germany would have to face the risks of a war on two fronts and could no longer rely on the economic resources of eastern Europe. But an alliance with Poland and Roumania would have little strategical value for the Western Powers unless it brought about the constitution of a 'long, solid and durable front' in the east, and this would imply help from Russia to Poland and Roumania, at least in the form of guns, ammunition and tanks. As regards the Russian armed forces, it was uncertain whether Russia's two neighbours would grant them passage, and the effectiveness of the Russian army, at any rate for offensive action, after the 'purge' of 1937, was considered doubtful. Turkish help would be most valuable, particularly in tightening the economic stranglehold on Italy by cutting her off from the Black Sea. At the other end of the Mediterranean, importance was attached to the neutrality of Spain.

The implications of the Polish alliance should war break out were further discussed during the summer. It held certain obvious advantages for the Western Powers: at worst it would force Germany to retain some thirty to thirty-five divisions in the east, while, should Germany attack Poland first, as the British Chiefs of Staff thought most likely, it would increase the time available for preparation and might even seriously weaken Germany's striking power. But the eventual collapse of Poland appeared certain unless the Western Powers could bring sufficient pressure on Germany to force her to relax her own pressure on Poland, and here was the difficulty.

On land it seemed clear that the French would not be diverted from their intention of aiming their main offensive against Italy to a precipitate assault on the Siegfried Line, the fortified position defending the German frontier; the most that could be expected in the first weeks was offensives with limited objectives, and these could hardly create for Germany the embarrassment of a war on two fronts.

In the air it would be difficult for the Western Powers to attack Germany with any considerable advantage to Poland so long as they adhered to their agreed policy of confining themselves to 'military objectives' in the narrowest sense.

All this pointed to the conclusion that 'the fate of Poland will depend upon the ultimate outcome of the war, and that this, in turn, will depend upon our ability to bring about the eventual defeat of Germany, and not on our ability to relieve pressure on Poland at the outset'.

The appreciations summarised above had assumed the active participation of Italy in the war as an enemy. As the summer advanced it seemed possible that she might not adopt this role from the outset; it was not obvious, however, that her neutrality would be to the Allies' advantage. In July the British Chiefs of Staff had discussed the strategical effect of Italy remaining neutral and had agreed that although a neutral Italy would to some extent hamper the application of economic pressure on Germany (since Germany in that case would not be bound to supply Italy with war material), Italian neutrality would appreciably reduce our military commitments and military risks; in particular the Mediterranean would remain open as a line of communication. Nor was it reasonable to suppose that any action which Great Britain or the French could take against Italy by sea, land or air could materially relieve German pressure on Poland. The upshot was that the longer Italy remained neutral, even if her neutrality showed benevolence toward Germany, the better it would be for the Allies, and only if her neutrality were strained to an extreme point would it be to their interest to antagonise her. On the other hand, this conclusion meant the abandonment of the only counter-offensive measures on the part of the Allies contemplated by them in the early stages of the war, apart from economic pressure.

As war came to appear imminent at the end of August, the British Government confirmed their opinion that Italy's neutrality was desirable; Commanders-in-Chief abroad were instructed to be careful, while taking all necessary precautions, not to provoke her. The Foreign Office were by now convinced that she did not intend to enter the war at present. This proved to be the case, and Italy's non-belligerency, as Mussolini chose to call it, was viewed with considerable relief. The attitude of Turkey also was satisfactory, and the British Government hoped that the Anglo-Turkish declaration of 12 May, stating the readiness of the two countries to co-operate alike in the event of aggression leading to war in the Mediterranean and in order to ensure the security of the Balkans, would be expanded

Plate 1: Mr. Chamberlain's War Cabinet, 1939, with Sir John Anderson, Mr. Eden and Sir Edward Bridges.

From left to right, Back row: Sir John Anderson, Lord Hankey, Mr. Hore-Belisha, Mr. Churchill, Sir Kingsley Wood, Mr. Eden, Sir Edward Bridges.

Front row: Lord Halifax, Sir John Simon, Mr. Chamberlain, Sir Samuel Hoare, Lord Chatfield.

into the treaty to which it pointed.[1] These blessings were far out-weighed by the failure of the protracted negotiations with the Soviet Union and the announcement of August 22 that it was about to conclude an anti-aggression pact with Germany. All hope of a 'long, solid and durable eastern front' thus vanished. But the Prime Minister had immediately announced that British engagements to Poland remained unaffected.

The British and French staffs had also agreed with regard to Allied strategy in the event of Japanese intervention. The question was essentially one of the correct distribution of naval forces. They recognised that 'the integrity of Singapore' was 'the key to the strategical situation in the Indian Ocean, Far East and Australasia', and also that we must be prepared at some time to send naval reinforcements to Singapore.

> 'On the other hand, if the Allies were defeated in the West, the collapse of our position in the Far East would automatically follow. Moreover, we have to consider our guarantees to the Eastern Mediterranean Powers and the hope that operations against Italy will offer prospects of early results.
>
> It is thus a question of balancing risks, and the issue cannot be decided in advance; but the weakening of the British Eastern Mediterranean Fleet should not lightly be undertaken.
>
> It must be for His Majesty's Government to decide in consultation with the French Government at the time on the redistribution of British naval forces to meet the situation with which the Allies are faced. Meanwhile plans for Anglo-French co-operation must provide for a number of possible situations, including the two extremes: the practical abandonment temporarily of the naval control in the Far East, or the Eastern Mediterranean.'

This indecision as to the respective priorities of the Mediterranean and the Far East implied an important change from British naval strategy as conceived in 1937; indeed British strategy had varied in the last years of peace according as first one and then another of the three Powers, Italy, Germany and Japan, seemed the most threatening.

In the last fortnight before war broke out in the West British relations with Japan were strained. But Japan had her hands too full with troubles in China to contemplate immediate intervention. Apart from that, the recent Russo-German agreement was bound to arouse her apprehensions, and in any case prudence counselled delay until the probable outcome of the war in the West became clearer.

---

[1] See below, p. 66.

C

The British and French staff delegations had dealt also with a number of matters of more limited scope, though of the first importance: such as the naval measures to be taken for the protection of trade, the assistance which Britain could offer in the event of a German attack on France, the time-table for the despatch of the proposed expeditionary force, the conditions of a German advance through the Low Countries, and the employment of British and French air forces. The results of these discussions, in so far as they affected the general conduct of the war, must be shortly reviewed.

The essential naval task was to protect the merchant ships carrying the cargoes on which depended the economy of the Allied Powers and their capacity to make war. In 1914 the need had been the same, but there had then been a formidable High Seas Fleet in German waters ready to sally out and challenge British control at any moment when it might hope to enjoy a temporary advantage. Now the Germans had no High Seas Fleet—only a few capital ships in number insignificant compared with those of the Allies; but the last war had shown how much damage could be done to commerce by a few raiders skilfully employed. The British Admiralty expected that Germany would exploit this form of warfare to the full. Their policy was to place the main fleet where it could give covering protection to shipping, and accordingly the strongest British naval concentration, including most of the heavy ships, was based, as in the earlier war, at Scapa Flow in the Orkneys. The normal zones of operations for the surface vessels of the Allied navies had been agreed upon with respect to the Channel, the Atlantic—where the French proposed to maintain a powerful '*force de raid*'—and the Mediterranean. It had been agreed further that, if Germany practised unrestricted submarine or air warfare on trade, convoy would be necessary in the Channel and North Atlantic; in the Bay of Biscay and Western Mediterranean, where convoy would not be adopted, the French would protect British trade as well as their own. The two navies would enjoy the use of one another's bases, and the secrets of the British anti-submarine device, the asdic, were imparted to the French.[1]

On land, it had been agreed that 'Anglo-French strategy should aim primarily at maintaining the integrity of French territory. Should the Low Countries be invaded, the Allies will attempt to stop the enemy and will form a front as far forward as circumstances permit.' Allied troops would not be able to enter Belgium unless invited by the Belgian Government, but 'chances of successful intervention would be enhanced if previous arrangements had been made

---

[1] The asdic was so named from the initials of the Allied Submarine Detector Investigation Committee.

with Belgium . . .' It was now agreed that a British army should again fight in France; but, if its task was to be similar to that of Sir John French's expeditionary force of 1914, the political antecedents were very different. Reaction against the scale of our losses in France and Flanders in the last war, financial stringency, the increased share of the funds available for defence now assigned to the Royal Air Force, dissatisfaction with French foreign policy and the hesitations of our own—all had fought against the resumption of a Continental military commitment, and until a few months before the outbreak of war no approval had been given for plans or preparations to be made specifically for sending an army to France. Not till February 1939 did the Cabinet decide that any part even of the Regular Army should be equipped on the scale necessary for warfare against a first-class Power.[1]

However much British official views may have differed as to whether we should send an expeditionary force to France, there had been no dispute as to the need of maintaining an adequate army in the Middle East—a phrase now used to include the Mediterranean regions hitherto known to geographers as the Near East—and in the Mediterranean itself.

When, in February 1939, the Chiefs of Staff presented their comprehensive report known as the 'European Appreciation', from the Army and Air aspect Egypt was put first in strategic importance. Control of the Suez Canal depended on control of Egypt and, since the defences of Malta against air attack were inadequate, Alexandria, though only moderately supplied with docking and repair facilities, was required as an operational base for the fleet. Under the Anglo-Egyptian treaty of 1936 Great Britain had the right to maintain a limited number of troops in the Canal Zone in peace, and the two countries were bound to help one another in war. Owing to the unrest in Palestine we had considerably increased our forces in the Middle East in recent months, and it was thought in February that we should have sufficient troops in Egypt to repel an Italian attack across the western desert.

Palestine, apart from British responsibilities under the Mandate, was strategically important from various aspects: as a buffer against invasion of Egypt from the north, as a *place d'armes* from which Egypt could be reinforced, as lying athwart the land route from the Persian Gulf, and as providing the Navy with an operational base at Haifa, the terminal of one of the oil pipe-lines from Iraq. The outlet of the northern pipe-line was at Tripoli in Syria, which was a French responsibility.

At sea the French and British fleets should be able to control

---

[1] See Mr. Hore-Belisha's speech on the Army Estimates, 8 March 1939, *House of Commons Debates* vol. 344, cols. 2161 ff.

respectively the western and eastern areas of the Mediterranean, and perhaps the Aegean. As for the central Mediterranean, we could only conjecture the extent to which the Italian Air Force would be able to interfere with our operations. We could not count therefore on being able to send reinforcements to Egypt through the Mediterranean if Italy were hostile, and garrisons and reserves of supplies must be provided for on the assumption that we should not. But the Chiefs of Staff reckoned in February that, even if a British fleet had to be despatched to the Far East—as they then assumed would be the case if Japan joined our enemies—Egypt and Palestine would have little to fear from Italy, granted that proposals for the defence of Egypt were approved and the reinforcements sent. In this case, however, Italy might gain control of sea communications in the Central and Eastern Mediterranean, since French assistance in those areas could not be assumed.

Unless and until she could conquer Egypt, Italy's only communication with her East African Empire would be by air; and so long as Italian forces remained in East Africa they would no doubt seek to deny us the Red Sea route and to weaken us in Egypt by a diversion in the Sudan. The first task of our air forces in the Sudan, Aden and East Africa would be, in co-operation with the Navy, to counter Italian attack in the Red Sea.

With regard to India, it was not thought that there was any immediate danger to her frontiers or coasts, though the possibility could not be ignored. Her security depended on British control of the routes across the Indian Ocean and therefore on the maintenance of British naval power. Her role would be rather that of a base on the grand scale and a provider of troops and supplies.

The conversations between the British and French staff delegations in London had been followed and supplemented by a series of conferences between British and French commanders abroad. By the beginning of September the French intentions in respect of operations in North Africa and the role of our own forces in Egypt had been discussed and co-ordinated, and conferences had been held at Jerusalem, Aden and Singapore.

Discussions had also taken place between the Allies as to the areas in which each should exercise the chief command. There was to be a French Commander-in-Chief of the land forces on the Western Front in Europe, and a British in the Middle East, excluding the French Mandate territories; a British Admiral would command in the Eastern Mediterranean, a French in the Western. Corresponding arrangements were to be made for other possible theatres.

The most effective use of the Allied air power in the common cause had also been considered in the course of the London conversations. The British delegation had sought to relieve the French 'dismay' at the smallness of the proposed initial British contribution on land by pointing out that, apart from the current increase of the Navy, 'Great Britain was now making a greater effort in the expansion of the Royal Air Force than she had ever made before . . . She was on the way to obtaining a bomber force comparable to Germany's.' So long, however, as the Low Countries preserved their neutrality, British bombers would find it more difficult than their German rivals to reach important targets in the enemy country. This disadvantage could be countered by basing British bombers in France, and the two Governments had agreed in April 1938 that an advanced air striking force should move from England to French airfields on the outbreak of war.

How this striking force, whether based in England or in France, could be most profitably employed had been the subject of much discussion. The British and French staffs had agreed in March that the Allies would 'not initiate air action against any but purely "military" objectives in the narrowest sense of the word, i.e., Naval, Army and Air Forces and Establishments', and as far as possible would confine it to 'objectives attack on which would not involve loss of civil life'. This principle would be followed during the first phase of the war. In the second phase the Allied bombers would whenever possible be directed against 'economic and industrial objectives in Germany, with the object of contributing to the ultimate breakdown of her resistance'. It was later agreed that, in the event of the Germans concentrating their efforts against France and attacking her by land and air through the Low Countries, the primary commitment of Bomber Command would be to stem the invasion in collaboration with the French Army and Air Force by striking at the German armies and their supply services.

In August, when war between Germany and Poland was imminent, it became urgently necessary to adopt a positive policy. Provisional instructions, conforming strictly to the narrow interpretation of 'military objectives', were issued by the British Chiefs of Staff on August 22 and a declaration of their intention to adopt this policy was issued by the two Governments.

Ever since in 1934 the rearmament of Germany in the air forced itself on British notice, the minds of the people had been prepared for a 'knock-out blow' by German bombers aimed at the commercial and industrial centres of Great Britain, and in particular at the sprawling mass of London. The Air Staff estimated in May 1939 that for a fortnight the Germans could maintain an attack on London by 1,000 bombers daily.

The scheme for the air defence of Great Britain in force at the outbreak of war was essentially that approved by the Cabinet in

November 1938. It was based on co-operation, under the control of Royal Air Force Fighter Command, between fighter aircraft, anti-aircraft artillery, searchlight companies and balloons. Guns aided by searchlights were to protect London and other vital industrial areas and ports against high-flying aircraft, while balloons would force low-flying aircraft to heights where they could be more conveniently engaged by fighters or gunfire. The manning of the guns and search-lights was the responsibility of the Territorial Army, and the Army was further responsible for the defence of airfields and a number of 'key points', mostly of industrial importance. Information of approaching aircraft would be received from the posts of the Observer Corps and from the new radar stations to be erected at points along the south and east coasts. It was hoped to make use of this invaluable device (known at the time as R.D.F.—Radio Direction Finding) for the ranging of anti-aircraft guns and also of searchlights, but such developments were not yet practical.

The guarding of the coasts and coastal waters of the United Kingdom was a task in which all three Services played their part; it included the defence of the coasts against sea-borne raids, the detection and removal of mines, the protection of shipping in home waters and the provision of security for naval bases and the direct defence of the principal commercial ports. The troops for manning the fixed defences of the twenty-eight defended ports were drawn from the Territorial Army.

One of the obvious changes brought about by air warfare is the more immediate impact of war on the civil population. Not only the risks of such warfare affect them, but also the necessary measures of defence. The experience of 1914–18 had shown that a modern war calls for an effort on the part of the whole people and blurs the distinction between fighting men and civilians. It was frequently an accident whether a particular war-worker wore uniform or not. Still more was this the case in the second war. Even in 1939 the military organisation known as the Air Defence of Great Britain, with its civilian observers, was closely related to the civilian organisation known as Air Raid Precautions, controlled by the Minister of Home Security.

In the event it was many months before the defences of the United Kingdom against air attack were tested, and the country was allowed to adapt itself without interference to a war economy in accordance with the planned procedure. The machinery of Civil Defence started to work smoothly.[1] The Regional Commissioners took up their posts, their headquarters linked up to the central Home Security war room

---

[1] See Mr. T. H. O'Brien's volume on this subject in the series of Civil Histories (H.M.S.O. 1955).

in London.[1] The Air Raid Precautions and auxiliary fire services had been mobilised; respirators had been supplied and blast-proof shelters were being constructed; the system of air-raid warning and 'blackout' which for five years were to play so large a part in the life of the nation was established; some 1,200,000 schoolchildren and others were evacuated in the first ten days of war to areas deemed safer than their homes; hospitals in threatened areas were cleared to receive casualties, of whom 35,000 a day were expected for the first few weeks. Road vehicles and premises were requisitioned for public services, and the Government, through the Railway Executive, took over control of the railways. Tankers and other vessels were also requisitioned; the Prime Minister announced on September 13 that a Ministry of Shipping would be set up at an early date. Oil and coal were rationed.[2]

Another lesson from the former war, and one reinforced by the use made of it by Nazi Germany, was the importance of propaganda. The Chiefs of Staff in their European Appreciation had advised that 'propaganda for home, enemy and neutral consumption would be of the utmost importance, particularly in the opening stages of the war'. They had been impressed by the reluctance in September 1938 of some of the population of Germany and Italy to face the prospect of war with Great Britain and they held that preparations to exploit similar feelings in a future war should be pressed on with. In the course of the year a department was organised under the Foreign Office, but its formation was not made public, to conduct propaganda in enemy countries. Its head, Sir Campbell Stuart, was in touch with the Ministry of Information, the British Broadcasting Corporation, the Fighting Services, the Ministry of Economic Warfare and various refugee bodies. The European Appreciation had also suggested the dissemination of propaganda by aircraft passing over enemy countries, and the new organisation, known as 'Electra House' from its first London headquarters, was charged with the preparation of leaflets, which took the form of warnings to the German people. The department was 'mobilised' on September 1, and the War Cabinet at their first meeting on September 3 authorised the dropping of leaflets that very night. This was the beginning of what came to be known as political or psychological warfare. Its effectiveness suffered in the early years of the war from the rivalry of the numerous bodies interested in the propagation of news, and still more from the inability of the Allies to provide victories to support it.

The first meeting of the Supreme War Council was held on British

---

[1] The functions of the Regional Commissioners will be explained later.
[2] *House of Commons Debates* vol. 351, col. 630.

initiative on September 12 at Abbeville, the United Kingdom being
represented by the Prime Minister and Lord Chatfield, France by
M. Daladier and General Gamelin. Three further meetings were held
in the course of 1939 and sixteen in all before the French armistice.
The main purpose of the first meeting was to advertise Franco-British
unity and supply mutual encouragement, and so to forestall the
enemy's efforts to divide the Allies. Mr. Chamberlain referred to the
British Government's recent announcement that they intended to
prepare for a three years war. In spite of the catastrophe in Poland
both parties seem to have shown a certain complacency in view of
the unmolested completion of French mobilisation and their belief
that time was on the side of the Allies. It was not possible, however,
to ignore Poland. Gamelin had authorised minor operations on the
eastern frontier of France with a view to creating a diversion, but in
no case did he intend to throw his army against the enemy's main
defences. In bombing policy too the Prime Ministers agreed to adhere
to the decision not to attack objectives within Germany at present.
The British Chiefs of Staff, reviewing the situation after the first ten
days of war, had noted that in spite of rumours to the contrary there
was as yet no definite proof that the German Air Force had attacked
other than military targets and that 'entirely contrary to expectation'
it was taking no action whatever against the United Kingdom.
Relatively the Allies had more to gain from a continuance of the
present calm than the enemy, and on balance they recommended
adherence to the existing policy of restriction. It may be remarked
that they assumed that, even were Great Britain to adopt unrestricted
air warfare, she would always observe the principle of 'refraining from
attack on civil population as such for the purpose of demoralisation'.[1]

The Prime Ministers were also optimistic with respect to relations
with Italy, agreeing that her continued neutrality was desirable and
that any provocation should be avoided. Even more important than
the attitude of Italy was the attitude of the United States, and in
particular her willingness to supply war material.

The original Anglo-French staff appreciation of April 4 had urged
that 'all the resources of diplomacy should be directed to securing the
benevolent neutrality or active assistance of other powers, particularly the United States of America'. Of active assistance from America
there seemed in 1939 little hope. The mass of the American people
detested the dictators and all their works, but in spite of the efforts
of the President to arouse them from their isolationism they saw little
immediate danger to themselves; the behaviour of the Western
democracies at the time of the Sudeten crisis had done nothing to
shake America's resolve not be drawn into war. This resolve was

---

[1] See Appendix I(a).

reflected in the Neutrality Acts of 1935–37, the effect of which was to prohibit the export to foreign belligerents not only of war material but of any goods for which they had not actually paid; further, no goods whatever might be carried to belligerent countries in United States ships. The granting of loans or credits to belligerents was also prohibited. Moreover, the Johnson Act of 1934, which forbade loans from any American citizen to foreign States which had defaulted on their payments to the United States, was still in force, and Great Britain was one of the countries thus penalised. President Roosevelt tried hard early in 1939 to secure the relaxation of these measures, which allowed no discrimination between an aggressor State and its victims, but without success. As things stood in September, they seemed to rule out not only all active assistance on the part of the United States to Great Britain and France but most forms of bene-volent neutrality. M. Daladier, however, expected an early revision of the Neutrality Law; he said that France had already sent a mission to America to arrange for the purchase of aircraft and that the results had been satisfactory. The matter was pursued further at the next meeting of the Supreme War Council on September 22 with the intention of co-ordinating the approaches of the two countries to the United States.

M. Daladier's expectations were justified. On the outbreak of war President Roosevelt summoned a Special Session of Congress with a view to a modification of the Neutrality Acts, and a new measure eventually became law on November 4; it repealed the embargo on war material to belligerents, allowing them to procure American goods on a cash-and-carry basis. Lord Lothian, the British Am-bassador at Washington, summed up the position at the time the new Act was signed by saying that the debates in Congress had shown two clear-cut decisions by the American people. The first was that they wanted the Allies to win and would help them by making available the resources of American industry of every kind on a cash-and-carry basis; the second was their determination to keep out of the war themselves. These decisions would probably remain the funda-mentals of America's foreign policy unless and until some change in the international situation confronted her with a threat to her own vital national interests.

CHAPTER II

THE FORCES AND THE PLANS
FOR THEIR EXPANSION

ON SEPTEMBER 9 the Cabinet (so the War Cabinet will henceforward be referred to) announced that the Government's plans were based on the assumption that the war would last at least three years; they announced further that they were mobilising the entire resources of the country. These decisions naturally implied a review of the programmes for the expansion of the armed forces. It will be convenient to set out first, in broad outline, the state which our rearmament had reached and our strength at home and overseas.

For the Navy, no scheme devised to meet the possibility of war against two Great Powers simultaneously had ever been accepted by the Government. Volume I will show how the construction of capital ships and cruisers was limited by treaty until the end of 1936, and how the assumption that an enemy was to be looked for only in the Far East broke down under the mounting threat from Nazi Germany. Still less had any scheme been devised for a war against three Powers, although Italy had been the potential enemy in 1935 and was still viewed as such in 1939. Fortunately the Italian navy could for the present be regarded as roughly balanced by the French; if for the present only, since their relative strengths would soon change for the worse.[1] But even if the Italian navy were ignored the policies and the estimated building capacities of Germany and Japan were such as to cause apprehension for the future, and the Admiralty had pressed since at least 1935 for the adoption of a two-power standard for the Royal Navy. Each year's programme had tended to be a compromise between the Admiralty's demands and the Treasury's resistance.

The Admiralty's immediate preoccupation was the German navy. It comprised two battle-cruisers (*Gneisenau* and *Scharnhorst*) each nominally of 26,000 tons but in fact considerably larger, three 'pocket-battleships' (*Deutschland*, *Admiral Graf Spee* and *Admiral Scheer*) each of 10,000 tons, two heavy cruisers (*Blücher* and *Hipper*), five light cruisers and 57 submarines. All these were of recent construction.

---

[1] The French had five battleships and two battle-cruisers, the latter fairly modern; the Italians had only two capital ships in the summer of 1939, but were expected to possess six, new or modernised, by the end of 1940.

In addition the Germans had two very powerful battleships (*Bismarck* and *Tirpitz*) and one heavy cruiser (*Prince Eugen*) nearing completion. Further, the British Admiralty calculated that by the end of 1944 the Germans would have the equivalent of nine capital ships (counting the three pocket-battleships as the equivalent of one capital ship) and Japan sixteen. Japan was understood to have ten capital ships at the outbreak of war.[1]

The view of the Admiralty, as stated to the Committee of Imperial Defence, had long been that the safety of the Empire required a superiority of three capital ships over Germany in home waters and of one capital ship over Japan. In 1939 the Royal Navy was short of this superiority by four ships. The actual position at the outbreak of war was that we had available ten battleships and three battle-cruisers. Of these only the *Nelson*, the *Rodney* and the battle-cruiser *Hood* had been completed since the last war; the *Warspite*, *Malaya*, *Barham*, and *Royal Oak* and the battle-cruisers *Renown* and *Repulse* had been modernised to a greater or lesser extent, while the remainder (*Royal Sovereign*, *Revenge*, *Resolution* and *Ramillies*) had not been modernised at all. The *Valiant* and the *Queen Elizabeth*, which were undergoing modernisation, were expected to bring the number of capital ships up to fifteen by the end of 1940. The four un-modernised battleships were considered fit for convoy work but not for operations against the modern ships of other Powers, and in particular not for action in the Far East. As to the future, there were five battleships building, of the *King George V* class, which were expected to complete in 1940–42; four ships of the *Lion* class had been approved but had not yet been laid down. Quite recently, in July 1939, the Committee of Imperial Defence had recommended the necessary preliminary measures for building three more capital ships in 1940–41 and had instructed the Admiralty and Treasury to consider the implications of building three capital ships a year from 1941 onwards.

Thus from the point of view of the Admiralty, in the light of the rival building programmes, Hitler's resort to war in September 1939, premature as regards not only his potential allies but his own navy, was an uncovenanted mercy.

It was obvious that with such disparity as existed in September 1939 the Germans would not risk a fleet action, but their large ships were well designed for raiding commerce. It was also expected that they would arm merchant ships to act as raiders, and they had in fact arranged to convert twenty-six.[2]

---

[1] A fuller account of the strength of the enemy and Allied fleets is given in Captain S. W. Roskill's work in this series, *The War at Sea* I (H.M.S.O. 1954), ch. iv, referred to henceforward as 'Roskill'.

[2] *Führer Conferences on Naval Affairs, 1939–1945*, published in *Brassey's Naval Annual, 1948* (henceforward referred to as *F.N.C.*) p. 34.

The story will show how difficult it proved, in spite of the enormous existing disproportion in capital ships, to counter the activities of the battle-cruisers; the other ships it was hoped to contain by skilful disposition and concentration of our cruisers, but of these there was a sad deficiency. The Admiralty, even before they came to demand a two-power standard, had thought a minimum of seventy cruisers necessary. At the outbreak of war there were in fact about fifty in service including Australian and New Zealand ships; eighteen were old ships of the first war not suitable for fleet work. The shortage of destroyers was also serious, and was found, when the U-boat war waxed hotter, to be even more serious than had been expected. Very few ships were at this time equipped with radar.

Within the first few weeks of war all previous naval programmes were reviewed with the intention of giving priority to construction which could produce results before 1942. Some ships building for foreign Powers were requisitioned and high priority was assigned to fitting out auxiliary war vessels, in particular armed merchant cruisers and trawlers, and to the arming of merchant ships.

The principle of maintaining during war an annual output of not less than 1,100,000 tons of merchant shipping, subject to Treasury approval, was accepted by the Cabinet in September and the Board of Trade were authorised to order 200,000 tons at once. In January 1940 the Cabinet approved proposals for raising the output of merchant shipping within twelve months to 1,500,000 tons and for transferring the responsibility for merchant ship-building to the Admiralty.

In March the Cabinet discussed and in general approved the programme of new construction for the financial year 1940–41 proposed by the Admiralty. The only capital ship with which it was now proposed to proceed, apart from the five already building, was the battleship, or 'battleship-cruiser', *Vanguard*; it was hoped to complete this ship in three and a half years. The Admiralty were concerned, however, on the long view, about the relative strengths of the British and Japanese navies after the eventual defeat of Germany, and wished the Government to reconsider in the autumn whether the construction of other battleships should or should not be proceeded with.

Nothing has been said so far of the Navy's air weapon. The Admiralty had only very recently reassumed complete control of the Fleet Air Arm; it was small and ill equipped, especially with regard to fighters, and its possibilities were as yet a matter of conjecture. At the outbreak of war there were four large (or fleet) aircraft-carriers fit for operations: *Ark Royal*, *Courageous*, *Furious*, and *Glorious*, and two smaller, *Eagle* and *Hermes*. Five fleet carriers were building, and a sixth had been authorised. When war broke out, the total first-line strength was 232 aircraft in seventeen squadrons. By American or

Japanese standards the Fleet Air Arm, as regards equipment, was backward. As it happened, the German navy was even worse provided, not possessing a single carrier, though it was using catapult aircraft. But the British naval aircraft were ill matched against the fighters of the Luftwaffe.

The dispositions of the Fleet when war broke out are fully set out elsewhere.[1] In accordance with the plans outlined in the last chapter, the Home Fleet, under Admiral Sir Charles Forbes, was based at Scapa; it included five battleships, two battle-cruisers, the aircraft-carrier *Ark Royal*, and a dozen cruisers.[2] At Rosyth was the carrier *Furious*. Outside the Home Fleet there were two cruisers in the Humber, and two unmodernised battleships, two carriers, and three cruisers at Portland.[3] The America and West Indies station comprised four cruisers; the North Atlantic force, based on Gibraltar, had two; spread over the South Atlantic, and controlled from Freetown, were eight.

In the Mediterranean Admiral Sir Andrew Cunningham, long experienced in those waters, had succeeded Sir Dudley Pound as Commander-in-Chief in June. His command included three battle-ships,[4] the carrier *Glorious* and seven cruisers; a floating dock had been towed out to Alexandria from Portsmouth in the summer, and by the end of October it was in use for docking capital ships. The only fully equipped naval base, however, in the Mediterranean was at Malta; the island would clearly be of great offensive value if and when Italy became an enemy, and the Admiralty would have liked to make use of it. But first it must be rendered safe from air attack. The Committee of Imperial Defence had agreed at the end of July that the scale of its totally inadequate defences should be increased, but shortly afterwards they recommended that as an immediate measure anti-aircraft guns should be diverted from Malta, and also from Gibraltar, to strengthen the fleet's present base, Alexandria. The only warships which remained at Malta in September 1939 were submarines and small surface craft.

The greater part of the French fleet, including three capital ships and ten cruisers, was also stationed in the Mediterranean, based on Toulon, Oran and Bizerta.

South and east of Suez there was the Red Sea escort force of destroyers and sloops, based on Aden; they could be supported if necessary by cruisers from the East Indies command, whose head-quarters were at Colombo. On the China station, under Admiral

---

[1] See Roskill I ch. iv.

[2] Battleships: *Nelson, Rodney, Royal Oak, Royal Sovereign, Ramillies*. Battle-cruisers: *Hood, Repulse*, to which *Renown* was soon added.

[3] Battleships: *Resolution, Revenge*. Carriers: *Courageous, Hermes*.

[4] *Warspite, Barham, Malaya*.

Sir Percy Noble, were four cruisers and one carrier, besides two French cruisers.

The Army in the few months preceding the outbreak of war had been subjected to a series of revolutionary changes. On March 29, after the occupation of Czechoslovakia, the Government had announced the doubling of the Territorial Army from thirteen to twenty-six divisions, which with the six Regular divisions would produce an army of thirty-two divisions.[1] In May Parliament passed the Compulsory Training Act, and this was followed on the first day of the war by the National Service (Armed Forces) Act, which introduced conscription. The British contribution to the Allied forces in the West was also substantially increased and the programme accelerated.

Just before war broke out the French were told that the First Contingent of the British Field Force, including four Regular infantry divisions, would be concentrated in France within thirty-three days of mobilisation; the first of the two Regular armoured (formerly 'mobile') divisions would be available in about eight months; the role of the Territorial Army had not been decided, but it was expected that two infantry divisions would be ready for despatch overseas in four months, a further three and one motor division in five months, and one horsed cavalry division in from four to six months from mobilisation. The dates when the remaining divisions would be available could not as yet be foreseen.

The force actually despatched within the first five weeks of war consisted of two corps each of two divisions, with ancillary troops. It included an Air Component, whose task would be to provide air reconnaissance and protection, composed of four fighter and eight reconnaissance squadrons, with two communication flights.

Surprising as it may well appear, the commander of the British Expeditionary Force had not been selected in peacetime. This important decision had now to be made by the new War Cabinet, and it was made at their first meeting. The officer who in the opinion of many seemed marked out for this post was Lieutenant-General Sir John Dill, holding the Aldershot command and regarded as our leading strategist. Others expected the appointment of General Sir Edmund Ironside, the Inspector-General of Overseas Forces, who had commanded the British troops in North Russia in 1918–19 and possessed varied experience of the Middle East. But the War Cabinet

---

[1] See Mr. Hore-Belisha's speech on the Army Estimates, 8 March, and the Prime Minister's statement of 29 March 1939, *House of Commons Debates* vol. 344, cols. 2161 ff.; vol. 345, cols. 2048–50. Only twelve of the projected Territorial divisions were in fact formed, so that, when doubled, they made twenty-four.

appointed instead General Viscount Gort, V.C., the Chief of the Imperial General Staff, replacing him in this post by General Ironside. Lord Gort's valour in the Great War was legendary; he was known as a fine fighting soldier; and the story will show how well his courage and resolution served his country in the dangers yet to come; but he was junior in length of service to Dill and in many eyes his qualities and experience fitted him rather for the role of a corps or army commander than for that of Commander-in-Chief in a European war.

The rapid changes of plan with regard to the purpose, size and composition of our land forces threw a severe strain on the Army generally, on the War Office, and on the recently created Ministry of Supply. Existing units were milked of officers and non-commissioned officers to train the new Territorial formations; production programmes had to be hastily expanded and the whole elaborate mobilisation scheme recast. The revised mobilisation instructions did not reach those concerned with carrying them out until the first week of August, and they were due to take effect from September 1, the very day on which general mobilisation of the army was ordered. Further, however valuable the decision to double the Territorial Army might be as a gesture, it was not accompanied by the necessary provision for training, or for constituting a properly balanced force, with its essential air component. The administrative units required for the new formations were not included and, though the number of divisions had been increased, there was no corresponding provision for an expansion of corps or army troops. All these remained to be found after mobilisation.

The legislation of May and September spared the War Office the anxieties of the previous war in respect of recruiting, but it did not solve the problem of equipment. Indeed it had been foreseen for some time that for a period of many months after the outbreak of war the supply of munitions and equipment, and not of men, would set the limit to the rate of expansion of the Army. Even with regard to the small expeditionary force the sudden decision to increase the initial contingent from two divisions to four, with their proportions of corps and army troops, had resulted in a shortage which meant that hardly a unit went to France completely equipped. Speaking of the enlarged Field Force of the future, the representative of the War Office had admitted at an August meeting of the Committee of Imperial Defence that 'the position regarding its despatch overseas was bad. The main deficiencies were in guns and tanks. Not until the middle of 1942 would there be sufficient 25-pounder equipments for thirty-two divisions. As regards tanks we had at present 60 infantry tanks, against a total requirement of 1,646.'

Meanwhile, as a result of the decision to send all Regular units abroad, the army at home was reduced to what has been described as a token force of semi-trained troops, and the policy of giving priority in every kind of equipment to the Field Force meant that these troops would remain seriously short of equipment even for purposes of training.

The two main tasks which the Chiefs of Staff had thought likely to fall on the army in the United Kingdom were the manning of the anti-aircraft defences and the maintenance of order among the civil population in the case of air attack.[1] At the outbreak of war Anti-Aircraft Command, Territorial Army, was organised in five divisions, under Lieutenant-General F. A. Pile, whose headquarters were at Stanmore, alongside those of Fighter Command, Royal Air Force; two additional divisions had been authorised but not yet formed.[2] Nowhere was the deficiency of equipment more painfully evident. Similarly the twenty-eight defended ports were far below their approved requirements in armament.

Before the decision was taken to send the flower of the Army at home to the Continent, the most likely theatre of operations for our land forces was the so-called Middle East. Even after the decision had been taken, the Chiefs of Staff, thinking both of possible Arab disaffection and of Italian invasion from Libya, had concluded that a considerable increase was required in the reserves of troops and materials normally kept in the Middle East in peace; this was in accordance with the Government's intention, announced by the Secretary of State in March 1939, to form there a second strategic reserve in addition to the traditional one in the United Kingdom.[3]

In August 1939 General Sir Archibald Wavell had taken up the new appointment of General Officer Commanding-in-Chief, Middle East. He was a soldier of strong character and tried ability, familiar with the background of Near-Eastern strategy alike by personal experience and as the biographer of Allenby, his former chief. He had been instructed to co-ordinate policy with the naval and air commanders, and the formation of a joint staff for planning and intelligence was authorised. The land forces in Egypt, under Wavell's supreme authority, were commanded by Lieutenant-General Sir Henry Maitland Wilson; these consisted in the main of an armoured division still in process of formation, three British infantry brigades, including one recently moved from Palestine, and a number of artillery and engineer units; additional to these was the

---

[1] A fuller account of the organisation of the Air Defence of Great Britain is given by Basil Collier, *The Defence of the United Kingdom* (in preparation) chaps. iv and v.

[2] The Anti-Aircraft divisions were not included in the Territorial Army formations previously mentioned.

[3] *House of Commons Debates* vol. 344, col. 2169.

D

11th Indian Brigade Group just arrived from India.[1] In Palestine, under Lieutenant-General M. G. H. Barker, there were the Head-quarters of the 7th and 8th Infantry Divisions and three infantry brigades, along with other troops.

In Syria the French, under General Maxime Weygand, Foch's former Chief of Staff, were getting together an expeditionary force; at the outbreak of war it consisted of two ill-equipped *brigades mixtes*, with no air support, but in September a division arrived from North Africa.[2]

There were small British garrisons in Malta and at Gibraltar; south of Egypt, in the Sudan, Uganda, Kenya and British Somali-land, the troops were mainly African, but there were two British battalions in the Sudan.

The French had asked in August 1939 for information about the recruiting of African troops from the British Colonies and were told of a plan to double the number in war. As from 1 September the War Office took over control of all African colonial forces, and by the end of the year the numbers serving had been largely increased. In January the Cabinet gave general approval to a report from the Colonial Office, with which the War Office concurred, on the best use to be made of the man-power of the colonial empire during the war. The Report argued that 'for at least the next two years the raising of new combatant units in the Colonial Dependencies will not on strict military merits be practicable, because all the available supplies of equipment will be required for units considered to be of superior fighting quality, raised in this country or the Dominions'. The possibilities of each colony were considered in turn, largely from the point of view of local defence and of forming pioneer units. In the King's African Rifles and the Royal West African Frontier Force, however, there were now five infantry brigades and some units of other arms, though not yet equipped even to the standard desirable for secondary theatres.

The part which India might play in a war outside her borders had recently been considered by the committee which, with Lord Chatfield as its chairman, had visited the country in 1938.[3] They had recommended that India should be invited to accept at least partial responsibility for maintaining forces adequate not only for local defence but for security against threats from without. This would imply that for the first time forces for external and for internal duties should form an integral part of the forces of India as a whole and

---

[1] A brigade group is an infantry brigade with troops of other arms attached for a special purpose.

[2] M. Weygand, *Rappelé au Service* (Paris 1950) pp. 30–33.

[3] Its report was published on 4 September 1939, with an announcement that H.M.G. had accepted it with minor modifications.

should not be two separate entities. The army in India would thus include a specially designated External Defence Force, equipped on a somewhat higher scale than the local defence units. For the air forces in India the Committee recommended a similar distinction between units intended for local and external defence respectively. The basis for the reorganisation of the Royal Indian Navy was an agreement of January 1938 whereby India undertook to maintain a sea-going squadron of modern escort vessels to co-operate with the Royal Navy in the defence of the country. But these, in their complete form at least, were only plans. The process of 'modernisation' would take years, and the great bulk of the armament, which would have to come from the United Kingdom, could not receive a priority equal to the latter's own. Beginnings had been made, however, in modernising the army, and, though the External Defence Force as such had not been formed, about two-thirds of the troops classified for this purpose by the Chatfield Committee had been sent abroad before the outbreak of war; there remained a divisional Headquarters and one brigade group earmarked for despatch overseas, and on September 7 the Cabinet decided that with the concurrence of the Secretary of State for India these also should move to Egypt.

In Malaya there were two infantry brigades (one British and one Indian); the Committee of Imperial Defence had recommended in July that Singapore should be stocked on a scale ample enough to enable it to hold out for a period of ninety days before relief arrived from Europe or the Mediterranean, and that the possibility of maintaining stocks to support the garrison and civil population of Malaya for six months should be explored. Eastward of Malaya there were an infantry brigade (mainly British) and an Indian infantry battalion at Hong Kong, and a British infantry brigade distributed between Shanghai and Tientsin. The troops in China were maintained in strategically indefensible positions for political reasons, and the same might be said of the gunboats of the Navy in Chinese waters.[1]

Such being the strength and disposition of the Army at the outbreak of war, the plans of the Government for its expansion must next be considered. On September 6 the Cabinet's attention was called to the fact that, so far as the Ministry of Supply could judge, the existing output of arms and equipment would not furnish more than sixteen divisions for service abroad in the first year, whereas

---

[1] No attempt has been made to do more than indicate the general distribution of the Army overseas; the R.A. and R.E. units have not been mentioned, nor have the small garrisons of Cyprus, Burma and Ceylon. Fuller particulars are given in the volumes of this history concerned with the campaigns in the Middle and Far East.

the present intention was to send thirty-two, and that any advance on this figure would mean an immediate and large increase in factory programmes. Allowance must also be made for the needs of the Dominions, the French and other allies whom it might be necessary to equip. Faced with the need of deciding the total land forces to be provided for and the dates by which they must be ready to move overseas, the Cabinet appointed a committee, with Sir Samuel Hoare as chairman.[1]

The 'Land Forces Committee', reporting on 8 September, recommended that the aim should be to equip fifty-five divisions by the end of the second year, viz. September 1941. The figure fifty-five was to include thirty-two divisions from the United Kingdom, fourteen from the Dominions, and four from India, plus a reserve of 10 per cent (five divisions) 'for assistance to Allies and so forth'. At least twenty divisions should be equipped within the first twelve months, subject always to priority for the needs of the Royal Air Force and some at any rate of those of the Navy.

The Cabinet, after full consideration of the needs of all the three Services and of the financial implications of their demands, eventually authorised the Minister of Supply to plan for the supply of fifty-five divisions on the full British scale within two years; they sanctioned the supply programmes of the Navy and Mercantile Marine on the existing basis, that of the Army as recently proposed, and that of the Royal Air Force for a monthly output of 2,550 aircraft, subject to the necessary examination from the points of view of finance and labour. The Government did not bind themselves to carry out the full programme; nevertheless the decision to aim at supplying arms and equipment for an army of fifty-five divisions was a notable landmark, and this figure continued as the accepted target long after the original intention of sending twenty divisions overseas in the first year had been rendered pointless by the course of events.

The number of fifty-five was not conveyed to the French, but in October 1939, after General Gamelin had urged the formation of more British divisions than the thirty-two promised, the Chief of the Imperial General Staff was authorised to inform him that thirty-two was not the limit of the number of divisions which it was intended to raise. The French General Staff were perturbed by the disproportion between the Allied and German forces which might be expected on the Western front in the spring; they seemed to the Cabinet to be unaware of the magnitude of the British war effort, including the extended Air programme, and of the other factors limiting the rapid expansion of the Army.

On 13 February 1940, after a general review of the supply pro-

---

[1] See Viscount Templewood, *Nine Troubled Years* (1954) p. 398.

gramme, which will be referred to later, the Cabinet adhered to the programme of fifty-five divisions as an object to be realised, now 'by the earliest possible date', and authorised the Minister of Supply to start at once, on this basis, on the construction of such factories as could not be completed in less than eighteen months. It was clear that on the present scales of equipment and wastage rates allowed by the War Office there was no possibility of turning out this number of divisions by the end of the second year, and doubtful whether even the thirty-six divisions 'now in existence' could be adequately equipped[1]; but some members of the Military Co-ordination Committee were of opinion that these scales were unrealistically high and that on a review they might well be reduced to a figure which would enable considerably more than thirty-six divisions to be maintained overseas by September 1941. Attention was called to the importance of not adopting an unreasonably lavish scale of equipment and ammunition for the British Expeditionary Force and the Air Defence of Great Britain, and of not giving the French any ground for complaining that we were not doing our fair share. It seemed clear, however, that even if the War Office scales were drastically cut down the amount of essential equipment which could be provided by September 1941 would not suffice for anything like fifty-five divisions.

The Royal Air Force when war broke out was working to a programme (Scheme M) approved by the Cabinet in November 1938; it envisaged a Metropolitan Air Force of 163 Squadrons (2,549 first-line aircraft), including 50 fighter and 85 heavy bomber squadrons (800 and 1,360 first-line aircraft); it envisaged also forty-nine squadrons (636 aircraft) for overseas stations. This programme was not due for completion, however, until March 1942; the actual strength available in September 1939 was very different—a Metropolitan Air Force with not more than 1,460 first-line aircraft, of which 536 were bombers, 608 fighters, 96 for army co-operation and 216 for coastal reconnaissance. These were supported by 2,000 reserve aircraft, those of fighter and coastal reconnaissance type amounting to little more than 50 per cent of the first line.

Compared with these numbers the French were understood to have 1,735 first-line aircraft (463 bombers, 634 fighters) and about 1,600 reserves.

Against these the Germans were believed to dispose of over 4,000 first-line aircraft (2,130 bombers, 1,215 fighters) in addition to 500 transport aircraft, with ample reserves. Figures now available show

---

[1] The figure 36 included three Dominion divisions, one Canadian, one Australian, one from New Zealand.

that the Luftwaffe's first-line strength was in fact about 3,600 (excluding 550 transport aircraft) of which 1,180 were long-distance bombers and 366 dive bombers; the reserves however were very much less than the British estimates, though some 3,000 aircraft were retained for training purposes.

The German bomber types were at this time superior to those of the Allies, while the single-engined Messerschmitt fighter excelled all Allied fighters except the eight-gun Spitfire and possibly the Hurricane. The French bombers were largely obsolescent types and were regarded as of doubtful operational value.

The headquarters of Bomber Command, under Air Chief Marshal Sir Edgar Ludlow-Hewitt, were at High Wycombe. Ten of its squadrons, armed with Battle aircraft, started to cross to France on September 2, to form the Advanced Air Striking Force; it had been intended to send double this number, but airfield accommodation was not available for more than ten. Two Blenheim squadrons formed part of the Air Component of the British Expeditionary Force. Besides these twelve, Bomber Command was able to mobilise twenty-five squadrons (352 aircraft), of which eight were armed with Blenheims and the rest with Whitleys, Hampdens and Wellingtons.

More British bomber squadrons could have been mobilised but for the policy of 'rolling up' some squadrons to supply reserves for those mobilised and to form operatonal training units. The question of the right proportion of reserve to first line was a difficult one, especially when the wastage to be allowed for operations had to be a matter of guesswork. Further, when criticisms were made in the Cabinet of the disproportion between the numbers of aircraft produced and the numbers which figured in first-line squadrons, the Air representatives declared that nine-tenths of our fighter squadrons had been re-equipped with modern aircraft during the previous twelve months, and that the constant change to a new programme before the previous one had been completed was responsible for a good deal of our present difficulties. As each successive scheme had been authorised, more and more of our resources had to be directed from operational units to the training organisation necessary to produce increased first-line strength.

The nineteen squadrons of Coastal Command were organised in three Groups, with headquarters at Donibristle (Fife), Chatham and Plymouth, all under the command of Air Marshal Sir Frederick Bowhill, who had his own headquarters at Northwood. Close co-operation with the Navy was assured by the formation of Area Combined Headquarters at Rosyth, the Nore and Plymouth; combined exercises had taken place from August 15 to 21, and on August 23 the squadrons were deployed to their war stations.

Fighter Command, under Air Chief Marshal Sir Hugh Dowding,

mobilised thirty-nine fighter squadrons, of which twenty-six were armed with Spitfires or Hurricanes.

As regards equipment other than aircraft in the Air Defence of Great Britain, there was a very serious shortage of guns, both heavy and light. Searchlights also were deficient. The 450 cable-carrying balloons authorised for the London area were ready, but such was not the case elsewhere. Much confidence was placed, however, in the fact that of the chain of secret radar stations twenty out of twenty-two had been completed. These were established along the coast from the Isle of Wight to the Firth of Tay, and there were two in the far north. Twenty-eight out of thirty-two proposed Observer Corps districts for tracing aircraft inland had been organised.

So far we have been considering the Metropolitan Air Force only. Seeing that it was in north-western Europe that the British high command believed that decisive damage might be both suffered and inflicted, it was natural that in the general stringency other theatres should have to rest content with what they could get. The total number of squadrons overseas was thirty-four and a half (with an initial establishment of 425 aircraft) as against the forty-nine provided for by Scheme M.

In the Middle East, including the Sudan and Aden, there were under the command of Air Chief Marshal Sir William Mitchell four fighter squadrons, eleven bomber, two bomber-transport, one general reconnaissance and one army-co-operation—nineteen in all, not counting a squadron of flying-boats in the Mediterranean. In India, after two bomber squadrons had been sent to Singapore, there remained only two bomber and three army-co-operation squadrons, and one bomber-transport; there was also the one not yet completed squadron of the Indian Air Force. In Malaya there were rather more than eight squadrons—four bomber, recently arrived from India and the United Kingdom, two torpedo-bomber and two general reconnaissance. The bombers were chiefly Blenheims, and there were two squadrons of flying-boats, but most of the other types were obsolescent. The Anglo-French Staff Conference which met at Singapore in June had 'viewed with great concern the inadequacy of the Allied forces in the Far East' and pressed for a largely increased strength to be permanently stationed there. This demand did not go altogether unheeded, but all that it was found possible to send before the outbreak of war was the four medium bomber squadrons mentioned. It will be noticed that there was no fighter squadron in India or in the Far East.

The expansion plan in force when war broke out provided for 12,000 aircraft by the end of March 1940, and for 5,500 more to be delivered thereafter. Shortly before the outbreak contractors were urged to speed up production, and it was hoped that the monthly output of air frames would soon rise from about 750 to 1,000 and within 18 months to 2,000. The possibility of raising this figure to 3,000 was considered by the Air Council on 10 September, with the Ministers of Labour and Supply present; the scheme was found impracticable, by reason of the shortage of machine-tools, of labour, and of some raw materials and also of the dollar cost involved. It was agreed that the maximum monthly increase attainable was 300 in the United Kingdom in addition to some 250 from Canada and Australia, and accordingly on September 22 after considering the Second Report of the Land Forces Committee the Cabinet authorised a programme aiming at 2,550 aircraft monthly, of which 250 should be built in the Dominions.

When the Cabinet decision was reported to the Air Council on September 26, with the information that a general priority for such items as machine-tools had been granted to the Air Ministry, an interesting discussion followed concerning the types of aircraft on which production should be concentrated. It was pointed out that the main bottleneck in production was the supply of light alloys and raw aluminium, and that certain types required more material than others. On the other hand it was urged that, although the diversion of effort to new types, such as the Stirling, would cause some falling off in production in the next twelve months, it was essential to provide the most efficient machines, and the Air Member for Personnel insisted that the morale of the aircrews depended on the efficiency of their aircraft.

Within the general expansion of the Royal Air Force, the growth of Fighter Command in particular deserves attention. Scheme M envisaged fifty fighter squadrons, of which fourteen would be Auxiliary Squadrons, to be formed by April 1941. Four squadrons had been earmarked since December 1935 for service with the British Expeditionary Force; the rest were intended for the defence of London and the industrial areas of Great Britain. In the course of 1939 the approved establishment of Fighter Command had been augmented by seven squadrons for special purposes, four to escort coastal shipping between the Forth and Southampton, two for the defence of the naval base at Scapa and one for the defence of Belfast. Thus the total in view at the outbreak of war was 57, of which 46 were intended for the main scheme of air defence at home.

We have seen that the number of fighter squadrons which actually had been formed by September 1939 was 39. Four of these promptly flew to France to join the Air Component of the British Expeditionary Force, so Sir Hugh Dowding was left with 35 squadrons to perform a task for which 46 had been accepted as the minimum figure, or 53, counting the recent commitments mentioned above. It had long been the common opinion that the Germans might start the war with a full-scale air attack on England; such an attack seemed again likely after the Prime Minister's rejection on October 12 of Hitler's peace offer, and indeed for several months it remained an alternative which German strategy might well adopt. The Air Marshal was naturally therefore reluctant to allow any of his squadrons to be diverted from their appointed task until at least the minimum of forty-six had been assured.

On the other hand it was inevitable that, as the size of the projected Field Force increased, the number of fighter squadrons which had been thought adequate in 1935 should no longer appear so, and in May 1939 the Chief of the Air Staff decided that six additional single-seater fighter squadrons should be established on a mobile basis by the beginning of 1940 so that they could be transferred to France at short notice. No promise however was made. In August, discussions between the War Office and the Air Ministry led to an agreement relating largely to future expansion: it was accepted that thirty-two divisions on the Continent would need fourteen squadrons, and that a reserve of two squadrons should be added to the expansion programme; in the meantime six Regular squadrons of Fighter Command should be placed on a mobile basis before the end of 1939; the decision to send any of them overseas must rest with the Cabinet.

Sir Hugh Dowding had protested against the immediate despatch of the four squadrons to France; he foresaw a steady drain on his resources as soon as fighting there began (the long period of inaction could not be foreseen); accordingly he promptly put forward a demand for more squadrons, eventually deciding to ask for eight. The discussion which followed between the Air Marshal and the Air Council as to the relative priority to be assigned to defence and offence in the British air strategy at this time is hardly relevant here. What is relevant is that, whereas on the one hand two Gladiator squadrons were sent to France in November and preparations were made for the despatch of more if necessary, Fighter Command was compensated by the step-by-step authorisation during October of eighteen more squadrons, and that all these (most of them Blenheims) were formed by 18 December, thus raising the total in the United Kingdom and France from 39 to 57; this total includes the four squadrons for the protection of trade, which were formed in October and transferred to Coastal Command in February 1940. Six of the 57 squadrons were in France. This left 47 squadrons for the defence of Great Britain, and that is the number at the disposal of Fighter Command at the beginning of May 1940; but it included three or four not immediately serviceable, and the reserves of aircraft were low. Further, two squadrons were earmarked for the Norwegian campaign, and four for reinforcing France.

In the meantime, in March 1940, the resources of Fighter Command had been reviewed by the Air Council in the light of the Command's increased commitments; these were threefold, due in the first place to extended demands for protection of coastal convoys, in the second place to the fresh areas in Scotland and the West of England which now claimed to be included in the scheme of defence, and in the third place to the estimated increase in the German long-range bomber force. The review led to recommendations that the strength of the Command should be raised to sixty fighter squadrons by 1 September 1940 and to eighty by 1 April 1941; the immediate addition of seven squadrons was urged, but action was forestalled by the intensification of war on the Continent.

Even so, the addition of eighteen squadrons to Fighter Command in the first four months of the war, raising the total to fifty-seven, was a striking readjustment of the balance in relation to the thirty-seven squadrons of Bomber Command. The events of the summer were to show that it was in no way an over-insurance.

Later in the war complaints were made of the failure of the Air Ministry to provide for the construction of other types of aircraft, notably transport and long-range fighter. An estimate of monthly production for the next quarter presented to the Cabinet in October 1939 showed not more than four bomber-transport aircraft, as against 260, rising to 280, bombers for the Striking Force.

The expansion of the Royal Air Force meant more than the construction of additional aircraft. The Secretary of State told the Cabinet in October 1938 that by the beginning of 1940 the factor limiting the number of squadrons that could be mobilised would be the trained crews available. The annual output of trained pilots was then about 1,600 (compared with a German output of over 4,000); it was intended to raise the rate on the outbreak of war to 5,600 pilots, with 8,000 observers and air gunners.

The training course for pilots when war broke out lasted about nine months and included only some 150 hours' flying time; elementary instruction was given at civil schools and more advanced training at the fifteen Flying Training Schools, of which one was in Egypt. Observers were trained in navigation at civil schools, and other aircrew in the squadrons. Flying was every day becoming a more complicated art in view of technical developments and more distant objectives, while reluctance to divert pilots and aircraft, or money, from the all too few squadrons to instructional work prevented the provision of the more elaborate training which a sound policy now demanded. The tendency was to send the pilot only partly trained to his squadron and let him complete his training there. The device of Group Pools (later known as Operational Training Units) to give more advanced instruction than at the schools, and also to serve as reservoirs for replacing casualties in war, had not gone far when war broke out, and it was criticised after that as reducing the number of first-line squadrons.

The provision for expansion of training facilities in wartime in the matter of buildings, airfields and aircraft was quite inadequate. When war broke out, various restrictions added new difficulties to training. There were obvious objections to depleting the mobilised squadrons in order to provide instructors, or to using them as schools of instruction, and although Bomber Command converted some of the squadrons they could not mobilise into Operational Training Units, and other Commands followed suit, this expedient was only possible so long as wastage remained low.

The shortage of trainer aircraft and instructors caused serious difficulties in 1940 and 1941, and was said by some critics to have resulted in a lower standard of training; this was only a temporary phase, however, and early in 1942 conditions improved; in that year the output of aircrew for service with the Royal Air Force was raised to 60,000 and a pilot's flying experience before he joined his squadron to anything from 300 to 350 hours.

Until the outbreak of war, plans for expanding the training organisation were mainly confined to the United Kingdom, but owing to its closeness to enemy bases and the congestion of its population Great Britain was not a satisfactory training ground. Much time and thought had been devoted to the possibility of using less crowded and less vulnerable countries, yet the only concrete result at the beginning of September 1939 was the one long-established flying school in Egypt. Before the end of December, however, a grand scheme had been approved by which the bulk of school training came to be given in the secure open lands of the Empire overseas and from 1941 onwards a steady flow of trained pilots was provided.

The decision to aim at a monthly output of 2,500 aircraft involved a corresponding supply of some 20,000 pilots and 30,000 other air-crew annually, and this would mean an immense increase in flying-training establishments, far beyond the capacity of the United Kingdom. It was this need that led to the British Commonwealth Air Training plan.[1] Under the scheme there were to be linked training organisations in Canada, Australia and New Zealand: men from the Dominions were to be trained in their home countries up to the Royal Air Force standards, and a certain number of men from the United Kingdom, Australia and New Zealand were to receive

---

[1] Also known as the 'Dominions' or 'Empire Air Training Scheme'.

training in Canada. There were to be twenty-five Elementary Flying Training Schools for pilots, twenty-five Service Training Schools for advanced pilot training, and in addition schools for aircrew who were not pilots. These schools were to supply every year some 11,000 pilots, 6,300 observers, and 10,700 wireless-operator air gunners; they were controlled by the Governments of the Dominions in which they were set up, the United Kingdom at first supplying nearly all the aircraft. The scheme was officially proposed on September 26 in communications from Mr. Chamberlain to the Dominion Governments; agreement in principle was announced on October 10, and final terms embodying certain modifications were settled by the Riverdale agreement of 17 December, so named from the head of the British Mission to Ottawa which negotiated it.[1]

The Union of South Africa was not a party to the scheme; it planned to train its own Air Force on separate lines, but allowed pupils from the United Kingdom to share in its expanded organisation. Southern Rhodesia also contributed flying schools, aircraft for which, along with most of the instructors and staff, were provided by the Royal Air Force. Later on a number of Royal Air Force schools were transferred from the United Kingdom to Canada and South Africa; they were eventually incorporated in the Dominion schemes.

American help also was forthcoming: by the summer of 1941 a variety of schemes for providing basic training for British pilots in the United States had been agreed to and some were already producing results.

The basis of the expansion of the forces, so far as the manpower of the United Kingdom was concerned, was the wartime National Service Act, which superseded the Military Training Act of May 1939. The supply of militiamen who became liable to service under the latter act was exhausted by the beginning of December, and the first registration of those liable under the National Service Act commenced on October 21; those affected were young men of 20 and 21; they were expected to number 250,000, of whom 200,000 should be available for the armed forces. It was found that there was a preference in nearly half the cases for the Navy or Royal Air Force, while some two per cent claimed to be conscientious objectors.

From the outset it was often hard to decide whether a particular man, qualified as a 'tradesman', was the more urgently needed in the forces or in civil life. Such cases had no doubt often arisen in the past when the mass of the population was still agricultural, but the diffi-

---

[1] *House of Commons Debates* vol. 352, col. 182.

culty was accentuated when a mechanised national economy demanded a mechanised army: in 1914, so Mr. Hore-Belisha told the
House of Commons, nearly sixty per cent of the army were infantry-
men, whereas now the proportion had shrunk to twenty per cent.[1]
Mechanisation meant a far greater demand from the army for
skilled tradesmen, some of whom might well be 'key men' in
industry, essential for war production. Mechanical aptitude and
training were proportionately even more desirable for the Royal
Air Force. Attempts had been made before the outbreak of war to
forestall this competition by producing a 'schedule of reserved occupations', but, even so, large numbers of skilled men sorely needed
in industry had joined the forces, and the War Office were naturally
unwilling to release them. The Admiralty represented in the autumn
that work on their requirements was to some extent delayed by the
call-up of Army reservists and Territorials employed in peacetime
on skilled work, and the same cause was responsible for a temporary
slowing down of the rate of aircraft production. The matter was
referred to the 'Manpower Committee', of which Mr. W. S. Morrison
was chairman; they produced a compromise report recommending
the permanent release of some 2,900 tradesmen from the Territorial
Army and a continuation of the 'comb out'. The Cabinet approved
the report, but decided that on the other hand all Army reservists
must rejoin the Army within three months.

In these early months the problem touched skilled labour only,
but it was growing; there was as yet no fear of the whole of the
country's manpower being insufficient for the combined needs of
industry and the forces. Still less was any anxiety felt as to the supply
of women for war work. Not only were women playing an essential
role in the factories, but already there was a women's organisation
associated with each of the three Fighting Services, of which it was
soon to be recognised as an integral and indispensable part. In all
these enterprises the women of the United Kingdom were pioneers.

The various proposals for the expansion of the forces were jealously
scrutinised, as was natural and right, by the Treasury from the
financial point of view, especially those of them which incurred
expenditure in hard currency countries, as for instance on aircraft,
machine tools, manufactured steel or raw materials from America.
The Treasury had pointed out in September that we were already
spending more (£210 million monthly) and raising more money out
of revenue (£80 million) than we had in 1918, and that, though
prices were now much lower than then; further, that we had
started the war of 1914–18 with greater resources in dollar exchange,
actual and potential, than we had today. Our gold resources at the

[1] *ibid.* col. 344.

outbreak of the present war were down to £450 million; by requisitioning securities this amount could be raised to £700 million, out of which we owed £100 million to other countries in banking debts. Their conclusion was that to equip fifty-five divisions in addition to providing 2,550 aircraft monthly would bring our resources very low by the end of the second year.

In February the Cabinet had before them a survey by Lord Stamp of the national resources in relation to the war effort, prepared for the ministerial committee on economic policy. After considering the prospects for the first year of the war under the heads of foreign exchange and industrial labour, Lord Stamp came to the conclusion that the present objectives could not be attained within the time set and recommended 'a revision of general plans to dimensions consonant with particular limiting factors of equipment, material, shipping and the transferability of man-power'.

The Cabinet, as we have seen, adhered to the fifty-five division objective and in general accepted the recommendations of the Military Co-ordination Committee, which they had before them at the same session.[1]

At the second meeting of the Supreme War Council, on 22 September, M. Daladier brought up the question of Anglo-French collaboration with respect to the manufacture of armaments, and it was formally agreed 'that it was most important that the Allies should pool their resources as regards credit, foreign orders etc., and that, in particular, any approaches to the United States of America should be made in a way which did not separate the interests of the two countries'. For these purposes M. Dautry, the French Minister of Munitions, was to make contact with the British Minister of Supply, and M. Jean Monnet was to help in co-ordinating the activities of the various French and British missions; this led to the setting up in the United States of a joint Anglo-French Purchasing Board, under Mr. Arthur Purvis. At home the Prime Minister appointed an interdepartmental committee, with Sir Arthur Robinson as chairman, 'to examine and co-ordinate all Anglo-French activities connected with the supply and purchase of war material etc.', including a general supervision over the activities of missions in North America.[2]

The Air Training Plan was the most spectacular contribution

---

[1] Above, p. 33.

[2] For a full critical account of the difficulties encountered and surmounted on the side of production and supply and of the financing of purchases from abroad the reader must be referred to the volumes of the Civil History, and in particular, to those of Sir Keith Hancock and Mrs. Gowing, *British War Economy* (1949), M. M. Postan, *British War Production* (1952), and H. Duncan Hall, *North American Supply* (1955).

from the overseas countries of the British Commonwealth to the Allied cause in the early part of the war, but it was far from the only one. Even before war broke out the Canadian Government inquired what help from Canada would be the most acceptable. On 17 October the Secretary of State for the Dominions was able to report that, on the naval side, the six destroyers of the Royal Canadian Navy would work in close co-operation with the Royal Navy; the Royal Australian Navy had six cruisers, one flotilla leader and four destroyers in commission[1]; both Canada and Australia intended to fit out ships as armed merchant cruisers; the two cruisers of the New Zealand Division of the Royal Navy had been transferred to the operational control of the Admiralty; the Union of South Africa had fitted out trawlers for mine sweeping; even Eire, he said, while remaining neutral, had shown a willingness to help with regard to the activities of German submarines in her coastal waters.

In respect of land forces, Canada had announced her decision to organise a force available for overseas service, consisting in the first instance of one division, and to make preparations for despatching another as well as technical units. Australia was raising a special force of 20,000 men for active service, besides mobilising the militia in two batches of 40,000 each. New Zealand was proposing to raise one infantry division, South Africa to expand her special service battalion to two brigades. The Union Defence Force was only bound to serve in defence of the Union, and for some time it was uncertain how this phrase was to be interpreted geographically; but in December General Smuts was known to be ready to send troops as far north as Kenya.[2]

As regards the Air, apart from the Commonwealth Training Scheme, the Royal Canadian Air Force was expected to provide at least fifteen squadrons; Australia had offered six squadrons for service overseas and was forming a flying-boat squadron in Wales for service with Coastal Command; New Zealand had put the New Zealand flight at Marham at the disposal of the Royal Air Force.

Practical questions were discussed with the representatives of the Dominions during their visit to London in November. It was settled that the first Canadian division, destined eventually for France, would assemble in England in January. Canadian Military Headquarters were set up in London, and nearly the whole of the division, under Major-General A. G. L. McNaughton, arrived before the end of 1939.[3]

The relations between the Canadian force and the United

---

[1] In November all the Australian warships then in commission were placed at the disposal of the Admiralty.

[2] See below, p. 559.

[3] C. P. Stacey, *Six Years of War* in the *Official History of the Canadian Army in the Second World War*, Vol. I, ch. vi (Ottawa 1955).

Kingdom authorities were governed by the Visiting Forces Acts of 1933. These statutes drew a distinction between occasions when forces of the two nations were 'serving together' and when they were 'acting in combination'. In the former case, which covered periods of training in the United Kingdom, the Canadian force was independent of War Office control; in the latter, which applied to active operations, the forces concerned would pass under higher British command. The instructions which General McNaughton received before leaving Canada merely provided that 'all matters concerning military operations and discipline in the Field, being the direct responsibility of the Commander-in-Chief of the British Army in the theatre of operations, will be dealt with by the General Officer Commanding, Canadian Forces in the Field, through the Commander-in-Chief, whose powers in this regard are exercisable within the limitations laid down in the Visiting Forces Acts'.[1]

The Australian and New Zealand Governments had been advised by the United Kingdom not to venture their troops overseas while Japan's attitude was uncertain. But, in view of the encouraging opinions of the Chiefs of Staff and of the British Ambassador in Washington and of a reassuring undertaking by the United Kingdom Government, before the end of November first the New Zealand Government and then that of the Commonwealth announced its intention to send a division overseas.[2] The first contingents of these two divisions sailed during January for the Middle East, where they were to complete their training.[3]

The principles governing the control and administration of the Australian expeditionary force (the Second Australian Imperial Force) were agreed upon with the War Office, London, in March 1940. The force was to be a separate force under its own commander, who would be responsible to the Commonwealth Government and entitled to communicate with it direct; questions of policy regarding its employment should be decided by the two Governments in consultation, the commander having the right to make his own decision in an emergency. The force would however come under the operational control of the Commander-in-Chief of the theatre in which it was serving.[4]

---

[1] *ibid.* p. 255.

[2] See p. 324 below: also Gavin Long, *To Benghazi* p. 64, and Paul Hasluck, *The Government and the People* pp. 167–170, both in the series *Australia in the War of 1939–1945* (Canberra 1952).

[3] The second brigade group from New Zealand came to the United Kingdom in June 1940; it moved to the Middle East in March 1941.

[4] The 'Charter' issued by the Commonwealth Government to General Blamey on these lines is printed in Long, *op. cit.* p. 101. The similar New Zealand charter to General Freyberg, dated 5 January 1940, is in the *Official History of New Zealand in the Second World War* (Wellington 1949), *Documents, Vol. I.*

The Dominions, even more than the United Kingdom, suffered from a shortage of equipment, and Britain was called upon to supply items of which she had no surplus from her own needs. The scheme of the Land Forces Committee for fifty-five divisions envisaged, as we have seen, fourteen from the Dominions; these would have to be equipped in the main by the United Kingdom, and it would be long before this could be done.

The same expansion scheme included four divisions from India. The equivalent of one Indian division had already been sent or promised, and the Government of India had offered early in September to raise two additional brigade groups for service in Burma and perhaps for the protection of the Middle-Eastern oilfields. The Government of India had moreover placed five escort vessels of the Royal Indian Navy at the disposal of the Commander-in-Chief, East Indies, and they offered to increase the output of Indian munition factories to the maximum. The Rulers of Indian States had gone further and had placed all their resources at the disposal of the British Government, and independent Nepal offered eight battalions for garrison duty in India.

The Cabinet considered a proposal to bring back British units from India, as had been done in the earlier war, and replace them by Territorial units from home, but preferred a gradual interchange of individuals between units at home and in India: the number of British troops in India in 1914 had been much greater than now, and the present question was really one of equipment.

To trace the development of British policy for India and of events in the sub-continent, except in so far as they bore on the prosecution of the war, falls outside the scope of this history. It may be remarked on the one hand that the possibility of civil disobedience on a large scale was recognised as a danger threatening the war effort; on the other hand that Indian volunteers for the fighting Services, up to the limit of the available equipment, continued to come forward.

E

CHAPTER III

THE GERMAN WAR MACHINE.
THE POLISH CAMPAIGN.
THE NEAR EAST

VOLUME I will show how in the course of the nineteen-thirties the German people yielded themselves to the allurements and menaces of the National-Socialist party; how Hitler and his associates succeeded, by propaganda and terror, in reshaping the German State and its institutions in conformity with the party's creed and in submitting them to its discipline; and how the will of the Führer was accepted as the supreme embodiment of the German ideal and of the sovereignty of the German people. By the Enabling Act of 24 March 1934 the two Chambers of the Weimar Republic with the necessary constitutional majority virtually destroyed the constitution and transferred legislative authority to the Chancellor and his Ministers, which soon came to mean the Führer alone. By successive stages between 1933 and 1935 the limitations set by a feeble federalism to the powers of the central Government of the Reich were swept away. Meanwhile the National-Socialist party was declared the only political party in Germany, and in November 1933 a controlled general election returned a parliament representing that party alone. After the death of President Hindenburg in August 1934 Hitler became undisputed head of the Reich and supreme commander of its armed forces; in February 1938 he assumed direct control of them, making himself at the same time his own Minister of War.

The dual organisation of the German State and the Nazi Party was highly complicated and subject to frequent changes of detail. But these minutiae were of no importance as concerned the higher direction of the war. There was a Cabinet of the Reich, but it never met during the war; there was a small Ministerial Council for National Defence, appointed at the outbreak of war, which passed a number of legislative decrees, but this body abstained from military and from major questions and held its last meeting in December 1939, after which, like the Cabinet of the Reich, it legislated only by the circulation of proposals in writing. More important than this council was its chairman, Field-Marshal Hermann Göring, Hitler's designated successor, who, apart from his military role, held several important civil posts, including that of Commissioner of the Four Years Plan for economic development. Under the party's 'Leader principle' the man was preferred to the committee, and Hitler's tendency was to detail new men to special tasks without regard for the existing organisation. Many of the numerous Ministries, moreover, were grouped under the permanent control of new-fangled officials called Plenipotentiaries-General. The initiation of German policy, however, and the central direction of the war were the responsibility of Hitler alone, influenced by such of his advisers or entourage as were at the time in favour and enjoyed his confidence. It was not realised in some countries during the war how completely Hitler dominated his subordinates, both civil and military.

As there was nothing in Germany corresponding to the British War Cabinet, so there was no parallel to the British Chiefs of Staff Committee. Its nearest equivalent would at first sight appear to be the *Oberkommando der Wehrmacht (OKW)*, the High Command of the Defence Force, or of the Armed Forces, with its chief, Colonel-General Wilhelm Keitel, reporting direct to the Führer. This body was intended to co-ordinate the activities of the three fighting Services, the civil administration and the production authorities; but it became in effect, and progressively, the military headquarters of the Führer, staffed by military advisers who were picked rather for their personal qualities than in accordance with any rational scheme of inter-Service teamwork. As one of its leading members, General Warlimont, remarked later, 'the development of an organisation devised to exercise uniform powers of command over the entire *Wehrmacht* by means of the *OKW* staff had been arrested in its initial stage. This organisation was, in consequence, vastly inferior to the General Staffs of the Services. The demarcation of virtually all powers in the fields of command and administration was very hazy, with the result that neither the staff of *OKW* nor any one of the High Commands of the Services had a clear understanding of its role.' *OKW* was in short a mixture of War Ministry, Combined General Staff, and personal headquarters of Hitler as Commander-in-Chief, Armed Forces. One of its weaknesses was that though the members of the staff were drawn from the three Services they had no status or responsibility in their respective Ministries or Departments, were not intended to represent them and were not in intimate touch with them.

The most important section of *OKW* was the Operations Staff under General Alfred Jodl, a much abler man than Keitel and probably possessed of greater influence with Hitler. There was also a staff, under General Georg Thomas, concerned with munitions and economic questions. Both Thomas and Admiral Canaris, the head of Counter-espionage Intelligence, were, as is now known, frankly disloyal to the regime to the extent of plotting its downfall; but their treasonable activities had, at this time at any rate, little effect on the conduct of the war.[1]

The Supreme or High Commands of the Army, Navy and Air Force, directly responsible to the Führer and always jealous of *OKW*, were in theory coequal but in fact conceded pre-eminence to the Army.[2] Both in numbers and in rank the Army representatives on the staff of *OKW* far surpassed those of the other Services. As between these, Göring's personal popularity and the driving force which he still possessed in the early years of the war assured a certain prestige and independence to the Luftwaffe, whereas the importance of the Navy in the event of an early war with the Western Powers was consistently underrated, in spite of the high regard which Hitler felt for Grand Admiral Raeder. This Service profited however from the fact that the Führer did not pretend to knowledge of naval affairs and interfered only in times of stress when reverses at sea threatened German prestige.

After the outbreak of war *OKW* and the High Commands of the Services each split into advanced and rear echelons, and the main decisions of policy were taken at the Führer's headquarters; daily discussions were held at which the Commanders-in-Chief and others were summoned to attend as required. When operations on a grand scale were in view, the practice was for Hitler to communicate his broad plan, orally or in writing, to the Service staffs, who then, working in liaison with one another, would produce draft orders. These, as approved or modified by the Führer, would subsequently be incorporated in general *OKW* Directives laying down his intentions.[3] There was, however, no joint and continuous consideration of problems by the responsible heads of the three staffs. It was in accordance with Hitler's suspicious, egotistical character to favour separate consultations and individual interventions, and these proclivities of his, as the war went on, led to growing confusion of function and inconsistency of decision.

The German Army, the *Heer*, of 1939, now as always the mirror of the nation, reflected the political and social changes which had transformed Germany in the last twenty-five years. The army which swept through Belgium into France in August 1914 was the creation of Roon and Moltke; it preened itself in the prestige of three victorious wars and more than forty years of unquestioned pre-eminence; in equipment, in discipline and in training it seemed to

---

[1] See J. W. Wheeler-Bennett, *The Nemesis of Power* (1953) p. 457.

[2] The three commands are regularly referred to as *OKH*, *OKM*, and *OKL*, standing for *Oberkommando des Heeres, der Marine*, and *der Luftwaffe* respectively.

[3] The originals of most of these Directives, signed by Hitler or by Keitel on his behalf, are now (1955) in Allied possession. Most of them have been made public; they are here referred to as *F.D.*, the American version being used: *Führer Directives and other top-level Directives of the German Armed Forces, 1939–1941* (1948).

have achieved perfection. The army of the years between the wars, though its foundations had been skilfully laid in the twenties by von Seeckt, remained to outward appearance a mere token force of 100,000 men until it rose above ground in 1935, when Hitler threw off the shackles of Versailles and reintroduced conscription.

By 1 September 1939 the Germans were able to mobilise, besides fortress and frontier units, 105 divisions—6 panzer or armoured, 4 'light', 4 motorised, 3 mountain, and the remaining 88 infantry. Of these, the original formations of the Regular army (referred to as the 'first wave'), namely all the mechanised, the three mountain, and thirty-five of the infantry divisions, were fully trained and of high quality. A second wave of eighteen[1] infantry divisions, consisting of young reservists, provided a solid backing for the Regular divisions, to be relied upon for large-scale operations in both attack and defence. The remaining formations, by reason of their age or inadequate training, were regarded as suitable for positional warfare only.

The Army was short in non-commissioned officers and in officers of the rank of Captain and Major, but its weapons were new and good and so, as its enemies found to their discomfiture, were its tactics. As regards discipline and fighting spirit, if the old semi-feudal loyalty to the head of the State no longer permeated all members of the Officer Corps, many of the younger men were animated by a fanatical resolve to avenge the humiliations of the recent past and demonstrate the conquering qualities of the resurgent German *Volk*. Plots against Hitler were afoot among certain of the Army chiefs in the autumn of 1938, and some of them might still feel distrust of his extravagances;[2] but it could hardly be doubted that on the field of battle all ranks of the German army would stand true to the Supreme Commander to whom they had sworn a personal allegiance.

Neither the Commander-in-Chief of the Army, Colonel-General Walther von Brauchitsch, nor his Chief of the General Staff, General of Artillery Franz Halder, was sympathetic to Nazism: Hitler is reported to have said that he had a conservative army, a National-Socialist Luftwaffe and an imperial navy.

The Navy certainly, in the names of such ships as the *Bismarck*, *Tirpitz*, *Hipper* and *von Scheer*, recalled the most recent as well as the more successful days of the Second Reich, and men like Grand Admiral Raeder, the Commander-in-Chief, and Langsdorff, the Captain of the *Admiral Graf Spee*, were officers of the old school; it is probable that owing to the influence of Raeder, who since 1928 had been in control of the Navy, this Service was less impregnated with

---

[1] Originally sixteen.
[2] See Wheeler-Bennett, *Nemesis of Power* pt. iii, ch. iii.

politics than the other two, but this does not mean that it was in any way lacking in loyalty to the Third Reich. Hitler had intended to create a powerful navy. In the winter of 1938–39 an elaborate programme (known as 'Z' programme) for a strong surface fleet had been approved for completion by 1944 and the following years. It would have then constituted a most formidable threat to the Royal Navy, but Hitler's decision to precipitate war in 1939 diverted to the construction of U-boats such resources as could be spared for naval shipbuilding.[1]

The Luftwaffe, like the Army, owed its resurrection in its earliest stages to the foresight and guile of General von Seeckt. In the thirties, however, it was built up mainly through the energies of two former members of the imperial Flying Corps, Erhard Milch and his superior, Hermann Göring. In March 1935, when the Luftwaffe came into the open as an independent branch of the Armed Forces, Göring became its Commander-in-Chief and Milch his Chief of Staff. No step was spared to make Germany air-minded and air-proud, and the Luftwaffe was wholeheartedly devoted to the Nazi regime.

Although the German Air Force was an independent Service and although independent strategic missions were not ruled out, its main function, as was perhaps natural in Germany, was to support the Army. No plan existed for dealing a 'knock-out blow' to Britain. Air policy was no doubt coloured by the general assumption that Germany's wars would be short and decisive. Unlike their Army colleagues, Air officers had had recent experience of operations; the Spanish Civil War had demonstrated the possibilities of close-support tactics, especially by dive-bombers, and the occupations of Austria and Czechoslovakia had shown that use might be made of aircraft in conveying troops.

While the statesmen of the Allied Powers and their advisers set themselves to speed up preparations for a three years war, Germany was reaping the fruits of premeditated aggression.

Hitler's guiding ideas, one of the chief of which was the need of eastern expansion, are clearly set out in *Mein Kampf*, but it is usual to date his decision to force the issue within a definite time by the solemn and secret pronouncement which he made to a select group of high officials on 5 November 1937.[2] The German people of 85 millions, he declared, needed more living space in Europe, and, since

---

[1] For the development of the re-born German Navy see Roskill, *The War at Sea* I 51 ff. and Appendix G giving the list of the ships in commission at the outbreak of war.

[2] Nuremberg document 386-PS, *Trial of the Major War Criminals before the International Military Tribunal, Nuremberg, 14 November 1945–1 October 1946* (Nuremberg 1947). This source is henceforward referred to as *N.D.*

he was convinced that the 'German question' could be solved only by force, it was his irrevocable decision to solve it so not later than 1943–45; possibly earlier, if France were either paralysed by an internal crisis or engaged in war with Italy. It was clear that in the first instance he intended to attack and annex Austria and Czechoslovakia; he is not reported as having given any specific indication of what further living space he would seek to conquer; he was concerned with improving his position for a settlement with the West.

By the end of March 1939 both Austria and Czechoslovakia had been disposed of; on the other hand Great Britain and France had just given their guarantee to Poland and the British decision to double the Territorial Army had been announced. In spite of this, or perhaps in response to what he may have considered as acts of defiance, Hitler early in April issued directives to the armed forces with regard to three eventualities: the defence of the frontiers against attack from east or west; the elimination of Poland; and a surprise occupation of Danzig.[1] Plans against Poland (Operation 'White') must allow for their execution at any date from 1 September 1939. Should it prove necessary, owing to a threatening attitude on Poland's part, to 'settle the account for good', the aim would be to smash the Polish armed forces and 'create in the East a situation corresponding to the requirements of Germany's defence'.

On May 23 he announced at another conference to his chief subordinates his decision to attack Poland at the first suitable opportunity, mentioning among his reasons the backwardness of British rearmament.[2] Poland would always take the side of Germany's enemies and exploit any chances of doing her harm. Danzig was not the point at issue at all; it was a question of expanding Germany's living space in the East. Hitler realised that this time it would be war. Poland must therefore be isolated, so as to avoid a conflict with England and France at the same time. Nevertheless it might prove impossible to avoid such a war, and he expressed his views as to the form a war against England would take. It would be a life-and-death struggle. England would need to bring the war as near to the Ruhr basin as possible, since the possession of this region would determine the duration of Germany's resistance. Germany on the other hand must defeat England by cutting off her food supply. Though the destruction of the British fleet by a surprise attack would settle matters, this could not be counted on and preparations must be made for a long war. From the point of view of both defence and offence Germany would be forced to occupy Holland and Belgium; declarations of neutrality must be ignored. 'The Army', said the Führer,

---

[1] *F.D.*; Directives of April 3, 11.
[2] *N.D.*, 79–L.

'will have to hold positions essential to the Navy and Air Force. If Holland and Belgium are successfully occupied and held, and if France is also defeated, the fundamental conditions for a successful war against England will have been secured. England can then be blockaded from Western France at close quarters by the Air Force, while the Navy with its submarines can extend the range of the blockade.' It is remarkable how accurately Hitler foretold the situation that was to arise in the summer of 1940; there was no suggestion, however, of invading the British Isles.

Hitler continued to hope, and intermittently to believe, that the Western Powers would not when it came to the point declare war on Germany should she attack Poland. By the middle of August, as he told Count Ciano, the Italian Foreign Minister, his mind was made up to begin operations against Poland by the end of the month at latest; they must be completed by October 15.[1] At this time the attitude of the Soviet Union was not clear, but from May onwards the prospect of improved relations with Russia must have encouraged the hope that an invasion of Poland would not necessarily mean war with Russia. This hope was more than realised by Hitler's diplomatic master-stroke in concluding a pact of non-aggression with the Soviet Union on August 23. On the 21st he could feel assured that the pact would be signed, and next day he explained to his Commanders-in-Chief in long harangues the personal and political factors which had influenced him in forcing a conflict with Poland now. He had earlier intended to turn first against the West 'in a few years', but Poland would always be hostile and he had decided to settle with her at once while circumstances were favourable—while he himself, Mussolini and Franco were in control and while there was 'no outstanding personality in England or France'. The political and military position, too, of both Britain and France had worsened and neither country was ready for war. 'There is no actual rearmament in England, just propaganda.' The construction programme of the British Navy was behindhand; little had been done on land; England was still vulnerable from the air, but this could change in two to three years. The difficulties the British had made about giving Poland a loan for rearmament showed that they did not really want to support her. France too, with her declining birthrate, did not desire war and had done little in the way of rearmament. Germany need not fear a blockade; the east would supply grain, cattle, coal, lead, zinc. In the Balkans there was an equilibrium of power favourable to her. And now, with Russia squared, 'Poland is in the position

---

[1] *N.D.* 1871–PS; *Nazi Conspiracy and Aggression* (Washington 1946) VIII 516, 77–TC; *Ciano's Diplomatic Papers*, ed. M. Muggeridge (1948) pp. 297–304; *The Ciano Diaries 1939–43*, ed. H. Gibson (New York 1945), 11–13 Aug. 1939.

in which I wanted her'. Hitler had made the political preparations
and 'the way is open for the soldier'.[1]

Next day, the 23rd, the time for the advance into Poland was set
for the morning of August 26, but it was postponed on the 25th, after
receipt of news of the signing of the Anglo-Polish treaty and of a
message from Mussolini that Italy was not ready for war. The time
was finally fixed, for the following morning, on the 31st, on which day
Hitler issued his first 'Directive for the Conduct of the War'.[2]

The outlines of the Polish plan of campaign to meet an attack by
Germany had been made known to the British Chiefs of Staff in the
summer, after a British delegation representing the three Services had
discussed matters with the Polish military authorities in Warsaw at
the end of May. It had not changed when General Ironside paid a
visit to Poland two months later. The Poles were convinced that in
the impending war Germany would throw her whole weight against
their country, acting on the defensive elsewhere, and they were
resigned to heavy losses and the abandonment of much territory.
They believed that even so they could always maintain a front some-
where in Poland and that the Germans would eventually succumb to
the forces of France and Great Britain. The Poles were most unwilling
to have Russian troops in Poland, or even to enter into direct relations with Russia in peacetime; they were less averse to the acceptance of Russian air help, and they hoped to be supplied with Russian
munitions in time of war, as well as with the raw material they
already received.

The Poles expected some 61 Active and Reserve and 16 *Landwehr*
German divisions to be disposed against them. Their own land forces
consisted of 30 Active and 10 Reserve divisions, with 11 horsed
cavalry brigades and one armoured brigade. They were short of
heavy artillery and tanks, and above all weak in the air: their air
force consisted mainly of medium range bombers, intended for army
co-operation work. Fighters, and they of poor quality, composed only
30 per cent of the whole. The Poles did not envisage a prolonged
defence of the huge salient formed by their western frontier; they
were prepared to be driven back within a month to a shorter line, of
rivers and lakes, running roughly north and south 100 miles west of
Warsaw, but including Bromberg (Bydgoszez) in the north and
Katowice in the south.[3] Marshal Smigly-Rydz, the Commander-in-
Chief, intended to keep under his own control near Warsaw a central

---

[1] *Nazi-Soviet Relations 1939–1941* (Washington 1948) p. 69: *N.D.* 798–PS; cf. *N.D.*
1014–PS.
[2] *F.D.* p. 49. See L. B. Namier, *Diplomatic Prelude* (1948) 303, 329; *The Ciano Diaries.*
[3] See Map 1.

reserve of ten divisions, which would be available for a counter-offensive.

The British delegation reported that the Polish army was believed to have increased in efficiency of late, and they testified to the fine spirit of both army and people. They were struck, however, by the prevalence of a lighthearted optimism which undervalued the German strength. The real weakness of the Polish army, apart from inferior numbers, was the shortage of equipment, which would not suffice to arm all the trained men, and the lack of industrial resources. The Poles had reserves for forty divisions for three months but no longer, and in spite of immense efforts made in the last two or three years the factories could expect to cover only part of the expected war wastage. Accordingly without Allied help Poland would probably be out of the war in six months at longest.

If the Polish army was to be kept in the field, help would be required in some or all of the following forms: the immediate provision of war material, especially guns and fighter aircraft; the organisation of the supply of munitions of war and raw material from outside, which really meant from Russia; and the granting of credits or loans. The Poles were informed of the difficulty of providing direct British military help, either by sea or by air, in the absence of any secure naval base in the Baltic or of British ground staffs in Poland. In June a Polish technical and financial mission came to England, but negotiations intended to secure supplies of money and materials did not run smoothly. Aircraft which were eventually ordered and packed never reached Poland at all. The possibility of land assistance in the form of operations against the western frontier of Germany was not discussed with the Poles by the British delegation. It had, however, been discussed earlier between British and French staffs in London; it was understood that there could be no question of hurried attack on the Siegfried Line or '*Westwall*'—the continuous defence with which the Germans were fortifying their western frontier. Somewhat later, in May, the matter was discussed between General Gamelin and the Polish War Minister in Paris; Gamelin undertook that, as soon as the main German attack gathered force against Poland, France would open an offensive against Germany with '*les gros de ses forces*' starting on the fifteenth day after the first day of mobilisation. The General states in his book that he made it clear to M. Kasprzyski that '*les gros*' (the main bodies) was a different matter from '*le gros*' (the bulk) and that an assault on the Siegfried Line was not promised. It appears also that the entry into force of the military convention was made dependent on the signature of the political agreement then in the course of preparation—which in fact was never signed until after the war had broken out.[1]

---

[1] See Gamelin II 410–429; Namier, *op. cit.* p. 246.

The British authorities were informed of the general trend of these conversations and of the impression received by our Military Attaché in Paris that 'the Poles were a little disappointed that the French were not prepared to go bald-headed for the Germans'. Indeed it was doubtful whether the Allied armies in the west would or could do much more than contain the lowest number of German divisions required to man the Siegfried Line and the rest of the western frontier —a number which the Poles put at 25–28 divisions and their allies at 30–35.[1]

The British Chiefs of Staff had given clear warning in July to the Committee of Imperial Defence that the fate of Poland must depend on the ultimate outcome of the war, and that this would depend on the Allies' ability to defeat Germany in the long run, not to relieve pressure on Poland at the outset. Such must be the over-riding consideration in our choice of action, and indeed it seems to have been accepted, at least in theory, by the Poles, however much they hoped for some more effective immediate help. Nevertheless, granted that there was little the British could do to help Poland by sea or land, it did not follow that they could not give her at least indirect aid in the air, and the Chiefs of Staff had proceeded to consider possible ways of doing so. This raised the whole question of bombing policy, and the decision now taken governed Allied policy throughout the following winter and spring.

The Chiefs of Staff submitted to the Committee of Imperial Defence four possible 'broad courses of action' from which to choose, with their respective advantages and disadvantages. All four were based on the assumption that all measures of economic pressure on Germany would immediately be enforced. The first course was 'not to initiate any offensive action in the air, except against warships at sea'. The second was 'to initiate air action against purely "military" objectives in the narrowest sense of the word—e.g. the German Fleet and its bases, air force units and establishments, and the German Army on the Western Front'. The third course was 'to extend our air action to cover objectives which, while as closely related as possible to purely military establishments, will have a more important effect in reducing the enemy's capacity to carry on the war. In this category the most suitable objectives appear to be stocks of oil fuel and plant for manufacturing synthetic oil.' The fourth course was 'to "take the gloves off" from the outset, and attack those objectives best calculated to reduce the enemy's war effort, irrespective of whether or not such action will cause heavy loss of life to enemy civilians'. The Chiefs of Staffs' arguments showed that it would be difficult to afford any serious relief to the Poles without, on the one hand, drawing retaliation in more dangerous degree on the Allies'

---

[1] For actual figures see page 60 below.

own cities and industries and, on the other, risking the alienation of neutral opinion.

The Committee of Imperial Defence approved this report as a basis for discussion with the French and with the Poles, whom it was thought important to deter from any 'impetuous action' which might give the Germans an excuse for indiscriminate retaliation. The French were consulted, and replied that they intended to confine themselves to objectives as defined in Class B in the memorandum of the United Kingdom delegation—namely purely 'military' objectives in the narrowest sense of the word. It was agreed that the other allies should be asked to adopt a common policy, and that as an immediate step Poland should be informed of the restrictions accepted by the French. The fact was that both the French and British Governments were conscious of their inferiority to Germany in the air and most unwilling to provoke indiscriminate bombing.

The consequent Declaration of the two Governments made mention of President Roosevelt's appeal and dealt also with maritime warfare and other points included in humanitarian conventions.[1]

Throughout her history Poland's long and exposed frontiers have invited invasion; the German subjugation of Czechoslovakia rendered Poland's position even more hopeless stategically, while the unusual drought of the summer of 1939 was a godsend to the German tanks. The first weeks of September showed that in every respect, except the courage of her inhabitants, she was utterly unprepared for war with Germany.

The German plan was to take full advantage of Poland's geographical weakness and overwhelm her forces by a double envelopment. Two Groups of Armies, the southern commanded by Colonel-General von Rundstedt, the northern by Colonel-General von Bock, based respectively on Silesia and Slovakia and on Pomerania and East Prussia, were to launch attacks converging on Warsaw or a little east of the capital; they would trap and crush the Polish armies before they could retreat behind the line of the rivers San, Vistula and Narew, which would mean entering the region claimed by Russia as her sphere of influence.[2] The plan allowed for a second, outer envelopment, further east, of such Polish armies as could escape the jaws of the inner trap. The Germans put into the field a total of fifty-four divisions at the outset of the campaign, including all their armoured, light, motorised and mountain divisions and about two-thirds of their 'first wave' infantry; these were reinforced or replaced

---

[1] This document is printed in Appendix I(a).
[2] See Secret Additional Protocol of 23 August, *Nazi-Soviet Relations* p. 78, and Map 1.

by five further divisions in the course of the next three weeks. The land forces were supported by some 1,600 aircraft, disposed in two fleets, south and north, under the command of Generals Loehr and Kesselring.

The plan was almost completely successful. The Poles, far inferior in numbers and equipment and caught with ten of their forty divisions not yet mobilised, were overwhelmed by the momentum of the German onrush, and particularly by the skilful use of air power and armour. The German bombers first paralysed the Polish air force by destroying its airfields and its factories, then broke up communications and headquarters and afforded efficient close support to the advancing armies. The armoured formations, pushing ahead of the infantry, drove through and far in rear of the Polish armies, upsetting their enemy's calculations and nerves and not troubling about their own flanks. The Polish high command, having failed to withdraw the divisions holding the Posznan (Posen) salient in time, and having failed also to hold the Narew–Vistula–San line or any other, decided on September 14 as a desperate measure to withdraw to the south-eastern corner of Poland, behind the Dniester and Stryj rivers, in order to keep open their only remaining line of communication, through Roumania. The German columns had in places exhausted their supplies of fuel and the Poles had obtained one or two minor successes, when the Soviet forces destroyed their neighbours' last hope of resistance by invading their territory with some twenty divisions on the morning of September 17; the Russians had been surprised, it seems, by the speed of the German advance.[1] The following night the Polish Government and Commander-in-Chief crossed the frontier into Roumania and organised resistance was at an end, though Warsaw did not surrender until September 27. On the night of the 28th the German and Soviet Governments signed a treaty agreeing on the boundary between their respective spheres of influence, and Poland was once again partitioned.[2]

During the campaign Marshal Smigly-Rydz had made appeals, obviously futile as things turned out, for the despatch of Allied war material to replace his losses; he also urged the Allies to sharpen their bombing policy, but General Gamelin was strongly against provoking retaliation in the west until the French and British armies had completed their concentration. Moreover, it was the settled policy of the British Air Ministry not to fritter away our own bomber strength on minor objectives, but to reserve it until it could undertake projects which might have a decisive effect on the war.

If any consolation was to be found in the events of this disastrous

---

[1] *Nazi-Soviet Relations* p. 91.
[2] *ibid.* p. 105.

month, it was something that three Polish destroyers and two submarines had escaped to join the Royal Navy, and that some at least
of the gallant Polish soldiers, sailors and airmen would be able to
continue to fight from Allied soil; also that the Russian advance had
deprived the Germans of the East Galician oilfield.

The German losses were small and there was plenty of time to
replace them. At a comparatively trifling cost the Germans had re-
established the prestige of their country as a great military Power,
had justified confidence in their new weapons and tactics, had freed
themselves for the present from the nightmare of a war on two fronts
and had demonstrated the worthlessness of an Allied guarantee. On
the other hand they had now acquired a much more formidable
neighbour in Russia, and Hitler's agreement with the Soviet Government to remove the long-established German population from the
Baltic lands shocked some patriotic Germans.[1] How far the natural
Nazi exultation at the success of their first war was generally shared
by the German people is doubtful.

It now seems clear that German confidence was not shaken by the
propaganda dropped over Germany by British bombers on various
occasions, from the first night of the war onwards. Such a measure
had been advocated by the Air Ministry in September 1938 and it
appealed to those Ministers who believed that a substantial section
of the German people might be induced to disown Hitler. The
Cabinet thought that the leaflets would have an important effect on
German public opinion, by reason both of their contents and of the
defiance which they represented to Germany's air defences, and, in
spite of advice from neutral and other sources that they diminished
rather than exalted British prestige, adhered to the opinion that they
were useful and should be continued. Their chief value was probably
the practice they gave to Bomber Command in navigating over
Germany at night.

It would seem that some opponents of Nazism in Germany were in
fact less interested in the leaflets than in the question why the Allies
did not seize the opportunity of the bulk of the German army being
engaged in Poland to attack in the west.[2] The Polish campaign was
in fact over before the events in the west could affect its course, nor
were Gamelin's plans much affected by events in the east. The
Cabinet were not sure what these plans were, and the new Chief of
the Imperial General Staff, General Ironside, and Air Chief Marshal
Newall, the Chief of the Air Staff, had flown over on September 4 to

---

[1] See *The von Hassell Diaries* (1948) p. 72.
[2] See H. B. Gisevius, '*To the Bitter End*' (1948) p. 375.

discover them, and to concert with the French the best means of relieving the pressure on Poland. They reported next day that Gamelin intended, after his armies had completed their concentration, to open a limited offensive with this object between the Rhine and the Moselle; the first phase would be to move forward up to the Siegfried Line; he would then, from the 17th onwards, proceed to 'lean against it' to test its strength. It was possible that a breakthrough might be achieved, but Gamelin had no intention of risking precious divisions in a precipitate assault on so strongly fortified a position. The Cabinet took note of Gamelin's plan and agreed that British bombers might be used to exploit any successes against the Siegfried Line.[1]

The Siegfried Line included a formidable concrete tank obstacle covered by a series of pill-boxes. It was organised in considerable depth, and was understood by the French to have been completed throughout its length between the Rhine and Trèves (Trier), while work was continuing further north.[2] The French Intelligence allowed for forty German divisions on the Western front, and thought that some twenty might soon be holding the Rhine–Moselle sector.[3] We now know that there were 33 German divisions in the west, including all the first-wave divisions not in Poland, besides frontier troops, on September 3, when France declared war, and that the total had risen to 46 or 47 divisions by September 21, when the Polish campaign was virtually over.

On 11 September the Cabinet were told that the French had established a line of infantry close up to the Siegfried Line, but the speed of the German advance in Poland spared General Gamelin the necessity of deciding whether or not the nature of the enemy's resistance justified a serious attack upon it. The opportunity of meeting only weak holding forces passed, and the General tells us that on September 21 he gave up any further thoughts of an offensive. By the end of the month he was convinced that the Germans were moving their fighting troops westwards, and he ordered that the armies which had advanced into enemy territory should retire to their original positions, leaving only a light screen.[4]

The Germans had in fact begun to replace good by inferior troops in the east in mid-September; by November 7 there were only eleven divisions on that front, all of low category. On October 16 and 17 a minor German attack between the Rhine and the Moselle drove in

---

[1] General Gamelin refers to these conversations in *Servir* III (1947) 47–50.

[2] Hitler told Ciano on August 12 that the Siegfried Line had now been completed, running 'from the Swiss frontier to the point where the Rhine enters Dutch territory'. *Ciano Diplomatic Papers* p. 299. See Map 6.

[3] Gamelin, *Servir* III 34.

[4] *ibid.* pp. 71, 88.

the French advanced troops, which withdrew without serious fighting to the positions covering the Maginot forts. This was the end of operations on the Western front, except for raids and patrolling, until May 1940.

Meanwhile the Germans were continuing to transfer the main weight of their forces to the west, or giving them further training at home; 'light' divisions were being converted into armoured, and new divisions created, including three of the S.S. (*Schutzstaffel*) divisions especially connected with the National-Socialist party. By 4 December 1939 the German field army numbered 116 divisions with two motorised infantry regiments, and over 80 of these were included in the Army Groups now concentrated in the Western theatre.

Official indications of German policy after the conquest of Poland were awaited with interest, and 'some attractive peace proposal' was expected. No such proposal was to be found in the speech delivered by the Führer at Danzig on 19 September. Poland, he said, would never rise again in the form given her by the Versailles treaty. Germany had no war aims against France and Great Britain. If they continued to fight, they were the warmongers. Great Britain had already begun war at sea against women and children. Let them beware. Germany had a weapon by which she could not be attacked. If she used it, as very soon she might, it was to be hoped that people would not then suddenly bethink themselves of 'humanity'.[1] On September 28, having agreed on the boundary partitioning 'the former Polish State', the German and Soviet Governments issued a declaration of their desire to put an end to the war; if they failed, France and Great Britain would be clearly responsible for its continuance, and the eastern Powers would consult with regard to the necessary measures.[2]

Hitler's peace offer was not long delayed. Rendering account to the Reichstag on October 6 he restated Germany's desire to live at peace with the rest of the world. She had no demands on France. From Great Britain she did indeed demand the restoration of her colonies, but not by way of ultimatum. She proposed negotiation for a settlement of economic problems, for a reduction of armaments and for the further humanising of war. But if Churchill and his friends wanted a war which would reduce Europe to ruins, they should have it.[3]

---

[1] The German text of the speech has no reference to a 'secret weapon', as it was reported in the British Press. What Hitler meant by the weapon which could not be used against Germany can only be guessed; German air power seems the most plausible suggestion, but the magnetic mine is a possibility.

[2] *Nazi-Soviet Relations* pp. 105, 108.

[3] *The Times* 7 Oct. 1939.

F

In vain the net is spread in the sight of any bird. Austria, Czecho-slovakia, Memel, Poland were too visible reminders of Hitler's method. The Cabinet agreed, however, that the speech needed a serious answer. The Prime Minister had felt for some time that Hitler's 'most formidable tactic would be a skilfully timed, carefully planned attack' on the home front. He had feared a peace offensive more than an air raid. 'One can see already', he wrote on September 23, 'how this war twilight is trying people's nerves.' In three days of the first week of October he received not far short of nineteen hundred letters which said 'stop the war' in one form or another. But Hitler's actual proposals had justified his expectation that they would be plainly unacceptable.[1]

Mr. Chamberlain delayed his reply until October 12, after views had been exchanged with the Dominions and the French. Some skill was required in reconciling their respective standpoints since the Dominion Governments felt strongly that a purely negative answer would be a mistake; they would have liked a statement of our war aims with a hint of willingness to invite neutral powers to the eventual peace conference. The Cabinet, who still thought it possible to divide the German Government and people, wished to take account of the point of view of the average German. The reply should end on a note of inquiry rather than of flat rejection. But the final version, stiffened by the knowledge that Hitler's speech had had a bad press in neutral countries, emphasised the impossibility of trusting the German word unless backed by actions and guarantees.

Hitler did not wait long for a favourable answer. It is unlikely that he expected one, and perhaps he did not desire one. He had already on September 27 instructed his Service chiefs to prepare plans for an attack in the west with the shortest possible delay, and there are indications that his intention was to launch it.[2] The 'peace offer' may have been meant merely to justify in the eyes of his own people a continuation of the war against an impenitent and inveterate enemy. At any rate on October 9 Hitler issued a Directive announcing that, if it should become apparent in the near future that Britain and, under her influence, France also were unwilling to end the war, he was determined to go over to the offensive without much delay. On the same day he issued for the personal information of the three Commanders-in-Chief and the Chief of Staff of *OKW* a lengthy memorandum setting forth the ideas and arguments which had led to the issue of the Directive.[3] The aim of Germany's enemies was to

---

[1] Private letters, some quoted by Feiling, *Life of Neville Chamberlain* p. 424.

[2] There are three contemporary accounts of Hitler's conference with his Service chiefs on September 27: two are in Halder's *Notes on Führer and General Staff Conferences, 27 September to 16 October 1942*; the third consists of extracts from the *OKW* Operations Staff war diary. See also Wheeler-Bennett pp. 463–464.

[3] *F.D.* pp. 57–66.

dissolve and destroy the German Reich, in accordance with the secular policy of the balance of power, and Germany's aim must consequently be 'the final military liquidation (*Erledigung*) of the West'.

The development of Plan 'Yellow' will be discussed in a later chapter. It is enough to say here that from 7 November onwards a series of orders from Hitler put back the opening date on grounds of weather for short periods, until on January 13 it was postponed indefinitely.

Addressing his Commanders-in-Chief once more on November 23 Hitler had insisted that everything was determined by the fact that the moment was favourable now; in six months it might not be so any more. After 1918 Germany's enemies had disarmed of their own accord and they were still behind in their rearmament. Nevertheless he was disturbed by the stronger and stronger appearance of the English. The English were a tough enemy. Germany had an 'Achilles' heel' in the Ruhr, and the loss of it would lead to the paralysing of her power of resistance. However, there was no doubt that Germany's armed forces were the best, even though the infantry in Poland had not accomplished what one should have expected from it; and after the occupation of Belgium and Holland the continuous sowing of mines, from the air, on the English coasts would bring England to her knees.[1]

In the light of after-knowledge Hitler's confidence does not look absurd. But there were important elements in Germany, and in the German army, which strongly disapproved of his plans for an offensive in the west and were very doubtful of the outcome of a war against France and Britain: there were in fact plots for displacing him.[2] The revelation of German defeatism makes it more possible to understand the feelings of Mr. Chamberlain in these early months. 'Until [Hitler] disappears and his system collapses there can be no peace. But what I hope for is not a military victory—I very much doubt the feasibility of that—but a collapse of the German home front. For that it is necessary to convince the Germans that they cannot win . . . On this theory one must weigh every action in the light of its probable effect on German mentality.'[3] We know better now how completely the German people had delivered themselves into the hands of their Führer and how futile were the efforts of the few who wished to remove or counteract him.

It seemed by no means certain to the British Chiefs of Staff that

---

[1] *N.D.* 789–PS.
[2] See Wheeler-Bennett pp. 465–474.
[3] Feiling p. 418.

after the elimination of Poland Germany would turn west. They pointed out, in an appreciation of 18 September, that she had three alternatives open to her. She could content herself with consolidating her position in Poland and adopt a defensive attitude towards the western Powers; this was unlikely, since a long war was clearly against her interest. Secondly, leaving some fifteen divisions to hold down Poland, she might concentrate on an offensive in the west, where she could make anything up to 100 divisions available, rising in the future to 130, against an Allied total of 64 (excluding French fortress troops and troops in North Africa); in the air she could muster 2,000 bombers against a Franco-British total of some 950.[1] If she adopted this policy, she could either concentrate against Great Britain by means of unrestricted air attack on our aircraft and aircraft factories, our supply and distribution system, our shipping, ports and inland communications, combined with naval measures against our trade; or else she could concentrate against France by land and sea, probably turning the Maginot line by an advance through Holland and Belgium. Germany's third course would be to continue on the defensive in the west while extending her political and military control in south-eastern Europe, in which case Roumania would probably be her next victim; after dealing with Roumania she might risk Russia's displeasure and strike towards the Bosphorus and Aegean; in this event Turkey might be expected to resist, and should be encouraged and assisted to do so, as a first step towards the building up of a Balkan front against Germany.[2] If Italy were hostile, the Mediterranean could not be used for the transport of Allied troops or material until her sea and air forces had been disposed of; on the other hand, Turkey would in this case be more likely to join the Allies.

The Cabinet approved the report; they directed that the views of the French military authorities on it should be requested and that the broad military strategy to be adopted in the Near East, and especially the Balkans, should be studied. General Gamelin in fact found it difficult to foresee at the moment which alternative Germany would adopt: to continue on the path of easy conquest in the Balkans or to attack France, violating the neutrality of Luxemburg and Belgium and eventually Holland.

Public opinion in the Balkan countries was believed to be in general in favour of the Western Allies, but these peoples lived in mortal fear of the Axis Powers and were anxious to remain neutral. Roumania and Greece had accepted guarantees from the Western Powers in April after the Italian occupation of Albania, but Roumania was clearly outside any direct assistance from them, and

---

[1] Germany had in fact at this time 1,200 long-range bombers, of which just under 1,000 were fit for service; the corresponding figures for dive-bombers are 344 and 286.

[2] See Map 2.

both she and Yugoslavia had declared their neutrality on September 5. Turkey, who in reputation for military strength excelled her Balkan neighbours, had signed a declaration of friendship with Great Britain in May, but she was known in September to be negotiating with Russia and her action could not be foretold. Moreover, between Turkey and Roumania—the latter endangered both by her nearness to Germany and by her resources of oil and grain—lay Bulgaria; and Bulgaria, who hoped to regain the territory lost in 1913 to Roumania and Greece, looked to the Axis Powers rather than to the Western Allies for her restoration. Near-Eastern policy in any case required extreme tact and skill; it was greatly complicated by Italy's unexpected neutrality. Italy, after her absorption of Albania in March, was more than ever interested in the Balkans and was certain to be antagonised by any forcible French or British intervention in that sphere. The Chiefs of Staff had agreed that Italy's neutrality was greatly to the Allies' advantage, and they had advised that Turkish, Greek and Roumanian belligerency would be too dearly bought at the price of Italian hostility. The Foreign Office also had recently issued the warning that we could not at one and the same time pursue a policy of keeping Italy neutral and a policy of mobilising the Balkan States against Germany; it seemed that the correct course in present circumstances was to encourage the formation of a neutral *bloc* in the Balkans.

Before the French and British staffs presented the joint appreciation required, the subject of a south-eastern front was discussed at the second meeting of the Supreme War Council. It appeared that the French were anxious to send at least a token force either to Salonika or, with Turkish consent, to Constantinople, as a moral encouragement to the Balkan peoples. They had two weak divisions ready in Syria, said M. Daladier, and were reinforcing them by a complete division from Morocco. General Weygand, whose appointment as Commander-in-Chief of French forces in the Eastern Mediterranean has been mentioned, was already at Beyrout.[1]

The French recognised that troops could not be sent to Salonika in the face of a hostile and undefeated Italian fleet, but to the British it seemed that they treated the probable Italian reaction to any Allied moves in the Balkans rather complacently, and did not realise the strain that would be thrown on shipping. It was agreed, however, that the possibility of sending and maintaining the suggested expeditions should be studied by the staffs and that the Italian and Turkish Governments should be sounded. A more fundamental difference was General Gamelin's desire to open up new theatres which would draw away German troops from the Western front, contrasted with

---

[1] See Gamelin III pt. ii, ch. iv; Weygand, *Rappelé au Service* (Paris 1950) pt. i *passim*.

the British Chiefs of Staff's desire to restrict the actual area of military operations at least until the resources of the Empire had been further mobilised.[1]

The views of the two staffs were reconciled in a joint paper issued by the Permanent Military Representatives on 28 September, which examined the four hypotheses of Germany attacking or not attacking in south-eastern Europe with Italy in either case neutral or hostile. It recommended that our present policy should be to maintain the neutrality of Italy and consolidate the Balkan States into a benevolently neutral *bloc*. No military commitment should be undertaken at Salonika except at the invitation of Greece and with the prior agreement of Italy. The only Balkan State which could resist a first-class Power was Turkey, and that not until she had received considerable material support. Turkey was, moreover, for geographical reasons, the only Balkan State to which the Allies could be sure of being able to send assistance. Everything therefore pointed to devoting what resources we had to the support of Turkey, while building up a strategic reserve in Egypt and Syria as men and munitions became available. Turkey was, in fact, and was long to remain, the key to our whole position in the Near East.

This policy was approved by the Cabinet on October 6; at the same time they favoured a diplomatic approach to Italy with a view to an improvement of relations; this should ease the situation in the Mediterranean, where a substantial part of our naval strength was stationed to keep watch on her.

Relations with Turkey were passing through a delicate phase: as the prospects of Italian aggression receded, the Turks were apparently less eager to convert the Declaration of 12 May into a treaty and seemed determined to insist on awkward economic and financial conditions. There was a Turkish military mission in London in October, and the Turkish Foreign Minister was during the first half of the month in Moscow, where he was subject to strong pressure to accept, as the price of a Turkish-Soviet pact, modifications of the draft treaty such as to weaken Turkey's obligations to the Allies. The Moscow negotiations, however, led to no result. A treaty of mutual assistance between Great Britain, France and Turkey, which had been initialled, along with a military convention, on September 28, was eventually signed on October 19. The treaty was to run for fifteen years; the most important articles of the political agreement were the first three, which provided for French and British assistance to Turkey in the event of aggression by a European Power either against Turkey direct or leading to a war in the Mediterranean area in which Turkey became involved; they provided also for Turkey

---

[1] See Gamelin III 206.

coming to the assistance of Great Britain and France should they become involved in war in the Mediterranean area as a result of aggression by a European Power, or of their guarantees to Greece and Roumania. By a secret protocol, which was communicated to the Russians, it was agreed that Turkey's obligations could not compel her to make war on the Soviet Union, and by secret notes the British and French Governments promised to come to the help of Turkey, at her request, 'as soon as military action started by a European Power reaches the frontiers of Bulgaria or Greece'. The military convention, which did not go into details, was concerned among other matters with the containment of Bulgaria, the reduction of the Dodecanese and the defence of Salonika. The treaty was however further accompanied by a 'special agreement' providing that the treaty should not come into force until Turkey had received the stipulated war materials (for which she had previously been granted credits) and certain loans. This 'suspensive clause', as it came to be known, was extremely unwelcome to the Western Powers because of their shortage of the articles required by the Turks, especially anti-tank guns, and their unwillingness to confess how bare their cupboard was. It was not until 8 January 1940 that it was agreed that the suspensive clause should be raised as soon as the gold promised to Turkey arrived at Ankara.

In their appreciation of September 18 on the possible future course of the war, drafted before Russia had invaded Poland, the Chiefs of Staff had not attempted to estimate the future action of Russia and its consequences for the Allies. They had merely noted that in the opinion of the Foreign Office the British guarantee to Poland did not cover aggression by Russia, and that if Russia declared war on Great Britain the number of enemy submarines would be increased by some 200, while Russian aircraft might reinforce the German Air Force. But on October 2 and 6 they were asked, in view of an inquiry from the Prime Minister of Australia, and as a corollary to their Balkan report, to prepare appreciations of the effects of Russia making war on Britain in concert with Germany and of the possibilities of Russian action in the Balkans.

The Chiefs of Staff did not expect direct co-operation between Russia and Germany to any appreciable extent by land and air; at sea Russian submarines operating from German bases would add to our shipping losses, and German raiders would have the use of the ice-free port of Murmansk. In south-eastern Europe Russia had possibly blocked the way to German penetration, but to some extent she also protected Germany's flank and rear; for both reasons the Western front was more likely than ever to be the decisive one. Economic help from Russia to Germany would slow down the effect of our blockade and postpone the day when the Allies could pass to the offensive. But it was in secondary theatres, by penetration into southern Asia, that Russia could cause us the most serious embarrassment; we could not disregard a threat to the oilfields of Iran and Iraq or to the peace of India. The Chiefs of Staff pointed out that while remaining nominally neutral Russia could do the Allies harm in many ways, e.g. by propaganda, but that on the other hand a partnership between Nazi Germany and Bolshevik Russia must be an uneasy one.

The Cabinet on October 12 authorised the despatch of a telegram to the Dominion Prime Ministers on the above lines, prefacing it with a reasoned statement of the improbability of Russia co-operating actively with Germany.

We now know that, by a Secret Protocol signed on the same night (23 August) as the German-Russian non-aggression pact, while Russia declared her special interest in Bessarabia, Germany stated that she had no political interests in 'these areas', a phrase which, so Ribbentrop later informed Hitler, was intended to cover 'the South-East of Europe'; Ribbentrop said that he had duly stressed Germany's economic interests in this region. Further by a trade agreement of August 19 Germany had granted to the Soviet Union a credit of 200 million Reichsmarks, to be devoted to the supply of raw materials.[1] The Germans also pressed Russia to use her influence to keep Turkey from agreeing to the proposed treaty with Great Britain and France, and Molotov explained that this was Russia's object.[2] As we have seen, however, Turkey refused to accept the Russian conditions.

By the end of September General Gamelin was convinced that German forces in large numbers were being transferred to the Western front, and the likelihood of an immediate German drive in the Balkans diminished.[3] Nevertheless the conclusion of the Turkish treaty created new commitments in the Near East and the technical aspects were referred to the Chiefs of Staff. Their report, which assumed the firm neutrality of Italy, pointed out that before effective British help could be given to Turkey work would be required on the defence of her ports and the development of bases; so far as the army was concerned, the limiting factor would be administrative; it would be 'a matter of months' before we could send an armoured division and an infantry division from the Middle East forces, while the amount of air support would depend on the Russian threat to India. The report was discussed by a committee of Ministers, and the Cabinet on 31 October approved their recommendations; these included an assurance to the Turks that were they threatened with aggression we should probably be able to send immediate naval assistance, since it had been found that the Turkish Aegean ports

---

[1] *Nazi-Soviet Relations* pp. 78, 83, 157.

[2] *ibid.* 110, 113, 120.

[3] Gamelin III 88, 210.

were better defended than had been supposed; in order, however, that this should be effective it was essential that the Turks should, in such an event, invite our naval forces to pass through the Straits—a contingency which Russia had tried to prevent in the Moscow negotiations.

Balkan policy came under review again in December. The revival of Russian expansionism, as shown in the treatment of the Baltic countries, had cast a shadow over south-eastern Europe, but it contributed to hopes of improved relations with Italy.[1] Even the possibility of Italy making common cause with the Western Powers was not wholly ruled out. Except for a few cruisers and destroyers the entire British Mediterranean fleet had now been withdrawn. It remained the policy of the British Chiefs of Staff and Cabinet to keep war out of the Balkans as long as possible. They recognised that German or Russian action might frustrate this policy in the spring, but the Allies should do nothing to precipitate events. After a conference of the French and British staffs and commanders held at Gamelin's headquarters on the 11th, the Cabinet decided on December 14 that the right policy was to go ahead with preparations for intervention in the Balkans, so far as this could be done without offending Italy. At the Supreme War Council on December 19 it was agreed to do all that was possible, by way of diplomatic action and the despatch of what war material was available, to encourage the Balkan states to resist aggression; it was agreed also to prepare for the organisation of bases.

Mr. Chamberlain made it clear on this occasion that direct help to Yugoslavia or Roumania was not practicable. We had indeed given pledges in peacetime to Roumania and Greece, but we were now at war in fulfilment of a pledge to another country and were doing all we could. To an inquiry from the Roumanian Government whether the guarantee to Roumania applied to aggression from Russia as well as from Germany, the British Government had replied on December 11, after consulting the French, that they could not give the required guarantee against Russia unless they were assured of Italy's neutrality and of Turkey's readiness—which did not at present exist—to collaborate. We shall see in the next chapter what special importance attached to relations with Roumania in view of her resources in oil.

Early in the new year (15 January 1940) the Cabinet, on the recommendation of the Ministerial Committee on Military Coordination, approved in principle the proposals for strengthening our position in the Middle East which the Chiefs of Staff had put forward in December. They aimed at building up in the Middle East a reserve of land and air forces and, as the immediate preliminary, developing

---

[1] For Russia's treatment of the Baltic States, see chapter v below.

the necessary bases and communications. The reserve should consist of nine divisions, including the present garrison, in Egypt and Palestine, three in India, and twenty-two bomber and fighter squadrons in the Middle East and ten in India. The administrative development implied by this scheme was of course in full accordance with the recent decisions of the Supreme War Council. The Committee further made the important recommendation that industrial capacity should be developed in countries east of the Mediterranean to enable the forces in the Middle East and India to draw their supplies as far as possible from this region.

Thus during the last months of 1939 the two crucial questions from the point of view of the Allies were the respective attitudes of Italy and Turkey. The hostility of Italy would make it impossible to maintain any forces in the Balkans until she had been eliminated; but hopes were cherished, fantastic as they now appear, that she might move over into the Allied camp. In the meantime the only possible foundation for an active Allied policy was the goodwill of Turkey. Turkey, however, was not prepared for war and was unwilling to incur the danger of German or Russian enmity until her deficiencies had been made good, nor was she ready even to allow the indispensable naval and air bases to be prepared in her territory. The Allies were willing enough to supply her deficiencies, but not to the neglect of their own urgent needs.

'We desire to emphasise', said the Chiefs of Staff at the end of November, 'that apart from the military point of view we are at present in no position to undertake any adventures in the Balkans. The over-riding consideration of Italy's neutrality has not yet been achieved. The administrative facilities required for the operation of large forces in this theatre are at present totally lacking, and would require development on a large scale, while the strain which the maintenance of these forces would impose on our resources of shipping would be very heavy. Any commitment once started would inevitably grow; and in this connection it must be remembered that any diversion of force to the Middle East must result in a corresponding diminution of our military effort in France.'[1]

---

[1] General Weygand's views on Balkan policy are given in *Rappelé au Service*, chaps. ii–iv; he appears hardly to have realised at the time the Allied shortages in trained men, munitions and shipping.

CHAPTER IV

THE ECONOMIC WAR: THE
FIRST PHASE

THE ALLIED staff paper of April 1939 on 'broad strategic
pol cy' had recognised that in the first phase of the war the
only offensive weapon which the Allies could use effectively
was the economic. As later chapters of this history will show, the
British Government long continued to rely, though with varying
emphasis, on the eventual success of economic pressure on Germany.
Such pressure was envisaged under two forms: the prevention of the
supply from without of articles essential to the German war effort,
and the destruction of economic life within Germany. The latter task
was to be the concern of Bomber Command of the Royal Air Force,
but nothing to this end could even be attempted so long as the
decision stood to restrict air attack to purely military objectives in the
narrowest sense. It was necessary therefore to concentrate on the
blockade of Germany. Reviewing the general situation at the end of
October for the benefit of the Dominion Prime Ministers, the Chiefs
of Staff restated their conviction that the only sphere in which we
could take the offensive was the economic, and they claimed that by
using our superiority at sea, combined with diplomatic and financial
action, we were already exercising such pressure. It is with the
exploitation of our superiority at sea that this chapter is principally
concerned, but naval, air and diplomatic activities reacted on one
another, and it is desirable to see the problem and the policy as a
whole.

The Chiefs of Staff, when framing their European Appreciation,
had before them a paper prepared by the Industrial Intelligence
Centre of the Department of Overseas Trade on the economic situation in Germany, Italy and Japan on 1st April, 1939. We are concerned here only with the parts dealing with Germany. The situation
in Germany, the paper pointed out, was more favourable to her now
than in 1914–18 in that she was not now, as then, encircled by a ring
of enemy Powers which could enforce a continuous blockade. On the
other hand her economic system was vulnerable in two particular
ways: the major part of her heavy industries was concentrated in the
exposed Ruhr–Rhineland–Saar area and she needed, in spite of her
recent efforts to attain self-sufficiency, to import in bulk certain key
commodities which could not be supplied by countries accessible to
her.

Soon after the outbreak of war the Ministry of Economic Warfare summed up the chief defects of the German economy as a shortage of certain essential raw materials; a shortage of labour, particularly skilled and agricultural labour; the unsatisfactory condition of the railways; and grave financial weakness. The Ministry believed that the visible supplies of certain highly important raw materials, such as iron, chrome, nickel, copper, tin, pyrites, petroleum and jute would not suffice for more than six months' wartime consumption. They believed further that transportation difficulties and lack of surplus production should prevent the U.S.S.R. from making good these deficiencies.

With this British appreciation it is interesting to compare a speech in which in May 1939 General Thomas, head of *OKW* War Economy Branch, surveyed the respective war potentials of Germany and Britain.[1] Germany held indeed, he said, a decided lead in weapons, trained manpower and economic organisation, and so in immediate striking power, but she was not in a position to sustain her forces over a long period; her armament was not 'in depth'. 'Almost certainly after the outbreak of hostilities new formations would be needed, and all economic resources devoted to making them available. There would be a simultaneous demand for increased munitions and other necessities, and the war industry, by reason of insufficient factories and raw materials, could not adequately meet the demands on it.' The General believed that, if a serious arms race began, Germany's lead would be overtaken in a year or a year-and-a-half, and in a long-term trial of strength the Powers with armament in depth would win. His summary of his country's economic weakness was very similar to the British estimate mentioned in the last paragraph: raw materials, shortage of labour, the inadequate capacity of certain branches of industry and general financial strain. These problems resulted, not from rearmament, but from the immense increase in economic activity in the last five years. The German economy was overtaxed: instead of running at 100 per cent of its capacity it was running at 125 per cent.

The British experts had called particular attention to the importance to Germany of the supply of iron ore from Sweden and of mineral oil from Poland, Roumania and Russia. Germany's requirements in iron and oil played a prominent part in the Second World War. Her need for iron ore will bulk large in Chapter V, and we are not concerned with it here.

As regards oil, an inter-departmental committee, of which Mr. Geoffrey Lloyd, the Secretary for Mines, was chairman, using the best available evidence as to fact but on certain points admittedly

[1] *N.D.* 28–EC.

having recourse to conjecture, calculated in October that Germany would need for the first six months of the year about 5 million tons of petroleum products and for the first twelve months about $10\frac{1}{4}$ million. Towards this she was believed to have held on 1st September stocks of not more than 3 million tons. Her probable sources of supply were estimated for the first six months as 1,200,000 tons from domestic production, and rather more than one million from Russia, Poland and Roumania, making a total, including original stocks, of $5\frac{1}{4}$ million; even if imports from Roumania were doubled to the very improbable figure of 1,600,000 tons, the total would be only a little above 6 million for the first six months.

These figures pointed to the conclusion that 'in the spring of 1940 Germany's oil position is likely to be critical, as she will by then have expended an amount equivalent to all her incoming supplies and, even taking the maximum supply figures, two-thirds of her war reserves'. This conclusion was based 'on the assumption that contraband control measures are successful in preventing the re-export of petroleum to Germany from adjacent neutral countries and that means can be found of dealing satisfactorily with the potential transit trade through Italy'.

The accuracy of this and other early British forecasts of the state of Germany's oil supplies will be considered later.[1] It may be remarked here in passing that in the light of evidence now available their perennial optimism does not appear as unreasonable as events soon suggested. They were falsified first by her unexpectedly low consumption of oil in the first year of war and then by the rich booty secured by her early conquests. It is of interest, however, to note that in July 1939 the War Economy and Armaments Branch of *OKW* calculated that unless Germany could increase her imports she would be forced to eat into her existing stocks at the rate of over 200,000 tons monthly. And these stocks were in fact nearly a million tons smaller than the British estimate. Moreover, in March 1940 Göring declared that by May of that year oil for the Army and for industry would be exhausted, and by July oil for the Air Force also; he insisted that the Navy must help by making over part of its considerable supplies of Diesel oil.[2]

To return to the Lloyd committee's report, it appeared that the only countries from which Germany could hope to import oil were Poland, Russia and Roumania. Of these Roumania was much the most promising. The average annual Polish production in recent years had been only half a million tons, and nearly the whole of the oil-bearing area was now under Russian control. Russia's exports of

---

[1] In chapter xvii.
[2] *F.N.C.* p. 89.

oil in 1938 had been well below one million tons and were expected 'practically to disappear' by 1940; apart from transport difficulties, which were serious, it was most unlikely that she would sacrifice her own economic development for Germany's sake. It was safe to assume that Russia and Poland could not provide more than half a million tons for Germany in the first twelve months, or quarter of a million in the first six. Roumania on the other hand had produced about 6½ million tons in 1938 and her exportable surplus might be expected to be 4½ million. The most that Germany could obtain out of this in the first year was probably two million tons (800,000 in the first six months); conceivably she might obtain four million. But in this case too transport was likely to be a limiting factor.

The committee ended by calling attention to 'the great importance of Roumania as the only petroleum producing country in Europe from which Germany can get any substantial quantities of oil products'.

The Cabinet, after discussing the report, invited Lord Chatfield and Lord Hankey to keep under constant review the action being taken to prevent oil supplies from reaching Germany, and our organisation for this purpose. The Cabinet accordingly received a succession of comprehensive studies of the whole question from a committee of which Lord Hankey was chairman.

Roumania had accepted an Allied guarantee in the spring, but realisation in the course of the summer and autumn of German strength and Allied weakness made her more and more reluctant to compromise her neutrality, until in July 1940 she fell into the grip of the Axis. The Allies aimed at buying up as much as possible of Roumania's oil production for themselves and allowing as little as possible for the Axis, at denying to Germany all available means of oil transport by land and river, and at arranging, with the Roumanian Government's approval, for the destruction of the oil wells in the event of a German invasion. Plans for the latter purpose and for blocking the Danube came to nothing; plans for denying river transport to Germany obtained a considerable measure of success; while protracted purchase negotiations succeeded in limiting Germany's ration of Roumanian oil to 150,000 tons monthly (she in fact received about half this quantity) and in substantially increasing our own. German documents reveal the counter-measures taken by the German Secret Service from December 1939 onwards, particularly with a view to the prevention of sabotage by the Allies. By the summer of 1940, when the country had fallen under Axis control, all Allied measures for denying Roumanian oil to Germany had come to a standstill and there seemed little prospect of reviving them.

If Sweden and Roumania occupied exceptional positions, there were other neutral Powers whose policy might count for much in the economic war, and from the first days after the outbreak of hostilities the Allies conducted a series of negotiations with neutral countries, hoping to secure, by what were called war-trade agreements, for themselves the maximum and for Germany the minimum of each country's desirable products. The first of these to be achieved was the secret agreement signed with Sweden on 7th December 1939, and it was soon followed by others. Hard bargaining was naturally required to induce the uneasy neutrals to agree to arrangements by hypothesis prejudicial to their formidable continental neighbour.

The persuasions of the civilian negotiators were supported and supplemented by the action of the Navy enforcing the control of contraband in co-operation with the Ministry of Economic Warfare.

Professor Medlicott has described at length the machinery of the blockade and has explained how in course of time many changes of method were introduced, chiefly out of consideration for neutral interests.[1] The main features in the basic or traditional system of controlling contraband were, as he puts it, four: the interception of vessels suspected of carrying contraband and their diversion to bases for examination; the collection and scrutiny by the Ministry's officials of information concerning the nature, ownership and destination of the cargoes detained; decision by the Contraband Committee whether the cargo should be seized and submitted to Prize Court procedure; and lastly the procedure of the Prize Court. It was the first feature or phase which called for action by the Navy.

The Admiralty's War Plan, in a section entitled 'Action against enemy sea-borne trade', explained the forms of pressure permissible under international law; it stated that 'whereas enemy vessels are liable to seizure anywhere outside neutral waters, action against neutral ships trading with the enemy is limited to those which carry contraband, except in so far as it is possible to establish a close blockade of some part of the enemy's coast'. This limitation to ships carrying contraband was not likely to be of much practical importance, since probably 'the contraband list in force will be so comprehensive as to cover practically everything of any value to the enemy in wartime'. This was in fact the case. The list of 'conditional contraband' issued by the Government on 4 September actually included foodstuffs, and their inclusion was justified by the Prime Minister on the ground that 'in this respect a naval blockade is in no way different from a land siege, and no one has ever suggested that a besieging commander should allow free rations to a besieged town'.[2]

---

[1] W. N. Medlicott, *The Economic Blockade* vol. I (H.M.S.O. 1952) chaps. i, ii.

[2] *London Gazette* 4 Sept. 1939, cited L. Oppenheim, *International Law* (ed. H. Lauterpacht) vol. II (7th ed. 1952) p. 804; *House of Commons Debates* vol. 351, col. 1237 (26 Sept.).

The Naval War Plan explained, however, that it would not be permissible to seize enemy exports carried in neutral vessels, except where a close blockade had been established, 'unless His Majesty's Government should decide to take action against enemy exports in retaliation for some breach of international law'—as they had done in 1915 and as they were in fact to do in November 1939.

The reference to a 'close blockade' meant little, since close blockades in the old technical sense, that is to say the interception at close quarters of all traffic with a defined part of the enemy's coastline, had become normally impracticable under modern conditions; on the other hand the system of total war, or war with a totalitarian power, was bound eventually to obliterate the distinctions both between absolute and conditional contraband and in the treatment of imports and exports. Blockade had become, as the Prime Minister asserted, the equivalent of siege.

It remained for the Navy to perform its task in accordance with the policy of the Government and the rules of international law. Much the heaviest part of this burden fell on the fleet in home waters, on which, second only to the duty of bringing the enemy to action 'wherever and whenever his forces can be met', the duty had been imposed of closing the North Sea to all movements of enemy shipping and of contraband control over neutral shipping; it is with this offensive side of the Navy's work that we are at the moment concerned, though in reality it was acting at the same time in defence of our own shipping. The command of the sea, or control of sea communications in the modern phrase, serves its possessor as both sword and shield.

The Home Fleet, under the command of Admiral Sir Charles Forbes, was based on Scapa Flow; Scapa was eventually rendered secure, but not till after the loss of a capital ship (the *Royal Oak*, sunk by U-boat on October 14) had shown up the inadequacy of its anti-submarine defences.[1] Fortunately at the time of the disaster the greater part of the fleet was absent; for one reason or another it did not become permanently based at Scapa until March 1940, Loch Ewe, the Clyde and Rosyth being all used as temporary homes, at the cost of damage to other important warships, the *Nelson* and the *Belfast*. These dangerous wanderings, however, did not substantially affect the execution of the plans for closing the North Sea to Germany's commerce.

The shortest and most obvious line (about 220 miles) on which to intercept shipping at the northern entry to this sea is one drawn from the Shetlands to the Norwegian coast near Bergen, and it was here that the Germans expected us to establish the blockade; but so

---

[1] For the reasons why Scapa was not made secure earlier, see Roskill, *The War at Sea* I 76–82.

southerly a line was rejected, not only by reason of the danger from enemy surface ships and aircraft to vessels engaged on interception but because it would not prevent inward traffic from reaching north Norwegian ports and thence proceeding southwards through Norwegian territorial waters. The interception of commerce was carried out further north and further west, between the Orkneys and Iceland and in the Denmark Strait between Iceland and the Greenland pack-ice.[1] It had been proved in the earlier war that under modern conditions the traditional method of examining at sea vessels suspected of carrying contraband was impracticable, and that examination could normally be conducted only in port. Accordingly a contraband control base was established at Kirkwall.

There were some holes in the net. Much time and thought, as we shall see in the next chapter, were devoted, but without much success, to the possibility of stopping the flow of commerce, especially of Swedish iron ore, down the Norwegian coast; ships used the 'Inner Leads', the territorial waters between the islands and the mainland, and the points at which they were likely to venture outside were few. As regards the Baltic, the Admiralty had taken the view that it was not worth while attempting to stop the enemy's trade in those enclosed waters. Mr. Churchill, however, from the outset was caught with the idea of sending in a force of old 'R Class' battleships, specially armoured and 'blistered' for the purpose; they might succeed in isolating Germany from Scandinavia and in particular in cutting the Swedish iron trade, but what perhaps chiefly appealed to the First Lord in operation 'Catherine' was the chance of singeing the German Führer's moustache by a stroke so daring and direct at a time when there were but slight possibilities of bringing off a large-scale naval offensive. Mr. Churchill did not lack distinguished naval backing, but his responsible advisers were convinced that in the absence of fighter protection and of a friendly Russian base the despatch of a surface force into the Baltic, while the German fleet outside was still capable of mischief, would be altogether unsound. The despatch of a strong force of submarines, on the other hand, at the proper time, might well prove feasible and obtain valuable results.

The blocking of the southern entrance to the North Sea was a much simpler affair. The Straits of Dover were closed by a minefield except for two passages, the one patrolled by vessels from Dover, the other guarded by the French; the main control base was established at Ramsgate.

The control of the Mediterranean exits was enforced by patrol vessels based in the west on Gibraltar, in the east on Haifa and Port

---

[1] See Maps 3 and 8.

G

Said, but it was found impossible to stop traffic from the Black Sea effectively while Greece and Turkey remained neutral.

The number of German merchantmen which fell into the meshes of the net was comparatively small. Some were caught in the Atlantic by British hunting-groups in pursuit of bigger game and some scuttled themselves; but the majority, in accordance with orders issued from Germany, made for the nearest port. From time to time they ventured to break out and in the early months not a few succeeded, but as late as April 1940 there were nearly 250 German ships so immobilised.[1] The control of neutral ships, however, was very effective, except in the Eastern Mediterranean. The work was heavy; on a single day at the end of October there were 92 neutral ships in the control ports of Kirkwall, Ramsgate and Weymouth. By the end of November the Ministry of Economic Warfare thought they had evidence that the effects of the blockade were beginning to be felt in Germany, and that apprehension about the future was influencing her policy. Reviewing economic conditions in Germany at the end of the year they found that, while her war potential was still on the upgrade, her economy was 'brittle', in that it might be brought down by a failure in any of a number of particular components. On 27th November a British Order in Council, justified by the Prime Minister as retaliation for illegal German minelaying and action by submarines, had ordered the seizure of Germany's exports, and this might be expected in due course to deprive her of the most valuable part of her export trade.[2]

The exercise of belligerent rights at sea has never been popular with neutrals. British statesmen and officials were not likely to forget the bickerings with the United States of America which had occurred in the early period of the previous war. Naturally in the later war too there were protests even from well-wishers at what seemed unnecessary delays or lack of consideration or high-handed procedure. It was obviously in the Allies' interest to avoid such friction and all superfluous use of force by enlisting the co-operation of neutral Governments and traders. The two neutrals who mattered most were the United States, whose goodwill it was important to maintain and exploit, and Italy, whose official illwill it was important to restrain on this side of belligerency.

The United States, as we have seen, were on the one hand desirous to see an Allied victory and on the other resolved not to be drawn into war. President Roosevelt had felt bound to declare his desire to keep America neutral, but short of war he showed that he would do all in his power to help the Allies; he had however to take account of

---

[1] See Roskill I 151.
[2] *House of Commons Debates* vol. 353, col. 1034; Order in Council of 27 Nov. 1939.

popular feeling including that of pacifists and of business men. The State Department acted against a background of neutrality legislation superimposed on the rules of international law.[1] The United States Neutrality Act of 4th November 1939, while allowing the Allies access to United States goods on a cash-and-carry basis, among its numerous provisions forbade United States ships to ply to France, Great Britain, Ireland, Germany, the Low Countries, Denmark, Sweden or Norway south of Bergen. Early in October the Foreign Ministers of the American States, in conference at Panama, announced their intention to establish a security zone of several hundred miles round their coasts, within which no belligerent activities would be allowed. This gesture was entirely in accordance with British interests, provided that the intentions of the American States were effectively enforced by patrols and that German raiders were not allowed to use the safety zone as a sanctuary from which to sally forth on their prey. The proposal was in due course accepted by France and Germany, though by them also with reservations, but it could not be strictly enforced and it was dropped towards the end of 1940.[2]

Immediately on the outbreak of war Mr. Cordell Hull, the Secretary of State, proposed conferences for the purpose of arranging by friendly understanding that the exercise of British contraband control should be made as little irksome as possible to Americans.[3] He suggested, in the case of exports from the United States to certain other neutral countries, the issue of navicerts—an invention of the earlier war—or certificates that ships concerned did not carry contraband; a voluntary system of navicerts, though not quite on the lines suggested by Mr. Hull, was brought into operation in December with regard to the United States and some South American countries. Nevertheless these friendly discussions did not prevent the irritation caused by certain British measures, such as the diversion of United States ships to Kirkwall in belligerent waters and the examination of neutral mails ostensibly in search of contraband but in fact as a means of obtaining economic intelligence. American wrath came to a head at the end of January and again a month later. On both occasions concessions were made to meet American objections.[4] Useful work was done in this connection by the Anglo-French economic mission sent over to co-ordinate Allied purchases as well as by the Ambassador's tactful mediation.

In the case of Italy objection centred chiefly on the British decision

---

[1] See W. L. Langer and S. E. Gleason, *The Challenge to Isolation* (London, 1952) chaps. vi, viii.

[2] See the *Memoirs of Cordell Hull* (London 1948) I 690.

[3] *ibid.* I 679–681.

[4] *ibid.* I 734–736.

at the end of November to seize German exports, Italy being largely dependent on German coal. In her case too concessions were made, as the result of discussions carried on in Rome by an Anglo-Italian committee, of which Sir Wilfred Greene, the Master of the Rolls, was the British chairman. In this matter as in others Count Ciano, the Foreign Minister, was found much more accommodating than his father-in-law, the Duce.

In this sketch of the first moves in the Allied economic offensive nothing has so far been said of the forces of the enemy or of the methods by which the Führer intended to use them. It must not be supposed, however, that these moves were not interfered with by the enemy or that his fleet and air force were not engaged in a vigorous and relentless offensive against the commerce of the Allies and the ships of war which protected it. For the Royal Navy, it should be remembered, there was no twilight period, no phoney war.

On 10 May 1939 Hitler issued directives for economic warfare. The Navy and Air Force were the most important instruments for attacking the enemy economy; they were to direct their preparations primarily against Britain and secondarily against France and must be careful not to violate the sovereignty of neutral states. The 'battle instructions for the Navy', as issued in the same month, elaborated this policy.[1] Assuming 'the most unfavourable case', that of a war on two fronts, for which admittedly the Navy was not ready, they pointed out that, since it was vain to attempt to keep open Germany's North Sea communications, naval forces would be available for attacking the enemy's merchant ships, and the only area where this could be successfully done was 'on the oceans'. The German navy could not hope to use the English Channel, but it could interrupt British efforts to blockade the northern exits from the North Sea and it could facilitate raiding operations in the Atlantic by occasionally passing surface ships through the blockade and creating diversions. Small-scale warfare, surprise attacks on inferior forces and constant harassing action must be the order of the day. Close co-operation with the Luftwaffe was essential.

In foreign waters the task of the German navy was to attack merchant shipping, in order to deprive the enemy of both cargoes and ships. The risks of action against warships, even of inferior strength, were to be avoided. Surface ships would operate on the high seas, leaving the enemy's coastal waters to the submarines. Surface ships would achieve success by 'surprise appearances, followed by immediate withdrawal, and constant shifting of areas of activity'; even the

---

[1] *F.D.* pp. 21–23, 29.

moral effect of such ubiquity would suffice to dislocate the enemy's trade and discourage neutrals from sailing. Efforts would be made to send out raiders and supply ships in good time before war broke out; two of the pocket-battleships and twenty-one submarines were in fact in the Atlantic at the end of August. Submarines could obtain best results near ports and round focal points of merchant shipping; if in course of time forced out into 'remote areas', they must make defence more difficult for the enemy by working at widely separated points, e.g. the West Indies and the Cape Verde Islands as well as the east coast of Great Britain.[1]

The German chain of command ran from the Chief of the Naval Staff, Grand Admiral Raeder, to two Commanders-in-Chief ashore, the one responsible for the Baltic, which was in no event to be denuded of all naval forces, and the other, with headquarters at Wilhelmshaven, for the North Sea including the Skagerrak and 'the approaches to the Atlantic'. The Naval Staff assumed direct responsibility for 'foreign waters'.[2]

Even though a war on two fronts, so far as Russia was to be feared, had been avoided, Admiral Raeder was by no means confident about the outcome of a contest so precipitately ordained by the Führer. On the day war broke out with Britain and France he wrote down his feelings as follows in a remarkable document, which was countersigned by one of his staff: 'As far as the Navy is concerned, obviously it is in no way very adequately equipped for the great struggle with Great Britain by autumn 1939. It is true that in the short period since 1935 . . . it has built up a well-trained, suitably organised submarine arm, of which at the moment about twenty-six boats are capable of operations in the Atlantic; the submarine arm is still much too weak, however, to have any decisive effect on the war. The surface forces, moreover, are so inferior in number and strength to those of the British Fleet that, even at full strength, they can do no more than show that they know how to die gallantly and thus are willing to create the foundations for later reconstruction.'[3] The pocket-battleships should, Raeder thought, be able to carry out cruiser warfare on the high seas for some time, but their action could not be decisive, either, for the outcome of the war. It would be the duty of the two battle cruisers, the *Scharnhorst* and *Gneisenau*, to contain enemy capital ships in home waters, but they were not as yet reliable or ready for action.

---

[1] *F.D.* pp. 37, 38.

[2] *F.D.* p. 27. By the beginning of September, in view of the pact with Russia and the withdrawal of Polish vessels to British bases, the Germans found it necessary to keep only minimum forces in the Baltic.

[3] *F.N.C.* p. 37.

Two days earlier Commodore Dönitz, in command of the submarine force, had expressed his misgivings as to the chances of exerting any serious pressure on the enemy within a reasonable time unless the building programme were greatly increased. As against the existing total of 57 submarines, he pleaded for a total of at least 300 of long-range types so as to enable 90 to work in the North Atlantic at the same time.[1] This increase was approved in principle, but shortages of men and materials and the demands of the other Services postponed action. It was not till July 1940 that the Führer sanctioned immediate measures for the completion of 312 submarines by the beginning of 1942.

In the first weeks of war Hitler was anxious to limit operations in the West; in particular no provocation was to be offered to France. British merchant shipping might be attacked, but for the present the Prize Regulations must be observed: that is to say, merchant ships might be sunk only after they had been stopped and searched and steps had been taken to ensure the safety of the crews.[2] Submarines, in view of the danger they must incur in conforming to these rules, were instructed to attack ships which under international law might be sunk without warning, namely troopships, vessels escorted by enemy warships or aircraft, and vessels taking any action, such as passing information, which might aid the enemy or jeopardise the submarine. To this class armed merchantmen were soon added. It was thus contrary to orders that the unarmed liner *Athenia* was sunk by *U 30* on 3 September, and as the result of this mischance special respect was paid to passenger ships until August 1940. Further, the pocket-battleships were ordered at the outset to refrain from raiding for the present, and the Luftwaffe was not to take the initiative in attacking even British naval forces.

On 23 October 1939, however, Hitler gave orders for a special staff for economic warfare to be formed in *OKW*, for the purpose of co-ordinating departmental action, and Admiral Schuster was appointed its chief.[3] On 29 November a directive laid down principles for the conduct of the war against the enemy's economy, designating Great Britain as the driving spirit among the Allies and assigning to the Navy and Air Force the joint tasks which would fall to them after the defeat of the Anglo-French field army and the occupation of 'a part of the coast facing England'. The first task would be to render useless the main British transhipment ports by mining and otherwise blocking their approaches; the destruction of British war industries was included also.[4]

---

[1] *F.N.C.* p. 36.

[2] *F.N.C.* pp. 40, 35; *Führer Directives* Nos. 1, 2.

[3] *F.N.C.* p. 53.

[4] *F.D.* p. 74.

Raeder chafed at the restrictions imposed by the Führer and brought constant pressure on him to allow a 'naval siege of the British Isles'—a phrase which was to replace 'the notorious expression "unrestricted submarine warfare"; such a method of warfare would free us from having to observe any restrictions whatever on account of objections based on International Law'.[1] It may be noted that Raeder and his master anticipated by a few days the British Prime Minister's discovery of the convenience of the 'siege' formula for stretching the accepted rules.[2] In the long run Raeder prevailed, practice outrunning declared intention, since 'previous experience has shown that gradual intensification without special proclamation is the best method'.[3] The restrictions were relaxed gradually by extensions of the classes of ships, such as ships sailing without lights or ships identified as enemy, which might be attacked without warning, and of the areas in which such attacks were allowed.

Hitler was unwilling to approve the final lifting of restrictions, the stage of 'naval siege', until the launching of the grand offensive in the West, first announced to his Commanders-in-Chief on 27 September; this might be expected to have important political repercussions and to call forth neutral protests in any case. Its victorious execution would moreover allow of more intensive pressure by sea and air against Great Britain. Eventually on 17 August 1940 Germany declared a total blockade of the British Isles, warning neutrals of the danger incurred by every ship using British waters, since the whole area had been mined and German aircraft would attack all shipping.

The British Naval War Plan recalled that the traditional methods of protecting trade were two: the dispersion of our shipping by evasive routeing, combined with a patrol of 'focal areas' by our warships; and the arrangement of convoys under adequate escort. It was intended to rely on these methods again, but some time might elapse before all was in working order.

The indication, erroneous though it was, given by the sinking of the *Athenia* on 3 September that the enemy proposed immediately to adopt unrestricted submarine warfare impelled the Admiralty to introduce at once, so far as possible, the convoy system for merchant ships: that is to say, combined sailings of merchant ships with escort on particular routes at regular intervals.[4] The Admiralty had at the end of August taken over the direction of the movements of British merchant ships, through its Trade Division, but it had of course

---

[1] *F.N.C.* p. 42, 23 Sept. 1939.
[2] See above, p. 75; *F.N.C.* p. 73.
[3] *F.N.C.* p. 71, 30 Dec. 1939.
[4] For fuller information on the convoy system, see Roskill I ch. vi.

no control over neutral ships (unless under charter to Britain), great numbers of which were needed to maintain the necessary volume of imports into the United Kingdom, and neutral ships could not always be induced to sail in convoy. Troop convoys always received special protection, the close escort being covered by more powerful ships.

Owing to the shortage of destroyers and lack of advanced fuelling bases—the technique of fuelling at sea had not yet been developed—the ocean convoys could not be escorted beyond some 200 miles from the west coast of Ireland, and in some cases ships had to be sailed in groups without escort. The Admiralty were continually pointing out that the use of Berehaven would enable us to extend protection 200 miles further west and urging that all possible steps should be taken to secure it.[1] But neither at this nor at any later time would the Government of Eire meet our wishes.

By the end of 1939, out of 5,756 ships which sailed in convoys only four were sunk by submarines. This small number is the more impressive if compared with the total of all ships (114) sunk by submarines in the same period.[2] Apart from the sinking of the fleet carrier *Courageous* in the Western Approaches on 17 September, the submarines' successes were mostly gained against merchant ships sailing independently; but in fact, after the first onslaught, Dönitz did not expect to have more than eight or nine U-boats regularly available for the Atlantic, and the average number at sea daily was less than seven. The total of nine sunk by the Royal Navy in the first four months of the war was a substantial proportion of the enemy's strength, and by the end of the year Germany had only thirty-three U-boats available for operations in all waters as against forty-nine on 1 September. In the first four months of 1940 the German submarines sank 115 ships (only eight in convoy), while thirteen U-boats were sunk.[3]

Grim as were the memories of the submarine menace in the earlier war, the Admiralty, trusting largely to the escorts' new under-water detecting instrument, the asdic, believed they had the measure of these assailants; it was from surface ships that they apprehended the most trouble. These could penetrate into the oceans beyond the present range of the German submarines or aircraft, and for protection against them destroyers were inadequate, while we were very short in cruisers. The Admiralty hoped it would suffice to direct our merchantmen to follow unusual routes, while cruisers patrolled the 'focal areas' where routes converged. If this expedient failed, convoys would have to be formed and escorted either for part of their journey

---

[1] See Map 8.

[2] See Appendix II.

[3] Roskill, I, Appendix K, gives a complete list and analysis of the sinkings of U-boats.

by warships or for the whole of it by armed merchant cruisers. But arrangements were also made for 'hunting groups' of cruisers and heavier ships to assemble and pursue any raider known to be on the prowl.

To watch for raiders attempting to break out northwards from the North Sea was the special duty of the reconnaissance patrols of Coastal Command. In their main task of spotting surface ships the aircraft were often foiled by the North Sea weather and the lack of means of detection at night, as well as by the crews' inexperience in sea reconnaissance, but they sometimes sighted surfaced submarines on passage; unfortunately they did not at this time carry charges capable of destroying them.

The only German ships available for distant ocean-raiding in the first months of war were in fact the three pocket-battleships, though the conversion of suitable merchantmen into armed raiders was in process, and only two of the three actually set out; these were the *Admiral Graf Spee* and the *Deutschland*, both of which left German ports, unknown to the Admiralty, a week before the outbreak of war. They were not authorised to start operations until the last week of September, and it was not till 1 October that the Admiralty learnt that a pocket-battleship (believed to be the *Admiral Scheer*, in fact the *Graf Spee*) had sunk a British ship off Pernambuco on the previous day. Then began the long hunt which ended so ingloriously for the German ship, but so triumphantly for her assailants—the three more lightly armed British cruisers under Commodore Harwood—with her suicide in the estuary of the River Plate on 17 December.[1] In the interval the *Graf Spee* had sunk nine British merchantmen, ranging from the coastal waters of northern Brazil to the Mozambique Channel; while the Admiralty assembled for her destruction from the Home Fleet, from the Mediterranean, from China and from the French bases an overwhelming preponderance of powerful ships. It was the first, and a most impressive, demonstration of how effectively the far-flung resources of the Empire could be centrally directed by the Admiralty relying on the trained initiative of commanders in distant waters, and the enemy be deceived as to our ships' whereabouts; it demonstrated also the dislocation of our naval equilibrium which might be caused by 'two ill-constructed heavy cruisers' (the First Lord's phrase) and suggested that we were fortunate that the other German heavy ships were not more adventurously employed.

Meanwhile the second pocket-battleship, the *Deutschland*, whose presence in the Atlantic was not known to the Admiralty until 21 October, returned unscathed to her German base on 15 November, after accounting for only two British ships; the Führer, unwilling to

---

[1] The three cruisers were *Exeter*, *Achilles* and *Ajax*.

risk the moral effect of the sinking of a ship so named, insisted that she should henceforward be known as the *Lützow*.[1]

One result of the activities of those two raiders was to denude the British Home Fleet of several valuable ships for what might have been a critical time. So long as the *Gneisenau* and *Scharnhorst* were unaccounted for, Germany had two ships which could outgun all British vessels except capital ships and in speed outstrip all our heavy ships except possibly the *Hood*. They could choose their moment for a pounce or a feint. In the wild weather of the North Sea it was idle to count on prompt or accurate information of their movements, and the heavy ships of the Home Fleet sailed on many fruitless attempts, east, north and west, to bring them to battle. It was decided after the end of October that capital ships should not venture into the southern waters of the North Sea unless there was good reason to believe that they would meet the heavy ships of the enemy.

Round the coasts of the United Kingdom it was mines and aircraft which gave trouble; both these had of course been foreseen as likely forms of attack, though it had not been foreseen that mines would be laid by aircraft. Both Britain and Germany early in the war had for purposes of defence declared large areas of the North Sea to be mined (though this does not mean that mines were actually laid over the whole of the declared areas immediately, or at all), and the Admiralty had promptly decided to increase their programme of minesweepers besides requisitioning further trawlers for the same purpose. The type of automatic submarine mine referred to in the Eighth Hague Convention is that which needs contact to explode it. In the previous war, however, a new type, exploded without contact by magnetic influence, was invented by the British, and it was this type, used offensively in our coastal waters by the Germans, which was to cause us extreme inconvenience until an efficient counter was at length produced. The secret of the mechanism was only detected after a German magnetic ground-mine, dropped from the air, had been discovered on a mudbank on 23 November, 1939, and it was not till the end of March 1940 that our new sweeping devices became really effective.

We now know from German documents that owing to a shortage of mines all the minefields planned could not be laid, and that only a small proportion of the mines available at the outbreak of war were of the magnetic type.[2] Nevertheless by the end of the year the enemy had destroyed 79 ships by mines and had put out of action for seven months no less a victim than the flagship of the Home Fleet, H.M.S. *Nelson*, mined in Loch Ewe on 4 December. In the first four months

[1] *F.N.C.* p. 54.
[2] *F.D.* p. 36.

of 1940 61 more ships were sunk by mines. To these losses should be
added the expenditure of time and effort caused to the Navy by
diversions and minesweeping and the technical process of affording
ships partial immunity from magnetic mines. The enemy's minelaying expeditions were not, however, without serious loss to him; in
December two of his cruisers covering such an operation were
torpedoed and put out of action for many months.

It was partly on the ground of illegal minelaying by the Germans
that the Prime Minister justified the retaliatory measure against
enemy exports. Though the Hague Convention does not mention
magnetic mines, there was as much humanitarian reason for applying
its restrictions to these as to contact mines.[1] The Germans used both
kinds and there is no doubt that they violated both the spirit and the
letter of the Convention.

The part played by the German Air Force in these early months
must now be further considered. In his first Directive, of 31 August
1939, Hitler ordered that preparations should be made for the Luftwaffe to disrupt Britain's imports and her armament industry, but
only if she and France began hostilities. On 3 September, after the
British declaration of war, he still held his hand, not allowing air
attacks even on British naval forces and troop transports unless the
Royal Air Force had taken comparable action first and the chances
of success were particularly good.[2] On the same day the British
Cabinet authorised the immediate despatch of a bomber force to
attack the German fleet reported to have sailed from Wilhelmshaven;
the operation was carried out on the 4th, but although several hits
were made no serious damage was done to the ships, while seven of
the 29 bombers were lost. So disappointing were the results that no
further such attacks were made for some time.

Restrictions on the activities of the Luftwaffe were gradually
relaxed by Hitler, as in the case of the Navy. On 16 and 17 October
the bases at Rosyth and Scapa were raided by a few Junker 88
bombers, which in the one case hit the cruiser *Southampton* without
crippling her and in the other caused the beaching of Jellicoe's old
flagship, the *Iron Duke*. When on 16 March, after the return of the
fleet, the Germans again raided Scapa, its anti-aircraft defences had
been greatly strengthened and little damage was done; a British
return raid on the island of Sylt, for which satisfactory results were
claimed, was even more innocuous. Neither the British nor the
German Air Force had by this date fulfilled expectations of what
bombers might effect against armoured ships. On the British side
inadequate attention had been devoted in peacetime to the training

---

[1] *House of Commons Debates* vol. 353, col. 1034; L. Oppenheim, *International Law* II (ed.
Lauterpacht, 1952) 471–3.

[2] *F.D.* pp. 50, 51.

of bomber crews in attacking naval targets: Coastal Command lacked a striking force, and the bombs in use were ineffective. On the German side more could have been achieved had the Air Force or the Naval Air Arm received such training. Other activities of the Luftwaffe, such as minelaying, were more successful, though co-operation with the Navy was not as rewarding as it could have been if relations between the heads of the two Services had been more friendly.

On 30 September Hitler authorised the German Air Force 'to carry on the war against merchant shipping according to prize law', but he later allowed attacks without warning.[1] How difficult it was to apply to aircraft regulations analogous to those devised for the very different circumstances of control by ships was proved by the Royal Air Force early in the war; German aircraft seem to have paid little heed to the restrictions and in October were attacking unarmed coasting vessels and trawlers off the east coast, though without much effect.[2] In December they sank ten ships and in January twelve, and for the next few months the protection of the east coast convoys raised a difficult problem. Anticipating such attacks the Committee of Imperial Defence had in August recommended the formation of four additional fighter squadrons in order to protect the convoys running between the Firth of Forth and Southampton.

The same Committee had before the war recommended other measures for the protection of merchant shipping against attack from the air, such as the conversion of existing guns to high-angle low-angle use and the manufacture of new ones. These measures, however, could only bear fruit in the future, and for the present there was a serious shortage of anti-aircraft armament.

The diversion of inward bound shipping from ports and routes especially exposed to enemy interference was naturally also considered. The Air Ministry favoured the policy throughout but it had drawbacks as well as advantages: it was found that, apart from the difficulty of increasing facilities for berthing, discharging and storing at west coast ports, much confusion, delay and expense were caused by departure from normal trade routine. The Committee of Imperial Defence had recommended before the war that in the early days after it broke out (when an attempt to knock out London was expected) ocean-going traffic should be diverted from the Thames and east coast ports generally. In accordance with these recommendations a considerable measure of diversion of shipping from the east to the west coast was effected during September and October, but extreme inconvenience was caused to consignees and ship-owners, and on 25 November the Cabinet approved recommendations, in

---

[1] *F.D.* pp. 55, 86.
[2] See Oppenheim, *op. cit.* II 531.

which the Ministry of Transport and the Chiefs of Staff joined, that ships should not henceforward be diverted from their usual ports except for strong reason. The Cabinet discussed the matter again in March and April, after the attacks by the German Air Force on shipping had become troublesome, but reaffirmed their previous decision that large-scale diversion of shipping from east coast ports should be adopted only if forced on us by enemy action; they were determined, however, to press on with plans for increasing the capacity of the western ports.

Throughout the winter, despite efforts to charter neutral tonnage and to make the most economical use of what tonnage we had, the shipping situation caused anxiety; this was not so much by reason of actual losses due to the enemy, which were to a great extent offset by captures and new construction, as because it seemed clear that war-time sailing conditions, the requirements of the forces and of the French, the reluctance of neutrals to face the dangers of trade to the United Kingdom, and probable delay in turning out new cargo ships, taken together, would prevent the achievement of the current import programmes. In November the new Ministry of Shipping had estimated the amount we could import in the first year of the war as 47 million tons (as against an average of 55 millions in the years 1934–38), whereas in the following February our existing importing capacity was taken to amount to only 32·7 million tons in British ships, to which foreign shipping might contribute between nine and twelve million tons in addition; a deficiency of between two and five million tons must therefore be expected in the first year. Difficulties would increase when we maintained overseas larger armies more actively engaged and in the event of full-scale attacks on our ports. The Cabinet discussed the problem in all its bearings on 22 December and after receiving a series of reports from Sir Samuel Hoare, the Lord Privy Seal, it gave instructions on 1 March for a review of the import programme, including the food programme, and for an examination whether the best possible use was being made of the shipping at our disposal.[1]

The heavy strain under which the Navy already laboured is well brought out in a letter which the First Sea Lord wrote on 15 January 1940 to the Secretary of State for Air, who had referred to our great

---

[1] For a full treatment of the highly complicated question of shipping the reader is referred to the volume on the subject by Miss C. B. A. Behrens, *Merchant Shipping and the Demands of War* (H.M.S.O. and Longmans 1955). Miss Behrens states (p. 36, fn 2) that in fact the average annual rate of importation until the French collapse was 47 million tons, of which probably about 10 million came in foreign ships. None of the figures given include petroleum products.

preponderance of naval forces over those of Germany. Sir Dudley Pound replied:

> 'Relatively, our preponderance is enormous except in the case of submarines which does not matter. In other types of vessels our requirements are, however, as in the case of fighter aircraft, absolute and not relative.'

Ever since the beginning of the war, he said, we had had to provide forces simultaneously for the following tasks: (a) control of all shipping entering the North Sea, and lately of shipping leaving it; (b) protection for Norwegian convoys; (c) protection for East Coast convoys; (d) protection for outgoing convoys from London and Irish Sea ports; (e) protection for homeward convoys (i) Gibraltar to the United Kingdom, (ii) Sierra Leone to the United Kingdom, (iii) Halifax (N.S.) to the United Kingdom; (f) protection for dispersed shipping in the Pacific, South Atlantic, Indian Ocean and China Seas; (g) protection for our own troop movements, in the Channel, the Mediterranean and the Indian Ocean; (h) protection for Canadian and Australian expeditionary forces; (i) contraband control in the Mediterranean; (j) hunting groups in the outer seas.

At present we could not be sure of detecting all enemy warships attempting to break out. Except for the convoys from Halifax which had a battleship escort, and where we had strong units, we might take a nasty knock anywhere. Two-thirds of the Halifax convoys were at the mercy of a pocket-battleship or battle-cruiser. We were very short in destroyers too. 'This shortage is due to the fact that all the various stages of the Great War have come on us simultaneously in this war.'

CHAPTER V

THE NORTHERN IRON: FINLAND

THE TWO essential substances, it was said in the last chapter, which Germany needed to import in large quantities in order to carry on the war were oil and iron. It was a far cry to the Roumanian oilfields, but vital supplies of iron passed to Germany through northern waters, and in part under the nose of the Royal Navy. The present chapter is concerned with the attempt to deprive her of these supplies.[1]

According to the best information available to the Ministry of Economic Warfare in December 1939, Germany had in 1938 imported 22 million tons of iron ore, of which $9\frac{1}{2}$ million came from sources now closed to her. We had no precise knowledge of her stocks of ore, but they were believed to be low: probably not more than 2 million tons. In order to avoid a 'major industrial break-down', it was estimated, she must import during the first year of war at least 9 million tons (750,000 tons monthly) from Sweden. The chief Swedish ironfield was the Kiruna-Gällivare district in the north, near the Finnish frontier; the ore was shipped partly from Narvik on the Norwegian coast, partly from the Baltic port of Lulea; Lulea, however, was normally closed by ice from mid-December to mid-April, while Narvik was ice-free. There was a smaller ironfield further to the south, some 100 miles north-west of Stockholm, and there were southerly ports of which the most important were Oxelösund and Gävle, but the maximum monthly rate of delivery during the winter from these ports was 500,000 tons, the limiting factor being the capacity of the railways. Accordingly, should it prove possible to cut off Germany's supplies through Narvik, she would in each of the four winter months receive 250,000 tons less than the required minimum and by the end of April would find herself a million tons short—a predicament which, to put it at the lowest, would cause her 'acute industrial embarrassment'. After April she might make up her deficiency by resumed deliveries from Lulea; should, however, means be found of cutting off the Lulea exports as well as those from Narvik, German industry might well be brought to a standstill. Unfortunately the Baltic was at present denied to British surface ships, so that to close the route through

---

[1] See Map 4 for this chapter and the next.

Lulea or through the southern port of Oxelösund would require no small ingenuity. Stoppage of the Narvik route was made difficult by the fact that ships could proceed south through Norwegian territorial waters, in which acts of war were forbidden by international law. Nevertheless the temptation to a strong naval power to interrupt this important traffic was great, and any sound excuse for doing so would obviously be welcome to the British Government.

It is interesting to compare with the Ministry of Economic Warfare's estimate of nine million tons, as the amount of Swedish ore needed by Germany in the first year, the figures contained in a document which was prepared in February 1940 by the economic section of *OKW* for the use of the German Naval Staff.[1] It states that the Swedes had agreed to supply to Germany ten million tons during 1940, while one to two million tons of ore of inferior quality were due from Norway, mainly via Kirkenes. Of the Swedish supply two to three million tons would naturally come through Narvik, though this amount might be reduced to one million if arrangements could be made for storing the mined ore at the Baltic ports during the winter months. But for various reasons the Germans could not count on obtaining, through Baltic ports, as much as nine million of the ten million tons they desired in 1940, and this obviously increased the importance of the Narvik route. Raeder himself told Hitler that the interruption of this traffic would mean a loss of two and a half to three and a half million tons annually. It would seem therefore that the British Ministry's figures were on the conservative side, unless the German figure of about eleven million tons (ten million from Sweden) represents a larger amount than was strictly necessary.

It is not surprising, therefore, that it was as a measure in the economic war that Allied operations in Scandinavia were first seriously conceived, and that they were then conceived as a purely naval affair. The conception opened out to include land operations to secure the northern Swedish orefields and soon became involved with the idea of helping Finland. The probability of German reaction to such operations made it necessary to envisage extended operations in central Norway and Sweden. After the collapse of Finland the project shrank to its former limited proportions as a naval measure, though the likelihood of German counter-measures on a large scale was appreciated. As Norway and Sweden were neutrals the affair had obviously also a diplomatic side; in fact the economic, the military and the diplomatic aspects were closely connected throughout.

The first move was made by the Foreign Office. A week before the

---

[1] See *F.N.C.* p. 79.

outbreak of war Lord Halifax asked the Chiefs of Staff how they would view the commitments implied in a proposed confidential intimation to the Norwegian Government that we should regard a German attack on Norway as tantamount to an attack on the United Kingdom. The Chiefs of Staff's reply raised many of the points which evoked so much discussion later; they considered that Germany, in view of Norway's economic importance to her, was un-likely to violate Norwegian neutrality, except as an act of reprisal against such a degree of benevolence towards the Allies on Norway's part as to interfere with iron ore supplies. Should Germany in such circumstances take action, it would be to our interests to come to Norway's assistance. A communication on these lines was accord-ingly made to the Norwegians; no reply was received. The Chiefs of Staff had pointed out that we could give Norway no direct help against air attack; but the Foreign Office ruled that this information was not to be passed on to the Norwegians unless they raised the question. Some weeks later the Cabinet approved the Chiefs of Staff's recommendation that any assistance we could provide for Norway must be limited to naval action, and that no assurance on the subject of German aggression should be given to Sweden.[1] It may be noted that the Chiefs of Staff considered that the idea of any German seaborne operations against the western sea-board of Norway might be 'dismissed as impracticable' in view of the risks from superior British naval forces. This assumption appears to have governed British military thought on the subject throughout. It turned out to be a miscalculation of critical importance.

The next move was made by Mr. Churchill. On September 19 the First Lord called the attention of the Cabinet to the desirability of preventing the importation of Swedish iron ore to Germany from Narvik in winter, when the northern Baltic was frozen. If diplo-matic pressure on Norway failed, he would be in favour of laying mines in Norwegian territorial waters to force the iron ships out to where they could be stopped by the Royal Navy.

When Mr. Churchill raised the matter again on September 29, it appeared less urgent, since the sailing of iron ore ships from Narvik had ceased for the time being, and no immediate action was thought necessary. There were, moreover, hopes at this time of chartering the whole of Norway's spare tonnage and of inducing the Swedes to limit the supply of ore to Germany. These hopes, in the case of Sweden, were not directly fulfilled, but on November 2, as a con-dition of securing what the Ministry of Economic Warfare regarded as a satisfactory War Trade Agreement, the Cabinet approved a proposal of the Minister to accept 'a somewhat indefinite assurance'

---

[1] These decisions were taken on November 22 and December 7.

H

from the Swedes that, while unable to agree to reduce their exports of iron to Germany, they would deny her any additional facilities and in fact make the supply difficult for her.[1]

It was not until the end of November that the Cabinet determined that the question of closing the route for ore ships from Narvik through Norwegian territorial waters should be fully examined, from both the military and the economic angles, and it was then discussed in connection with a proposal of the Admiralty's to repeat the measure adopted in 1918 of laying a continuous barrage of mines across the North Sea from the Orkneys to Norway immediately south of Bergen. The primary purpose of this project was the protection of allied trade by 'cooping in' enemy surface raiders and submarines, but it should also assist our contraband control. A Foreign Office paper recalled the reluctance Norway had shown in 1918 to allow the extension of the barrage into her territorial waters; it was only when Germany's defeat seemed imminent that she had acquiesced, and even then mines were not actually laid. It was claimed, however, by the Admiralty that the barrage would be of great use even if it stopped at the edge of the three-mile limit. The Cabinet agreed that preparations should be made at once for the laying of the 60,000 mines which the barrage would require; it was not expected that it could be completed in less than six months, and eventually in July 1940, owing to the course of events, this ambitious project was replaced by another to lay a chain of mines from the north of Scotland to Iceland.

Before the reports called for by the Cabinet were ready for discussion important new considerations had been introduced by the Russian invasion of Finland.

On the night of September 28–29 the German and Soviet authorities had signed a 'Boundary and Friendship Treaty' laying down the line along which Poland was to be partitioned between them; immediately afterwards the Soviet Government concluded pacts with the Baltic States, Esthonia, Latvia and Lithuania, which had now fallen within the Russian sphere of influence; the U.S.S.R. was to have the right to construct military bases on their territory.[2] Soon afterwards the Soviet Government made even more exacting demands on Finland: as well as the cession of certain islands and of the Finnish part of the Kola peninsula they asked for a naval base at the outlet of the Gulf of Finland and for an extension of the Soviet frontier in the Karelian isthmus north of Leningrad in exchange for some Karelian territory of little value further north.

[1] See W. N. Medlicott, *The Economic Blockade* I ch. iv.
[2] See *Nazi-Soviet Relations* pp. 102–107.

If the Russo-German pact of August 23 created the impression
that the Soviet Union had disinterested itself in central Europe,
the negotiations with the Baltic States showed a more positive
attitude. Surprised by the speed of the German advance in Poland,
Russia had quickened her own pace in taking measures which, if
defensive from her point of view, appeared in a different light to
other peoples. So far as British relations with the U.S.S.R. were concerned, an official British expression of disapproval of the Soviet
invasion of Poland, and a declaration by the signatories of the
German-Soviet Boundary Treaty that they would hold England and
France responsible for the continuation of the war, had not prevented
the conclusion on October 10 of an Anglo-Soviet trade agreement
for an exchange of rubber and tin and machinery for Russian timber.[1]
On the same day the Cabinet discussed an appreciation by the Chiefs
of Staff of the military implications of the U.S.S.R joining the war
against us or showing benevolent neutrality to Germany.[2]

Later in the month of October, when knowledge of the Soviet
demands on Finland was causing indignation in informed circles, the
Cabinet asked for another appreciation from the Chiefs of Staff, on
'the relative advantages and disadvantages which would accrue to
us if, either formally or informally, we were to declare war on the
U.S.S.R. as the result of Soviet aggression against Finland or any
of the other Scandinavian countries'.

The Chiefs of Staff reported that the invasion of Finland by itself
would be no military threat to the Allies, nor could the Allies give
any assistance to Finland. Such action on Russia's part might, however, be preparatory to an invasion of Sweden and perhaps of North
Norway, which would be a much more serious matter from our
point of view. The establishment of Russian bases in Norway on
the model of the recent Soviet-Esthonian pact would progressively
threaten our security. A Russian invasion of northern Scandinavia
might well provoke a German invasion in the south, and we should
be compelled to resist a German-Soviet domination of the peninsula.
But so heavy a commitment must be considered from a broad point
of view. The one strong argument for action was that it should win
us the sympathy of neutrals all over the world. The open support
of the U.S.A. would outweigh the enmity of Russia. But without
American support France and Britain were in no position to undertake additional commitments. The Cabinet on November 1 approved
this common-sense conclusion.

At this time war between the U.S.S.R. and Finland seemed unlikely, but during the month of November the danger to Finland

---

[1] *ibid.* p. 108.
[2] See above, p. 67.

increased and on November 30 Soviet troops and aircraft crossed the
Finnish frontier; relations between the U.S.S.R. and Great Britain
had also become worse. The official British view of the Soviet action
against Finland was stated by the Prime Minister in the House of
Commons.[1] Owing to our inability to give effective help to Finland
his words were studiously moderate, but the Cabinet recognised that
the mood of the country was one of deep sympathy for the Finns and
indignation against their invaders and that a more open condemna-
tion of Soviet action might be demanded. Further, the Russian
aggression in the north, though perhaps of no direct menace to us,
might presage expansionist schemes, which we should be forced to
resist, in South-East Europe and Asia.

The Finnish appeal to the League of Nations on December 2 was
embarrassing: the thought of economic sanctions made little appeal,
particularly to the Powers anxious to conciliate Italy. The British
Government supported, however, without enthusiasm a resolution
pressed by the States of Latin America to the effect that the U.S.S.R.
had excluded itself from the League, and with less hesitation one
urging members of the League to give what help they could to
Finland. French opinion also was profoundly stirred.

It was in these circumstances that the question of depriving
Germany of her supplies of Swedish iron was discussed at considerable length by the British authorities. Interest in the question had
been stimulated not only by the invasion of Finland but by reports of
the illegal and inhumane methods, such as the machine-gunning of
merchant ships from the air, which Germany was now adopting in
her conduct of the maritime war: in particular the Admiralty had
reported on December 14 that she had sunk three ships in three days
within neutral waters, though the Norwegian Government did not
admit that two of these ships had in fact been attacked within their
territorial waters.

The Military Co-ordination Committee had before them on
December 20 papers produced by the Ministry of Economic Warfare,
by the First Lord of the Admiralty, by the Foreign Office, and by the
Chiefs of Staff.

The Ministry of Economic Warfare stated the economic point of
view, with the conclusions summarised at the beginning of this
chapter. It is desirable to quote the crucial paragraphs in full:

> 'The conclusion which may be reached as to the effect on Ger-
> many's economy of a stoppage of iron ore exports from Narvik
> to Germany is that, whereas there can be no certainty that such
> action alone would be decisive, there is a strong prima facie case
> to suppose that, if immediately brought about and if the usual

---

[1] *House of Commons Debates* 30 Nov., vol. 355, col. 255.

ice conditions are experienced at Lulea, it would be likely to cause by next spring such a substantial curtailment of German steel production as to have an extremely serious repercussion on German industrial output. From the purely economic stand-point, in fact, her position would, in that event, be so serious as to appear to justify the risk of considerable handicaps to our-selves in the spheres of Politics and Supply in order to bring it about.

Nevertheless, valuable as would be the closure of the Narvik route in itself, the full benefit of this action would only be secured if it were followed up by impeding exports via Lulea as well when the ice melts next April. For, whereas the closure of Narvik alone might not cause more than acute embarrassment to Germany, the closure of Narvik followed by a stoppage of exports via Lulea might well bring German industry to a standstill and would in any case have a profound effect on the duration of the war.'

The paper proceeded to consider the economic effect of German counter-measures since we at present depended on Norway and Sweden for ferro-alloys and certain other materials; moreover, we ourselves received some $2\frac{1}{2}$ million tons of Swedish iron ore annually through Narvik. The Ministry of Economic Warfare were more optimistic than the other Government Departments which they had consulted as to the net advantages of the proposed Allied action.

Mr. Churchill's opinion was that every effort should be made to cut off *all* Germany's supplies of Scandinavian ore by the end of 1940. Such an achievement would be equal to a first-class victory in the field or from the air and might indeed be immediately decisive. The Narvik source should accordingly be stopped at once by mines laid in Norwegian waters; the supply from the ice-free port of Oxelösund by 'methods which will be neither diplomatic nor military'; the case of Lulea would not become urgent until April. Mr. Churchill was not deterred by the prospect of an extension of the war by Ger-many to Sweden and Norway; he believed we had more to gain than lose by such a development; and he had no doubt that we could take and hold bases on the Norwegian coast. He ended by justifying the breach of international law implied in the mining of the Leads by appeals to the righteousness of the Allied cause. 'Acting in the name of the Covenant, and as virtual mandatories of the League and all it stands for' (the Council and Assembly of the League of Nations had just been meeting for the last time), 'we have a right, and, indeed, are bound in duty, to abrogate for a space some of the conventions of the very laws we seek to consolidate and re-affirm. Small nations must not tie our hands when we are fighting for their rights and freedom. The letter of the law must not in supreme emergency obstruct those who are charged with its protec-tion and enforcement. It would not be right or rational that the

Aggressor Power should gain one set of advantages by tearing up all laws, and another by sheltering behind the innate respect for law of their opponents. Humanity, rather than legality, must be our guide.'[1]

Commenting on this paper the Foreign Office agreed that we could not be expected to fight the war on the basis of allowing Germany to break all the rules while we kept them, and hoped that, even in countries desiring to remain neutral, there was now a growing readiness 'to recognise the broad issues involved in this struggle and perhaps, therefore, to judge more leniently of our disregard of rules which could justly claim observance only so long as that observance was general'.

Mr. Churchill's standpoint was one from which many supporters of the Allied cause were bound, now and later, to regard the attitude of strict neutrality adopted by the potential victims of German aggression. 'Small nations must not tie our hands when we are fighting for their rights and freedom.' But was it not reasonable, on the other hand, to recognise the fact that we were calling on small nations to undertake heavier risks, entailing more immediate and more certain, if not ultimately greater, sufferings than we seemed called upon to endure ourselves? Their unpreparedness and weakness might invite aggression, but so did our own, and because of our weakness we could not ensure to them even so much protection as we could provide for ourselves. Might they not fear, with some justice, that before their rights and freedom were secured their national existence would be destroyed? In Mr. Churchill's case indignation at German methods worked along with his inherent combativeness, and his desire to exploit the offensive powers of the splendid Service over which he presided, to demand some immediate action.

Important new factors were suggested by an earlier Foreign Office paper (of December 15). It reviewed possible developments in Scandinavia in the light of the Soviet invasion of Finland: no complications directly affecting the Allies were expected so long as the Finns maintained their resistance, but if the Russians should succeed in overrunning Finland the threat to northern Sweden and Norway might well stir Germany to take counter-measures and the Allies might then be called upon to help the Scandinavian powers against either Russian or German aggression.

Thus the subject had now been widened to include both the transport of Swedish iron ore to Germany through every outlet and the general policy of the Allies towards the Scandinavian States, should matters develop as they well might. More than merely naval action might now be involved. The Chiefs of Staff accordingly presented

---

[1] Churchill I 490–492.

their report in two parts, the first dealing with the Narvik issue only, the second with the larger question.

The Naval Staff, it appeared, were convinced that the Narvik traffic could not be stopped without a violation of Norwegian neutrality but they suggested that this might be justified as a measure of retaliation against the recent German attacks on merchant ships in neutral waters. Of the two possible methods of interference, by mines or by naval patrols, the Foreign Office preferred the latter as being more easily justifiable as a retaliation in kind, but the Admiralty had come back to the former, as being less likely to lead to a clash with Norwegian ships of war. Sabotage, another possibility, was not lightly to be undertaken: it would injure our own economy if directed against the very vulnerable railway connecting the ore fields with Norway, whereas no lasting effects could be expected from sabotage by the Allies elsewhere unless covered by a military force in the north of Sweden; such a force would have to be based on Narvik.

This contingency led to the second part of the report. While mere minelaying was unlikely to bring German troops into Scandinavia, an Allied landing at Narvik would probably provoke a German invasion of South Sweden or South Norway, neither of which we could prevent, and might also lead to hostilities with the U.S.S.R. A British military expedition to support the Swedes could only be based on the Trondheim–Östersund–Stockholm railway, and our formations as at present equipped were unsuitable for operating in the difficult terrain of southern Scandinavia at any time of the year. On the other hand, in order to dispute our control of the northern Swedish ore fields, Germany would have to send a considerably larger force than ours and this would mean an appreciable dispersion of her effective strength. The possibility of Russia attempting to seize Narvik or the northern Swedish ore fields was also discussed. Our only effective retort would be to anticipate her, in which case we might expect Swedish approval.

The Chiefs of Staff pointed out that the alternative policies of laying mines or sending an expedition through Narvik to the ore fields could not be considered independently of one another, since the adoption of the first might alienate Norwegian goodwill and so prejudice the success of the second; they emphasised finally the need of obtaining 'a really firm estimate . . . of the precise effect which the stoppage of these supplies will have on the German war effort'.

On December 19, the day before the Military Co-ordination Committee considered these four papers, their Chairman, Lord Chatfield, and the Chief of the Imperial General Staff had been present at a meeting of the Supreme War Council, at which M. Daladier had referred to a memorandum presented to Hitler by the German industrialist Thyssen emphasising the extreme importance to Germany of the Swedish ore deposits. Extracts from a report on this memorandum were read to the Committee and evidently impressed them. The representative of the Ministry of Economic Warfare was now doubtful whether the stoppage of the Narvik exports alone was worth while; it would produce only a limited effect—perhaps an embarrassment to the enemy for a few weeks by about May 1940, and it would be a serious matter for ourselves if our own imports from Scandinavia were cut off. But the Committee agreed that it was worth while taking a big risk in order to stop Germany's supplies of Swedish ore and, to start with, they judged the present moment opportune for closing the outlet through Narvik by naval action and for interfering if possible with the Oxelösund supply by other means. But they also seriously considered the suggestion of sending a picked Anglo-French force of 3,000–4,000 men accustomed to snow conditions to land at Narvik and seize the North Swedish ore fields. General Ironside took the view that such a limited 'sideshow' was justifiable; the remoteness of the place would make it difficult for the enemy to use a large force against it.

It was at this point that the idea was mooted of using the sympathies of the Swedish and Norwegian peoples for Finland as a means of securing the consent of their Governments for the entry of Allied troops, it being understood that the purpose of these troops was to join with them in assisting Finland and repelling the Soviet attack which might ensue. The French had urged at the meeting of the Supreme War Council the danger of allowing either the Russians or the Germans to obtain possession of the Swedish ore deposits; they had also proposed a joint approach to Oslo and Stockholm assuring the two Governments of Franco-British help against the possible consequences to them of assisting Finland, and the Council had agreed as to 'the importance of rendering all possible assistance to Finland and of taking diplomatic action in Sweden and Norway' in the sense of the French proposal. The draft instructions prepared by the French as the basis of such an approach seemed however to pledge us to more than diplomatic action; it appeared that

'our promise to co-operate with Sweden and Norway, if accepted, might be developed into the despatch of an expeditionary force, which in that case would be able to occupy Narvik and the Swedish iron ore fields as part of the process of assisting Finland and defending Sweden. And all this would arise as a result of our having carried out the resolution adopted by the League of Nations at its last meeting, calling upon Member States to assist Finland.'

The idea was plausible but it proved in the event a will-o'-the-wisp.

The matter came before the Cabinet on December 22 and 27, and it had to be considered from both the diplomatic and the military points of view.

Clearly very wide issues were involved. The opening of a Scandinavian front might prevent the German activities in the Balkans; but, if it did not, it might impose an intolerable strain on our own shipping. The Prime Minister thought we had perhaps come to one of the turning-points of the war. There were now two distinct projects: the original limited proposal to stop the traffic from Narvik by naval action, whether by mines or patrols, and the major one of securing the ore fields by a land expedition. It was more or less agreed that for success in the larger project the consent of Norway and Sweden was essential, but there was little doubt that the minor operation would be unpalatable to Norway and disturbing to Sweden. This seemed a strong reason for not queering the pitch for the major operation by attempting the minor one first; but the whole point of the latter was to stop the Narvik traffic immediately while the northern Baltic was frozen, whereas the blocking of the outlet through Lulea could wait until the ice broke in April. Thus the good was the enemy of the best, and for the next three months a contest was waged between them. In the December Cabinets the issue lay between those who wished to take immediate action, justifying it on the grounds of recent German violations of law and humanity and trusting that circumstances would develop in such a way as to make larger measures possible later, and those who held that it was not worth while to stop the Narvik traffic at the risk of spoiling the chances of coming to an understanding with the Swedes based on their fear of Russia and on our common sympathy with Finland. Mr. Churchill has made it clear that his own desire was for immediate action by the Navy;[1] the majority of the Cabinet, however, took the other view and a more tentative order of proceedings was adopted on December 27, by which date the immediate prospect of a Russian advance into Sweden had receded. It was decided to inform the Swedish and Norwegian Governments at once that Great Britain and France were prepared to help them against the consequences which might result should they send help to Finland; they were further to be informed, somewhat later, in general terms that we intended to send ships into Norwegian waters to stop coastwise traffic from Norwegian ports to Germany; but it was decided not to execute the threatened operations until the Scandinavian Governments' reactions to the latter communication were known; in the

---

[1] Churchill I 492.

meantime the Chiefs of Staff should report fully on the military implications of stopping the export of Swedish iron ore to Germany and the War Office should proceed with preliminary measures for the despatch of a force to Narvik.

The Chiefs of Staff's report of 31 December contained the first comprehensive estimate of what operations in Scandinavia would entail; it was based on two vital assumptions: that the interruption of the export of Swedish ore to Germany—say for a year—would really be decisive, and that Swedish and Norwegian co-operation would be forthcoming. On these assumptions they were now prepared to recommend intervention in Scandinavia: 'the opportunity is a great one and we see no prospect of an equal chance being afforded us elsewhere'. Some six weeks previously the Chiefs of Staff, revising a still earlier opinion, had decided, on the ground that it might be extremely difficult to limit our commitment, that they could not recommend the despatch of a small expedition to Scandinavia; now, however, that the stakes had been raised they thought the gamble justifiable.

In an accompanying paper the Chiefs of Staff gave their opinion that, if the Cabinet decided in accordance with their advice to undertake the major project—to deprive Germany entirely of Swedish ore—which could not be executed till March, it would be unsound to attempt the minor one in the interval.

In yet another paper the Chiefs of Staff, on the instructions of the Cabinet, considered more in detail the military consequences of the Germans establishing themselves in south Norway. In view of later events their conclusions have special interest. Assuming still that we should never seek to forestall the Germans by occupying Norwegian territory without the previous consent of its Government, the Chiefs of Staff advised that we could not prevent an initial German landing at Oslo or Kristiansand; we might be able to anticipate the enemy at Stavanger, though not if he used airborne troops, and we should hope to succeed in doing so at Bergen and Trondheim; a German sea-borne invasion of either port in the early stages was thought 'extremely improbable'. The British forces designed to occupy the three latter places, with the necessary shipping, should be held ready for instant despatch from the moment we decided to stop the Narvik traffic; we could not however be ready to land forces at Narvik for the protection of the railway to Gällivare against sabotage until the end of March.

The Chiefs of Staff were not prepared to recommend the acceptance of these risks 'if the issue at stake were the cutting off of a mere $\frac{3}{4}$ million tons of ore from Germany'; but should this minor stoppage not only not prejudice but actually facilitate the major project, that would put a different complexion on the matter.

The possibility of the Germans establishing themselves in *north* Norway before us was still not taken into account.

It was now for the Cabinet to satisfy themselves, first, that the economic prize was worth the risk and, secondly, that the co-operation of the Scandinavian Governments, which the Chiefs of Staff regarded as essential for the success of the larger project, could reasonably be counted upon.

On the first point, after hearing the views of the Ministry of Economic Warfare, the Cabinet, meeting on 2nd and 3rd January, 1940, were of the opinion that, although the effect of cutting off Swedish ore would be gradual and the time taken to bring about a collapse would be long, nevertheless in the end it would be decisive. Discussion was concerned, however, mainly with the question of the Narvik traffic and the possible German seizure of bases in south Norway as retaliation, and this risk the Cabinet were prepared to accept. Eventual operations in Sweden were not seriously considered at this time. It was decided to inform the Norwegians now, if the French concurred, that, having regard to the violation by German naval forces of Norwegian territorial waters, we were taking appropriate dispositions to prevent the use of these waters by German trade and that for this purpose it would be necessary for our naval forces at times to enter and operate in them. (The idea of laying mines had now been dropped.) But the necessary orders were not to be issued until the reactions of the Norwegian Government were known. In the meantime detailed plans were to be prepared for the occupation of Stavanger, Bergen and Trondheim. The French approved and gave orders for a special brigade to be formed.[1]

The communications to the Scandinavian Governments were made on January 6; protests followed from both so emphatic that after prolonged discussion of the whole question in its political bearings, including many alternative suggestions, the Cabinet decided on January 12 to take no action against the Narvik traffic at present; they feared that such action might imperil the complete stoppage from the northern ore fields at a later date. The Scandinavian Governments, however, were not to be informed of this decision. The Chiefs of Staff, it should be stated, were doubtful of the expediency of carrying out the smaller project at this time and they reiterated their conviction that the active co-operation of the two Scandinavian countries was essential for the success of the larger project.

This decision of the Cabinet marks the end of the first phase of the Scandinavian episode; the purely naval project had been

---

[1] Gamelin III 197.

dropped, and future action was dependent on the will of two weak States which lived in terror of their powerful neighbours.[1]

It is time to take note of the attitude of the enemy.[2]

The occupation of the Scandinavian countries was not part of Hitler's original design of aggression but was suggested to him by the Chief of the Naval staff, Admiral Raeder. On October 10 the Admiral pointed out how advantageous it would be, for submarine warfare, to obtain bases on the Norwegian coast, for instance at Trondheim, with the help of pressure from the U.S.S.R.[3] Nevertheless, even in the view of the Naval Staff, there were strong arguments against the occupation of Norway. Although it would extend the operational base for naval and air action against England, it would not directly affect operations in the decisive area, the Atlantic; on the other hand it would cause at least a temporary stoppage of the Narvik traffic, owing to the inevitable British reaction, and to guard the long Norwegian coast-line against the superior British naval power would be difficult. Consequently the continuation of Norwegian neutrality, with a covered way assured through territorial waters, might well be in Germany's interest. In no circumstances, however, could Germany tolerate a British occupation of Norway, which might bring Sweden under British influence and endanger German control of the Baltic, nor yet an interruption of the ore traffic from Narvik. In fact the Naval Staff, we are told on good authority, considered that the loss of Norway to England would be tantamount to losing the war. Should there be reason to suppose that the British were intending such measures, Germany must act to prevent them, and in the meantime she must keep a close watch for any indications of the British attitude.

When Raeder brought to Hitler's notice in October the advantages of securing submarine bases on the Norwegian coast, he received a non-committal reply. In December he raised the matter again, and he now had support from another quarter. *Reichsleiter* Alfred Rosenberg, Director of the Foreign Affairs Bureau of the Nazi Party, was in touch with a group of pro-Nazi Norwegians headed by the former Minister of War, Vidkun Quisling, which had in mind a *coup d'état* to be carried out with German help. Raeder and Rosenberg worked together and arranged an interview between Quisling and Hitler. According to Rosenberg, Hitler assured Quisling that he would

---

[1] Mr. Churchill's dissatisfaction is expressed in his letter of 15 January to a colleague; *The Second World War* I 498. See also his broadcast to the neutral Powers of 20 January (*The Times* 22 Jan. 1940).

[2] See *Nazi Conspiracy and Aggression* I 735 ff.

[3] *F.N.C.* p. 47.

prefer that the Scandinavian States should remain neutral but that attempts by the enemy to strangle Germany by an extension of the war must be countered.[1] At any rate Hitler was by the middle of December persuaded to authorise the preparation of a plan for the occupation of Norway; two alternative schemes were to be submitted, one for a *coup de main* engineered from within by Quisling with military assistance from Germany on a minor scale only; the other a joint naval, land and air operation in case the political scheme should fail.[2] Planning thereupon commenced under the auspices of *OKW*. Raeder had pointed out to Hitler that a German seizure of Norwegian bases would naturally occasion strong British counter-measures in order to interrupt the Narvik ore traffic. Thus the Germans had no retaliatory scheme in their pigeonholes at this time, had the British Cabinet decided for action in Norwegian waters; what measures they might have improvised, one can only speculate.

On the Allied side the two months following the British Government's decision on January 12 to drop the intended measures against the Narvik ore ships were dominated by the Finnish struggle. In the first weeks of the war the U.S.S.R. had seriously underestimated the Finnish will and power to resist; they had succeeded in capturing the small Finnish port of Petsamo on the Arctic, but everywhere else, and notably in the Karelian isthmus, between Lake Ladoga and the Gulf of Finland, where the frontier ran only some 15–30 miles north of Leningrad, their attacks had been foiled by Finnish mobility and tenacity making full use of the terrain and the climate. The Soviet Air Force despite its immense numerical superiority had inflicted little military damage and its attempt to terrorise the Finns by indiscriminate bombing had been in the main unsuccessful. But at the beginning of February the Russians renewed their attacks on the Finnish defences in the Karelian isthmus in greater strength and with improved tactics; there were signs that the Finns, whose vastly inferior forces were kept at full stretch, were now tiring.[3]

The admiration and sympathy of the non-Communist world for the Finns had been increased by the unexpected stoutness of their resistance to aggression, and in view of the inactivity on other land fronts it was inevitable, if not reasonable, that public opinion in many countries should demand that sympathy should show itself in substantial help. This was particularly the case in France.[4] The

---

[1] *N.D.* 004–PS and *Nazi Conspiracy and Aggression* I 742, 66–C.

[2] *F.N.C.* pp. 47, 62–67.

[3] See *The Memoirs of Marshal Mannerheim* (tr. E. Lewenhaupt, 1953) chaps. xiv, xv.

[4] See Reynaud, *La France a sauvé l'Europe* II 24.

French had been much dissatisfied by the decision of the British to drop the intended naval measures against the ore traffic, and the two questions—of help to Finland and of cutting off the German ore supplies—became closely entwined.

The Cabinet's decision of January 12 had not indeed been merely negative. The threat of naval action was kept suspended above the heads of the two Scandinavian Governments and it was hoped to win them round by moral pressure; moreover, planning for the major operation continued.

The Anglo-French military committee in London, in an appreciation of possible German action in the spring, took the view that Germany would not invade Scandinavia unless in fear of being forestalled by the Allies. But the Chiefs of Staff disagreed; they estimated, in a paper of January 28, that before launching an offensive in the west Germany was likely to take action to secure her supplies of oil and iron and might well attempt to seize the Gällivare deposits as soon as the Baltic became free. The northern Baltic should be free for shipping not later than the end of April, and Allied troops, if they went at all, ought therefore to reach Narvik by 20 March—a date which thus became important. The necessary Allied forces were put at two infantry brigades and one fighter squadron for Narvik; the Southern Sweden force, including the troops to seize Trondheim and Namsos (80 miles to the northward of Trondheim), which would be required as bases, and also Bergen and the Stavanger airfield, would need some five divisions in all, with two fighter, two bomber and one army co-operation squadron; an advanced base would also have to be maintained for four heavy bomber squadrons operating from Britain. The naval commitment would be substantial: some forty destroyers for continuous escort duties for two months, together with many trawlers and patrol vessels, besides a large quantity of merchant shipping. Nevertheless in spite of all difficulties the Chiefs of Staff considered the prize so great that, if an opportunity to occupy the ore fields should be presented, or could be created, 'we should seize it with both hands'. They added a warning: unless our preparations were timely and complete, we should be unable to do so.

It was obviously desirable to clear up Scandinavian policy with the French. The two staffs exchanged ideas and a meeting of the Supreme War Council was arranged. The staffs agreed in principle on the strategy for securing the ore fields and on the necessity of obtaining the previous consent of the two neutral Governments. On the best way of helping the Finns there was difference of opinion, since the French were inclined to give priority over the Narvik plan to what seemed to the British an ill-thought-out and quite unrealistic project of a landing at the Finnish Arctic port of Petsamo, now in Russian hands; this operation was to be combined with an expedition by the Finnish army, which for this purpose would be reinforced by some thirty to forty thousand Allied volunteers, to be introduced into Finland through the neutral countries.

When the Supreme War Council met on February 5 the two Governments agreed on a common policy.[1] Both were determined that Finland must be saved, declaring that her capitulation to Russia would be a major defeat for the Allies, most damaging to their prestige throughout the world. It was clear that the despatch of arms and equipment would not be enough: Field-Marshal Mannerheim, the Finnish Commander-in-Chief, had asked for reinforcements of 30,000 men. As to the course of action to be pursued, Mr. Chamberlain urged that in the Allies' determination to save Finland they must not lose sight of their principal aim, the defeat of Germany, towards which the seizure of the Swedish ore fields would be an important step. The ideal therefore would be an operation which combined assistance to Finland with control of the ore fields, and this ideal might be realised by an expedition proceeding from Norwegian ports to the Finnish frontier via Gällivare and Boden; such an expedition, 'ostensibly and nominally designed for the assistance of Finland', would 'kill two birds with one stone'. Mr. Chamberlain believed that the effect on the Germans would be one of 'consternation'. The British plan, so expounded, was accepted by M. Daladier. It was agreed that the forces required must be units of the Allied armies, though they might be disguised as volunteers after the example of the Italian 'non-intervention' in Spain; the bulk of the troops would be British, and the French agreed in principle to the diversion of formations from the British Expeditionary Force; the imminent despatch of the 42nd and 44th Divisions to France was therefore cancelled. Responsibility for co-ordinating arrangements, and the command of operations in the Scandinavian theatre, were assigned to the British.

So far, so good; but what of the neutral States through whose territories these camouflaged forces were to pass? This difficulty, too, it was proposed to meet in an ingenious manner. As soon as the Allied expeditions were ready, but not until then, the Finns should be advised to appeal to the world in general, and to Norway and Sweden in particular, to save them from their invaders; the Allies would use this moral lever to overcome the opposition of the neutral Powers to allow them passage, assuring the neutrals that a force stood ready to assist them against German retaliation. The possibility that they might remain obdurate and put a stop to the whole affair could not be evaded; sabotage of the Narvik railway might ruin

---

[1] The British Ministers present were the Prime Minister, the Foreign Secretary and the three Service Ministers.

everything; but active opposition on their part was in Mr. Chamberlain's view a very remote contingency. M. Daladier shared Mr. Chamberlain's hopes, but was less ready to let the execution of the great project depend on the consent of the neutrals; he won agreement to his proposal that if neutral opposition prevented us from securing the ore fields the alternative Petsamo project might be reconsidered.

In the light of later events an air of unreality pervades the proceedings of this conference, as shown in the readiness to lock up troops and equipment in Finland when so urgently needed elsewhere, in the underestimation of the administrative difficulties of such a campaign, in the slight regard paid to the danger of provoking Soviet hostility, in the miscalculation of German efficiency and resource, and finally in the wishful thinking which discounted the determination of the neutral Governments to maintain their neutrality. Desirous though her Scandinavian sisters might be to preserve the independence and integrity of Finland, they were still more desirous not to be drawn into war.

In the weeks following the conference the Allied Governments pressed on simultaneously with plans for helping Finland, with the preparation of the dual-purpose operation authorised by the Supreme War Council and with the diplomatic manœuvres intended to clear the way for it. It is not proposed in the course of this history to mention all or most of the numerous plans devised and discussed for operations which were never executed, but the projected expedition to Finland has exceptional interest: it was the first of the major schemes in time, for many weeks it occupied a large part of the attention of the Cabinet and their advisers, it reached the stage of the commanders being warned and receiving instructions from the Government, and most important of all, it formed the basis for an operation which was actually executed and which cannot be rightly understood without some knowledge of the earlier project.

Assistance to Finland was a daily item on the Cabinet's agenda. Much thought was given to the possibility of infiltrating volunteers into Norway and Sweden, but on 10 February the Cabinet were informed that the Finns now laid comparatively small emphasis on the need for men as against their urgent need for munitions, especially for fighter aircraft and heavy anti-aircraft artillery. With the enemy's advance in the Karelian isthmus, however, the prospect of Finnish resistance continuing until the spring became remote, and on February 22 the Finnish President appealed to the Allies, as the only hope of immediate relief in view of the military situation, to bring pressure on the U.S.S.R. to agree to peace negotiations. This suggestion was not at all to the liking of the Allies; they desired neither war with Russia nor a patched-up peace between Russia and

Finland which would enable Russia to give more extensive economic help to Germany.

A tentative request from the Finns for 100 bombers now and for 50,000 men before the end of March was considered by the Chiefs of Staff quite impracticable, but the despatch of 50 Blenheims by March 20 had been provisionally approved when it was learnt on March 9 that the Finns were treating for peace. By this time 144 British aircraft had been promised to the Finns, of which 53 were known to have arrived.[1]

In the eyes of the Allied Governments and Chiefs of Staff the despatch of munitions and volunteers to Finland had all along been of very secondary importance compared with the large-scale enterprise, preparations for which were being hurried on.

The Cabinet on February 7 authorised the measures recommended by the Chiefs of Staff in their paper of January 28 and the Chiefs of Staff next day provided for the necessary inter-Service planning to be begun.

The scale of the expedition now proposed was as follows: a demi-brigade (three battalions) of *Chasseurs Alpins* and one British Regular brigade, strengthened by three companies of skiers, were to land at Narvik and move up the railway to secure the Gällivare mines; a mixed force, probably of two or three brigades, was to operate in support of the Finns in Finland, but for administrative reasons not further south than the head of the Gulf of Bothnia; five battalions of the 49th (Territorial) Division were to occupy the southern Norwegian ports; and three divisions, one Regular and two Territorial, withdrawn from the British force assigned to France, with one Territorial brigade of the 49th Division on the lines of communication, were to help the Swedes to resist a German invasion. The move involved 100,000 troops and 11,000 vehicles in all and was expected to take eleven weeks.

The basis of planning was to disembark the troops at the fastest rate at which they could be absorbed by the transportation facilities in the country. The principal base port would be Trondheim, from which there was only a single-line railway running east; and this line would have in addition to carry the imports needed by the people of Sweden should Germany blockade her Baltic ports. It was pointed out that stores took longer to load than troops. Thirty-six destroyers would be required for escort duty, and it was proposed to sail the parties for Bergen and Stavanger in four cruisers. An aircraft-carrier would be used in order that the Gladiators and Lysanders of the air component might be flown to airfields in Scandinavia at the earliest possible moment.

---

[1] Marshal Mannerheim states that 11,500 foreign volunteers in all reached Finland; *op. cit.* p. 359.

I

The air aspect of the expedition, at any rate in the south, caused some concern, now and later, as well it might. The Germans, according to the Chief of the Air Staff, had 1,300 heavy bombers within range of Trondheim, through which port we might need to pass voluminous traffic. Should we fail to deny them Stavanger aerodrome, the danger would be greatly increased. The air forces we ourselves could send were limited by the airfields available in Scandinavia; Trondheim itself possessed only a small one, and there was none elsewhere from which modern fighters could operate. Nevertheless the Chiefs of Staff were of opinion that these risks might be reasonably accepted as part of the price to be paid for 'seizing the ore fields and thus hastening the end of the war'. The northern expedition would not be exposed to similar hazards from the air, but even so the railway from Narvik into Sweden was but a precarious line of communication.

Misgivings were certainly aroused in the Cabinet by the large scale of the enterprise now envisaged, and doubts were expressed whether the Territorial divisions which it was proposed to employ were sufficiently trained for mobile operations. But there was no serious suggestion that the scheme as a whole should be reconsidered.

In settling the date for the expedition there were many points to be thought over, and the Chiefs of Staff and Foreign Office presented a joint report which the Cabinet discussed on 18 February. The earliest day on which troops could be equipped and ready to land in north Norway was March 20, in which case the store-ships would have to sail on March 12. The latest day, to make sure of forestalling the Germans at Lulea, was April 3, which would mean that the store-ships must sail on March 26. The force intended for Stavanger, Bergen and Trondheim (Force 'Stratford'), however, could start earlier, by February 28. (It is interesting to note that the Chiefs of Staff still did not believe it practicable for the Germans to forestall us at Trondheim.) On military grounds the earlier the date chosen for the Narvik expedition within these limits the better. On the diplomatic side, time must be allowed for the necessary consents to be obtained, first from the Finns to sanction the use of Allied Regular troops and to appeal to Norway and Sweden, and then from these two Powers for passage through their territory; on the other hand any delay in action would increase the risk of a leakage of information, and the Supreme War Council had agreed that the neutrals should not be appealed to until military preparations were complete. It was a nice balance of arguments, on the continuing assumption that the expedition could not succeed, and would not be attempted, in the face of Scandinavian opposition.

Meanwhile an incident had occurred in Norwegian waters which directed the attention of the world to the issues raised by Scandinavian neutrality. On 17 February the First Lord of the Admiralty reported to the Cabinet that the German tanker *Altmark*, which had acted as supply ship to the *Graf Spee* in the Atlantic and had relieved her of her captured British crews, had been identified by a British aircraft on her homeward journey. On the approach of a destroyer she had taken refuge in the Jössing Fiord, on the south-west coast of Norway, whither she had been followed by Captain Philip Vian of H.M.S. *Cossack*, the leader of the flotilla. When he demanded the release of the prisoners Captain Vian had been informed by the commander of one of two Norwegian torpedo boats standing by that the *Altmark* had been examined in Bergen and authorised to proceed homeward through territorial waters as being an unarmed ship; nothing was known of prisoners. Captain Vian's signal to this effect crossed with one from the Admiralty instructing him that, unless the Norwegians agreed to convoy the *Altmark* to Bergen with a joint British and Norwegian guard and escort, he was to board her and free the prisoners. This he did, displaying the dash and skill expected of the Royal Navy. The Admiralty signal had been made with the concurrence of the Foreign Office and the Cabinet highly commended Captain Vian's exploit.

The Norwegian Government, 'quivering under the German terror', as Mr. Churchill puts it,[1] protested vehemently against the *Cossack*'s action in attacking the *Altmark* in territorial waters; the British Government resented the negligence of the Norwegians in failing to detect the presence of the prisoners and took the incident as confirming their claim that Norwegian neutrality was being improperly and illegally exploited to the advantage of the Germans.[2] In a former war a British Foreign Secretary had protested that 'if Danish neutrality consists in mere assertion and . . . remonstrance against England, and in the most unqualified acquiescence in every extravagant demand of the enemy', the King would take 'such measures as may be necessary to secure his own honour and his country's welfare'.[3] On similar lines the First Lord vigorously urged that an excellent opportunity now offered for laying the minefield for which he had so long been pressing; he did not believe that the Norwegian reaction would go beyond words, and he still viewed without misgiving the possibility of the war with Germany extending to the Scandinavian peninsula. The Cabinet discussed the proposal at length; immediate naval preparations were authorised, but after

---

[1] Churchill I 508.

[2] For the communications exchanged between the two Governments see Cmd. 8012 (1950) and the Norwegian official publication *Altmark-Saken 1940*, ed. R. Omang (Oslo 1953), with summary in English; for the legal aspect see C. H. M. Waldock, in *The British Year Book of International Law 1947*, and Oppenheim, *op. cit.* II 693–695, 730.

[3] Lord Howick to the Danish Minister, 17 March 1807, cited H. W. V. Temperley, *Life of Canning* (1905) p. 73.

mature consideration of the legal and economic arguments and of the probable reaction of neutrals, and after consulting the leaders of the Opposition and the Dominion Governments, they decided on February 29 not to proceed 'for the time being' with the measures proposed. One point which might perhaps have received more emphasis in favour of their decision was that only two months now remained of the period during which the Narvik traffic was of vital importance to Germany, so that the economic loss which could be inflicted on her was of but a minor order.

At the same meeting at which this decision was taken the Chiefs of Staff reported that the force (Stratford) for the three southern bases had been ready since February 26 and that the commanders designate of all the three expeditionary forces had received their detailed instructions. But the prospect that the larger operation would take place had now for some time become remote.

On the diplomatic side nothing went right. The Swedish Government declared roundly on February 16 that they would not in any circumstances allow foreign troops to cross Swedish soil to the help of Finland. They were willing enough to send her volunteers and material *sub rosa*, but they were not prepared, thought our Minister at Stockholm, to provoke either Russian or German hostility until satisfied that the Allies could protect them against both—which was far from being the case at present.

A fortnight later the Cabinet none the less informed both the Swedish and Norwegian Governments that an Allied force had been prepared for despatch to Finland and that we should presently request passage for it and co-operation. Should compliance involve them in war with Germany we could afford extensive military support, but to make this effective there must be staff conversations. The Swedes refused both passage and staff conversations, and the Norwegians took the same line. Nor could the Finns be induced to make such a formal appeal to us for armed assistance as might shame their Scandinavian neighbours into allowing us to pass through. The Finns were in fact well aware of the Swedish attitude and were now thinking seriously of negotiating with the Russians unless the Allies could meet their quite impossible demands for the immediate despatch of material, and especially bombers, on a large scale.[1]

On March 9 it was known that a Finnish peace delegation was in Moscow. To give the Finns moral support, and at their request, the Prime Minister made a statement in the House of Commons on

---

[1] See above, p. 109.

March 11; it was to the effect that the French and British Governments had sent and were continuing to send material assistance to the Finns and had informed them that, in response to an appeal for further aid, they would immediately come to their help with all available resources.[1] Still hoping for the appeal which never came, and convinced that the two neutral Governments, under the influence of fear, were acting in a manner contrary to the real sympathies of their peoples, the Cabinet now considered the suggestion, pressed by the French, that we should not accept a mere diplomatic refusal of permission to land but should test on the Norwegian beaches the firmness of the opposition. After receiving a report from the Chiefs of Staff they decided next day, March 12, to prepare for a landing under such conditions, in the first instance at Narvik only; if this landing was successful, it was to be followed by one at Trondheim. The forces for Bergen and Stavanger were to be held ready but not despatched. The commanders for Narvik were approved, Admiral Sir Edward Evans and Major-General P. J. Mackesy, commanding 49th Division, and that evening they received their instructions at a special meeting of Ministers and the Chiefs of Staff. Their instructions were of an unusual, not to say embarrassing, nature. The object of the campaign, they were told, was to render assistance to Finland, while ensuring that the North Swedish ore fields were denied to Germany and Russia for the longest possible period. The first task was to establish a force at Narvik; the second, to secure with the utmost despatch the railway into Sweden; the third, to concentrate the force in Swedish territory in the most suitable place that circumstances allowed for the execution of its ultimate role. The attitude of the Norwegians at Narvik was uncertain; it was the Government's intention that the force should land provided it could do so without serious fighting; it was not the intention of the Government that it should fight its way through either Norway or Sweden. The commanders were not to be deterred by a mere show of resistance or by minor opposition even if it entailed some casualties; on the other hand they were only to use force 'as an ultimate measure of self-defence should their forces be in jeopardy'. This delicate experiment, as it turned out, was never made, since the Finns accepted the Russian terms on the night of March 12–13. The pretext or cover of assistance to Finland was now no longer available to mask designs on the Gällivare ore fields and orders were given to disperse the forces prepared. The normal flow of reinforcements to France could accordingly be resumed.

One can only guess what would have been the immediate, and

---

[1] *House of Commons Debates* vol. 358, col. 836.

what the later consequences of such a semi-peaceable invasion of Norway. In Whitehall the prospect of at last seizing the initiative had been exhilarating, and the cancellation of the plan had a depressing effect. 'Our second defeat has come about', commented one of the Cabinet's advisers, 'and we must now look about for something else.'

The Cabinet had in fact had something else in view, but it too had to be dropped, at any rate for the moment. This was an ingenious proposal which had first been submitted to them in November as a method of retaliation against illegal German minelaying. Known by the code name of 'Royal Marine' or 'R.M. Operation', the project was the special child of Mr. Churchill.[1] It was a scheme to lay floating mines, either from French territory or from the air, in German waterways and, in the first instance, in the Rhine; they would be so constructed as to become harmless before they reached neutral waters. The Cabinet had authorised work to be started, and on March 6, after discussion with the Air Ministry, the War Office and General Gamelin, Mr. Churchill had presented the plan to the Cabinet as ripe for execution: the release of mines from the bank could begin on March 12, but the Royal Air Force would not be ready till the middle of April. The Chiefs of Staff smiled on the operation; it might have important results and should be carried out as soon as possible. The Cabinet approved, subject to French agreement, and the necessary warning to neutrals was drafted. The idea was now to launch 300 to 400 'fluvial mines' on the night of the 14th. The French Government, however, asked for delay, fearing the effect of German retaliation on an assemblage of French aircraft, and so the matter stood when the Finns sued for peace.[2]

The enemy's intelligence service had given him a fair idea during these last weeks of what was in the wind, and it had not escaped him that the Finnish resistance, blessed as it was by the League of Nations, offered the Allies a plausible pretext for intervention in Scandinavia. The *Altmark* incident was taken by the Naval Staff as a warning that Norwegian territorial waters would not be safe in the future, and the Norwegian Government were believed by the Rosenberg group (though this belief was not shared by the German Legation at Oslo) to have an understanding with the British.[3]

Planning for the occupation of Norway, on two hypotheses, had been ordered by Hitler in December.[4] On January 27 Keitel, by

---

[1] See Churchill I 456–458, 517.
[2] For French reactions, see Gamelin III 216–220.
[3] *N.D.* 004–PS.
[4] See above, p. 105.

command of the Führer, had taken over direction of further preparations; a working staff had been formed at *OKW* and detailed
planning had begun. On February 21, a few days after the *Altmark*
episode, Hitler put General von Falkenhorst in charge of the execution of the project, which, according to a statement made by the
General in 1945, he regarded as of the highest importance and
urgent. Its purpose was to cover the right flank of the German
armies on the Continent, to allow free movement to the fleet and to
secure the supply of iron ore. Falkenhorst would be under the
direct orders of the Führer; he had six divisions placed at his disposal
and was provided with an inter-Service planning staff.[1] At length on
March 1 Hitler issued a directive for *Fall Weserübung* (operation
Weser Exercise).[2] By this time the idea of a non-violent coup had
been abandoned and Hitler had decided that Denmark too must be
occupied; the occupation of both countries was to be represented as
a 'peaceful' measure, intended to protect Scandinavian neutrality,
but resistance would be broken by all military means; surprise was
essential.

The Germans were now apprehensive that action by the British
was imminent; on March 3 Hitler decided finally that *Weserübung*
was to precede the operation in the West, and next day orders were
issued with his approval for pushing on preparations so that by
March 10 the attack could be launched with four days' notice.
Raeder pointed out that from the naval aspect the project was risky
in the extreme and contrary to all the rules of war; nevertheless
complete surprise should bring off success. All the modern warships
must be employed, the most difficult part of the operation being the
return voyage, when they must expect to have to break through the
British fleet. The situation continued tense until the signature of the
Russo-Finnish treaty, after which the Naval Staff were of opinion
that the danger of a British landing was no longer acute.[3] This made
it more difficult to justify drastic action by Germany. 'The conclusion of peace', Jodl noted, 'deprives England, but us too, of any
political basis for occupying Norway.'[4]

It was just before the Finnish capitulation that Mr. Sumner
Welles visited London as President Roosevelt's representative on a
mission of inquiry which he afterwards described as a forlorn hope.[5]

---

[1] *N.D.* 1809–PS, (Jodl's Diary); also *Nazi Conspiracy and Aggression* Supplement B
pp. 1534 ff.; see Wheeler-Bennett, *The Nemesis of Power* p. 494, for the opposition of the
Army chiefs.

[2] *F.D.* pp. 88–90.

[3] *F.N.C.* pp. 84–88.

[4] *N.D.* 1809–PS, 12 March 1940 (Jodl's Diary).

[5] *The Time for Decision* (1944) p. 105.

He had already visited Rome, Berlin and Paris. 'American public opinion', he wrote later, 'had at this moment, except in one or two sections of the country, reached another climax of out-and-out isolationism. Popular feeling demanded that this government refrain from any action, and even from any gesture, which might conceivably involve the United States with the warring powers.' This being so, the President wished his representative merely to find out 'what the views of the four governments might be as to the present possibilities of concluding any just and permanent peace'. Mr. Welles soon discovered that there were none. The Germans had informed him, so the Prime Minister gathered, of their intention to launch a tremendous offensive directed entirely against Great Britain in the near future, whereas in London Mr. Welles received from all parties the impression of a 'relentless determination' to see the war through to the bitter end.[1]

A few days after this, much speculation was aroused as to the purpose and outcome of a meeting of the two Dictators on the Brenner Pass on March 18. In fact, no important decisions were taken, Mussolini merely confirming his intention to move with Germany when he judged the moment to be ripe. Hitler, we are told, returned beaming with joy.[2]

The collapse of Finnish resistance was generally recognised as a severe blow to the prestige of the Allies. Speaking in the House of Commons on March 19 the Prime Minister was at pains to assure the House that the Allies had not failed in their obligations to help Finland.[3] Finland would never have been invaded but for the Nazi-Soviet pact, and it was 'only German threats which terrified the Scandinavian countries into withholding the help which might, perhaps, have saved her'. Even so, no appeal from the Finns to us had gone unanswered: the only actual request for the despatch of land forces had been that made in January for 30,000 trained men in May, and we had made preparations to send much larger forces by an earlier date. The Finns, however, had not made by March 5 the formal appeal which we had asked for. The Opposition did not claim that more could have been sent with safety, but several Members suggested that there had been unnecessary delays. Several spoke also of a sense of boredom and bewilderment in the country and urged greater vigour and a stronger initiative in the conduct of the war. But no division was taken.

---

[1] *The Time for Decision* (1944) pp. 61 ff., 108.
[2] Ciano *Diaries* 18 March 1940, *Diplomatic Papers* p. 361; *N.D.* 1809–PS.
[3] *House of Commons Debates* vol. 358 cols. 1834 ff.

In France the consequences were more serious. The Government had for some time been anxious as to their own position, while General Gamelin would not have been sorry to see the Germans involved in a troublesome campaign at a safe distance from French soil. The French had advocated several measures in the last few weeks which to the British seemed unsound, whereas they had considered the British over-cautious and slow.[1] The time had evidently come for taking stock of the new situation and the British Government pressed for a meeting of the Supreme War Council. But on March 20 it was known that M. Daladier and his Cabinet had resigned; the defeat of Finland had dealt it a mortal blow.

That the effect of the Finnish débâcle should have been regarded as so disastrous to the prestige of the Allies may now appear surprising. Why should Great Britain and France, engaged in a life-and-death struggle against a formidable and far better prepared enemy who threatened invasion, at a time when they were still grievously short in trained men and munitions, have been expected to send help to a remote ice-bound neutral country and thereby risk war with a second Great Power? It should be remembered that in 1940 the Allies were still pictured as the champions of the League of Nations and the enemies of all aggressors; in December 1939 they had joined in a general appeal for help to Finland and they had more recently made a public declaration of their intention to help the Finns to the utmost of their power. The deliberations of these months show British Ministers acutely sensitive to public opinion abroad as well as at home, as though the consciousness of material weakness made the maintenance of moral integrity all the more essential. That being so, this new exhibition of impotence, following on the failure to give any appreciable help to Poland, was bound to create a sense of despondency and, to some extent, of humiliation.

---

[1] See Reynaud II 26.

CHAPTER VI

THE NORWEGIAN CAMPAIGN

SIX MONTHS and more had now passed since the outbreak of war, and it was natural that the Allied Governments should consider how they stood; the fact that in France a new administration was in office made a survey of policy the more necessary. It was indeed a '*drôle de guerre*': so much had not happened. No knock-out blow had been attempted by the Luftwaffe against London or Paris; there had been no invasion of France or Belgium; the U-boats had not seriously endangered our essential supplies; Italy, Japan and Russia had not made war on us. We had been allowed, for the building up of our resources, a much longer period of grace than we had ever expected. The Prime Minister felt justified in claiming that Hitler had missed the bus.[1]

But there was little positive on which the Allies could plume themselves. If the sinking of the *Graf Spee* and the *Altmark* incident were feathers in the cap of the Royal Navy, these successes could hardly outweigh the collapse of Poland and Finland, to whom we had pledged our support, and our obvious incapacity to supply Turkey, our prospective ally, and other countries too, with the munitions they needed. The French Chamber had shown its dissatisfaction with the Daladier Government, and French Ministers evidently felt strongly that something drastic must be done to fortify the national morale. A meeting of the Supreme War Council was fixed for March 28, and on the 25th M. Reynaud, the new President of the Council, addressed to the British Government a note in which he urged that among other things a revision of methods of directing the war was required; the present procedure of discussion, he maintained, did not secure the necessary speed of decision. The Allies moreover were too legalistic in their concept of neutrality: they must be prepared to disregard formalities and act, if need be dictatorially, in accordance with the common and lasting interests of the free peoples. The general conduct of the war, he continued, was at present dominated by two fundamental problems, the one physical—how to cut off Germany's supplies, especially of iron and oil; the other psychological—how to assert our initiative so forcibly as to regain the confidence of the neutrals in our eventual victory. The solution lay in resolute action:

---

[1] On April 4; see Churchill I 526; Mr. Chamberlain had used this phrase in his correspondence on earlier occasions with reference to the crisis of September 1938, when, as he thought, Hitler had been baulked of his great opportunity.

the Allies should proceed at once to take control of navigation in Norwegian territorial waters, occupying the vantage points on land required to make this control fully effective; they should also take the necessary steps to cut off German supplies from the Caucasian oilfields, even at the cost of a rupture with the U.S.S.R., and as an immediate measure they should study the possibility of passing submarines into the Black Sea. The French Government would like their proposals examined in a new spirit of realism and authority. It must not be assumed that time was on our side.

On this point the Chiefs of Staff were in agreement: time was on our side only if we took the fullest possible advantage of it. This meant not that we should yield to a demand for spectacular but unsound projects but that we should 'intensify and accelerate the building up of our resources' with a view to passing to 'a general offensive strategy' at the earliest possible moment. Such was the conclusion of the report—in fact an interim appreciation of the present military situation—which in March they submitted to the Cabinet. The position at sea they regarded as not unsatisfactory, though an aggravation of air attack on our shipping in home waters might have serious results; our economic pressure was telling on Germany, but there were holes in the blockade through Italy and in the Black Sea and in the Far East, while German exploitation of Russian resources, particularly of oil, might during 1941 largely nullify its effects. In the air it would still be some time before the Allies could wisely initiate an offensive on an effective scale. On land the Chiefs of Staff believed that with the support of the frontier fortifications the Allied forces in France should be able to stop a German offensive. Italy's continued neutrality was most desirable, and in the Near East our policy should still be to strengthen Turkey, 'our northern bastion', and create a benevolently neutral *bloc* of Balkan States.

The Cabinet had also before them on the day before the meeting of the Supreme War Council a Foreign Office paper on the Scandinavian issue replying to an earlier exhortation, received from the Daladier Government. The Foreign Office proposed that we should warn the Swedish and Norwegian Governments that we reserved the right to take more vigorous measures in future in certain eventualities and, in particular, to prevent Germany from exploiting the resources or the facilities of their countries. In the meantime no announcement should be made of the dispersal of the force intended for Finland. Such a policy of vague menace would be a new departure, but it would provide a basis for future action at the right moment. The Foreign Office were as previously hesitant about approving such a breach of neutrality as the mining of the Leads, pointing out that at this time of year, when spring would soon allow the resumption of shipments from Lulea, the stoppage of the Narvik traffic would produce but limited results. They preferred to strike at Germany direct and suggested that the French should again be invited to sanction the sowing of mines in German waterways, as an operation to which the British Government attached high importance.

The Cabinet saw strong practical objections to M. Reynaud's proposals: they were not prepared to occupy strategic points on Norwegian soil, and his suggestions for action against Germany's oil supplies ignored the fact of Turkish neutrality. But the Cabinet were in favour of mining the Rhine at the earliest possible date, and thought that as a lever to secure French consent we might use our willingness to take naval action against the Narvik traffic after warning the Scandinavian States; they might be told that we did not propose indefinitely to allow Germany to make profit out of their neutrality. The Allied case, as the Prime Minister stated it next day to the French, was that these neutrals were not free agents.

At this meeting, on March 28, Mr. Chamberlain laid great stress on the need of keeping up the spirits of our own people and impressing neutrals with our offensive capacity while striking a blow at German morale. He referred to the respective effects on British public opinion, far greater than their intrinsic importance justified, of the German air-raid on Scapa Flow on March 16 and the British retaliation against the island of Sylt.[1] He commended the 'Royal Marine' operation as combining the psychological merit of surprise with the practical one of increasing the strain on the German railways. He did not believe it would lead to retaliatory air attacks on France. The Allies' main weapon was, however, economic pressure, and Germany's two weak spots were still iron and oil. With regard to iron, he spoke in general terms of the vulnerability of both the Narvik and the Lulea sea-routes; the key to the oil problem was Roumania, and the only method of ensuring her resistance to German demands was to provide Turkey with the means of giving her effective help. The possibility of cutting off supplies from Baku should also be studied.

M. Reynaud likewise referred to the need of combating the prevalent sense of frustration, embittered as it was by skilful German propaganda seeking to persuade the French that England was responsible for the war. He was in favour of mining the Norwegian Leads with the least possible delay and the Lulea approaches, by aircraft, later; he was not hopeful of stiffening Roumania against German pressure, but agreed that the possibilities of action in the Caucasus should be studied and preliminary measures taken. As for the fluvial mines project, M. Reynaud said that on a previous occasion the French War Committee had rejected it by reason of the

---

[1] See above, p. 87.

expected reprisals against France, but he thought that if combined with other operations it might be sanctioned.[1]

It was eventually agreed that a warning on the lines proposed by the British Foreign Office should be addressed to the Governments of Norway and Sweden on April 1 and that minefields should be laid in Norwegian waters on April 5 with a view to forcing German shipping into the high seas; plans should be prepared for interrupting the Lulea traffic in the spring. Further, subject to the concurrence of the French War Committee, the 'Royal Marine' operation should be started on the evening of April 4, in the form of launching mines from land; the second phase, the dropping of mines from the air, was to follow on April 15. If this time-table had been adhered to, the Allies would have laid their mines in Scandinavia two days before the enemy struck.

At the same meeting the two Governments agreed to issue a 'solemn declaration' to the effect that 'during the present war they will neither negotiate nor conclude an armistice or treaty of peace except by mutual agreement'. The fate of this declaration will be recounted later.

Now at long last action against the ore traffic had been approved. Next day, March 29, the Cabinet confirmed the decisions of the Supreme War Council and discussed the details and timing of the warnings to be given to neutral Governments with regard to the mining of the Scandinavian waters and of the Rhine respectively, and the form of the public announcements intended to justify our action to public opinion at home and abroad. They also noted that a German reaction to our proposed measures might give us an opportunity of landing forces in Norway with the consent of the Norwegian Government. The Chiefs of Staff had already instructed the Joint Planning Sub-Committee to study the whole question and prepare a directive on which the inter-Service planning staffs could proceed. The problem appeared indeed essentially the same as that envisaged last December. There would be no question of landing in Norwegian ports unless the Germans made some move which turned Norway into a theatre of operations—in which case Norwegian co-operation with us might be expected.

At their next meeting, on April 1, the Cabinet approved the report and directive submitted by the Chiefs of Staff. The report tabulated the possible German reactions, among which it envisaged a decision to establish air and naval bases in Norway; in this case 'the moment the Germans set foot on Norwegian soil, or there is clear evidence that they intend to do so, our object should be (a) to despatch a force

---

[1] The War Committee consisted of the President of the Republic, the President of the Council (Prime Minister), the Ministers of War, Marine, Air and the Colonies, Admiral Darlan, and Generals Gamelin, Vuillemin, and Georges.

to Narvik to secure the port and, subsequently, the railway inland as far as the Norwegian-Swedish frontier, and to pave the way to the Gällivare ore fields; (b) as a defensive measure, to despatch forces to occupy Stavanger, Bergen and Trondheim, in order to deny their use to the Germans as naval and/or air bases'. If, as seemed possible, the Germans should have forestalled us at Stavanger, the proposed landing would probably be impossible; none of the landings could take place if the Norwegians were hostile. We should then be reduced to action by sea and air. It was not expected that the Germans would invade Sweden except as a last resort with a view to securing her ore; if they did, there was no immediate action which we could take, but the reconstitution of a force, such as had been proposed before the Finnish collapse, was being studied.

But the same day the Cabinet learnt of a hitch; the French War Committee had refused to sanction the 'Royal Marine' Operation and proposed its postponement for three months, by which time their factories engaged on aircraft and munitions should be less vulnerable to air reprisals. The Cabinet were disappointed and annoyed; they had hoped much from the moral effect of mining the Rhine, and our Allies now seemed to be backing out of a bargain. Hoping that the French might be induced to change their mind the Cabinet decided to hold up the presentation of Notes to the Scandinavian Govern-ments and wait for a day or two; some members feared the effect on public opinion of a violation of a small nation's neutrality if unac-companied by a more direct defiance of Germany.

On April 3 nothing had been heard from the French, but reports had been received to the effect that German troops had been con-centrated and embarked at Baltic ports; objectives in Scandinavia had been mentioned. It was not believed, however, in Stockholm, whence the most specific of these reports emanated, that the Germans would land this force in Norway or Sweden if we were merely to make use of Norwegian territorial waters or to stop ore shipments. The Cabinet decided, whether or not the French agreed to the execution of the 'Royal Marine' operation, to have the warning Notes handed to the Scandinavian Governments on April 5 and the minefields laid on the 8th—a delay of three days on the date originally fixed.

The chief difficulty on the French side was understood to lie with M. Daladier, who although no longer President of the Council was still Minister of National Defence, but the President of the Republic took the same line. Mr. Churchill, who saw Daladier in Paris on the 5th, was convinced that it would be unwise to press the French to agree to the Rhine operation at the present time, and the Cabinet reaffirmed that day their decision to proceed with the mining of the Leads. It would seem that no serious damage to German economy was expected to result from this measure so late in the winter, and for this very reason it was thought unlikely that Germany would 'take dangerous retaliatory action'; it was advocated largely on psychological grounds—to gratify French opinion and to show the world that we were after all capable of taking the initiative.

At their meeting on April 5 the Cabinet approved proposals from the Chiefs of Staff intended to avoid delay in starting the expeditions on the first news of a German move against Scandinavia and to prepare for the despatch of additional forces to Norway if necessary. The Cabinet also, on the 6th, approved the instructions for the commanders of the forces held ready to sail immediately, the Chief of the Imperial General Staff explaining that the only change of substance between these instructions and those drafted before the Finnish collapse was that the Narvik force was now not to cross the Swedish frontier without further orders.[1] It was our intention that it should land only with the general co-operation of the Norwegian Government, but it was thought possible that a perfunctory resistance might be encountered locally during the period of disembarkation; such resistance should be disregarded and brushed aside, but it was not intended that the Allied troops should fight their way through against serious Norwegian opposition. In any case the force detailed for Stavanger was not meant to do more than raid and destroy the aerodrome. It was considered unlikely that the enemy could forestall us at Bergen or Trondheim; the possibility of his doing so at Narvik was never contemplated at all. The commander of each of the forces was to act under the direct orders of the War Office. The Cabinet at the same time approved the instructions for the naval commanders.

It remained the policy of the Government that no Allied troops should land in Norway unless and until the Germans had done so or had made it clear that such was their intention. Nor was it by any means taken for granted that the Germans would react in this way.

The reports of German military preparations were, however, well founded. On March 26 Admiral Raeder gave as his opinion to the Führer that, although the danger of a British landing in Norway was no longer acute, the enemy would make further attempts to disrupt German trade in neutral waters and might try to create a pretext for action against Norway. Sooner or later, he insisted, Germany would be obliged to occupy the Norwegian coast, and he urged that she should do so as soon as possible; after April 15 the nights would be too short. Hitler agreed to the operation taking place about the time of the new moon (April 7). On April 2 the date was fixed for the

---

[1] See chapter v, p. 113. The new instructions are printed by T. K. Derry, *The Campaign in Norway* (H.M.S.O. 1952) Appendix A(1). The reader is referred to this work for an account of the campaign.

9th, and the first movements by sea began in the small hours of the 3rd.[1]

Hitler's intention was, in Denmark, to occupy Jutland and the island of Fuenen by surprise and proceed to the occupation of Zealand; in Norway, to seize important points on the coast by surprise landings from the sea and air. The plan was daring and original. The troops would be conveyed to the several Norwegian landing-points in warships, their artillery, equipment and supplies being carried in transports disguised as cargo-ships, which would start earlier so as to arrive at the same time as the troops. Airborne troops would be used at Oslo and Stavanger. Almost the entire German surface fleet, divided into six groups, would be required for the operation; ten destroyers carrying 2,000 mountain troops to Narvik would be accompanied till near their destination by the battle-cruisers *Gneisenau* and *Scharnhorst*, which would break off at an agreed point and create a diversion in the Arctic.

The German Naval Command were well aware of the hazardous nature of the task assigned to them. Admiral Carls, Group Commander, East, expected that about half the warships used would be lost if there were Norwegian or British resistance, but the prize was held to be worth the risk and much was hoped from surprise and speed.

The Naval Staff were now convinced that British action in Scandinavian waters was imminent; they commented on April 4 that a race was beginning for Scandinavia between Great Britain and Germany. The Germans were indeed on this day already off their marks, since the first of the ships carrying equipment sailed during the night of the 2nd/3rd. Four nights later the warships of the Narvik and Trondheim groups put out to sea.

On April 8 the British Cabinet were informed that the more northerly of the projected minefields had been laid that morning off the eastern shore of the Vest Fiord, an arm of the sea leading to Narvik; the force which was to have laid the southern minefield had been ordered back in view of the movements of the German fleet.

On April 4 aircraft had located two large German warships at Wilhelmshaven. Weather was bad on the 5th. During the night of the 6th/7th great activity had been observed on the wharves and roads of the north German coast near Kiel, Hamburg, and Lübeck. On the morning of the 7th enemy warships had been sighted moving north off the coast of Jutland, and later in the day British bombers had

---

[1] *F.N.C.* p. 87; *N.D.* 1809–PS, 3 April 1940 (Jodl's Diary).

attacked a considerable force which they reported as including two large units. The Home Fleet, under Sir Charles Forbes, and the Second Cruiser Squadron had accordingly sailed from Scapa and Rosyth that evening. The First Cruiser Squadron, which had been embarking troops at Rosyth for Bergen and Stavanger, had been ordered to disembark them and would be sailing shortly, so the Cabinet were told on the 8th, without them. The four cruisers put to sea in fact in such haste that there was no time to remove the men's equipment and these four battalions were immobilised for five days. The escort for the troopships intended for Narvik and Trondheim had also been ordered from the Clyde to Scapa. 'The Admiralty had judged it desirable to do everything they could to ensure that the German ships would not be able to return home. Everything possible had therefore been ordered out.' In other words, the whole combined operation, known as R4, had been abandoned.

The Commander-in-Chief, it is now known, was surprised at the decision to abandon 'R4', having himself no doubt that the German invasion of Norway was actually under way. At the Admiralty, however, the intelligence received on the 8th was still thought to indicate a major break-out of the German fleet, which must be countered by the fullest possible strength. It is an honourable tradition of the Royal Navy that a British fleet shall seek to bring the enemy's strongest force to battle at the first opportunity. It is possible, however, that by doing so it may be playing the enemy's game, and such turned out to be the case in the present instance. It is unlikely, nevertheless, that even if the main British fleet had been used to cover the sailing of the troops the latter could have anticipated the German landings; the enemy had obtained too long a start, and no preparation had been made on the British side for landing against serious opposition from the shore. Still less can it be assumed that if we had secured Norwegian bases we should have been able permanently to hold them.[1]

On the morning of Tuesday April 9 the Allied Governments learnt that they had delayed too long. Before the day was over it was known that the Germans had occupied Copenhagen and Oslo, Stavanger, Bergen, Trondheim and—hardly believable—Narvik. The Danish Government had capitulated before the invaders, but the Norwegian King and Government, whom the Germans had failed to capture, were resisting, and they had appealed to the Allies for help.

For an account of the operations of the Home Fleet the reader must be referred to Captain Roskill's volume.[2] Here it need only be said that owing to defective information, due largely to rough weather and bad visibility, it was unable either to bring the German heavy

---

[1] For particulars of how the crucial decisions were taken, see Roskill I 161.
[2] *The War at Sea* I ch. x.

ships to action, apart from the brief inconclusive engagement between the *Renown* and the *Gneisenau* and *Scharnhorst* on the morning of April 9, or to prevent the landing of the German troops at their selected ports. The two enemy battle-cruisers proceeded to execute their sortie to north and west and reached home safely but not unscathed by the evening of the 12th, the *Hipper*—also damaged—joining them at sea early that day on her return from Trondheim. The German ships covering the landings further south were not so fortunate, though projected attacks on Trondheim and Bergen by British surface ships on the 9th were called off by the Admiralty. The *Koenigsberg*, of the Bergen group, was damaged by the shore batteries during the landing on the 9th and destroyed in harbour by Skuas of the Fleet Air Arm next day. The *Karlsruhe*, after a successful disembarkation at Kristiansand, was torpedoed by the submarine *Truant* on the evening of the 9th and sunk later. The new heavy cruiser *Blücher* was destroyed by shore batteries while penetrating Oslo fiord. The pocket-battleship *Lützow*, after performing her appointed task at Oslo, was torpedoed by the submarine *Spearfish* early on the 11th but was, with difficulty, got back to Kiel.

The Germans thus lost in these operations three cruisers and, as we shall see, ten destroyers, besides the damage done to the *Lützow*, the *Scharnhorst*, and the *Hipper*, but these losses were not heavier than they were prepared for. On the other hand their air attacks on the 9th, in which the *Rodney* was hit and the destroyer *Ghurka* sunk, brought the British Commander-in-Chief to the opinion that the correct policy was to attack the enemy in the north with surface forces and assistance from the Army, while leaving the southern area mostly to submarines.

From this decision, which was endorsed by the Admiralty, it followed that there was little chance of stopping the flow of reinforcements from German and Danish ports to Oslo during the Norwegian campaign despite the efforts of our submarines and mine-laying aircraft in the Skagerrak and Kattegat. Moreover, in view of Germany's superiority on land and in the air, it was only a question of time when she would contrive to pass her troops from Oslo to whatever point she wished in southern or central Norway.

April 9 was a day of many and difficult meetings for the Allies. They had again lost the initiative; they were ill informed as to how things stood both in Norway and in the North Sea; their planned expeditions had been called off and in the whole United Kingdom there were only eleven battalions capable of being sent abroad, of which four were at present useless owing to the precipitate departure of the cruisers with their equipment. The view was nevertheless expressed in the Cabinet that the termination of Norwegian neutrality had greatly improved our position and that our overwhelming sea power should enable us to dispose of the German landing-parties 'in a week or two'.

The French Ministers were much perturbed. After a meeting of the War Committee MM. Reynaud and Daladier came over in the afternoon to propose that, provided Belgian co-operation was forth-coming, the Allied armies on the Western front should move forward at once into Belgium—a proposal with a long history which will be treated in the next chapter; on this condition the French would consent to the immediate release of the fluvial mines.[1] Nothing came of this, but it was agreed to occupy the Danish outpost of the Faroë Islands without delay and to approach the independent Government of Iceland with an offer of help against German aggression and a request for naval and air facilities. The Faroës were occupied on April 13 but the decision to send troops to Iceland was not taken until May 6.

Touching the immediate question of operations in Scandinavia, it was held to be dangerous to despatch troops overseas until the naval situation had been cleared up. But granted that they might be despatched, it was now to be expected that they would have to land against German opposition—a contingency which had not been allowed for either in estimating the quantity or quality of the troops required or in the loading of the ships to convey them. The serious-ness of this last difficulty does not seem to have been appreciated in high quarters; but it was soon seen that the troops available were no longer adequate to secure all the objectives formerly proposed and that a choice would have to be made between them.

At first indeed the Cabinet had hoped that we should turn the Germans out of Bergen and Trondheim and also occupy Narvik, which they were at that time not known to have reached. When it was learnt that they were there, the Chiefs of Staff considered the recapture of the two southern ports the more urgent from the military point of view, but not more than one British battalion could sail before April 12. At the meeting of the Supreme War Council on the 9th M. Daladier said that in the French view Narvik should be attacked first; the division of *Chasseurs Alpins* which had been made ready for Finland would be available for this operation. It was evident that both Governments still cherished hopes of obtaining control of the ore fields, since they believed that, willing or not, Sweden would be drawn into the war. When the Military Co-ordination Committee met in the evening fresh intelligence indicated that the Germans might have three to four thousand men at Narvik besides six destroyers. It was agreed that consequently the Allied forces ought not to attempt to eject the enemy from more than one

---

[1] See Reynaud II 29 ff.; Gamelin III 314–318.

lodgement at a time and, despite the opinion of the Chiefs of Staff that morning, the Committee resolved that, having regard to the strategic importance of Narvik in relation to the Gällivare ore fields and to the attitude adopted by the French at the Supreme War Council that afternoon, our plan should be to concentrate attack on Narvik whilst masking the other ports. The Chief of the Imperial General Staff emphasised that the success of the operation depended on the most careful preparation, and that it would be doomed to failure if it were rushed. The Cabinet endorsed the Committee's decision next morning.

With the opening of the Norwegian campaign the distinction between the higher direction of the war and local strategy became blurred in practice. This was due partly to the geography of the theatre of operations, partly to the facts that the nature and development of the campaign had not been foreseen, no proper organisation of command had been effected and consequently confusion of functions ensued.

In the *Manual of Combined Operations, 1938*, it is written:

> 'one of the earliest decisions to be made on a declaration of war is the system of command in each theatre of war. The Cabinet decides in what form control is to be exercised and advice on this point will be tendered by the Chiefs of Staff as part of the war plan. Normally, if each Service is carrying out a distinct strategical role and if adequate co-ordination is possible from Whitehall, the responsibility for carrying out the tasks of the Navy, the Army and the Air Force rests with their respective Commanders-in-Chief in each theatre of operations . . . There may however be cases where a war zone is extensive and a number of widely spread operations are being undertaken concurrently either in the form of single Service or combined operations but where adequate co-ordination from Whitehall is not possible. In these cases a system of general control through a supreme command may prove necessary. Generally speaking, the greater the distance from home the more it is probable that it will be necessary to have a Supreme Commander responsible for local co-ordination.'

In the case of Norway it does not appear that the question was specifically referred to or decided by the Cabinet; in view of the minor and contingent character of the operations originally envisaged, their dispersion over hundreds of miles of coast and their comparative nearness to the United Kingdom, it was no doubt taken for granted that Whitehall would 'co-ordinate'. There was indeed no place in Norway suitable for headquarters even of one

Service and, when a single commander was eventually appointed for the land forces in central Norway alone, he and his staff could only hope to control them from London, and consequently they remained there. With regard to the Navy, it would hardly have been possible to appoint a commander for operations in Norway as a whole other than the Commander-in-Chief of the Home Fleet, and he had many other concerns besides Norway and the North Sea. So it was probably inevitable that strategy should be co-ordinated from Whitehall. But the fact remains that no machinery for the effective direction and execution of a combined campaign in such circumstances had at this time been created, nor do the consequences of the lack of it seem to have been appreciated.

An important part in the direction of the campaign was played by the Military Co-ordination Committee. Lord Chatfield, its original chairman, had recently resigned office and the Committee now normally consisted of the three Service ministers, Mr. Churchill, Major Oliver Stanley and Sir Samuel Hoare, and the Minister of Supply (Mr. Burgin), with the three Chiefs of Staff as expert advisers.[1] The chairman was Mr. Churchill. His unrivalled experience, his technical knowledge, his force of character and his many great qualities assured him a unique pre-eminence, and his interests ranged far beyond the merely naval field. Nevertheless the arrangement was an anomalous one, since the Committee might be called upon to decide between the respective urgency of the claims of the Admiralty and other Services, and it did not work well. Nor did it last long; from the 16th until the end of the month the Prime Minister himself was persuaded to preside at every meeting but one. Mr. Churchill has written scathingly of the Committee's earlier deliberations—'a copious flow of polite conversation' leading to 'a tactful report'—and compared them unfavourably with the prompt methods of the Admiralty.[2] As one Service member saw it, the Committee caused undue civilian interference in purely military affairs and waste of time in explaining them. The Prime Minister's belief was that Mr. Churchill in his enthusiasm put more intense pressure on his advisers than he realised, and reduced them to silent acquiescence. Mr. Chamberlain noted at this time that the Chiefs of Staff were 'all over-driven', and took credit for having 'double-banked' them by the employment of three Vice-Chiefs of Staff; one of these was General Sir John Dill, brought back for the purpose from France, whose 'able brain' he had long wished to have at headquarters. These

[1] See Chatfield, *It might happen again* p. 187; Churchill I 528–530. Major Stanley had replaced Mr. Hore-Belisha in January, and on April 4 Sir Kingsley Wood had exchanged offices with Sir Samuel Hoare, Lord Privy Seal. See Appendix V.

[2] Churchill I 529; reference is there made to frequent meetings of the 'Defence Committee of the War Cabinet'; in fact the first meeting of this body was on May 10, from which time it superseded the Military Co-ordination Committee.

officers acted as substitutes for their chiefs when absent, but also relieved them of much departmental work. Meetings of the Vice-Chiefs counted equally as meetings of the Chiefs of Staff Committee.[1]

At the beginning of May, in circumstances which he has described, Mr. Churchill was made the Prime Minister's deputy, with special responsibility 'for giving guidance and direction to the Chiefs of Staff Committee'; he was to be assisted by a central staff, the senior officer of which, Major-General Ismay, was to become an additional member of the Committee in his own right.[2] A less lop-sided arrangement would have been to make Mr. Churchill Minister of Defence, but the Prime Minister was not prepared to give him authority over the other two Service Departments. However, Mr. Churchill had not many days to wait.

The conclusions of the Military Co-ordination Committee were normally reported in the form of recommendations to the Cabinet, but during these critical days they also took decisions, which they reported to the Cabinet for confirmation. Neither the Co-ordination Committee, however, nor the Cabinet was a suitable body to take rapid decisions and still less to supervise their execution, nor did the Chiefs of Staff supply the need of a Combined Headquarters. All three bodies were continuously occupied with the most varied matters affecting our interests at home and abroad, and their picture of what was happening in Norway was usually incomplete and out of date. Yet Norway is not far distant from Britain, and it is perhaps unfortunate that no member of any of them could find time to visit this theatre and see for himself the conditions under which the campaign was being fought. What happened was that from April 9 onwards there followed a rapid and bewildering succession of plans; the administrative confusion which resulted was not foreseen, nor was due care taken to ensure mutual understanding between the Services concerned.

The Cabinet, as we have seen, on the morning of April 10 approved the recommendation of the Military Co-ordination Committee to concentrate on the capture of Narvik. The Committee, discussing that afternoon the steps required, agreed that our first object in seizing the place was to establish a naval base for ourselves, the second to use the port as a base from which to reach out to the Gällivare ore fields; they agreed further that the first step would be to establish an advanced base in the vicinity of Narvik where the troops could be sorted out with a view to operations against the

---

[1] The first meeting of the Vice-Chiefs as such was on April 27; the other two officers were Vice-Admiral T. S. V. Phillips and Air Marshal R. E. C. Peirse.

[2] Churchill I 576–579.

Germans in Narvik itself. Two battalions were immediately available to establish the advanced base; they would be reinforced by the balance of the troops intended for the landings in Norway, namely six battalions; the French *Chasseurs* would follow, but could not arrive until April 23 or 25. The First Lord reported these arrangements to the Cabinet on the morning of the 11th; it was proposed to make a lodgement at Harstad (a small port on an island over sixty miles distant from Narvik by road and ferry), where our troops could reorganise and prepare for an attack against Narvik.

The command of the troops for 'Rupert', as the expedition was now designated, was entrusted to Major-General P. J. Mackesy. It had been intended that the naval commander of the Narvik expedition should be Admiral Sir Edward Evans; he was now replaced by Admiral of the Fleet the Earl of Cork and Orrery, whose appointment as Commander-in-Chief, Portsmouth, had recently expired. It was unusual to select an officer of such high rank—higher in fact than that of the Commander-in-Chief of the Home Fleet—for so small a command; but Lord Cork enjoyed the First Lord's particular confidence and had been in close consultation with him during the winter in connection with operation 'Catherine', the proposed employment of specially strengthened surface ships in the Baltic. Lord Cork received orders direct from the Admiralty and was independent of the Commander-in-Chief Home Fleet, but in the main depended on him for the provision of the necessary naval forces. Owing to the lateness of his appointment he had never met his Army colleague, and it soon appeared that the instructions they had respectively received were far from identical.

Lord Cork was given no written orders, but he was present at the meeting of the Co-ordination Committee on April 10, and his 'impression on leaving London was quite clear that it was desired by His Majesty's Government to turn the enemy out of Narvik at the earliest possible moment' and that he 'was to act with all promptitude in order to attain this result'.[1] No representative of General Mackesy was present on the 10th, but the Chief of the Imperial General Staff sent him fresh orders that day, stating that the object of his force was to eject the Germans from the Narvik area; his initial task would be to establish his force at Harstad, arrange for co-operation with any Norwegian forces present and obtain the information necessary to enable him to plan his further operations; for these, reinforcements would be sent. It was not intended that he should land in the face of opposition. These 'instructions' were handed to General Mackesy at Scapa on April 11 by Brigadier Lund, the Deputy Director of

---

[1] Lord Cork's *Despatch*, published as Supplement to the *London Gazette* of 8 July 1947.

Military Operations, along with a letter from General Ironside, which included the following sentences:

> 'Latest information is that there are 3,000 Germans in Narvik. They must have been knocked about by naval action. You will have sufficient troops to allow you to make preliminary preparation and reconnaissances . . . You may have a chance of taking advantage of naval action and you should do so if you can. Boldness is required.'[1]

The naval action referred to was the attack ordered by the Admiralty on the 9th and carried out the following morning by Captain Warburton-Lee and five destroyers against the German force in the fiords round Narvik. The heroic exploit of Captain Warburton-Lee and his small force, in atrocious weather conditions, resulted in the sinking of two of the ten German destroyers besides an ammunition ship and six merchantmen at the cost of one British destroyer sunk and one beached. This success was followed up on April 13, when under Admiral Whitworth's command the *Warspite* and nine destroyers, in concert with aircraft from the *Furious,* disposed of the remaining German destroyers and sank a submarine without the loss of any British ship.

There remained in or near Narvik the two thousand German troops—three to four thousand as the Chiefs of Staff believed—besides the 2,500 survivors of the ships' crews; cut off from relief by land and sea but supplied to some extent by air and by the railway from Sweden and encouraged by bomber help, this small force under Major-General Dietl held the town until May 28 against increasingly superior numbers supported by the Royal Navy and its guns. A chance of ejecting them directly after the second naval action (April 13) was missed because no troops had then arrived. When the advance party appeared in the *Southampton* next day, precious time was lost owing to difficulties in wireless transmission. General Mackesy's force, however, had been neither embarked nor equipped for an opposed landing, and in the opinion of the army officers and of Lord Cork's Chief of Staff, Captain Maund, an expert on the organisation of combined operations, an early assault against an enemy in position was impracticable by reason of the deep snow, the lie of the land and the absence of proper landing-craft. Lord Cork on the other hand did not accept the soldiers' opinion but was convinced that with greater determination on their part an assault against the ill-found garrison might well have succeeded.[2]

---

[1] The instructions and the letter are printed by Dr. Derry, *The Campaign in Norway* Appendix A.

[2] See L. E. H. Maund, *Assault from the Sea* (1949) ch. ii; also Derry, *op. cit* ch. x.

The realisation that the capture of Narvik might be a slower affair than they had expected was deeply disappointing and vexing to the authorities at home and especially to the First Lord of the Admiralty.

In the meantime the naval success at Narvik had led to the first change of the strategic plan for the campaign, and one improvisation now followed another. In the ten days next after April 10, when the Cabinet had decided to concentrate on Narvik, strong reasons were adduced on political as well as military grounds for securing Trondheim, the ancient capital of Norway, in view of its importance both for the encouragement of the Norwegians and as a centre of communications with access by rail to Sweden. The Germans for their part spoke of the decisive importance of Trondheim.[1]

The Military Co-ordination Committee had agreed on April 11 that an operation against Trondheim, to which the code name 'Maurice' was assigned, should be studied in detail but that no actual preparations should begin until it was known what would be needed for Narvik. On the 13th after receiving the news of Admiral Whitworth's success they agreed that 'if the information from Narvik in the opinion of the First Lord of the Admiralty justified the assumption that the occupation of the town would not be seriously opposed, the War Office and Admiralty in consultation should, without further reference to the Committee, make arrangements for diverting the second brigade of the Narvik force to Namsos'. Namsos, some 80 miles north-north-east of Trondheim, was a small port at which it had already been decided to land a naval party, as well as at Aalesund, another small port 150 miles south-west of Trondheim.[2] The possibility of a landing direct at Trondheim was also considered at this meeting. The Cabinet were told next morning of these new ideas and were further informed that M. Reynaud allowed them a free hand in the employment of the *Chasseurs Alpins* hitherto earmarked for Narvik.

The Chiefs of Staff had remarked on the 13th that it would not be possible to divert any part of the Narvik force, except perhaps the French contingent, to Trondheim, since the ships were believed to have been loaded for a single disembarkation;[3] nor, said General Ironside next day, had the force been furnished with maps of the

---

[1] *F.D.* 18 April.

[2] Operations 'Henry' and 'Primrose'.

[3] According to an Aide-Memoire of April 11 by D.C.I.G.S. to C.I.G.S. 'the loading of personnel and M/T has been so arranged as to facilitate separation of the old Avonmouth (24 Guards Bde.) and Stratford (146 Inf. Bde.), into two parties should this prove necessary'.

Trondheim area. Nevertheless, as the result of the discussion in the Co-ordination Committee the Chiefs of Staff decided on the 14th that the 146th Territorial brigade could and should be so diverted while at sea. These troops eventually landed at or near Namsos on the 16th and 17th, without some 100 tons of their stores and without their Brigadier, whose ship had gone on to Narvik.

The command of 'Mauriceforce' had been entrusted to Major-General A. Carton de Wiart, V.C., who was first warned for overseas service on the 12th; his instructions, given him on the 14th, explained the objects of the expedition to Central Norway as being (a) to provide encouragement for the Norwegian Government, (b) to form a rallying point for the Norwegian Government and armed forces, (c) to secure a base for any subsequent operations in Scandinavia. His role would be to secure the Trondheim area, but his force was not organised for a landing in face of opposition. The General would be directly under the War Office.

General Carton de Wiart was flown out next day (15th) to Namsos, but without a staff. Namsos was found to be anything but a satisfactory landing-place for a considerable force: it had poor berthing facilities, it was short of fresh water, it lay under four feet of snow and it offered no concealment against the air bombardments which had already begun. Further, as was explained to the Cabinet, the incomplete training of the troops added to the hazards of the affair.

The implications of a direct attack on Trondheim were meanwhile being examined. The Joint Planners advised that such an operation would be costly in execution and unlikely to succeed; they suggested that we should aim rather at isolating the garrison by converging advances from Namsos and Aandelsnes, which latter port was now preferred to Aalesund as a base. Air Commodore Slessor drew attention to the vulnerability of Trondheim to air attack and to the inadequacy of its small aerodrome at Vaernes. The Chiefs of Staff, however, while approving the principle of the converging movements, would not abandon the idea of direct attack. The Co-ordination Committee, with the Prime Minister in the chair, confirmed these conclusions next day (16th); the risky nature of a direct attack was impressed on them, and they agreed that only troops of good quality should be used, going so far as to sanction the recall of a Regular brigade from France for this purpose and its replacement by a Territorial brigade from the United Kingdom. No date was fixed, but the Chiefs of Staff later in the day agreed that April 24 'would not be too late', though April 22 might be possible.

On the 17th came disappointing news from Narvik. The commanders evidently did not expect to take the place under existing conditions for some weeks and were awaiting the reinforcements referred to in General Mackesy's instructions of April 10.[1] But Narvik had now fallen to second place in the Allied strategy, and the General was told that he must expect no further mobile troops. On the 18th a new disquieting feature was reported: the Norwegians guarding the land approach from Oslo to Trondheim were hard pressed and were calling for help; the attempt to meet this call was shortly to put an intolerable strain on the force ('Sickleforce') which began to land that night at Aandelsnes with orders to push south to Dombaas in the Gudbrandsdal.

In the meantime Sir Charles Forbes, at sea in the *Rodney*, had been asked to consider the naval aspect of a landing at Trondheim, now referred to as 'Operation Hammer'; he had replied that he did not regard it as feasible without very heavy losses in troops and transports from air attack, first in the narrow sea approaches and later during the landing. He did not see the same objection to conveying the troops in warships, but he estimated the naval force required as larger than could well be found, and further consideration did not alter his dislike of the whole plan. His apprehension of danger from the air was confirmed by the severe damage suffered by the cruiser *Suffolk* on the 17th after bombarding the aerodrome at Stavanger.

The question was not put to the proof. On April 19 the Chiefs of Staff and their Deputies unanimously endorsed the naval view that the prospective gains from 'Hammer' did not justify its undoubted risks, especially to the fleet; they were encouraged by the successful landing of 8,000 men at Namsos and Aandelsnes to hope that an 'enveloping operation' from these two bases would achieve the capture of Trondheim by more certain if slower and less spectacular methods. They were also influenced by the appearance in the press of reports that we intended a direct attack on Trondheim. Mr. Churchill felt reluctantly bound to accept this conclusion on the part of the responsible professional advisers of the Government and obtained an immediate decision to this effect from the Prime Minister. The Co-ordination Committee were informed of the change of plan that night, and the Cabinet approved it next morning.[2]

The optimism engendered by the success of the first landings at Namsos and Aandelsnes was short-lived. On the 21st the Cabinet

---

[1] It is difficult to reconcile the statement (in the Minutes of the Chiefs of Staff meeting held on the morning of 17 April) that 'General Mackesy had no justification for expecting the Demi-Brigade of *Chasseurs Alpins*' with the statement in his Instructions of 10 April (printed in Derry pp. 247–248) that it was 'intended to reinforce [him] with a view to subsequent operations' and that these reinforcements would include a 'leading échelon *Chasseurs Alpins*' which might be made available between 21st and 25th April.

[2] See Churchill I 563–565. It is clear from the records that the change of view took place on the *19th*, and that it was on the afternoon of that day, not, as he states, on the 18th, that Mr. Churchill reported it to the Prime Minister. The abandonment of 'Hammer' is discussed by Dr. Derry, *op. cit.* pp. 74–77, where the references are to the first edition of Mr. Churchill's book.

learnt that owing to prolonged air bombardment of Namsos on the previous day, immediately following the arrival of the first contingent of *Chasseurs Alpins*, no more men or supplies could be landed for the present and lack of motor transport prevented an effective advance towards Trondheim. At Aandelsnes Brigadier Morgan, commanding 148th Infantry Brigade, had also lost his transport and four precious Bofors guns, sunk by a submarine; his two battalions were in touch with the Norwegians south of Dombaas, but they were without artillery and until the German advance from Oslo was halted they were in no position to move against Trondheim. The War Office were accordingly constrained to admit that the capture of Trondheim was 'not now immediately possible', since 'the anticipated pressure cannot be supplied either from the north or south'. They were still determined, however, to press on with operations for Trondheim and hoped it would be possible to employ all the six battalions of the French 1st Light Division of *Chasseurs Alpins* in the Namsos area while the 15th (Regular) Infantry Brigade reinforced Morgan's brigade at Aandelsnes. The devastating effect of the German bombers and the incapacity of our exiguous anti-aircraft artillery to deal with them were not yet realised in Whitehall.

It had now been decided to appoint a single commander for all the land forces in Norway except those at Narvik; this was Lieutenant-General H. R. S. Massy, who as Deputy Chief of the Imperial General Staff was familiar with the views of the Chiefs of Staff. His improvised headquarters and he himself, however, in view of the dispersion of his command and the poverty of his communications, remained in London; yet he was only once invited to attend meetings of the Co-ordination Committee. Shortly afterwards Major-General B. C. T. Paget was appointed to command 'Sickleforce'; after appealing vainly, before he sailed, for air support he arrived at Aandelsnes on the night of the 25th/26th.

At the same meeting at which they approved the proposal to abandon the direct attack on Trondheim the Co-ordination Committee discussed a letter of April 18 which the Prime Minister had received from M. Reynaud. The French Ministers were disquieted by the slowness of our progress in Scandinavia. To M. Reynaud the denial of the ore fields to the Germans was still the vital object and he still hoped for Swedish co-operation. He believed further that if more energy were shown by the two great Allies they could send larger forces to Norway at a faster rate; the French were now prepared to send three Light divisions, besides six battalions composed of their own Foreign Legion and of Polish troops.

The published apologias of M. Reynaud and General Gamelin show how unsatisfactory were the relations between the President of the Council and his Minister of Defence, M. Daladier, who supported the General, and Admiral Darlan. After a chilly *Cabinet de Guerre* on April 12 Gamelin had offered his resignation but had been persuaded by M. Daladier and the President of the Republic to remain at his post.[1]

One of the two specific requests contained in M. Reynaud's letter was for British shipping to convey the 3rd French Light Division to Norway. To the British it appeared that the French did not realise that the factor limiting the despatch of reinforcements was not lack of sea transport but the inadequacy of our present bases in Norway for disembarking and maintaining large forces. M. Reynaud's other request was for an early meeting of the Supreme War Council, and this was arranged for April 22 in Paris.

The first session was devoted to the Scandinavian campaign.[2] From a gloomy exposition of the German superiority in land forces and armaments M. Reynaud drew the moral that the most hopeful Allied weapon was the blockade and that the difficulty of stopping Germany's supplies of oil made the denial to her of Swedish iron supremely important. This meant that we must be ready to support Sweden in case of German invasion, and for this purpose it was urgent to capture Trondheim. Mr. Chamberlain explained the British plans and the practical difficulties in the way of carrying them out. It was agreed that the campaign should be prosecuted with the utmost vigour, and that the immediate military objectives should be (a) the capture of Trondheim, (b) the capture of Narvik and the concentration of an adequate Allied force on the Swedish frontier. The French were prepared to allow part of their contingent to be used on the Narvik front, and the British promised to make every effort to provide shipping for the 3rd French Light Division, base facilities permitting.

The Prime Minister was well pleased with the outcome of the discussions with the French, but in the next few days the news was bad.

North of Trondheim the thawing of the fiord had allowed a small German force to land on the 21st on the flank of our advanced troops and to drive them back; Namsos itself, largely destroyed by bombing and deserted by the population, was an utterly inadequate base and General Carton de Wiart had suggested that evacuation might become necessary.

South of Trondheim the Allies had been forced to withdraw up the Gudbrandsdal, where the Germans were attacking with tanks as well as from the air. In the Osterdal, the parallel valley to the east, the enemy were advancing towards Trondheim against little opposition

---

[1] See Reynaud II 22–43; Gamelin III pt. iii, ch. ii.
[2] See Churchill I 573–577.

from the Norwegians. On the 26th it was learnt that most of the Gladiators sent out to restore a desperate air situation had been destroyed on the frozen lake which had been cleared to receive them.

On April 24 the Chiefs of Staff considered a proposal for the revival of 'Hammer' in a modified form as the last chance of capturing Trondheim and so maintaining communications with Sweden, whose Government might otherwise yield to German demands for the control of the ore fields; such an operation could only be executed by two Regular brigades from France, and in any case there must be a fortnight's delay. The proposal was killed by a paper from the Joint Planners which forced the Chiefs of Staff and the Co-ordination Committee to the conclusion that even if we captured Trondheim we should be unable to afford the anti-aircraft resources required to defend it. It had been consolingly suggested earlier that apart from the question of support to the Norwegian people our only need in southern Norway was a lodgement on the coast to which the projected mine barrage could be 'hooked', and at length on the 26th the Co-ordination Committee decided in principle on the evacuation of the forces in central Norway; this was not to be ordered, however, until absolutely necessary and, if possible, not until after the capture of Narvik. The Cabinet were perturbed by the thought of the probable effect of withdrawal on Allied and on neutral opinion, but hoped to create the impression that we had landed forces in central Norway as a diversion only.

The new policy meant of course a reversal of the recent decision by the Supreme War Council. The French protested, and MM. Reynaud and Daladier, General Gamelin and Admiral Darlan came over on the 27th to have the continuing strain on the Navy explained to them, as well as the devastating effect of the enemy's air superiority, which aircraft based on the United Kingdom had not the range to challenge.[1] Mr. Chamberlain emphasised also the imminent danger of war with Italy, in which case our naval and air strength clearly could not be drawn on at the same time for central Scandinavia.

The Supreme War Council agreed that the idea of taking Trondheim must be given up and that the evacuation of 'Sickleforce' might become urgent at any moment, but they accepted Gamelin's suggestion that the force at Namsos should be withdrawn northwards gradually in order to hold up as long as possible the enemy's advance on Narvik. The General's other proposal, for the establishment of a wide bridgehead south of Trondheim based on a number of small ports, was judged impracticable by the British Admiralty. It became

---

[1] See Reynaud II 42; Gamelin III 365–370.

apparent, however, in the next few hours from information received from Aandelsnes that to delay the departure from central Norway would be to court disaster, and on the evening of the 27th the Co-ordination Committee accepted General Massy's recommendation to evacuate 'Sickleforce' on the night of April 30/May 1 and the Namsos force likewise. Guerrilla operations, for which special companies were already being organised by the War Office, were to be started in Norway as soon as possible. Any Norwegian troops who wished were to be taken off at the same time as the French and British. The situation was explained to General Gamelin who was still in London.

The story of the successful withdrawals from Aandelsnes and Namsos, including General Paget's skilful extrication of 'Sickleforce' in the face of the advancing enemy, has been told elsewhere.[1] The last ships left Aandelsnes on the night of May 1/2 and Namsos on the following night. The King of Norway and his Government had been previously embarked from Molde for passage to Tromso in north Norway. One of the most unsatisfactory features of the expeditions to central Norway had been the lack of cordial relations with the Norwegian army, whose Commander-in-Chief was bitterly disappointed by the absence of effective support from the British and by their final decision to withdraw. The British for their part were disappointed that more effective resistance was not offered by the Norwegians, and in particular by their failure to carry out important demolitions. The Norwegians were in fact caught with their small army only half mobilised, and the German swoop on their country had a paralysing effect.

Although the evacuation from Namsos was not to take place till the night of May 2 the Prime Minister judged it necessary, in view of the rumours circulating, to tell the House of Commons that evening that we had withdrawn from Aandelsnes; he expressed his belief that even now the weight of advantage lay with the Allies, pointing out that the German supplies of ore through Narvik had been indefinitely suspended and that the entire balance of naval power had been altered. As things now stood, we had no intention of letting Norway become a sideshow nor of being trapped into dispersing our forces.[2]

British strategy in Norway was now comparatively simple in plan —to capture Narvik at the earliest possible moment and to harass the enemy in the country between Narvik and Namsos by guerrilla warfare. It was not so simple, however, in execution, since German air superiority was still the dominant fact and we had not the continuous

---

[1] Derry ch. ix.
[2] *House of Commons Debates* vol. 360, cols. 906 ff.

local maritime control required to prevent the German troops from forcing their way up the coast.

At Narvik, the failure to eject a small and isolated garrison disappointed and puzzled politicians and staff officers in London who seemed unable to appreciate the difficulties of climate and terrain as well as those due to the inadequate preparation of the expedition. A landing would have to be made from open boats through several feet of snow against troops armed with machine-guns who would be defiladed from the fire of the ships' guns.[1] These difficulties were increased by a lack of co-operation between the two commanders, due partly to defective initial briefing (their instructions, as we have seen, were conflicting and they had never met until they arrived at Narvik), partly to their having separate headquarters, one ashore and one afloat, but also to a more personal factor.

It was laid down in the *Manual of Combined Operations* that for the effective working of the system of joint command (such as was first prescribed for the Narvik expedition) 'the commanders must be suited both by temperament and experience to co-operate with each other. They must not only be able to enjoy each other's confidence and to work as a team but each commander should also have a broad knowledge of the capabilities and limitations of the other Services.' This condition was unfortunately not fulfilled at Narvik. Between the naval and army commanders there soon appeared a complete incompatibility of view and temperament. Lord Cork, impressed by the Government's desire, frequently and forcibly urged by the First Lord, to capture Narvik and its railway as soon as possible, was eager to risk an assault under cover of the guns of the fleet. The soldiers believed that in the existing conditions such an attack would be 'sheer bloody murder'. The difference of opinion was complicated by the fact that, as originally sent out, Lord Cork and General Mackesy were independent of one another; but it is clear that by April 17 or 18 for one reason or another the General had lost the confidence of the Chief of the Imperial General Staff as well as of the First Lord of the Admiralty; on the 20th he was put under the Admiral's orders and might henceforward communicate direct with the War Office on administrative matters only. While of course ready to obey orders, General Mackesy protested against Lord Cork's proposals and against the danger to the civilian population which they seemed to imply. After a compromise project—a naval bombardment intended to pave the way for an unopposed landing—had proved ineffective on April 24, weather forced an interval, in which French *Chasseurs* and other reinforcements arrived for the Allies. On May 3 Lord Cork gave orders for a direct attack on Narvik to be carried out on the 8th; but

---

[1] See Maund, *Assault from the Sea* p. 34.

L

in deference to Army opinion that, in view of insufficiency of landing-craft and the impossibility of achieving surprise, such an adventure could only result in disaster, he referred the matter home and in the meantime postponed the attack. By the time that the Cabinet had urged him to press on with the capture of the place and promised him their support whatever risk he decided to take, Lord Cork had decided on an indirect approach. The preliminary operation was successfully carried out in full daylight on the night of May 12/13 by French troops in co-operation with the Norwegians advancing from further north and with the help of tanks landed (for the first time) from mechanised landing-craft (L.C.M.s).

Meanwhile the Co-ordination Committee had had before them on May 6 a report by the Chiefs of Staff on the strategic implications of the capture of Narvik. It summarised the advantages which its capture and control would bring to the Allies under five headings.

> (i) We stop the ore reaching Germany via Narvik. We increase our chances of stopping the supply via Lulea, by providing a base for aircraft attack on the Lulea area and for the despatch of demolition parties to Sweden if opportunity offers.
> (ii) With the Norwegian coast largely in German hands it will be an advantage to possess a naval advanced base in Northern Norway for ships operating against German naval forces and sea communications along the Norwegian coast and in northern waters.
> (iii) It is through Narvik alone that we would be able to maintain a line of communication with Sweden.
> (iv) By retaining a foothold on Norwegian soil, we may hope to keep Norway as an ally, in the same way as Belgium in 1914–1918.
> (v) The loss of prestige that the withdrawal from the Trondheim area may involve will be lessened by a secure control of the Narvik area.

Experience in central Norway had convinced the Chiefs of Staff that 'the crux of the Narvik operations would be our ability to establish the necessary anti-aircraft defences and to operate fighters from a shore aerodrome'.

Accordingly the report argued that besides Narvik itself it would be necessary among other things to secure the Bardufoss aerodromes (55 miles north of Narvik) and establish two others. Speed was of first importance, since the enemy were developing aerodromes and otherwise consolidating their position to the south; moreover, the short nights were getting shorter and by mid-May the unfreezing of the Gulf of Bothnia would enable the Germans to establish themselves in the north of Sweden and bomb us from there.

The report proceeded to estimate the forces required. The army commitment, other than an anti-aircraft unit, was not regarded as serious. The naval commitment, though heavy, was just acceptable, even in the event of war with Italy. The really serious demand would be for anti-aircraft defence; were it met in full, the total allotment to Narvik would amount to 10 per cent of the heavy guns, and 30 per cent of the light guns now held for the Air Defence of Great Britain.

The estimated requirements for Narvik limited the scale of defence which could be spared for the anti-aircraft protection of points on the coast to the south. The Chiefs of Staff had on May 1 rejected a proposal by General Massy that a base should be established to the south of Narvik, and Lord Cork was told on May 5 that the most that could be done was to establish a forward landing ground at Bodo (some 120 miles south-west of Narvik) from which British fighters based further north could operate and to provide it with anti-aircraft guns on a small scale.

There was also the question of command. As early as April 28 the Chiefs of Staff had decided that, while the existing system of a single command (Lord Cork's) was right in present circumstances, the time would come, as the forces in the Narvik area expanded, when it would be 'necessary once more to split the command among the three Service commanders—thus reverting to the normal system for large scale combined operations'. To avoid delay it was decided to send out Lieutenant-General C. J. E. Auchinleck with a senior Air officer to Narvik forthwith. His instructions, dated May 5, stated that the Government's purpose in northern Norway was to secure and maintain a base from which we could (a) deny iron ore supplies to Germany via Narvik; (b) interfere with her supplies via Lulea; (c) preserve part of Norway as a seat for the King and Government. On arrival the General was to report, in conjunction with Lord Cork, on the forces required to attain the objects mentioned and the area to be occupied; in due course he was to take over the command of the land force.

General Auchinleck arrived at Narvik on May 11; in view of the difficult relations existing between the naval and army commanders he decided, as he was empowered to do, to take over General Mackesy's command, in subordination to Lord Cork, at once. But by this time Norway had after all become a sideshow.

It had been arranged that the Prime Minister's short statement in the House of Commons on May 2 should be followed by a debate in the following week. The debate took place on May 7 and 8, and its results were momentous.[1]

---

[1] *House of Commons Debates* vol. 360.

The Government case was presented by the Prime Minister and the three Service Ministers. They admitted that the Allies had sustained a reverse but begged the House not to exaggerate it. The Germans had suffered heavy losses; it was impossible to say yet which side would prove to have gained. It was true that the Germans had surprised us by occupying the western as well as the southern ports of Norway, but we could not have prevented this without Norwegian co-operation. Ministers made much of the weakness and folly of the neutrals and of the aid given to treacherous Germans by traitorous Norwegians: coast defences had been handed over and railways left intact. It was true that the greater part of the British force designed to help Finland had been dispersed, but the advance troops had been kept available and the reinforcements could be despatched as quickly from France as from the United Kingdom; the shipping could not have been left idle indefinitely. As for Trondheim, we had been forced to try to recapture the city by the appeal of the Norwegians, who might otherwise have collapsed. The direct attack on Trondheim had been abandoned on the unanimous advice of the Chiefs of Staff. We had no air base in Norway and we could not stop the move of German reinforcements from Oslo. The root of our troubles was our failure to gain parity in the air. As regards the future, the Prime Minister appealed to the country to close the ranks; his mind was not shut to changes of system, but he did not believe that a smaller Cabinet would be more efficient. He had, however, advanced Mr. Churchill to a position of great authority.

The usual spokesmen of the two Oppositions were reinforced by such Conservatives as Mr. Amery, Lord Winterton and Mr. Duff Cooper, as well as by critics from the Services—notably Sir Roger Keyes, appearing in his uniform as Admiral of the Fleet, who was known to have implored the Government to allow him to lead the assault on Trondheim. The failure in Scandinavia, many Members declared, was only symptomatic of a general complacency and lack of drive and leadership. Mr. Churchill's new duties as Chairman, it was said, put him in an impossible position. The Opposition made it clear that they would not co-operate with an administration led by Mr. Chamberlain. Mr. Amery on the first night ended impressively with Cromwell's 'In the name of God, go', and Mr. Herbert Morrison, opening the attack next day, announced that the Opposition would move a vote of censure and divide the House. The Prime Minister came under criticism for appealing to his 'friends in the House' to support him; the phrase was construed in a party sense, whereas the present emergency was felt to be more than a party matter.

The division on the 8th gave the Government a majority of 81 only (281 to 200); 33 Conservatives voted against them and some 60 abstained. The result convinced Mr. Chamberlain that he did not command such confidence as a Government needed to carry on such a war, and finding that Labour would not serve under him he resigned on May 10.[1] There was need in truth for a Government commanding all the trust and support which the country could give, for a few hours earlier the Germans had launched their offensive in the West.

The subsequent story of the campaign in Norway falls into three parts: the fighting retreat of the British up the coast, the operations leading to the capture of Narvik—or the ruins of Narvik—on May 28 by French, Polish and Norwegian troops, supported by the Royal Navy and shore-based fighters, and the skilfully concealed evacuation of north Norway a few days later. It was with the greatest reluctance that the new Government surrendered the fruits of such prolonged endeavours, but the growing danger on the Continent forbade the dispersion of the Allied forces.

It was the new Prime Minister, Mr. Churchill, himself who first, on May 20, suggested that it might be the right policy to evacuate Narvik after capturing it. A definite recommendation to this effect was first made by the Chiefs of Staff on May 22 after careful consideration of the pros and cons. They were impressed by the drain on the Navy, especially in destroyers, and the impossibility of providing the land and air forces which General Auchinleck thought necessary. They did not believe that a withdrawal from Norway would now influence the battle in France, but the forces it could release might be urgently needed in the United Kingdom and home waters. These considerations outweighed the arguments that, if we withdrew, the chances of our blocking the port of Lulea by air action (Operation 'Paul') were very slight and that after six months the Germans would be able to restore the outlet for ore through Narvik itself.

The Cabinet gave orders on May 23 for plans for withdrawal to be prepared and on the 25th they endorsed the instructions which, after a meeting of the Defence Committee on the previous day, had been sent to Lord Cork for the evacuation to take place at the earliest possible moment. They were not shaken from their decision by the contrary representations of the Commander-in-Chief, Home Fleet, and the French agreed to the evacuation at a meeting of the Supreme War Council on the 31st. As in the earlier case of Namsos embarrassment was caused by the conflicting duties of giving adequate notice to the Norwegians and of preserving secrecy; further complication, in the form of a plea for delay, was introduced by an abortive

[1] See Feiling pp. 438–441.

proposal, known as the 'Mowinckel plan', of Norwegian or Swedish origin, for the neutralisation of the north of Norway. Eventually King Haakon and his Government were persuaded to accept passage to England in order to carry on the war from there, and the evacuation of the Allied troops took place on the five nights ending June 7/8. Before withdrawing they dismantled the railway and other important installations and blocked the harbour; nevertheless a steamer with iron ore left Narvik in January 1941. The Norwegian forces laid down their arms on June 10.

The success of the evacuation was marred by the sinking of the aircraft-carrier *Glorious* and her two gallant escorting destroyers *Ardent* and *Acasta* on June 8, with heavy loss of life, including the pilots of the Fleet Air Arm and Royal Air Force who had rendered valuable service during the last weeks. These ships had the ill-luck to meet the battle-cruisers *Gneisenau* and *Scharnhorst* which had set out from Kiel on the 4th on a different mission. Both the enemy ships suffered serious damage in the course of this sortie and were disabled for several months, so that the German fleet ended the campaign with no major warship fit for sea.[1] On the other hand only one success was scored by the twenty-eight German submarines stationed to interrupt our traffic off Norway and in the northern waters of the North Sea.[2]

As for the German army, the British Chiefs of Staff estimated before the evacuation that eleven divisions were employed in Norway, whereas the British had only the equivalent of one and a half, besides eight French battalions and four Polish. In fact the Germans never had more than seven divisions in Norway during the campaign and two divisions and a motorised brigade in Denmark.

The Luftwaffe used for the invasion about 1,000 aircraft of which half were for transport; this represented the 'first operational employment of transport aircraft carrying airborne combat forces to the most forward areas of battle'. Thus in Norway, as in the previous year in Poland, the Germans may claim to have opened a new chapter in the history of war, as regards the help an air force can provide for an army. Of the remainder of the force the greater part were long-range bombers. Besides the Norwegian airfields which they captured in the first few hours of the invasion the Luftwaffe used those at Aalborg in Jutland and others in North Germany. The successive British attempts to wreck Stavanger airfield thus did not seriously hamper their activities.

This volume is concerned with the reasons for the failure of the Norwegian campaign in so far only as it was due to the defects in its

---

[1] Roskill I 201.

[2] The *Cedarbank*, on 21 April.

higher direction.[1] In the first place it is only just to recognise the superior efficiency of the Germans in planning and execution at a high level as well as in the training, equipment and, in many cases, the tactical handling of their troops. After the small German navy had by the clever, if unscrupulous, exploitation of the factor of surprise secured its immediate objectives, the Luftwaffe, greatly superior in numbers and operating from airfields far closer than those available to the Royal Air Force, established a supremacy which paralysed our efforts. The Polish campaign had demonstrated the crushing effect of the Luftwaffe's co-operation with the army in open country; the Norwegian campaign, besides showing how skilfully the Luftwaffe could adapt its methods to a land of deep fiords and glens, showed also, in the words of a German writer, that 'German air power has made it possible to eliminate Britain's seapower in a limited area' (the Kattegat) 'in which Germany possessed no corresponding naval strength'.

There seems no doubt, either, that the German Intelligence, whether derived from air reconnaissance or from other sources, was far superior to the British. We were taken by surprise not only by the enemy's plans and the efficiency of his execution but on matters of topography and local practice about which we must have had ample opportunities to acquire information. The enemy profited moreover from the lack of proper provision for security on the British side at this stage of the war.

But it is necessary to emphasise the fact that the Germans excelled us not least in unscrupulousness. They were prepared at their chosen moment to invade and occupy two unoffending neutral countries, to sink their ships and kill their inhabitants, while the Allies were not. The enemy had thus all the enormous advantages of the initiative; not only were his resources in men and munitions far superior, but his troops were armed and equipped for a pounce. Those of the Allies were not, though it is true that from the end of December and early in January detailed planning was authorised for a contingency which might never arise; it is true also that the enemy knew a good deal about the Allied preparations, but could not know the comparative innocence of their purpose.

Apart from the severe handicap imposed on the Allies by their desire to respect Scandinavian neutrality, the fact remains that throughout this period of the war at home, in France, in the Near East, in Scandinavia, their trained man-power, armament and equipment were insufficient to go round; it was a case of trying to get a quart out of a pint pot. The responsibility of the high command lies therefore in the first instance in having attempted what they did

---

[1] For a fuller discussion see Derry ch. xv.

attempt under such unfavourable conditions. How strong was the compulsion?

M. Reynaud claimed at the meeting of the Supreme War Council on April 27 that Allied intervention in Norway had two objects: first, to open a theatre of war where Germany would wear out her resources, including her precious reserves of oil, without strategic advantage and, secondly, to cut off her supplies of iron ore. The second motive is that which told with the British; those in this country who desired to extend the war to Scandinavia were probably few, though such a desire was expressed in high quarters, and many undoubtedly felt that our prestige demanded some offensive action, some striking success, to set against Germany's tale of victorious aggressions. But in fact our word was pledged: we had assured the Norwegians in the first few days of the war that we should regard an attack on them as tantamount to an attack on ourselves, and the Norwegian Government had on April 9 appealed to us for help. Though we were far from satisfied with that Government's interpretation of its duties as a neutral, the appeal could not be ignored.

There is a larger question here which challenges the historian: were the Allied Governments, for all their honourable scruples, in fact responsible for involving Norway in the horrors of war and an enemy occupation? It is true that when the matter was raised early in September the British Chiefs of Staff advised the Cabinet that 'it seems unlikely that Germany will initiate any attack on Norway except by way of reprisal and even then only if Norwegian neutrality were to assume such a degree of benevolence towards the Allies as to interfere with iron ore supplies'. It is also true that throughout the winter German opinion was undecided whether the maintenance of Norwegian neutrality was not in Germany's best interests.[1] But such considerations are unrealistic. Once the gloves were off in the economic war, once the German attacks on trade were pressed by illegal and inhumane methods, it was almost inevitable that the Allies should adopt reprisals and that in doing so they should accept the risk that weak neutrals, of whose independence they regarded themselves as the champions, might have to endure hard trials before their independence was assured. To the Germans Norway's neutrality was beneficial only so long as their iron supplies were undisturbed; rumours of Allied designs were frequent, and weeks before the British Cabinet had come to any decision Raeder (on December 8) advised the Führer that 'it is important to occupy Norway'; a few days later Quisling reported that 'there is a very real danger that Norway may be occupied by Britain, possibly soon', and thereupon Hitler gave orders for plans to be prepared; there was no pretence that

---

[1] See F.N.C. pp. 45, 63, 67, 70, 81.

Norwegian consent was required.[1] It is doubtful if the *Altmark* incident did more than add a sense of urgency. Even if there had been no reason to expect Allied interference with the ore traffic, it is likely that as Hitler's strategy expanded he would have felt it necessary to prevent the establishment of British air bases in Norway and to seize bases there himself for both the Luftwaffe and the Navy. As things turned out, the Germans were the patent aggressors. The Allies landed in Norway in fulfilment of an obligation and at the request of her Government.

It does not follow that the Allies, and particularly the British, on whom the main responsibility for the direction of the campaign had been placed, carried out their obligation in the best way. It can hardly be denied that the principle of maintaining the aim was flouted: there were far too many changes of plan, and the changed plans did not allow time for corresponding changes to be made in preparations at a lower level. The result was often chaos. Troops were used for purposes for which they had not been designed nor trained nor equipped; ports were found inadequate to maintain the forces assigned to them; ships were not loaded as they should have been and essential gear could not be disembarked in time. Commanders on land, with hardly an exception, felt that there had been a total lack of realistic planning, especially on the administrative side.

Besides these blunders, there were sheer miscalculations or failure of imagination: the likelihood of the Germans using their heavy ships as they did was not foreseen; the mobility of British and French troops unaccustomed to Arctic conditions was exaggerated; while the daring and performance of Germans of all three Services were underestimated, and in particular the shattering effect of the Luftwaffe when means of defence were lacking.

Mention has already been made of our failure to secure a proper integration of the three Services at the executive level. The need for this, along with the need for air defence on all occasions, was perhaps the most important lesson of the campaign, and the facts bear repetition. The Joint Planners planned together under conditions of extreme pressure, at least on the operations side; the Chiefs of Staff exercised their advisory function, though Mr. Churchill has suggested that they lacked proper direction from above.[2] But when it came to the execution of decisions the Service ministries issued separate orders to their own commanders; there was no combined headquarters representing all three Services nor any proper arrangement for harmonising the orders given. Another defect was the failure to

---

[1] *F.N.C.* pp. 62, 66.
[2] Churchill I 576.

ensure that commanders called upon to work together possessed the qualities that would make successful co-operation likely. And finally, on the point of individual characteristics, the guess may be hazarded that the Chiefs of Staff were sometimes induced by the forceful personality of the First Lord of the Admiralty to lend support to bold enterprises against their better judgement. Mr. Churchill, during the greater part of the Norwegian campaign, had not the responsibility of the final voice; when it came to him later, he showed how superbly he could rise to it. Mr. Chamberlain, though undoubtedly a strong personality, whose authority in his own Cabinet was unchallenged, often paid excessive attention to the probable effect of our measures on public opinion, while in the case of foreigners his failure to understand their psychology frequently led him into undue optimism.

Apart from its value in providing lessons for future combined operations, there is perhaps a danger of exaggerating the importance of our failure in Norway. Our forces engaged were small; Germany soon secured other sources of iron ore; against her acquisition of extended naval and air bases may be set the mauling of her fleet; while the serious damage to Allied prestige, even before the final withdrawal from Norway, was swallowed up in the vast catastrophe in France.

CHAPTER VII

THE BUILD-UP IN FRANCE

ALL THE TIME that the British high command had been preoccupied with Scandinavia, the Expeditionary Force had been building up its strength in France. The initial contingent had arrived by the first week of October. Covered by naval and air escorts, over 160,000 men and over 22,000 vehicles had crossed. Fears of interruption by the enemy, which had dictated the use of Cherbourg, Nantes and St Nazaire as the principal landing ports, proved to have been excessive; for, though Hitler had authorised offensive action by the German navy when Britain and France declared war, it was not his policy at this time to provoke them, and little attempt was made to interfere with the passage. Nevertheless it was a remarkable and unprecedented feat of organisation on the part of the Services to convey a fully mechanized army overseas without mishap.

It had been agreed that the Expeditionary Force should take over the Lille sector of the French defences along the Belgian frontier, a length of some 25 miles.[1] There were no fortifications in this area comparable with the elaborate works of the Maginot system further south: only a ditch and a line of concrete blockhouses with an incomplete wire obstacle. The position was improved during the wet, cold winter by much severe labour, but in the event its strength was never tested.

Anxiety as to the state of our field defences was expressed by Mr. Hore-Belisha, the Secretary of State for War, and also by some of the Dominion Ministers, on their return to London from visits to the forward area in November. The handling of the matter by the Secretary of State was resented at General Headquarters, while Mr. Hore-Belisha felt that his offers of mechanical assistance had not been properly appreciated by the Generals. After the Chief of the Imperial General Staff and the Prime Minister had themselves visited the army in France it was clear that relations between the Secretary of State and the higher officers were unsatisfactory and unlikely to improve. Early in January the Prime Minister, who had already in mind some reconstruction of the Government, took the opportunity to suggest to Mr. Hore-Belisha his transference to another Department. Mr. Chamberlain considered that his colleague

---

[1] See Maps 5 and 6.

had rendered great services to the Army but that a change at the War Office was desirable. 'Of course', he wrote on January 7, 'the enemies of the Government will do their best to exploit the incident by representing it as a victory for brass hats who don't like the democratisation of the Army. This is grossly unfair to them and I may say that none of the Generals have ever taken the initiative in complaining to me or asked directly or indirectly that he should be moved. The friction is due to personal incompatibility and not policy or administration'.[1]

The British Government had agreed that the direction of the land campaign should be a French responsibility, and in view of the recognised importance of a unified command and of the disparity of the respective forces it was natural that Lord Gort should be subordinated to a French General. His instructions placed him under the command of the Commander-in-Chief, North-East Theatre of Operations, and it was understood by the British authorities that his immediate superior was General Georges. In the course of February, however, it appeared that General Gamelin was unaware, and did not approve, of the devolution of his supreme authority over the British army to his subordinate, and some little time and trouble were required to correct the misunderstanding and clarify Lord Gort's position. It was then agreed that while he was officially under General Gamelin he would in fact, by delegation from him, continue to receive orders regarding operations from General Georges, with whom he was on excellent terms; he would, however, have direct access to Gamelin at his discretion. As it happened, after the battle had begun in May Lord Gort was subordinated to yet a third French General—General Billotte, commanding the First Group of Armies, whose zone of operations was adjacent to the British.[2] Lord Gort possessed also a specific right to appeal to his own Government in the event of a French order seeming to him to imperil his command; the general direction of the campaign might be left to the French, but no British Government could disclaim responsibility for the safety of British troops.[3]

Apart from questions of strategy, which will be discussed later, the Cabinet were principally concerned, as regards the British Expeditionary Force during the period of the 'twilight' war, with the completion of its equipment and with the organisation of effective air co-operation.

---

[1] Mr. Chamberlain's private papers; see Feiling, *Life of Neville Chamberlain* p. 434; Major-General Sir F. de Guingand, who was Military Assistant to Mr. Hore-Belisha, gives his account in *Operation Victory* (1947) pp. 38–42.

[2] See below, p. 185.

[3] For Lord Gort's instructions see Major L. F. Ellis, *The War in France and Flanders 1939–40* (H.M.S.O. 1953) p. 11 (henceforward referred to as Ellis).

The problem of equipment applied to the initial contingent, which was sent out deficient in several important respects, as well as to the total force of ten divisions promised to arrive in France by 1st March 1940.[1]

On 1 December 1939 the Cabinet considered a War Office memorandum showing in detail the shortages expected to obtain in the equipment of this latter force in the light of the forecasts of the Minister of Supply. Shortages were particularly noticeable in the case of infantry tanks, of which there were only 70 in France out of a requirement of 204; by the end of February there would still only be about 130 out of 461 required. Cruiser tanks for the Armoured Division now mobilising for overseas were also short. Other serious deficiencies appeared in respect of anti-tank guns, light anti-aircraft guns, ammunition of various types, and vehicles. In most items, so far as the first six divisions were concerned, the shortages were only in reserves and maintenance, but the later divisions were likely to be incomplete in their unit equipment also. These calculations were based, however, on estimates of normal wastage (suggested by 1917–1918 averages) beginning from November 15 in the case of divisions already in the field and, in the case of the rest, from the dates of their arrival. If operations were delayed, the position would be correspondingly better, and there was in fact, of course, a very considerable delay.

The Cabinet referred the general problem to the Military Co-ordination Committee, which discussed the several items at a series of meetings in conjunction with the Minister of Supply; it appears that little improvement was achieved before the end of the campaign.

The status of the units of the Royal Air Force serving in France was somewhat complicated. The Air Component, of thirteen squadrons, commanded by Air Vice-Marshal C. H. B. Blount, was under the orders of Lord Gort. On the other hand, the ten bomber squadrons of the Advanced Air Striking Force (A.A.S.F.), commanded by Air Vice-Marshal Playfair and stationed near Rheims, were independent alike of Lord Gort and of the French, receiving their orders direct from Bomber Command in England.[2] Liaison with the French was maintained at two levels: the Chief of the Air Staff was represented at the headquarters of General Vuillemin, Commander-in-Chief of the French Air Forces, by Air Marshal A. S. Barratt, while Bomber Command was represented at the headquarters of General Mouchard, commanding the First Air Army, by Air Commodore

---

[1] See above, p. 27; the destination of the Territorial divisions had not been fixed at the outbreak of war, but by November 15 the French had been given to understand that they would go to France.

[2] Above, p. 34.

F. P. Don. Air Marshal Barratt was authorised in a critical situation to assume control of the latter mission and to issue orders direct to the A.A.S.F., but there was no formal contact between him and Lord Gort; should the General want stronger bomber support than his own Air Component could provide, he must apply to the War Office, who would ask the Air Ministry to instruct Bomber Command to send the necessary orders to A.A.S.F. This arrangement was soon found to be insufferably clumsy; to the Army it seemed the *reductio ad absurdum* of the longstanding refusal of the Air Ministry to meet their peculiar needs.

Before the war the Air Ministry and the War Office had for some time been engaged in controversy as to the requirements of the Field Force in numbers and types of aircraft. The figure of twelve squadrons had been agreed upon as early as 1937 as suitable for the small Field Force then contemplated; in 1939 it became clear that larger numbers would be required as the force expanded, but in the existing shortage of aircraft the Air Ministry were naturally reluctant to divert more than absolutely necessary from the Commands at home which might be called upon to meet a full-scale air offensive against Great Britain. This, however, was not the whole of the dispute. Impressed by the important part played in the Polish campaign by the German Air Force in close support of the Army, and chafing at the delays which seemed bound to result from the roundabout methods prescribed for the British Expeditionary Force should further air assistance be wanted, the War Office demanded that the Commander-in-Chief should have larger air forces under his direct control. Accordingly they asked that, over and above the Air Component, the Army should have 250 first-line bomber aircraft, with reserves, put at its disposal by the spring. But even this was only a short-term measure; the War Office urged that the Army should be supplied with specially constructed aircraft and should train its own pilots; in fact they wanted an Army Air Arm. The Air Ministry on the other hand were determined to retain unity of control and argued that the permanent allocation to the Army of such a force as it demanded would cripple our existing resources for launching a bombing counter-offensive or for switching our air power to whatever might at any time be the most vital purpose. To allot 250 first-line bombers, with reserves, to the Army would reduce the present first-line strength of our main striking force by nearly half. Moreover the greatest effect achieved by the German Air Force in Poland had been due to long-range bombers operating far in rear of the Polish forward troops.

The broad issue, referred by the Cabinet to the Land Forces Committee, was referred back by them, and the Cabinet discussed it on November 8. They decided that the raising of an independent

Army Air Arm was inopportune; at present the whole Air striking force must be available for whatever purpose the strategy of the
moment required; it was desirable, however, that prototypes of a
mass-produced aircraft suitable for the Army's needs should be
developed, and with a view to operations in 1940 an adequate force
should be earmarked for work with the Army unless required elsewhere in an emergency.

The working out of a scheme in accordance with this last decision
was entrusted to Lord Chatfield in collaboration with the two
Ministries concerned. He reported a month later that the two staffs
had agreed on an arrangement, analogous to the relationship
between the Navy and Coastal Command of the Royal Air Force,
which should meet the immediate needs of the Army. The Advanced
Air Striking Force and the Air Component of the British Expeditionary Force were both to be brought under a new command, to be
known as British Air Forces in France (B.A.F.F.), though the Air
Component would continue under Lord Gort's operational control.
The new Air Commander-in-Chief would decide in consultation with
Gort how the British bomber squadrons in France should be used in
support of the army; only when some major operation of a different
character was in view, and with the sanction of the Cabinet, would
these aircraft pass under the direct control of Bomber Command.
It was judged that the ten squadrons of the Advanced Air Striking
Force reinforced by the remaining six squadrons of medium bombers
from the United Kingdom should provide sufficient support for the
Army for many months to come. The Cabinet approved the scheme,
and Air Marshal Barratt was appointed to the new command as
from 15 January.

Such were the arrangements for securing air support for the British
Expeditionary Force as they stood when the Germans launched their
offensive. But, as the representatives of the War Office and Air
Ministry pointed out, the allotment of British bombers in France was
intended to serve the Allied front as a whole, and for the working out
of the scheme the French high command must therefore be brought
into consultation. This was all the more important in that British
statesmen made a point of setting off against our small land contribution to the common strength the great efforts we were making in the
air as well as at sea.

It was with regard to fighters, however, that the sharpest controversy arose with our allies. When the French started to reorganise
their Air Force in 1938, they decided to give priority to fighters, but
at the outbreak of war their system of air defence was still weak;
from September onwards until the final catastrophe, repeated requests were received from them for the despatch of additional fighter
units to France from the United Kingdom.

The initial British contribution was the four squadrons of Hurricanes, forming part of the Air Component of the British Expeditionary Force; these were intended for protective work both on the front occupied by the army and in the area further south where the Advanced Air Striking Force were stationed. It had been agreed further between the War Office and Air Ministry that six additional squadrons should be placed on a mobile basis before the end of 1939, but none of these were to be sent overseas except by special decision of the Cabinet.[1] At a meeting of the Supreme War Council on September 22 the French representatives asked for six more British fighter squadrons (eighty aircraft) as well as for further anti-aircraft batteries. Gamelin was at this time expecting a German offensive before the middle of October and was anxious for an increase of fighter strength in Lorraine. He raised the matter again in the first week of October, when he still expected a German attack against the Maginot line or through Luxemburg, to be followed by a main thrust through the Low Countries. It was none the less possible that the Germans might at any time start a full-scale air offensive against the United Kingdom, and the resources of Fighter Command were seriously below the standard which had been judged necessary. Air Marshal Dowding had been reluctant to release even the four squadrons earmarked for the British Expeditionary Force and he protested against the despatch of more. The Cabinet were not prepared to accede to Gamelin's request in this respect, except to the extent of giving the Chief of the Air Staff discretion to send two further squadrons to France if the situation demanded, and two Gladiator squadrons were in fact sent in November.

General Gamelin had also pleaded for greater flexibility in our dispositions, and here it was found possible to meet him to some degree; two squadrons were moved south in October from the British Expeditionary Force to the Advanced Air Striking Force area and two 'Fighter Wing Servicing Units'—advanced bases, each available for the eventual maintenance of two squadrons—were established in France. This latter expedient was not developed further for various reasons, one of which was the conviction of the Air Ministry that owing to the inferiority of the French air-raid-reporting system our squadrons could operate with greater efficiency from British stations than from French. Accordingly when the Germans attacked in May we had six fighter squadrons in France with preparations made for the reception of four more.

As regards land forces, the British contingent increased from four divisions in October to ten in April; in addition the Royal Engineers and infantry of three further Territorial divisions were sent out for

---

[1] Above, p. 37.

pioneer and labour duties. Early in April a third corps was functioning. On May 10, when the German offensive began, one of the five complete Territorial divisions, the 51st, was doing a spell in the line in the Saar region, so that there were available for an advance into Belgium nine divisions organised in three corps.

In the sphere of strategy, two issues were under almost continuous consideration from September to May; these were the line on which the Allied armies should resist the expected German offensive and the use to be made of the Allied bomber force. The two issues differed in that on land the Allied force was preponderantly French, whereas the bombers were mainly British, so that the final decision would rest in the first case with Paris but in the second case with London. Both issues, however, were closely affected by the policy of weak neutral Powers whose pro-Ally sympathies were hardly in doubt but whose fears of the probable aggressor constrained them to a scrupulous interpretation of their neutrality; both were finally resolved by the German invasion of the Low Countries but not until then. As in the Scandinavian case, uncertainty about the future action of neutrals and failure to break down their reluctance to co-operate hampered all our planning and exposed our forces to serious risks.

The question of the line of Allied resistance will be treated first.

After the acquiescence of the French and British Governments in the reoccupation of the demilitarized zone in the Rhineland by the German army in March 1936, Belgium reverted to her traditional neutrality; France and Great Britain declared, nevertheless, that they held themselves bound to come to her assistance if she were attacked.[1] As the aggressive intentions of Nazi Germany disclosed themselves, the possibility of a war in which Belgium and Great Britain would be involved became a pressing matter. Consequently, when the British Cabinet decided in February 1939 to authorise staff conversations on a wider scale than formerly, they proposed that Belgium should be included, and perhaps the Netherlands also. The Belgian Government, however, were not willing to take part, and no approach was made to the Netherlands.

The Belgian refusal was particularly disconcerting by reason of the strategic situation: the French and British staffs assumed that Belgium would appeal for Allied help if and when the Germans attacked her, but the effectiveness of that help would depend on the Allies being previously taken into her confidence.

'The general conditions of a German offensive through Belgium and Holland' had formed the subject of a joint Anglo-French staff

[1] Anglo-French Declaration of 24 April 1937.

M

paper of 2 May 1939. It noted that the Belgian prepared line of defence was the river Meuse from Namur to Liège and thence the Albert canal to Antwerp, while that of the Dutch ran west of the marshes of the Peel (in the east of the province of North Brabant) and northwards to the Yssel Meer (Zuyder Zee).[1] The duration of Belgian and Dutch resistance would depend on its being organised in time and supported by French and British forces. Little, if anything, could be done to help the Dutch on land; as regards Belgium the dominant factors were the need of obtaining permission from her Government for the Allied forces to intervene, and the importance attached by the Allies to ensuring that their forces were not engaged in an encounter battle against superior numbers in unprepared positions and with insufficient reserves. There was no prepared position and no satisfactory water obstacle west of the Albert Canal until the river Scheldt (*Escaut*) was reached, and accordingly the choice would lie according to circumstances between reinforcing the Belgians on the Meuse–Albert Canal line and holding the Scheldt on the line Tournai–Audenarde, thus connecting the French defences at Maulde (ten miles north-west of Valenciennes) with the 'Belgian National Redoubt' covering Ghent and Antwerp.[2] The conclusion followed that, since without full knowledge of the Belgian plans the Allies could not count on occupying the Albert Canal position, the only safe assumption was that their initial defences after they entered Belgium would be organised on the Scheldt and that it was from there that they must prepare to launch their eventual offensive. This meant that all but a small part of Belgium must expect to be overrun by the enemy.

These conclusions were approved by General Gamelin and they formed the approved strategy when war broke out.[3] The Belgian attitude did not change, but on August 28, with war in sight, the British Government none the less renewed to Belgium their promise of assistance in the event of unprovoked aggression provided that she herself resisted, and they assured her that we should respect her neutrality so long as other Powers did so. A similar assurance was conveyed to the Netherlands on September 1.

Some weeks later, when the collapse of Poland seemed imminent, in their appreciation of 18 September on 'the possible future course of the war' the Chiefs of Staff brought the matter to the attention of the Cabinet. They pointed out that by attacking France through the

---

[1] See Maps 5 and 6. The main Belgian defence lines, shown in Map 6 as those of the winter of 1939–40, do not altogether correspond with the text above.

[2] The Belgian National Redoubt no longer existed in 1940.

[3] For the development of French strategic ideas, see Commandant P. Lyet in *Revue Historique de l'Armée*, reprinted as 'La Bataille de France, Mai-Juin 1940' (Paris 1947); also Gamelin, *Servir* I ch. iv.

Low Countries Germany would turn the most formidable part of the Maginot line and avoid the heavy casualties to be expected from an assault against very strong defences. They repeated the view expressed in the summer that the Allies could not check such an advance as far forward as the Peel line in Holland, but it would be in the Allied interest to stem it in Belgium. They understood that the French had in view two alternative lines: if the Belgians were still holding out on the Meuse, the French and British armies should occupy the line of the river from Givet to Namur, with the British on the left; alternatively, were it decided to hold the line of the Scheldt, the British Expeditionary Force should occupy the portion between Audenarde and Ghent, connecting at Ghent with the Belgians.

Commenting on these possibilities, the Chiefs of Staff took the view that the former of the two alternatives would be unsound unless plans were concerted in sufficient time before the German advance. The second had the disadvantage for the British that the position assigned to them would be parallel to their communications with their existing bases, whereas a shift of bases to the Channel coast would be unsatisfactory from the point of view both of port and road facilities and of air attack. Unless therefore plans could be concerted with the Belgians for the early occupation of the Givet–Namur line, 'we must press the French to agree to meeting the German advance in prepared positions on the French frontier'.

At a meeting in Paris on September 20 between two members of the British Cabinet, Lord Hankey and Mr. Hore-Belisha, and the French Prime Minister and Commander-in-Chief, General Gamelin was found to hold very similar views. He had determined to avoid an encounter battle on the Belgian plains. It would not be possible to send large French forces to co-operate with the Belgians on their Meuse–Albert Canal line without previous conversations, though he would not hesitate to establish *points d'appui* in Belgium in advance of his main position on the French frontier. He thought, however, that the Belgians might hold up the Germans long enough to enable the Allies to occupy the line of the Scheldt, so covering the Belgian ports; he did not press for the stationing of British troops on the Scheldt. Writing to General Ironside on September 23 he said that in any case he did not propose to bring the British left further north than the Courtrai canal (ten miles south-west of Audenarde). Discussing the question of assisting the Belgians some days later (September 27) the Cabinet expressed their reluctance to allow British troops to leave their prepared positions if there were a risk of their being caught in the open, but agreed that the matter was a technical one to be discussed by the commanders on both sides.

On September 30 General Gamelin sent to Lord Gort copies of two 'Instructions' for General Georges, dated September 30 and 29, dealing with the situations which would arise according as the Belgians did or did not invite in the Allied forces '*en temps utile*', that is to say in sufficient time to establish themselves in defensive positions before the Germans attacked in force.[1] If they did, the Allies would advance into Belgium in order to support the Belgians on their line of resistance, River Meuse–Albert Canal–Antwerp; if they did not, the Allies would meet the German attack in their organised defences, though it might be desirable to establish an advanced line of resistance on the Scheldt.

Meanwhile at the instance of the Chiefs of Staff the British Government had asked the Belgian Government to authorise staff conversations, but an official refusal was received on September 29. The Belgians said they did not expect the Germans to attack through their country, and in any case they themselves were putting the necessary measures of defence into effect. It seemed possible, however, that unofficial talks through civilian intermediaries might be allowed, and on the French side General Gamelin, so he tells us, was authorised to discuss matters informally with the Belgian staff, and came to an understanding with them on certain points.[2] Thus, as in the Scandinavian affair, strategy was closely entangled with diplomacy.

In the first week of October General Gamelin expected a main thrust by the German armies through Belgium and Holland to develop between October 22 and November 10. The Belgian attitude, however, showed no change till the end of October when, according to Gamelin, M. Spaak, the Foreign Minister, asked the French Ambassador what would be the reaction of the Allies should Germany invade Holland, and how the Allies proposed to carry out their promise to help Belgium if she were the victim of German aggression. M. Daladier in his reply on the latter point explained that the effectiveness of the help would depend on the degree of previous preparation.[3]

The implications of an invasion of the Netherlands now received much attention. Both the Belgian and the Dutch Governments appear to have believed that a German attack was imminent early in November—the 11th was mentioned; the two Sovereigns appealed on the 7th, without result, to the belligerents to accept mediation, and the Belgians showed readiness to allow discussions through the British Military Attaché, Colonel Blake, in Brussels and the Belgian Military Attaché in Paris; but otherwise things remained as they were. As the critical days passed without an explosion, the Belgians returned to their former silence.

---

[1] Gamelin III 82–85.
[2] *ibid.* I 86.
[3] *ibid.* III 138.

One result of the attention now devoted to the possibility of a German invasion of Holland was to suggest to Gamelin the adoption of a more ambitious strategy. He conceived the idea, in the event of the Belgians welcoming in the Allies, of pushing forward a French motorised force on his left flank to occupy the Dutch territory on both shores of the Scheldt estuary, including the islands of Walcheren and South Beveland, and so to link up with the Belgian garrison of Antwerp. On the right the Allies would move up, as previously contemplated, to the left bank of the Scheldt from the Franco-Belgian frontier to Ghent. Further to the east French troops would advance along the Meuse from Givet to Namur. In the centre, between the Sambre and the Scheldt, an Allied cavalry screen would, if the Germans did not attack Belgium, move forward in the direction of Brussels. But a plan so limited would leave the Belgian army to defend the important part of Belgium forming a re-entrant north of the Sambre and east and south of the Scheldt, and Gamelin became more and more impressed with the advantage of occupying a new line of resistance intermediate between the Albert Canal and the middle Scheldt. He was attracted by the shortening of the front by 70 or 80 kilometres which the new line offered, by the greater depth it would allow for anti-aircraft defence, by the prospect of saving the French and Belgian industrial regions and by the increased chance of linking up with the twenty divisions of the Belgian field army which would help to reduce the disparity in numbers.[1]

On November 9, while communications were still passing between the French and the Belgian staffs, a conference was held at Vincennes at which, besides Generals Gamelin and Georges, the Chief of the Imperial Staff, the Chief of the Air Staff, Lord Gort and other British officers were present. After Gamelin had said that he and Georges expected a move by the Germans, probably 'a blitz-krieg against Holland', in the near future, Georges explained the plan which he had worked out on the lines of Gamelin's idea described above. In the centre light troops would be sent forward first to the line of the Dendre and then to the line Namur–Wavre–Louvain–Malines–Antwerp; there was no question, however, of fighting a battle on the line of the Dendre; it must be either on the Scheldt or on the Namur–Wavre–Antwerp line. The British representatives raised no objection; military opinion had for some time favoured the stationing of French troops on the left of the British Expeditionary Force; and the conference then proceeded to discuss bombing policy and other matters.

The same evening the two British Chiefs of Staff reported to the Cabinet on their visit; the Chancellor of the Exchequer presided in

---

[1] See Gamelin I 89–108, III 139 ff.; Lyet pp. 16 ff.

the absence of the Prime Minister. The French proposals for a contingent advance of the Allied forces were explained; the Cabinet were told that the Belgians were believed (erroneously, as it was soon learnt) to be hard at work on the construction of defences on the sector of the more advanced line (between Namur and Wavre) which was protected by no water obstacle. When asked if he thought the British army ought to advance, General Ironside reminded the Cabinet that the Commander-in-Chief had been expressly put under the orders of the French commander; he had the right of protest to the Cabinet, but until he protested—which he had no intention of doing—they would be ill-advised to intervene. Gort had agreed to the proposed advance and he himself had accepted it. This assurance seems to have satisfied the Cabinet.

Gamelin tells us that it was after receiving an assurance on November 13 that the Belgian military authorities would fulfil the conditions which he judged necessary (as regards mobilisation and construction of defences) that he expounded the new plan to the French and British chiefs at Georges' headquarters on the 14th. Thereupon he issued his 'personal and secret instruction No. 8' with a view to an advance to the Namur–Antwerp position without halting on the Scheldt. The French Ninth and First Armies would hold respectively the Meuse from Givet to Namur and the Namur–Wavre 'gap'; the British would hold the line of the river Dyle, covering Brussels, from Wavre to Louvain; the Belgians would occupy the sector between Louvain and their National Redoubt [sic], which included Antwerp and Ghent, while the French Seventh Army, hitherto intended to form a general reserve, would come up on the extreme left to guard the southern shore of the West Scheldt estuary and to connect, if possible, with the Dutch forces.

No objection to the proposed advance to the Dyle seems to have been raised from the British side at this stage either. The Chiefs of Staff were clearly in favour of it, and for General Gamelin's reasons. They actually believed that the shortening of the line would release about twenty divisions to reserve. They felt sure, they said, that the French high command were alive to the time factor and would not commit the British Expeditionary Force to an encounter battle. The part of Gamelin's plan relating to the islands at the mouth of the Scheldt did not, however, commend itself to the British Chiefs of Staff; but since he intended to carry out the operation with French troops they acquiesced and agreed to lend British naval and air assistance on a small scale.

The new strategy was endorsed at a meeting of the Supreme War Council on November 17. This meeting dealt mainly with the question of air policy in the event of a German invasion of the Low Countries. Comparatively little discussion seems to have been devoted to the movement of the armies, but both Prime Ministers spoke strongly in favour of the new plan, Mr. Chamberlain urging the importance of saving as much as possible of Belgium from German occupation. M. Daladier is even reported as having said that he regarded the defence of Antwerp–Namur as quite as essential as the defence of France itself.

The strategy thus approved by the two Governments held the field until the actual invasion: it consisted, it may be repeated, of two alternative plans, one, known as Plan E, for an advance to the Scheldt (*Escaut*) between Maulde and Ghent, the other, Plan D, for a drive to the line Namur–Antwerp, of which the central sector, along the river Dyle between Wavre and Louvain, would be held by the British. Plan D was to be put into execution if circumstances allowed.

Plan D was not without its risks. The risk foreseen at the time was that even if the Allied columns won the race to their assigned positions against the advancing Germans they might suffer heavy casualties from the air while on the move or might not arrive in time to reconnoitre and organise their new defence line. The even greater risk, which was not fully realised, was that if the enemy broke through the Allied positions further south the divisions in Belgium might be unable to move back in time to avoid encirclement. But it was never expected that the main thrust of the enemy would be made through the difficult country of the Ardennes or that the troops set to guard the crossings of the Meuse above Namur would prove unequal to their task.[1]

There was another feature of General Gamelin's plan, the gravity of which was not realised by the British. It was connected not with preference for the Dyle position but with the advance of the left flank into Holland, to the Scheldt estuary and beyond. This operation was to be executed by the Seventh Army, under General Giraud, which had hitherto been in strategic reserve. As things turned out these divisions achieved no useful result and their place as central reserve was never adequately filled.

The adoption of Plan D made it more important than ever that the Allies should receive a timely invitation from the Belgians and march at the moment of their own choice, not the Germans'. There were two occasions between November and May when it seemed possible that acute fear of an invasion might prevail over their chronic dread of precipitating one to induce the Belgians to extend this invitation.[2] The first was in January, when rumours that some

---

[1] Gamelin's defence is given in *Servir* I 81–108; Georges felt some misgivings; Lyet, *op. cit.* 22, 24, 28.

[2] For the November alarm see p. 160 above.

German action was impending were confirmed by the capture on the 10th of two German staff officers, with the plans for an offensive, who had made a forced landing in Belgium.[1] The Belgians expected to be attacked on the 14th and informal conversations were held in high quarters. Even now, however, the Belgians did not invite the Allies in, and it appeared later on that they had never thought of doing so until the Germans actually invaded them; thus, when the expected attack again did not occur, all that the Allies could secure was a promise that necessary military information would be supplied. The second occasion was on April 9, the day of the German invasion of Denmark and Norway, when MM. Reynaud and Daladier came over for a meeting of the Supreme War Council in London. M. Reynaud said that the French War Committee had decided in principle in favour of advancing into Belgium forthwith if the co-operation of the Belgian army could be secured. He declares in his book that he was himself strongly opposed to such action, but he does not appear to have given his hearers any inkling of this, any more than he had done on March 28 at the first Supreme War Council to be held after he became Prime Minister.[2] It was agreed to renew pressure on the Belgian Government through both diplomatic and military channels to invite the Allied armies in immediately, but again the Belgians refused. Their Minister for Foreign Affairs said, however, that his Government would certainly issue the invitation the moment they were sure that an invasion was imminent.

Meanwhile the contingency of the Germans attacking Holland but not Belgium had been discussed by the Allies. The action of the Belgians in such an event must be important, but it was not clear what it would be; in the soldiers' opinion the despatch of Allied forces through Belgium without Belgian co-operation would be dangerous, if not impossible. At the meeting of the Supreme War Council on March 28, after dealing in the morning with questions affecting Scandinavia and South-East Europe, the Allied leaders proceeded to formulate their policy as regards Holland and Belgium. If Germany invaded Belgium, the Allies would immediately move into Belgium without waiting for a formal invitation; if Germany invaded Holland and the Belgians helped Holland, the Allies would move to Belgium's support at once; if Germany invaded Holland but Belgium remained neutral, the Allies would feel justified in entering Belgium in order to help the Dutch, but they did not pledge themselves to any specific action.

The Allied attitude was finally declared at the Supreme War

---

[1] A full account of this incident is given by J. Vanwelkenhuyzen, *L'alerte du 10 Janvier 1940*, in *Revue d'histoire de la deuxième guerre mondiale* Oct. 1953.

[2] Reynaud II 44: cf. Gamelin I 88, III 315, *The Private Diaries of Paul Baudouin*; tr. Petrie (1948) p. 10.

Council on April 23 when the general military situation was reviewed. The two Governments agreed that in this case their armies should forthwith advance into Belgium irrespective of the Belgian Government's attitude and that it was undesirable to ask for Belgian consent previously. The extent of the armies' advance, however, would depend on the Belgian attitude. If Belgium with her twenty divisions joined the Allies they would be justified in pushing forward to the Namur–Antwerp line (Plan D); if not, the move would take place under much less favourable conditions and it would not be safe to set the first bound further east than the Scheldt.

So the matter rested until all doubts were ended by the German invasion of both Belgium and Holland on May 10 and the immediate appeal of the victims of aggression for Allied help.

Besides the question of the conditions and extent of the advance of the Allied land forces there was another important strategic issue on which the two Governments held lengthy discussions during these months, and it was one on which they found it harder to agree, though it was less complicated by the uncertainties of neutral action. At the meeting of the Supreme War Council on April 23, which has just been referred to, Mr. Chamberlain said that this very uncertainty made it all the more imperative that the Allies should take action other than a land advance to hamper the German occupation of Holland; and it was agreed that in the event of a German aggression against either or both of the two neutral countries the Royal Air Force should be authorised, without further consultation between either the Allied Governments or the Allied high commands, immediately to attack marshalling yards and oil refineries in the Ruhr. This decision was an important achievement from the British point of view; but it meant no more than it said and by no means amounted to permission for a general air offensive even against targets of direct military importance.

It is necessary to turn back to earlier episodes in a long story. The French and British staffs had agreed in March 1939 that, in the event of a main German attack on land and in the air being concentrated against France, the object of all the available bombers would be to contribute to the success of the battle on land.[1] No distinction appears to have been mentioned at this stage between the medium bombers which it was proposed to send to France as the Advanced Air Striking Force and the heavy bombers of Bomber Command which would form our main weapon of attack. This distinction is, however, one which it is important to bear in mind.

---

[1] See above, p. 17.

When war became imminent the two Governments discussed their bombing policy afresh, and on September 2 they announced to the world their intention to prohibit bombardment of any but strictly military objectives in the narrowest sense of the word.[1] Thus, only if Germany initiated unrestricted air action from the outset, should we proceed to attack even objectives so vital to her war effort as her oil resources.

On September 5 the Cabinet learnt that the Chief of the Imperial General Staff and the Chief of the Air Staff had agreed with General Gamelin that the ten squadrons of the Advanced Air Striking Force should support the French army in their proposed advance against the Siegfried Line, but our representatives were insistent that the heavy bombers of Bomber Command should not be 'frittered away' on minor targets; we must not risk leaving ourselves so weak in bombers that we should be unable to take effective air action to defend ourselves later on. 'The French Air Force, which was barely equipped, had no air plan other than limited operations in co-operation with the general plan of the French army.'

On September 11 the Cabinet considered whether their current policy should be modified in view of recent developments in Poland and elsewhere, but on the advice of the Chiefs of Staff decided to maintain it.[2]

Up to this point the French and British authorities were in agreement; neither wished to precipitate unrestricted bombing. The divergence arose over the policy to be adopted at a later stage, which might begin very soon, when the Germans passed to the offensive in the west.

In order to understand the attitudes of the two Governments, it is necessary to take account of their respective states of preparation. The French had concentrated on their army, in which respect of course they far outdistanced the British; their air preparations were backward, both offensive and defensive, and they were anxious about the safety of their towns in general and their aircraft factories in particular; the British, though their land contribution was so small, were comparatively well advanced as regards the efficiency of their bomber and fighter resources; they believed that a German air offensive against the United Kingdom would be severely handled and believed also, however mistakenly, that we were in a position to retaliate with effect on German communications and industrial installations. It soon appeared that the French were most reluctant to take any step, even when the German forces invaded, which might bring air retaliation against French soil. In their view the main role of the Allied air forces would be to support the armies,

---

[1] See above, p. 56.
[2] See Appendix I(a).

and they could appeal to the acceptance by the British staff representatives in the spring of 1939 of the principle that in the circumstances envisaged the object of all the available bombers would be to contribute to the success of the battle on land. Even then, however, the British officers had remarked that if heavy air attacks were simultaneously being made against Great Britain it would be necessary to answer them by a bombing counter-offensive against selected targets in Germany.

Soon after the outbreak of war it appeared that the French and British authorities differed as to how Allied bombers could best support the armies in the land battle. The British Chiefs of Staff in a paper of 22 September pointed out that in the event of a German advance through the Low Countries it would be essential for our aircraft to seize 'the fleeting opportunity' presented by the enemy's columns, but that such action would inevitably involve casualties to Dutch and Belgian soldiers and civilians; they therefore asked the Cabinet's authority to issue the necessary orders should the need arise. The Cabinet postponed their decision until after the hoped-for staff conversations with the Belgians, which were expected to reveal more about their plans. After an interval the Chiefs of Staff pressed again for authority (October 12) and on the following day they received it; the Cabinet took the view that the action proposed was comparable to the bombardment of towns of military importance which contained civilians and was therefore permissible.

At their next meeting (October 14) the Cabinet discussed air policy in a wider context; they gave general approval to the recommendations of a committee composed of the Chiefs of Staff and certain Ministers to the effect that while our air strength remained inferior to Germany's we should not be the first 'to take the gloves off', but that if Germany initiated action against either ourselves or France which threatened to be 'decisive' we must use our striking force in whatever way offered 'decisive' results; from this point of view the Ruhr region, containing some sixty per cent of Germany's vital industry in an area about the size of Greater London, was the most promising target, but it included of course a large civilian population. The Cabinet discussed how far an attack on the Ruhr would be an appropriate counter-stroke to an invasion of Belgium, but came to no decision except the negative one that an attack on the Ruhr or any but strictly military objectives would not be justified unless and until Germany either killed large numbers of civilians by air attack on one of the Allied countries or perpetrated a violation of Belgium. These views were conveyed to Gamelin and Vuillemin on 24 October with the rider that, should Germany give provocation in the second of the ways specified, it would be for the British Cabinet to decide immediately whether our bombers should not attack the Ruhr as well as the advancing German forces.

A sharp difference between the Allies now showed itself.[1] The French high command were averse from authorising a bombardment of the Ruhr until the spring, when the disproportion between Allied and enemy air strengths should have been reduced, and in any event considered that the most effective response to a German invasion of Belgium would be to concentrate all the Allied bombers, heavy as well as medium, on the enemy columns and such direct military objectives as railways and airfields. The British Chiefs of Staff, on the other hand, advised the Cabinet that a German occupation of Belgium would give such important advantages to the German air and naval forces that it ought to be prevented by the immediate use of all means at our disposal; with regard to the most effective use of our air power, it was common ground that medium bombers might profitably act, and should act, directly against the advancing enemy, but in the view of the Chiefs of Staff it would be 'grossly uneconomical' to use heavy bombers for this purpose, whereas their concentration against the Ruhr offered prospects of bringing its industry 'practically to a standstill' as well as of eventually dislocating an important part of the enemy's line of communication through Belgium. They admitted that the bombardment of the Ruhr must entail civilian casualties and that it was contrary to the current policy of the Cabinet that we should be the first to assume this responsibility. They urged however that the action of the German Air Force in Poland, 'where they attacked factories, power stations, railway communications etc.,' amply justified the bombardment of the Ruhr, and in view of the military advantage of attacking the German army in the early stages of its advance they asked for discretion to bomb specified military objectives in the Ruhr immediately Belgium was invaded, without further reference to the War Cabinet.

The Chiefs of Staff recommended the same action in the event of Holland alone being invaded, if the Belgians invited us in; if the Belgians did not invite us in, we should merely attack from the air such military objectives as would help the Dutch to delay the German advance.

These reports were thoroughly discussed by the Military Co-ordination Committee on November 13, and by the Cabinet next day. Particular attention was devoted to the question whether the battle for Belgium was likely to be 'decisive' for the whole course of the war. The conclusion was reached that it was not possible to authorise in advance of the event any specific policy for the employment of the main Air Striking Force, and that the decision must be

---

[1] See Gamelin III 144.

taken by the War Cabinet, in the light of the facts existing at the time. In the meantime we should explain our attitude to the French.

A meeting of the Supreme War Council was accordingly held on November 17. After Mr. Chamberlain had expounded the Air Ministry's plan, which he envisaged as continual waves of small forces flying low, prepared to accept very heavy losses (possibly from twenty to fifty per cent), M. Daladier expressed his doubts of the wisdom of risking such losses at a time when the German Air Force exceeded ours by three to one and when the French factories were still concentrated in industrial areas and inadequately defended; the situation might be very different in a few months' time. Moreover, he did not believe that the bombing of the Ruhr would prevent an occupation of Belgium. In view of the French opposition Mr. Chamberlain did not press the British policy and it was agreed that if, but only if, the Germans should bomb Allied aircraft factories or similar objectives the British heavy bombers could at once retaliate at the discretion of the Cabinet without further reference to the French; otherwise, even if the Germans invaded Belgium in the next few months, our air reaction should still be confined to military objectives in the strictest sense. This was the meeting at which the two Governments agreed that the Allied armies should, if possible, move forward to the Namur–Antwerp line; the extreme importance attached to this advance by the two Prime Ministers was largely due to their acceptance of the arguments in favour of preserving as much as possible of Belgian soil, while rejecting the method of doing so, namely bombing the Ruhr, preferred by the British.

So the matter rested until the spring; it was reopened by Mr. Churchill in the Military Co-ordination Committee, of which he was now chairman, on April 8, the day before the German invasion of Denmark and Norway. By this time the British Air Forces in France had been reorganised under the command of Air Marshal Barratt, and an inter-allied staff, known as the Allied Central Air Bureau (A.C.A.B.), had been formed to facilitate the prompt assignment of aircraft to the objectives chosen. In addition to the ten squadrons of the Advanced Air Striking Force in France the four squadrons of Blenheims of No. 2 Bomber Group were held ready in England, and should Barratt require further bomber support he could apply to Bomber Command. There were now twenty squadrons of heavy bombers in this Command; they formed the 'last reserve' available to the Allies in an emergency, and it was obvious that there might be other calls upon them, e.g. from the Admiralty or for retaliatory action against Germany, besides the summons to the land battle. In the event of conflicting demands the decision would lie with the Cabinet.

At the meeting of the Committee it appeared that several members had come nearer to the French view. With a German offensive perhaps imminent, the General Staff, and not they only, were now of opinion that our heavy bombers should intervene more directly in the main battle than merely by bombing the Ruhr; they could be better employed in attacking vital rail or road junctions such as Aachen, München-Gladbach or Düren west of the Rhine. The Committee reported in this sense to the Cabinet, and the Cabinet gave their approval on April 14, it being understood that, if it was intended to take some action which went beyond the general policy laid down by the Cabinet, or to use the whole bomber force for some operation which might be decisive, the sanction of the Cabinet as a whole would be necessary.

At this time the Cabinet were considering the general question of the action to be taken by the Allies in the event of a German invasion of the Low Countries. They had agreed on April 12th to seek French concurrence in the proposal that if and when Germany invaded either neutral country the Allied air forces without further reference to their Governments should immediately attack military objectives in Germany, such as troop concentrations, marshalling yards, communications and oil refineries. In view of French objections they decided on the 14th to instruct Air Marshal Barratt to try to reach an agreed plan with the French high command to cover the opening phase of air operations in the case under consideration. The result of the Air Marshal's conversations with Generals Gamelin and Vuillemin was unsatisfactory: not only were the French still unwilling that we should attack industrial targets until the enemy had done so, but Gamelin seemed opposed even to our taking the initiative in bombing German lines of communication west of the Rhine. Moreover, the French evidently took a less serious view than the British of the danger to the Allied cause which would result from a German occupation of Holland. The Chiefs of Staff were gravely perturbed and appealed to the Cabinet to take the matter up with the French Government. The Prime Minister accordingly pressed the point at the meeting of the Supreme War Council on April 23. On this occasion the French accepted the British point of view, stipulating only against the inclusion of factories among permissible targets. So the matter stood between the Allies when the wholesale German irruption on May 10 rendered all fine-drawn distinctions obsolete.

The Chiefs of Staff and the Cabinet had discussed at some length in the preceding few days the capacity of our bomber force. Our total first-line long-range bomber strength was 450 (including about 100 Blenheims, which would not be used for an attack on the Ruhr), but in view of casualties in the Norwegian campaign (75) and the unreadiness of many of the aircraft in reserve the Air Ministry could not feel sure of being able to use more than 240 heavy bombers (excluding Blenheims), 'of which only half would be actually serviceable on any given day'. With this force we should be able to drop twenty-eight tons of bombs nightly on oil refineries, marshalling yards and vital plants, and 'at this rate we should theoretically be able to destroy the objectives in 11–18 days'. The Air Ministry estimated that we should be able to carry on operations at the planned intensity for six weeks, after which it would be reduced by about half. The German first-line heavy bomber strength, on the other hand, was estimated at about 1,900, as against our 450, and they should be able to replace losses quicker than we could.

The reference to night bombing is of interest. It marks a decision which, though not conveyed by a formal directive, was of the utmost importance in the development of British air tactics and continued to guide the policy of Bomber Command. Owing to the grievous losses suffered by our heavy bombers in daylight operations over the North Sea in the winter, night bombing came to be regarded as tactically necessary.

In the light of later experience the results hoped for from the small bomber force of May 1940 must appear fantastic, and indeed the attitude of the Air Staff was not that it was desirable to open up the air war now but rather that, seeing that a German invasion of Holland—the contingency then under consideration—would be merely a preliminary to an air war against the United Kingdom, it was preferable to take the initiative at the moment most favourable to ourselves.

As we approach the day which focused the eyes of the world on north-west Europe we may attempt to gather up some of the threads. The Allied forces at Aandelsnes and Namsos had been safely evacuated and a new general was being sent to Narvik to report on the situation. But confidence in the Allied direction of the war had been severely shaken. The Chamberlain Government stood its trial in the House of Commons on May 7 and 8, and in Paris M. Reynaud, now determined to replace Gamelin, decided in view of Daladier's opposition to resign office.[1] The attitude of Italy had for some time caused anxiety; it was felt that further German successes might at any moment encourage Mussolini to hasten to the assistance of the victor. In the latter half of April indications mounted up that Italy meant to take the plunge fairly soon—a descent on Dalmatia was thought likely—and attention had been devoted to measures which might deter her. Various precautionary steps were approved, and strong naval reinforcements, including the three battleships *Royal*

---

[1] Reynaud II 54.

Sovereign, Malaya and *Warspite*, along with three French battleships, were moved to Alexandria. By the end of the first week of May, however, the tension had relaxed. British Balkan policy continued to be governed by the attitude of Italy; discussions had been held in London at the time of the invasion of Norway with our diplomatic representatives in the Balkan countries, at which possibilities of supporting Turkey and Greece were considered. But there were no indications of an imminent German offensive in the Balkans.

The strategical situation as a whole resulting from the German invasion of the two Scandinavian countries was reviewed by the Chiefs of Staff early in May on the assumption that the invasion was 'a first step in a major plan aimed at seeking a decision this year'. The Germans might try to achieve their object in one of two ways, by a major attack directed either against Great Britain or against France. Of the two alternatives the Chiefs of Staff thought the former the more likely, for four reasons: France could not resist alone after the defeat of Great Britain; a full-scale attack on France would involve heavy losses which might have a serious effect on German morale; British support to France under attack was likely to prove more effective than French support to Great Britain; and lastly, by use of her air force alone against this country Germany would exploit her relatively strongest weapon with the least expenditure of life and economic resources.

A major attack directed against Great Britain would probably take the form of an air offensive, which might prepare the way for invasion; the occupation of Danish and Norwegian bases had increased the scale of attack on our naval forces and shipping and an occupation of the Low Countries would increase it still further. Every possible step should therefore be taken to hasten the production of anti-aircraft equipment, particularly Bofors guns, bomber and fighter aircraft and fully trained crews, even at the temporary expense of our long-range programme. Moreover it was vitally important to prepare for the diversion of sea-traffic to western ports and for drastic reduction of unessential imports. Plans for dealing with invasion should be reviewed; the public should be instructed as to the reality of the air threat and passive defence measures should be made effective.

If the Germans on the other hand directed their main attack against France, they could make 160 divisions available for the Western front against 104 of the Allies, fortress troops on each side excluded.[1] Granted adequate air defence, France should be reasonably secure, even with this disparity, against land attack by both

---

[1] The figure for the Germans excluded divisions in Scandinavia; that for the Allies counted French and British divisions only. For the actual figures see below, p. 177.

Germany and Italy; it was not certain, however, that air defence would be adequate to cover both the armies and the French vital centres in view of Allied deficiencies in fighter and bomber aircraft alike.

In the Balkan, Mediterranean and Middle East areas we must expect Germany to seek to embarrass us by diversions, with the collaboration of Italy and perhaps of Spain and Russia. Our strategy in countering them must be mainly defensive, with the possible exception of air attack on Italy's north-western industrial area.

This report was discussed at length by the Cabinet on May 9, the day before the German invasion of the Low Countries falsified one of its major expectations; unfortunately the first week of the campaign was to falsify another, the effectiveness of the French resistance. The Cabinet gave the report their general approval; they agreed on the importance of perfecting civil defence and of counteracting public apathy with regard to the air menace. They did not regard the financial implications as alarming: difficulties of production rather than of payment were the governing factors. But it did not fall to Mr. Chamberlain's Government to supervise the execution of the measures proposed.

CHAPTER VIII

THE CAMPAIGN IN THE LOW COUNTRIES AND FRANCE

THE BELIEF in an imminent German offensive which had harassed the Belgians and their would-be rescuers at intervals throughout the winter and spring was not without foundation. Early in October Hitler decided that 'the attack cannot begin soon enough'; the actual date would depend 'on the operational readiness of the tank and motorised units and on weather conditions'. The attack should if possible be carried out during the autumn; if successfully begun it could continue 'into the coldest part of the winter'.[1] Zero day was in fact twice fixed, for November 12 and for January 17, and in each case the troop movements had begun before the operation was postponed; these, it will be remembered, were the two occasions when the Allies definitely expected an immediate invasion of Belgium.[2] Apart from these two specific dates German preparations for the offensive remained in a state of readiness, though subject to frequent postponements. Hitler in after years blamed the General Staff for delaying the offensive. Brauchitsch, the Commander-in-Chief of the Army, and Halder, his Chief of the General Staff, were certainly opposed on broad grounds to its being launched before the spring. The postponement in January, however, was due mainly to the weather, though perhaps to some extent to the leakage of information resulting from the capture of the two staff officers. Eventually on May 1 the Führer ordered that as from May 4 all should be ready daily for a start within 24 hours, and on May 9 zero hour was finally set for 0535 next morning.

By this time the plans for 'Operation Yellow', as the western offensive was known, had been subject to various alterations, of which one was of the greatest moment.[3] Hitler's intention had always been to strike 'at the northern flank of the Western Front, through the area of Luxemburg, Belgium, and the Netherlands'. His purpose was 'to defeat as large a portion as possible of the French field army, together with the allies fighting at their side, and at the same time to conquer as large an area as possible in Holland, Belgium and

---

[1] *Führer Directives*, pp. 63–67: see above, p. 62.

[2] See above, ch. vii, pp. 160, 163.

[3] A full account of the German planning of the campaign is given in the Supplement to Ellis, *The War in France and Flanders 1939–40*.

Northern France, to serve as a base for air and sea warfare against Britain, and as a wide protective belt for the vitally important Ruhr area'.[1]

The army plan drawn up in October provided for the execution of the Führer's purpose by two groups of armies, Army Group B in the north and Army Group A in the south; a third force, Army Group C, would stand on the defensive or begin feint operations on the Franco-German frontier still further south. This general scheme remained unaltered, but the roles assigned respectively to Army Groups B and A underwent changes of supreme importance. According to the original plan the object of the offensive was to destroy the Allied forces north of the Somme and to penetrate as far as the Channel coast. The main attack would be delivered by Army Group B in a westerly direction towards the general line Ghent–Charleroi in the first instance.[2] The role of Army Group A would be secondary, to cover Army Group B against enemy action from the south and south-west.

This plan was from an early date criticised on the German side as unimaginative and unlikely to achieve surprise or to have a decisive effect on the war. In essence it was a frontal attack, and even if it succeeded in forcing back the Allied armies to the Somme it would only win a limited area of coast and hinterland for the extended operations of the Navy and Luftwaffe. The German aim should be more ambitious; to annihilate all the Allied land and air forces in France and secure the whole northern coastline of the country. An essential step towards this end would be to attack in force *south* of the Sambre after crossing the Meuse between Namur and Sedan, with the double object of cutting off the Allied armies in retreat towards the Somme and crushing the forces 'preparing to counter-attack between the Meuse and the Oise'. It was therefore proposed by the able commander and chief of staff of Army Group A (Colonel-General von Rundstedt and Lieutenant-General von Manstein) that the main weight of the attack, the *Schwerpunkt* or decisive point, should be transferred to the southern wing, and after much discussion a revised plan was approved by the Führer in the second half of February. Army Group A, strengthened by a concentration of armour, was now to strike in force through the Ardennes and across the Meuse between Dinant and Sedan towards the lower valley of the Somme, and not only to guard the left flank of the advancing German columns against a French attack from the south. The task of Army Group B should be the subsidiary one of breaking through the Belgian frontier defences, freeing the Ruhr from immediate danger

---

[1] Directive No. 6 of 9 Oct. 1939. *F.D.* p. 67.
[2] Map 5.

and drawing on itself 'as strong elements as possible of the Franco-British army'. With regard to the Netherlands there were several changes of plan; eventually it was proposed to attack and seize the whole of the country.

The allocation of divisions in the final plan was as follows: Army Group B, twenty-eight, including three armoured and one motorised; Army Group A, forty-four, including seven armoured and three motorised; Army Group C, seventeen; *OKH* Reserve, forty-five, including one motorised; making a total of 134 divisions.

Against this formidable array the Allies too could produce for the North-Eastern front on May 10 the equivalent of rather more than 130 divisions; this figure includes twenty-two Belgian, ten British, one Polish, some eight Dutch, and ninety-four French. Apart from the disadvantages inherent in the co-operation of mixed national forces, the Allied troops were by no means all trained up to the level of most of the German, nor were they so effectively equipped. Of the French infantry divisions only sixty-seven were recognised as field (as distinguished from fortress) divisions, and even these were of very varying quality. Moreover as against the ten German *Panzer* divisions the Allies had ready only three fully armoured (*cuirassées*) and three light mechanised divisions; the British 1st Armoured and the French 4th did not enter the battle till later. Altogether the French put into the field at the beginning of May about 2,500 tanks; the enemy numbers were hardly greater, but the German armour was concentrated in the *Panzer* divisions whereas the French was dispersed over various formations and units.[1]

The general disposition of the Allied forces had remained the same since Gamelin's decision to transfer the Seventh Army from strategic reserve to link up, on the extreme left flank, with the Dutch.[2] On the Allied right, from the Swiss frontier to Longuyon at the northern end of the Maginot line, were the Third and Second Army Groups; in the centre, from Longuyon to Namur, with their junction about Sedan, were the Second and Ninth Armies, forming part of the First Army Group. Further to the left, the First Army, composed of seven divisions, including three motorised, of good quality, under General Blanchard, was prepared to advance rapidly to the open country between Namur and Wavre, behind a screen of two divisions of mechanised cavalry. On their left would be nine British divisions (the tenth doing duty on the Saar front), and on the British left, covering Antwerp, so much of the Belgian field army as was not occupying advanced positions in the Ardennes or along the Albert canal.

---

[1] The figures are taken from Lyet pp. 31–32; those given by General Gamelin in vol. I of *Servir* (pp. 309–317) do not differ to any important extent. For the numbers of German tanks see Guderian, *Panzer Leader*, tr. Fitzgibbon (1952) app. iii.

[2] Above, p. 163.

North of Antwerp, extending into Holland, General Giraud's Seventh Army of six divisions, including two motorised, would be in contact with the Dutch, covered by the remaining division of mechanised cavalry.

Thus a high proportion of the best trained and most mobile formations would be found on the left flank, between Namur and the coast. This was explained partly by the wide wheeling movement assigned to them and the need of beating the enemy to the Scheldt estuary and to the Dyle position, but also partly by the conviction of the high command that the main German thrust would be made, as in 1914 and as originally intended by Hitler and Brauchitsch, over the Belgian plain. To guard the difficult, broken country of the Ardennes and the deep-cut valley of the Meuse above Namur, it was thought that troops of less good quality would suffice.

In reserve, but widely dispersed, General Georges had two armoured divisions and thirteen infantry, of which three were in process of formation. Three further divisions, held available for the South-Eastern front, were promptly put at his disposal by Gamelin.[1]

Such in broad outlines were the strengths and dispositions of the land forces. The role of the Luftwaffe was to disrupt the Allied air forces by concentrated attacks on their ground installations and then to provide direct support for the operations of the armies; it would also undertake the transport of the airborne forces intended to secure important strategic points in Belgium and Holland. The forces employed in the campaign amounted to some 3,530 operational aircraft out of a total first-line strength of about 4,800 when the attack was launched, together with some 470 transport aircraft and 45 gliders for operations in Holland.

The French air force available in France for battle consisted of some 1,000 aircraft, of which about 800 were in the north-east theatre; these 800 included rather more than 400 fighters and about 100 bombers.[2]

The Royal Air Force in France consisted of the ten medium bomber squadrons and two fighter squadrons of the Advanced Air Striking Force and the thirteen squadrons of the Air Component, something over 400 aircraft in all. It had been arranged that, if and when the Germans invaded, four more fighter squadrons were to fly out from England, two for duty with the Air Component, two with the Advanced Air Striking Force.[3] We have also noted the arrangement made for assistance from the medium bomber squadrons in England and the discussions as to the best use of the heavy bombers.[4]

---

[1] Lyet p. 42; Gamelin I 313.
[2] Lyet pp. 34, 35.
[3] See above, p. 156.
[4] Above, pp. 155, 165 ff.

In the early morning of Friday 10 May, without a declaration of hostilities, the German armies, preceded by an intense air attack, began the invasion of Holland, Belgium and Luxemburg; Hitler had once again set in motion the huge machine of aggression and let loose the horrors of war on three more unoffending neutral countries. The Dutch and Belgian Governments immediately appealed for help to London and Paris. Soon after six Lord Gort received from French Headquarters the order to put Plan D into effect and at 1 p.m. the leading British troops, the 12th Royal Lancers, crossed the Belgian frontier.

May 10 was a day of high political as well as military importance. M. Reynaud, who had decided that Gamelin must be replaced and had in consequence offered the resignation of his Cabinet, felt that the moment of the German invasion was no time for a domestic crisis; accordingly the President of the Council and the Commander-in-Chief shook hands in the presence of the enemy.[1] Mr. Chamberlain's first instinct was in the same direction. He had been convinced by the Commons debate of May 7 and 8 that a National Government must be formed and he doubted whether it could be formed under himself. The news on the morning of the 10th prompted the thought that at such a moment it was his duty to remain at his post. Being assured, however, that the Labour leaders would not serve under him he resigned office, and at six o'clock that evening the King sent for Mr. Winston Churchill.[2]

Seeing that it was the failure of the Norwegian campaign which was primarily responsible for the fall of the Government and that in the direction of that campaign Mr. Churchill had played, as he has put it, an 'exceptionally prominent part', it may at first seem surprising that his accession to the supreme post was greeted with popular acclamation. The reason is not obscure. The failure in Norway was the occasion rather than the cause of the Government's defeat. Its defeat was due to more general causes. Rightly or wrongly there was a strong feeling in the country that the Chamberlain administration stood condemned, on its pre-war record, of a lack of judgement and drive; and this feeling was reinforced by a widespread opinion that the higher direction of the war in these early months showed similar defects. Slowness and failure on the part of the Allies contrasted unhappily with Hitler's audacious initiative and swift successes. The contrast was of course largely to be accounted for by the fact that the Germans were prepared for war, in mind and in

---

[1] Reynaud II 54.
[2] Feiling p. 441; Churchill I 595 ff; L. S. Amery, *My Political Life* III (1955) 371–374.

material resources, while the Allies were not. Rearmament in the United Kingdom was still in its early years; only in the last few months had compulsory military service been introduced, against bitter parliamentary opposition; and both the British and the French Governments had envisaged a period of defensive strategy in which to build up their military strength. Resources for any effective stroke on land or in the air were patently lacking. On the other hand the postponement of the expected air attacks on our great cities produced in the people a sense of anti-climax and boredom, resulting in a demand for bolder leadership. The story of rearmament will be found in Volume I of this series; with purely political issues a military history such as this cannot attempt to deal. The fact remains that in large and important sections of the country and the House of Commons the Government was now held guilty of having pursued a futile foreign policy in the past, of having made inadequate provision for rearmament in the last few years, and more recently of slackness in harnessing the national energies to the war effort. Of that policy and that inadequacy Mr. Churchill had been the most consistent and outstanding critic, and slackness was not a sin which could be laid to his charge. Of him it might have been said, as of the Athenians of old, that his nature was such as to allow no rest either to himself or to other men; and this, if they did not know it already, both Whitehall and the country were soon to discover.

The National Government formed by Mr. Churchill as Prime Minister had the support of all three parties. His War Cabinet retained Mr. Chamberlain and Lord Halifax as Lord President and Foreign Secretary and included two leaders of the Labour Opposition, Mr. Attlee and Mr. Greenwood, as Lord Privy Seal and Minister without portfolio. It had no other members. Thus the new War Cabinet was smaller than the old, five members as against eight (Lord Chatfield not having been replaced), and only the Foreign Secretary held departmental office.

Mr. Churchill has stated his opinion that 'the key-change' made by him was 'the supervision and direction of the Chiefs of Staff Committee by a Minister of Defence with undefined powers' who was also Prime Minister. 'Thus for the first time the Chiefs of Staff Committee assumed its due and proper place in direct daily contact with the executive head of the Government, and in accord with him had full control over the conduct of the war and the armed forces.'[1]

Mr. Churchill himself thus became Minister of Defence, but he saw no need to complicate the machinery by creating a Ministry of Defence additional to the three Service Departments; his necessary staff was provided by the military wing of the War Cabinet

---

[1] Churchill II 15.

Secretariat—which was also the secretariat of the Chiefs of Staff—with General Ismay as its head and Colonel L. C. Hollis and Lieutenant-Colonel E. I. C. Jacob as his chief assistants.[1]

The Military Co-ordination Committee was renamed the Defence Committee; it worked in two panels, according as it was concerned with Operations and Supply. The Minister of Defence presided over both. Meetings dealing with Operations were regularly attended by the three Service Ministers and the Chiefs of Staff, with General Ismay, but there was at first no strict line drawn between permanent and occasional members.[2] Later there was a permanent nucleus of Ministers, including Mr. Attlee and the Foreign Secretary. Meetings dealing with Supply were attended by the chief personages of that Ministry and of the Service Departments immediately concerned.

On May 13 the House of Commons gave the new Government a unanimous vote of confidence; it was then that the Prime Minister struck the note which was to mark the character of his administration. He would say to the House, as he had said to his colleagues in the Government:

> 'I have nothing to offer but blood, toil, tears and sweat . . . You ask, what is our policy? I will say: It is to wage war, by sea, land and air, with all our might and with all the strength that God can give us; to wage war against a monstrous tyranny, never surpassed in the dark, lamentable catalogue of human crime. That is our policy. You ask what is our aim? I can answer in one word: It is victory, victory at all costs, victory in spite of terror, victory, however long and hard the road may be; for without victory, there is no survival. Let that be realised; no survival for the British Empire, no survival for all that the British Empire has stood for, no survival for the urge and impulse of the ages, that mankind will move forward towards its goal. But I take up my task with buoyancy and hope. I feel sure that our cause will not be suffered to fail among men. At this time I feel entitled to claim the aid of all, and I say, "Come then, let us go forward together with our united strength" '[3]

Before the new Cabinet held its first formal meeting on May 13 a number of important decisions had been taken. The unleashing of the Expeditionary Force for the race to the Dyle needed no British decision; the word, as we have seen, came from French Headquarters. At Lord Gort's request the Government resolved to send out the Armoured Division to France at once. It had been agreed with the French that the mines of the 'Royal Marine' operation were to be

---

[1] See Churchill II 16–21.

[2] Its Minutes were at first headed as those of 'a Meeting of Ministers and Chiefs of Staff'; the form 'Defence Committee (Operations)' first appears in July.

[3] *House of Commons Debates* vol. 360, col. 1502.

released into the Rhine as soon as the German offensive started, and this was now done; photographs showed soon afterwards that the river barrage near Karlsruhe had been damaged. Demolition parties were sent to Belgium and Holland in accordance with plans previously made, to be ready to block ports and destroy their installations. Fighters from England patrolled the coast of the Low Countries, and four Hurricane squadrons flew over to reinforce the Air Component and the Advanced Air Striking Force. The ten medium bomber squadrons of the latter, supported by others from England, proceeded to operate as desired by the French, but it was soon discovered that they could do little to stop an advancing army; the Battle aircraft in particular were very vulnerable in day fighting, and losses were heavy, especially on May 14. On the 17th it was found necessary to reorganise the ten squadrons as six.

The use to be made of the heavy bombers of Bomber Command, apart from two squadrons detached to bomb enemy communications west of the Rhine, was a more debatable matter. On May 10 the Government announced publicly, in agreement with the French, that they reserved to themselves the right to take action which they considered 'appropriate in the event of bombing by the enemy of civil populations, whether in the United Kingdom, France or in countries assisted by the United Kingdom'. It was not, however, till May 15, the day after the Germans had bombed the city of Rotterdam, that after long discussions the Cabinet authorised an attack on the Ruhr and the Strategic Air Offensive began.[1] That night over a hundred heavy bombers attacked, the great majority in the Ruhr; but the damage done was in fact slight, as indeed in the conditions of that time was bound to be the case.

It may be mentioned, in anticipation, that on May 31 the Chiefs of Staff pointed out to the Cabinet that the opening up of the war in the West had forced us to adopt a much wider interpretation of the term 'military objective' than that contained in the current instructions still binding on commanders in other possible theatres. They proposed therefore, and the Cabinet approved, the issue of fresh instructions which extended the meaning to be attached to 'military objectives'. The intentional bombardment of civilian populations, as such, remained illegal; it must be possible to identify the objective and 'reasonable care' must be taken 'to avoid undue loss of civil life in the vicinity of the target'.

Until the night of the 13th the situation in the land battle did not appear particularly alarming. The British Expeditionary Force had

---

[1] For the bombing of Rotterdam see Appendix I(b).

reached their appointed position on the Dyle more or less unmolested, the bulk of the Luftwaffe being engaged elsewhere, and the French First Army were in place on their right. Little was known of what was happening on the far side of the Meuse. The Belgians holding their forward defences had failed to destroy all the bridges and were complaining of lack of air support. There were calls for air support all round, and thirty-two Hurricanes were sent over as replacements on the 13th; but the Air Ministry insisted on the danger of sending more fighter squadrons out of the country. The Air Staff, said the Secretary of State, had considered sixty squadrons to be necessary for defence against bombers based on Germany; now we had only thirty-nine, and the enemy might soon acquire nearer bases.

The news of the next few days (May 14–16) was very different. The Cabinet learnt on the 14th that the Germans had crossed the Meuse at Dinant and broken through at Sedan. On the 16th they learnt that the French had ordered the withdrawal of the right of the British line to conform with the movement of their own troops further south, the enemy having driven forward between Hirson and Mezières. The Chief of the Imperial General Staff reported that the situation was most critical. The Dutch, overwhelmed by the German attack, had ceased fighting on the 15th.

During these momentous days Ministers and their professional advisers had many other matters of first-rate importance on their minds. The Cabinet had decided on May 9 that plans for dealing with an invasion should be reviewed and passive defence against air attack rendered efficient. Next day, after receiving the news of the German aggression, they gave orders for the Civil Defence organisation to be brought to the 'highest state of readiness', and the War Office took similar measures with regard to the coast defences and home forces. The use of German parachutists in the invasion of the Low Countries naturally turned attention to this danger, and volunteers, the forerunners of the Home Guard, were enrolled to deal with them.

There were also the operations in North Norway, where the German troops were creeping up the coast towards Narvik; Lord Cork was told that he must expect no more reinforcements in fighters or anti-aircraft guns.

More disturbing were the probable intentions of Italy with their effect on the safety of the Mediterranean and Red Sea routes. Reports were frequent and contradictory, but Mussolini's reply on May 18 to a personal appeal from the Prime Minister, sent on the 16th at the request of the Cabinet, had an ominous ring.

Everything depended on the result of the battle in France. On the afternoon of the 14th the French Prime Minister made one of a series of desperate appeals for fighter reinforcements, asking for ten more squadrons to be sent that day; he renewed his appeal in a tone of deep despondency next morning, the 15th, saying that the road to Paris lay open for the enemy. Mr. Churchill, however, telephoning direct to General Georges, received a rather less disquieting report. At the meeting of the Chiefs of Staff Committee which then discussed the matter Sir Hugh Dowding, Air Officer Commanding-in-Chief, Fighter Command, pointed out the seriousness of granting M. Reynaud's request: a German success on the Continent might be followed by an air attack against Great Britain, and while he was confident that with the Air Defence of Great Britain at its present strength the Navy and Royal Air Force should be able to prevent an invasion he was absolutely opposed to parting with a single additional Hurricane. This attitude was maintained by Dowding throughout, and that day the Cabinet supported him: the Prime Minister explained to M. Reynaud that our fighter squadrons were 'in effect our Maginot Line'. But on the following day, the 16th, in view of Air Marshal Barratt's report of the severe difficulties under which his fighters were working, every pilot carrying out four or five sorties a day, and of his recommendation that the equivalent of four squadrons should be sent at once, the Cabinet decided to despatch these squadrons and they further authorised preparations for the despatch of two more at very short notice.

But this was not all. Mr. Churchill could not understand why penetration by a comparatively small number of tanks should have made it necessary to order the withdrawal of the British Expeditionary Force from their positions, and he decided to fly over to Paris that day, May 16.[1] It was only then and there, looking out on the archives of the Quai d'Orsay burning in the garden and hearing Gamelin's appalling admission that he had no strategic reserve, that he realised the full gravity of what had happened. The French, believing that the Germans would now strike direct at Paris, saw no means of stopping the onslaught of their armoured formations preceded by dive-bombers and followed up by 'the whole German army in motors'. The French armour, Mr. Churchill was told, was utterly inadequate; they had lost much of their best artillery, and of the 650 fighters with which they had begun the battle there were only 150 left. They cherished hopes, which Mr. Churchill thought delusive, of the moral and physical effect of a few British fighter squadrons and evidently thought it unreasonable and selfish that the bulk of our fighter force should be kept at home inactive when France was in such dire straits. The trouble was, said M. Reynaud, that the British and French were fighting separately. Mr. Churchill was not

---

[1] Mr. Churchill's account of his visit is given in *The Second World War* II 41–46. See also *The Private Diaries of Paul Baudouin* pp. 31–33.

persuaded that the best use of aircraft was to attack tanks, and in the hope of giving time for a reserve to be scraped together, or at least of restoring French spirits, he recommended to the Cabinet that six more fighter squadrons should be sent to France and that a larger part of our heavy bombers should attack the German masses crossing the Meuse into the bulge in the French line. His colleagues in London, meeting late the same night, agreed.

This decision left only some thirty fighter squadrons for the defence of the United Kingdom, compared with twenty now assigned to France. There were not enough available airfields, however, in France to receive the six new squadrons, so they worked from aerodromes in Kent, and in fact within the next few days all the fighter squadrons assigned to France, except the three with the Advanced Air Striking Force, had similarly to work from England. On the 20th the Cabinet decided, on urgent representations from the Air Staff, that no additional fighter squadrons should be withdrawn from the Air Defence of Great Britain save for occasional support from English bases. The German advance compelled the Advanced Air Striking Force also to abandon their airfields, and for a few days their bombers were out of action. Owing to the severe casualties suffered in day fighting the Air Staff wished to restrict their use to moonlit nights, but in view of our commitments to the French it was decided that they might be used by day with adequate fighter escort.

The leading infantry of the British Expeditionary Force had reached their positions on the Dyle on May 11; they were able to organise their front before the afternoon of the 14th, when they were in contact with the enemy along the whole seventeen miles of it.[1] At a meeting on the 12th, near Mons, at which Lieutenant-General H. R. Pownall, his Chief of the General Staff, represented Lord Gort, it was agreed that General Billotte, commanding the First Army Group, should 'co-ordinate' the operations of the British and Belgian forces as well as his own. Some such arrangement, implying at least 'a common doctrine', was rendered necessary by the fact that the Allied forces in the north now included the Belgian Army, under the independent command of its King, besides the British force which received orders direct from General Georges.[2] But matters did not work smoothly, the French general did not prove an effective coordinator, and one of Lord Gort's chief difficulties was the lack of orders and information from the French. At length on the 16th, after the French line on the British right had been bent back the previous day by heavy pressure, orders came from Billotte for a withdrawal to begin that night; the move to the Scheldt was completed on the 19th.

---

[1] The story of the British Expeditionary Force is told by Major Ellis. See also Lord Gort's Despatch, issued as supplement to the *London Gazette* of 10 October 1941.

[2] See above p. 152.

On the 17th General Headquarters, apprehensive of the danger to the British right and rear from the German spearheads, had started to organise a southern flank. By the 19th the enemy was threatening our line of communications through Amiens and it was clear that his first objective was not Paris but the sea and the Channel ports. On the 20th the Germans occupied Amiens and Abbeville; Lord Gort's force was now altogether and, as it turned out, finally severed from its base south of the Somme.

The weak points of the Allied strategy were now revealed. The advance into Belgium had many points in its favour, but its soundness depended on the fulfilment of three conditions: the advancing outer flank must have time (Gamelin's '*temps utile*') to reach and organise its new positions before it was attacked; the centre must be strong enough to stand firm while the flank was advancing; the arrangements must be flexible enough to allow of a regrouping of forces should things go wrong. None of these conditions were fulfilled. The Belgian resistance in the forward areas did not last as long as had been hoped and the French troops on the right (the inner sector) of the advancing flank did not have time to establish themselves. The centre did not hold, because, assigning the cream of the army to the Belgian plains and discounting the possibility of a strong enemy attack through the Ardennes, the French high command had entrusted the defence of the Meuse between Namur and Sedan to troops mostly of inferior quality. Thirdly, there were no adequate reserves at the proper points and failure promptly to grasp the situation ruled out the possibility of providing them in time. It is doubtful if in any case the forces under Billotte could have been drawn back in time to avoid envelopment, but the French orders to withdraw came certainly too late. Reserves, while reserves still existed, also started too late, and were thrown into the battle piecemeal; their lateral movement was delayed by the bombing of communications, and one of the features of the whole campaign was the flooding of the roads by masses of refugees. Hence the mobile first-line divisions in the north were, later on, cut off and attacked in flank and threatened from the rear, while no powerful counter-attacks were carried out against the lengthening southern flank of Army Group A.[1]

The speed and force and width and depth of the German offensive were something new in war. Students of former campaigns could not understand why such distant penetrations were not blocked or counter-attacked in flank; surely the initial momentum must eventually flag. Such, however, was the rapidity of the enemy's movements

---

[1] See Lyet pp. 71–76; Lyet states (pp. 50, 66) that of the eighteen divisions forming the general reserve on May 10 the last had been spent by May 17 with the formation of a new Seventh Army to block the Oise valley; the Sixth Army was in process of formation on the Aisne.

that the high command and the two Governments were usually applying their minds to a situation several hours or even days out of date.

The discovery that not only had the defences of the Meuse given way but Gamelin had no strategic reserve available came as a terrible shock to the British. It may excite surprise that in view of the crucial importance of these points we had not satisfied ourselves by previous inquiry that proper preparations had been made. General Howard-Vyse, General Ironside's representative with Gamelin, reported afterwards that 'partly on account of reticence, and partly because of the confusion between the G.Q.G. and H.Q. Nord-Est it was never easy to ascertain the composition of the French reserves'. With regard to the quality of the troops on the Meuse, we had no liaison with the armies concerned, which were far removed from our own sector. In short visits to the Lorraine and Luxemburg fronts in January and March General Ironside had noted nothing amiss. The failure of the British General Staff to insist on further information on points not directly concerning our own forces was due no doubt largely to the prestige acquired for the French command by the victories of Foch, but also to the delicacy which any British officer must have felt in questioning French dispositions when our own contribution on land was so small in comparison. Nevertheless Mr. Churchill has admitted that we were in error.[1] Henceforward, at any rate, he decided to maintain better touch and Sir John Dill, formerly commanding I Corps in France, now Vice-Chief of the Imperial General Staff, was sent out on May 19th to spend some days at General Georges' headquarters; he was to submit for Georges' consideration the plans which it was the duty of the War Office and Lord Gort to concert for the action of the British Expeditionary Force in various contingencies.

It was in the concerting of these plans that the first difficulty arose. On the afternoon of Sunday the 19th General Pownall telephoned to the War Office that in view of the gap on his right Lord Gort was examining the question of a withdrawal towards Dunkirk, should that be forced upon him, as a necessity, by the failure of the operations to close the gap further south.[2] Alike military theory and the experience of 1918 taught the supreme importance of allies maintaining an unbroken front in such conditions as the present, and the suggestion from General Headquarters, though as yet only tentative, was sharply criticised by the Cabinet and the Chief of the Imperial General Staff. Withdrawal to the Channel ports would mean being

---

[1] Churchill II 43.

[2] On May 17 the Prime Minister had invited the Lord President to examine 'the problems which would arise if it were necessary to withdraw the B.E.F. from France, either along its communications or by the Belgian and Channel ports'. See below, p. 193.

caught in a bomb-trap; the British force should at all costs move south-west towards Amiens and join the French on the line of the Somme. We must if necessary abandon the Channel ports and our cohesion with the Belgians; the sacrifice of our army would not help Belgium. This decision was confirmed at a meeting of the Defence Committee (Operations) held in the Admiralty that night, after a letter had been read from Dill describing a conference at which he had been present that day with Gamelin and Georges; unfortunately a rumour had reached the French that Lord Gort was 'contemplating taking action independent of . . . General Billotte and withdrawing on Boulogne'. Such action, said Dill, would *'at this moment'* have a disastrous psychological effect. The Prime Minister accordingly dictated instructions which the Chief of the Imperial Staff was to take to Gort forthwith; he was to 'move southwards upon Amiens attacking all enemy forces encountered, and to take station on the left of the French army'. The War Office would inform Georges. Some at least of those present at this meeting were convinced that the proposed action was quite impracticable, and, further, that it was 'dangerous . . . to try and command the British Expeditionary Force from London'.

The incident is an example of the difficulty, referred to above, in keeping abreast of events, for when General Ironside reached Lord Gort's headquarters next morning (20th) it was explained to him that, with seven of our nine divisions in close contact with the enemy on the Scheldt, with the area between the British Army and the Somme occupied by strong enemy columns, and with supplies of ammunition limited, the orders of the Cabinet could not possibly be executed. It is doubtful whether, in telephoning to the Prime Minister and Secretary of State that morning, he made sufficiently clear that this was so, but Lord Gort stated the position to the Secretary of State in a telegram. The best that Gort could do was to operate south of Arras with a small force on the 21st: elements of two British infantry divisions (5th and 50th) and the 1st Army Tank Brigade, co-operating with French mechanised cavalry, gained ground against superior German numbers but were unable to maintain their momentum or the ground they had won. A more ambitious project for an Allied counter-attack southwards came to nothing.[1]

Much as they disliked the idea, the British Cabinet accepted the fact that the Expeditionary Force might have no option but to make its way to the Channel ports. Dill, who was still in Paris on the 20th, warned the French of this possibility; the Admiralty had already the previous night given instructions for an outline plan to be prepared, in order to cover all eventualities, 'for embarking a large number of

---

[1] See Ellis ch. vi.

personnel from Boulogne, Calais, Dunkerque and neighbouring ports'.

Meanwhile Reynaud had on May 18 taken over the Ministry of National Defence from Daladier and had sent for General Weygand from Beyrout to replace Gamelin; he also took the fateful step of summoning the aged Marshal Pétain to join his ministry. He was bitterly to regret the appointment of these two ghosts of the ancient glories of France, but at the time he felt that their immense prestige, as nothing else, might revive the waning confidence of their countrymen.

Sir John Dill was impressed by Weygand's 'energy and decision': 'a breath of fresh air coming amid all the tired men' he had been meeting. He was physically vigorous far beyond his 73 years, and it was fondly hoped that on his shoulders rested the mantle of his master Foch. But it was not in him to restore the lost battle, a battle probably by this time lost irretrievably. In any case the orders he issued were tardy and unrealistic, appropriate to situations which no longer existed. The plan, he tells us, which commended itself to him when he took over command on the 20th was to attack the gap created by the enemy at its narrowest point, namely the twenty-five miles between Arras and the Somme valley; this involved simultaneous attacks by the French First Army in the north and by the new Seventh Army which was forming south of the Somme.[1]

Before issuing orders the Generalissimo determined to discuss matters with King Leopold, General Billotte and Lord Gort. A meeting was duly held at Ypres on the 21st, but it did not secure the desired co-ordination.[2] Lord Gort was not precisely informed of the rendezvous and did not arrive until after Weygand had left. Billotte met with a fatal motor accident on his return journey, and his successor, General Blanchard, hitherto in command of First Army, was not present at Ypres. The Belgians expressed doubt of their ability to withdraw to the Yser as proposed by Weygand.

There had not been sufficient time or opportunity for relations to be properly established between the Belgian high command and the British, and they did not improve with adversity. The Belgian army was hopelessly inferior in equipment to the German and it had soon been driven back to the Dyle and the defences of Antwerp. The French decision to withdraw to the Scheldt uncovered Brussels and a further Allied withdrawal meant the occupation of practically the whole of Belgium by the enemy. It was improbable that the Belgians would, even if they could, continue to retreat indefinitely. Already on

---

[1] See Weygand, *Rappelé au Service* p. 92.

[2] There were in fact several meetings and various accounts exist: see Ellis p. 107; also Weygand, *op. cit.* pp. 97–102.

O

the 20th there was talk at their headquarters of desertion by the British Expeditionary Force, and a warning came that if the British moved south the King might feel compelled to capitulate.

On the night of the 22nd/23rd the main body of the British Expeditionary Force fell back from the Scheldt to the French frontier defences, the Belgians holding the river Lys on their left and forming a sharp re-entrant. In view of the growing danger to the British rear, a defence line, very thin at first but developing into a second front, was organised from the 20th onwards along the canals connecting with the sea at Gravelines through La Bassée, Aire, St. Omer. For reasons which are discussed elsewhere the German armour did not press the attack against this line on May 24, when such pressure would have been very dangerous to the defenders.[1]

General Weygand expounded his plan to the French and British Prime Ministers at Vincennes on May 22. The Belgians should withdraw to the Yser, as he understood that they now had agreed to do; the British and the French First Army should attack south-westwards towards Bapaume and Cambrai at the earliest moment; a new French Army Group [*sic*] should strike north from south of the Somme to meet them; and the Royal Air Force should give all possible help by day and night while the battle lasted. The plan was approved.[2] Unfortunately it bore no relation to the facts: no French initiative followed, and it was soon clear that the Belgians would not move further west than to the Lys. Far from attacking again southwards from Arras, the British troops holding it only just avoided encirclement by withdrawing from the city on the night of the 23rd/24th. Finally, when another Allied attack from the north had been agreed on for the 26th, Gort was compelled on the evening of the 25th to use the two British divisions assigned for this operation in order to stop a gap which had been opened near Ypres at the point where the British and Belgian lines should have met. The necessity for these moves was not understood by those at a distance, and some time and trouble were needed to straighten out matters with the French. Co-ordination was not found more effective under General Billotte's successor than before the accident. Liaison between the two Governments, however, was improved by Mr. Churchill sending Major-General E. L. Spears to Paris as his personal representative with Reynaud.[3]

---

[1] See Ellis pp. 138–139, 347–351; the order to halt was issued by Rundstedt on May 23 and confirmed by Hitler next day.

[2] Weygand states (*Rappelé au Service* p. 108) that the phrase (in the conclusions forming an addendum to the Minutes of the Supreme War Council relating to the attack from the north) 'certainly tomorrow with about eight Divisions' was not authorised by him. The conclusions were drafted by Mr. Churchill and approved by M. Reynaud.

[3] Churchill II 96; Sir E. L. Spears, *Assignment to Catastrophe* vol I. *Prelude to Dunkirk* (1954) ch. xvi.

Meanwhile the swift German armoured columns, with their southern flank well guarded, had been sweeping to the sea and northwards up the coast. Troops were hastily assembled and sent out from England to garrison Boulogne and Calais, but Boulogne fell on the 25th and Calais on the evening of the 26th, in each case after desperate fighting. The whole of the British Expeditionary Force had been on half-rations since the 23rd and ammunition threatened to run short, though a new supply line had been organised across the Channel, partly by air.

Late on the night of the 25th General Blanchard ordered the retirement of the Allied forces in the north behind the Lys, in order to form a large bridgehead covering Dunkirk; he had no intention of retreating further.[1] On the same night however the British Defence Committee, convinced that the Weygand plan was impracticable, concluded that Lord Gort should march north to the coast and that the Navy should prepare all possible means for re-embarkation, not only at the ports but at the beaches. This decision was approved by the Cabinet next morning and, after Reynaud's assent had been secured, was conveyed to Lord Gort.[2] Thus was set in motion the machinery, which had been preparing since the 20th, for evacuating the army, and the Admiralty ordered the commencement of Operation 'Dynamo' for that evening, the 26th. Lord Gort was instructed by the Secretary of State that his sole task was now to evacuate to England as large as possible a proportion of his force, and he decided to start the retirement from the Lys line on the evening of the 28th. Blanchard was informed of this decision that morning (28th), but orders for the evacuation of the First Army did not arrive from General Weygand until next day. As a result of this delay and also of German pressure part of the First Army was cut off in the Lille area and other French troops arrived on the beaches too late.[3]

On May 25 an unhappy meeting of the French War Committee had been held, with the President of the Republic in the chair. Though accounts of it differ, it is clear that they discussed the possibility of France having to make peace, with the consequent need of sounding the British.[4] Next day M. Reynaud came over for a private talk with Mr. Churchill. The French, he said, were ready to go on fighting, but in view of the disproportion of forces on the front between the Maginot line and the sea—50 divisions to 150—Weygand did not believe that resistance could last very long. In such an

---

[1] Lyet p. 103.

[2] See Ellis p. 174 for the failure of the French high command to inform either Blanchard or the Admiral at Dunkirk that evacuation was intended.

[3] See General Pownall's record quoted in Churchill II 81–83; Ellis p. 219; Lyet pp. 109–111.

[4] Reynaud II 180–182; Baudouin 50–56; Weygand, *Rappelé au Service* pp. 145–148 and app. ix.

extremity no method of readjusting the balance should be neglected and an attempt should be made to release the ten divisions on the Italian front. M. Reynaud's purpose was to lay the situation as the French saw it before Mr. Churchill and in particular to suggest a joint approach to Italy in the hope of buying her neutrality or her mediation, or at least postponing the *coup de grâce*. It would be necessary to offer her specific concessions in the Mediterranean.

The British Government had quite recently been in favour of approaching Italy both directly, and indirectly through President Roosevelt, with a view to settling differences. But these approaches were on general lines. The Cabinet now decided, after long discussion, that such offers as the French had in mind could obtain no benefits to compensate for the moral risks of setting foot on the slippery slope of negotiations with a triumphant enemy. The one hope of saving France was to remain unbeaten ourselves. M. Reynaud was answered accordingly.[1] The same day, May 28, Count Ciano made it clear to the British Ambassador in Rome that Italy's belligerency was imminent.

The condition of France was now extremely grave; General Weygand expected that resistance would soon collapse before a determined German attack. The British Cabinet had for the first time to consider seriously the possibility of France abandoning the contest. On May 27 they had before them an important paper by the Chiefs of Staff on 'British strategy in a certain eventuality'. The points raised by the paper and the decisions taken will be discussed in the next chapter.

May 27 and 28 were dark days indeed. The Belgian army ceased fighting and it was by the narrowest margin that a German irruption through the fifteen-mile gap on our left was prevented.[2] The French were urging concessions to Italy and President Roosevelt was becoming anxious about the disposal of the British Fleet. The Germans were overwhelming our garrisons at Hazebrouck and Cassel. Evacuation was not going well, and our fighter defences were reported by Fighter Command as 'almost at cracking point'.

On the 28th the Prime Minister thought it necessary to prepare the country for 'hard and heavy tidings'[3] and on the 29th he telegraphed to Gort that if he were cut from all communication with the Government and all evacuation from Dunkirk and the beaches had in his judgement been finally prevented he would become sole judge of when it was impossible to inflict further damage on the enemy. The Government were sure that the repute of the British army was

---

[1] See Reynaud II 200–213.

[2] For the circumstances of the Belgian capitulation see Ellis pp. 198–199.

[3] *House of Commons Debates* vol. 361, col. 422.

safe in his hands.[1] But the Prime Minister's spirit never wavered. His fortitude equalled that of his great predecessor in the days

> When Europe crouch'd to France's yoke,
> And Austria bent and Prussia broke;

it stimulated and expressed the resolution of his colleagues and the whole country.

During this anxious period, while it was still uncertain whether any appreciable fraction of our trained army would be salved from the Continent, while the Royal Navy, the Merchant Navy, and Fighter Command were suffering heavy losses in the attempt to rescue it, and while it was the opinion of many that the victorious Germans would make this island their next objective, to those behind the scenes, though probably not yet to the population at large, invasion might well seem an imminent danger.

As early as May 17, at the Prime Minister's request, Mr. Chamberlain, the Lord President, had called a meeting of Ministers and officials to consider problems which might arise if things went badly in France. Not concerning themselves with purely military questions, they urged that the Government should take powers from Parliament to exercise control over property, business, labour and the whole life of the nation in a supreme emergency; the Cabinet had approved, and a short Bill to this effect, as drastic a measure as the country had ever known, had passed through all its stages and become law on May 22. The Cabinet had also approved a scheme proposed by the Minister of Labour and National Service, Mr. Ernest Bevin, which established a Production Council and gave the Minister full responsibility for controlling the supply of labour in all industries and the use to be made of it. Many other important measures of home defence had been authorised.

On the strictly military side, the Chiefs of Staff warned the Cabinet (on May 29) that they thought it highly probable that Germany was now 'setting the stage for delivering a full-scale attack on England'; they were not satisfied that the country had been sufficiently warned or organised to meet the threat. It might take the form of a seaborne raid on a large scale by motorboats combined with air-borne raids, and they recommended that the present plan of defence should be reviewed. In another paper the Chiefs of Staff pointed out the strategic advantages which the Germans would gain from an occupation of Eire and the weakness of her armed forces, which might well expose her to the fate of Holland. They emphasised above all the

---

[1] Lord Gort's *Despatch* col. 5929a.

harm we suffered from the refusal to us of the use of Berehaven as a naval base.

On the 27th General Ironside was succeeded as Chief of the Imperial General Staff by Sir John Dill. General Ironside at the same time was appointed to succeed Sir Walter Kirke in the more than ever responsible post of Commander-in-Chief, Home Forces.

The story is told elsewhere of how the difficult combined operation known as 'Dynamo' was carried out; of how the British and French troops marched through the shortening and narrowing corridor of safety to the defended perimeter enclosing Dunkirk and seventeen miles of beaches to the east; of how under the direction of Admiral Ramsay at Dover the skill and gallantry of the Navy, assisted by an armada of small craft, contrived despite gunfire from the shore, bombs, mines, torpedoes and capricious weather, to remove from harbour and beach a number of men far exceeding expectations; of how Fighter Command, working to the limits of endurance, provided such air cover as was possible, in defiance of the efforts of the Luftwaffe.[1]

East and west our flankguards were assailed by the onslaught of two German Army Groups. By midday on the 30th nearly all our retiring forces were within the perimeter, and the perimeter had for some time been within artillery, indeed within mortar, range of the enemy. That day Lord Gort received his final orders from the Cabinet; as soon as his force was reduced to three divisions, he was to hand over his command to a corps commander, who was authorised, when in his judgement no further organised evacuation was possible and no further proportionate damage could be inflicted on the enemy, in consultation with the senior French commander to capitulate formally to avoid useless slaughter.

The last British troops were taken away, however, in the early hours of June 3, and Major-General the Hon. H. R. L. G. Alexander, to whom the honour of commanding the rearguard had been entrusted, sailed for England, followed later by Captain W. G. Tennant, the senior naval officer at Dunkirk. Over 50,000 French troops were taken off during the following night, and it was then agreed with the French authorities that enemy fire prevented further embarkation.

The atmosphere of gloom at home was marvellously changed by the success of 'Dynamo'. Not only were over 200,000 trained men restored to the country, but the feeling that, after a long succession of failures, the resources of the nation had been tried in a supreme

---

[1] See Ellis, chaps. xiv–xvi; Roskill I xi.

effort and not found wanting caused profound relief and satisfaction. The dramatic circumstances of the evacuation and the knowledge that hundreds of private individuals and small craft had played their part along with the Royal and Merchant Navies added a peculiar flavour to the national rejoicing.

Satisfaction at the rescue of so large a proportion of the British Expeditionary Force was tempered by regret that many thousands of Frenchmen had been left behind. Orders were given on the night of the 30th that equal numbers of British and French were thenceforward to be embarked, but over 70,000 British had already left.[1]

On June 4 the Prime Minister, in the exhilaration of 'a miracle of deliverance' and also of impending invasion, rendered account to the country in terms more cheerful than those of his solemn warning of a week before. It is not possible in these volumes to take note of all the eloquent utterances with which he rallied his countrymen and all those who in any part of the world cared for the cause of freedom. But no chronicle of the war can avoid mention of some of these historic documents, and, of them all, his speech in the House of Commons on June 4 can least be passed over.

'I have, myself, full confidence that if all do their duty, if nothing is neglected, and if the best arrangements are made, as they are being made, we shall prove ourselves once again able to defend our island home, to ride out the storm of war, and to outlive the menace of tyranny, if necessary for years, if necessary alone. At any rate that is what we are going to try to do. This is the resolve of His Majesty's Government—every man of them. That is the will of Parliament and the nation. The British Empire and the French Republic, linked together in their cause and in their need, will defend to the death their native soil, aiding each other like good comrades to the utmost of their strength. Even though large tracts of Europe and many old and famous States have fallen or may fall into the grip of the Gestapo and all the odious apparatus of Nazi rule, we shall not flag or fail. We shall go on to the end. We shall fight in France, we shall fight on the seas and oceans, we shall fight with growing confidence and growing strength in the air, we shall defend our island, whatever the cost may be. We shall fight on the beaches, we shall fight on the landing grounds, we shall fight in the fields and in the streets, we shall fight in the hills; we shall never surrender, and even if, which I do not for a moment believe, this island or a large part of it were subjugated and starving, then our Empire beyond the seas, armed and guarded by the British Fleet, would carry on the struggle, until, in God's good time, the new world, with all its

---

[1] The total number evacuated in Operation 'Dynamo' was 338,226 including 139,097 of our allies. According to 'the most detailed estimate' about 40,000 of the French were left behind (Ellis pp. 246–248).

power and might, steps forth to the rescue and the liberation of the old.'[1]

It was a great deliverance. But, as Mr. Churchill reminded the country, wars are not won by evacuations; certainly not by evacuations in which the army leaves its guns, its tanks and its vehicles behind and returns to find the cupboard bare. What had happened was 'a colossal military disaster'. For the moment the prospect of winning this war was remote. Two needs were urgent: to keep France at our side and to prepare for invasion.

The German high command were surprised by the extent and the speed of their successes in the north. They had failed, it is true, 'to prevent the escape of the British forces across the Channel', but otherwise all their aims in the north were achieved. They had eliminated nearly forty French and British divisions, to say nothing of Dutch and Belgian forces, and though they suffered heavy losses they were able to regroup their armies without delay for their next task. This was the destruction of the remaining enemy forces in France; operations were to begin in the shortest possible time and were to be prepared in three sectors.

The first phase, which in fact started on June 5, was to be an advance between the Oise and the sea to the lower Seine below Paris; the second, the main operation, which followed on June 9, was to be an offensive east of Paris in a south-easterly direction, 'with the aim of defeating the bulk of the French army in the Paris–Metz–Belfort triangle and of bringing about the collapse of the Maginot line'. Thirdly, a subsidiary operation was to pierce the Maginot line in the direction of Nancy–Lunéville.

Independently of its support of the army, the Luftwaffe would be given 'unlimited freedom of action against the British homeland as soon as sufficient forces were available'. This operation was to be 'started with a crushing attack in retaliation for the British raids on the Ruhr area'. The German navy was at the same time authorised to wage unrestricted warfare in the waters round the British Isles and along the French coast.

Plans based on this directive were to be submitted to the Führer by the three Commanders-in-Chief.[2]

The success of 'Dynamo' brought little relief to the French. They were convinced that within a few days the regrouped and replenished German armies would turn against their own forces strung out along the river lines of the Somme and Aisne. Naturally

---

[1] *House of Commons Debates* vol. 361, col. 795.
[2] Directive No. 13 of 24 May; *F.D.* pp. 96–98

they were insistent on obtaining all possible help from their ally, both on land and especially in the air. During the next fortnight, which saw the overrunning of the thin French line of defence first west and then east of Paris and the occupation of Paris itself (June 14), the question how to help France in her desperate need was under discussion in London. Unfortunately the desire to help and the efforts made did not prevent the growth of mutual disappointment and distrust between the two Governments. It was inevitable that France in her agony should view things differently from a Britain still awaiting the supreme test and determined not to strip herself of the vital weapons; a Britain who believed it still possible to save herself by her exertions and Europe by her example.[1]

The demand for further help had been pressed at the Supreme War Council on May 31, during the Dunkirk evacuation, when Mr. Churchill and Mr. Attlee went over to secure French consent to the withdrawal of the remaining Allied forces from North Norway. After Dunkirk there remained in France two formed divisions, the 51st (Highland), which was serving in the Saar region on May 10, and the 1st Armoured, recently disembarked at Cherbourg, without its supporting infantry; there were also a number of independent battalions employed on the Lines of Communication. In Great Britain, as was explained by Sir John Dill, there were only three divisions available, and they not fully equipped. Other troops would soon be arriving from overseas, but at the moment our resources were very low, and some force must be kept in the country to meet the risk of invasion. As for the air Mr. Churchill promised to maintain in France the six bomber and three fighter squadrons of the British Air Forces in France but he could give no pledge of further drafts on Fighter Command.

Shortly afterwards, on June 2, three days before the blow fell in the western sector, the French asked in no very tactful manner for the immediate despatch of three divisions and 320 fighter aircraft (twenty squadrons) to be based in France besides bomber assistance 'at least as powerful' as that recently given in the northern fighting. The Chiefs of Staff, to whom these requests were referred, gave as their opinion that the United Kingdom was 'already insufficiently insured against full-scale air attack or invasion, and the despatch of any forces to France at this juncture must further increase these risks to a dangerous degree'. Nevertheless, in view of the military importance of preventing a French capitulation, they recommended that the

---

[1] The story of the events leading to the armistice is told in Churchill vol. II and Reynaud vol. II; by General Weygand in *Rappelé au Service* and, less fully, in *The Role of General Weygand* (1948); and by Sir E. L. Spears in *Assignment to Catastrophe* vol. II, *The Fall of France*, (1954). See also L. Marin in *Revue d'histoire de la deuxième guerre mondiale* No. 3 (June 1951); A. Kammerer, *La Vérité sur L'Armistice* (2nd ed. Paris 1945), prints many documents in his 150 pages of Annexes.

Headquarters of an expeditionary force should be established in France at once, with two Territorial divisions to follow within a few weeks. The limiting factor was lack of equipment and in particular of artillery. This force should be supplied with an appropriate air component, but in view of the needs of Home Defence they did not recommend the despatch of any additional fighter squadrons.

It was only after long discussion that the Cabinet accepted this estimate of the maximum support we could give the French. The number of army formations was governed, as has just been said, by the available equipment, but on the air side Air Chief Marshal Dowding, as well as the Chief of the Air Staff, was called upon to explain the strain which the fighting in France, as well as more recently over Dunkirk, had thrown on our fighter resources. The earlier operations had cost us twenty-five Hurricanes a day, against four a day received from production; the later battle had drawn on all the squadrons of Fighter Command, and these consequently needed reorganisation. We must not squander the capital of our fighter aircraft by sending to France more squadrons than we could see our way to maintain. At the present time the bottleneck was trained fighter pilots. On the subject of bombers, the Chief of the Air Staff said that during the 'battle of the Bulge'[1] the whole of the activities of our long-range bombers had been diverted to the attack of targets directly connected with the land battle, though this was a procedure which in his own opinion could not be justified on military, but only on psychological grounds. The Cabinet agreed that the bomber force not required to maintain the six squadrons now in France should remain based in England but should continue to give support as in the past, with priority for the land battle.

Next day, after hearing encouraging figures of aircraft production and of the number of squadrons (forty-five) now available in Fighter Command, the Cabinet gave the French some hope that in time additional fighter help might be provided. They also agreed to sub-stitute a re-formed Regular division for the second of the Territorial divisions. Later still, after the Battle of France had begun, it was decided to send instead the newly-arrived Canadian division—'the best trained reserve we had for defence against invasion'—as the second of the divisions (starting 11 June) and, after further desperate appeals, to reinforce British Air Forces in France with two more fighter squadrons (making five); up to six others might also operate from airfields in this country in support of the French.

The British authorities were induced to make these efforts in order to meet the requests of their allies to the limit of the possible and to maintain their fighting spirit, but they were under no illusion that

---

[1] See pp. 183–184.

such support as they could provide would seriously affect the result of the disastrous campaign. The Prime Minister, however, hoped that, at worst, the French would 'continue a gigantic guerrilla'.[1]

On June 11, the day Italy at length entered the war, Mr. Churchill and Mr. Eden, with Sir John Dill and General Ismay, flew to General Weygand's new headquarters near Briare on the Loire for a meeting of the Supreme War Council. The French commanders drew a depressing picture of the military situation. The divisions in the west had been fighting for over six days without rest and were exhausted. The whole army was now engaged from the sea to the Maginot line. There were no reserves and no reliefs. The enemy had at points crossed the lower Seine and the Marne. The end, said Weygand, might come at any moment. The Allies had entered on the war lightly and with no realization of the overwhelming strength of Germany. Not very plausibly, however, Reynaud and Georges argued that even now a large-scale air attack against the advancing German forces might completely reverse the situation and save the day. Mr. Churchill restated the British point of view but promised to examine yet further the possibility of increasing air support to France.

The meeting considered also and approved in principle the idea of establishing a strategic bridgehead or national redoubt on the Atlantic coast, in Brittany. M. Reynaud had on May 29 asked General Weygand to study this question, and something had been done, but Weygand explained that the military difficulties were great.

The British representatives returned on the 12th after a further meeting with little faith that French resistance would be prolonged. The tragic sacrifice of the 51st division at St. Valéry and the refusal of the French to allow our heavy bombers to take off from the south of France to attack Italian factories had not created a favourable impression. But Reynaud himself seemed determined to fight on and he had promised that if things became seriously worse the French would take no decisive action without consulting their allies.

That very night occasion arose for the redemption of the promise. At a meeting of the French Council of Ministers near Tours Weygand, supported by Pétain, urged the Government to start armistice negotiations. On the 13th the British Prime Minister, the Foreign Secretary and Lord Beaverbrook, the Minister for Aircraft Production, flew by invitation to Tours. M. Reynaud, the only French Minister of authority present, said that the French armies were at their last gasp and that Weygand had told him that it would soon be necessary to ask for an armistice; to which he had replied that he did not consider the situation yet desperate. But in order to carry his Government with him he needed an assurance of immediate help

---

[1] Churchill II 123.

from America. The possibility of a separate peace had to be faced. The French recognised that by the declaration of March 28 they were pledged not to discuss or conclude an armistice or peace except by agreement with Great Britain.[1] In the circumstances what would be the attitude of their ally?

The British Ministers were not prepared to release France from her pledge, at any rate until the result of a joint appeal to President Roosevelt had been received. Whatever happened Britain would eschew reproaches and recriminations, but she would fight on to the end herself.

The thought of help from America had for some time been in the minds of both Governments. As early as May 15 Mr. Churchill had warned the President that the scene had darkened swiftly, that the danger of a Nazified Europe might be imminent, and that the voice and force of the United States might count for nothing if they were withheld too long. He asked that the President should proclaim 'non-belligerency', which in practice, he thought, might cover the loan of forty or fifty of the older American destroyers and of several hundred modern aircraft as well as other forms of help. Later he had emphasised on the one hand the determination of the present British Government to fight to the very end, but on the other hand the danger to the United States should some later Quisling administration, under the pressure of defeat, use the Fleet as a bargaining counter with a victorious enemy.[2]

M. Reynaud had been dissuaded earlier from appealing to Mr. Roosevelt, but at length on June 10, on leaving Paris, he had sent him an urgent request for a public announcement that America would give France all possible moral and material aid short of sending an expeditionary force.[3] As for the French, they would fight before Paris, behind Paris, they would shut themselves up in a province, and if they were driven thence they would go to North Africa or, if need be, to one of their possessions in America. The President replied to this appeal on the 13th, to the effect that his Government were doing everything in their power to make available to the Allies the material they needed, and were redoubling their efforts. This was so because of their faith in and support of the ideals for which the Allies were fighting. He applauded the Allies' determination to continue the struggle and made an encouraging reference to naval power.

Mr. Churchill, who both before and after the meetings of the Supreme War Council on June 11 and 12 had urged the President

---

[1] See above, p. 122.

[2] See Churchill II 22, 50.

[3] See *The Memoirs of Cordell Hull* (London, 1948) ch. 57; Reynaud II 295. W. L. Langer and S. E. Gleason, *The Challenge to Isolation 1937–1940* (London, 1952) pp. 480 ff.

to do anything he could to put heart into the French, learnt of this reply on his return from Tours on the night of the 13th. With the Cabinet's support he pressed Reynaud to accept it as the favourable answer required to justify continued resistance; indeed he strained its language to persuade the French that America was now committed beyond recall to entering the war: the President had gone as far in words as the Constitution allowed. Accordingly in reporting to Mr. Roosevelt the upshot of the Tours meeting, of which he could not exaggerate the critical character, he urged him most forcibly to allow his 'magnificent message' to be published.[1]

In fact, however, the hope of any such dramatic American intervention was illusory. The political situation entirely excluded the possibility of the United States entering the war in the near future, and no help that she could send could stay the advance of the German armour, which was the real nightmare of the French. The President's stirring message was not intended to commit his country to military action and he did not even allow its publication. He made his position clear in his reply to a final appeal sent by Reynaud on June 14 for armed help. Accordingly the question which the French Ministers had put to Mr. Churchill, whether the British Government would release France from her obligation not to enter on separate negotiations with the enemy, now became urgent.

At this sad time a further misunderstanding helped to embitter Anglo-French relations. The Cabinet intended that Lord Gort should command the reconstituted British Expeditionary Force as soon as its strength rose to four divisions, but meanwhile the command of the troops in France was entrusted to Lieutenant-General A. F. Brooke, who had greatly distinguished himself in the handling of II Corps in the fighting in Flanders. General Brooke understood from Weygand on the 14th that organised resistance on the part of the French armies had ceased; he was also assured—incorrectly, as it turned out—by Weygand and Georges that the two Governments had decided to organise an Atlantic redoubt in Brittany, and on this understanding he agreed to the concentration at Rennes of the British troops newly arriving; those already fighting in the coastal area under the command of the French Tenth Army should so continue. Being convinced, as were the French generals, that the defence of Brittany was in present circumstances impracticable, General Brooke explained the situation by telephone to his Government, and was authorised that evening by the Prime Minister, after a meeting at which the Chiefs of Staff and Vice-Chiefs were present, to act henceforth independently of the French forces, though he was still to co-operate with any that might yet be resisting in his vicinity. Air Marshal

---

[1] Churchill II 163–164.

Barratt was instructed at the same time to concert action henceforward with Brooke rather than with Georges. No further British forces were to land in France until further notice. The French were informed, but in spite of the admitted disintegration of their army they were deeply chagrined.[1]

The sands were fast running out. The final orders for the evacuation of the British forces from France were given on June 16 and 17[2]; on the 17th the Pétain Government approached the Germans with a view to an armistice.

On June 14 the French Government had moved to Bordeaux. On the following afternoon the Council of Ministers met. M. Reynaud was now completely at variance with the Commander-in-Chief and was determined to dismiss him. He tells us how against his own pleadings the majority of his colleagues decided to ask the British to release them from the pledge of March 28, in order that they might inquire the terms on which the enemy would grant an armistice. Weygand rejected as dishonourable the suggestion that the French army should, like the Dutch, lay down its arms while the Government carried on the war from overseas.

Next morning, Sunday June 16, the British Cabinet considered their answer. The issues now raised were of vital interest to the Commonwealth as a whole, but the Cabinet agreed that the emergency was too pressing to allow of prior consultation with the Dominions. They were above all concerned with the future of the French fleet. They eventually decided to reply that, while the agreement forbidding separate negotiations must be understood to be binding not on any particular individual or Government but on the French Republic, we did not object to the French asking the terms of an armistice; on this one condition, however, that the French fleet sailed to British harbours at once and remained there during negotiations. It was to be understood that His Majesty's Government dissociated themselves entirely from the proposed inquiries, but they expected to be consulted as soon as any armistice terms were received. They expected also that the French would take all possible

---

[1] See General Brooke's despatch in *Supplement to London Gazette of* 21 May 1946; Weygand, *Rappelé au Service* pp. 222, 230; Churchill II 169; Ellis pp. 295–300. Sir Alan Brooke states in his despatch that he was informed by the C.I.G.S. that neither he nor the Prime Minister knew anything of the Brittany plan. This information was not literally correct, since both Governments had agreed on June 11 that the preparation of a plan for organising a redoubt in Brittany was of great importance. But it is true that no decision had been taken, and Reynaud had stated on the 13th that it was already too late to organise a redoubt in Brittany.

[2] The evacuation of British troops ceased officially on June 25, but many were taken away after that date. The total number of Allied troops evacuated by the Royal Navy from the area south of the Somme adds up to 191,870, of whom 144,171 were British (Ellis p. 305).

steps to transfer the Polish, Belgian and Czech troops in France to North Africa. The two telegrams embodying this reply had a curious history.

Meeting again in the afternoon the Cabinet were told that since their morning session the question had been raised of strengthening M. Reynaud's hand by some striking gesture. They had already on the 13th made to the French Government a solemn declaration of 'the indissoluble union of our two peoples and of our two Empires' and pledged our resolve to continue the conflict until France stood 'safe and erect in all her grandeur' and all the enslaved peoples were freed from the nightmare of Nazi tyranny. A manifesto going further and couched in even more dramatic terms had now been drafted by some prominent persons of both countries, and as a measure justified by the existing emergency the Cabinet approved the celebrated Declaration of Union between the two nations. It was to be telephoned to M. Reynaud at once, and further, to give it every chance of succeeding in its immediate object, the Prime Minister had instructed Sir Ronald Campbell, the British Ambassador now at Bordeaux, to suspend action on the two stern telegrams recently despatched.[1] The Cabinet also urged that the Prime Minister and some of his colleagues should meet M. Reynaud at the earliest possible moment. A rendezvous off the coast of Brittany had been proposed and, as Mr. Churchill has described, his party had actually taken their seats in the train when everything was changed by a message from Bordeaux.[2]

The decisive Council of Ministers had met at five o'clock. M. Reynaud had previously received the earlier messages declaring the British insistence in the matter of the fleet, which he thought unpractical, and also the later one offering the political union, which he eagerly welcomed. The Council however were deeply divided. The political proposal did not achieve its object; it was brushed aside as, in the opinion of the majority, hardly relevant in the immediate crisis, and debate was concentrated on the question of an armistice. Considering that it was impossible to carry on the Government with the majority of his colleagues against him, M. Reynaud resigned that evening, and the President of the Republic chose as his successor Marshal Pétain, an arch-defeatist, who had long been in favour of an armistice. General Weygand became Minister of Defence, Admiral Darlan Minister of Marine.[3]

The requests for the terms on which an armistice might be concluded were sent to the German and Italian Governments early next

---

[1] Churchill II 180–184, where the text of the Declaration is printed.
[2] *ibid.* p. 186.
[3] Reynaud II 347 ff.; Marin, *op. cit.* p. 17; Baudouin pp. 114 ff.

morning, the 17th, without consultation with London, and the French armies on the greater part of the front ceased fire soon afterwards. It would seem that the new Government sought to justify the breach of the pact with Great Britain by the argument that her refusal to throw all her forces into the common battle destroyed any moral right she might have to insist on its observance.[1]

To the British Cabinet the vital issue was the future of the French fleet, and they considered it of the highest importance that the ships should be sailed to British ports *before* the discussion of terms with the enemy. After the meeting of the Supreme War Council at Briare on the 12th Admiral Darlan had solemnly promised Mr. Churchill that he would never let them fall into German hands, and on the night of the 16th he had repeated this assurance to Sir Ronald Campbell.[2] M. Baudouin, the new Minister of Foreign Affairs, and Marshal Pétain himself gave similar undertakings on the 17th, on which day our Ambassador brought the suspended telegrams to the attention of the Marshal and his colleagues. On the 19th Sir Dudley Pound, who had flown to Bordeaux on the previous day with the First Lord, reported that Admiral Darlan had reaffirmed his promise that in no circumstances would the fleet be surrendered but had objected to the ships being sailed to British ports. Reynaud had made similar objection on the 16th, on the ground that such action would leave North Africa a prey to the Italian fleet. The British object was of course to prevent all possibility of the Germans compelling the French to bring the disposal of the fleet into the armistice negotiations.

The Cabinet also considered the possibility of securing for ourselves or at least denying to the enemy other French resources of various kinds, such as shipping, war equipment, raw materials, and especially oil. Elaborate plans had been long under preparation, under Lord Hankey's auspices, for ensuring by removal or destruction that the Germans should obtain as little loot as possible should they succeed in overruning western Europe, and in May and June 1940 these plans bore fruit.

The most important prize was the French colonial empire; it was still hoped that the Government might continue the war from North Africa.

Another matter which caused anxiety was the attitude of the new French Government with regard to the captured German air pilots, over 400 in number, most of whom had been shot down by the Royal Air Force. M. Reynaud had promised Mr. Churchill on June 13 that

---

[1] Reynaud II 361; cf. Pétain's remarks as reported in the *procès-verbal* of 25 May, Weygand, *Rappelé au Service* app. ix.

[2] Churchill II 140, 203.

they should be handed over to the British, but in spite of urgent demands the promise was not honoured by his successors.[1]

On the evening of June 22 the Cabinet learnt the German armistice terms and learnt that they had been accepted by the French. A large part of France, including all the northern and Atlantic coast, was to be occupied by the Germans.[2] All French armed forces, except such as were needed to maintain internal order, would be demobilised and disarmed. The French fleet, and here was the crucial point, with the exception of such part as was left at the disposal of the Government to safeguard French interests in the colonies, was to be assembled in its normal peace-time ports and demobilised and disarmed under German or Italian supervision (*contrôle*). The German Government solemnly declared that they did not intend to use during the war for their own purposes the French warships berthed in the ports under German supervision, except such as were required for coast watching and mine-sweeping. They also declared solemnly and formally that they did not intend to make claims with regard to the French fleet at the conclusion of peace. All warships outside French territorial waters, except those assigned to the colonies, were to be recalled to France. The French Government must henceforth take part in no action hostile to Germany and must prevent members of their armed forces from leaving French territory; they must forbid French nationals to fight against Germany in the service of States at war with her, and must exercise vigilance to secure that no material of war was transferred to England or elsewhere abroad.

This convention could be denounced at any time by Germany if the French Government did not fulfil its obligations. As a last humiliation, it was not to come into force until the French had concluded a similar agreement with Italy—Italy, whose forces had hardly gained a yard, even in the moment of French collapse, against vastly inferior numbers.[3]

The armistice conventions did not require the surrender of the fleet nor the surrender or occupation by enemy troops of any portion of the French colonial empire except parts of French Somaliland; this moderation is explained by the fact that while Hitler hoped to bring the war to an end forthwith by a satisfactory agreement with Britain —he was the gambler, Ciano said, who had made a big scoop and would like to get up from the table—the war was not finished yet and might continue. In this case it was of primary importance to secure that the French fleet did not fall into British hands; therefore the

---

[1] Churchill II 161.

[2] See last endpaper.

[3] The French texts of both armistice conventions are printed in A. Kammerer, *La Vérité sur l'Armistice* pp. 442, 454.

P

French Government must not be provoked by unacceptably harsh terms to prolong the hopeless struggle. Hitler had moreover no desire to be burdened with the administration of the whole of France or her colonies. So Mussolini's greed and desire for glory without risk must be restrained. What terms Hitler might have decided to impose on France after defeating the British Empire is of course a different question. In any case it was open to him to denounce the armistice convention at will on the pretext that the French had failed to fulfil some of its terms.[1]

A corollary of the acceptance of the armistice terms was the decision of the Pétain Government not to move to North Africa and establish themselves there. This they had been pressed to do by the British Government—as it had been Reynaud's purpose—and transport had been offered. For some days they, or some of them, hesitated. But Pétain and Weygand had no intention of going, and the seductive terms of the armistice decided their colleagues. They persuaded themselves that their duty was to remain in France and obtain for her from the conqueror the best treatment they could.[2] On July 1 they set up house at Vichy.

These were unhappy days for Anglo-French relations. Nevertheless even when the clouds were darkest two voices struck notes of courage and hope. In the House of Commons on June 18, after recounting briefly the story of the Allied defeat on the Continent, Mr. Churchill gave reasons why his countrymen might face the imminent threat of invasion without dismay. He concluded:

> 'What General Weygand called the "Battle of France" is over. I expect that the battle of Britain is about to begin. Upon this battle depends the survival of Christian civilisation. Upon it depends our own British life and the long continuity of our institutions and our Empire. The whole fury and might of the enemy must very soon be turned on us. Hitler knows that he will have to break us in this island or lose the war. If we can stand up to him all Europe may be free, and the life of the world may move forward into broad, sunlit uplands; but if we fail then the whole world, including the United States, and all that we have known

---

[1] See the account of the Munich meeting of the Dictators on June 18 in Ciano, *Diplomatic Papers* 372–375; *Diary* p. 265.

[2] For a discussion of the case for and against a continuance of the war from North Africa see Weygand, *Rappelé au Service* pp. 280–284 and *En lisant les Mémoires de Guerre du Général de Gaulle* (Paris, 1955), ch. v; Baudouin, *Private Diaries*, pp. 110, 140–142, and articles by A. Truchet and L. Marin in *Revue d'Histoire de la deuxième guerre mondiale* Nos. 3 and 8, June 1951 and Oct. 1952; also A. Truchet, *L'armistice de 1940 et l'Afrique du Nord* (Paris, 1955). It seems that on the British side the matter was never comprehensively discussed, no doubt because until June 22 we were preoccupied with the larger issue of inducing the French to fight on, whereas after June 22 the question, so far as the French Government were concerned, was not a practical one.

and cared for, will sink into the abyss of a new dark age made more sinister, and perhaps more prolonged, by the lights of a perverted science. Let us therefore brace ourselves to our duty and so bear ourselves that if the British Commonwealth and Empire lasts for a thousand years men will still say, "This was their finest hour." '[1]

On the same evening another voice, a French voice speaking from London, announced to the world that not all Frenchmen accepted the necessity of capitulating to triumphant Germany. General Charles de Gaulle, one of the youngest of his rank in the French army, was known before the war for his unconventional views on military policy and his vigour in expounding them. He had long urged the need of a professional and mechanised army. In the recent fighting he had commanded an armoured division with distinction in an offensive role south of the Somme. When Reynaud reconstructed his Ministry on June 5 he made de Gaulle his Under-Secretary of State for National Defence. The new Minister had been charged with measures for continuing the war in North Africa and with this end in view had been sent to make contacts in London. He had been present in a junior capacity at the meetings of the Supreme War Council on June 11 and 13, where his resolution had impressed Mr. Churchill, and he had been one of the group concerned in producing the abortive Declaration of Union. Now, by his broadcast on June 18, he set up a standard of resistance to which his countrymen were invited to rally.

It was the end of a chapter, a chapter which had opened twenty-one years before, when France and Britain, the signatories of a victorious peace, failed to give to the new Europe the strong united leadership it needed. While Germany remained weak, France and Britain were at variance. When Germany began to renew her strength, France and Britain, despite their common interests and apprehensions, lacked the will to meet her repeated challenges with a firm resistance. In the last year danger had drawn them closer together, but adversity had revived old sentiments of disapproval and distrust. Now the alliance was dissolved and Britain was called upon to make good the assertion of her chosen chief that she was ready, with the support of the Empire-Commonwealth, to carry on the fight 'if necessary for years, if necessary alone'.

---

[1] *House of Commons Debates* vol. 362, col. 60.

CHAPTER IX

THE IMMEDIATE
CONSEQUENCES OF THE
FRENCH COLLAPSE (1)

THE DEFECTION of France meant the ruin of the strategy so laboriously planned in the previous year. Not only in Europe but in all parts of the world it had been based on the sharing of French and British responsibilities and resources. Now the whole burden fell on the British Commonwealth, and this at the moment when a new enemy had declared himself in the Mediterranean. A suggestion to Moscow from Mr. Churchill that the success of German's 'bid for the hegemony of Europe' might not be wholly in the interests of the Soviet Union met with no response.[1] Not since the days of Napoleon had we faced such an accumulation of enemy strength and it was a new thing to find ourselves ranged without an ally against even a single European power. A review of our plans was clearly needed.

As early as May 19 the Chiefs of Staff considered a draft report on 'British strategy in a certain eventuality'. The contingency thus ominously veiled was the complete collapse of French resistance followed by a separate peace between France and Germany. The report as amended and approved by the Chiefs of Staff was discussed by the Cabinet on May 27 at what seemed the lowest point of our fortunes, when it was doubtful whether more than a fraction of our army could be extricated from the Continent.

It would be wrong to regard this appreciation as expressing the matured views of the Chiefs of Staff at this time. The officers who prepared it emphasised later that the relevant paragraphs 'were not designed to serve as a precise definition of our future strategy and were included primarily to illustrate our ability to continue the war and to argue the urgent measures it was considered desirable to institute'; and we are told that when the Chiefs of Staff came to consider the draft their attention was 'mainly focused on the recommendations for immediate action'. Nevertheless it seems worth while to devote some space to this paper: it represented the first facing up to the new strategic situation and formed the basis for subsequent appreciations in the next twelve months.

---

[1] Churchill II 119.

The report assumed on the one hand that Italy would come into the war against us, that eventually all French territory in North Africa would be accessible to the enemy, and that Spain, Portugal and all the Balkan States except Turkey would fall under enemy control; it assumed on the other hand that we could count on the full economic and financial support of the United States, possibly extending to active participation on our side, and that Russia would be alarmed by the increasing might of Germany. On these assumptions it posed two questions: could the United Kingdom hold out until assistance from the Empire and America made itself felt? And could we ultimately bring sufficient economic pressure to bear on Germany to ensure her defeat?

The continuance of our blockade must force Germany to make it her main object to break down the resistance of the United Kingdom. This she could hope to effect by 'three broad methods': unrestricted air attack aimed at breaking down public morale; starvation of this country by attack on shipping and ports; and occupation of the United Kingdom by invasion. On a longer view, in concert with Italy German strategy would strive ultimately to overthrow our position in Egypt and the Middle East and to open a trade route through the Red Sea.

Dealing first with the security of the United Kingdom and its approaches, the report pointed out that within a few weeks of a French collapse these would be exposed at short range to the concentrated attack of the whole of the German naval and air forces working from bases extending from Trondheim to Brest and that the threat of invasion would be ever-present. Our ability to avoid defeat would depend on three factors: the capacity of the people as a whole to withstand air bombardment, the continued importation of the necessary food and war material, and our success in resisting invasion. On the first point, the report stated the frank opinion that the existing 'quasi-peace-time organisation' of Civil Defence was not sufficient to grapple with the problems which might face us in the new circumstances, which included the menace of Fifth Column activities. On the invasion issue it said with equal frankness that, should the enemy succeed in establishing a powerful force, with vehicles, firmly ashore, the army in the United Kingdom would not have the offensive power to drive it out. The Navy, though still committed to the Narvik adventure, was adequate to protect our overseas supplies, but its ability to defeat a seaborne attack would depend on its power to operate in the face of heavy air attack against both ships and bases. We could not count on maintaining effective naval forces in east and south coast bases or indeed on operating surface forces in strength in the southern part of the North Sea and the Channel at all. So with regard to supplies: we might have to depend on west coast ports entirely, and we must cut down unessential imports 'such as bananas and children's toys'. We could subsist and maintain our war industries on 60 per cent of our present imports.

The upshot of all this was that everything in the last resort depended on the ability of our fighter defences to reduce the scale of attack to reasonable bounds, though for the repulse of an invader an effective force of bombers would also be important. We must therefore concentrate our energies primarily on the production of fighter aircraft and crews and should give priority to the defence of the essential factories. At the same time we must not neglect or waste our bomber force.

The Air had come into its own as the essential partner of the Navy in the defence of the nation's life. The possibility of a 'knock-out blow' aimed from bases in Germany had of course long been accepted by British minds. But the vast extension of the area from which the blow might fall, the belief that it might actually fall in a few weeks, and the cool calculation of our chances of parrying it, were together something new. The Air, of course, could not keep us in food and weapons; only sea-power could do that; but the grim fact, long recognised in theory, that without air protection neither ships nor ports nor factories might perhaps be of any use now forced itself on the Government's attention.

The point was emphasised in a later report which the Cabinet considered on the same day, May 27. In reply to a direct question from the Prime Minister, the Chiefs of Staff gave their opinion on the prospects of our being able to continue the war alone. 'The crux of the matter', they answered, 'is air superiority'; Germany could not gain this 'unless she could knock out our air force, and the aircraft industries, some vital portions of which are concentrated at Coventry and Birmingham.' We should be able to prevent serious damage to these by day, but not by night, and the measure of the enemy's success would depend not only on the material damage he could do but on the degree to which he could terrorise the workpeople into ceasing production. If therefore the enemy pressed home night attacks on our aircraft industry, he was likely to achieve such material and moral damage within the industrial area concerned as to bring all work to a standstill. Their conclusion was that '*prima facie* Germany has most of the cards; but the real test is whether the morale of our fighting personnel and civil population will counterbalance the numerical and material advantage which Germany enjoys. We believe it will.'

Even so, the outlook was obviously of extreme gravity; but in the opinion of the Prime Minister the Chiefs of Staff exaggerated the danger. They had based their conclusions on an estimate of the respective air strengths of ourselves and Germany which gave the enemy a superiority of four to one. Mr. Churchill challenged these figures. He claimed that the true proportion was more like two-and-a-half to one, and it was agreed that the point should be more closely investigated. It was recognised none the less that the danger to our aircraft industries, especially at night, was very serious. We had no adequate reply against night attack by German bombers, said the Chief of the Air Staff; the anti-aircraft gun was a deterrent only and we had insufficient experience at present of the efficacy of fighters in co-operation with searchlights. The Cabinet could only agree in general to concentrate every effort on the needs of the Fighting and Civil Defence Services and on the maintenance of the civil population under wartime conditions. In particular they approved with certain modifications fourteen specific proposals of the Chiefs of Staff; these included the tightening up of the Civil Defence organisation and the control of possibly dangerous persons; the cutting down of imports and the distribution about the country of stocks of food and fuel and raw materials; the procurement of aircraft and warships from the United States of America, and the opening of negotiations with Eire for the use of Berehaven. The measures taken will be mentioned later in this and following chapters.

The earlier appreciation dealt also with prospects overseas. A French collapse would at once destroy the basis of our strategy in the Mediterranean. Italy would be free to concentrate all her strength against Malta, Gibraltar and Egypt. Malta could probably withstand one serious seaborne assault but no more and could not be used as a naval base. We could continue to use Gibraltar as such until Spain became hostile, and the fortress could probably hold out for a couple of months longer. But we could not hope to control sea communications in the Western as well as in the Eastern Mediterranean. 'To contain the Italian fleet and secure Egypt a capital ship fleet should be based on Alexandria'; but eventually, as the result of a successful Axis attack from Libya, we might have to withdraw this fleet to Aden and block the Suez Canal after us. In the Far East Japan's attitude would be opportunist; she would hope to exploit the general situation 'but with a watchful eye on the United States of America'. It was most improbable that we could send any naval forces to the Far East.[1] Therefore we must rely on the United States to safeguard our interests in that region. As over the coasts of Great Britain, so in eastern waters the collapse of France would mean unforeseen dangers to the British peoples.

The Chiefs of Staff proceeded to discuss our prospects of winning the war. It is worth while quoting their relevant paragraphs in full.

'The defeat of Germany might be achieved by a combination

---

[1] The importance of this conclusion is discussed in chapter xiv.

of economic pressure, air attack on economic objectives in Germany and on German morale and the creation of widespread revolt in her conquered territories.

ECONOMIC PRESSURE

The following general conclusions which we have reached on this wide economic problem have been arrived at after consultation with a representative of the Ministry of Economic Warfare.

German control of the resources of Western Europe and a part of Northern Africa will secure for her a number of immediate economic assets. Nevertheless Germany and the area under her control will still depend on outside sources for certain essential commodities, particularly natural fibres for clothing and footwear, rubber, tin, nickel and cobalt. Moreover the occupied territories of Western Europe will aggravate the food shortage which is already a serious problem in the Reich; and the whole oil output of Roumania, Poland and Germany together with such supplies as are likely to be available from Russia will not suffice to maintain German and Italian stocks, which would have to be drawn on from the outset.

With genuine and extensive pan-American co-operation and with the Dutch, Belgian and French Empires at our disposal, we shall be in a strong position to control all deficiency commodities at source, as except for Japan and Russia and a few isolated territories there will be no neutrals. It will no longer be practicable by normal contraband control methods involving visit and search.

Our ability to apply economic pressure of this nature will depend primarily upon American co-operation. On this assumption, and provided that we can maintain control over the Allied Overseas Empires and naval control of the wider oceans and focal points leading to the blockaded area, the trickle of supplies reaching Germany by blockade running will be negligible.

The effect of the denial of overseas supplies to Germany will manifest itself in the following ways. Firstly, food shortage. Dependent upon the yield of the harvests in 1940, which are expected to be low, German-controlled Europe will be somewhat short of bread-stuffs. There will also be a widespread scarcity of essential fats and fruits. Life will be sustained for a period by the heavy slaughtering of immature animals. This will be necessary because, after the end of the grazing season, there will be a dearth of feeding stuffs. It will probably be only a matter of months before hoarding by the peasant population creates a really acute shortage of food in the industrial areas, including parts of Germany herself.

Secondly, Germany's war potential itself must be expected to decline through deficiency in oil. The whole of her own and of Italian stocks of petrol plus the whole output of Roumania and small supplies from Russia will nearly suffice to provide the lubricants and petrol needed to maintain orderly administration and the minimum industrial activity in the Continent as a whole. As soon as the initial stocks are exhausted, and if synthetic plants can be destroyed, the German garrisons would be largely immobilised and her striking power cumulatively decreased.

A third effect will be on the quality of Germany's war equipment. It is impossible to estimate the amount of war material that the German fighting forces will have to consume under the conditions postulated. But it is certain that deprived of all imports of certain essential non-ferrous metals, alloys, rubber and cotton and wool, Germany will not be able to maintain a high rate of replacement and the quality of her war equipment, including aeroplanes, must be expected to decline. Even with practically no consumption of war equipment a large part of the industrial plant of Europe will stand still, throwing upon the German administration an immense unemployment problem to handle.

With regard to the time factor, effective denial of these supplies is, we are advised, likely to produce widespread starvation in many of the industrial areas including parts of Germany, before the winter of 1940 (assuming an early French collapse). By the same date the depletion of oil stocks will force Germany to weaken her military control in Europe or to immobilise her armed forces. By the middle of 1941, Germany will find it hard to replace her military equipments. This process of exhaustion would be somewhat hastened by destruction of Germany's synthetic oil plants and of Roumanian wells, by blockage of the Danube and the diversion of Russian oil supplies.

AIR ATTACK ON ECONOMIC OBJECTIVES IN GERMANY

Economic factors have shewn that the primary objective for our air attack should be the enemy's oil resources and focal points in his transport system. We have already made progress in the systematic elimination of the key objectives (the effects of which have not been allowed for in the estimate of supplies above) and if we can maintain these attacks, even on a light scale, an important contribution will be made towards the enemy's defeat. Moreover, shortage of lubricating oils and petrol may have a very important effect on the intensity of the air offensive against this country in the ensuing months.

The pressure we could exert by air action would for some time be extremely limited, owing to the effects of the enemy's offensive and the need for conserving a proportion of our striking power to deal with the contingency of invasion. We could not expect to do more than maintain a very limited scale of attack until we could obtain additional resources from the Dominions and from the United States. In the course of time we could hope to bring a heavier scale of attack on Germany by developing the United Kingdom as an advanced base for the operation of large long range bombers flown from production centres across the Atlantic.

SUBVERSIVE ACTION

The only other method of bringing about the downfall of Germany is by stimulating the seeds of revolt within the conquered territories. The occupied countries are likely to prove a fruitful ground for these operations, particularly when economic conditions begin to deteriorate.

In the circumstances envisaged, we regard this form of activity as of the very highest importance. A special organisation will be required and plans to put these operations into effect should be prepared, and all the necessary preparations and training should be proceeded with as a matter of urgency.

POLITICAL ASPECTS OF ECONOMIC PRESSURE

The political and moral issues involved in imposing on the mass of Europe the severe effects of economic pressure may present serious difficulties. It will be necessary to realise, however, that it is only by this pressure that we can ensure the defeat of Germany, and that by holding out we shall remain as a nucleus on which the rebuilding of European civilisation may be attempted.

If, on the other hand, we do not persevere, the economic collapse of Europe and the United Kingdom under a corrupt Nazi administration would only be postponed for a short while, and we should have no chance of contributing to Europe's reconstruction.'

Of the three proposed methods of warfare the Chiefs of Staff not unnaturally considered economic pressure the vital one. The air offensive was to be directed primarily against economic objectives, and economic pressure would stimulate insurrection. Indeed the report said squarely that upon the economic factor depended our only hope of bringing about the downfall of Germany, and thus its authors could not emphasise too strongly the importance of the substantial accuracy of the forecast derived from the Ministry of Economic Warfare.

On this the historian of the Economic Blockade has something to say.[1] Professor Medlicott remarks that 'the Services in effect posed two questions to the Ministry of Economic Warfare': was there, in the conditions now envisaged, any strategic advantage in continuing economic warfare, or would German's supply position now become invulnerable? and secondly, assuming the continuance of economic warfare, could supplies reaching Europe be controlled in some other way than by naval patrols? The reply to the first question was

---

[1] W. M. Medlicott, *The Economic Blockade* I (H.M.S.O. 1952) 60, 417–421.

emphatically yes; the second was answered by the method of increased control at source, of which mention will be made later.

Referring again specifically to the Chiefs of Staff's report, Professor Medlicott writes: 'All that the Ministry's representative seems really to have advanced on this occasion in the way of a general estimate is that if certain conditions were fulfilled the Germans would after a year be in approximately the same economic difficulties that they were believed to have been in in the spring of 1940. There was no suggestion that Germany would collapse, and in any case the postulated conditions were not carried out. The line of argument had been that, in spite of a great increase in resources and, in some cases, of stocks, Germany would be faced with new difficulties of administration and distribution, and that her sources of overseas supply would be reduced, in the main, to two, namely Russia and the French Empire.' Since, however, we were unable to close these two supply routes, or to conduct an effective air offensive, or to bring about resistance by the occupied populations, or to deny to the enemy the use of 'waterways round Europe or of the Danube' or 'to ensure by military action a sufficiently rapid wastage of German production', there was no possibility of the hoped for results being obtained. 'The Ministry's estimate, wild or otherwise, was not, in fact, put to the test.'

Professor Medlicott explains however that the papers produced at this time for the Cabinet 'were, under instructions from the Chiefs of Staff, prepared under conditions of great speed and secrecy' which ruled out adequate consultation with the Ministry of Economic Warfare. He admits also that in the absence of exact information as to stocks and consumption the estimates of Germany's economic strength had to be based on a large element of guesswork. We now know that the Ministry's guesses during this early period of the war tended to be far too optimistic. One reason was that Germany was not working her war industries as hard as the British experts then supposed, and consequently the basis on which they calculated the date when her stocks would be exhausted was incorrect. Another was that our experts made too little allowance for the capacity of a highly organised and intelligent nation to adapt its economy to the changed conditions of war. But we know also that similar miscalculations—on the pessimistic side—were made by the Germans themselves.[1]

There is one surprising omission in the list of factors which might contribute to German's defeat: it will be remarked that there is no reference to offensive operations by a reconstituted British army. But the circumstances of the time must be remembered. In the last days of May 1940 such a suggestion might well have appeared

---

[1] Germany's economic position is discussed rather more fully in chapter xvii below.

unrealistic. 'It is unlikely', said the report, 'that more than a small portion of the British Expeditionary Force could be extricated from France.' At home we should not, in the next two or three months, have more than three and a half divisions trained, equipped and mobilised, five partly trained and equipped, five relatively untrained and with little equipment, besides two armoured divisions, of which the equivalent of about two brigades could be mobilised. There were also fifty-seven Home Defence battalions. But there was certainly never any intention on the part of the Chiefs of Staff or the Government not to build up an effective striking force, though its proposed size varied from time to time. The Chiefs of Staff a month later approved an *aide-mémoire* for discussion with the Americans which, while admitting that our strategy for the defeat of Germany would be exercised mainly through the medium of naval and air power, insisted that land forces would be needed not only for defence purposes and to harass the enemy and exploit any successes so gained but also for the ultimate occupation of enemy territory to enforce terms of peace; while Mr. Churchill spoke to General Smuts of the possibility of large-scale amphibious operations in 1940–41. We may suppose that it was always assumed that at some stage land operations on a considerable scale would be required to consummate Germany's downfall, but so many prior conditions would have to be fulfilled that to mention the matter in May 1940 would have served no practical purpose. Indeed, as has been suggested earlier, it would be a mistake to attach very much importance to the section of the report dealing with our prospects of eventually defeating Germany. That could wait; success must depend on many unpredictable factors, above all on the nature and degree of American co-operation. This was of special importance in the Far East, now that the Chiefs of Staff had expressed the opinion that we should be unable to send a fleet there ourselves. In any case there was never any thought of surrender or negotiation with the enemy. The practical question was how we were to survive the next few months. It was the Chiefs of Staff's recommendations on this matter, apart from the disputed estimates of relative air strengths, which interested the Cabinet and were generally approved by them on May 27. As the Chief of the Air Staff had put it, our ability to carry on the war single-handed would depend, so far as the air was concerned, not on our obtaining air superiority over the Germans (as one Minister had suggested) but on our preventing the Germans from achieving such air superiority as would enable them to invade this country.

By May 27 however it was by no means certain that the dread eventuality would become actual, and for some weeks the prime object of the Cabinet, apart from preparing for the defence of the island, was to salvage all that was possible from the wreck of French resistance. On June 11, when there were still hopes of some co-operation from a French Government, the Chiefs of Staff presented a report dealing with this subject as well as with the possibility of help from the United States. In the section headed 'Denial of French resources to the Germans' the first item was naturally the French Navy: it was thought that any peace terms would certainly include a demand for its surrender and that an armistice would not be granted until after its surrender. This would upset the whole balance of power at sea, not only in the Mediterranean. 'We could not afford to see French ships and submarines added to the German and Italian navies. It seems to us therefore that we have only two alternatives: (a) to attempt to persuade as many French ships as possible to join our own Fleet'—an attempt which was not thought likely to succeed—and '(b), if (a) fails, to press the French to sink the whole of their Fleet.'

It was on the following day, June 12, that Mr. Churchill obtained from Admiral Darlan a promise that he would never let the Fleet fall into German hands;[1] the promise was renewed on several occasions by members of the new French Government, but the ships were not sailed before armistice negotiations began, as we had required, to ports outside German control. The French had agreed that their ships should join the British or scuttle themselves *only* if the Germans demanded their surrender—as many of the French Ministers, like the British Chiefs of Staff, expected that they would. But the Germans did not demand the surrender of the French Fleet, and by not doing so they drove a skilful wedge in Franco-British relations. It now appears that, in considering what terms to concede, Hitler was not so much interested in seizing the French Fleet for himself as in preventing its joining the British; he was anxious only to secure its neutralisation, possibly by internment in a neutral country, such as Spain, or better still its self-scuttling. Thus both the Germans and the British would have accepted the solution of neutralisation, though the choice of neutral ports favoured by Hitler would certainly not have satisfied the British. Mussolini, on the other hand, would have liked to demand the surrender of the ships, but felt bound to bow to Hitler's policy when the two Dictators met at Munich on June 18th.[2] Hitler was at this time hoping to conclude an early peace with Britain in order to consolidate his gains; should this prove impossible, he desired to keep in being a French Government that would be prepared to work with him; for both reasons he

---

[1] See above, p. 204.
[2] See above, p. 206.

wished to appear moderate. Hence the specious terms of the armistice, which might be taken to spare the honour of the French Navy; but this was only a policy of the moment; the Germans might well have attempted, and perhaps contrived, to seize the ships later on if an opportunity came. This danger was very present to the British; after their outwitting in Norway they were unlikely again to underestimate either the unscrupulousness or the ingenuity of the Germans. In any case they did not know what was in the Dictators' minds and they could not but regard the French action in opening negotiations with the enemy as the breach of a solemn agreement.

On the night of June 22 the Cabinet learnt that an armistice had been signed, but they did not know the exact terms. Discussing the danger with regard to the Fleet, they were informed that the two new battleships, the *Richelieu*, described by the First Sea Lord as 'the most powerful battleship afloat in the world today', but not yet worked up, and the *Jean Bart*, which was some way off completion, had sailed for Dakar and Casablanca respectively. The two modern battle-cruisers *Dunkerque* and *Strasbourg*, with an aircraft-transport and six large destroyers (*contre-torpilleurs*) lay at the naval port of Mers-el-Kebir near Oran in Algeria. Four 8-inch cruisers were at Toulon, and others with the British fleet at Alexandria; there were certain less important French ships of war at Portsmouth and Plymouth.

The Cabinet were determined that at no cost must the two new battleships fall into enemy hands and add their strength to the menace to be apprehended from the expected commissioning of the *Bismarck* in August. We had Darlan's word, it was true, and the Cabinet had just learnt in garbled form that Darlan had recently issued orders for the transmission of the command, in the event of his own inability to exercise it freely, to four named admirals in succession. His signal had in fact (on the 20th) instructed all naval commanders to conform to the following orders: they were to fight fiercely to the end as long as a regular French Government, independent of the enemy, had issued no orders to the contrary; they were to disobey all other Governments; and whatever orders were received they were not to allow the enemy to take possession of any warship intact. On the 24th, after the armistice, Darlan made a final cypher signal to the Fleet in the following terms:

1. The demobilised warships are to (*doivent*) stay French, under the French flag, with reduced French crews, remaining in French metropolitan or colonial ports.

2. Secret preparations for auto-sabotage are to be made in order that an enemy or foreigner seizing a vessel by force shall not be able to make use of it.

3. Should the Armistice Commission charged with interpreting

the text come to a decision different from that in para. 1, as soon as action is taken on any such decision, warships are without further orders to be despatched to the United States, or alternatively scuttled, provided that no other action is possible to preserve them from the enemy. Under no circumstances are they to fall into enemy hands intact.

4. Ships that seek refuge abroad are not to be used in operations of war against Germany or Italy without prior orders from the Commander-in-Chief of the French Navy.

This later signal, of June 24, was not seen by British eyes, and if Admiral Odend'hal, the head of the French Naval Mission in the United Kingdom, gave the gist of it (*commenta*) to the British naval officers with whom he was in contact, he certainly did not impress its importance on them. His immediate concern was to secure the return to French waters of the warships detained at Portsmouth and Plymouth. Darlan had resented the restrictions placed earlier by the British on merchantmen bound for French ports, and his annoyance was increased by the detention of the warships both in the United Kingdom and at Alexandria. On the 25th Odend'hal assured Admiral Pound that the French had accepted the armistice only on condition that the French Fleet must remain French under the French flag with a French reduced complement. Pound, however, was anxious to know the exact terms of the armistice, as finally agreed on with both the Germans and the Italians. The French were pressing for modifications of these, and on the 30th Darlan telegraphed to Odend'hal that the Italian Government authorised the stationing of the 'effective fleet' either at Toulon or in North Africa, and that he hoped the German Government, whose reply was awaited, would agree. But the signal arrived in a corrupt form, and as late as July 1 Odend'hal could only say that his Government had firm hopes of obtaining permission to station the Fleet at Toulon and in North Africa. In the view of the Cabinet, however, not even North African ports, and still less Toulon, could be regarded as outside the German reach. This was indeed the crux, and the fact that this concession with regard to the ports was, as it happens, made by the enemy before the action at Mers-el-Kebir is therefore of minor importance.

More significant from the British standpoint was the clause in Darlan's signal of June 24 directing French warships, in certain circumstances, to make for the United States as an alternative to scuttling themselves. But this signal, as we have seen, was never shown to the British, and in any case the Cabinet did not consider the intentions, and probably would not have considered the orders, of a single Frenchman, even were he Commander-in-Chief or Minister, sufficient insurance against so extreme a risk; the capture of the

Richelieu and *Jean Bart* alone might 'alter the whole course of the war'. The Admiralty had evidence, moreover, that the Germans were in possession of French naval codes and were issuing instructions to French ships purporting to come from Darlan.

Reports which reached the Cabinet on June 24 indicated that the French ships at Alexandria and in North Africa were likely to obey the orders of their Government and make for, or remain in, French African ports; they would not be allowed to fall into enemy hands, but they would not fight on with the British. The general view of the Cabinet was that we should do all we could to get hold of the four big ships or at least make sure that they were scuttled.[1] Meeting again in the evening they took the view that no time must be lost, since within a few hours of the conclusion of the armistice with Italy (which was announced during the session) the Germans might at once fly over personnel to the French North African ports; it was therefore agreed that the Prime Minister and Foreign Secretary should draft a communication to Bordeaux demanding, in view of the risk of their falling into German hands, that the ships should be scuttled within a time to be specified. It was clear that the French Government had taken umbrage at British encouragement of General de Gaulle, who on the 23rd had broadcast proposals for the formation of a French National Committee or Council of Liberation, and were in no friendly mood. At a third meeting, held that night, the First Sea Lord presented an appreciation by the Naval Staff which, all things considered, deprecated an operation directed against the *Force de Raid* in Algerian waters, on the ground that the serious losses we might suffer seemed a heavy price to pay for the elimination or partial elimination of the French fleet. The only real chance of success lay in a surprise attack carried out at dawn and without any form of prior notification. In the discussion stress was laid on the ease with which the Germans could evade the pledges given in the armistice conditions, but a decision was deferred, and the proposed ultimatum to Bordeaux was not sent. A diversion was caused next day (25th) by the news that the *Richelieu* had left Dakar, but on the following day she headed back for that port. On the 27th the Cabinet decided in principle that the French ships at Mers-el-Kebir should be presented on July 3 with certain alternative proposals designed to ensure that they would never fall into German hands; failing acceptance of these, they would be attacked by a superior British naval force.

The execution of this policy was the first task of the new fleet,

---

[1] *Richelieu, Jean Bart, Dunkerque, Strasbourg.*

known as Force H, which was now assembled at Gibraltar under the flag of Vice-Admiral Sir James Somerville. It had been formed in order to restore the balance, so far as possible, in the western Mediterranean, and it included the battleships *Valiant* and *Resolution*, the battle-cruiser *Hood* and the carrier *Ark Royal*.

The decisive meeting of the Cabinet was held on the evening of July 1, the First Sea Lord and Admiral Phillips, Vice-Chief of Naval Staff, both being present. They had before them an *aide-mémoire* approved by the Chiefs of Staff the previous evening and a request from Darlan that we should reserve final judgement pending the discussions on the armistice conditions which were starting at Wiesbaden that morning.

The Naval Staff had on June 24 advised against an attack on the French ships in Algerian waters. Now, on the 30th, the Chiefs of Staff, with the three Vice-Chiefs, agreed without a dissentient voice that from the military point of view this operation, known as 'Catapult', should be carried out as soon as possible. 'In the light of recent events' we could not rely on French assurances, and once the ships had reached French metropolitan ports we could be certain that sooner or later the Germans would use them against us. 'Recent events' must have included the collapse of the will to resist in North Africa and Syria, the rebuff sustained by Mr. Duff Cooper and Lord Gort at Rabat,[1] and a mendacious account, issued from Bordeaux, of the British Government's behaviour in the past. Further, it was of vital importance to ensure, as far as possible, the concentration of the maximum naval strength in home waters, and that the ships now shadowing the French fleet should be released for duties elsewhere. The action contemplated might indeed lead to France becoming actively hostile, but it was thought to be only a matter of time before the proposed extension of the blockade to France would have this result in any case.

The Cabinet did not believe that the armistice negotiations could affect the real facts of the situation, since no promises would prevent the Germans from seizing the ships if they had a mind to. The operation must go forward; discussion centred on the alternatives to be offered to the French Admiral Gensoul, the arguments to be used to him, and the instructions for Admiral Somerville. The Chiefs of Staff had suggested that Gensoul should be presented with four alternatives: to join with us actively against Germany, to sail his ships to British ports on the understanding that they would not be used against the Germans unless the latter broke the terms of the armistice, to demilitarise the ships under our supervision, or to sink them. The Cabinet were not wholly satisfied with regard to the

---

[1] See below, p. 229.

third alternative, and decided that, while we would accept demilitarisation if offered, we should not ourselves propose it.

The final drafting of the message and instructions for the French and British admirals were to be settled by the Prime Minister and First Lord that night. Accordingly the following signal was approved for communication to Admiral Gensoul:

'His Majesty's Government have commanded me to inform you as follows:

'They agreed to the French Government approaching the German Government only on condition that, if an armistice was concluded, the French Fleet should be sent to British ports. The Council of Ministers declared on 18th June that, before capitulating on land, the French Fleet would join up with the British or sink itself.[1]

Whilst the present French Government may consider the terms of the Armistice with Germany and Italy are reconcilable with these undertakings, H.M. Government finds it impossible from their previous experience to believe that Germany and Italy will not at any moment which suits them seize French warships and use them against Britain and Allies. Italian Armistice prescribes that French ships should return to metropolitan ports, and under armistice France is required to yield up units for coast defence and minesweeping.

It is impossible for us, your comrades up to now, to allow your fine ships to fall into the power of the German or Italian enemy. We are determined to fight on until the end; if we win, as we think we shall, we shall never forget that France was our Ally, that our interests are the same as hers, and that our common enemy is Germany. Should we conquer, we solemnly declare we shall restore the greatness and territory of France. For this purpose we must be sure that the best ships of the French Navy will not be used against us by the common foe.

In these circumstances, H.M. Government have instructed me to demand that the French Fleet now at Mers-el-Kebir and Oran shall act in accordance with one of the following alternatives:

A. Sail with us and continue to fight for victory against the Germans and Italians.

B. Sail with reduced crews under our control to a British port. The reduced crews will be repatriated at the earliest moment. If either of these courses is adopted by you we will restore your ships to France at the conclusion of the war, or pay full compensation if they are damaged meanwhile.

C. Alternatively, if you feel bound to stipulate that your

---

[1] This sentence is inaccurate; it was based on a misreading of a telegram of June 18 from the British Ambassador at Bordeaux. The information given him that day was that the Council of Ministers had been discussing the action they would take if presented with terms requiring the French Fleet to be surrendered. This contingency did not arise, so the 'declaration' never became operative.

ships should not be used against Germans or Italians, since this would break the Armistice, then sail them with us with reduced crews to some French port in the West Indies—Martinique, for instance,—where they can be demilitarised to our satisfaction, or perhaps be entrusted to the United States of America, and remain safely until the end of the war, the crews being repatriated.

If you refuse these fair offers, I must with profound regret require you to sink your ships within six hours. Finally, failing the above, I have the orders of His Majesty's Government to use whatever force may be necessary to prevent your ships from falling into German or Italian hands.'[1]

At the same time Admiral Somerville was instructed that if Gensoul accepted the second alternative, but insisted that we should not use the ships during the war, this condition might be accepted for so long as the enemy observed the armistice terms. Should Gensoul refuse all the alternatives offered and suggest that he should demilitarise his ships at their present berths, this too might be accepted but only on the condition—a most exacting one—that the necessary measures could be carried out in six hours under Somerville's supervision and would be such as would prevent the ships being brought into service for at least one year, even at a fully equipped dockyard port. If none of these alternatives were accepted, the French ships at Mers-el-Kebir were to be destroyed, particularly the *Dunkerque* and the *Strasbourg*. Speed and surprise were judged essential, with the result that when the British terms were conveyed to Admiral Gensoul on the morning of July 3 he was already within sight and virtually under the guns of the British fleet. To an ultimatum backed by a show of force French honour, he felt, could only return one answer, and this, according to his statement made after the war, accounts for the extraordinary fact that his signal to the French Admiralty mentioned none of the British alternative demands except that his ships should be sunk within six hours; to this signal he received the reply that all available forces in the Mediterranean had been ordered to rally to him. The course of events at Mers-el-Kebir on that unhappy day has been described elsewhere.[2] Messages passed at frequent intervals between Ministers in the Cabinet Room and British ships off the African coast—a notable example of the change brought about by the wireless telegraph in the balance of responsibility. Late in the afternoon Gensoul, who may have been playing

---

[1] Paragraphs three and following are printed in Churchill II 208. The earlier paragraphs appear to have been drafted in the Admiralty.

[2] Maj.-Gen. I. S. O. Playfair, *The Mediterranean and Middle East, I* (H.M.S.O. 1954) 131–138, Roskill I 240–245; Churchill II 209 ff. See also Gensoul's evidence before the French parliamentary Commission of Enquiry, 28 June 1949.

for time, informed Somerville, through Captain C. S. Holland, the the British intermediary, that he proposed to demilitarise all his ships at Mers-el-Kebir and, in the event of any enemy threat, to sail them for Martinique or the United States; the reduction of crews had actually begun. But it was too late: Somerville had instructions to finish off the affair before nightfall, and shortly afterwards Force H opened fire. The action resulted in the disablement of the *Dunkerque* and two older battleships and a large destroyer, with the loss of nearly 1,300 French lives. The *Strasbourg* with the remaining large destroyers made her escape to Toulon.

Proceedings at Alexandria had a happier issue, thanks largely to the tact of Admiral Cunningham and the good relations existing between the officers of the two fleets; it was easier too to reach agreement in a port under British control.[1] The British Cabinet learnt on July 5 that the French Admiral, Godfroy, had agreed to discharge oil fuel and to demilitarise his ships at once, and they instructed Cunningham to avoid giving any undertaking that after the ships had passed into our charge we should not make use of them. On July 7 the two Admirals agreed that the French would not scuttle their ships, try to leave harbour, or commit any act hostile to the British; while the British would not attempt to seize the ships. In the event of French warships elsewhere being taken over by the enemy, the agreement would be reconsidered and, if war broke out between Great Britain and France, it would lapse.

The French ships at Plymouth and Portsmouth were boarded and seized in harbour on the morning of July 3 with the loss of two lives.

There remained the menace of the *Richelieu* at Dakar. After an ultimatum similar to that of July 3 had been presented and ignored, she was attacked on July 8, first with depth charges, by a motor-boat from the aircraft-carrier *Hermes*, and later by aircraft with torpedoes; these attacks did not succeed in damaging the *Richelieu* past repair, but she did not in fact move from Dakar.

The First Lord of the Admiralty was accordingly able to inform the House of Commons on July 9 that, of the nine French capital ships, seven had now been put outside the power of the enemy; the *Jean Bart* at Casablanca would not be fit for operations for some months.[2] On July 14 the Prime Minister followed this statement with a broadcast in which he announced that we regarded this phase of the war as at an end and proposed to take no further action against French ships in North African or colonial ports. This policy was in accordance with the advice of the Admiralty; the immunity would

---

[1] See Viscount Cunningham of Hyndhope, *A Sailor's Odyssey* (1951) ch. xxi.

[2] *House of Commons Debates* vol. 362, col. 1087.

not of course apply to French ships making for ports in enemy control.

The question whether the destruction of the ships at Mers-el-Kebir was justified will no doubt be debated for years to come. It is now clear that on both sides vital decisions were taken at the highest level without full knowledge of the facts: the British Cabinet did not know of Darlan's final orders to the Fleet nor of the final text of the armistice terms; the French Government did not know the text of the British ultimatum. Whether fuller knowledge would have prevented the tragedy one can only speculate. In view of the tense emotional atmosphere then enveloping both parties it seems unlikely. The British Government distrusted the new rulers of France, they feared German duplicity and German resourcefulness, and they believed that the whole strength of the Royal Navy might very soon be needed to repel invasion; to these facts was due also the sense of urgency, perhaps the precipitancy, shown in their reluctance to await precise information of the final armistice conditions and in their disregard of the consideration that even if the Germans secured the French ships some months must elapse before they could make effective use of them. On the side of the French there was anger at the British Government's attitude and the threat of violence, and also anxiety not to expose their homes and families to the consequences of a breach of the armistice.

Certainly no more distasteful decision was ever taken by a British Cabinet, and its execution went sorely against the grain of the Navy. Mr. Churchill was not a man lacking in respect or indeed affection for France, while in the eyes of many British naval officers, including Admirals Cunningham, North and Somerville and all the liaison officers in the Mediterranean, the affair was a deplorable blunder. They had no fear that their late colleagues would ever allow their ships to fall into German or Italian hands, and the self-scuttling of the fleet at Toulon in November 1942, though admittedly in very different circumstances, to some extent justifies their optimism. They took most seriously, moreover, the naval consequences which might follow from a French declaration of war. Sentiment apart, it was from the British point of view a balance of risks: the risk of allowing these all-important ships to fall into enemy hands against the risk of driving France into the enemy camp. It is not surprising that to the British Government the former risk appeared the less acceptable. Even granting that their present commanders were resolved not to allow the Germans to use the ships, how could the Cabinet be satisfied that some French Government, dominated, perhaps, by such a man as Laval, would not issue orders which French officers, with their deep respect for legal authority, would feel bound to obey? Or else that the Germans, who had swooped on Oslo and Narvik and the bridges in Holland, might not bring off a similar daring and treacherous *coup* against the French in North Africa? Compared with such a danger the possibility of a despondent and war-weary French Government declaring war against its late allies might well seem negligible.

Denmark's 'safety', wrote George Canning in July 1807, 'is to be found, under the present circumstances of the world, only in a balance of opposite dangers. For it is not to be disguised that the influence which France has acquired from recent events over the north of Europe, might, unless balanced and controlled by the naval power of Great Britain, leave to Denmark no other option than that of complaisance with the demands of Bonaparte, however extravagant in their nature or repugnant to the feelings and interests of the Danish Government.'[1]

Read France for Denmark, Germany for France, west of Europe for north of Europe, Hitler for Bonaparte, and the parallel is striking. It was as essential in 1940 as in 1807 that the naval power of Great Britain should not be endangered.

Such were the considerations which eventually prevailed with the British Cabinet and Chiefs of Staff. Unquestionably their decision aroused deep and lasting resentment in the French Navy and among many other Frenchmen. But the moral effect of the decision was by no means wholly damaging. It afforded to the neutral world, and especially to the United States of America, a proof that Britain at bay under her new Government could be tough to the point of ruthlessness. The Prime Minister was sure the country was behind him. He knew also that President Roosevelt would approve vigorous action.[2] The bombardment of July 3 drew a line of blood between Pétainist France and Britain; it also drew a line of demarcation between the new spirit of the British people and the temper of the twilight war. We were beginning to 'imitate the action of the tiger'.

---

[1] F.O. Denmark No. 53, cited J. H. Rose, *English Historical Review* Oct. 1901, p. 717 reprinted in *Napoleonic Studies*.

[2] See W. L. Langer and S. E. Gleason, *The Challenge to Isolation* p. 573.

CHAPTER X

THE IMMEDIATE CONSEQUENCES OF THE FRENCH COLLAPSE (2)

SECOND in importance only to the French Fleet were the French oversea possessions. Just before the fall of the Reynaud Government the Chiefs of Staff expressed their hope that the French would continue the fight from North Africa, using the abundant shipping at Marseilles to convey all the troops and material possible, with priority for specialists and technical units. But on the same day they advised on the action to be taken in the event of a total French collapse, involving the whole of the army and colonial empire. Much would depend on the attitude of local French authorities, but the general conclusions of the report were that we should intensify the blockade by controlling produce at source and deny the use of French colonial bases to the enemy; there could be no question of taking over the French possessions for ourselves. The Mediterranean coast of French Africa would be outside our control but we should press the French to allow us the use of Casablanca as a naval base should Gibraltar become untenable. By every means the enemy must be kept out of Syria. In the Far East the French defeat might tempt the Japanese to occupy Indo-China, whence they could threaten Singapore by both sea and air; we ought to do nothing which might disturb the status quo. Here, as elsewhere, American co-operation was most desirable. We should also try to induce Turkey to declare herself a belligerent. In any case, should the Government at Bordeaux make terms with the enemy, we should appeal to the local administrations to disregard a surrender made under duress and fight on with us.

The Cabinet on June 17 approved both reports. For some days it seemed that the French colonial authorities might respond favourably, but even those who had protested against surrender were reluctant to disobey lawful authority and show a divided front. On the 22nd the British Cabinet authorised a further appeal, but General Noguès, Commander-in-Chief in French North Africa, had accepted defeat by the 25th. He refused to meet Mr. Duff Cooper, Minister of Information, and Lord Gort, who flew to Rabat on the 26th, and they were not allowed to make contact with members of the Reynaud

Government.[1] By June 27th it seemed clear in London that there was little hope of resistance in the African colonies. The news from the Levant too was bad. Nowhere, it seemed, in the French overseas empire was anyone of commanding repute prepared to give a lead.[2] General de Gaulle was not as yet a national figure. His broadcasts, especially that of June 23, challenging the authority of the Pétain Government to speak for France, and the British declaration in support of him had naturally incensed Bordeaux, and his initiative was by no means universally applauded even by patriots determined to resist. Nevertheless on June 28 he was recognised by the British Government as 'the Leader of all Free Frenchmen, wherever they may be, who rally to him in support of the Allied cause'.

For a few days after the incident at Mers-el-Kebir it was touch and go whether the Government, now installed at Vichy, would be provoked into declaring war on Great Britain. A few French bombs were in fact half-heartedly dropped over Gibraltar and the French Government broke off diplomatic relations. A strategical appreciation of the implications of French hostility was clearly called for, and on July 16 the Chiefs of Staff issued a report on this subject, assuming the worst possible case, of a France actively hostile.

The most serious military results were likely to appear in the first place in the altered balance of naval strengths in the Mediterranean and the eastern Atlantic, particularly if the enemy used French West African ports. This danger, of the enemy using French bases, came next, and thirdly there was the increased risk to some of our own overseas possessions. Gibraltar might become unusable if attacked from North Africa, and it might become very difficult to reinforce Malta. The use of either Casablanca or Dakar by the enemy, especially Dakar, would be most serious, nor could we tolerate the use of Diego Suarez in Madagascar as a base for enemy raiders in the Indian Ocean. On the other hand we were in a good position to influence by economic pressure the attitude of the more isolated French colonies.

Steps had already been taken to strengthen the defences of Gibraltar. The local anti-aircraft defences were derisory, a mere eight guns, when the Chiefs of Staff decided on June 19 to send sixteen heavy anti-aircraft guns as a matter of urgency. The importance of Gibraltar as 'the only capital ship dock between the United King-

---

[1] See Viscount Norwich, *Old Men Forget* (1953) pp. 282–284.
[2] For the Levant, see below, p. 302. General Catroux, Governor-General of Indo-China, who afterwards joined de Gaulle, was recalled in July.

dom and Durban' was stressed at meetings a month later, and also the danger to ships in harbour from the Spanish 12-inch howitzers known to be mounted near by. It was agreed that the fortress must be defended to the last, but the Chiefs of Staff recognised that in the absence of facilities for fighter aircraft it could not be used indefinitely as a base for the fleet in the face of heavy air attack from Africa or Spain.

Should Gibraltar become unusable, Freetown in Sierra Leone would become 'vitally important' as a bunkering station and a port where convoys could be assembled and routed.[1] Even with Gibraltar still available, Freetown's importance had been greatly increased by the closure of the Mediterranean, since most supply ships and transports for the Middle East called at Freetown for water, fuel and stores. This port was also the headquarters of Commander-in-Chief, South Atlantic, who had a small force of cruisers at his disposal as escorts and for the protection of trade. The Chiefs of Staff recognised that Freetown might be bombarded in the course of raids by German or Italian ships, but they did not consider serious attack likely unless France became hostile, and they thought it unnecessary to send British troops to Freetown at present. They merely recommended that the coastal and anti-aircraft defences should be strengthened and accommodation prepared for an infantry brigade and a squadron of fighter aircraft. As an alternative to Freetown, the possible use of Takoradi in the Gold Coast as assembly port for convoys should be investigated, and it might be feasible to route some part of the Australian and New Zealand trade by the Pacific and Panama, whilst a small proportion of the Cape traffic could be routed via Trinidad; this would however greatly increase the distance and the demand for escorts. Freetown would in any case continue to be a link of the first importance in our sea communications.

The recommendations of the Report of July 16 included the maintenance of a capital ship fleet at Gibraltar, as well as of the existing fleet in the Eastern Mediterranean; also immediate action to improve the defences of Malta. On July 22 the Cabinet approved the recommendations and later the same day the Defence Committee paid special attention to the defence of Gibraltar against a surprise attack.

Happily the worst did not occur. Marshal Pétain did not declare war on his old ally. The remaining French warships did not fall into enemy hands. The Germans did not seize the Mediterranean or West African ports. Spain did not admit German troops from France, and German attempts later on to make use of Syria merely gave the Allies an opportunity to occupy it. Neither Gibraltar nor Freetown

---

[1] See Map 8.

was seriously attacked, while Malta resisted all assaults from the air. Nor indeed did the whole of the French Empire adhere to Vichy; before the end of 1940 the vast regions of French Equatorial Africa joined General de Gaulle.[1]

But our good fortune went further. The Vichy Government itself was neither so uniformly ill-disposed nor so incapable of taking a line of its own as was commonly assumed in London. There were many shades of grey between the black malevolence of Laval, the vacillations of the senile chief, and the latent sympathies of Weygand. Moreover there were limits to the pressure which the conqueror would put on them. Hitler explained to Ciano on July 7 that a separate peace with France was undesirable for two reasons; Germany could not at present occupy the French African colonies which she proposed to annex when peace was signed, and it was better to leave them meanwhile in French possession; secondly, the Atlantic coast of France must be retained in German hands for the double purpose of intensifying the war against England and maintaining communications with Spain, 'a country which was most useful for the Axis game whatever happened, and indispensable should one wish to make an attempt on Gibraltar'.[2] Hitler evidently thought that in the meantime French official goodwill would be a considerable convenience, and he preferred therefore not to humiliate the Pétain Government beyond a certain measure. A further argument, which may have influenced him, for treating France with some leniency was the emergence of the Free French movement; so long as Britain was undefeated nothing must be done to encourage resistance or, least of all, to drive the French colonies into the Gaullist camp. Vichy had in fact a good many counters to bargain with.

The first test of the relationship between victor and vanquished came on July 16. On the previous day the Germans had demanded military facilities in North Africa: eight air bases in Morocco, the use of the railway from Tunis to Rabat, the use of French ports and French ships to convey German air units to Africa. This demand far exceeded the terms of the armistice and Pétain successfully resisted it.[3] We can now see that, while in the last resort Vichy must obey the crack of the German whip, the Germans would be loth to crack it, or at any rate to use it, more often than necessary. This was not, however, fully understood in England at the time.

It falls outside the scope of a military history to recount the political negotiations conducted by the British Government with Vichy on the

---

[1] See below, p. 317, and Map 12.

[2] *Ciano's Diplomatic Papers* p. 376.

[3] Weygand, *Rappelé au Service* p. 320. Baudouin 172–174.

one hand and with General de Gaulle on the other. The Cabinet's aims were two: on a long view, to restore France as a Great Power; on a short view, to defeat Germany by any honourable means. For the latter purpose it was often necessary to seem ruthless in our treatment of the French people, but the British no less than the Germans had to refrain from provoking Vichy unduly; a further complication lay in the fact that the United States hoped for more from Vichy, and less from de Gaulle, than did the British. Controversies with Vichy, after bitterness over the Fleet had abated, turned largely on economic questions; the enforcement of the blockade had been made infinitely more difficult, and the Ministry of Economic Warfare were anxious to stop the leakages. The greater part of the resources of Western Europe was now under enemy control and all the Continental ports from the North Cape to Bordeaux were at Germany's disposal, while the existence of the as yet unbeaten Italian fleet in the Mediterranean made the maintenance of an effective blockade in those waters henceforward impossible. The Prime Minister went so far as to remark on July 8: 'The blockade is broken, and Hitler has Asia and probably Africa to draw from.'[1]

A paper hastily prepared for the Cabinet and circulated by Mr. Greenwood, Minister without Portfolio, just before the armistice, estimated the economic consequences of a French collapse as follows. Germany had acquired certain stocks (especially oil, some metals, textile materials, feeding stuffs and fats) and control of certain sources of supply (food, raw materials and manufactured articles) including manufacturing capacity and manpower; the export surplus of iron ore from metropolitan France was about 15 million metric tons, and Belgium and northern France contained much industrial plant. But Germany would still need to import various non-ferrous metals for herself, and also coal for other countries. While she had obtained considerable stocks of petroleum, she would not be able to use the whole of them for her own purposes. As regards ourselves, we should suffer through the loss of imports (eggs, butter, margarine, bacon, iron ore, steel, timber, aluminium, flax, calcium carbide) and of importing capacity, the latter by reason not of the lack of shipping but of the need to divert shipping to west coast ports. The necessity of reducing imports might compel us to bring in more goods in manufactured form and so increase the strain on our foreign purchasing power. On the other hand we should for a time have more shipping under our control and should enjoy, along with the United States, an almost complete monopoly of the world's tankers. The resources of the French, Dutch and Belgian colonial empires should be of great value, particularly in earning hard currencies by their exports.

---

[1] Churchill II 567.

In a second paper, primarily devoted to the ways in which the Americans might help us, Mr. Greenwood submitted certain conclusions to which the Ministry of Economic Warfare had agreed. Assuming that we could still hold the Eastern Mediterranean, could deny the enemy the Mosul oilfields, and could maintain the air offensive on German key industrial installations and transport centres, it was probable that by March 1941 the enemy would not possess enough petroleum products to make possible a war effort on the same scale as hitherto. Much would depend, however, on the extent to which Germany would be forced to expend her oil supplies on the military measures needed to hold down subject populations becoming increasingly hostile. The next few months were likely to see widespread disorganisation of industry leading to unemployment, in the recently conquered regions. Hence followed two main conclusions, in which the Ministry concurred: first, the maintenance and, so far as possible, the intensification of the blockade must be regarded as constituting an essential element in any plan for the ultimate defeat of the enemy; secondly, 'the weapon of blockade, though of great importance, is essentially a subsidiary arm; it is not one which by itself is capable of achieving victory. This will not be obtained until our resources are such as to enable us to force an issue by battle.'

There is certainly some discrepancy between this view and that of the Chiefs of Staff quoted earlier, to the effect that our only hope of defeating Germany lay in the economic weapon. It appears as if the economists put their faith in battle and the Fighting Services in the blockade. But the discrepancy should not be exaggerated; nowhere was it doubted that economic pressure was necessary and that the army would have a part to play, though in the summer of 1940 it was impossible to tell what that part would be.[1]

To return to the economic prospect, the Cabinet had before them on July 18 expert reports from committees presided over by Lord Hankey and Mr. Geoffrey Lloyd on Germany's oil position. These pointed out that her problem had been completely altered by her domination of continental Europe and the need for maintaining the economic life of this vast area, which included territories productive of little oil themselves and hitherto dependent on importation from overseas. The conclusion drawn was that, in spite of the stocks she had captured, oil represented a very weak link in the economy of the European system under Germany's hegemony; she might have sufficient supplies for any major military operation she might wish to carry out before the end of September, but difficulties in distribution were already being experienced, and Germany's plans, possibly for

[1] See above, p. 217.

an invasion of England, might be diverted by effective attack on her supplies.[1] The Cabinet agreed that the destruction of German hydrogenation and synthetic plants and refineries was of primary importance; also the immediate destruction of Italian and French refineries and stocks adjacent, before present stocks of crude oil were refined; also that communications from Roumania, Italy and France should be attacked, as well as, in second priority, storage installations, depots and loaded tankers. The question had of course to be considered in connexion with the existing bombing policy.

It was to be long, however, before Bomber Command could make any serious impression on Germany's economy, and we may turn to the methods by which the blockade of the lands under German control was henceforward enforced.[2] Here too the French collapse is a landmark. It is not merely that French co-operation in the control of contraband in the Channel, in the Mediterranean, and from West African ports, and in the issue of navicerts came to an end. The problems and the methods were largely transformed as the result of the German conquests. In the first place, while the area to be guarded by the Royal Navy was vastly increased, the extent of neutral territory was greatly reduced. It was therefore both economical and possible to introduce a simpler and more drastic procedure, aiming at the control at source of exports to countries under German domination and bringing the world's shipping also under our control. The new methods were threefold: they involved the introduction of compulsory navicerts for cargoes and ships, of ship warrants, and of rationing. These innovations were given legal form by the Reprisals Order of 31 July 1940.

The navicert has been described as a commercial passport; it was issued by British officials abroad, on the instructions of the Ministry of Economic Warfare, to cover goods or ships whose owners had satisfied the Ministry that they would not be used for the benefit of the enemy. The Cabinet agreed in July that ships sailing without navicerts should henceforth be presumed to have an enemy destination and be treated as blockade-runners; the new policy, which had been made feasible by the changed attitude of the United States, was to apply to both contraband and the control of exports from Europe.[3] The ship-warrant was a device intended to restrict the use of certain privileges, such as bunkering and watering at British ports and insuring on the British market, to vessels whose owners had similarly satisfied the Ministry. Rationing, another expedient of the earlier war, meant the restriction of an 'adjacent neutral's' imports of certain

---

[1] The accuracy of these and other reports on Germany's oil position will be discussed in chapter xvii.

[2] See W. N. Medlicott, *The Economic Blockade* I chaps. xii, xiii.

[3] *ibid*. pp. 94, 436, 452.

goods to the amount judged by British authorities to be necessary for his own needs.[1]

It was hoped that these measures would act as deterrents to intending blockade-runners, but they would be enforced by the Navy; a special war zone was defined off the west coasts of Europe and north-west Africa in which blockade-runners would be liable to seizure. The new system took some time to introduce and make effective, but by February 1941, it is claimed, the compulsory navicert system was firmly established as 'the mainstay of the blockade', and the ship-warrant scheme had also justified itself.[2] Nevertheless the results achieved by the new measures must not be over-estimated. To quote the historian of the Economic Blockade,[3]

> 'The situation in the east remained virtually unchanged; the Russian leak in the blockade was never closed until the Germans attacked in June 1941 . . . In the west a new leak appeared through Morocco and Vichy France, and although the principle of forcible rationing was now applied to the smaller European neutrals (Sweden, Switzerland, Greece, Turkey, Spain and Portugal), and although various forms of economic aid were employed as a positive inducement to prevent exports to the Axis, the leaks continued. So the distinctive new plans of the Ministry, if well-conceived, were imperfectly executed, and it was only when, in the summer of 1941, the Soviet Union found itself at war and the United States by its freezing agreements against Japan entered vigorously into the economic struggle, that it really became possible to plan economic warfare against Germany, Italy, and Japan on a global basis . . .
>
> Compulsory navicerting did not prevent blockade running with valuable cargoes; compulsory rationing could be, and was, twisted by German and Falangist propaganda into a scheme to starve Spain; there was a campaign inside the United States for the supply of foodstuffs and other forms of relief for civilian populations within the blockade area; the Royal Navy almost ceased to function in the provision of patrols, and the Ministry had to watch more or less helplessly the great leak—almost a flood—of shipping and goods to Vichy French ports.'

The failure to establish effective patrols was due partly to the policy of not provoking the French overmuch, partly to the blockade-runners' ability to keep close in to the African shore, but mainly to the extreme strain to which the Navy was subject at this time. We had had six destroyers sunk at Dunkirk and nineteen damaged; heavy demands on this type of ship were now made for the defence of the

---

[1] By 'adjacent neutral' was meant a country, such as Spain, having a common frontier with a country under enemy control.

[2] Medlicott I 448.

[3] ibid. I 417, 423.

British Isles against invasion. None the less the Royal Navy, without the help of its late French ally and indeed under the constant possibility of his opposition, was called upon to protect our troopships and merchantmen against increased dangers. The first German submarine arrived at Lorient on the west coast of France in July, but already in June Allied and neutral shipping losses from U-boats had risen to 284,000 tons from a mere 55,580 in May, and the four months following were referred to by U-boat commanders as 'the happy time'.[1] Not only were their present bases much nearer to the scene of their depredations but they were spared the slow, perilous passage through the North Sea at the beginning and end of each sortie. Northern waters, however, also saw them active, and in June three armed merchant cruisers of the Northern Patrol were torpedoed and sunk.[2]

On the British side the conversion of such great ship-owning nations as Norway and the Netherlands from neutrals to belligerents and the capture of ships from nations which had made terms with the enemy meant a large but non-recurrent access of merchant tonnage.[3] But for several reasons the aggregate carrying capacity of the tonnage at our disposal declined. This was so even before the needs of our forces in the Mediterranean became a serious burden. The closure of the Mediterranean to through shipping in June after Italy's entry into the war involved the diversion of ships to the much longer passage round the Cape; from early in July all deep-sea shipping approaching the British Isles was similarly diverted from the Channel to west- and north-about routes, with serious delays to vessels bound for London and the east coast. But it was not only that vessels carrying supplies or troops were forced to take longer voyages. The historian of Shipping points out that

> 'because the cargoes that had to be carried were often of unaccustomed types and were destined for places not equipped to receive them; because ships had to sail on routes and to carry cargoes for which they were not designed, many operations all over the world were thrown into confusion, and even when the confusion had been overcome often took longer to perform. Moreover these difficulties, caused because Europe was occupied by the enemy and the Mediterranean closed, were increased by various time-consuming expedients required to protect ships from attack. . . . The result of these manœuvres, together with all the dislocation they caused, was to save ships at the expense

---

[1] See Appendix II.
[2] Roskill I 265.
[3] See C. B. A. Behrens, *Merchant Shipping and the Demands of War* ch. v, sec. (i).

R

of their carrying-capacity; and it was the loss of carrying-capacity in the second year of war that was the principal cause of the shipping shortage, not the loss of ships or the rise in the demands of the Services.'[1]

To this it may be added that the loss of the use of Continental repair yards increased the demands on our own yards, causing an accumulation of ships awaiting repair; delays occurred in the turn-round of ships in port owing to inadequate provision for clearing and disposing of cargoes; while a heavy strain was imposed on the railway system now called upon to move goods in directions for which it was not designed.

The conduct of the British blockade under the Conditions described in this chapter was a matter of close concern to Spain and Portugal, and in other ways too the French collapse greatly increased the strategic importance of these countries. Spain no longer marched, along her Pyrenean and African frontiers, with a Power that was our ally; no longer could our forces at Gibraltar look for support to Casablanca or Oran. Moreover the belligerency of Italy might perhaps encourage General Franco to follow Mussolini's example. Franco had joined the anti-Comintern group in March 1939, he had expressed himself as sympathetic to the Axis, and he had struck a pact of friendship with Germany in November. If Spain welcomed in the German divisions now close to her frontier or opened her Atlantic ports to German submarines, the result for the British would be grave. But it was far from certain or even probable that Franco would throw in his lot with the Axis. He might well covet Gibraltar and a larger slice of North Africa; but the crucial fact since the end of the civil war had been the exhaustion and poverty of his country, and the western Powers were in a position to supply its needs as the Axis Powers were not.

On 3 September 1939 Franco had declared Spain's neutrality. In March 1940 the British Government had concluded a war trade agreement assuring her a credit of £2 million for purchases in the sterling area. On June 12, the day after Italy entered the war, Franco announced that Spain was no longer neutral but 'non-belligerent', but the change of phrase meant no real change of attitude. Spain's occupation on June 15 of the neutral Tangier zone was, if anything, to our advantage. Nevertheless the task of the new British Ambassador at Madrid, Sir Samuel Hoare, lately a member of the

---

[1] Behrens, *op. cit.* pp. 109, 110; and see p. 18 for a provisional definition of 'carrying-capacity', in the case of the dry-cargo fleet: 'the amount of commodities . . . which the existing fleet could carry, in a given period of time, in response to the needs in the various areas which it had to serve'.

Chamberlain War Cabinet, was an exceedingly delicate one: he was to counteract the all-pervading German influence and keep Spain neutral in fact.[1]

From the military point of view the contingency of Spain helping the Axis had of course been discussed during the period of the French alliance and counter measures had been considered; these had included a possible occupation of the Grand Canary. The discussions had also embraced the possibility that Portugal, with whose attitude of benevolent neutrality we were well content, might fall under Axis domination. The Azores and Cape Verde Islands were of too great strategic importance to be allowed to fall into enemy hands: they lay athwart our trade routes from the South Atlantic and contained British cable stations, as did Madeira.[2] The Chiefs of Staff pointed out, however, that unless there were clear indications that Spain intended to enter the war against us it would not be to our advantage to precipitate Spanish and Portuguese hostility by occupying the Atlantic Islands simply because Gibraltar had become unusable to us. The Cabinet accordingly agreed on July 22 that it would be desirable to seize certain of the islands only in the event of Spanish or Portuguese hostility, or if it became clear beyond reasonable doubt that either of these Powers intended to intervene against us. Mere convenience for the purposes of the blockade would not be sufficient reason. In any case the actual decision to send the expeditions, for which preparations had already been begun, would be taken by the Cabinet. The forces earmarked for these operations were two composite brigades consisting mainly of Royal Marines.

Reference has been made above to the changed attitude of the United States as rendering possible the new method of conducting the blockade. We saw earlier that in their strategic review of May 25 the Chiefs of Staff rested their hopes of victory and indeed survival on the assumption that 'we could count on the full economic and financial support of the United States of America, possibly extending to active participation on our side'. Mr. Churchill had no doubt that such active participation would be forthcoming eventually, and he had proclaimed his faith, though in tactful phrasing, in his great speech of June 4.[3] It is one of his chief services to the cause of freedom that, while none was tougher than he in asserting and upholding British rights, he realised, perhaps earlier and more constantly than

---

[1] See Sir S. Hoare (Viscount Templewood), *Ambassador on Special Mission* (1946).

[2] The Canary Islands were Spanish: the Azores, Madeira and the Cape Verde Islands were Portuguese. See Map 8.

[3] p. 195 above; see also his telegram of 16 June to the Dominion Prime Ministers, Churchill II 172.

any other British statesman, not only the fundamental harmony of British and American interests but the need of explaining and commending British policy to responsible opinion in the United States. Mr. Churchill had inherited from the Chamberlain Government, in Lord Lothian, an ambassador at Washington peculiarly fitted by temperament and knowledge to win the confidence of the American people and interpret their feelings; but he had seen the importance of direct contact with the President and had been inspired at the outset of the war to initiate, as Naval Person, an informal confidential correspondence with him. This he had continued as Prime Minister, and from May 19 he had arranged for copies of the daily telegrams about military operations compiled for the Dominion Premiers to be sent to the President for his private information. The value of this intimate exchange of knowledge and ideas, to which it would be difficult to find a parallel in history, though Mr. Churchill may possibly have had in mind his great ancestor's correspondence with Heinsius, can hardly be exaggerated.

Some things however were impossible. The United States was in June 1940 totally unprepared for war, in material, in manpower and in mind. To many Americans Europe meant little and one country in that remote continent was much as another. But the successive German victories came as a severe shock to the self-confidence of all concerned with international affairs and responsible for the safety of the nation. Naturally men reacted in different ways, according as they thought it possible or probable that Britain would hold out. Many asked whether, if France had collapsed under the Germans, Britain might not be expected to collapse likewise. If Britain had been prudent in not risking her fighter reserves in a dying cause, might not a similar abstention be prudent for America too? To others, including the President, it seemed that British resistance was essential for America's own security during the period that must elapse before the vigorous measures of rearmament now being put in hand could bear fruit. In any case, with a presidential election imminent in November it was out of the question for any party or practical politician to advocate belligerency or even, as Mr. Churchill urged on May 15, 'non-belligerency'. 'The great majority of the American public', writes Mr. Cordell Hull, the Secretary of State, 'were behind our efforts to aid the Allies in all ways possible, but they were equally resolved that we should stay out of the war.' [1] Nevertheless, speaking at Charlottesville on June 10, the day Italy announced her belligerency, the President promised to 'extend to the opponents of force the material resources' of his country. With his approval 500,000 rifles and 500 75-mm. field guns [2] with a quantity of other 'surplus'

---

[1] *The Memoirs of Cordell Hull* I 803.
[2] Eventually 900 field guns were received.

munitions were sold to private companies for resale to the Allies, and on the collapse of France the whole of the French orders were, with French consent, transferred to Britain.[1]

For some weeks or months even friends of Britain in America believed that her defeat was probable. They were naturally concerned for the future of the British Fleet, as were we for the future of the French Fleet. On May 25, in our darkest hours, Roosevelt spoke to Lothian, not for the first time, of the importance, 'if things came to the worst', of transferring the British Navy, with aircraft and merchant ships, before they could be captured or surrendered, to Canada or Australia. Such a suggestion, so it seemed to Lord Lothian and to Mr. Churchill, implied a dangerous misconception on the American side, namely that the United States could afford to wait until the British Isles had been liquidated and still count on the assistance of the British Fleet. They set themselves to destroy this fallacy. Mr. Churchill had already assured the President on May 20:

> 'Our intention is whatever happens to fight on to the end in this Island and, provided we get the help for which we ask, we hope to run [the enemy] pretty close in the air battles in view of individual superiority. Members of the present Administration would likely go down during this process should it result adversely, but in no conceivable circumstances will we consent to surrender. If members of the present Administration were finished and others came in to parley amid the ruins, you must not be blind to the fact that the sole remaining bargaining counter with Germany would be the fleet, and if this country was left by the United States to its fate no one would have the right to blame those then responsible if they made the best terms they could for the surviving inhabitants. Excuse me, Mr. President, putting this nightmare bluntly. Evidently I could not answer for my successors who in utter despair and helplessness might well have to accommodate themselves to the German will. However, there is happily no need at present to dwell upon such ideas'.[2]

Lord Lothian, in his conversation with the President on May 25, had remarked that the British decision would probably be profoundly influenced by whether, 'if such a catastrophe impended', the United States itself would be in the war on our side. The President replied, so Lothian reported, that, 'as the decision rested not with him but with Congress, he could give no definite answer, but he thought it probable. As things were going, it seemed likely that Germany would

---

[1] On June 17; Hancock and Gowing, *British War Economy* p. 194; H. Duncan Hall, *North American Supply* pp. 146–155.

[2] See Churchill II 50, 51; also R. E. Sherwood, *The White House Papers of Harry L. Hopkins* (1948), published in America as *Roosevelt and Hopkins*, ch. vi.

challenge some vital American interest in the near future, which was the condition necessary to make the United States enter the war with the necessary popular support, and that opinion was rapidly changing as to what United States vital interests were.'

Shortly before the French request for an armistice, the British Cabinet approved an *aide-mémoire* of June 13 which the Chiefs of Staff had drawn up for Lothian's use. It summarised their previous appreciations of our chances of victory; this might still be achieved, but 'only by a combination of economic pressure, air attack on economic objectives in Germany, with its resultant effect on German morale, and the creation of widespread revolt in the conquered territories'.

> 'Without the full economic and financial co-operation of the whole of the American Continent, the task might in the event prove too great for the British Empire single-handed. Nevertheless, even if the hope of victory in these circumstances appeared remote, we should continue to fight as long as it was humanly possible to do so.
>
> It has been suggested that, in the event of the United Kingdom being overrun by the enemy, the struggle could be continued by the British Fleet from the American Continent. In resisting invasion, however, the whole of our naval resources in home waters would be thrown into the defence and a successful invasion would automatically imply the loss of a large proportion of our fleet. The remaining forces, operating from America, would be faced by considerable problems of maintenance, supply, and manning, and the combined German and Italian fleets, possibly strengthened by captured units of the French navy, might extend their activities well beyond the confines of Europe. Without our air weapon, and with our ability to exert economic pressure through seapower considerably reduced, our chances of victory would be virtually at an end, even with the full military and economic assistance of the American Continent.'

As regards the Far East, 'we see no hope of being able to despatch a fleet to Singapore. It will therefore be vital that the United States of America should publicly declare her intention to regard any alteration of the *status quo* in the Far East as a *casus belli*.' As for the American hemisphere, the Chiefs of Staff welcomed a recent resolution of Congress to the effect that the United States could not tolerate the transfer to any non-American Power of a European Power's colonial possessions in America.

It was evidently this *aide-mémoire* which the Ambassador brought to the notice of the State Department on June 27, following it up a few days later with further memoranda urging, in connection with the help America could render on the economic side, the importance of a reorganisation of American industry for war production and of an amendment of the Neutrality Act.[1] The President had in fact for the last month been consulting his military advisers on how far the war material asked for by London could be spared, while a bill was being drafted for Congress for the purpose of legalising any transfers which the military advisers might recommend.

The President had further agreed, so Lothian reported on June 17, that secret staff talks should take place at once between the navies, and if necessary the air forces, of the two countries. On the British side the Admiralty had a few days previously set up a committee, with Admiral Sir Sydney Bailey as chairman, to consider questions which would arise if naval co-operation with the United States eventually came about, and at the end of June the Chiefs of Staff approved the draft of a further *aide-mémoire* for the use of our representatives. This paper was not confined to merely technical points; it contemplated possible assistance from the United States armed forces, and suggested, as the 'guiding principle' in their employment, that they should 'reinforce or even replace British forces in those areas where America's own interests lie and where they can thus also contribute to the defence of those interests. A second principle might be that United States forces should be used in those areas where they have bases of their own from which they could secure British interests within their orbit.' But here the planners were looking some way into the future. On 4 July the Cabinet were merely informed that the President had agreed to technical naval discussions in London.

In his telegram to the President of May 15, his first as Prime Minister, Mr. Churchill listed our immediate needs under six headings, of which the first was the loan of forty or fifty of America's older destroyers; the second, several hundred of the latest types of aircraft now becoming available. In the third place, he asked for an assurance that when our dollars ran out we should still be able to obtain essential materials, such as steel, from America. His fifth suggestion was the visit of a United States naval squadron to Irish ports. Finally, he was looking to America to keep the Japanese quiet in the Pacific, using Singapore in any way convenient.[2]

Our shortage of destroyers has been already mentioned: they were sorely needed as escort vessels to 'bridge the gap' until the ships built under the new construction programme were ready for service.[3] The President replied that only Congress could sanction such a transfer, and that he judged it inadvisable to approach them at present. But

---

[1] *Cordell Hull* ch. 58.

[2] See Churchill II 22 and ch. xx.

[3] In May a welcome reinforcement of four destroyers had been received from Canada, but on June 15 we had only 68 fit for service, out of 133 in commission in home waters. In 1918 some 433 destroyers were in service.

Mr. Churchill continued to press on him the vital importance to us of obtaining these destroyers, while demanding also 200 Curtiss P40 fighters.

The passing of the National Defence Act did not meet the difficulty with regard to the destroyers, since the transfer of any military material to a foreign Government was forbidden unless the Chief of Staff or Chief of Naval Operations had certified that it was not essential for the defence of the United States. The prohibitive clause might seem vexatious in the circumstances, but it illustrated the fact that the President had to consider the interests of his country from two points of view. If it was clear to him that he could help America by helping Britain, it was obvious that America would help both Britain and herself by strengthening her own armament. While the war lasted, American policy had to be so adjusted as to keep these two purposes in proper balance.[1] The British need for the destroyers was, however, very urgent, and the President was eventually persuaded that constitutional difficulties could be met by connecting the transfer of the ships with an assurance as to the fleet and another offer from the British Government undoubtedly promoting the defence of the United States.

It had often been urged by Americans that their country's security demanded that it should acquire strategic bases in the western Atlantic, and in the summer of 1939 the British Government had informally agreed to grant the United States facilities in Trinidad, St. Lucia and Bermuda. The Americans however had not availed themselves of this concession and the question had lapsed, when on May 24 Lord Lothian proposed that we should make a formal offer to Washington stating that, while we were not prepared to discuss any question of sovereignty, we should be willing to lease to the United States landing-grounds on British territory, in view of the importance of such facilities to American security; he mentioned particularly Trinidad, Newfoundland, and Bermuda. 'Lord Lothian believed that an offer of this kind made by us would make a deep impression in the United States and add to our security. If we acted quickly, our action would have the advantage also of spontaneity.' Evidently many interests were involved. The Chiefs of Staff, to whom the matter was referred, strongly recommended the proposal as obviously to the advantage of both parties, but the Cabinet's reaction was at first unfavourable. They considered at this time that no such concessions should be made without a definite assurance of American assistance, and it was remarked that the Americans had

---

[1] Sherwood, *White House Papers* I 175. See also M. S. Watson, *Chief of Staff; Pre-War Plans and Preparations* (Washington 1950) ch. x, and M. Matloff and E. M. Snell, *Strategic Planning for Coalition Warfare, 1941–1942* (Washington 1953) ch. ii, both in the series *United States Army in World War II*; also W. L. Langer and S. E. Gleason, *The Challenge to Isolation 1937–1940*.

refused to sell us their destroyers. But on July 18 the Foreign Office revived the proposal in a more restricted form, calling attention to the various ways in which America was now helping us without asking for anything in return: it was with America's consent, and very much against her immediate economic advantage, that we maintained our contraband control. The Cabinet were persuaded, and agreed on July 29 that we should, without demanding a *quid pro quo*, grant the facilities especially desired. The climate of opinion in America had now come to favour the release of the destroyers, provided some compensating advantage was forthcoming, and on August 14 the Cabinet had before them an offer from the President to hand over at least fifty destroyers and other material of war in exchange for a long lease of land for the construction of naval and air bases in certain British territories in the Western Hemisphere, combined with an assurance that the British Fleet would never be handed over to the Germans or scuttled. On the latter point only a confirmation of the Prime Minister's speech of June 4 was asked for;[1] as regards the concession of bases, the Admiralty, who had formerly demurred, now took the view that to get fifty destroyers would be of inestimable benefit to us, and the Cabinet accepted the President's proposals in principle, subject to consultation with the Governments of Newfoundland and Canada.

It is clear that the Cabinet had broader considerations in mind than the need of destroyers. It was remarked that, if the present proposal went through, the United States would have made a long step towards coming into the war on our side. To sell destroyers to a belligerent was certainly not a neutral action. And its consequences might outlast the war. This might well prove to be the first step in constituting an Anglo-Saxon *bloc* or indeed a decisive point in history.

It is unnecessary to recount here the difficulties in finding a suitable formula for the announcement of this happy event. Thankful as they were for the material help, the Cabinet were unwilling to represent as a 'deal' a transaction in which the British Empire made such wide and lasting concessions against a temporary benefit; they would have preferred that both should appear as simple acts of goodwill. On the other hand it was essential for the President to show that the United States was receiving valuable consideration for its gifts. A compromise was eventually arrived at and notes were exchanged on September 2. It should be recorded however that only nine of the destroyers were in service by the end of 1940, and agreement on the exact facilities to be allowed the Americans was not reached until the following March.[2]

---

[1] See above, p. 195.

[2] The bases in Newfoundland and Bermuda were treated as a free gift; the others as part of a bargain: see Map 8. On the other side, for reasons somewhat obscure, only the

Long before this, American foresight and American goodwill to Britain had shown themselves in other practical ways. At home the President was building up his war organisation, the 'defence agencies', as they were then known. On May 16 he had asked Congress for enormous defence appropriations, setting a production target of 50,000 aircraft a year and asking for no delays in deliveries to foreign nations; on July 10 he demanded greatly increased appropriations, aiming at a mechanised army of two million men, and on July 19 he introduced the Selective Service Bill. By now the first consignments of the large quantities of rifles and field guns already mentioned were arriving in Britain. In August the promised staff conversations began in London, and as the result of a conference between the President and Mr. MacKenzie King a Permanent Joint Board on Defence was set up representing the United States and Canada.[1]

It was on August 20 that the Prime Minister, after informing the House of Commons of the proposed lease of bases in the western Atlantic, prophesied that 'undoubtedly this process means that these two great organisations of the English-speaking democracies, the British Empire and the United States, will have to be somewhat mixed up together in some of their affairs for mutual and general advantage'. 'For my part,' he continued, 'looking out upon the future, I do not view the process with any misgivings. I could not stop it if I wished; no one can stop it. Like the Mississippi, it just keeps rolling along. Let it roll. Let it roll on full flood, inexorable, irresistible, benignant, to broader lands and better days.'[2]

---

destroyers and not the other desiderata were mentioned in the notes of September 2. For the whole transaction see Churchill II ch. xx, Cordell Hull ch. 60, Sherwood I 175–177, *The Challenge to Isolation* ch. xxii.

[1] For the Ogdensburg Conference see C. P. Stacey in the *International Journal*, Spring 1954, also Langer and Gleason, *op. cit.* 704.

[2] *House of Commons Debates* vol. 364, col. 1171, Aug. 20.

CHAPTER XI

REORGANISATION AND REARMAMENT, MAY–AUGUST 1940

SO SWIFT was the rush of events in the two months following the German eruption in the west, so crowded and pressing the matters to be decided by the new British Government, that there has been little opportunity to describe the changes taking place in the Government itself and its plans for meeting the impending dangers.

In the summer of 1915 Sir William Robertson, soon to become Chief of the Imperial General Staff, wrote these prophetic words:

> 'The responsibility for co-ordinating the many and varied aspects of military policy rests with the Prime Minister, who is ex-officio Minister of Defence. When conflicting views are expressed, as must necessarily often be the case, it is the duty of the Prime Minister to weigh arguments and formulate the policy to be laid before the Cabinet. Only by the firm exercise of these functions by the Prime Minister can a consistent policy be assured.' [1]

Under the system introduced in May 1940 these requirements were met. 'The responsibility for co-ordinating' rested with Mr. Churchill; but he had to help him two organs which the soldier of the first war had not foreseen: the Defence Committees of the War Cabinet and the Committee of the Chiefs of Staff, the latter available for consultation in both their corporate and their individual capacities. But the supreme executive authority remained the War Cabinet; to it Mr. Churchill was careful to refer all major questions of policy, reporting to it after decision in cases of extreme urgency. He was careful also to pay due respect to the House of Commons, while his broadcasts rallied the nation and were the most effective weapons of Allied propaganda.

The three Service Ministers remained responsible to Parliament for all the business of their Departments, and as members of the Defence Committee were concerned with strategy, but within their Departments they were now mainly occupied with matters of organisation and administration. [2]

---

[1] *Soldiers and Statesmen 1914–1918* (1926) I 161.

[2] Mr. A. V. Alexander was First Lord of the Admiralty, Mr. Anthony Eden and Sir Archibald Sinclair Secretaries of State for War and the Air. For the other members of the Defence Committee see above, p. 181.

The Chiefs of Staff Committee, from the end of May onward, consisted of Sir Cyril Newall, Sir Dudley Pound, and Sir John Dill, together with General Ismay, the Prime Minister's staff officer and representative. They were now relieved of part of their burden by the Vice-Chiefs,[1] but their range of responsibilities remained vast, and they had to focus their attention alike on points needing immediate decision and on the broad questions of future policy. The variety of their agenda was impressive; apart from matters of finance and domestic administration and narrowly political issues, which did not concern them, they were called upon to deal not only with strictly military problems all over the world—strategy, organisation, and allocation of men and materials in short supply—but with frequent points submitted by the Foreign Office and the Departments of Propaganda and Information. Towards the end of June proposals by their Secretary, Colonel L. C. Hollis, for lightening and speeding up their work were discussed and approved: the papers to be considered by the Chiefs should be confined as far as possible to those concerned with major strategy, the rest being dealt with by the Vice-Chiefs meeting three days a week. But there was no hard and fast line between the provinces of the two groups, and the reform made no important change.

The Chiefs of Staff's usual practice was to refer questions, either of their own motion or on inquiry from the Minister of Defence, to the Joint Planning Sub-Committee, composed of the Directors of Plans of the three Services; where detailed inter-Service examination of a particular project was called for, the Joint Planners would nominate an *ad hoc* Inter-Service Planning Staff, with appropriate assistance from outside. The Joint Intelligence Sub-Committee reported direct to the Cabinet and Chiefs of Staff on matters of importance; they also advised the Joint Planning Staff, and the two bodies would on occasion submit joint reports. Their members worked mainly in their respective Service Departments, drawing their material from the relevant sections of the three staffs. The Chiefs of Staff would accept their reports with or without amendment or return them for revision or sometimes reject them, and would eventually make their own report to the Minister of Defence or Cabinet, unless the case was one in which they could take executive action themselves. The machinery was made to work smoothly by the existence of the single War Cabinet secretariat directed by Sir Edward Bridges and General Ismay, which ensured liaison between the various Service committees and the numerous other bodies concerned with every aspect of the war effort.[2]

---

[1] See above, p. 130.

[2] See Churchill II 17; for the membership of the principal bodies mentioned, see Appendix V.

It was customary for the Chiefs of Staff Committee to meet in the morning, first by themselves and later with the Minister of Defence in the chair, shortly before the session of the War Cabinet. The meetings of the Defence Committee (Operations) usually took place in the afternoon or evening. All these bodies however were liable to meet at any time and several times a day.

Mr. Lloyd George in the earlier war had found it convenient to have at his elbow an independent undepartmental secretariat of his own, working in the famous 'garden suburb'. It appears that Mr. Churchill in the first weeks of his premiership entertained the similar idea of employing a personal staff, under the superintendence of General Ismay, to keep him in touch with developments in home defence, in British and enemy munitions production, in foreign and Free French affairs, and in Secret Service activities. But the only outcome of lasting importance was the installation in Downing Street of the physicist, Professor F. A. Lindemann (later Lord Cherwell), as head of a team of scientists and statisticians who acted as the Prime Minister's eyes and ears, assembling, checking, comparing and criticising the departmental figures and arguments.[1] So primed and briefed, and enriched by his long study and experience of the arts of war and politics, Mr. Churchill's ubiquitous interest and energy enabled him to dominate the whole war effort and by his personal intervention to give when necessary, in his own words, 'extreme priority and impulse'. 'Action this day' was a frequent superscription on his minutes, while his practice of authenticating in writing all his instructions on matters relating to national defence served the interests as well of present efficiency as of future historians. The drive at once imparted to the public service by Mr. Churchill's leadership was very soon reinforced by the people's sense of emergency. The two stimuli together created a mood of resolution, of exhilaration, which resulted in an intensification of national effort probably without precedent.

The combination of Mr. Churchill in his dual capacity and the Chiefs of Staff proved highly effective. Besides his main function of supplying central direction, his great merits may perhaps be summarised as his constancy in subordinating minor points to those of permanent and supreme importance (such as the need of a good understanding with the United States of America); his fertility in suggesting, and his readiness to entertain, new ideas; and his refusal to tolerate obstruction and delay. The Chiefs of Staff on the other hand, with the prestige of their expert knowledge and experience, could temper the Prime Minister's impatience and restrain the flights of his fancy. It must not be supposed that relations were

---

[1] Churchill I 420, II 338.

always easy. Mr. Churchill would not readily take no for an answer. Using all his great powers of argument he could bring extreme pressure to bear on his advisers. Describing a statesman of a bygone age, he once wrote of 'the compulsive violence of a vital mind', and perhaps the words apply as aptly to himself as to Bolingbroke.[1] Moreover Mr. Churchill has explained his methods of work: they included dictation from bed in the morning, a nap in the afternoon, and midnight discussions and decisions. On the Chiefs of Staff, who were expected to take part in these after a full day's work, the strain was severe and tempers might well be frayed. But fundamentally the statesmen and the Service experts understood and trusted one another. For this all-important fact, so different from the state of things in Germany, no one deserves more credit than General Ismay. As a tactful go-between, as 'an interpreter, one among a thousand', he explained, he soothed, he suggested, he harmonised, and thereby made a notable contribution to the successful conduct of the war. To do Mr. Churchill justice, in spite of his strong views and the force and tenacity with which he expressed them, he was loth to overrule his Service advisers on a military matter in which they stood firm in their opinion. But it was important that they should stand firm, and some were better fitted to do so than others.

On the civil side the more important questions were dealt with on behalf of the Cabinet, at this time, by five ministerial committees: the Production Council, the Economic Policy Committee, the Food Policy Committee, the Home Policy Committee and the Civil Defence Committee. The work of these five committees was 'concerted and directed' by yet another body, the Lord President's Committee, which took decisions on general policy and relieved the Cabinet of much work. Its chairman was Mr. Chamberlain, the Lord President; its other members were the chairmen of the five committees mentioned (Mr. Attlee, Mr. Greenwood and Sir John Anderson) together with the Chancellor of the Exchequer, Sir Kingsley Wood.[2]

Of the Departments engaged in providing material of war the production branch of the Admiralty, under the Controller of the Navy, Rear-Admiral B. A. Fraser, and the Ministry of Supply, under Mr. Herbert Morrison, underwent no spectacular changes; but within a few days of assuming the premiership Mr. Churchill appointed Lord Beaverbrook to take charge of a new Ministry of Aircraft Production.

---

[1] *Marlborough: his Life and Times* (1947 ed.) II 884. In *The World Crisis, 1915* (1923) pp. 165–166, referring to his argument with Lord Fisher on the Dardanelles project at the meeting of Mr. Asquith's War Council on 28 June 1915, Mr. Churchill had written: 'I am in no way concealing the great and continuous pressure which I put upon the old Admiral . . . Was it wrong to put this pressure upon the First Sea Lord? I cannot think so. War is a business of terrible pressures and persons who take part in it must fail if they are not strong enough to withstand them.'

[2] *House of Commons Debates* 4 June 1940, vol. 361, col. 769. See the diagram in Appendix VII, which refers, however, to the spring of 1941.

During the period covered by this volume there was no central ministry of war production balancing and supplying the needs of all three Services, though there were frequent demands for one. That no such body was created is no doubt due, as Professor Postan has argued, to the Prime Minister's conviction that his own activities, exerted through the Defence Committee (Supply) and his individual advisers, official and unofficial, were doing all that was necessary.[1]

It is outside the scope of a book on Grand Strategy to attempt to describe the methods by which munitions were procured. That story has been told in broad outline by Professor Postan, to whose account the present volume is deeply indebted. This book is concerned, however, with the major decisions of the Government and their advisers when faced with the problems of what munitions were required, and in what priority, and how they should be allocated when ready for use.

As Professor Postan shows, in the period between the Dunkirk evacuation and the entry of America into the war, in which 'both its ambitions and its performances rose to a height which only a few months previously had appeared impossible', the British war industry was called upon for a dual effort; it had at the same time to implement 'the immense long-term programmes of rearmament' and 'to meet a succession of immediate demands from the front lines of battle'.[2]

Even before the Germans opened up the war in the West, the Chiefs of Staff, expecting an early full-scale attack on the United Kingdom, had made it their first recommendation to the Chamberlain War Cabinet that every possible step should be taken to hasten the production of anti-aircraft equipment, particularly Bofors guns, bomber and fighter aircraft, and fully trained crews, even at the temporary expense of our long-term programmes. The report received general approval from the Cabinet. The events of the next few weeks made this policy even more urgent, and the Materials and Production Priority Committee, after the change of Government, worked on the principle that precedence should be given to armament and equipment capable of being used against the enemy in the next three months.[3]

The Chief of the Air Staff came to feel misgivings that this policy might be pressed too far; that in concentration on immediate needs

---

[1] See M. M. Postan, *British War Production* (H.M.S.O. 1952) especially ch. iv, 'From Dunkirk to Pearl Harbour'.

[2] *ibid.* p. 115.

[3] This committee of the Production Council was an amalgamation of the Materials and Production Sub-Committees of the former Ministerial Priority Committee.

we might mortgage the future and endanger our prospect of winning the war. He was also anxious that the programmes of the three Services should be 'kept in phase', to mature at the same target date. It was possible that if the enemy could be held till the end of October he might be unable to last out another winter—the influence of the optimistic economic forecasts of this period is observable—and the three months of our immediate concentration should therefore be extended to five. But this happy result could not be counted on and a later target date should be fixed for our maximum effort. Our industry had hitherto been working to a three-year war, but September 1942 was 'manifestly too far ahead'. The Air Marshal suggested therefore that the target date for all three Services should be June 1941. This would mean that if the war went on into 1942 our production would be inferior in quantity and quality to what it would be under the present plan; but we could not eat our cake and have it.

The Chiefs of Staff, after discussion, were not in favour of immediately extending the three months emergency period so recently announced, but otherwise they accepted the Air Marshal's views and so reported on June 4. The Prime Minister on the other hand approved the five months extension, but could see no reason whatever for altering the existing scheme for a three years' war. The Chiefs of Staff appear to have expected that the quickening tempo of the war would lead to a decision before the end of 1941.

In the most pressing matter of all, the speeding up of the turn-out of operational aircraft, the vital decisions had already been taken. On May 15 representatives of the new Ministry and of the Air Staff agreed that at least until the end of September all efforts should be concentrated on the production of two fighter and three bomber types, with special emphasis on the former. Lord Beaverbrook immediately applied his 'ruthless energy' to the task, using what Professor Postan has called methods of 'direct action'. On May 31 the Production Council 'both legalised and also broadened Lord Beaverbrook's overriding priorities'. Firms were instructed to give first priority (1A) to fighter or bomber aircraft, to instruments or equipment for such aircraft, to anti-aircraft equipment, especially Bofors guns, to small arms and small arms ammunition and to bombs. Anti-tank weapons, tanks, machine-guns and corresponding classes of ammunition were given priority 1B. Two weeks later a revised Priority of Production directive included trainer aircraft among the items to receive priority 1A and field artillery among those to be accorded priority 1B.[1]

Soon afterwards Lord Beaverbrook presented a detailed programme showing the numbers of the various types of aircraft he hoped

---

[1] See Postan p. 116.

to turn out, month by month, by June 1941; he explained that the shortage of certain raw materials, such as aluminium, was a limiting factor. While welcoming this 'splendid programme', the Air Ministry criticised as inadequate, in view of the need for a balanced force, the provision of trainer and bomber aircraft. They were perturbed by the proposal to produce in the Air Force in the United Kingdom by August 1941 a first-line strength of only about 1,000 bombers as against 2,000 fighters.

This and other points were discussed by the Defence Committee (Supply) on July 8, after which the Ministry of Aircraft Production revised their estimate to show a closer balance of fighters and bombers. The Committee had agreed that 'everything possible should be done to increase the production of bombers, and particularly of modern heavy bombers, so as to build up a large striking force'. As the Prime Minister put it, 'in the fierce light of the present emergency the fighter is the need, and the output of fighters must be the prime consideration till we have broken the enemy's attack'; but the only way to win the war was by an overwhelming bombing offensive.[1] Bombers were in fact also wanted for a more immediate task, to break up the forces soon to gather for the invasion of Great Britain, and their existing strength was far from impressive. After the recall of the Advanced Air Striking Force from France the five first-line Groups of Bomber Command were returned as numbering, as an average for the month of July, 491 aircraft 'serviceable' but only 376 'available with crews'.

In the matter of fighters the new campaign, as the event proved, was immediately effective. 'Output of the favoured types soon responded to this preferential treatment and to the Minister's revivalist influence. The delivery of new fighters rose from 256 in April to 467 in September—more than enough to cover the losses— and Fighter Command emerged from the Battle in the autumn with more aircraft than it had possessed at the beginning. The most spectacular, as well as the most important, single incident in the history of war production was thus crowned with success.'[2]

These outstanding results were not secured without friction and acrimonious wranglings between the Air Ministry and the Ministry of Aircraft Production. Each bitterly resented the claims and methods of the other. The flood of Lord Beaverbrook's forceful, personal onset foamed against what he considered the obstruction of the Civil Service and the Air Marshals, and the Prime Minister was not infrequently called in to mediate.

More serious for the future was the effect on later deliveries of the

---

[1] Churchill II 567.
[2] See Postan p. 116.

S

decision to concentrate all effort on the needs of the moment. 'The success of the mid-1940 spurt', writes Professor Postan, 'had not been bought without disturbing for a while the normal flow of aircraft production. Stocks of materials and components and reserves of production capacity were drawn upon for immediate use, and the whole cycle of production was brought forward in a manner which sacrificed future prospects to current output. The sacrifice was well understood and willingly made.'[1]

It was in the shortage of pilots rather than aircraft, as the next chapter will show, that the strain on Fighter Command in the next few months came nearest breaking-point. On July 1 the Secretary of State for Air informed the Cabinet of the steps already taken to increase the store of pilots in the immediate emergency and for the future. With a view to meeting the needs of the current summer, training courses had been shortened, the capacity of training units increased, pilots borrowed from the Navy and non-operational establishments and units combed. A Polish bomber squadron had been formed and arrangements were in hand for training pilots of other Allied nations. For the future, in view of increasing output of aircraft and of the fact that the course of the war had made the United Kingdom less and less suitable for training, more and more reliance must be placed on facilities overseas.

A second report followed a month later. The steps to accelerate the output of pilots mentioned in the previous report were being taken and improved upon: Allied crews were being trained, and it was proposed to establish new flying training schools overseas and to transfer existing schools from the United Kingdom to the Dominions. The report explained what an expansion of first-line strength meant in terms of instructors and equipment, and how long in advance the necessary arrangements must be made; for every 100 aircraft added to squadrons, 40 trainer aircraft were required six months beforehand.

This report was thoroughly discussed at meetings of the Defence Committee, with the object of expediting by every possible means the output of pilots for the first-line squadrons. The proposal of the Air Ministry to transfer schools from Great Britain overseas led to sharp conflict of opinion, and was eventually referred to the Cabinet. They decided not to send out of the country at the present time resources which might be needed to stem the enemy's attack but to postpone decision for three months; a number of practical measures were approved for easing in the meantime the very real difficulties and dangers of flying training in the United Kingdom under present conditions.

The Army also had both its immediate or emergency requirements

---

[1] See Postan p. 123.

and those of its long-term programme. It was necessary in the first place to arm and equip a sufficient force to defend the country against invasion. Professor Postan estimates that 'the whole of the army equipment available at home on the morrow of Dunkirk was barely sufficient to equip two divisions'.[1] Moreover, the emergency demanded not merely the rearming of the Field Force but the equipment of a large and miscellaneous home defence army to meet invasion. Here the munitions sent from America in July came in very useful as a stop-gap.

The long-term programme was that sanctioned by the Cabinet in February:[2] the objective was to remain an army of 55 divisions, but no date was mentioned for its attainment. In the meantime plans were made, in accordance with what the Ministry of Supply found possible, for the equipment by September 1941 of a force which came to be defined as 36 divisions. The probable employment of the Army had greatly changed when the new Government considered its requirements on June 19. There was no near prospect of our being able to send a large force to the Continent and it was doubtful if we should ever want to employ abroad an army of such proportions as it had been intended to send to fight alongside the French. On the other hand, we should want a well-trained and equipped army to resist invasion, and Italy's recent declaration of belligerency would involve operations in the Middle East. As to the nature of the equipment, the experience of France confirmed that of Poland, that our need of tanks, anti-tank guns and anti-aircraft artillery was pre-eminent.

The Defence Committee (Supply) had before them a memorandum jointly sponsored by the War Office and the Ministry of Supply; it suggested, as a basis for delivery by June 1941, the requirements of 36 divisions, supplemented by the replacement of 'recent capital losses' as soon as possible, by the satisfaction of the special requirements of Home Defence, and by the need to produce as many heavy tanks as possible. The memorandum mentioned no ultimate objective; this could be discussed later. The Committee agreed with the proposals of the Departments, but laid down that these should be regarded as being 'within the framework of a 55 division objective, which should be reached as soon as possible after Z + 21', viz. the end of May 1941. The immediate task was to expedite delivery during the next five months of everything required to make good deficiencies in essential items of equipment. Large supplementary orders should be placed in North America to insure against interruption of output in this country through enemy action.

---

[1] *op. cit.* p. 117.
[2] See chapter ii, p. 33.

This was the Government's answer to the Chiefs of Staff's recommendations of June 4.[1] The Prime Minister accepted the date of June 1941 as a suitable target date, but was not prepared to abandon the objective of a 55-division army. The two Departments agreed, in fact, after the meeting, to aim at having the equipment and maintenance of the 55 divisions provided by $Z + 27$ months, viz. the end of November 1941. The 55 divisions, as Professor Postan puts it, now became 'the firm basis of all planning', whereas previously it had been only a vague aspiration.[2]

The Defence Committee (Supply) had already, since their first meeting on June 6, devoted attention to increasing the production of specific army weapons and the ammunition for them. As the summer went on, particular attention was paid to tank production.[3] On June 10 we had only 103 cruiser and 114 infantry tanks in the United Kingdom, of which the heaviest (Mark II) weighed 24 tons and were armed with 2-pounder guns. Much interest was taken in the production of a new heavy tank, A.22 (known afterwards as 'Churchill'), of which type 500 were desired by the end of March 1941. It was pointed out that production suffered from the fact that tanks did not receive 1A priority, but the Cabinet, in view of the predominant needs of air defence, declined to accord to tanks equal precedence;[4] certain other items, however, hitherto enjoying the highest priority, were degraded to Priority 2.

It had been recognised that the success of the German tanks in France had been due to their concentration in armoured formations, and the Prime Minister's thoughts were running in this direction. He considered that our new tank programme should be sufficient to equip seven armoured divisions by the summer of 1941. The army programme as roughly forecast to the Cabinet on August 1 was not so ambitious, nor so specific. Of the eventual 55 divisions, 44 were noted as 'existing'; they comprised 34 from the United Kingdom including three armoured and one cavalry; about five from the Dominions (two Canadian, two Australian, one New Zealand and a brigade from South Africa); three from India, one from the African colonies, and the equivalent of one from the Allied nations. The remaining eleven were 'in sight'; one (armoured) from the United Kingdom, one from Canada, one from Australia, six from India and two from East and West Africa.[5]

---

[1] See p. 252 above.

[2] *op. cit.* p. 128.

[3] *ibid.* pp. 183 ff.

[4] See p. 252 above.

[5] A satisfactory computation of the formations existing at a given date during a period of expansion is difficult. Of the United Kingdom infantry divisions three were in fact organised as (ten) brigade groups; the formation of the third Canadian division had been announced in May, and a fourth was 'in sight'; the third (8th) Australian division had been formed by August 1, and a fourth (9th) was 'in sight'.

The occasion for this statement was a recommendation from the Chiefs of Staff that the Government of India should be asked to prepare for overseas service the equivalent of three divisions by May 1941 and three more by the end of 1941. The limiting factor in India, as at this period of the war in the United Kingdom, was not manpower but equipment; it was accepted moreover in London that the despatch of forces from India must not be allowed to prejudice defence of the North-West frontier or internal security.

Remembering the splendid and prompt contribution made by India to the Allied forces in the earlier war, the Prime Minister fumed at what he considered our failure hitherto to draw on her resources, alike in British and in Indian units, in large enough quantities or with sufficient speed. Comparison of the total number of divisions which we had put in the field by the end of the first year of the 1914 war—47 divisions of 13 battalions each—with our present figures led him to write in private of 'a feeble and weary departmentalism'. But Mr. Churchill knew well enough that any comparison must allow for greatly altered circumstances. If on the one hand the United Kingdom now contained six million more men and women of ages ranging from 18 to 65, on the other hand the Royal Air Force and Air Defence of Great Britain now made demands which either did not exist or were infinitely less twenty-five years before, while Army formations now comprised a far larger amount of technical and non-divisional troops.

The needs of the Navy have been left till last because the French collapse led to no such dramatic spurt or diversion in naval construction as in the case of the other Services. 'In a sense,' Professor Postan has written, 'the entire war-time programme of the Navy in the first year of war was made up of urgent short-term requirements.' One naval emergency-need and its satisfaction by means other than new construction have already been referred to: the acquisition of the fifty American over-age destroyers for the escort of Atlantic convoys. At home naval needs received only a low degree of priority; 'a proportion of the existing capacity for armour plate reserved for the Admiralty was diverted to supply the Army tank programme'.[1] Apart from this, naval construction suffered from the competing claims of merchant shipbuilding, the conversion of ships to naval use, and the mounting need of repairs. As early as May 27 the Admiralty decided on a drastic reshaping of its building programme: work was being held up on ships whose completion was a long-term affair, in order to concentrate on the production of smaller craft and on repair work.

The question of manpower, too, was becoming serious, though as

---

[1] Postan pp. 115, 65; see generally his pp. 59–66 and his table on p. 470.

yet mainly in respect of skilled craftsmen. There was no question of the Services being starved. Mr. Ernest Bevin, the Minister of Labour and National Service, assured the Cabinet on July 4 that his Department had consistently been in the position to meet all requirements made upon it by the armed forces for new recruits. Not only had many more men expressed a preference for the Navy and Air Force than those Services could absorb, but the number of men available for the Army was now ahead of what it could take. What was required was more skilled workmen for industry—it was on the numbers of skilled men available that opportunities for the employment of women largely depended—and forty training centres had been authorised.

Figures were produced giving the total male population, from 20 to 41 years, as 7·35 millions, of whom 3⅔ millions were in reserved occupations, including the Mercantile Marine, and over 700,000 were unfit. This left slightly under 3 millions available for the armed forces: 1·43 millions were in the Army, 173,000 in the Navy, 243,000 in the Royal Air Force, 100,000 in the Air Raid Precautions and Fire Services, while 200,000 had been allowed to defer service—a total of 2·146 millions, leaving a balance of about 800,000.

The war, as it was now developing, called for troops, as well as weapons, different from those who had proved victorious in the war of 1914–18. The War Office plans at the time of the French armistice included the ultimate formation of fifty special companies of 'storm troops' drawn from all units of the Army. These 'Leopards', as he characteristically called them, Mr. Churchill envisaged as 'ready to spring at the throat of any small landings or descents' on the coasts of the British Isles; we had always in the past, he said, set our faces against the idea of such special troops, but the Germans certainly gained in the last war by adopting it, and this time it had been a leading cause of their victory.[1] The War Office had already started to raise ten 'Independent Companies', and half of them had been employed in Norway. Mr. Churchill's instinct for the offensive and daemonic energy were now to expand this experiment with remarkable results.

Towards the end of the evacuation from Dunkirk he urged on the Chiefs of Staff through General Ismay the importance of not allowing 'the completely defensive habit of mind . . . to ruin all our initiative.' We ought to organise raiding forces and keep the Germans guessing at what points along the hundreds of miles of coast under their control we should strike them next. Plans should be made for transporting and landing tanks and for the raising of 5,000 parachute troops.

[1] See Churchill II 147.

Experience in Norway was suggesting similar ideas in the War Office, and on June 11 the Chiefs of Staff proposed to the Prime Minister the appointment of a Commander, Offensive Operations, with a small inter-Service staff, 'to prepare, as a matter of urgency, plans which he should subsequently execute'. This was the origin of Combined Operations.[1] Lieutenant-General A. G. B. Bourne, Royal Marines, was accordingly appointed, and his directive was approved.

General Bourne was to have a dual function. As 'Commander of Raiding Operations' his duty would be 'to harass the enemy and cause him to disperse his forces, and to create material damage', especially on his western coast-line. He would have under him the War Office's six Independent Companies and 'the irregular commandos now being raised', and in addition a proportion of the parachutist volunteers in prospect. Certain raids by the Independent Companies had already been planned, and he should assume control of any of these he thought proper. As the Chiefs of Staff's adviser on Combined Operations, he would take over command of the Inter-Service Training and Development Centres and advise on the organisation required for opposed landings; three brigade groups were to be specially trained for Combined Operations, which were evidently envisaged as more ambitious affairs than 'purely raiding operations'. General Bourne was also to press on with the development and production of special landing craft.

The first Inter-Service Training and Development Centre had been started in 1938 near Portsmouth with Captain L. E. H. Maund, R.N., as Commandant; it had studied the subject of combined operations in all its aspects including parachute descents and the use of amphibious tanks, and had obtained authorisation for the construction of a few landing-craft to convey small parties of infantry and vehicles; vessels of the Glen Line were considered suitable for adaptation as Infantry Assault Ships. On the outbreak of war the Centre had been disbanded, but it was revived after a few months.

On June 20 the Chiefs of Staff gave general approval to Bourne's scheme for the organisation and equipment of the Directorate of Combined Operations, as it was now renamed. Among his naval requirements he asked for four ships to serve as landing-craft carriers and depot ships, for a total (including vessels already ordered) of some 200 landing-craft, and 100 motor boats. On the Army side he envisaged ten Independent Companies, including several composed of Allied troops, each of about 200 men, and ten Commandos of 500 men each. On the Air side a parachute training centre was to be formed at once, and enough Whitley bombers adapted to carry 720 fully armed men and 60,000 lb. of stores.

---

[1] See Churchill II 214, 217; also Dudley Clarke, *Seven Assignments* (1948) pp. 205 ff.

General Bourne explained that there were three main types of offensive operations in view: small raids intended to compel the enemy to disperse his resources and maintain defence along his entire coastline; demolition raids, which would normally be carried out by somewhat larger forces; and operations to seize and secure points of importance to ourselves. For operations other than raids proposals would be received from the Joint Planning and Inter-Service Planning Staffs, who would have submitted drafts of directives to the Chiefs of Staff for approval.

Only two actual raids were carried out during the summer, at Le Touquet in June and in Guernsey in July. They were small affairs, described slightingly by the Prime Minister as pinpricks, and they were not successful except in gaining experience. For operations of a larger type, a brigade of Royal Marines was already formed and in training for the seizure of the Azores and Cape Verde Islands, if Spain should join in the war against us.

A month later the Chiefs of Staff were informed that General Bourne had been succeeded as Director of Combined Operations by Admiral of the Fleet Sir Roger Keyes. No reflection on the previous Director was meant, but the Prime Minister felt that it was essential to have an officer of higher rank in charge, owing to the larger scope now to be given to these operations. On August 6 Keyes reported that arrangements had been made for training regular formations in combined operations at Inveraray; four of the ten Independent Companies were now trained, and twelve Commandos had been raised. Five hundred specially selected volunteers were being trained as parachute troops. Three fast 10,000-ton ships were being adapted for the launching of landing-craft. But no further operations took place in 1940, and in September all Independent Companies and Commandos were placed at the disposal of Home Forces for resistance to an invasion.

On 3 July General Bourne, while still Director of Combined Operations, represented to the Chiefs of Staff that there existed a good deal of overlapping, with the risk of confusion in execution, between the activities of a number of Government Departments and agencies all concerned with 'the one aim of undermining the enemy'; he suggested that they should be co-ordinated under a single Cabinet Minister. The need for some co-ordination had been under discussion in various interested circles for some weeks; this was natural in view of the importance attached by the Chiefs of Staff in their report of May 25 to subversive action, with the purpose of stimulating the seeds of revolt within the conquered countries. As the result of a fruitful meeting held on July 1, with the Foreign Secretary in the Chair and with several Ministers present, the Prime Minister invited Mr. Hugh Dalton, head of the Ministry of Economic Warfare, to preside over a new organisation formed to co-ordinate all action, by way of subversion and sabotage, against the enemy overseas. It was to be known as the Special Operations Executive. Mr. Dalton's position was to be analogous to that of Lord Swinton, who had been appointed at the end of May to co-ordinate Home Defence 'security' measures; the member of the Cabinet to whom both these Ministers would if necessary refer matters of doubt or dispute was to be Mr. Chamberlain. The Cabinet on July 22 approved the constitution of the new body and its proposed activities.

The planning and direction of raids by formed bodies of British or Allied ships, troops or aircraft would remain the function of the military authorities, but Mr. Dalton would maintain touch with Departments planning such raids. In order that the general plan for irregular offensive operations should be in step with the general strategical conduct of the war, he was to consult the Chiefs of Staff as necessary, keeping them informed of his plans and, in turn, receiving from them the broad strategic picture. Accordingly on August 21 the Vice-Chiefs of Staff discussed with Mr. Dalton the manner of their co-operation. There was general agreement that his organisation should be responsible for offensive subversive activities which did not involve the use of officers or men wearing uniform.

As the new Executive was closely connected on the one side with regular military activities, so it was on the other with political. The weapons of politics are negotiation and propaganda, and in the latter field there were already several competitors—the Ministry of Information, the British Broadcasting Corporation, and the mysterious body controlled by Sir Campbell Stuart and known as Electra House.[1] The functions of this last, in so far as they were concerned with clandestine propaganda to foreign countries, were now taken over by Mr. Dalton to form a separate branch of the Special Operations Executive.

Thus during the weeks between the Dunkirk evacuation and the Battle of Britain there were born a cluster of organisations destined to win renown hereafter: the Home Guard, formerly Local Defence Volunteers, had been formed already and more will be said of them in the next chapter; but we have remarked here the first beginnings of Combined Operations, the Commandos, the parachute regiment, the airborne divisions, the Special Operations and the Political Warfare Executives. These were all notable points in the development of the British war-machine.

The disasters in Europe had the result of intensifying the effort of the other nations of the British Commonwealth likewise.

---

[1] See p. 19 above.

The 1st Canadian Division had been in England since the end of 1939 and had begun to cross to Brittany when the French resistance collapsed. On 10 May 1940 the Government at Ottawa decided to hasten the movement of the 2nd Canadian Division to Great Britain, and a few days afterwards the formation of a third division was announced and the rifle battalions of a fourth were mobilised.[1] For some months a Canadian infantry brigade provided the garrison for Iceland.

Instalments of Australian and New Zealand troops had arrived in the Near East in February, and early in March the Commonwealth Government decided to raise a second division (7th Australian) for overseas. The bad news in May caused a review of their whole programme, and on the 22nd Mr. Menzies, the Prime Minister, announced that, among other important measures, a third division would be raised for service abroad.[2]

Complaints were expressed from time to time by the Dominion Governments that they were not kept sufficiently informed of the views of the high command in the United Kingdom as to how the military situation was likely to develop. This defect was due partly to distance, partly to the pressure of events in Europe, partly to the need for extreme secrecy. It had been customary ever since the outbreak of the war to send to the Prime Ministers of Canada, Australia, New Zealand and South Africa, 'for their most secret and personal information', a daily telegram recording the progress of operations; since the German invasion of the Low Countries these telegrams had been sent twice daily. Copies had also been sent of the Chiefs of Staff's *Weekly Résumé* supplied for the Cabinet, but it had been thought necessary to send these by ocean mail, and they might well be stale when they arrived. Apart from such communications the Secretary of State for the Dominions met the High Commissioners daily. These expedients could not however present a complete picture of the strategic position as a whole nor, except within narrow limits, of how it might be expected to develop. Special appreciations by the Chiefs of Staff had indeed been sent in February and May, but it was unreasonable to expect them to be prepared very frequently, while with regard to future operations it was of course undesirable to extend in the least degree the risk to security.

As the best that could be done, the Cabinet agreed on June 5 that the Dominions Office should, with the approval of the Service Departments in important cases, communicate to the Prime Ministers, for their secret and personal information, the substance

---

[1] C. P. Stacey, *The Canadian Army 1939–1945* (Ottawa 1948) chs. i and ii.

[2] P. Hasluck, *The Government and the People 1939–1941* (Canberra 1952) 167 ff., 213 ff.

of Cabinet papers of special interest relating to the military aspects of the war. Mr. Churchill may have had this discussion in mind when he reported to the four Prime Ministers on his return from Tours on the night of June 14, and again on the 16th gave them a cheering review of the situation as he saw it.[1] With General Smuts he was on particularly intimate terms, greatly respecting the judgement of his 'old and valiant friend'.

Something should also be said about the contributions of the Allies. Although so many famous countries of Europe had been over-run and subjugated by German aggression, the Governments of most of them had found their way to London and were playing their part in the prosecution of the war. The Norwegians and Dutch con-tributed their fine merchant navies; the colonial possessions of the Netherlands and Belgium, as well as those French colonies which had adhered to General de Gaulle, were of great economic importance; the Poles, long accustomed to nurse their ardent patriotism in exile, had given a signal proof of their gallantry and skill in the escape of their warships from the Baltic in September 1939; the Czech National Committee, evacuated from France in June 1940 in British ships, like the Polish and Belgian Governments, were at length recognised by Downing Street in July as the provisional Government of their country.

The Prime Minister was most anxious to make full use of the man-power of the Allies, both for its value in arms and as an advertisement of the fact that Britain was fighting not only for herself but to restore the freedom of Europe. In June he was thinking of a foreign legion; we were also, he said, to have in this country a Polish division, and Dutch, Belgian, and Norwegian brigades. It was 'the settled policy of His Majesty's Government', he wrote later, 'to make good strong French contingents for land, sea, and air service, to encourage these men to volunteer to fight on with us or with de Gaulle, to look after them well, to indulge their sentiments about the French flag . . . The same principle also applies to Polish, Dutch, Czech, Norwegian and Belgian contingents in this country, as well as to the Foreign Legion of anti-Nazi Germans.'[2] A weekly report to the Cabinet on the pro-gress and conditions of foreign contingents was demanded, and inter-departmental committees were set up to keep their affairs under review.[3] The project of a foreign legion never took shape, but many foreigners, including anti-Nazi Germans, served in the Auxiliary Military Pioneer Corps.[4]

---

[1] Churchill II 172.

[2] Printed with slight verbal differences in Churchill II 569.

[3] The Committee on Foreign (Allied) Resistance (C.F.R.), formerly the Committee on French Resistance; and the Allied forces (official) Sub-Committee (A.F.O.).

[4] See *House of Commons Debates* vol. 363, col. 583.

The position of Frenchmen abroad was peculiar, in that rival authorities claimed their allegiance. The British policy was to help all those wishing to join General de Gaulle, wherever they might be, but to allow no coercion; French troops in British territory who did not wish to fight were to be repatriated without their equipment. There were other Frenchmen who preferred to join the British forces. At the beginning of August the Cabinet approved General de Gaulle's proposal to form a Council of Defence, composed of representatives of French overseas territories which decided to adhere to him, and they also approved the draft of an agreement on the constitution of the Free French Forces. Briefly, this permitted de Gaulle to recruit, and provide a civil administration for, a volunteer French force of all arms to be used against the common enemies; it would be under the general direction of the British high command, de Gaulle undertaking when necessary to delegate immediate command to British officers of appropriate rank, but it would never be required to take up arms against France. In a covering letter the Prime Minister declared that it was the determination of the British Government, when victory had been gained, to secure the full restoration of the independence and greatness of France. In another, unpublished, letter the Prime Minister explained that this latter expression could have no precise relation to frontiers, which we were unable to guarantee, and that the stipulation about not taking up arms against France would not apply to Vichyite France. At the end of August, the Free French land forces in the United Kingdom numbered about 4,500 men, while about 1,500 had joined the Free French Navy under Admiral Muselier.

Agreements were negotiated from time to time with the exiled Governments of the other Allied nations with regard to the principles controlling the co-operation of their armed forces. The common formula was that these should be employed under British command 'in its character as the Allied High Command'; in the case of Norway it was stipulated that the Norwegian armed forces in Great Britain should be used either for the defence of the United Kingdom or for the liberation of their own country.[1]

Not to mention the important part played by all the Dutch Services in the Far East, the Polish, Norwegian, Dutch and Belgian navies all gave assistance in European waters; Poland, Czechoslovakia, the Netherlands, Norway and Belgium all contributed air units—the Polish contingent amounting by June 1941 to eight fighter and four bomber squadrons. On land, Polish troops fought at Narvik

---

[1] The Governments with which agreements were signed in the period covered by this volume were those of Czechoslovakia, Poland and Norway; agreements with Greece, the Netherlands and Belgium followed in 1942.

and in the Middle East, and all the nations mentioned had troops training in the United Kingdom.

It is time to turn to the enemy. The Germans likewise were reorganising and rearming their forces during June and July, but on very different lines from the British. The inconsequence in the German plans reflected the fluid nature of Hitler's grand strategy in the weeks following the French armistice. The main work of the land forces—the defeat of the French and British armies on the Continent —had been accomplished. Hitler hoped, and it seemed possible, that the war might now come to an end with Britain's acceptance of the moderate terms, as he regarded them, which he was prepared to offer her: she must return the German colonies and acquiesce in Germany's hegemony on the Continent, but she would not be further weakened or humiliated. These hopes Hitler seems to have cherished, with declining assurance, until July 19, when he rendered account of his victories to the Reichstag.

But even if the war had to continue, there was no call for land forces on the scale of May 1940, and the Army was not the only claimant for Germany's resources. Admiral Raeder was complaining of the delay in building submarines and pressing for the release of material to carry out the 'modified' programme, sanctioned in December 1939, of a total of 372 U-boats by the end of 1941. His appeal no longer fell on deaf ears. Even before the battle of France was won, Hitler with well-judged confidence had assured him, on June 4, that he intended to reduce the size of the Army after the defeat of France; the needs of the Navy and the Air Force would then come first, since the further prosecution of the war would be mainly the concern of these two Services.[1] There were further the claims of German industry as a whole, which was crying out for skilled men, and also of agriculture. A decrease in the numerical strength of the field army would achieve the twofold object of reducing its demand on the armaments industry and of releasing men for a new armaments programme. It must have been evident too to Hitler that only limited forces would be required, and indeed could be transported, should he finally decide on the invasion of Great Britain, a plan which he was now turning over in his mind. Until he knew whether the war against Britain could be brought to an early conclusion, he was not likely to consider military intervention in any part of the Continent such as Gibraltar or the Balkans.

On June 14, the day the Germans entered Paris, *OKW* ordered that the Army should be reduced from a total of 159 divisions to a

---

[1] *Führer Conferences on Naval Affairs* p. 109.

new level of 120. Thirty-nine infantry divisions were to be disbanded, but the mechanised forces would be increased to a total of thirty divisions—twenty *Panzer* and ten motorised. The Polish and French campaigns had proved the disproportionate value of such formations; these thirty mobile divisions would form the spearhead of the new army.

The Führer also had to reckon in these days of premature triumph with the possibility of an early demobilisation of the field army, to be succeeded by a smaller peacetime force, perhaps of 60–80 divisions, and this scheme influenced the proposed measures of immediate reorganisation. But the whole policy of reduction was reversed by Hitler's decision, announced to a small circle at the end of July, to attack Russia; in view of his new designs the strength of the Army, so far from being diminished, was to be increased to 180 divisions, of which 36 were to be armoured or motorised. At the same time Hitler cancelled all restrictions on materials for the construction of U-boats; he had already on July 10 ordered immediate measures for completing the modified programme of December 1939.

Meanwhile plans for an invasion of England had been conceived and given shape. On August 1 Hitler issued a directive beginning with the words: 'In order to establish conditions favourable to the final conquest of Britain, I intend to continue the air and naval war against the British homeland more intensively than heretofore'.[1]

---

[1] *Führer Directive* No. 17.

CHAPTER XII

THE DEFENCE OF THE ISLAND

(i)

Preparations

THE INHABITANTS of the United Kingdom passed through periods of extreme peril in 1941 and 1942 before the Battle of the Atlantic was won, when U-boats in increasing numbers were raising the total of ships sunk to an alarming degree. But the danger of defeat was never so imminent as in the summer of 1940. Certainly to the people who lived through those years the time of greatest tension was the four critical months between the Dunkirk evacuation and the uncertain weather of October, just as it was the 'blitz' of the winter of 1940–41 which brought the war nearest to them.

On the day before the Germans launched their attack against the Low Countries the Chamberlain Cabinet discussed a review of the strategical situation by the Chiefs of Staff.[1] It was based on the assumption that Germany had resolved to seek a decision in 1940. Her most likely course, said the report, would be to launch a major offensive against Britain, and the main threat to the United Kingdom was an intensive air offensive which, if successful, might culminate in an attempt at actual invasion. An enemy occupation of the Low Countries would seriously aggravate this menace. The Chiefs of Staff recommended that the plans already prepared for dealing with invasion of this country should be reviewed forthwith and requirements met, and that active steps should be taken to educate public opinion to the reality of the air threat and to develop to the highest pitch of efficiency our measures of passive defence. Henceforward the invasion of Great Britain was a constant item on the Cabinet agenda; the belief in the imminence of an attempt to invade was only temporarily interrupted by events on the Continent, which in their turn suggested the new methods which German ingenuity might devise. Parachute landings, aircraft alighting in open spaces, raids by motor-boats, amphibious tanks, Fifth Column activities, all received attention.

On May 29, while the successs of the evacuation of the British

---

[1] See above, p. 173.

Expeditionary Force was still doubtful and there were but few trained soldiers in the country, the Chiefs of Staff warned the Cabinet that in their view it was highly probable that Germany was now setting the stage for delivering a full-scale attack on England. The late Commander-in-Chief, Home Forces, General Sir Walter Kirke, had asked them to inform him when they considered that an attack was imminent; they thought that his successor, General Ironside, should be so informed now. They were not satisfied, from the military point of view, that in face of this danger the country as a whole had been sufficiently warned, or adequately organised, 'to meet the threat on which the fate of our land and Empire may depend'. They therefore recommended that the country should be warned and roused to face the danger, and that the Army at home should be brought to a high degree of alertness, particularly at night. The Cabinet took note that the necessary measures were being set in train. The Chiefs of Staff's apprehension at this time seems to have been based on general probability rather than specific evidence; as the weeks wore on, the term 'imminent' was found too elastic and distinctions had to be drawn between the various grades of imminence to which current information pointed.

Prospects of an immediate invasion receded when the British divisions returned from Dunkirk and the German armies redeployed for the Battle of France; but a fortnight later, with the French suing for an armistice, the Cabinet expected that the enemy would attempt an invasion, whether on a larger or a smaller scale, within the next few weeks. Again no specific evidence was quoted. On July 3 the Defence Committee were told that in the view of the Joint Intelligence Committee there were grounds for supposing that invasion was imminent. On being pressed for their evidence the Intelligence staffs could only say that they thought large-scale raids, involving all three arms, might be made on the British Isles any day, but that a full-scale invasion was unlikely before the middle of July. They had strong indications that behind the Dutch and French coasts the German Air Force was being reorganised and regrouped and that the process was nearly complete; most units, however, would not have finished their refitting for about a fortnight.

At the end of May the Director of Naval Intelligence had called the attention of the Committee to the need of strengthening our intelligence system, which was not devised to meet so wide-reaching a threat as was now presented by the German occupation of the whole coastline from Norway to the Pyrenees. The Committee urged the need of extensive and regular visual and photographic air reconnaissance and recommended that a special inter-Service staff should be formed to collate and evaluate all information bearing on the possibility of an invasion. A Combined Intelligence Committee of junior officers was accordingly set up in the Admiralty and proceeded to issue daily reports. Nevertheless it was difficult to discover what was afoot in the ports and on the coasts of the North Sea and, still more, of the Baltic. Some of the usual sources of intelligence were lacking, and weather over the North Sea was not propitious to continuous observation.

The British high command, as we now know, gave the enemy credit for being much more far-sighted and advanced in his preparations than was in fact the case. The error was a natural one. In view of the careful planning which had paved the way for Germany's previous campaigns, how could it be supposed that *OKW* had not in its pigeonholes some masterpiece of staffwork providing in minutest detail for the successive stages of an invasion of England? Yet until months afterwards no such plan existed.

The destruction of the British Empire had never in itself been one of Hitler's objectives. Indeed he regarded this institution with mixed feelings. It had, of course, borne its part in the outrage of Versailles; it had ravished, and still held, some of Germany's colonies: it was deeply tainted with liberalism, democracy and pacificism. On the other hand it was a creation of Nordic genius and enterprise; in the late war it had proved that it still possessed the martial virtues; it showed little sympathy for Bolshevism; and, its main interests lying outside the Continent of Europe, there seemed no reason why its policy and that of the Third Reich should collide. One can only guess what grandiose schemes of world-domination would have emerged in time from the megalomaniac's mind; but at any rate until June 1940 he would have been glad to come to an agreement with Britain based on a recognition of their respective spheres of interest.[1] Asssuming, however, that Britain forced a war on Germany Hitler had long before thought out the method of winning it and in May 1939 had explained his ideas to his subordinates.[2] Germany would defeat England by cutting off her supplies: she would subject her to a blockade by sea and air which after the occupation of the Low Countries and the French coast could count on success. There was no hint of invasion. It was the same in October and in November,[3] and indeed there is no satisfactory evidence that the Führer ever contemplated invading England until May 1940.

On May 21, when the German armoured divisions were reaching the Channel coast, the naval records mention briefly a conversation

---

[1] For information used in this chapter with regard to German plans and preparations I am greatly indebted to an unpublished monograph by Mr. R. R. A. Wheatley.

[2] Above, p. 52.

[3] *Führer Directives* Nos. 6, 9, pp. 66, 73.

T

between Hitler and Admiral Raeder on the possibility of a landing in England; the results of the conversation are not stated. On June 14, however, a directive issued by General Keitel contained the statement that with the imminent collapse of France 'the task of the Army in this war will be essentially fulfilled . . . The Navy and the Luftwaffe must be reorganised so that after the defeat of France the war against England will be continued by sea and air.' And as late as June 17, according to the naval records, Colonel Warlimont, Deputy Chief of the *OKW* Operations Staff, informed his naval colleague that no preparatory work of any kind had been carried out in *OKW* with a view to an invasion, since the Führer had so far expressed no such intention, being fully aware of the unusual difficulties of an enterprise of this kind.

It seems clear also that at this time Hitler genuinely desired to bring the war in the West to an end and secure his winnings, and he continued to hope for such a result until the third week of July. Nevertheless he was beginning to think about the possibility of an invasion. He discussed it in private with Mussolini at Munich on June 18, and with Raeder two days later, when the naval conditions for success were explained to him: air superiority was essential.[1] At length on July 2 he issued his first instructions to the Services for preparations to be made for a contingent operation.[2] A landing in England, he said, was feasible, provided that air superiority could be attained and certain other conditions satisfied. But the plan had taken no sort of definite shape, and as few people as possible should be told of it. The Services were asked for information on certain points. Evidently a large-scale operation was in view.

It is of interest that, a few days before this, General Jodl, Chief of the *OKW* Operations Staff, Hitler's personal adviser on operational matters, had produced an appreciation of possible courses of action should the war continue. He relied for the defeat of Britain on air war directed at the destruction of the Royal Air Force and the air industry, supplemented by attacks on shipping. Only after air supremacy had been achieved and British will to resist broken should invasion be attempted. Its purpose would be not to inflict military defeat—that could be left to the Luftwaffe and Navy—but rather 'to finish off a country, economically paralysed and practically incapable of fighting in the air—if this is still necessary'. This 'finishing off' (*Todesstoss*) conception of an invasion is important.

The next fortnight was critical. The staffs worked in accordance with the Führer's directive. Reporting to him on July 11, Raeder stressed the naval difficulties. Invasion should only be considered as

---

[1] See *Hitler e Mussolini: Lettere e Documenti* (Milan 1946) p. 54; Halder's Diary July 13; *F.N.C.* p. 111.

[2] *F.D.* p. 105.

a last resort to force Britain to sue for peace; the correct strategy was blockade reinforced by air attacks. Hitler is recorded as agreeing that air superiority was necessary; he too viewed invasion as a last resort. But the strategists of *OKW* and *OKH* were now more optimistic: the operation would be only 'a river-crossing in force on a broad front', the part of the artillery being played by the Luftwaffe. Hitler's hopes of an early peace were waning, and on July 16 he issued his Directive No. 16: *Preparations for a landing operation against England.*[1] 'Since England,' he said, 'despite the hopelessness of her military situation, still shows no signs of a desire to come to terms, I have decided to prepare and, if necessary, to carry out a landing operation against her. The aim of this operation is to eliminate the English homeland as a base from which the war against Germany can be continued and, should it prove necessary, to occupy the country completely.' Preparations were to be completed by mid-August. The code name for the operation would be 'Sea Lion'.

Three days later, on July 19, Hitler in a speech to the Reichstag made his final appeal for peace.[2]

Here, for the present, we may leave the German preparations and return to the British counter-measures.

There had been no parallel since Napoleonic times to the predicament in which the people of the United Kingdom now found themselves; if our shores were no longer, as in the days of sail, at the mercy of a wind favouring the invader, there was now the new peril from the air, a peril whose effect on our swollen and congested population could not be foretold.[3]

No attempt will be made in this volume to describe at length the preparations for the defence of the country against air attack or invasion.[4] It is not easy, however, to draw an acceptable line between the central direction of the war and the domain of the theatre commander when the United Kingdom itself, including the capital of the Empire, formed the stage; when the battle headquarters of the Commander-in-Chief, Home Forces, were within a few feet of the Cabinet room; when civil and military administration were intimately linked; and when, it may be added, the Prime Minister was a man profoundly interested in every detail of the art of war and confident in his ability to supervise its conduct. It will be sufficient here to sketch the military organisation created to execute

---

[1] *F.D.* p. 107.
[2] *The Times* 20 July 1940.
[3] See Churchill II 248.
[4] See Basil Collier, *The Defence of the United Kingdom.*

the general policy of the Government, and the main features of the scheme of defence.

The policy had been set forth in unforgettable terms by the Prime Minister's speech of June 4: we should defend our island to the last and never surrender. Whatever apathy may have existed in the country before, from then onwards the mood of the whole people, with insignificant exceptions, was one of resolution. When Hitler launched his peace offensive in the Reichstag on July 19, the Cabinet took the view that there was nothing in it which called for answer or debate in Parliament. Public morale, it was said, was so good that no formal expression of it was necessary at the present time. The Foreign Secretary, however, replied in a broadcast on July 22: 'We shall not stop fighting till freedom, for ourselves and others, is secured.'[1]

On the side of organisation, machinery for co-operation between the civil and military powers was provided, under the supreme authority of the Cabinet, by the Ministry of Home Security; this Department was an emanation from the Home office, with which it shared, in Sir John Anderson, a single ministerial head. Co-operation was secured both at the centre and in the country at large.

At the centre, a start was made with the formation of the Home Defence Executive. In November 1939 the Chiefs of Staff had recommended certain precautionary measures to counter the possibility of an invasion, unlikely as such an attempt then appeared. Reviewing the situation early in May in consultation with Sir Hugh Elles, Chief of the Operational Staff of the Ministry of Home Security, they issued a directive for the purpose of ensuring that plans to meet sea-borne and air-borne attack on the United Kingdom were co-ordinated by the Commander-in-Chief, Home Forces, and the Regional Commissioners concerned. Their recommendations included the immediate setting up of a 'Home Defence Executive' under the chairmanship of the Commander-in-Chief. The members would be the Air Officers Commanding-in-Chief, Bomber, Fighter and Coastal Commands, and representatives of the Admiralty, Air Ministry and the operational staff of the Ministry of Home Security, as the Department concerned with Civil Defence. They would be jointly responsible to the Chiefs of Staff, while remaining individually responsible to their own Ministers, to whom they would apply for any additional authority required in furtherance of their common plans. The directive proceeded to enumerate various aspects of the problem—such as the security of communications, the preparation of demolition plans, the evacuation of the civil population, the combating of Fifth Column activities—which deserved the particular attention of the new body.

---

[1] *The Times* 23 July 1940.

Experience soon showed that the Executive required strengthening on the civil side, and the Cabinet on May 28 approved the addition to it of three civil servants, including one of particular distinction, Sir Findlater Stewart of the India Office, to represent the civil power as a whole. The Executive should now be able, said Mr. Chamberlain in proposing these modifications, to give directions for action on all matters which were the responsibility of civil Departments; but it should no longer be responsible to the Chiefs of Staff, though on military matters it would still receive direction from them. Matters requiring higher decision would be referred in the first place to the Secretary of State for War and the Minister of Home Security in consultation, and in the last resort to the Cabinet.

Mr. Chamberlain was of the opinion that a body so composed could deal quickly and efficiently, and without reference to any other authority, with most of the problems arising during the period of planning and preparation before an attack took place. The Chiefs of Staff, however, were not satisfied that it would be suitable for the conduct of active operations. The United Kingdom, said the Chief of the Air Staff in a paper addressed to his colleagues, must now be regarded as a fortress awaiting attack; 'the present system on which the war is fought by committees, conferences and conversations on the telephone is far too slow and cumbrous to meet a situation in which we shall be fighting for our lives against direct assault by an enemy whose strategy is marked by the utmost speed of decision and ruthlessness in action'. In his view it was essential to centralise authority yet further, and he drew the conclusion that 'one Super Commander-in-Chief must be appointed to command all forces, sea, land, air and civil defence, that are placed at his disposal by the Government, on the advice of the Chiefs of Staff'. This commander would have a small combined staff and a headquarters linked by direct line to the headquarters of all operational Commands in the country. The actual conduct of operations would be left to the Commanders-in-Chief concerned, but 'they would receive their directions from a single Super Commander who would be responsible direct to the Prime Minister. The latter would, of course, be advised as at present by the Chiefs of Staff, and the Super Commander would not take their place in any way . . . But he must have a special status, far higher than that of an ordinary Commander-in-Chief, since he will command not only all three Services, but also the civil defence forces.'

This novel and bold proposal, anticipating the institution, later in the war, of a Supreme Commander, was discussed by the Chiefs of Staff. The scheme which they put forward to the Cabinet, and which the Cabinet accepted, was less drastic. There was no suggestion of a Super Commander, but the Commander-in-Chief, Home Forces, would have beside him, along with his own Chief of General Staff, a Rear-Admiral, an Air Vice-Marshal, and Sir Findlater Stewart as chief Civil Staff Officer; this staff would keep him 'fully informed of the state and availability of the forces' and would convey his wishes to the commanders and departments concerned. He would occupy an Advanced Headquarters in the Cabinet War Room and would have direct access to the Prime Minister. In the meantime, until active operations began, the Home Defence Executive would continue as at present.

This organisation synchronised with the appointment of General Sir Edmund Ironside as Commander-in-Chief, Home Forces; it was a post more congenial to him than his table at the War Office, and he had as his Chief of General Staff Major-General B. C. T. Paget, who by his skilful withdrawal from Norway had added to his high reputation.

Such was the arrangement for unified control at the centre. In the country co-operation was secured through the institution of Regional Commissioners. These functionaries, who had no parallel in the British Isles but bore a certain resemblance to Prefects on the Continent, had been designated before the outbreak of war. They were selected from men of light and leading, not necessarily politicians or civil servants, to act in their respective Regions—the twelve areas into which the United Kingdom had been divided for the purpose—as the local representatives of the central Government. Responsible to the Minister of Home Security, they had on their staffs representatives of the various Departments in Whitehall and so provided in each area a single civil authority to which the local military commanders could refer. Should their own headquarters be cut off from Whitehall, they were empowered to decide and act, and in case of invasion would take their orders from the military authorities.

It was at this grim period at the end of May that the Cabinet approved the important staff paper, already referred to, envisaging the collapse of France.[1] On June 19 the Chiefs of Staff pointed out that the danger then foreseen now actually confronted us, and pressed that such of their recommendations as had not been carried out should at once be put into force. They were particularly concerned with what they regarded as the inadequate measures taken to control aliens and other potential Fifth Columnists and to cut out unnecessary imports.

The German occupation of the northern and Atlantic coasts of France drew special attention to the Channel Isles and to Ireland. Jersey lies less than twenty miles from the west coast of Normandy

---

[1] Above, p. 209.

and about ninety from Portland Bill; the islands had no coast defences and no anti-aircraft guns. The Chiefs of Staff reported on June 11 that they were then of no great strategic importance either to ourselves or to the enemy, and would be of none at all when the enemy reached the coast. The Cabinet at first decided to send two battalions to the islands for their defence against raids, but, when the Chiefs of Staff advised on June 18 that they should be demilitarised as soon as their airfields were no longer required, the Cabinet reluctantly acquiesced. It was impossible to protect them by air or by naval means. So the military garrison was evacuated, along with such of the civil population of about 100,000 as wished to accompany them. The Germans soon proceeded to occupy the islands—a distressing fate for a people who for nearly nine hundred years had been associated with the English Crown.

The case of Ireland was very different. Her strategic importance was twofold. In the first place, as had long been foreseen, the use of certain ports in Eire would be of enormous value to the Navy in its task of protecting commerce.[1] Under the Anglo-Irish treaty of December 1921 the right to make use of Queenstown, Berehaven, and Lough Swilly had been reserved for Great Britain; but in April 1938, as part of a general settlement of outstanding questions and with the approval of the Chiefs of Staff, the Chamberlain Government had surrendered this right unconditionally, in the hope of obtaining better relations, including co-operation in defence, with the Dublin Government. Under the constitution of 1937 Eire remained nominally a member of the British Commonwealth, but her Government had declared neutrality in September 1939 and indeed maintained diplomatic relations with Germany. Though in various minor matters they showed themselves not unhelpful to us, they had not allowed us the use of the ports. The Naval Staff had, in October, explained very forcibly the benefit derived by German U-boats from the inability of our escort craft and flying boats to cover, from English bases, a sufficient area of sea in the Western Approaches. We should press for the use of one or more of the Irish ports, Berehaven being the most suitable. The British Government had approached Mr. De Valera but found him inflexible; he maintained that the great majority of the people of Eire were resolved to maintain their neutrality and would react violently to any concession of the kind suggested. So the matter had rested until the acquisition of French Atlantic bases widely extended the possibilities of U-boat activity.

The second danger was that the Germans would treat neutral Eire as they had treated neutral Norway and use her territory as a

---

[1] See Map 8.

base for the bombing of Great Britain and the invasion of Northern Ireland.

The Chiefs of Staff reopened the question at the end of May. It was in the Western Approaches that our trade was most vulnerable to submarine attack. Our light forces could not operate from their present bases at Plymouth and Milford Haven further than 14° West; using Berehaven they could operate 180 miles further west. On May 23 Mr. De Valera had assured the British Government that Eire would fight if attacked by Germany and would call in British help the moment it became necessary, but there could be no question of inviting in British troops before an actual German descent and before fighting had begun. The Cabinet on June 1 approved the measures already taken by the Chiefs of Staff and their recommendation that military support should be provided to Eire as soon as her Government asked for it. The Chiefs of Staff pointed out, however, that so long as Eire remained neutral she could not fully safeguard herself against enemy activities from without or from within. So long as her present policy held, Eire would remain a serious weakness in the defence of these islands.

This intractable affair was brought before the Cabinet again in the middle of June, and discussions continued until July 6. Alarming reports had been received of German preparations in Southern Ireland, and the Cabinet were by no means satisfied with the arrangements made by the Government of Eire to deal either with a surprise attack by sea or air or with the plottings of the Irish Republican Army or uninterned Germans. In the view of the Chiefs of Staff it was almost a foregone conclusion that, simultaneously with air attack and perhaps also seaborne invasion on our east and south coasts, we should be faced with a Nazi descent upon Eire. They were not content with our present plan to hold troops in Northern Ireland and Wales ready to intervene; they held it essential to station strong British forces in the south of Ireland before an invasion took place. The Government again approached De Valera, to find out what were the smallest political concessions which would induce him to admit British troops and ships forthwith, but it became clear that the gulf between the two points of view was far too wide to be bridged. Nevertheless the Cabinet agreed on July 26, in spite of Eire's continued neutrality, to supply her with a certain amount of military equipment.

It would be tedious and unprofitable to follow in detail the many appreciations estimating the probable method and scale of a German assault on Fortress Britain, but the more important may be briefly noticed.

Examining the question, on instruction from the Cabinet, in November 1939, the Chiefs of Staff had reaffirmed their predecessors' view (of 1937) that, whereas small-scale raids, though possible, would not be a serious threat, 'the large-scale overseas invasion of one major Power by another is one of the most hazardous and difficult operations of war that can be attempted'. For success the enemy would need to control the sea-routes and to neutralise the defending air forces, both for an indefinite period, while the first wave of invaders would need tactical surprise to make certain of getting ashore. The conclusion was drawn that it was conceivable that the Germans might attempt invasion by means of a combined airborne and seaborne expedition, but that our security was not seriously threatened so long as our naval and air forces remained in being and provided the necessary precautions were effectively maintained.

This appreciation held the field until May, when the German successes in Denmark and Norway, offset indeed to some extent by their naval losses, called for a review. The resulting report was approved by the Cabinet on May 21. A seaborne and airborne attack was now considered quite possible, but the conclusion of the previous appreciation still held good. Air superiority was the crux of the problem, since, if the Germans succeeded in neutralising our air forces, it might be impossible for our naval forces to prevent the establishment and maintenance of considerable German forces in this country.

We must expect at the outset an air offensive, combined with sabotage, against our air force and air industry and also against our naval ports and ships on the south and east coasts. The area selected for airborne or seaborne landings, apart from mere raids, would presumably be that in which the full weight of the enemy's short-range bombers and fighters could be brought to bear; the most vulnerable area was therefore first judged to be between the Wash and Folkestone, but with the advance of the Germans in northern France it was extended to any part of our southern coasts within 200 miles of German airfields. Initial landings by parachute or airborne troops must be expected in the vicinity of ports; the first requirement of a seaborne invasion would be landing-places where vehicles could be put ashore; their selection would depend partly on the avoidance of our mined areas. The inception of an air offensive would give us some warning, but the only positive information would be the concentration of the ships and troops. The actual date of sailing and the points of attack would not be revealed except by reconnaissance.

On July 17 the Chiefs of Staff approved for transmission to the Commanders-in-Chief a report by the Joint Intelligence Committee on the probable scale of attack. This was estimated under the heads of air attack, naval action, sabotage, diversions, an attack on Ireland, and invasion proper. The principal objective of the latter was likely to be the capture of London, and the main seaborne invasion would probably be made between the Wash and Newhaven. Beaches would be selected for the landing of a wave of tanks carried in small flat-bottomed craft, supported by troops in specially equipped merchant ships which could be run ashore. Large numbers of small craft of all types were likely to be used in addition. The most probable areas for beach landings were near Southwold in Suffolk and in east Kent. Simultaneous landings must be expected with a view to a pincer movement on London. As regards numbers, up to 15,000 men lightly equipped might be dropped from the air in one day in East Anglia or Kent. By sea, up to five divisions might be landed as an initial striking force. The limiting factor would be neither troops nor shipping but the extent to which shipping for the first attack could be concentrated without being detected, or interfered with, by our naval and air forces; the manœuvrability of the convoys would also be important.

Just at this time the Chiefs of Staff were asked by the Prime Minister to review the plans for meeting invasion. The First Sea Lord had presented a memorandum arguing that, while the Germans could not possibly sustain an invading force until they had defeated both our air and naval forces, modern conditions made feasible its landing in greater numbers than formerly. Hitler's disregard of probable losses, the dive-bombing of ships, the possible use of small fast craft, and the long extent of coastline from which the invaders might put out, must all be taken into account. The enemy could approach our shores from almost any point, and the chances of his getting considerable numbers of men ashore depended almost entirely on weather conditions. After reviewing the various sections of the European coast from Norway to the Bay of Biscay the paper suggested that some 100,000 men, with some tanks, might land undetected, with the hope of forcing capitulation by a rush on London.[1]

General Paget explained that the defence had already been disposed, as far as resources would permit, to meet a scale of attack of this magnitude. It would be unsound to withdraw further formations into reserve, and thereby give them a counter-offensive role, as suggested by the Prime Minister, until there were sufficient guns available to allow them the necessary fire support.

The use to be made of the Army against invasion was conditioned by the state partly of their equipment and partly of their training. Since Dunkirk there had been no lack of men, and after the French armistice there was of course no question of sending more troops to the Continent, though an infantry brigade was despatched to Iceland at the end of June to reinforce the Canadian troops then

---

[1] For the Prime Minister's comments on the Admiralty paper see Churchill II 252.

garrisoning the island. Apart from men in training units, in holding battalions and in Anti-Aircraft Command, there were at home three categories of troops: the Field Force, Home Defence units, and the Local Defence Volunteers, first raised in mid-May and in July renamed the Home Guard. On May 31 General Ironside said that, besides smaller formations and units, there were fifteen divisions available for home defence, including the 2nd Armoured and the 1st Canadian; but a large proportion of this force was insufficiently trained and equipped, especially with transport, and therefore unsuitable for offensive operations. Dunkirk added trained men but not equipment, and the Cabinet approved on June 10 a War Office scheme for the reorganisation of the Field Force. Its strength was henceforward twenty-four infantry plus two armoured divisions, exclusive of forces from the Dominions.[1]

The developing strategy of defence on land is described elsewhere.[2] It was naturally moulded by recent experience in France, especially of the devastating effect of armoured columns. Airborne landings also were very much in mind. As is usually the case when a long front has to be held by inadequate forces, whether the inadequacy is in numbers, in training, in armament, or in mobility, there was controversy as to the proportion of field troops to be allotted to the beaches or held in reserve to counter-attack, and as to the distance from the coast at which reserves should be stationed. General Ironside maintained that if we had four armoured divisions in the United Kingdom the whole problem of the defence of the country would be solved. The controversy reached high levels at the end of June, but as deficiencies of training and equipment were met and more formations became available it settled itself.

On July 19 the War Office announced that General Sir Alan Brooke would succeed General Ironside; it was considered 'essential to place the command of Home Forces in the hands of a Commander-in-Chief who has had immediate experience of command in France and Belgium.'[3]

On August 8 at the Prime Minister's request the Chiefs of Staff considered the dispositions of the home army (reckoned at twenty-six divisions) with relation to the vulnerability of the several sectors of the coast, taking account of the time within which heavy counter-attacks could be mounted. It was found that the Commander-in-Chief's actual dispositions conformed very closely to the theoretical scale propounded by the Prime Minister.[4]

---

[1] For the progressive re-equipment of these formations see the diagrams in Churchill II 243.

[2] See Collier, *Defence of the United Kingdom*.

[3] *The Times* 20 July 1940.

[4] See Churchill II 260.

The parts to be played by the three Services in the event of invasion were reviewed at a special meeting of the Chiefs of Staff on July 26, at which the principal commanders concerned with the defence of the island were present. They discussed a memorandum by the Air Staff dealing primarily with the respective roles of the three operational commands of the Metropolitan Air Force, but amounting in fact to an appreciation of the probable form and order of an invasion and an indication of the action to be taken by the three Services. It was approved, subject to certain modifications and amplifications, and circulated to the Commanders-in-Chief concerned as 'their principal directive'.

The paper maintained that, until Germany had defeated our fighter force, invasion by sea was not a practical operation of war. Consequently the preliminary stage of an invasion was likely to be a large-scale air offensive against the fighter defences, viz, fighters in the air, fighter aerodromes and organisation and the aircraft industry. A heavy air attack might simultaneously be made on our naval forces and their bases, particularly those on the east and south-east coasts.

Should the enemy decide to risk a seaborne invasion, this must comprise three principal phases: the concentration of shipping and troops at points of departure; the voyage; and the establishment of a bridge-head in this country. Airborne landings might be used to create diversions or, alternatively, to seize a port of disembarkation. In any event the close approach of the expedition to our coast and the attempt at landing a force by air presupposed an effort by the German Air Force to establish virtual air superiority over the area.

By reason of the all-embracing effects of a seaborne invasion, the predominant and first task of the armed forces must always be to direct all their energies against the invaders; next in importance would come the protection of our aircraft industry and fighter organisation; third in importance would be the defeat of the airborne landings.

The naval problem arose from the fact that the two equally vital tasks of the Navy—to repel invasion and to safeguard our supplies—made conflicting demands on inadequate resources. It was agreed that, if and when invasion was actually attempted, the first task of the Navy would be to prevent it; but the safeguarding of our supplies would remain a no less important responsibility, and a premature diversion of warships from their ceaseless task in the Atlantic might have very serious results.[1]

The immediate naval responsibility for repelling an invasion rested on the Commanders-in-Chief of the Home Fleet and the

---

[1] For the 'general naval appreciation of possible invasion' issued by the Admiralty at the end of May and brought up to date, see Roskill, *The War at Sea* I ch. xiii.

Nore and on the Vice-Admiral, Dover.[1] The Home Fleet was in June and July being denuded for various purposes connected with the French collapse, whereas the current strength of the German fleet was over-estimated by the Admiralty. Sir Charles Forbes accordingly felt misgivings about stationing his heavy ships away from their base at Scapa, and was gravely perturbed at the rising losses of shipping in the North-West Approaches due to the diversion of escort vessels to invasion waters. Moreover he accepted the Air Staff view that until the Germans had acquired the necessary air supremacy by destroying our fighter force an invasion was not feasible. Sir Charles Forbes was informed however at the beginning of July that his major responsibility was now the defeat of invasion. During that month and the next, cruisers of the Home Fleet were by Admiralty order disposed round the east and south coasts. Capital ships, on the other hand, were not to venture into the southern waters of the North Sea unless the enemy's heavy ships had done so. The destruction of an invading fleet was normally to be regarded as the task of cruisers and smaller ships, and the Nore Command was strengthened in these respects.

Sir Reginald Drax was not so willing as Sir Charles Forbes to reject the possibility of a sudden invasion of Great Britain. In his view the advent of airborne troops, of dive-bombers and tanks had greatly increased the difficulties of the defence and he stood out for the maintenance of what he considered an adequate strength in cruisers and light vessels in southern waters.

The parts to be played by the three operational Commands of the Royal Air Force were explained at the meeting on July 26. Each was assigned its appropriate task according to the form and the successive phases which an attempt to conquer the country might take—whether a full-scale air attack on the fighter defences and the fleet, a descent of parachute troops with guns and tanks, a seaborne invasion, or a combination of all methods.

We left Fighter Command depleted first by the operations in northern France, then by its cover of the evacuation from Dunkirk, and finally by the last efforts to succour our ally in the decisive battle.[2] But the number of squadrons had not been reduced, and at the time of the French armistice some fifty-eight were in existence, though not all of these were fit for operations. This total of fifty-eight was only two short of the number which the Air Staff had approved in principle in the spring as essential for defence against a German Air Force using the bases then available to them. But the

---

[1] Home Fleet, Admiral of the Fleet Sir Charles Forbes; Nore, Admiral the Hon. Sir Reginald Drax; Dover, Vice-Admiral Sir Bertram Ramsay.

[2] See chapter viii. See also Sir Hugh Dowding's Despatch (of 1941) on the Battle of Britain.

French collapse had vastly aggravated the task of Fighter Command. The whole of the Luftwaffe was now free to concentrate against the United Kingdom from an arc extending from Norway to Brittany. 'German long-range bombers could reach virtually every part of the country in considerable strength: German fighters and dive-bombers could operate over the Western Approaches [eastward of] the eighth meridian, and over all England to the south of a line between South Wales and the Humber; and inside that area bombers could be given a fighter escort.' This last point was the one which most critically affected Fighter Command: it meant that German bombers could now attack by day protected by short-range fighters. 'In short, the general effect of the German occupation of western Europe upon the air defence of Great Britain was to extend the area that was open to air bombardment and intensify the scale of attack that was to be expected.'

The first obvious precaution was to extend the system of air defence to the parts of the island not previously threatened. The measures taken were for the benefit of the west of England, the north of Scotland and the area round Belfast. But the immediate expansion of Fighter Command was governed by the available resources of pilots and aircraft, and these were largely committed to the refitting of the squadrons which had suffered in the French campaign. Nearly 300 pilots had been lost in that fighting, and it was decided in July not to increase the number of squadrons but to add a flight of four aircraft to all the thirty Hurricane squadrons of the Command and to six of the Spitfire squadrons. This measure had been completed by the third week in July. Throughout the period July–September only four new squadrons were added to the operational strength of Fighter Command: one Canadian, two Polish and one Czechoslovakian. By 8 August the number of squadrons reckoned fit for operations had risen to fifty-five, but there was still a considerable shortage on the establishment of pilots. In the intense fighting that was about to begin Sir Hugh Dowding could not count on putting more than six or seven hundred aircraft into action at the same time.[1]

Anti-Aircraft Command, which worked in close co-operation with Fighter Command, now comprised seven divisions. It was still far below its authorised scale of equipment. At the end of July it held little more than half the number of heavy, and less than a third of the light, guns authorised in May 1939.[2]

In its chain of coastal radar stations, however, Fighter Command possessed a potent weapon of defence which proved adequate for the

---

[1] The greatest number of fighters actually airborne at one time was between two and three hundred.

[2] 1,280 heavy and 517 light as against 2,232 and 1940 authorised.

emergencies of the summer. Warning of attacks, whether flying high or low, could now usually be given in time, if only just in time, for Controllers to launch their squadrons into the air to meet them. The effectiveness of this device was not expected by the enemy; combined with the efficient system of communication and control, it now became our salvation.

Coastal Command may be mentioned next. This Command, under Air Chief Marshal Sir Frederick Bowhill, was, with the Navy, responsible for the reconnaissance of airfields, ports and estuaries from which the invading forces might issue and of the waters they must traverse. For this task, which further embraced attacks on shipping, the Command could call on fifteen or sixteen squadrons of its own besides loans from Bomber Command and the Fleet Air Arm. Visual observation was supplemented by the Photographic Reconnaissance Unit, which revealed to skilled interpreters the waxing and waning strength of the craft assembled for invasion.

Bomber Command, under Air Marshal C. F. A. Portal, could count in July a total of forty squadrons, of which thirty-five were operationally fit. Of these, fifteen were medium squadrons, armed with Battles and Blenheims, while the remaining twenty, comprising Wellingtons, Whitleys and Hampdens, then ranked as heavy. All of these were available to counter an invader, whether by actually attacking his ships, barges and docks or by destroying his communications inland and the factories serving his aircraft industry.

Such, in outline, was the scheme of defence against a German invasion in the summer of 1940.[1] How the Government's arrangements for the conduct of the war in such conditions, in London and in the country, would have worked had they been put to the test, we cannot tell. No German forces landed; Regional headquarters were never isolated from Whitehall. Thus there was no occasion for Sir Alan Brooke to leave St. Paul's School for his command post adjacent to the Cabinet War Room, or for Regional Commissioners to assume their dormant powers. The Royal Air Force indeed was tried to the limit, and the Navy to a lesser degree, and neither was found wanting.

The defeat of the German plans was naturally the chief preoccupation of the Government, as of the people, of the United Kingdom during this fateful summer. But before we turn to those plans, and to their failure, it is well to remember that the directors of policy had many other calls on their attention, from all parts of the world. In particular it was in these very months, when invasion was believed to be impending at home, that decisions of the utmost gravity had to be taken as to the diversion of reinforcements to Egypt.[2]

---

[1] See Map 9.
[2] See below, ch. xiii.

(ii)

The Crisis

We left the German high-level plans at the point when Hitler, on July 16, had informed his subordinates in his first directive for 'Sea Lion' that he had 'decided to prepare and, if necessary, to carry out a landing operation', and that they must complete their preparations by the middle of August. They set to work, but from now onwards their conflicting views as to the proper areas, the proper date, and the proper hour, for a landing, and indeed as to the feasibility of the operation as a whole, as well as the different lengths of time required for their elaborate preparations—all these, to say nothing of the weather, made decision very difficult for the Führer and led to postponements. Only five days after the issue of the directive he was uncertain whether invasion could be brought off that autumn or should be set back to May 1941.

It may be that these doubts of an early defeat of Britain induced Hitler to extend his outlook and play with the idea of an invasion of Russia this year or next. His motives for such an adventure will be discussed hereafter; but it is of interest that his first recorded hint of it to his henchmen dates from July 21, while ten days later he told them definitely that Russia must be finished off in the course of the the struggle, and the sooner the better. This year would have been best, but now it was not possible; so let it be the spring of 1941. This purpose is not to be taken as having interfered with 'Sea Lion'; it was rather a reason for hurrying it on. But it meant that 'Sea Lion' could not be Hitler's sole preoccupation.

On July 31 the Führer carried matters a step further. 'The air war will start now.' If its results were not satisfactory, invasion preparations would be stopped, but if things went well the invasion would take place. Present preparations must continue and, if possible, be completed by September 15. A new directive followed next day, August 1.[1] In order to establish conditions favourable to the final conquest of the country, he intended to continue the air and naval war against the British homeland more intensively than heretofore. The Luftwaffe was to defeat the British Air Force with all means at its disposal; after temporary or local air superiority had been achieved, ports and inland towns, especially those concerned with the food supply, were to be attacked, but south coast ports were to be spared as far as possible in view of the projected operations. He added that the Luftwaffe must be available in fighting strength for 'Sea Lion'.

---

[1] *Führer Directive* No. 17.

The air offensive might begin at any date from August 5 onward; the actual day was to be chosen by Göring when its preparations were complete and the weather favourable. On August 2 Göring issued his own directive for operation 'Eagle'. The Royal Air Force was to be destroyed as the Polish and French air forces had been destroyed; he believed that the British fighter defences in the south could be smashed in four days, and the Royal Air Force completely defeated within two to four weeks.

The operational plans of the three Services for the invasion can only be outlined here.

In the case of the Army the original plan as proposed at the end of July came to be modified in a less ambitious sense as the result of naval criticism. The main geographical objectives however remained the same; to secure first the area south-east of a line drawn from the Thames estuary to Portsmouth or Southampton, and then to extend it to a line from Maldon in Essex to the estuary of the Severn.[1] The chief differences lay in the number and extent of landing areas, the number of divisions to be used in the first wave, and the rate of their reinforcement.

The final plan provided for a series of landings between Folke-stone and Brighton by twenty-three divisions of Sixteenth and Ninth Armies, besides airborne troops. The first wave would consist of nine divisions and two airborne formations. Tanks would accompany the first landing, while four *Panzer* divisions would form part of the second wave. About 120,000 men were to get ashore, complete with their equipment, within three days. Ten complete divisions were to arrive within eleven days, but the whole three waves of twenty-three divisions not until six weeks from S Day, the day of the first landing. In addition, two divisions were held ready for a descent on Lyme Bay, further west. This modified plan fell far short of what Brauchitsch thought necessary.

The air forces most directly concerned would be the Second and Third Air Fleets; their four main tasks were to provide direct air support for the armies, to prevent interference by the Royal Navy, to interrupt the movement of British reserve divisions from a distance, and to frustrate the intervention of the Royal Air Force. The VIII Air Corps, controlling some 200 dive-bombers, would supply close support to the 16th Army.

The ships conveying the troops would consist partly of large river barges—some self-propelled, some not, but all needing a tow across the open waters of the Channel—partly of steamers averaging 4,000 tons,[2] partly of motor boats and auxiliary sailing vessels, partly of

---

[1] See Map 10.
[2] Gross registered tonnage.

U

tugs and trawlers. Protection would be afforded by destroyers, torpedo-boats and U-boats, besides patrol and mine-sweeping flotillas and a specially laid minefield; the heavier vessels of the diminished German Navy, still suffering from its losses in the Norwegian campaign, would be used to create diversions further north.

Elaborate deception plans were also prepared.

Unfortunately from the German point of view, the differences between the Services went deeper than mere matters of tactics or strategy, and the close co-ordination demanded by so intricate an enterprise was lacking. The Army suspected, moreover, that the hearts of the Navy and Luftwaffe were not in the job. Indeed invasion could not appear in the same light to all three. To the victorious land forces, taught to chant *Wir fahren gegen England* as their war song, it was the obvious, dramatic consummation of their triumphs. To the Navy it was merely a highly precarious and perhaps unnecessary appendage to a surer, if slower, form of warfare to which they had long been committed. Concentration on invasion, by reason of its disturbance of existing priorities, was bound to hamper the older strategy. As for the Luftwaffe, its ambitious chief, Reichsmarschall Göring, was more interested in the delivery of a knockout blow from the air than in supporting the sister Services, and this may have caused his squadrons to pay more attention to the independent than to the co-operative side of their two-fold mission.

The opening of the Battle of Britain was heralded by nothing so spectacular as an artillery barrage and no obvious date can be fixed for it. British historians distinguish a preliminary phase beginning July 10, but the official start of the great offensive was on August 13, the Eagle Day (*Adlertag*) of the Luftwaffe.[1]

The regrouping of the German air formations after the Battle of France was completed by the third week of July. Facing the south-east and south coasts of England were Air Fleets (*Luftflotten*) 2 and 3; *Luftflotte* 5, based on Norway and Denmark, threatened a diversion in the north-east of the island, but after one unsuccessful day (August 15) played little part in the battle. On August 10 *Luftflotten* 2 and 3 are reckoned to have had available for use against the United Kingdom, counting serviceable aircraft only, 875 long-range bombers, 316 dive-bombers, 702 single-engined fighters, 227 twin-engined fighters and fighter-bombers; *Luftflotte* 5 had 123 long-range bombers and 34 twin-engined fighters. R.A.F. Fighter

---

[1] The Luftwaffe General Adolf Galland, who played a prominent part in the Battle of Britain, speaks of it as beginning on July 24. For an account of the battle see Collier, chaps. x, xii–xv; also D. Richards, *The Fight at Odds* (H.M.S.O., 1953) ch. vi.

Command, as we have seen, could not have put into the air more than 600–700 aircraft at a time.[1]

Some time before Hitler issued his directive of August 1 for the intensification of air and naval warfare against Great Britain, the Luftwaffe had started on their share of the work. During the month prior to Eagle Day they had attacked shipping and ports in the Channel, seeking to wear down Fighter Command and threatening to render Dover useless as a naval base. From August 12 they attacked Fighter Command directly—its aerodromes, sector stations and, at first, its radar installations. From August 24 onwards they continued their attacks, with strong fighter escorts, and, as time went on, an increasing proportion of their effort was made at night.

The chief burden of the defence fell on the score or so of squadrons of No. 11 Group under Air Vice-Marshal Park, whose headquarters were at Uxbridge. It was on August 20, only a week after Eagle Day, that the Prime Minister paid to Fighter Command the historic tribute that 'never in the field of human conflict was so much owed by so many to so few'.[2] The most exacting days, however, were to come just afterwards: during the fortnight August 23 to September 6 casualties in Spitfires and Hurricanes totalled 295 destroyed and 171 badly damaged (as against an accession of 269 from production and repair), while 103 pilots were lost (killed or missing) and 128 wounded. The enemy likewise were suffering grievously: in the same fortnight between August 23 and September 6 they lost 214 fighters and 138 bombers, amounting with other types to a total loss of 385 aircraft.

The battle reached its climax in September. The Royal Air Force had not been defeated, but they had sustained heavy losses and the time in which an invasion was possible was passing. Quick results were required. On the 5th Hitler directed that the Luftwaffe should launch harassing attacks on the inhabitants and defences of the large cities, particularly London, by day and night, and accordingly a new phase of the air offensive opened on September 7. On that afternoon a force of more than 300 long-range bombers attacked the thickly populated areas of the docks in East London, and the same night about 250 bombers followed to the same objective, guided by the still blazing fires. Hitler began to think that the destruction of the capital might by itself bring victory without the hazards of an invasion. The onslaught of the 7th was in fact the heaviest single blow which London was to suffer until the spring of 1941, but it was the attack on the 15th which is most famous in the annals of the Royal Air Force. On this day, which has been chosen for the commemoration of the winning of the Battle of Britain, our fighter squadrons

---

[1] Collier App. 19.

[2] *House of Commons Debates* vol. 364, col. 1167.

claimed 174 aircraft destroyed, and the anti-aircraft gunners another eleven. As is now known the real number destroyed was nearer 60, as against 26 British fighters lost; both British and German pilots consistently over-estimated the other side's casualties. But the tale of British victories constituted none the less a glorious achievement, and the nation was justified in believing that the German attempt to defeat the Royal Air Force had failed.

It was in these same early days of September that the enemy's assembly of craft for invasion became observable. On the afternoon of the 7th the Chiefs of Staff, in the light of the most recent intelligence 'agreed that the possibility of invasion had become imminent and that the defence forces should stand by at immediate notice'. Their information was derived partly from reports of concentrations of barges in ports from Havre to Ostend, partly from the completion in the last few days of aerodromes and gun emplacements in and behind the Channel coast, partly from the redeployment of bomber groups, and partly from the statements of captured spies. Moon and tides during the period 8–10 September were thought to be favourable for a seaborne invasion on the south-east coast, and the Chiefs of Staff concluded that the stage was set for an attempt at invasion during this period, and that 'the main attack would probably be made by barges covered by bomber aircraft escorted by fighters and was to be expected anywhere on the coast between Southwold and Beachy Head'.

The necessary orders were issued by Home Forces: that evening (September 7) troops immediately concerned received the code-word 'Cromwell', and the unauthorised ringing of church bells in some parts of the country gave rise to reports that German parachutists were actually dropping.[1] There was never any stronger evidence of an imminent invasion than on this day; but for a fortnight tension was high. On the 13th the *Nelson* and the *Hood* were moved from Scapa to Rosyth, and during these weeks Bomber Command paid special attention to barges and shipping in French and Belgian harbours; on the night of the 17th they succeeded in causing serious damage. After September 19 the numbers of these craft were seen to be gradually decreasing and, though on October 3 the Prime Minister warned the Defence Committee that it could not be said that the risk of invasion had greatly diminished, the prospect of broken weather during that month did in fact make an attempt much less probable.

The pilots of Fighter Command, and their colleagues below who guided and served them, had foiled the German strategy in its first

---

[1] 'On receipt of the code-word "CROMWELL" troops will take up battle stations . . .' G.H.Q. Operation Instruction No. 1 (5 June 1940). See Collier ch. xiv; Churchill II 276.

phase—the elimination of the Royal Air Force in the air and on the ground and the destruction of our aircraft industry. Hitler's instructions of September 5 to attack the large cities were to that extent a confession of failure. But the alternative object remained—to break down the British people's resolution by incessant bombing and so to force the Government to surrender. In spite of the heavy losses they inflicted on Fighter Command the Luftwaffe were unable to secure this result in September and, though daylight operations did not cease afterwards, their scale was reduced both by the Germans' own losses and by worse weather. Henceforward the Luftwaffe's most effective efforts were devoted to massed night attacks on industrial towns and ports, combined with attacks on shipping and the laying of mines.

The successive decisions and indecisions of the German high command, which form the background to these events, are now known to us. Their shifting course is in marked contrast to the clear-cut decisions and smooth inter-Service planning which characterised the German invasion of Denmark and Norway.

On September 3 the earliest date for the sailing of the transports was announced as September 20; S Day, the day of the first landings, would in that case be September 21; the order for the operation to proceed would be issued ten days before S Day, and would be confirmed seven days later.[1] The basic directive for 'Sea Lion' is known to have been ready for issue on September 11.[2] But on the 14th it was announced that a further postponement had been ordered, though all preparations were to continue.

The next few days were crucial. On the 13th Hitler, expecting great results from the recent bombardment of London, was inclined to trust to the air war alone for victory and cancel 'Sea Lion'. Next day, the 14th, he changed his mind. At a conference that afternoon he decided, apparently in view of the paramount advantages of not prolonging the war in the West, to let 'Sea Lion' stand. The Navy had done its preparatory work, he said, the coastal artillery was in place, the operations of the Luftwaffe were above all praise. But the enemy fighters had not yet been completely eliminated and, in spite of the great successes obtained, the necessary preconditions for an invasion did not exist. Four to five days of good weather should make decisive results possible. He would then, it seems, drive home the blow with 'Sea Lion', since invasion was the only certain means of ending the war promptly.

But this was in fact the turning point. The stout resistance of fighters by day, backed up by the aggressiveness of British bombers

---

[1] *F.D.* p. 113.

[2] This directive is missing from the captured archives.

by night, forced the Germans to recognise the fact that air superiority was not in sight after all, and the weather forecast was not encouraging. Accordingly on the 17th Hitler postponed 'Sea Lion' till further notice. It was not however cancelled, and preparations continued, though the need of dispersing invasion shipping in order to reduce losses in fact extended the necessary period of warning before S day. The next favourable moon and tide period fell in the second week of October, and before the end of September the chances of an invasion being attempted in 1940 became remote. On October 12 'Sea Lion' was definitely called off.[1] During the winter, preparations were to be kept up merely as a means of exerting political and military pressure; the British must suppose that a landing on a broad front was still intended. Hitler's purpose was so far realised that for many months to come British forces were held in the island ready to repel an invasion. But this was the limit of his success. To his enemies, to his allies and to neutrals it was evident that he had met with his first major failure.

Historians are not called upon to answer hypothetical questions: whether, for instance, when it came to the point Hitler would ever have launched his thousand barges on so risky an adventure and, if he had, what would have been the result. One may reasonably enquire, however, how far material preparations for an invasion had actually proceeded, and what were Hitler's intentions. To the first question it is possible to give a rough and general answer based on the detailed researches of Mr. Wheatley.

In the case of the Army, the thirteen divisions intended, under the original plan,[2] for the first wave of the invasion arrived in the coastal area facing England between 28 July and 3 August; in the following weeks they were specially organised, equipped and trained for their unaccustomed task. The divisions for the later waves were not moved, since there was no point in assembling them too far forward. Some 250 amphibious tanks, organised in four battalions, were ready for use in September. The main framework of the army supply organisation was in existence by the time it was wanted. It is true that General Warlimont reported to *OKW* on September 23, after a tour of the operational area, that 'even excluding the factor of enemy interference, the preparations for Operation "Sea Lion" are not yet finished; this is the result of taking decisions too late on a number of open questions affecting the three Services'. His criticisms were in fact directed chiefly against some of the Luftwaffe's preparations.

[1] *F.D.* p. 117.
[2] See above, p. 285.

But it is doubtful whether this report should be taken as meaning that arrangements were so far behindhand as to prevent the launching of the operation had it been ordered. The strategic deployment of the Luftwaffe in northern France and the Low Countries had, as we have seen, been accomplished by the middle of July.

Much the most difficult part of the preparations was Raeder's, whose task it was to organise and protect a sea crossing for more than twenty divisions and afterwards to maintain them, in the face of an undefeated and immensely superior navy. No wonder Raeder disliked the whole idea; but on September 6 we find him telling the Führer that, if air supremacy could be increasingly established, it would be possible to be ready by the new date (September 21),[1] while in a subsequent report of the *O.K.M.* Merchant Shipping Branch (of 5 July 1941), reviewing the development of German landing-craft, it is stated that 'in spite of all the difficulties the necessary landing fleet [for 'Sea Lion'] was successfully formed in time'. After examining the evidence concerning the different types of vessel Mr. Wheatley sums up as follows:

'Returns compiled by the *O.K.M.* Merchant Shipping Branch and the Naval Commander-in-Chief, France, show that by 19 September every kind of transport vessel had been converted and more than adequate numbers were on their way to the invasion ports. The question is whether these vessels would have reached the particular port where they were required in time for a landing on 24 September. When the shipping position on the 19th and other factors bearing on this problem have been examined, it can be tentatively estimated that over four-fifths of the transport fleet could have been assembled in time. By the 19th virtually all the steamers, including reserves, were available. Over 95% of the barges had been distributed between the invasion ports, even if the replacement of losses was questionable.[2] There is also little doubt that at least three-quarters of the tugs and trawlers could have been ready. Lastly, if only half the motor-boats and none of the small group of auxiliary sailing vessels had reached their final destinations by the 19th, it seems possible that considerably more could have been ready for operations by the 23rd. It would have rested with Hitler and the Naval Staff to determine whether this situation was satisfactory; but the trend of the evidence certainly suggests that, while "Sea-Lion" could not have been launched at the full strength planned, a transport fleet of sufficient numbers had been assembled for the purpose. All the essential naval preparations were thus completed for a landing on the 24th.'

---

[1] *F.N.C.* p. 133.

[2] By the 21st the loss amounted to at least 9 per cent of the numbers required; this figure can also be taken as an indication of the minimum loss to be expected up to the 24th.

In confirmation of this conclusion we have a written statement made by Raeder himself in 1944 to the effect that his opinion in 1940–41 had consistently been that in view of British naval strength the risk was very great and a landing was practicable only if the weather, tides etc., were favourable and above all if Germany had superiority in the air. Granted this latter condition, he believed that success was possible; he had consequently 'pressed on the preparations with the utmost urgency, and on the part of the Navy they were completed in sufficient time for an autumn landing'.[1]

There remains the question, what were the Führer's real intentions with regard to an invasion?

Some have suggested that despite his immense laborious preparations Hitler never seriously meant to invade England against opposition, but that the whole thing was a gigantic bluff intended to force the dispersion of our energies and to wear down our morale. The difficulty of fathoming the Führer's mind is greatly increased by the co-existence on the German side throughout this period of two distinct but not incompatible strategies—the strategy of 'Sea Lion' and the strategy of the Blitz.

On the one hand it is clear that Hitler never proposed to throw his legions ashore on an England unsoftened, materially and morally, by previous harassings from the air. The matador would not face the bull until its strength had been reduced by the attentions of his forerunners. The more effective the harassings, the easier would invasion be, and conceivably they would be so effective that no invasion need be launched at all. In this most favourable case the preliminaries which made a landing possible would make it unnecessary. But, short of this, invasion might be regarded as merely a *coup de grâce*. Halder is reported to have believed that, after the decision to reduce the frontage and scale of the landings, it could 'only be a question now of finishing off an enemy defeated by the air war'. And on September 14 Jodl is quoted as expressing the Führer's view that 'the Channel crossing would only come into question—as before—if it is a matter of finishing off a country already defeated by the air war'. Indeed it seems certain that as Hitler came more and more to realise the difficulties, and particularly after the Navy had declared its inability to carry out the Army's original plan, he hoped more and more that an invasion would not be necessary.

Nevertheless it seems against reason to suppose that Hitler never intended to invade a Britain still showing fight. For a mere victory march, and still more for a mere feint, it was quite unnecessary to draw so heavily on Germany's material resources, to divert shipping

---

[1] *N.D.* 066–C.

for months from its normal uses, to give special training to so many picked formations, to delay the reorganisation of the army, and to forgo attractive enterprises elsewhere in Europe.[1] We have seen that, after apparently pinning his hopes early in September to victory by air attack alone, Hitler decided on September 14 not to call off 'Sea Lion', because of the prospect it offered of a rapid ending of the war. It would seem then that, while he never intended to attempt an invasion until certain conditions had been fulfilled—of which the most important was the gaining of air superiority, followed, it was to be hoped, by a crumbling of British morale—he was prepared in those circumstances to make the attempt even in the face of opposition. But what precise degree of previous mastery he required it is impossible to say. Hitler was essentially a gambler: he required a strong probability of success, but he did not require a certainty.

By the end of October the immediate danger of invasion was generally believed in London to have passed. The *Nelson* and the *Hood* returned to Scapa. At a special meeting of the Defence Committee on the 31st, at which the Commanders-in-Chief at home stations of all three Services were present, the best employment of our forces during the winter months was considered. The Admiralty called attention to the very serious losses our shipping was suffering in the North-Western Approaches and to the consequent need of recalling all the light naval forces possible from anti-invasion duties. This was the view of the Commander-in-Chief, Home Fleet, who had always held that an invasion was not practicable so long as the Navy and the Royal Air Force were undefeated. Its adoption in principle by the Committee meant that henceforth the Army must be prepared to hold the beaches in south-east England with only local help from the Navy for twelve hours after the alarm had been received. Sir Alan Brooke pointed out that the reduction in light naval craft and patrols would mean surrendering 'no man's land'— the Channel—to the enemy, but he was prepared to accept this handicap provided that thorough air reconnaissance of the invasion ports was maintained whenever weather allowed. The Chief of the Imperial General Staff added the warning that, if the full burden of withstanding the first shock of invasion was to fall on the Army, we might have to reconsider the policy of sending the best-trained units abroad. 'We still had only an amateur army with an average of three pre-war officers per infantry battalion. Shortage of technical

---

[1] See for instance the following paragraph in Keitel's order of August 1: 'If a decision is made *against* the execution of "Sea Lion" in September, nevertheless all preparations should continue, but in a form which will not damage seriously the German economy through paralysing inland shipping.' This last clause implies that existing preparations *were* seriously damaging the German economy. *F.D.* p. 112.

equipment would prevent the early formation of new divisions in place of those sent overseas.'

Sir Hugh Dowding maintained that, though we had succeeded in defeating the German attacks by day, we had only done so with a narrow margin and it would be dangerous to assume that we could repeat this success in the face of sustained and determined German attacks unless the fighter force and training organisation behind it were both expanded.

Sir Charles Portal, who had recently succeeded Sir Cyril Newall as Chief of the Air Staff, said that in the formation of new squadrons preference would be given in the next few months to fighters, in order that we might be ready to meet a renewed German onslaught in the spring. New bomber squadrons would be formed with a view to full employment during the longer nights of autumn 1941. It was agreed that it would be wrong in the meantime to divert bombers from targets in Germany to possible invasion ports until there was good evidence that invasion was impending.

Thought at the highest levels was thus turning from the immediate problems of the summer and of the island to those of the future and of distant horizons. The danger of invasion had been reduced, the Prime Minister cautiously put it, by the successful outcome of the air battles and by the increases in the strength of the Army. The threat of airborne attack had been reduced by the raising and arming of the Home Guard. The danger during the winter months would remain relatively remote provided that we maintained our vigilance, and did not permit over confidence in the country. The march of events in south-east Europe compelled us to accept the risk of sending reinforcements to the Middle East to the limit of shipping capacity.

CHAPTER XIII

ITALY ENTERS THE WAR.
THE DAKAR EXPEDITION

PLANNING in the summer of 1939, the French and British staffs had assumed that Italy would be an enemy. Indeed, it was only against Italy that they had seen any early prospect of taking the offensive. But in fact, when in May of that year Mussolini joined his country's cause with Germany's by the Pact of Steel, he warned Hitler that Italy would not be ready for war for at least three years; and in August, when at length Hitler apprised him of his intentions against Poland, Mussolini replied that Italy could not enter the war at that time unless Germany supplied her with an impossibly long list of material requirements. Hitler made no protest, but Raeder, at least, regretted the absence of Italian co-operation.[1]

The Allies had welcomed the Italian decision, and their policy was to keep the country non-belligerent, if not neutral, as long as possible. On Italy's inactivity depended not only the free use of the Mediterranean and, it was believed, the Red Sea for our shipping but the hope of building up in the Balkans a neutral *bloc* of resistance to German penetration. An Italian attack against Egypt and the Canal from Libya would also be a serious matter.[2] For these reasons the British Government deliberately avoided giving Italy provocation: they felt obliged to relax the blockade for her benefit and sought to improve relations by a trade agreement.

It is not necessary to relate the ups and downs experienced by our diplomacy during the winter and spring. The line taken by the Government and people of the United Kingdom with regard to the imposition of economic sanctions against Italy at the time of her Abyssinian aggression had undoubtedly strained the traditional good will of the Italian people towards Britain; but the Italians felt still less good will towards Germany, and the mass of the nation, from the King and the Foreign Minister downwards, had no wish for war. All this however counted for little. The decision rested with the Duce alone. Mussolini's natural egotism and pugnacity, his desire for military glory and territorial expansion, his long-standing resentment at Britain's power in the Mediterranean and his admiration for Hitler, all urged him to draw the sword as Germany's ally. Only

---

[1] *Ciano's Diplomatic Papers* pp. 303, 314; *The Ciano Diaries*, 25, 26 August 1939.
[2] See Maps 11 and 12.

temporarily and fitfully was he restrained by his knowledge that Italy was unprepared for an immediate war or a long one. Those who knew his temperament could feel no confidence that it would not at any moment overcome his judgement. It would seem that eventually on 18 March 1940 he assured Hitler at their meeting on the Brenner that he would be ready in three or four months and would then 'form Germany's left flank'.

By this time the prestige of the Western Allies had been shaken by the collapse of Finland: it was much more severely shaken, and Germany's strengthened, by events in Scandinavia, the Low Countries and France, and on May 13 Mussolini told Ciano that he would take the decisive step within a month.[1] On the 29th, at a conference with the heads of the Services, he declared his intention to take up arms on or shortly after June 5, and he so informed Hitler. For military reasons the actual date was deferred, but on the 10th Mussolini announced to the Italian people from his Roman balcony that Italy would enter the war after midnight. Next morning Italian aircraft dropped a few bombs on Malta, and on the 12th the British cruiser *Calypso* was sunk by a submarine south of Crete.

Italy's weakness was recognised both by her own Government and by the Allies. She had calculated on a short war in which the Germans would win the victories while she herself did just enough to claim the fulfilment of her desires at the peace. Her weakness was in the first place economic: she lacked the raw materials required by her rearmament programme and she had formerly been, and might be again, largely dependent on Great Britain for her supplies of coal. In February 1939 the British experts had called attention to this fatal defect: in peacetime four-fifths of her imports came by sea and, although about three-quarters of the imports essential to her in war came from countries accessible by land, the limited carrying capacity of the railways across her northern frontiers would force her to rely for about 50 per cent of these imports on sea traffic. If the Dardanelles were closed to her, her economic position would soon become critical and the lack of petroleum products would prove decisive after the exhaustion of her present stocks. Since both the Axis countries were deficient in much the same classes of raw materials, they were bound to compete against each other in the reduced markets which would remain open to them. A further weakness lay in the concentration of over three-quarters of Italy's industrial capacity in Piedmont and Lombardy, in particular in the triangle Turin–Genoa–Milan. These considerations had led the Chiefs of Staff to the conclusion that Italy could not obtain sufficient raw materials to maintain land operations on a large scale and simultaneously conduct naval and air operations

---

[1] *The Ciano Diaries.*

at full intensity for long, while the curtailment of her Black Sea trade would shorten the period of her resistance.

Politically, all power centred in Mussolini, head of the Fascist Party and Head of the Government. Decree-laws issued by him in the name of the King were formally ratified by the Council of Ministers. In peacetime the important body, though endowed with none but advisory and deliberative functions, was the Fascist Grand Council of some twenty-four members, but after the outbreak of the World War it met only once, in December 1939, before the *coup d'état* of July 1943.

On 30 May 1940 the Duce informed the Führer that he had assumed supreme command of the armed forces; under him were Marshal Badoglio, Chief of the General Staff of the Armed Forces, Marshal Graziani, Chief of the Staff of the Army, General Roatta, Graziani's deputy and successor, Admiral Cavagnari, Chief of the Naval Staff, and General Pricolo, Chief of the Air Staff.

The Italian navy was considered by our experts to be the best prepared of the three Services and to be an efficient fighting force. With the two *Littorios*, which were expected to come into commission about July, it would comprise six battleships, seven 8-inch cruisers, twelve 6-inch cruisers, anything up to fifty fleet destroyers and over 100 submarines. As it turned out, the submarines proved much less effective than the German U-boats, but the superior numbers and superior speed of the surface ships, as well as their central position in the Mediterranean, rendered them, after the French collapse, a force which the British had to take very seriously. In the Red Sea the eight Italian submarines and seven destroyers based at Massawa might well have been expected, at least in the earlier months of the war, to render the passage hazardous for our convoys.[1]

Mussolini informed Hitler on May 30 that Italy had seventy army divisions available, of which twelve were overseas; he could have prepared another seventy, he boasted, but for the lack of equipment. In April the War Office had estimated the Italian army as comprising sixty-one divisions in Italy, including frontier guards; ten in the islands and Albania; one Regular division in the Dodecanese; the equivalent of fifteen or sixteen divisions in Libya; and in East Africa one Metropolitan (or Regular) division and the equivalent of one or two other white and of about seven weak African divisions. The Italian formations, the War Office thought, would not lack for men, but were less well provided in the heavier weapons and in transport; moreover, it was doubtful if any troops besides the fanatical Blackshirts would have much stomach for a fight against Great Britain.

---

[1] For the strength and condition of the Italian forces and for a full treatment of the war in this theatre see Maj.-Gen. I. S. O. Playfair, *The Mediterranean and Middle East* I (H.M.S.O. 1954) 38, 90–97, henceforward referred to as 'Playfair'. See also Roskill, *The War at Sea* I 61, 293 and appendix H for the actual strength and disposition of the Italian Navy in June 1940.

The Italian Air Force, the *Regia Aeronautica*, in the opinion of the British Air Ministry was not ready for war: the modern aircraft were good, and probably about one third of the pilots up to the standard of the Royal Air Force. But the remainder were thought to be definitely below it, and morale was expected to crack if heavy casualties were suffered at the outset. When war broke out, the Italians had a total of 313 aircraft disposed in Libya and the Dodecanese, with the ability to reinforce either theatre from home. In East Africa they had 325 aircraft, of which 142 were in reserve; the difficulty would be to replenish their stocks of fuel, spares and ammunition.

At the end of March Mussolini discussed Italy's war policy with his Chiefs of Staff. In Libya he intended to remain on the defensive equally against Tunisia and Egypt. In the Aegean too he would act on the defensive. But in East Africa he would take the offensive in the north to safeguard Eritrea and against French Somaliland (Jibuti) and, to a limited extent, against the Sudan. In the south, on the Kenya front, he would stand on the defensive but, 'if necessary', launch a counter-offensive. The Navy would take the offensive at all points in the Mediterranean and outside, while the Air Force would conform its activity to that of the other Services.

Two months later the Duce was still fairly modest, though still fairly indefinite. France had been hard hit, but was not yet defeated. On May 29 he confirmed his former intentions to his Chiefs of Staff. 'On the land front we cannot undertake anything spectacular, we shall remain on the defensive. We might undertake something in the east, possibly Yugoslavia. Our forces will concentrate on England—viz. on her positions and her naval forces in port and in the Mediterranean.'[1]

Mussolini's strategy grew more ambitious with the collapse of France. He decided to launch an offensive against Egypt, but the date was continually postponed. Writing on July 13 he told Hitler that his hope was to make it coincide with his attack on England. Mussolini was also eager to participate in the invasion of England, but the Führer was no more enthusiastic about receiving such support than the Duce was to accept the proffered help of German long-range bombers to attack the Suez Canal. The Dictators had their pride.

Mussolini's plans for aggrandisement in the Balkans will be considered later.

It was apparently not till mid-April, after the fall of the German blow in Scandinavia, that the Allied Governments began to pay much attention to the possibility of an early resort to war by Italy, and

---

[1] Hitler e Mussolini, *Lettere e Documenti* p. 45.

Greece or Yugoslavia was then thought to be her likeliest victim. But a month earlier, in the course of staff talks at Aleppo concerned with the help which Turkey might expect from the Allies, the Turkish delegates insisted on including in the agenda the action to be taken in the case of a hostile Italy. On April 6 the Chiefs of Staff approved a paper on our policy in that event; it had been prepared with a view to a meeting in London with the British diplomatic representatives in the Near East. Our policy was summed up as to render untenable the Italian position in Libya and eventually in East Africa. The British and Egyptian forces in Egypt would in the first instance act on the defensive, but would be prepared to take advantage of the French pressure from Tunisia to stage local offensives with limited objectives. At a much later stage if the Italians still held out it might be necessary to mount a major offensive from Egypt.

On April 18 the Cabinet instructed the Chiefs of Staff to consider the implications of our becoming involved in war with Italy at the present time. The most probable form of Italian action was regarded as an attack on Yugoslavia. With Scandinavia on our hands, any further military commitment was obviously most undesirable, and we had no treaty obligation to Yugoslavia, as we had to the Greeks; but the blow to our prestige in the Balkans if we remained passive had to be taken into account. In the view of the Chiefs of Staff this last consideration was decisive: Italian aggression in the Balkans must be resisted and we must cut our losses by withdrawing from Norway except from the Narvik region. Initially our major strategy against Italy would have to be defensive, and we must divert our shipping from the Mediterranean round the Cape of Good Hope. Our most promising immediate riposte would be to bomb the industrial towns in the north-west of Italy, and the implications of such action should be discussed with the French.

Discussions followed at the Supreme War Council. The French were apprehensive of the reactions on their own industry which might result from the proposed bombing; they greatly preferred the project of an Allied expedition to Salonika—a project which seemed to the British to be ruled out for administrative reasons. There was agreement on the naval measures to be taken in the Mediterranean, and it was promptly decided to send the battleships *Malaya* and *Royal Sovereign* (and later the *Warspite*) to Alexandria, to divert nearly all our shipping round the Cape, and to man the defences of Alexandria, Haifa, Malta and Gibraltar. Further defensive measures were taken in May, and detailed arrangements were made at the end of the month for an Anglo-French expedition to occupy Crete should Italy attack Greece, but not otherwise; the object of the expedition would be to deny the use of the island, and more especially of its airfield, to the Italians.

The strategic situation in the Mediterranean and the Near East was of course transformed by the defection of France. The foundation of our strategy had been naval control of the Mediterranean, a control jointly exerted by the French in the west and by ourselves in the east and based no less on Oran, Toulon and Bizerta than on Alexandria and Haifa and, if possible, Malta. We had intended, after establishing such control, to strike at Italy hard. On land French forces would threaten the Italian North African possessions from Tunisia and a French army in Syria would encourage the Turks and help to stabilise the Balkans. Now, such naval forces as we could spare for the Mediterranean would have to cope unaided with the entire Italian navy and a large part of the *Regia Aeronautica*. The loss of Bizerta would mean, at best, only occasional interference by our ships and aircraft with Italian control of the narrow waist of the Mediterranean between Sicily and Cape Bon and it might prove impossible to interrupt the flow of Italian reinforcements to Tripoli. Still less could we hope regularly to reinforce our own garrisons in the Middle East by the Mediterranean route. Malta certainly, and Gibraltar possibly, would be in grave danger.

So bleak did the prospect appear that the Chiefs of Staff, while noting that to contain the Italian fleet and secure Egypt a capital ship fleet should be based on Alexandria, had advised that preparations should be made for eventually withdrawing our ships to Aden and blocking the Canal, since the heavy attack which after a period of months the enemy should be able to launch from Libya might render our position untenable. In fact the Naval Staff on June 17 tentatively raised the question whether, as soon as it was clear that French control of the western Mediterranean was coming to an end, the fleet should not be moved from eastern waters to Gibraltar. From the standpoint of naval strategy, it was suggested, there was a strong case for such a measure. Alexandria was an unsatisfactory base, exposed, as it would probably be, to increasingly formidable attack from German as well as Italian aircraft and lacking proper repair facilities; thus the fleet would become less and less able to interfere with Italy's sea communications. But there was a weightier argument: since German raiders might now be able to operate from French, and possibly Spanish, Atlantic ports, we might soon be obliged to use more battleships for convoy purposes, and these could only be found from the fleet now at Alexandria. 'Atlantic trade', the First Sea Lord had signalled to Admiral Cunningham on the previous day, 'must be our first consideration.' On the other hand the economic and, still more, the military and political objections to a withdrawal of the fleet from the eastern Mediterranean were obvious. The suggestion was strongly opposed both by Admiral Cunningham and by the Prime Minister. Mr. Churchill urged that the fleet was well placed to sustain our interests in Turkey, to guard Egypt and the Canal; even if Spain declared war and we were forced out of Gibraltar it did not follow that we must quit the eastern Mediterranean, since an alternative base could be found in the Canaries which would still enable us to control the western exit.[1] The Chiefs of Staff, sensible of the extremely grave military and political implications of the proposal, deferred its consideration on June 18 and nothing more was heard of it. On July 3 they informed the Middle East, India and the Dominions that it was intended to retain the fleet in the eastern Mediterranean as long as possible. This decision was, as things turned out, one of immense importance.

The Naval Staff had also referred to the disappointing attitude of Turkey and Egypt, neither of which was willing to declare war on Italy.

Even before the conclusion of the Franco-German armistice, the Turkish Government decided to adopt an attitude of non-belligerency, invoking the provision in the Tripartite Treaty of 19 October 1939 that Turkey would not be required to take action likely to involve her in war with Russia.[2] Though Article 7 of the treaty declared that its provisions were binding as bilateral obligations between Turkey and each of the other Powers, the Turks could argue after the armistice that the French defection had entirely altered the circumstances in which the treaty had been agreed to. Their Prime Minister announced on June 26 that Turkey would preserve her present attitude of non-belligerency for the security and defence of the country, and she did not even break off diplomatic relations with Italy. The foundation of our Balkan strategy, as envisaged in London, had collapsed.

Egypt was differently placed, inasmuch as British armed forces had for years been stationed in her territory. By the treaty of 1936 Egypt was pledged as an ally to come to the aid of Britain if the latter became unavoidably engaged in war. The Cairo Government had evaded a declaration of war on Germany in September 1939, but had broken off diplomatic relations with her and had in fact taken all the practical measures required by the British. In June 1940 they were still reluctant to declare war, but—unlike the Turks—they broke off relations with Italy and they agreed to fulfil their treaty obligations. Egyptian troops did, moreover, play some part in the defence of their country. Strong pressure was needed, however, to induce King Farouk to send away the Italian diplomatic staff and to appoint a Prime Minister in whose co-operation the British authorities could feel confidence.

---

[1] See Churchill II 390, 392, 563; Cunningham, *A Sailor's Odyssey* p. 241; Roskill I 296.

[2] See above, p. 67.

x

In the French Mandated Territories of Syria and the Lebanon the High Commissioner and the new Commander-in-Chief, General Mittelhauser, at first stated their intentions of continuing the war; but in conformity with Pétain's policy the General soon declared that hostilities had ceased in his command. The British Government saw in this no immediate danger to our cause, but thought it well to announce, after consultation with the Turks, that 'they could not allow Syria or the Lebanon to be occupied by any hostile Power or to be used as a base for attacks upon those countries in the Middle East which they are pledged to defend, or to become the scene of such disorder as to constitute a danger to those countries'.

So we were left to our own resources.

The high command in the Mediterranean theatre rested with a triumvirate of Service chiefs of equal status. The naval Commander-in-Chief, Mediterranean, was Admiral Sir Andrew Cunningham, flying his flag in the *Warspite*; his command did not however extend over the Red Sea. On land, General Sir Archibald Wavell, now styled Commander-in-Chief, Middle East, included the Balkans, Turkey, Iraq, Aden, and East Africa in his responsibilities. The newly-arrived Air Officer Commanding-in-Chief, Air Marshal Sir Arthur Longmore, a recent Commandant of the Imperial Defence College, was responsible for Malta as well. An inter-Service planning and intelligence organisation had been established at Cairo, where the army and air chiefs, sharing a common headquarters, worked in extremely close co-operation. On political matters the commanders were directed to consult with the British Ambassador, Sir Miles Lampson.

On June 18 General Wavell, supported by his Air colleague, urged that, in view of the immense area over which operations might extend and the probable difficulty of obtaining prompt decisions from a distant Cabinet preoccupied with the defence of Great Britain, it was imperative to set up some form of War Council in Africa, with authority delegated from the Cabinet, 'to co-ordinate and direct the war effort and the utilisation of resources in the Middle East'. General Wavell suggested that the proposed body should possess, under the general direction of the Cabinet, full control in all matters of military operations, economic organisation, supplies and shipping within a certain area, which should include all Africa and extend to the frontiers of India. Its chairman might be taken from the present War Cabinet of the United Kingdom, the other members being chosen for their energy and ability from the United Kingdom or the Dominions. It should be advised by a Chiefs of Staff committee similar to that in London, but as the naval Commander-in-Chief might be afloat a separate naval adviser would probably be required. The proposal might be revolutionary, but some decentralisation was essential if prompt and resolute action were to be ensured. Admiral Cunningham agreed in principle, but felt that it would be difficult for the Admiralty, in view of the strategic mobility of naval forces, to delegate the executive naval power.

On further consideration General Wavell decided that events were moving too swiftly to allow of the delay which the setting up of such a body would entail; he suggested instead that a Cabinet Committee in England should keep a close watch on affairs in the Middle East. The Chiefs of Staff were of opinion that no such action was required, but a few days later, on July 11, the Prime Minister decided to create just such a body, consisting of the three Secretaries of State for War, India and the Colonies (Mr. Eden, Mr. Amery and Lord Lloyd). Its terms of reference were to keep the conduct of the war in the Middle East under review and to report to the Minister of Defence.

The new committee did not of course meet Wavell's desire for the delegation of control to a body on the spot. A year later, when Wavell himself was almost overwhelmed by the multiplicity of his responsibilities, not only military but political, relief as regards the latter was provided, if not for him, for his successor by the appointment of a Minister of State. But though Captain Lyttelton was to 'represent the War Cabinet on the spot', there was no such delegation of the control of the war effort, both operational and economic, as Wavell had originally suggested. Indeed, it may be doubted whether such a delegation of power over so vast an area would have been compatible with the sovereign control of the Cabinet and the Chiefs of Staff, or with the powers exercised by the Prime Minister and Minister of Defence in the general direction of the war.

In January 1940 the Cabinet had approved the Chiefs of Staff's proposals for building up in the Middle East a reserve of land and air forces, including nine divisions in Egypt and Palestine and some twenty-two bomber and fighter squadrons.[1] This programme was naturally far from accomplishment in June, and on the naval side too there were grave deficiencies.

The considerable fleet allotted to the Mediterranean in September 1939 had been gradually whittled away in view of the continued non-belligerency of Italy. But in April and May, as we have seen, its strength was rebuilt, and by June 9 Sir Andrew Cunningham had under his command four battleships,[2] six or more cruisers, twenty fleet destroyers, a dozen submarines and the aircraft carrier *Eagle*. This force, as the Admiral says,[3] was 'on paper, quite an imposing one', but two at least of the battleships were old and slow, the destroyers were too few, and there was a sad lack of escort vessels and minesweepers and, above all, of aircraft for reconnaissance.

---

[1] See p. 69.

[2] *Warspite, Malaya, Royal Sovereign, Ramillies.*

[3] *A Sailor's Odyssey* p. 234.

In the weeks preceding the Italian declaration of war there had been some discussion of the action to be taken by our Mediterranean fleet. Cunningham had received Admiralty approval of his intention to aim first at securing control of the communications in the eastern Mediterranean and Aegean and cutting off supplies from the enemy's bases in the Dodecanese. He did not at present contemplate the interruption of Italian sea communications with Libya: not only was he short of light surface forces and of air support, but the fact that the Allies were no longer thinking of land offensives against Libya made it more important to give Turkey the encouragement which a blow to the Italians in the Dodecanese would represent. He proposed however to carry out 'an extensive sweep' in the central Mediterranean.

To the Prime Minister, eager that the quality of the Italian Navy and Air Force should be tested without delay, a strategy which seemed to him purely defensive was unacceptable. We must be prepared to run risks in all theatres. The Chiefs of Staff did not accept this criticism: they were convinced that, while our forces in the Mediterranean would adopt a tactical offensive, strategically, owing to Italy's superiority in the air, we should have to remain on the defensive in the opening stages of a war with her. A month earlier the First Sea Lord had told the Supreme War Council that experience in Norway had shown the danger of placing big ships, without fighter protection, within 200 miles of enemy air bases. The Vice-Chiefs of Staff now reaffirmed this lesson and pointed out the difficulty of executing large-scale repairs at Alexandria. Admiral Cunningham moreover urged that his 'limited' proposal should not be regarded as defensive: it implied the destruction of enemy forces in the Dodecanese and the ultimate 'liquidation' of these islands. It was the 'burning desire' of himself and all his command to get at the Italian Fleet, but to do so implied possibilities of air reconnaissance which he did not at present possess.[1]

To a certain extent the successful action off Calabria on July 9 gave the Admiral the longed-for opportunity.[2] It was far less conclusive than he would have liked, but it had at least probed the enterprise of the Italian Navy. 'Never again did they willingly face up to the fire of British battleships, though on several subsequent occasions they were in a position to give battle with great preponderance in force.'[3] The Prime Minister was encouraged to hope for a more aggressive strategy on our part. Now that the Germans dominated northern Europe, we must look to the Mediterranean for action. He believed the time had come to bombard the Italian homeland both from the sea and from the air and considered that too much was

---

[1] See *A Sailor's Odyssey* pp. 230–233.
[2] See Roskill I ch. xv.
[3] *A Sailor's Odyssey* p. 263.

made of the risk to ships from aircraft. He recalled his own proposals of the previous autumn to reconstruct some of the older battleships with heavy deck armour, which would have given them some degree of immunity for the purpose now suggested.

Not the least of the factors hampering ambitious naval operations, as the Prime Minister well understood, was the precarious condition of Malta. Early in July 1940 the Chiefs of Staff took this matter in hand, on representations being made by the Governor, Lieutenant-General W. G. Dobbie, and the chiefs of the three Services in the island. Malta had not so far been bombed severely, but it was the obvious target for Italian aircraft based on Sicily. It comprised a civilian population of several hundred thousand, and apart from the matter of prestige it was of military importance both as a naval base, which Admiral Cunningham was anxious to maintain and use as such, and as a refuelling point for aircraft flying through the Mediterranean. The present defences against air attack were far below those authorised by the Committee of Imperial Defence in July 1939. The Chiefs of Staff now approved the despatch to Malta from the United Kingdom of a modest reinforcement of Hurricane fighters and anti-aircraft guns; the conveyance of this equipment to the island illustrated the difficulties attending every attempt at this time to use the Mediterranean sea-route.[1]

Our land forces in the Middle East at the end of May comprised some 36,000 men in Egypt, including New Zealand and Indian contingents. They were not, however, organised in complete formations, and equipment was short throughout, especially artillery of all sorts, ammunition, fighting vehicles and transport. In Palestine there were about 27,500 troops, including two Australian brigades and an incomplete horsed cavalry division; the greater part however were not fully equipped and trained, and one brigade might be required for service in Iraq. In the Sudan were three British battalions and the Sudan Defence Force, in Kenya two East African brigades and two light batteries. A brigade from the Union of South Africa arrived in June 1940.

Sir Arthur Longmore's force in Egypt and Palestine amounted to 205 aircraft—96 bombers and bomber transports, 75 fighters, 24 army co-operation Lysanders and 10 flying-boats; he had no modern fighters or long-range bombers, and was short of spares and other equipment.[2]

Our general policy in the Middle East was succinctly defined by the Chiefs of Staff in a telegram of which copies were sent to the

---

[1] For Operation 'Hurry' see Playfair I ch. viii.
[2] Playfair I 95.

Commanders-in-Chief at the beginning of July. The retention of our position there was still of the utmost military importance in view of the economic blockade of Europe and of our requirements for oil. The security of the Middle East depended on the defence of Egypt and the Sudan, Iraq, Palestine, Aden and Kenya. Kenya was our second line of defence in Africa; it was a base of operations against Italian East Africa and offered, through Mombasa, an alternative line of communication to Egypt. Another reinforcement route, for aircraft and light stores, was being opened across Africa from the Gold Coast.[1] Our strategy must for the present be in the main defensive, though local offensives should be started whenever possible. Our existing forces should be able to deal with any purely Italian attack on Egypt. A German attack would be a different matter, and German aircraft might render Alexandria untenable as a fleet base. It was hoped that Turkey would oppose a German or Italian advance on the Middle East through the Balkans; in any case the threat from this direction could not become serious for a longish time.

The need for strengthening our forces in the Middle East at the earliest possible moment was recognised, but our immediate concern must be the defence of the United Kingdom. We should hope to release equipment for the Middle East when the situation at home became clearer, but this might not be for two months. In the meantime we would send anything we could spare. A few days later the Dominions were told that we thought it unlikely that the enemy would be able to embark on large-scale operations in North Africa till the end of September, by which time we hoped to have defeated any attempts at invasion at home.

It was of course a grave handicap to us that the enemy could reinforce Libya in a few days whereas the voyage to Egypt round the Cape took two or three months.

The new Middle East Committee were soon seriously concerned at the shortages of men and equipment. After discussion with the Chiefs of Staff on July 25 they recommended to the Minister of Defence that the 5th Indian Division, due for despatch to Basra, should instead be placed at General Wavell's disposal, and that preparations should be made now for sending a second armoured division from England to the Middle East as soon as the threat of invasion might seem to have lessened. The War Office and Air Ministry should hasten the reinforcement of the Middle East with troops and equipment so fast as home needs allowed, and Australia and New Zealand should be asked to send thither any forces they could spare after meeting their commitments in the Far East. We should also press on with measures already begun for fomenting Abyssinian resistance to the Italians.

---

[1] See Map 12.

This report does not appear to have been discussed as a whole by the Cabinet or Defence Committee, but the Cabinet approved the Chiefs of Staff's recommendation for the diversion of the Indian division to Egypt.

Mr. Churchill was evidently not wholly satisfied with the use being made of our existing forces and, as he has told us, he asked that Wavell, whom he did not know personally, should be invited to England for consultation. A senior air staff officer, Group Captain Wigglesworth, accompanied the General. The situation in the Middle East was then discussed at length.[1]

General Wavell explained what he had done and what he intended to do. After scoring some minor successes in the Western Desert our main forces had withdrawn 125 miles east of the frontier to the position at Mersa Matruh where it was our plan to hold an enemy advance. The real danger, however, would be an attack by German armoured and motorised units. Owing to our pre-war policy of not offending the Italians we had neglected opportunities to maintain a system of intelligence in Libya, and had now no effective information of happenings there, while our few aircraft had not the range for distant reconnaissance; it would therefore be easy for the Germans to pass troops to North Africa without our knowledge. Reinforcements in both troops and equipment were urgently required, and it was important that they should be such as to make up complete units and formations—an ideal which shortages at home, exigencies of shipping and the multitude of commitments in the Middle East rendered difficult of attainment.

In the area of his command south of Egypt, the capture of Kassala in the Sudan by an Italian force from Eritrea was no serious matter; extensive operations against the Sudan could not begin before the end of the rainy season in October. In Kenya the loss of the post of Moyale on the Abyssinian escarpment was regrettable, and our plans for an early advance into Italian Somaliland had been set back, but Kenya itself should be in no danger. In British Somaliland an Italian force was advancing from Abyssinia. It had been our original intention to evacuate this dependency, which was of little strategic importance. The Chiefs of Staff had pointed out in a report of July 16 that the cessation of French resistance in Jibuti would increase the danger to our own territory and perhaps compel evacuation. From this we should suffer only in prestige. Wavell decided nevertheless to hold the Protectorate and moved a British battalion from Aden to reinforce the Indian and African troops forming the garrison; it was now hoped to hold Berbera on the coast. However, while Wavell was in England, evacuation of the whole Protectorate was made necessary, after heavy

---

[1] Churchill II 375, 376. For a full account of these discussions see Playfair I ch. x.

fighting in the hills, by the enemy's superiority in numbers and in artillery, and the Italians entered Berbera on August 19.[1] During the six months of their occupation they did us little harm.

The grave predicament disclosed by the conversations in London led to prompt decisions. As the result of discussions between the Prime Minister, the Secretary of State for War (Mr. Eden), the First Sea Lord and General Wavell it was resolved, in spite of the imminent danger at home, to send to the Middle East at the earliest possible date an armoured force of over 150 tanks—light, cruiser and infantry types—with full equipment, along with over 100 guns, field, anti-tank and anti-aircraft. Some air reinforcements had already been sent, and it was now decided to rearm with modern aircraft as many as possible of the squadrons already in the Middle East. It was an act of high courage to strip the country of so many precious weapons and trained men at a time when invasion threatened.[2]

But it was one thing to decide to send reinforcements to Egypt; it was another thing to get them there, and no small controversy ensued. The point at issue between Mr. Churchill and his advisers was what portion of the reinforcements should be exposed to the hazards of a Mediterranean passage; it was a balance between speed and safety. Mr. Churchill desired to take advantage of the elaborate naval plans for safeguarding the sailing of certain warships for Alexandria to despatch in their company some of the merchant vessels conveying the army reinforcements; this meant slowing down the rate of progress and so increasing the danger from the air. Crucial at the other end was the date by which Wavell must expect an attack from Libya. The Prime Minister could not tolerate the possibility that, by being sent round the Cape, the infantry tanks might not be available when needed, either in England or in Egypt.

General Wavell, however, did not consider that the chances of a successful passage through the Mediterranean justified the risk of losing valuable equipment, and the Chiefs of Staff recommended that only such reinforcements as could be conveyed in warships should go by that route and that the rest should be sent in fast merchant ships round the Cape. They reckoned that so the whole of the armoured brigade should be in Egypt by September 29, a delay of at most twenty-five days. Mr. Churchill was not convinced but, as he has told us, he did not ask the Cabinet to overrule professional opinion, and his colleagues decided accordingly, with his reluctant acquiescence. In the event both expeditions arrived safely; the naval reinforcements berthed at Alexandria on September 5 and, though the Italian

---

[1] For an account of this campaign see Playfair I ch. ix.

[2] Apart from the less valuable light tanks, probably not much more than 250 cruiser and infantry tanks remained at home.

offensive was launched before the appearance of the tanks at Suez, it came to a halt well short of Mersa Matruh.[1]

Just about the time of General Wavell's return to his command, Mr. Churchill, as Minister for Defence, submitted to the Chiefs of Staff for examination a draft general directive for Wavell's guidance; it was not to be regarded as precise instructions. Beginning with a statement of the relative strategic importance of the different possible areas of operations, it proceeded to suggest how by the end of September the maximum force should be assembled for the defence of the Delta against the major invasion of Egypt from Libya which must now be expected at any time. The last third of the document dealt with the tactical employment of the proposed force. After the all-important defence of the western frontier came the Sudan; Kenya could take only third place, and we could always reinforce Kenya faster than Italy could pass troops thither from Abyssinia or Italian Somaliland. Suggestions were therefore made for the movement of troops from Palestine to Egypt and from Kenya to the Sudan. The tactical paragraphs included directions for a main line of defence to be constructed along the western edge of the Delta; notes were added on the contamination of drinking water, on delayed-action mines and on the rendering of asphalt roads unusable.[2]

Certain points in this directive were criticised by the Chiefs of Staff, who suggested amendments; it should be made clear, they said, that the Delta position could only be regarded as a last ditch, the right strategy being to concentrate as far forward as possible and destroy the Italian army in the desert. A revised edition, as approved by the Defence Committee, was on August 22 sent to Wavell for his observations; Mr. Churchill explained to the Cabinet, who gave it their blessing, that it was not intended as an order to be carried out without modifications.

The observations of the three Commanders-in-Chief followed promptly. Wavell's first, and last, comment was that the successful defence of Egypt and especially of the naval base at Alexandria depended on air power. On land, it was material rather than men that was required, and especially artillery and anti-tank weapons. The enemy would not reach the Delta with large forces of infantry but only if he could bring superior armoured force. He urged that a second complete armoured division was needed as soon as possible; even with the reinforcements on the way the first would be incomplete. He could not agree that all the Prime Minister's suggestions for the disposition of his available forces were sound. Kenya was important; after our expulsion from British Somaliland we could not afford

---

[1] For operation 'Hats' and the discussions concerning it see Playfair I ch. x; Churchill II 394–400; Cunningham *op. cit.* 271–272.

[2] The directive, without the technical notes, is printed in Churchill II 379.

to see our prestige in Africa further weakened; he did not agree that we could reinforce that front quicker than the Italians could. Nor did he think it safe to denude Palestine to the extent proposed. He proceeded to explain his views on the defence of Egypt in the west.

Admiral Cunningham's comment was that the directive appeared largely to disregard the naval and air aspects of the situation. Any advance by the enemy beyond, or even as far as, Matruh would threaten the fleet base at Alexandria; Matruh must be held at all costs. The reply from the Prime Minister can hardly have been comforting to the Admiral, who inferred that his own part in this scheme must be to take energetic steps to increase the facilities of Port Said and Haifa for use as rearward bases from which the fleet could operate if Alexandria were denied to us, so as to put off leaving the Mediterranean as long as possible.

Air Marshal Longmore strongly supported a representation of Wavell's that the Sudan needed reinforcement even at the expense of Egypt, since an enemy advance from the north might endanger our air route from West Africa. He also emphasised his weakness in fighter squadrons, outnumbered by the Italians, as he claimed, on the Egyptian front by four to one.

The Chiefs of Staff, after considering this correspondence, found that, except as regards Kenya, there was no great difference between Wavell's intended dispositions and those of the directive, and expressed their general agreement with his proposals as a whole. The Defence Committee took the same line, while advising that the question of the proper garrison for Kenya should be reviewed at an early date.

This exchange of opinions is of great interest from the point of view of the higher direction of the war. So detailed a directive from a Minister to a commander in a distant theatre was to say the least unusual; to which it may be replied that Mr. Churchill was an unusual Minister, possessing an unusual interest, fortified by long study and experience, in the art of war, and unusual drive. At the same time it is clear that he was not wholly satisfied as to the General's capacity. 'While not in full agreement,' he tells us, with General Wavell's use of resources at his disposal, 'I thought it best to leave him in command. I admired his fine qualities and was impressed with the confidence so many people had in him.'[1] A note of hesitation is perceptible; it appears that he missed in the General a vigorous resolve to overcome obstacles. These misgivings continued. In the last week of September, complaining of the waste of troops in Kenya, in Palestine and in Egypt on 'mere police duty', Mr. Churchill spoke of 'the general slackness of the Middle East Command in concentrating

[1] Churchill II 376.

the maximum for battle, and in narrowing the gap between ration strength and fighting strength'.[1] This last criticism, which became chronic, will be referred to later, but it must be stated that the Secretary of State and the Chief of the Imperial General Staff did not share the Prime Minister's doubts of Wavell's determination and energy.

Rather in the same way Mr. Churchill thought it necessary to administer to Cunningham 'prods' which the Admiral resented.[2] Generous as he was of his praises in their moments of triumph and untiring in his endeavours to supply their needs, it is doubtful if the Prime Minister in those early days fully appreciated the quality of these two great commanders. Perhaps there was in each of them too much of the Scot, by birth or (in Wavell's case) by adoption, to respond acceptably to his exacting optimism; but, beyond this, in Wavell, so accomplished with the pen, there often appeared a peculiar inability to express his thoughts coherently in speech.

The Middle East directive had not forgotten Malta. It recorded the hope that the garrison when strengthened would play its part in the defence of Egypt by hampering the despatch of further reinforcements, Italian or German, to Africa. The much-discussed Operation 'Hats' included the convoying of storeships for the island from Alexandria. At this same time, towards the end of August, the Chiefs of Staff, on the initiative of the Ministerial Middle East Committee, considered the possibility of using the island as a base for bombing the Italian mainland. They concluded that such action could not be recommended at the present time; the important targets in Italy were in the north-west, where they could be more easily reached from England than from Malta, and in any case until its air defences were stronger it was undesirable to provoke retaliation on the island, now so useful as a staging point for aircraft on the route to Egypt. In assessing its claims for further air defences the Committee had to take account alike of Admiral Cunningham's desire to use the island as a fleet base and of the many other demands on our anti-aircraft supplies. They resolved that, in principle, the anti-aircraft defences of the island should by 1st April 1941 be brought up to the scale approved before the war and that in addition its fighter strength should be raised to four squadrons as soon as possible. A month later, on September 24, the Defence Committee, on the Prime Minister's motion, decided to reinforce the garrison by a sixth infantry battalion and a 25-pounder battery, to be carried in warships from Gibraltar in the last days of October.

The question of reinforcing Malta could, however, never sleep for

---

[1] *ibid.* II 442.
[2] *A Sailor's Odyssey* p. 231.

long, and decisions taken were subject to constant alteration as the result of happenings elsewhere. On October 15 the Defence Committee were again discussing the question, as a matter of urgency: the expedition last mentioned could not now sail till November, and it was decided that it should convey two batteries of field artillery with anti-aircraft guns and a few tanks (but not an infantry battalion) and that as part of the operation twelve Hurricanes should be flown into Malta off the carrier *Argus*: the necessary infantry should now be sent at the first opportunity from Egypt.

For the conveyance of men or material from Britain to Malta the co-operation of Force H at Gibraltar was essential. But these ships had other tasks; the postponement of the October convoy was due to events in the eastern Atlantic.

We must return to the early reactions of the British high command to the Franco-German armistice, as especially affecting our interests in West Africa and off its coasts, and that at a time when we still hoped that the French territories overseas would dissociate themselves from Vichy.[1] It gradually became clear, however, that no such general movement could be expected, while the amount of support which General de Gaulle could hope to receive in the several colonies was conjectural; on the other hand, as it also became clear that the Vichy Government did not wish to pick a quarrel with us, there was important backing in Whitehall for the view that we should not go out of our way to provoke it. It was obvious too that, with invasion threatening and the Navy at full stretch, we should not for some time be able to send any considerable force abroad.

On August 3rd the Colonial Office sketched 'the general West African background' as follows:

> 'Our first aim on the collapse of France was to induce the French colonies to fight on as our allies. We established close contact with the local French administrations and offered substantial financial inducements. The reaction leaves no doubt that there are French elements ready to rally to our side. But the Vichy government is in a position to exercise strong pressure on the local officials who have been in a defeatist and wavering frame of mind; and there is no doubt that the official policy of the local administrators is now one of obedience to Vichy and refusal to co-operate with us.'

The Colonial Office accordingly proposed that we should now adopt the policy of fostering and building up 'such dissident elements in the French territories as show themselves disposed to reject the

---

[1] Above, p. 230.

official French policy'. They remarked that the alternative of a direct show of force had hitherto been ruled out on military advice.

This was the case. In their appreciation of July 16 on the implications of French hostility the Chiefs of Staff had stressed the danger to our trade routes of enemy operations from the French West African ports, and had suggested that we should prepare plans for the destruction of the base at Dakar by naval action. But on the 29th they agreed that naval bombardment was out of the question, as being contrary to the Government's policy not to impair Anglo-French relations, whereas 'an occupation by land forces in face of French resistance would be an operation of some magnitude for which we have not at present the forces available'.

On August 5, however, the Prime Minister laid before the Cabinet a project which had been worked out by General de Gaulle, Major-General E. L. Spears and Major Desmond Morton.[1] It had the attraction of not involving the employment of any British land forces. General de Gaulle, who shared our desire to establish a French Government friendly to Britain and hostile to Germany in as many parts of the French Empire as possible, thought that a landing in West Africa offered better prospects than one in Algeria. Messages from Nigeria offered some confirmation of this opinion. Accordingly it was proposed that an expedition under his command should sail from England with the purpose of occupying Dakar and consolidating the French colonies in West and Equatorial Africa under the Free French flag. It was apparently assumed that the landing would be unopposed. The next objective would be to win over the French territories in North Africa, and General Catroux would be sent for from Indo-China to take command there eventually. Only French forces would land in French West Africa; their strength would be roughly that of a brigade group, with some aircraft; the British part would be to equip, transport and escort them. The only ports suitable were Dakar in Senegal, Conakry[2] in French Guinea, or (to a limited extent) Duala far to the east in French Cameroons. It was proposed that three agents selected by de Gaulle should be flown to Nigeria immediately to make contact with French and British authorities. The Cabinet agreed that operation 'Scipio' should be carried out and that preparations should be pressed forward.

The Chiefs of Staff, who had been consulted only at the last moment, thought it right, in view of the military implications of the success or failure of a revolt in West Africa, to express their opinions on the general question of our policy in respect of the French colonial

---

[1] See Churchill II ch. xxiv generally for the Dakar project; also C. de Gaulle, *Mémoires de Guerre, L'Appel 1940–42* (Paris 1954).

[2] Sometimes spelt Konakri. See Map 12.

possessions. They called attention to the inconsistency of the two parallel policies of improving our relations with Vichy and of encouraging any elements in the French Empire which were willing to fight against Germany. After reviewing conditions in the several territories and expressing their apprehensions of the enlarged commitments into which support of de Gaulle's expedition might lead us, they ended with a very guarded approval of it. They could only recommend it if reports from West Africa showed that it had reasonable prospects of success and was not likely to involve us in a considerable military commitment. Otherwise we should do well to seek a *modus vivendi* with the local French administrations and avoid an open breach with Vichy on the colonial issue.

The course of 'Scipio' never did run smooth. On the afternoon of the very day, August 5th, when the Cabinet sanctioned it, the Chiefs of Staff learnt that General de Gaulle had not taken account of the possibility of Vichyite naval forces interfering with his landing; his first reaction to this suggestion was that he would not attempt to land if air reconnaissance revealed the presence of French warships in the harbour; the expedition must proceed to the nearest British colony and move thence against Dakar overland; he felt also driven to stipulate that the British should guarantee his expedition against any forces sent by Vichy by sea. The plan was then radically revised, the General making it clear that he would have no part in fighting between Frenchmen, and a number of alternative landing schemes were considered.

The Prime Minister discussed the new situation with the Chiefs of Staff on the night of August 7. It was agreed that the only place where a landing could be really effective was Dakar, and after the meeting Mr. Churchill issued a directive for the preparation of a fresh plan forthwith: the operation was now to be carried through, whether or not de Gaulle's emissaries reported favourably of local opinion. The forces which might be called upon were Free French troops and warships, the ships of the Royal Navy, a Polish brigade, and a brigade of Royal Marines, now held ready for the capture, in certain circumstances, of Atlantic islands, or alternatively commandos from Combined Operations; there must be adequate air support. It was not intended to hold Dakar, once secured, with British forces. The possible reactions of Vichy were a matter for the Cabinet.

On August 13 the Cabinet's approval was asked, and provisionally given, for what the Prime Minister described as a drastic change of plan, to which the Chiefs of Staff had agreed. It was now proposed to establish de Gaulle at Dakar by a *coup de main*. Every endeavour would be made to secure the place without bloodshed, on the plea that an Allied force had come to prevent the Germans seizing Dakar, and to bring succour and help to the colony. The British commanders had been appointed: Vice-Admiral J. H. D. Cunningham and Major-General N. M. S. Irwin.[1] Once General de Gaulle's force had been successfully installed, the British would withdraw. It was improbable, though possible, that the Vichy Government would declare war on us; if they did, Mr. Churchill thought, it would perhaps not matter very much.

The character of the plan, as well as its code-name—henceforward 'Menace'—had now been completely altered. British forces would be openly used and the operation would be carried through in spite of opposition. Mr. Churchill has told us that he 'had now become set upon this venture' and 'undertook in an exceptional degree the initiation and advocacy of the expedition'.[2]

The commanders discussed plans with the Prime Minister, with the Chiefs of Staff and with General de Gaulle, and their directives as revised by the Chiefs of Staff on August 16 were approved by the Prime Minister; they were told that the Inter-Service Planning Staff, the Directorate of Combined Operations and the Service Departments were at their disposal for consultation, and with such help they were to draw up their own detailed plans; the date of the operation was now envisaged as September 12 or 13. But all sorts of difficulties arose, of a tactical, logistical, and topographical nature, suggesting at least a postponement of a month. The chances of a successful surprise now seemed remote, and on the night of August 20 the Vice-Chiefs of Staff, who were handling the matter, and General de Gaulle agreed to the Prime Minister's proposal to revert to the original plan. The garrison of Dakar should be invited to receive de Gaulle as liberator; the British force would remain in the background, and only if opposition were serious would the British ships open fire. The new proposal was explained to the commanders next morning, and they, after consulting de Gaulle, prepared a fresh plan; they were in agreement that it would be necessary for the expedition to break its journey at Freetown, and that it could not arrive before Dakar until September 18. This plan was approved. Finally, on August 27, the Cabinet sanctioned the venture in view of the importance of its objects; the danger of Vichy declaring war was not considered very serious. So on August 31 the transports and the commanders sailed. The British land forces comprised a brigade headquarters and four battalions of Royal Marines and one Independent Company (from Combined Operations), with two French battalions and a company of tanks. The naval force was assembled from many stations: it included the *Barham* and two cruisers from the Home Fleet, the *Resolution* and *Ark Royal* from Force H, the *Cumberland* from the South

---

[1] Vice-Admiral John Cunningham is not to be confused with Admiral Sir Andrew Cunningham, Commander-in-Chief, Mediterranean.

[2] Churchill II 422.

Atlantic squadron, besides three French sloops and some landing craft.

The omens for the success of the enterprise were unpropitious. A leakage of information was indicated; inquiry showed that there had been indiscreet talk—not in British circles—in England, and the movement of equipment, perhaps inevitably, had not been concealed though it might be that its actual destination had not been guessed. Then on August 24 General Irwin put on record his misgivings as to the adequacy of the air forces assigned and of the training of the troops in landing operations, should de Gaulle's advances not be favourably received; and it was not till the 26th that the British general met the men whom he was to command. Most serious of all was the arrival at the last moment, actually after the storeships had sailed, of first-hand information to the effect that the defences of Dakar were considerably stronger than we had believed, and that almost certainly any attempt by de Gaulle would be resolutely opposed. This disquieting intelligence—part fact, part opinion, and, so far as it was opinion, entirely contrary to the French leader's own information—was brought by the British naval and army liaison officers recently at Dakar; their journey from Lagos by air had been accidently delayed. Captain Poulter, the army officer, had indeed sent a copy of the French West Africa defence scheme to the War Office in June, but unfortunately it had not been communicated to the leaders of the expedition. The result was a hurried and unsatisfactory preparation and distribution of orders at sea and at Freetown—a result to which the failure to provide a headquarters ship for the land forces largely contributed.

While all this was happening, the situation in French Equatorial Africa—the vast region extending from the mouth of the Congo northwards to Lake Chad—had changed in a very favourable manner.[1] On August 16 the Chiefs of Staff passed on to the Prime Minister a telegram from General Giffard, General Officer Commanding, West Africa, giving the view of de Gaulle's emissaries that success in the Cameroons and Equatorial Africa was a prerequisite for any successful operation against Dakar. That afternoon they discussed the matter with de Gaulle; he approved the plan of operations to be carried through by small French forces for the capture of Duala in the Cameroons and Fort Lamy in the Chad territory, but saw no reason why these should delay or interfere with 'Menace'. The Prime Minister and the Chiefs of Staff agreed and General Giffard was urged to give every encouragement and help to the French operation against Duala. It was successfully carried out on the night of August 26/27 and the following day; and on the 28th Brazzaville,

[1] See Map 12.

the capital of French Equatorial Africa, was taken after two hours' fighting. Already on the 26th the Governor of Chad territory had proclaimed its adherence and that of its garrison to de Gaulle. By the beginning of September the only part of French Equatorial Africa still loyal to Vichy was Gabon in the south; this province, after at first rallying to de Gaulle, returned to its former obedience and remained faithful to Pétain until finally won over in November.

Further north, matters were not going so happily. While the Dakar expedition was at sea, three French cruisers and three large destroyers from Toulon passed through the Straits of Gibraltar on September 11 to Casablanca, whence they reached Dakar on the 14th—the day that the Allied troop convoy arrived at Freetown. A detailed account of the circumstances is given elsewhere; here they need only be mentioned briefly.[1] The Cabinet had decided on July 11, a week after the incident at Oran, to take no further action with regard to the French ships in colonial or North African ports, while reserving the right to deal with warships heading for ports under enemy control. On September 10 the French Marine informed the British Naval Attaché at Madrid of the intended move of six ships from Toulon, without mentioning their destination. Mr. Churchill has explained in his book how it came about that neither this warning, nor an earlier one from Tangier, led to effective action in London.[2] The naval authorities at Gibraltar, receiving no fresh instructions from the Admiralty, did not consider it their duty to attempt to stop the ships.[3] When at length, about noon on the 11th, the First Sea Lord learnt of the French intention, the Cabinet sent orders to Gibraltar that they should not be interfered with if their destination was Casablanca, but must be prevented from reaching the Atlantic ports of France or Dakar. It was then too late. We now know that the French ships did not, as was thought probable in London, carry reinforcements for Dakar—they were in fact bound for Libreville in Gabon, much further south—but it was natural at the time to suppose that they did, and in any case their arrival at Dakar may have 'stiffened the will of the local authorities to resist the British purpose with force'.

The Prime Minister accordingly on the afternoon of the 15th gave instructions for the Chiefs of Staff to be immediately convoked to consider the new situation; he directed that 'Menace', as at present proposed, should be cancelled, and a variant of 'Scipio' substituted; namely an expedition, which need not be wholly French, up the railway from Conakry in French Guinea so as to cut the communications of Dakar from the land. At the same time Dakar would be blockaded

---

[1] See Roskill I 309 ff., where the naval side of the Dakar expedition is fully treated.

[2] Churchill II 425–426.

[3] For current Admiralty policy see above, p. 225.

by a sufficient naval force. The Chiefs of Staff however reported that such an operation was not practicable, either on the land or on the naval side, adding that 'until the threat of invasion has either been dealt with or has receded, and until our reinforcements have reached the Middle East, we are definitely of the opinion that we must do nothing which might result in active hostilities with the Vichy Government.' They advised that de Gaulle should rather use his forces to consolidate the position in French Equatorial Africa, using Duala as his base. The Cabinet next morning accepted their report, with its implication that the bulk of the British troops should be made available for other employment, and approved a consequential signal to Admiral John Cunningham.

But General de Gaulle and the British commanders took a less gloomy view of the probable effect of the arrival of the French ships at Dakar, and were eager to put the matter to the proof. After full discussion the Cabinet reversed their previous decision and gave the men on the spot authority to go ahead with whatever plan they preferred. But, before the operation was eventually launched on September 23, an interruption was caused by the need to frustrate the attempt of some of the French warships in Dakar to work southward and interfere with Free French schemes in Equatorial Africa. According to M. Bouthillier, Pétain's Minister of Finance, the Vichy Government had information as early as September 8 that de Gaulle intended to make a landing in Africa with British support, but they did not realise until Cunningham tried to divert the French ships to Casablanca that the objective of the Allied expedition was Dakar.[1]

The plan adopted by the local commanders (Plan 'Charles') was as follows: if the attempt to enter the harbour unopposed should fail Free French troops should land on the beach at Rufisque (15 miles east of Dakar) and march thence on the fortress; British troops should be put ashore only if called upon after the French had secured a footing; it was realised that owing to difficulties with regard to landing craft the French attempt could hardly succeed against opposition. Only if the French failed to make a landing would an unrestricted bombardment by our ships follow as cover for a forcible British landing. As things turned out, resistance was in every respect much more vigorous than had been expected, both from the guns of the fortress and of the battleship *Richelieu* and at Rufisque when the French attempted to land; moreover a thick fog on the 23rd and 24th made accurate shooting by the Navy impossible and increased the difficulties of intercommunication between the Allies. Further, whereas little harm was done to the shore defences, the *Resolution* and the cruiser *Cumberland* suffered considerable damage.

---

[1] Y. Bouthillier, *Le Drame de Vichy* I (Paris 1950) 162.

On the 25th the authorities in London and on the spot came independently to the conclusion that the operation should not be proceeded with. To call it off was the lesser of evils. So the expedition returned to Freetown, arriving safely on September 29.

The fiasco at Dakar was a bitter blow to our prestige, in the Prime Minister's words. The prize had been tempting—so valuable a base, the *Richelieu*, certain deposits of Belgian and Polish gold—and worth considerable risk. Failure was due above all to the unexpected fighting spirit of the garrison, which completely refuted General de Gaulle's information and confirmed the warnings of the British liaison officers. The forces at our disposal were strictly limited by our commitments elsewhere and success depended on resistance being at most half-hearted. As one Cabinet Minister put it, 'Menace' was a justifiable gamble on the state of morale at Dakar. The other handicaps were secondary—the fog, and probably even the breaches of security and the arrival of the French warships; one can only guess to what extent the last factor had stimulated the garrison's determination to resist.

On the British side there were divided opinions; indeed the Prime Minister's own instinct had been to drop the direct assault as early as the 14th, when the arrival of the French ships at Dakar was known. Altogether there was much to recall Norway: the false political premises, the desire to meet the wishes of an ally, the frequent changes of plan, the dangerous delay, the hurried preparation of the final plans and orders, the faulty loading of ships, even the separation at sea of a general and his troops, sent in different ships in different directions.[1] But of course the failure of 'Menace' was on a much smaller scale, and little was lost save prestige.

The immediate result of the expedition and of its failure was to exasperate the Government at Vichy, who ordered their aircraft to bomb Gibraltar on September 24 and 25; it seems that this French reaction convinced the Germans that Pétain could be trusted to observe the terms of the armistice and defend French territory against any aggressor.[2] On the British side all hopes of winning over French North Africa by penetration from the south collapsed. On the other hand troops and ships were released for possible operations aiming at the acquisition of the Azores or Cape Verde Islands in case the fleet should be driven from Gibraltar. Meanwhile General de Gaulle and the Free French contingent proceeded to Duala.

Dakar was not, however, the only fiasco which marked that month

---

[1] General Irwin was carried north in the *Devonshire* on Sept. 14, as part of the operation designed to intercept the French ships, while his troops proceeded to Freetown.

[2] Bouthillier, *op. cit.* I 152, 162.

of September. The long-awaited Italian offensive was eventually launched on the 13th. A much earlier start had been intended. The Duce had told the Führer on July 13 that the offensive was meant to synchronise with the German attack on England. General Halder, Chief of the General Staff of the German Army, was informed at the end of that month that everything was to be ready by about August 5–7; on August 19 Mussolini, believing that the invasion of Britain would take place 'within a week or within a month', ordered Marshal Graziani to attack on the day that the first German platoon set foot on British soil. To achieve such exact conformity might have taxed the most experienced staff, but the Royal Navy and the Royal Air Force spared Graziani the need of attempting it. It was now time, continued the Duce, for the Marshal to attack the forces opposing him; no territorial objectives were set; it was 'not a question of heading for Alexandria or Sollum'; only let him attack. On the 29th the Duce gave orders for the offensive to be launched even if the Germans did not land in England; for the Germans might come to an agreement with the British, and Italy would not be able to take part in the negotiations unless she had fought 'at least one battle' against the enemy. So Graziani attacked on September 13, but a few days later the offensive came to a prolonged halt at Sidi Barrani, about fifty miles east of the Egyptian frontier.[1] Graziani reported to his master in December that its continuation was prevented by the poor state of the communications, by lack of water and by shortage of transport. The necessary preparations for a further advance to Mersa Matruh (70 miles) had been practically completed, he said, by the beginning of December, but more motor transport vehicles were awaited from Italy.

---

[1] For an account of operations see Playfair I ch. xi.

CHAPTER XIV

REPERCUSSIONS
IN THE FAR EAST

ITALY had entered the war. Japan was still neutral. But it was hardly to be expected that this unfriendly Power would not take advantage of the Allied defeats to extend and press its claims for aggrandisement in eastern Asia and thereby add to British embarrassments.[1]

Until the collapse of France encouraged a bolder policy, Japan's main object was to finish off the 'China Incident' and in the meantime incur no serious additional commitments. She had been at war with China for over two years, and though she controlled immense tracts of the country and from time to time won battles she saw no immediate prospect of securing the submission of Chiang Kai-Shek, the Chinese Generalissimo.[2] Until then it was not to her interest to disperse her energies in any other major contest; but, while she had for this reason been unwilling to break with the Western Allies, she could not afford to lose face by yielding on any of a number of minor points of difference. When war broke out in the west the Tientsin dispute with Great Britain was still unresolved, and within a few days, while proclaiming her 'independence' in the European conflict, she offered 'friendly advice' to the Western Powers to withdraw their armed forces from the parts of China occupied by her armies. In January 1940 fresh friction was caused by the action of a British warship in stopping a large Japanese ship, the *Asama Maru*, not far from the coast of Japan and taking off a number of German technicians. On the other hand Japan had long been on bad terms with the U.S.S.R., and the conclusion of the German-Soviet pact of August 1939 came as an unpleasant shock to her as to other of Germany's wellwishers. She was also on bad terms with the United States, who in July of that year had given notice to terminate in six months' time the Commercial Agreement of 1911 between the two countries.

In the case of Japan the issues of peace and war depended not on the unpredictable moods of an irresponsible dictator but on the ups

---

[1] For this chapter see Map 13. Events in the Far East are treated at length by Maj.-Gen. S. W. Kirby, *The War against Japan* (H.M.S.O., in preparation), henceforward referred to as 'Kirby'.

[2] See Map 14.

321

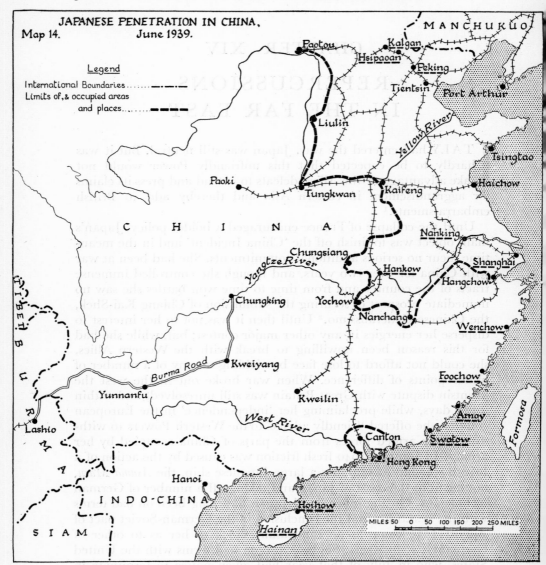

JAPANESE PENETRATION IN CHINA,
Map 14.   June 1939.

Legend

International Boundaries........ —·—·—·—
Limits of,& occupied areas
          and places.......... ▬▬▬▬▬

NOTE. Japan's control was confined principally to the lines of communication in the areas which her troops had overrun.

and downs of a contest between the recklessness of an extreme militarist party and the more moderate policies of their civilian rivals. Until July 1940 Cabinets of the latter type were in power, but there was no knowing how far they would be able to resist militarist pressure. It was the general policy of the Chamberlain Government to try to improve relations with Japan in so far as this was possible without antagonising the United States or abandoning General Chiang Kai-Shek or sacrificing British commercial interests in China. A struggle was going on in Japan between those who favoured a rapprochement with Germany and those who desired Japan to draw nearer to the democracies. Everything pointed to the near approach of a turning-point in Japanese policy, and it would be wrong to miss any chance of drawing Japan closer to our side. Such a policy had the backing of Sir Robert Craigie, our ambassador in Tokyo; but there were others who believed that we should find it impossible to satisfy everyone.

The question was discussed by the Cabinet at the end of November 1939. The Chiefs of Staff, asked for an appreciation of the Sino-Japanese military situation, reported on December 9, in brief, that if Japan was prepared to expend the men and munitions there was no part of China that her armies could not eventually overrun, though in the face of Chinese guerrilla fighting the subjugation of the country might exhaust her military and economic resources. But if she decided to limit her commitments she could make considerable military forces available for operations elsewhere and yet keep control of the chief communications and centres in China. The main Japanese fleet, they added, still retained complete freedom of action, though there were heavy demands on Japanese shipping.

So far as the United Kingdom was concerned, the matter might not appear very urgent, but the Dominion Ministers were in London at this time, and for the representatives of Australia and New Zealand it raised vital problems.[1] The Governments of these nations, who were considering the despatch of forces to the Middle East, wished to be reassured that by doing so they would not be exposing their own countries to danger. In a review of the strategical situation at the end of October the Chiefs of Staff had expressed the opinion that Japan, though deeply involved in China, must be expected to take every opportunity of exploiting the situation in Europe to her own advantage. They continued:

'Our naval strength at the present stage of re-armament coupled with the naval dispositions at present required to deal with commerce raiders, and taking into account our losses and possible future losses, would make it difficult quickly to concentrate a fleet in the Far East in the event of a Japanese threat to Singapore. This situation has always been foreseen and steps have already been taken to reinforce the garrison of the fortress and enlarge its reserves of supplies and stores, thereby increasing the

[1] See above, p. 44.

period for which it may be expected to hold out against attack. Until the Japanese had reduced Singapore and thus made it impracticable for the British Fleet to operate in the Far East, they could not contemplate large-scale operations against Australia or New Zealand. In any event such operations would involve very heavy military commitments which Japan is not at present in any condition to undertake.

If therefore Japan adopts a policy of aggression against the Allies, this seems most likely to be directed against Allied interests on the mainland, such as Shanghai, Hong Kong and ultimately perhaps Indo-China. We feel that the immediate danger to Australia and New Zealand is remote.'

This ground for confidence, so far as the Dominions were concerned, was strengthened by the opinion of the ambassador in Washington. Lord Lothian thought that if Japan started to expand outside the China Sea zone, in which her supremacy was recognised by the Washington treaties, there would be a powerful movement in the United States to stop her. He did not believe that public opinion would stand aside if the independence of the Philippines were challenged.

'If the Japanese action left the Philippines alone and concentrated on British possessions, and Dutch Islands, other than Australia and New Zealand, the reaction of American public opinion would be far slower. But partly because the Central Pacific is now regarded as a kind of American reserve [*sic*], partly because the expansion of Japan overseas would eventually threaten the Monroe Doctrine and partly because a war with Japan would probably not involve sending abroad vast armies of conscripts, I think that long before Japanese action threatened Australia or New Zealand, America would be at war.'

The argument of the Chiefs of Staff was expanded and supported in a memorandum drafted by the First Lord of the Admiralty. But, further to reassure the Australian representatives, he formally accepted, on behalf of his Department, the full responsibility of defending Australia or Singapore from a Japanese attack on a large scale.

'We wish to make it plain that we regard the defence of Australia, and of Singapore, as a stepping-stone to Australia, as ranking next to the mastering of the principal fleet to which we are opposed, and that if the choice were presented of defending Australia against serious attack, or sacrificing British interests in the Mediterranean, our duty to Australia would take precedence. It seems very unlikely, however, that this bleak choice will arise during the next year or two, which is what we have to consider at the present time.'

This paper raised an interesting discussion in the Cabinet. Did it, or did it not, go further than anything agreed upon by the Government in recent discussions before the war, or communicated to the Dominions? The Cabinet were reminded of the discussions that had taken place in 1937 and in March of the present year, 1939. There was no suggestion that His Majesty's Government should go back on the assurances then given; but it was pointed out that we had since concluded an alliance with Turkey, and that in our Military Convention with the Turks and in our staff conversations with the French we had expressed our intention of doing everything possible to neutralise Italian naval power in the Mediterranean and to maintain normal traffic through it. This made it very difficult to give any specific and detailed assurances to the Dominions. It was impossible to say in advance what size of fleet we should send, or when it could be collected and made ready to proceed to the East. The First Lord's memorandum, however, was concerned with 'a serious attack' against Australia, which was something different from a mere raid, and there was general agreement that in such case a fleet must and would be sent. The Cabinet accordingly approved the First Lord's memorandum on the understanding that it should be read in conjunction with previous assurances given to the Dominion Governments; and in particular with a C.I.D. Paper of 4 June 1937 and with the Prime Minister's telegram of the 20th March 1939 to the Prime Minister of Australia. The crucial paragraphs of the former paper are:

> 24. (*If war with Japan breaks out when we, allied with France, are already at war with Germany.*) '. . . The strength of the fleet for the Far East, and the time within which it would reach Singapore, must be variable factors, dependent both upon naval and political considerations. Nevertheless, the basis of our strategy will lie in establishing at Singapore, at the earliest possible moment after the outbreak of hostilities with Japan, a fleet whose strength, as a minimum, will enable it to act on the defensive and to serve as a strong deterrent against any threats to our interests in the Far East.'

> 33. (*Intervention of Italy.*) 'The intervention of Italy against us would at once impose conflicting demands on our fleet. In this situation our policy must be governed by the principle that no anxieties or risks connected with our interests in the Mediterranean can be allowed to interfere with the despatch of a fleet to the Far East.'

The relevant paragraph in Mr. Chamberlain's telegram was as follows:

> 'In the event of war with Germany and Italy, should Japan join in against us it would still be His Majesty's Government's full

intention to despatch a fleet to Singapore. If we were fighting against such a combination never envisaged in our earlier plans, the size of that fleet would necessarily be dependent on (a) the moment when Japan entered the war and (b) what losses if any our opponents or ourselves had previously sustained.

It would, however, be our intention to achieve three main objects:

    (i) The prevention of any major operation against Australia, New Zealand or India;

   (ii) To keep open our sea communications;

  (iii) To prevent the fall of Singapore.'

The Cabinet wished it to be made clear to the Dominion Ministers at the meeting to be held that afternoon (November 20) that the policy laid down in this telegram still held good, but that the precise action we should take in any particular circumstances would have to be decided by the Government at the time, in the light of prevailing conditions.

The First Lord's paper was then revised and approved and communicated to the Australian and New Zealand Governments and also to the French. In its revised form it applied to New Zealand as well as to Australia and included a paragraph envisaging 'an encroachment' by Japan on the Netherlands East Indies. In such an event—which was considered unlikely in view of the probable reaction of the United States—or in the event of Great Britain becoming involved in war with Japan,

> 'the Admiralty would make such preparatory dispositions as would enable them to offer timely resistance either to the serious attack upon Singapore or to the invasion of Australia or New Zealand. These dispositions would not necessarily take the form of stationing a fleet at Singapore, but would be of a character to enable the necessary concentrations to be made to the eastward in ample time to prevent a disaster. With our present limited forces we cannot afford to have any important portion of His Majesty's Fleet idle. All ships must play their part from day to day, and there are always the hazards of war to be faced, but the Admiralty can be trusted to make the appropriate dispositions to meet events as they emerge from imagination into reality.'

The question of the Dutch colonies was to provoke long discussions in the future, but that of Singapore was a closer anxiety, and it is necessary to see how matters stood at this time.

An account of the many changes of the British Government's policy with regard to the Singapore base during the years of peace, and the measures taken, or recommended but not taken, for its fulfilment, will be found in other volumes of this history.[1]

In June 1939 an Anglo-French Conference was held at Singapore. The delegates' terms of reference included a warning that the security of Singapore, as the key to our position in the Far East, was of first importance, but that the Allied naval forces in the Far East might, at the outset, not exceed their peace strength. Having considered the strategic situation and existing plans and means of defence, the Conference put on record their 'grave concern' at the present inadequacy of Allied naval and air forces in the Far East. We could neither ensure our essential communications in case of war with Japan nor prevent the enemy from occupying advanced bases directly threatening our vital interests. Since it seemed impossible to station sufficient naval forces in the Far East in peacetime, a substantial increase in the permanent air garrison was of 'paramount importance'. The land forces were also judged to be inadequate: an infantry brigade was required, additional to one already earmarked for despatch, and also armoured fighting vehicles and more artillery.

In July 1939 the Committee of Imperial Defence had agreed to extend the 'period before relief', for which the garrison must be able to maintain itself on its own resources, from seventy days to ninety. In July too it was decided to despatch to Singapore a brigade group and two bomber squadrons from India and two from the United Kingdom. The additional brigade recommended by the Anglo-French Conference was not sent—it is difficult to see where it could have come from—while the total of eight air squadrons thus provided was four less than the scale which had been approved by the Committee of Imperial Defence in May. At the end of September the Chiefs of Staff decided to extend the period before relief to 180 days.

So matters stood at, or soon after, the outbreak of war in the West. During the winter and spring nothing occurred to compel the Government to speed up their long-term plans. Sir Shenton Thomas, the Governor of the Straits Settlements, supporting a similar demand from the Air Officer Commanding, did indeed in January 1940 urge on the home Government the importance of providing 'a really strong air force' for Malaya. This would prevent the Japanese from establishing advanced bases within reach of the country and would allow reductions in the land garrison; moreover, by acting as a deterrent it might 'make all the difference between peace and war in the Far East'. But the Oversea Defence Committee, an interdepartmental body of which the Permanent Under-Secretary of

---

[1] Kirby vol. I; N. H. Gibbs, *Grand Strategy* I (in preparation).

State for the Colonies was chairman, agreed on March 9 that no proposal for an increase of air forces in Malaya in the foreseeable future could be entertained.[1] With regard to the allocation of civilian manpower, the authorities at Singapore, they said, must do the best they could to improve the efficiency of the local volunteer forces without prejudice to the production of tin and rubber which made Malaya, in the Governor's words, a real treasure-house in the accumulation of foreign exchange. A few days later the Cabinet went further; feeling that the risk of war with Japan had receded while trouble with Russia was possible over the Finnish issue, they decided to recall to India the two squadrons sent thence to Singapore in the autumn.

Two months after this the Cabinet had before them the Chiefs of Staff's report on 'British strategy in a certain eventuality'.[2] The paper assumed the intervention of Italy against us. The paragraphs on the Far East referred to the economic importance of Singapore and remarked that to counter Japanese action a fleet, adequately supported by air forces, was necessary there. 'What forces we can send can only be judged in the light of the situation at the time. It is most improbable that we can send any naval forces to the Far East. Therefore we must rely on the United States of America to safeguard our interests in the Far East. Australia should be asked to consider a reinforcement of the garrison at Singapore.' But the Cabinet had at the end of May more urgent dangers to think about than contingencies in the Far East.

Just about this time, as it happened, relations with Japan seemed easier. The Japanese Ambassador said on June 11 that even a change of Government in his country would not mean an abandonment of neutrality, and on the 13th a compromise settlement, though an unsatisfactory one, of the tiresome Tientsin dispute was arrived at. But the French collapse was bound to strengthen the Japanese extremists. The Tokyo Government soon changed its attitude and presented a series of demands, of which the most important was for the closing of the 'Burma Road'—the long precarious track through the mountains of Yunnan which now formed for Chiang Kai-Shek almost his only supply route from the friendly world.[3] Any measure to the disadvantage of China was bound to be unpopular in America,

---

[1] See Kirby, I ch. ii.

[2] See pp. 209 ff above.

[3] The 'Burma Road' extended for 712 miles from Kunming, the capital of the province of Yunnan, to Lashio, the terminus of the railway from Rangoon. Only 117 miles of it were in Burma. See Map 14.

and inquiries were made as to the support we might hope to receive from Washington if we resisted the Japanese requests. It soon appeared that only diplomatic support would be forthcoming, and the Chiefs of Staff urged strongly that we should not run the risk of becoming involved in war single-handed with Japan on points not of vital importance to ourselves, on points too on which we had no means of making our wishes prevail. The interests of Australia and New Zealand, for whose protection we could no longer send the promised fleet, must also be taken into account. Our two battalions at Shanghai, whose withdrawal the Japanese had requested, were hostages to fortune and would be much more useful at Singapore. We should rather seek a general settlement with Japan. The Cabinet eventually decided to suspend the transport of war material on the Burma Road for three months (that is to say, during the rainy season, when traffic would in any case be negligible) on the understanding that during this term special efforts would be made to bring about 'a just and equitable peace in the Far East'. The Governments of the Dominions had of course been consulted.

Precisely at this moment, 22 July 1940, the comparatively moderate Japanese Government fell and was succeeded by a more definitely pro-Axis one under Prince Konoye, Mr. Matsuoka becoming Minister of Foreign Affairs. In close association with Imperial General Headquarters the new Government adopted as its aims an early settlement of the China Incident and the solution of the 'Southern Region problem'. Certain general principles were approved for application as opportunity offered. French Indo-China would be requested to discontinue all aid to Chiang Kai-Shek and to provide supplies and facilities for Japanese troops. The Burma Road must be completely stopped, and the hostile attitude of Hong Kong and the Western settlements in China terminated. Armed force might be used in support of such purposes if circumstances were favourable. In employing armed force the Japanese would attempt to confine hostilities to the British as far as possible, but thorough preparations would be made for war against the United States, since this might be unavoidable.[1] Such were the secret decisions. A few days later, on August 1, the new Government issued a statement on national policy, in which the ultimate aims of Japan were declared to include 'the construction of a new order in Greater East Asia'. This pronouncement, and the new orientation of policy which it expressed, were ominous for peace, and

---

[1] See 'General Principles suitable for application in the changing world situation', accepted at the Liaison Conference between Imperial General Headquarters and the Government on 27 July 1940; *Japanese Monograph No. 146* App. 2, issued by The United States Army Forces, Far East. See also H. Feis, *The Road to Pearl Harbour* (Princeton 1950) ch. xi.

the British high command were well advised to consider their implications.

Some weeks previously, on June 25, the Chiefs of Staff had represented to the Cabinet that our inability to send a fleet to the Far East at this time made it all the more important that we should improve our land and air defences in Malaya as far as possible. Neither from the United Kingdom nor from the Middle East could equipped troops be spared; the only other sources were India and Australia. India could send one brigade now and could increase it to a division by September. These troops, however, were at present earmarked for Iraq or Iran; if not needed there, they would seem well suited for Africa. But Australia also would shortly have troops available and, following up their suggestion of a month earlier, the Chiefs of Staff recommended that the Canberra Government should be asked to despatch to Malaya as soon as possible one infantry division and two air squadrons, in addition to the squadron 'now being sent'. They were at this time in favour of keeping the two British battalions at Shanghai as a gesture, and also of retaining the garrison at Hong Kong 'to fight it out if war comes', while evacuating the British women and children. The Cabinet approved these proposals on June 26; they thought it important to explain to the Australian Government how the defection of the French fleet had altered the whole strategic situation and the whole balance of naval strength; this was accordingly done.

Canberra had already decided to send two more squadrons to Malaya, but the request for an infantry division was unwelcome. Apart from the fact that the next division (the 7th) due to go overseas was insufficiently equipped, it was a principle cherished alike by the Government and the military authorities in Australia that the forces of the Dominion should not be dissipated but should be concentrated in one theatre under one commander. By sending General Blamey as corps commander to Palestine they had confirmed their intention that the 7th division should eventually join the 6th in the Middle East. This principle seems to have been the basis of their refusal on July 3 to divert it to Malaya.[1]

A different objection was put forward by the Australian High Commissioner in London, Mr. S. M. Bruce, a former Prime Minister. Mr. Bruce could point out that when in November 1939 his Government had consented to send a division overseas it was accepted policy that if serious danger threatened from Japan the Admiralty

---

[1] See P. Hasluck, *The Government and the People 1939–1941* in *Australia in the War of 1939–1945* (Canberra 1952) p. 222.

would despatch a fleet of appropriate strength to the Far East. Now Canberra were told that no fleet at all could be sent and were at the same time asked to send a second division abroad. On behalf of the Chiefs of Staff General Ismay sought to reassure the High Commissioner. The General argued that the loss of French naval cooperation in the western Mediterranean not only had jeopardised our position in that sea but might enable the Italian fleet to join the Germans in threatening our vital communications in the Atlantic and home waters. This was something we had never foreseen and could not permit. Nevertheless the assurance given to the Dominions in November stood firm. In the opinion of the Chiefs of Staff Japan could not undertake a serious invasion of Australia so long as the British Fleet (wherever it might be) was in being and Singapore was secure. The first condition still held good, and it was to ensure the second that Australia was now asked to reinforce Malaya.

The High Commissioner's feelings can be well understood. The Dominions had indeed been warned as early as June 13, when France was near collapse, that if Japan declared war it was most improbable that we could send adequate naval reinforcements to the Far East in the altered circumstances. But it was none the less disquieting to be now definitely told that the fleet on whose immediate despatch in such an event the Australian Government had for years been counting could not possibly be sent. War, however, as was observed long ago by a great military historian, is a rough teacher; it taught the Australians that one cannot hope to foresee all its strange chances; it taught the mother-country, not once or twice in these years, the unwisdom of promising what one cannot be sure of being able to perform.

This, however, was not the end of the matter. The Australian and New Zealand Governments not unnaturally wished to receive from the Chiefs of Staff in London a full appreciation of the military situation in the Far East, taking account of the important changes which had come about in the West. No such review of our eastern policy had in fact been undertaken since June 1937. The Joint Planners set to work and by the end of July 1940 produced a comprehensive and masterly report.

The report began by pointing out that the two assumptions on which the staff assessment of our defence requirements in the Far East was based in 1937 were both now untenable: a threat to our interests need no longer be entirely seaborne, since Japan, by reason of her advance in South China and of French weakness in Indo-China, could now develop a dangerous overland threat to Malaya; and we should not now be able to send a powerful fleet to the Far East. The whole problem must therefore be studied afresh.

Japan's ultimate aim being the exclusion of Western influence from the Far East, she must be presumed to intend the eventual capture of Singapore; but in accordance with 'her traditional step-by-step policy' her immediate aim was probably the exclusion of British influence from China and Hong Kong; she was unlikely to risk an open breach with the British Empire and the United States of America until the situation in Europe was clearer. We likewise, with our commitments in Europe and without French help, must avoid an open clash with Japan and should work for a general settlement with her. Failing such a settlement we must play for time, conceding nothing until we must and building up our defences.

The foundation of our strategy must remain the basing of an adequate fleet at Singapore, as the only means of controlling the essential sea communications with India and Australasia. Until success in the West enabled us to do this, we must expect that our interests in the Far East would suffer. We must seek to limit the extent of the damage and in the last resort retain a foothold from which to retrieve the position later.

Four lines of aggression were open to the Japanese: a direct attack on British possessions; penetration into Indo-China or Siam; an attack on the Netherlands East Indies; seizure of the Philippines. Of these the second was the most likely initial move, and a Japanese penetration into Siam would undoubtedly threaten Singapore and make the defence of Burma and Malaya far more difficult. Even so, the threat to our vital interests would not be so direct as to justify us in going to war with Japan with our present resources. On the other hand the establishment of Japanese bases in the Netherlands East Indies would directly threaten our vital interests—our sea and air communications and the base at Singapore. Unfortunately we could not as things stood deny the Japanese a foothold in these islands, but with Dutch assistance we might succeed in checking them there. Dutch co-operation would simplify the whole problem of Far Eastern defence, and if the Dutch resisted we should offer them full military and economic support.

Our garrisons in North China, being strategically useless and tactically indefensible, should be withdrawn. Hong Kong was in a nearly similar position, but must be held as an outpost, though we could not hope to relieve it and ought not to reinforce it. Nor could we hope to defend British Borneo.

But matters would be different were the Japanese to undertake a major expedition against Australia or New Zealand while Singapore still remained to us as a possible base for a fleet; that would be an extremely hazardous operation; they might however attempt raids by sea or air or try to seize an advanced base in the Pacific, such as Suva in Fiji.

The conclusion of the report was therefore that we must concentrate on the defence of Malaya. In the absence of a fleet we should rely principally on air power. But the requisite air forces could not be provided for some time to come; substantial land reinforcements were needed. These could not at present be found from the United Kingdom or India; only Australia had available the trained troops who could be suitably equipped.

The Chiefs of Staff accordingly made detailed recommendations for the interim reinforcement of Malaya.[1] Food reserves for both the expected garrison and the civil population should be built up. They also recommended that our naval construction programme should be reviewed and the existing programme speeded up; that provision should be made by the end of 1941 for the increased air forces required in Malaya, Borneo and the Indian Ocean; that the Governments of India and Burma, in consultation with the Air Officer Commanding, Far East, should review their defence requirements in the light of a possible threat from Siam; that the views of our commanders in the Far East should be obtained as to the forces required until a fleet again became available; and that certain airfields in the north of the Malay Peninsula and in Sarawak should be prepared for demolition. The Government of New Zealand should be invited to hold a brigade ready for despatch to Fiji.

The Cabinet needed time to consider this weighty report; their immediate response on August 8 was to authorise the despatch of an encouraging telegram from the Prime Minister to the Prime Ministers of Australia and New Zealand by way of 'foreword'.

Mr. Churchill explained that we were trying our best to avoid war with Japan, both by yielding on points where the Japanese military clique could perhaps force a rupture and by standing up where the ground was less dangerous. He did not himself think Japan would declare war unless Germany could make a successful invasion of Britain.

'Should Japan nevertheless declare war on us her first objective outside the Yellow Sea would be the Dutch East Indies. Evidently the United States would not like this. What they would do we cannot tell. They give no undertaking of support, but their main fleet in the Pacific must be a grave pre-occupation to the Japanese Admiralty. In this first phase of an Anglo-Japanese war we should of course defend Singapore, which if attacked— which is unlikely—ought to stand a long siege. We should also be able to base on Ceylon a battle-cruiser and a fast aircraft-carrier, which, with all the Australian and New Zealand cruisers and destroyers, which would return to you, would act as a very powerful deterrent upon the hostile raiding cruisers.'

---

[1] See below, p. 336.

Z

He went on to say that the Eastern Mediterranean Fleet, which we were about to reinforce, could any time be sent through the Canal into the Indian Ocean or to relieve Singapore. In view of the Italian challenge we did not wish to do this, even if Japan declared war, until it was found to be vital to the Dominions' safety. He continued:

> 'A final question arises, whether Japan having declared war would attempt to invade Australia or New Zealand with a considerable army. We think this very unlikely, because Japan is first absorbed in China, secondly would be gathering rich prizes in the Dutch East Indies, and thirdly would fear very much to send an important part of her fleet far to the southward leaving the American fleet between it and home. If, however, contrary to prudence and self-interest, Japan set about invading Australia or New Zealand on a large scale, I have the explicit authority of the Cabinet to assure you that we should then cut our losses in the Mediterranean and proceed to your aid, sacrificing every interest except only the defence and feeding of this Island on which all depends.'[1]

Recognition of our inability for some time to send a fleet to Singapore had, as we have seen, drawn attention to the need to defend our interests in South-East Asia by other means. It may be worth while to stop for a moment to consider what exactly was the relation of Singapore to these interests. The latter were manifold: they included the economic resources of the Malay Peninsula and our political commitments to the British colony of the Straits Settlements and to the Malay States, Federated and Unfederated, which all enjoyed British protection. Looking further we note the immense importance of Singapore as a place of call for shipping, alike mercantile and naval, passing between the Indian Ocean and the China Seas, Indonesia and the Southern Pacific, and as a strategic point from which these communications could be controlled by a maritime power and their control denied to an enemy. It was this consideration which primarily had decided British Governments between the wars to build their eastern base at Singapore. No attack on this base was then apprehended, except from the sea; it was thought that the fleet, once arrived and supported by the coast defences, would protect itself, but, as it was never proposed to maintain a large fleet in Far Eastern waters in peace, the base had to be made capable of resistance until such time as the fleet could be counted on to arrive.

Whether Singapore was properly to be described as a 'fortress' is

---

[1] The whole telegram is printed in Churchill II pp. 385–386, with the sentence last quoted above slightly amplified.

doubtful. Both Mr. Churchill and the Chiefs of Staff regularly spoke of it as such, but its right to the title has been disputed. What, to begin with, is meant by Singapore? The island, with its area of 225 square miles and a population of over half a million? Or the naval base, on the northern shore of the island? Or the great city of Singapore ten miles away on the south side, with its docks and fuelling station? If by a fortress is meant a strategic point naturally or artificially defended on all sides, then a fortress Singapore was not—in any of the senses mentioned. True, there were coast defences at other points than at the naval establishment, but it is perhaps safest to think of Singapore, from the military point of view, as a fortified base.

The problem had been transformed after the French collapse, not only by our incapacity to challenge a Japanese naval expedition in force against Singapore or the neighbouring islands, but also by the possibility of a Japanese advance by land through a defeated or submissive Indo-China and Siam. The Chiefs of Staff's telegram to Canberra at the end of June had remarked that it would no longer do to confine ourselves to the defence of Singapore Island; we must consider the defence of Malaya as a whole and particularly the security of the up-country airfields. This need was emphasised by local differences between Army and Air commanders as to the proper disposition of the small forces available—differences for which reinforcements appeared the only solution.

The Chiefs of Staff were bound to refer to this local problem in their long report of July 31. They called attention to the need of preventing the establishment of shore-based aircraft within close range of the base at Singapore: they thought that the Japanese, even if they had not previously established themselves in Siam, were more likely to try to land up-country in Malaya and work southwards than to risk a direct assault on the island; they noted that the important rice-growing region was in the north, and they stated the necessity for maintaining food reserves for as long as possible for the garrison and civil population of Malaya. All these factors—the last, because it would be easier to break a Japanese blockade of the whole peninsula than one of Singapore only—pointed to the necessity for holding the whole of the Malayan peninsula; and this clearly involved larger land and air forces.

In order to supplement this strategic report the Chiefs of Staff soon afterwards called for a tactical appreciation by the commanders on the spot.

The story of the plans and preparations for the defence of Malaya is told at length elsewhere in this history;[1] something however must

---

[1] See Kirby vol. 1.

be said on the subject here, in so far as it affected policy in Whitehall and relations with other Governments.

The frontier of British Malaya with Siam (Thailand) ran about 400 miles north of Singapore—some 350 miles on the east coast, nearly 450 on the west.[1] At the latter point the peninsula is only about sixty miles wide; further south it broadens to 200 miles. A range of high mountains divides the western from the eastern side, and the interior, where not cultivated, is thick forest and jungle. There is no town of importance on the east side. Bangkok, the capital of Siam, is connected with British Malaya by a railway which runs down the eastern coast of the long narrow Isthmus of Kra; the distance by sea across the Gulf of Siam from Kota Bahru, the Malayan town lying furthest north on the east side, to the nearest point in French Indo-China, is about 250 miles.

The Chiefs of Staff reckoned that to hold Malaya in the absence of a battle-fleet we required twenty-two squadrons—a total of 336 first-line aircraft—as a minimum. Compared with this our present strength was 88 first-line aircraft, while the Dutch for the defence of their eastern possessions had 144. It was clearly impossible to attain the desired figure in the near future: it must be remembered that the Battle of Britain had not yet been fought, while an attack against Egypt was expected at any time. The Chiefs of Staff therefore asked that a reinforcement of two fighter and two general reconnaissance squadrons by, at latest, the end of 1940 should be authorised, in addition to the re-equipment of the existing squadrons, which must be brought up to establishment. We should aim at completing the full programme by the end of 1941.

The requisite strength of the army must depend on the arrival of air reinforcements. Even when the full air programme had been completed, the minimum garrison for holding the whole of Malaya must be taken as six brigades, with ancillary troops, whereas the present garrison, apart from coast defence and anti-aircraft troops, only equalled three brigades, with ancillary troops. But until the balance of air power had been made up an increase in the army would be required to a strength which the General on the spot had estimated as the equivalent of three divisions and attached troops; this figure could be progressively reduced as air reinforcements arrived. The anti-aircraft defences of Singapore were also 'well below the approved scale'.

Our naval forces on the China, Australia and New Zealand stations included no capital ships. Our best hopes for a naval war in the Far East lay in winning early successes against the Italians in the Mediterranean.

See Maps 13, 15.

Such was the problem. As for land forces, neither the United Kingdom nor India could supply even one division. Australia should therefore be asked to provide one and to equip it as far as possible. But preparations should be made to receive a second if and when it could be found from some source. As soon as we had been able to improve our position in Malaya, staff conversations should be begun with the Dutch in the Far East, in which Australia and New Zealand should be invited to take part. At present there was no substantial military help we could bring to the Dutch and, though economic pressure on the part of Great Britain and the United States would in time prove disastrous to Japan, she had sufficient stocks for the first six months. Meanwhile we could only instruct our commanders to study the problem of Anglo-Dutch defence.

After the Cabinet had received this appreciation on August 8, the Chiefs of Staff produced a comprehensive report on the Re-inforcement of Garrisons Abroad, covering all theatres. Though Home Defence still made its demands, the equipment of the forces and organisation of the defences in the United Kingdom, combined with the approach of weather unfavourable to invasion, had reduced anxiety on that score. With respect to the Far East the report in-corporated the recommendations of the earlier paper, but gave first priority to the needs of the Middle East. It was the intention of the Air Ministry, said the report, ultimately to equip and maintain the squadrons in the Far East with aircraft from America.

On August 28 the Chiefs of Staff were told that the Prime Minister had authorised action in accordance with the main recommendations of the Far Eastern Appreciation; the Air Ministry were to examine both the long-term air programme and the possibilities of meeting the immediate proposals. The North China garrisons had been with-drawn, the Australian and New Zealand Governments had been asked to provide respectively a division for Malaya and a brigade for Fiji, and the commanders in the Far East had been instructed to produce a joint tactical appreciation. The question of staff conversa-tions with the Dutch was at present held in abeyance.

So far there had been general agreement, but the destination of the (7th) division from Australia led to much discussion and an unresolved conflict of opinion between the Prime Minister and the Chiefs of Staff.

The Prime Minister showed little enthusiasm for the proposal to send an Australian division to Malaya. It should, he minuted, in any case only remain there until the tension with Japan relaxed, and then move on to the healthier climate of the Middle East. The needs of Malaya should be met by the two British battalions withdrawn from China and by four more Indian battalions. The Prime Minister's reluctance was reinforced by that of the Australian Government, which, while ready to send the division to Malaya if necessary, greatly preferred that it should train in India until ready to join its fellow in the Middle East. The Chiefs of Staff saw no advantages in the latter suggestion, but at repeated meetings discussed the alternative policies of despatching this division to Malaya—for which the Chief of the Imperial General Staff adduced technical reasons—or to the Middle East, as the Prime Minister strongly urged. Their considered opinion supported the General, but they did not convince the Prime Minister. Sir John Dill laid stress on the need of a mobile division to operate in the north of Malaya in case of a Japanese incursion; the Prime Minister held on the contrary that the defence of Singapore must depend primarily on the Fleet; it was vain to think that the presence of a single division could make any difference towards the defence of Malaya—a country nearly as large as England. The Prime Minister accordingly decided to ask Canberra to send the 7th Australian Division to Palestine, and it duly arrived in the Middle East in the course of the winter.[1]

After the decision had been taken the Chiefs of Staff discussed the defence of Singapore with the Prime Minister. They could not agree with him either that we might be able to concentrate a superior fleet in the Far East, or that the defence of Singapore should be based on a strong *local* garrison and that the defence of the Malay Peninsula as a whole could not be entertained.

All three Chiefs of Staff expressed their disagreement with the Prime Minister. Sir Dudley Pound declared that the despatch of a fleet superior to the Japanese to the Far East would mean sending both our fleets now stationed in the Mediterranean together with a major portion of the Home Fleet. At the present time this could not be done. Sir John Dill stressed the importance of denying the Malay Peninsula to the Japanese, and in particular the airfields, from which they could threaten the fortified base of Singapore; they would then be able to advance southwards and bring it under artillery fire. Sir Cyril Newall argued that the danger with regard to Singapore lay not so much in its capture by the Japanese as in the denial of its facilities to our own fleet, should the enemy secure a firm foothold on the mainland.

The Prime Minister was interested but unmoved. In present circumstances we had to accept risks in all parts of the Empire; in his view the threat to Singapore could not be regarded as unduly alarming compared with the dangers on the home front and in the Middle East. War with Japan was not a foregone conclusion; and even if she did declare war it was unlikely that she would be inclined or able

---

[1] See Churchill II 591 and Hasluck, *op. cit.* p. 225. Another Australian division, the 8th, was eventually sent to Malaya.

to mount an attack against Singapore. The Japanese had shown themselves consistently reluctant to send their fleet far afield, and an expedition 2,000 miles from home would court danger both from the American fleet on its flank and from the British fleet when it arrived. At present the despatch of a superior fleet was doubtless out of the question for us, but no one could tell how the situation might develop. In the air the Japanese had not proved themselves formidable antagonists, and the experience of London hardly suggested that a fortress of the strength of Singapore could have much to fear from Japanese air attacks.

This little controversy has a double interest. It provides a rare instance of the Prime Minister deciding in a military question in a sense contrary to the views of his professional advisers, though indeed the decision was based on a broad view of Japan's probable action. It is also interesting as perhaps showing the background of his strategical thinking with regard to the Far East, though it would be wrong to ignore the differences between September 1940 and the autumn of the following year. The Japanese did not, in fact, make war on us until fifteen months after the time we are now concerned with, whereas an Italian army was already on Egyptian soil.

Early in September the Cabinet had discussed the situation in the Far East as affected both by reports that the Japanese had demanded the right of passage for their troops through Indo-China and by the approach of the date after which we should be free to re-open the Burma Road. The Chiefs of Staff were asked for their opinion on the extent to which hostilities in Indo-China would be likely to cause military or economic embarrassment to Japan. They reported on the 9th that the Japanese could subjugate Indo-China and Yunnan and still have sufficient forces to constitute a serious danger to Singapore with its present garrison; economically Japan would in the long run gain definite economic advantage from the occupation of Indo-China.

The Japanese had in fact on August 30 signed an agreement with the Vichy Ambassador at Tokyo by which the French undertook to co-operate in securing Japan's economic and political aims in Asia and, in principle, to allow her to base troops in northern Indo-China for operations against Chiang Kai-Shek. After points of detail had been settled between the local authorities on September 22, Japanese troops crossed the frontier on the following day. On the 27th the substance of these agreements was made public.[1]

Some days before this, reports that the Japanese had forced some

---

[1] *Japanese Monograph No. 146*, U.S. Army Forces, Far East.

such concessions on French Indo-China were reaching London. This seemed one of several reasons for reopening the Burma Road for the benefit of the Chinese, and the Chiefs of Staff recommended that we should do this when the three months' closure expired on October 17; we should inform President Roosevelt and the Chinese Generalissimo at once of our intention, but not the Japanese. The Cabinet decided on October 3 not to prolong the closure of the road, if the Dominion Governments concurred—as they did—and to make a public announcement on October 8. They also decided to set up an interdepartmental committee on the Far East, with Mr. R. A. Butler as chairman, to keep under review our policy in that part of the world and consider counter-measures against the Japanese should they become our enemies.

Japan had recently concluded, on September 27, a tripartite pact of alliance with Germany and Italy recognising a New Order in Europe and the Far East. While the three signatories were not obliged to render each other assistance during the present war in Europe or in the Sino-Japanese war, they were bound to do so in the event of attack by a Power not already engaged. Such assistance, however, so Matsuoka declared, did not imply automatic belligerency. The treaty also provided that the mutual obligations of the three Powers should not affect their political relations with the Soviet Union.[1] Such an alliance had long been wished for by the Japanese Army, and Matsuoka eagerly took up the negotations. In order to press on with the policy of southward expansion it was desirable to secure German support and to improve relations with Russia, and above all to deter the United States from active belligerency. This was of course the side which appealed to Germany; as Ribbentrop explained to Molotov, the treaty was 'directed exclusively against American war-mongers'.[2] But the possibility that the pact might precipitate the war it professed to avoid did not escape the Japanese, and their acceptance followed a long debate in a committee of the Privy Council at which the country's readiness for war with America was discussed.

Mr. Matsuoka informed our Ambassador in November that 'his impelling motive in concluding this pact had been his conviction that the United States' entry into the war would inevitably involve other states including Japan. . . . Furthermore the entry of the United States into the war might well be the signal for general use of those terrible engines of destruction, such as thermite, which belligerents have hitherto abstained from employing.' The Japanese would have been wise to remember this possibility in December 1941.

---

[1] Text in W. L. Langer and S. E. Gleason, *The Undeclared War 1940–1941* (London 1953) p. 30. See Feis, *op. cit.* ch. xv.

[2] *Nazi-Soviet Relations* pp. 195, 197.

CHAPTER XV

STRATEGY AND RESOURCES REVIEWED, SEPTEMBER – OCTOBER 1940

B Y THE END of September the months of supreme crisis had passed. The Germans had not invaded England nor yet the Balkans; the Italian invasion of Egypt had come to an inglorious standstill; neither Spain nor the Vichy Government of France had joined in the war; our overseas supplies had not been cut off and the Royal Air Force had taken the measure of the Luftwaffe— at least by day. But any of the dangers hitherto avoided might threaten again: Germany had large armies available for employment anywhere on the Continent, the U-boats' challenge to our shipping had not been mastered, London and other vital areas were being continuously bombed at night, the behaviour of Russia and Japan was unpredictable. It was time for a review of our strategy and the disposition of our resources. The enemy also had to make crucial decisions.

As a convenient introduction we may take the discussions between high British and United States officers at the end of August, for which, for the sake of secrecy, the cover name of 'Standardisation of Arms Committee' was adopted.[1] The United States delegation represented all arms; their first duty was to report to the President on the likelihood of Britain holding out, but they were prepared for general discussions. Admiral Ghormley made it clear however that they were only observers and were not intended to act as a Joint Mission nor authorised to accept commitments. The conversations with the Chiefs of Staff began on August 29, when Sir Cyril Newall expounded the existing strategical situation and the British policy for the conduct of the war. Germany's only chance of avoiding decisive defeat, he believed, lay in either ending the war in the near future or breaking the blockade and obtaining new sources of outside supplies, especially oil. Germany and Italy would therefore be driven to further action in the autumn. There were three ways by which Germany might

---

[1] See above, p. 243, also Mark S. Watson, *Chief of Staff: Pre-war plans and preparations* pp. 113–114; Matloff and Snell, *Strategic Planning for Coalition Warfare*, pp. 22–25; S. E. Morison, *The Battle of the Atlantic* (Boston 1948) pp. 40–41. The principal American representatives were Rear-Admiral R. L. Ghormley, Major-General D. C. Emmons and Brigadier-General G. C. Strong.

hope to break down our resistance: by unrestricted air attack, by the destruction of our shipping and our ports, and by invasion. The last was now unlikely to succeed, and the enemy might be expected rather to intensify his efforts to achieve the two former. To a question, raised at a later meeting, whether any plans had been prepared to meet the possibility of a failure to withstand attacks on the United Kingdom, Sir Cyril Newall replied in the negative. 'Our whole strategy was based on the assumption that we should withstand attack, and it was the fixed determination of the whole nation to do so.'

Combined with air attack on the towns and on shipping we expected an early enemy offensive in the Middle East, with the objects of driving out our fleet, obtaining the cotton of Egypt and ensuring the supply of oil from the Black Sea. The enemy might also launch an attack through Spain in order to control the western Mediterranean; in south-east Europe, while Italy might move into Greece, we did not envisage a German advance through the Balkans as yet, but we were in no position to afford direct support at present against aggression on the part of either Germany, Italy or Russia. On a long view, our position in West Africa might be endangered and we were faced by 'a grave potential threat' from Japan in the Far East.

The foundation of our strategy was to wear Germany down by ever-increasing economic pressure. We believed that by next summer her morale would be lowered and her oil reserves expended, and that thereafter her military effort might be restricted by shortage of oil. A continuous and relentless air offensive against both our enemies, directed at their oil supplies, communications and industry, was also an essential part of our strategy, and we intended to build up our resources so as to be able to undertake major offensive operations on land when opportunity offered; in the meantime we possessed in our amphibious power a weapon with which to strike against their widely extended coastline. The elimination of Italy was a strategic aim of the first importance; her collapse would reduce the threat to the Middle East, render the blockade of Germany more effective, and free our hands to meet the menace of Japan. With regard to the Far East, the Americans were informed of the main conclusions of the recent report on that subject.[1] The support of the American battlefleet, they were told, would obviously transform the whole strategical situation. When Admiral Ghormley asked whether it was in the British interest that this fleet should remain in the Pacific, Sir Dudley Pound replied emphatically that it was. To a further question the answer was given that, while we were certainly relying

---

[1] See above, pp. 331 ff.

on the continued economic and industrial assistance of the United States in ever increasing volume, no account had been taken of her active co-operation, since this was clearly a matter of high policy.

The visitors were also informed of our production programme for all three Services; this depended on the productive potential of the United Kingdom, backed by the productive capacity of the United States. In order to achieve this programme by the spring of 1942 our short-term expansion in 1941 must needs be limited.

The Chiefs of Staff's statement to the Americans was based on a lengthy and elaborate appreciation on Future Strategy, which was ready for submission to the Cabinet on September 4. This document, however, was never accepted as Government policy, though it was communicated to the Dominions as a valuable staff study. It is of interest to the historian as the first full-scale review of grand strategy produced since the collapse of France, and also as giving a considered and balanced estimate of the reasonable requirements of the fighting Services.

The appreciation had been prepared 'with the object of examining, in the existing situation, the factors affecting our ability to defeat Germany, and to make recommendations from the military point of view as to the policy which should govern our war effort and the future conduct of the war'. Part I included a survey of the economic situation prepared with the help of the Ministry of Economic Warfare. Germany's basic economic problem, said the paper, was no easier than before the French collapse, since she would have to administer the greater part of the Continent under the conditions imposed by our blockade; her economy would depend largely on the degree to which she could exploit her conquests and impose her discipline upon them, extend her influence and obtain supplies from Russia. Her chief problems were still due to deficiency in certain essential commodities, coupled with serious difficulties of distribution. The weakest link in the economy of German-controlled Europe was oil. Apart from any interference by her enemies, Germany's oil resources were judged to be adequate until about June 1941; after that date the position in Germany would become precarious, even if she obtained all possible seaborne supplies from Roumania and Russia, and by the end of 1941 it might well become disastrous.

On the political side, a review of opinion in the various enemy and occupied countries led to the conclusion that risings were not likely to break out, still less to succeed, except as the outcome of careful plans and organisation controlled and assisted from Great Britain.

There followed next a detailed comparison of our own and the enemy's armed forces as at August 1940, August 1941, and 1942. At sea, the Germans would have their two new battleships (*Bismarck* and *Tirpitz*) in service by August 1941, and it was estimated that they might by then have 130 U-boats, and 235 by August 1942, in each case allowing for wastage. Prospects for our merchant shipping were unpleasant; we might have to face an annual net loss of between three and five million tons gross, involving a reduction of imports. By land we could not possibly strike with success at Germany in 1941, but in 1942 the mobility and efficiency of her army might have been considerably reduced by the blockade and by air attack and by commitments in occupied areas. Our air striking power should have substantially increased by the summer of 1941, and in 1942 it should be 'immensely formidable'.

The paper proceeded to call attention to the factors affecting the fulfilment and possible expansion of our Service programmes, such as labour, raw materials, machine tools and drop forgings, air attacks on industry, the competition of American rearmament and the need of foreign exchange. The general conclusion was that our existing programmes gave a reasonable target figure for industry, but that their achievement depended on adequate protection from air attack and on the amount of American productive capacity placed at our disposal. Further, there must be no violent change either in the programmes or in assigned priorities; and, if we were to make a large increase in the strength of our anti-aircraft force without cutting the programme of 55 divisions by the spring of 1942, we should have to extend the call-up to men between eighteen and fifty.

The forecast of our own and the enemy's strategy is summarised above in the account of the American conversations and need not be repeated. It was not our policy, said the Chiefs of Staff, to attempt to raise, and land on the Continent, an army comparable in size with that of Germany. We should aim, nevertheless, as soon as the blockade and air offensive had secured conditions when numerically inferior forces could be employed with good chance of success, to re-establish a striking force on the Continent with which we could enter Germany and impose our terms. Subversive operations and propaganda within the occupied countries, if properly controlled and timed, could make valuable contributions to this result. The general conclusion was that 'our strategy during 1941 must be one of attrition . . . Throughout 1941 we must accelerate to the utmost the building up of our resources. *But the general aim which should govern our strategy and determine the scope and rate of development of our expansion programmes should be to pass to the general offensive in all spheres and in all theatres with the utmost possible strength in the spring of 1942.*'

The final section of the appreciation was devoted to the consequent requirements of the fighting Services, attempting to set out a balanced programme in which our strategical requirements were related to the manpower and productive capacity likely to be at our disposal. The appreciation as a whole, however, was never discussed by the Cabinet, which had many preoccupations in the month of September, and when it was eventually considered by the Defence Committee on October 15 it was in certain respects, as the Prime Minister remarked, out of date. It will be better therefore to consider the Service programmes as they were severally discussed and determined.

At the end of August the Minister of Supply, Mr. Herbert Morrison, submitted a comprehensive memorandum on the munitions situation. The recent heavy losses of the army, he said, had largely been made good; we had now to consider how the enemy's immense superiority in stocks and steel output could be reduced and neutralised. In order to secure even local superiority at our chosen points of attack overseas we should need armoured vehicles and mobile guns in many thousands. While our output at the end of 1941 would be nearly equal to the peak output of the last war in field artillery, it would be appreciably less in small arms and very much less in medium and heavy artillery; on the other hand it would be very much greater in anti-aircraft guns of all types and of course in tanks and tank guns and anti-tank guns. The problem of ammunition was very different. To act on the assumption that there would be the same continuous demand from the army as in the siege conditions of the last war would involve much waste of time, labour, resources and storage space; but to be on the safe side we must create the capacity to meet heavy demands.

How large a force would our production enable us to maintain in 1942? On the triple assumption that our munition factories were not bombed too disastrously, that there was no heavy battle wastage in the meantime, and that labour and materials were available, the Minister estimated that we should have the initial equipment— except in anti-tank rifles and guns—for 55 divisions in advance of December 1941,[1] and we should be well able to maintain the weapons of such a force during 1942. The fulfilment of the tank programme, however, depended on the continuance of the partial moratorium on naval construction. For the right assignment of priorities in general an adequate statistical basis was essential.

The paper contained a section on munitions from North America. The United States had already sent us 820 field guns of ancient pattern with ammunition and over half a million rifles, which last

---

[1] Above, p. 256.

had been issued to the Home Guard. We counted on continuing and increased help, but there were difficulties. The Minister was not concerned with the dollar problem; the Defence Committee had given him a free hand; but there was the danger that as America's own war production grew the supplies for Britain would suffer. For safety we must either adopt a common type of weapon and share the output or else prevail on the Americans to produce the types we ordered. The difficulty was most acute in the matter of field artillery, and was not solved until it was agreed in London that certain British formations should be armed with American 105-mm. howitzers instead of our own 25-pounder guns.

North America of course included Canada. Professor Postan has explained why the British munitions programme before Dunkirk was kept 'within very narrow bounds'; but 'when, after Dunkirk, the British Government turned its eyes across the Atlantic. . . . the arguments which made for restraint in the ordering of American munitions applied with much less force to Canada . . . While progress in the United States was held up by long-drawn-out financial, technical and political negotiations, the Canadians went ahead to build up an armaments industry, the greater part of which was directly at British service. One-third of the original Army "insurance" programme was allotted to them and as time went on their share became steadily larger.'[1]

We may take next the Army programme of 14 September, which Mr. Eden, the Secretary of State, described as the War Office corollary to the paper we have just considered. It was the nearest approach to a comprehensive plan that could at the moment be framed, but for some time to come the limiting factor would be equipment. For this reason, instead of the fifty-five divisions agreed upon in June as the objective to be aimed at by December 1941 the War Office preferred to estimate the force which it would be possible to equip and maintain by the spring of 1942 as fifty divisions, or, more correctly, fifty divisions plus. This figure would comprise forty-five infantry divisions besides armoured formations equivalent to five armoured divisions and ten army tank brigades. The Prime Minister had demanded ten armoured divisions; but if our tanks were grouped into more divisions (than five) and fewer army tank brigades (than ten), this would merely be 'a redistribution of our assets'. The tank prospect was unsatisfactory. Our own output of cruiser tanks, the sort most useful for desert fighting, was very low, and indeed to reach the total of both cruiser and infantry tanks we should have to call on America. In any case the margin would be small.

---

[1] Postan, *op. cit.* pp. 229, 234–235. For the 'insurance' programme see above, p. 255.

We might, however, be able to equip more than fifty divisions by 1942, and the War Office proposed therefore to base their man-power requirements and recruiting scheme on the full programme of fifty-five; this would not include the men wanted for garrisons abroad, for training and Home Defence units, and for anti-aircraft and coastal defence at home, or for the Allied forces. Of this possible field force of fifty-five divisions, thirty-four might be expected to come from the United Kingdom, three from Canada, three from Australia, one each from New Zealand and the Union of South Africa, four from the African colonies and nine from India (or from India and the Allies).[1] After the spring of 1942 the output of equip-ment might suffice for still more divisions, but it would not do to 'risk an overdraft on our man-power assets'. It was clear that we should not have the men to build up an army much larger than that contemplated. We must therefore 'concentrate on bringing a force of this modest dimension to the highest pitch of fighting efficiency'.

Regarding the operational purpose which this army would serve, the War Office recalled that the Chiefs of Staff in their appreciation of Future Strategy had estimated the total force required for the defence of territories overseas, exclusive of India and the Dominions, as the equivalent of twenty-one divisions: namely, three for the Far East, one for Iceland and seventeen for the Middle East. But the Prime Minister had asked for not seventeen but twenty-seven divisions, of which fifteen would come from the United Kingdom, to make offensive operations possible in the Middle East, and the Secretary of State hoped that these ten additional divisions would be provided in due course. Home Defence, however, must have priority, and it was difficult to say what forces this would require at any given date: until the end of 1941 the number of mobile divisions needed could hardly be put at less than fourteen, but by 1942 it might be reduced to four.

The War Office concluded that by June 1941 the most we could do was to equip and maintain twenty-one divisions for oversea service; to equip and provide reserves for the troops needed for Home Defence; and to provide equipment on a training scale for the additional divisions then forming. Between June 1941 and the spring of 1942 we should be able to meet the maintenance requirements of the Middle East and find some divisions towards the additional ten demanded for that theatre. By the spring of 1942 we should have—trained and fully equipped except perhaps for anti-tank and medium artillery—fifty divisions in all.

Commenting on various points in the War Office proposals, the Prime Minister minuted that we must aim at not less than ten

---

[1] These figures do not exactly correspond with the estimate of 1 August; above, p. 256.

armoured divisions in 1941 and that at least twelve divisions, besides the troops on the beaches, should be in reserve in the United Kingdom. Both these points were approved in principle by the Defence Committee on October 15.

The War Office proposals implied a substantial contribution from India, considerably larger than that first envisaged. By August 1940 three Indian divisions were earmarked for oversea service, if not already despatched: two for Egypt, one distributed between Malaya and Aden. The offer of the Government of India to make three more available by April 1941 was gratefully accepted, but the Cabinet decided on the recommendation of the Chiefs of Staff to ask for a further three divisions, making nine in all, to be provided by the end of 1941, it being understood that their despatch must be conditional on the retention of sufficient forces in India for the defence of the North-West Frontier and for internal security.

The difficulty with regard to the Indian contributions was always equipment. The Chatfield report[1] had recognised that formations sent overseas must have a higher scale (known as E.D.T.—External Defence Troops) than those retained for service in the country, and it was now accepted that India could not possibly equip to the higher scale herself. It was agreed that any troops sent out from India 'to fight a first-class enemy' must be equipped to this scale, and that London should undertake to equip them, however uncertain it might be in August 1940 at what date the commitment could be honoured.

In September the Chiefs of Staff called attention to India's bareness and recommended that, as soon as the urgent needs of the Middle East and certain oversea garrisons had been satisfied, India should receive the minimum of equipment required for training purposes and that regular monthly shipments of stores should be sent her until her outstanding needs had been met. The Chiefs of Staff had taken up at the end of August the question of reinforcing the oversea garrisons, which had been largely neglected during the building up first of the British Expeditionary Force and afterwards of the Home Defence army; conditions were now somewhat easier, and they recommended that henceforward approximately 50 per cent of the army equipment produced should be allotted to garrisons abroad until all units had obtained their War Establishment and appropriate reserves. This recommendation had been accepted, and the monthly allotment to India was to be taken from the moiety assigned to overseas. Later, on the proposal of the Chief of the Imperial General Staff, it was agreed that India should receive regularly 10 per cent of the equipment produced in the United

---

[1] Above, p. 30.

Kingdom, and that this percentage should be taken from the moiety assigned to the army at home; the new principle was not to apply, however, to infanty tanks and cruiser tanks, or anti-tank and anti-aircraft guns—a considerable exception. Mr. Churchill noted that we must get fighting units from India in exchange for the equipment sent her.

The War Office paper mentioned a suggestion of Lord Beaver-brook's that the Army should have a separate Air Arm of its own. Mr. Eden agreed that in theory this was the right solution, but it was not feasible, 'starting from scratch', to raise, train or maintain such a force before 1942 at earliest; in the meantime the Army would have liked a less qualified right to the use of the aircraft available for close support than the Air Ministry were willing to admit. On one point there was no disagreement. When the American delegates had recently asked the British Chiefs of Staff 'whether experience showed that it was desirable to have a separate Air Force or whether the Force should be subordinated to the Army and Navy', Sir Cyril Newall had replied as follows with his colleagues' concurrence:

> While not necessarily subscribing to the view himself, he con-sidered that if a general consensus of opinion were taken on this subject it would probably be agreed that it was desirable, given unlimited resources, that there should be a separate Air Force and that the Navy and the Army should also be served with their own separate Air Forces. In the absence of unlimited resources it was necessary to cut one's coat to one's cloth. He thought that all were agreed that it was essential that there should be a separ-ate Air Force. Only in these conditions was it possible to foster the development of industry, science, research and technique. If the Air Force were subordinated to the Army and the Navy its freedom of development would inevitably be restricted.

The Prime Minister's immediate reaction to Mr. Morrison's paper on the munitions situation had been that, while the Navy could lose us the war, only the Air Force could win it. Our one hope, so far as could be seen at present, of overcoming the immense military strength of Germany lay in the power of the bomber to paralyse her economy. 'The Air Force and its action on the largest scale must therefore claim the first place over the Navy or the Army.' This principle need not, however, interfere with the production of anti-submarine craft, and we must aim at ten armoured divisions by the end of 1941.[1] The prerogative of the Air Force was asserted with no less emphasis a few days later by the Minister of Aircraft Production. Lord Beaverbrook, now a member of the War Cabinet, claimed for his Department not only 'a first helping of the raw materials required

---

[1] See Churchill II 405–408.

A A

in the manufacture of aircraft', but an absolute priority for the materials it needed—a 'right which must not be tampered with by any priority committees or other devices'. Supply of machines, however, would not by itself secure air supremacy. Pilot strength must be increased, and new fields of recruitment and training explored. 'Given freedom from hampering interference, asked no longer to defend his programme at every turn, given control of all components of manufacture not at present under his authority and with the right to exact from the Air Ministry Training Command a proper use of Training equipment, the Minister of Aircraft Production will undertake to supply enough Training machines for the Royal Air Force, the Navy and the Army, without impairing the supply of operational machines.'

The 'target programme' for the Air Force at the beginning of September, as proposed by the Air Ministry, gave first place to the Metropolitan Bomber Force. Its expansion had been postponed in May to the paramount need for fighters, and its rapid development, said the Chiefs of Staff, was an essential part of our strategy, if we were to break down 'within a reasonable time' Germany's resistance to the point at which 'a culminating offensive' could achieve her final defeat. This force should contain a high proportion of heavy bombers for the long-range offensive into Germany by night and, in suitable conditions, by day. The attainment of the old objective of numerical parity with Germany was, in present conditions, neither practical nor necessary: quality was more important than quantity. We should aim at a heavy bomber force of 1,600 first-line aircraft (as compared to our present figure of about 650 medium and heavy) and these should include as high a proportion as possible of the new types with greatly increased range and striking capacity. Hitherto, it must be remembered, heavy bombers had meant Wellingtons, Whitleys and Hampdens, not the Stirlings, Halifaxes and Manchesters of the future. But we ought also to have 400 bombers of a light type for day operations and for the support of the Army. The Chiefs of Staff urged that every effort should be made to complete the bomber programme as early as possible in 1942.

No comparable further expansion was envisaged in Fighter Command at home. It would be enough to raise our first-line strength from the existing figure of about 1,300 aircraft to 1,500 in the course of 1941. As regards other types, our total first-line strength in general reconnaissance aircraft should be doubled, and army co-operation machines would have to keep pace with whatever field force we decided to raise for operations on the Continent. It was recognised that 'small parachute and air landing forces' might be required in connexion with combined operations by land and sea, but nothing on a large scale was contemplated; in any case it was thought uneconomical to provide special types for such purposes, since heavy bombers could if necessary be diverted to this role.

British requirements overseas have been touched on in earlier chapters. The most urgent need was to make good our serious weakness in the Middle East: first to re-equip the bomber and fighter squadrons already in the theatre with modern aircraft—which should be completed by the end of October—and then to provide facilities for twelve reinforcing squadrons. Certain heavy bombers could fly direct from England to Egypt, but other aircraft, apart from the slow sea-passage to the Cape, must either break their journey at Malta or be disembarked at Takoradi to fly across Africa; both these routes had now been organised, but both were precarious. In the Far East, where we must now rely on air power for defence, we had only 88 aircraft, whereas the minimum judged necessary was 336; our capacity to meet the most immediate requirements must depend on the course of operations in Europe and the Middle East. In India there were at present only 78 aircraft, mostly obsolete, and no fighters. Nothing but a limited measure of re-equipment was practicable at present. There were also the needs of the Dominions to be considered, amounting to some sixty squadrons.

The target programme of the Air Ministry amounted in all to 270 squadrons (including 100 heavy bombers, 25 medium bombers, 93 fighters) for the Metropolitan Air Force, and 90 squadrons for overseas (excluding the Dominions)—a total of 360 Royal Air Force squadrons, with an initial establishment of 5,623 aircraft.

On September 30 the Cabinet devoted a meeting to a provisional discussion of the munitions situation in the light of the various departmental papers. In general the existing programmes of the three Services were reaffirmed. Every effort must be made to complete them by the dates due, but it would be better to accept some lag in their completion than to truncate the programmes themselves.

A few days after this, on October 2, the Ministry of Aircraft Production issued their ambitious programme for the turning out of just under 38,000 aircraft by the end of 1941, the monthly output rising from 1,620 in September 1940 to 2,762 in December 1941. Professor Postan has told how this and subsequent programmes were rendered impossible of fulfilment by 'the inexorable facts of industry and administration', to which German night bombing and the consequent dispersal of factories contributed.[1]

The Cabinet agreed on September 30 to continue their discussion at a further meeting to be held in the near future. This discussion, it seems, never took place, but on October 15 the Defence Committee considered and in general approved two important papers by the

---

[1] *British War Production* p. 124; details of the 'Hennessy programme' of October 1940 are given on p. 475.

Prime Minister on Priorities and on the reinforcement of the Mediterranean and Middle East. The 1A Priority, he said, must remain with aircraft production, but not in the sense that it should completely monopolise the supplies of any limited commodity. Allocations if necessary would be decided at Cabinet level.

The Admiralty's views on new construction had been stated at the beginning of September. Apart from the admitted need for small craft, which the enemy's acquisition of new bases had aggravated, the Naval Staff were anxious about the position with regard to capital ships, particularly in view of the possible deterioration of our relations with Japan. For a true comparison with our actual or potential enemies, one must exclude our unmodernized ships, namely the *Barham* and *Malaya*, the battle-cruiser *Repulse* and the four battleships of the *Royal Sovereign* class; the Prime Minister's repeated proposals for the strengthening of the decks of the latter had been carefully considered but judged unacceptable by reason of the long period (eighteen months) for which each ship would be out of action. Leaving out these seven old ships, we should have by the end of 1941, barring casualties, the seven other existing capital ships plus the four at present under construction—eleven capital ships in all.[1] As against these, Germany should have at the same time four new capital ships and Italy six, counting the modernised vessels of the *Cavour* class, while Japan was expected to have thirteen new or modernised capital ships and also three new small battle-cruisers. Similar estimates followed for the three subsequent years.

The Cabinet had decided at the end of May to suspend or defer work on one of the battleships of the 1937 programme (*Howe*), on both those of the 1938 programme (*Lion* and *Temeraire*), and on the 15-in.-gun *Vanguard* of the 1940 programme and on the aircraft-carrier *Indefatigable*. The Admiralty now asked that work should be resumed on all these vessels. But this alone would not be enough; it would only enable us to achieve parity in new ships with Germany and Italy by June 1945, assuming no further construction on their part, and made no allowance for Japan. They therefore pressed that the two battleships of our 1939 programme should be laid down as soon as possible, and an additional aircraft-carrier in March 1941.[2] They maintained that their proposals would not interfere with the construction of merchant ships at the rate of $1\frac{1}{4}$ million tons a year.

The Prime Minister's view was that, speaking generally, the speed of construction and early dates of completion must at this time be considered the greatest virtue in new building.[3] In the competition

---

[1] *Nelson, Rodney, Hood, Renown, Queen Elizabeth, Valiant, Warspite; King George V, Prince of Wales, Duke of York, Anson.*

[2] The four battleships of the 1938 and 1939 programmes were in fact never built.

[3] This minute is printed in full in Churchill II 592.

between the Services the Navy must exercise its existing priorities in respect of small-craft and anti-U-boat building, and the same applied to merchant ships and to landing-craft. He was satisfied, however, that the Naval Staff's proposals with regard to capital ships were sound.

The Cabinet on October 25 gave general approval to the naval programme with its multifarious items, subject to the normal consultations taking place with the Treasury and to the understanding that further delays might be imposed by shortages of steel and other materials.

The Prime Minister consistently urged the necessity of exploiting the scientific and technological ability which had already produced such remarkable results. This war, he minuted in September 1940, was not 'a war of masses of men hurling masses of shells at each other'.

> 'It is by devising new weapons, and above all, by scientific leadership, that we shall best cope with the enemy's superior strength. If, for instance, the series of inventions now being developed to find and hit enemy aircraft, both from the air and from the ground, irrespective of visibility, realise what is hoped from them, not only the strategic but the munitions situation would be profoundly altered . . . We must therefore regard the whole sphere of R.D.F., with its many refinements and measureless possibilities, as ranking in priority with the Air Force, of which it is in fact an essential part. The multiplication of the high-class scientific personnel, as well as the training of those who will handle the new weapons and research work connected with them, should be the very spearpoint of our thought and effort.'[1]

Six weeks later, in his note on priorities, he struck the same note.

Later chapters will mention the achievements of the research initiated or brought nearer to fulfilment in these months in the fields of anti-submarine warfare, of the location of surface vessels, of night-fighting in the air, of anti-aircraft and long-range gunnery by sea and land—all made possible through the discovery of means of utilising radar on very short wave-lengths. Indeed the invention of the cavity magnetron valve has been acclaimed as having 'had a more decisive effect on the outcome of the war than any other single scientific device evolved during the War'.[2] In a volume such as this only the general effect of these advances can be noted, but it is

---

[1] Churchill II 407.

[2] A. P. Rowe, *One Story of Radar* (Cambridge 1948) p. 35; see also J. G. Crowther and R. Whiddington, *Science at War* (H.M.S.O. 1947) pp. 31–49.

relevant to inquire how far they were made possible by organisation at a high level.

The country profited greatly from the attention paid before the war to scientific research for war purposes, though the number of scientists engaged on such inquiry was not very large. The Committee of Imperial Defence had always kept in touch with scientific developments affecting war, and it was natural that Mr. Chamberlain should charge Lord Hankey, for so long its Secretary, with special responsibility for ensuring co-ordination of scientific effort between Government Departments, outside organisations and individual scientists. All three Service Departments had their research organisations, each of which made its own contribution to the final victory. In the all-important field of radar the Air Ministry was the pioneer, with the creation in the winter of 1934–35 of the Committee for the Scientific Survey of Air Defence, under the chairmanship of Mr. H. T. Tizard.[1] Governmental support for the new venture was secured through a sub-committee of the Committee of Imperial Defence formed in the spring of 1935, with Sir Philip Cunliffe-Lister (later Viscount Swinton) as chairman, to deal with problems of air defence. At a lower level the first Inter-Service Committee on R.D.F. came into being on the initiative of the Air Ministry in September 1938. Individual scientists, too, kept the other Services informed of progress being made in one of them. There was however no organic connexion between the three scientific departments: priorities between competing demands were settled by agreement or by reference to a Minister.

In September 1940 the Royal Society suggested that closer cooperation of the scientific world in the war effort should be secured by the setting up of a committee under a Cabinet Minister, the members being representatives of the leading scientific societies. The Prime Minister was determined that the secret investigations then being conducted by the various departments must not be imparted to a new wide circle, but he approved the proposal on the understanding that 'we are to have an additional support from the outside, rather than an incursion into our interior'.[2] Accordingly a Scientific Advisory Committee was appointed, with Lord Hankey as chairman and six distinguished scientists as its members, representing the Royal Society, the Department of Scientific and Industrial Research, and the Medical and Agricultural Research Councils. Their function was to advise the Government on scientific problems, to suggest individual names for particular lines of scientific inquiry,

---

[1] The other members were Professors P. M. S. Blackett and A. V. Hill and Mr. H. E. Wimperis, with Mr. A. P. Rowe as secretary.

[2] Cited by Sir H. Tizard, *A Scientist in and out of the Civil Service*, Haldane Memorial Lecture 1953.

and to bring to the notice of the Government promising new scientific or technical developments which might be of importance to the war effort.[1] The Committee's normal channel of communication with the Cabinet was to be the Lord President of the Council. This body, however, as its composition showed, was not directly concerned with the day-to-day needs of the fighting Services; these were otherwise provided for.

Scientific geniuses, like others, are not particularly patient of organisation from above, but the course of the war showed the brilliant results attainable by teams of researchers drawn from Government research establishments, from the universities and from industry when provided with funds and facilities by authority and brought into close contact with representatives of the Services. With regard to radar, it is said, 'admirals, generals and air marshals came from the very first to see what was being done. They did not tell the scientists that they wanted this or that, but stated their problem and asked what science could do about it. The staff officers got into the habit of bringing rather diffuse problems to the scientists, and general discussions went on between admirals, air marshals, lieutenants, pilots, scientists, laboratory assistants, development engineers and anyone who could help.'[2] It was only gradually, it seems, that the Service chiefs learnt to 'state their problem' as a whole and 'ask what science could do about it', rather than ask the scientist to supply some specified requirements, but the change of approach led to their needs being met in unimagined ways of far wider scope. This informal co-operation obtained in other matters besides radar, and the benefit was reciprocal: commanders, from their practical experience, could make helpful suggestions to the scientists.

Another fruitful outcome of the closer contact between scientist and fighting man was the development of 'operational research'; this meant in practice the attachment of scientists to operational headquarters, where they could see for themselves the shortcomings of existing equipment and try to provide quantitative assessments of the results of methods and of types of operations with a view to improving them. This form of co-operation, which had its origin in the first war, was revived in Fighter Command in the late thirties and soon came to be extended throughout the Royal Air Force; from the autumn of 1940 onwards, under the guidance of Professor P. M. S. Blackett, it was developed with striking results in the Anti-Aircraft Command of the Army, and later in Coastal Command and in the Navy.[3]

---

[1] In May 1941 an Engineering Advisory Committee was set up, also with Lord Hankey as Chairman, 'to advise the Government upon engineering questions connected with the war effort'.

[2] *Science at War* p. 85.

[3] *ibid.* pp. 91–98; P. M. S. Blackett in *Brassey's Naval Annual 1953*, ch. ix, 'Operational Research'.

The possibility of using atomic energy for military purposes was realised by a few physicists in Britain and some other countries shortly before the outbreak of war. In April 1940, on receipt of reports that it might be possible to construct a bomb of unprecedented explosive force, a committee of scientists, with Professor G. P. Thomson as chairman, was set up under the auspices of the Air Ministry, to keep further developments in nuclear research under review.[1] But it was not till the late summer of 1941, after the period treated in this volume, that the Government formally adopted the project and entrusted its furtherance to a committee presided over by a Minister of Cabinet rank.

In order to present an intelligible story it is necessary to treat separately the different strands which composed it; but it must always be remembered that the sequences of events were contemporaneous and that one influenced another; also that the constant need for decisions on the various points must have pressed very severely on the directors of strategy. In the single month of September, besides the weighty matters mentioned in this chapter, they were concerned with defence against invasion and against the devastation of our cities and ports, with the threats to Egypt, Malta and Gibraltar, with the preparation of expeditions against Dakar and the Atlantic islands, with negotiations with the Americans over bases and destroyers, with the intentions of Vichy, of Spain and of Japan, and with the never-ceasing attrition of our seaborne supplies.

Subject to the approval, where appropriate, of the Cabinet and its Defence Committee, important strategical decisions were taken, as hitherto, by the Prime Minister and Minister of Defence, advised by the Chiefs of Staff who usually had before them reports drawn up by the Joint Planning staff. The Prime Minister had complained at the end of August that the existing machinery failed to initiate plans, and with the intention of overcoming 'the dead-weight of inertia and delay' he directed that the Joint Planners should henceforth work directly under his own orders and elaborate the details of such plans as he would communicate to them; they would still be at the service of the Chiefs of Staff Committee and would refer to them for their observations the results of their work.

'Thereafter should doubts and differences exist, or in important cases, all plans will be reviewed by the Defence Committee of the War Cabinet, which will consist of the Prime Minister, the Lord Privy Seal [Mr. Attlee] and Lord Beaverbrook, and the

---

[1] For the origin of the 'Maud Committee' see the article on 'Co-operation on Atomic Energy' by Prof. G. P. Thomson, in *American Scientist* Jan. 1953.

three Service Ministers; the three Chiefs of the Staff with General
Ismay being in attendance. The Prime Minister assumes the
responsibility of keeping the War Cabinet informed of what is
in hand; but the relation of the Chiefs of the Staff to the War
Cabinet is unaltered.'

This minute was approved by the Cabinet on August 26.[1]

On misgivings being expressed by the Chief of the Imperial
General Staff, Mr. Churchill explained that there was no question
of the Joint Planners submitting military advice to him. The Chiefs
of Staff would retain their collective responsibility for advising the
Cabinet as well as the Prime Minister or Minister of Defence, and he
proposed to work with and through them as heretofore.

It has seemed worth while to mention this incident because of
the importance of the subject, but it does not appear that in fact any
noteworthy change in procedure or in result took place. The outline
plan for any projected operation, together with directives to the
force commander, was normally prepared by the Joint Planning
staff assisted by the Joint Intelligence Sub-Committee.[2] The object
of the outline plan was to decide on the practicability of the operation,
to estimate the resources required, and to assess the implications of
providing these necessary resources. The outline plan was then submitted to the Chiefs of Staff who, provided that the conclusions in
the paper were favourable, and were approved, laid down the
degree of action to be taken regarding the appointment of the
commanders, the preparation of the forces, and the taking up of
shipping. The commander, once appointed, took over entire responsibility for operational planning, but the despatch and subsequent maintenance of the force, in accordance with the requirements
of the commander, remained a departmental commitment.

Such was the central machinery for the formulation and execution
of plans for the many expeditions under consideration at this period
of the war, and it worked smoothly, though provision for planning
on the administrative side may have been inadequate. 'The practice
of obtaining *ad hoc* administrative advice', it has been said, 'piecemeal
from the several Service ministries worked better than could have
been expected, but it was not a satisfactory method.'

Several personal changes which occurred about this time should
be recorded here. Mr. Neville Chamberlain resigned from the
Cabinet, his health having finally broken down; different views may
be taken of his judgement in matters of foreign policy and of his

---

[1] Churchill II 219–221.

[2] The Joint Planning Staff was reorganised, under the three Directors of Plans, in three
sections: Strategic Planning (the staff of the former Joint Planning Sub-Committee),
Executive Planning (the former Inter-Service Planning Staff), and a new Future Operational Planning Section. See diagram in Appendix VII.

suitability as a war-leader, but he devoted all his strength to the defeat of the enemy, once war had broken out, and in his selfless loyalty to Mr. Churchill's Government he rendered most valuable service. He was succeeded as Lord President of the Council by Sir John Anderson; Mr. Herbert Morrison became Home Secretary and Minister of Home Security in Sir John Anderson's stead, and Sir Andrew Duncan took Mr. Morrison's place as Minister of Supply.

On the enemy side too the autumn of 1940 made necessary a review of strategy. But Germany's difficulties were not the same as ours. Her superiority in numbers and armaments still gave her the initiative and she enjoyed the advantage of interior lines for the movement of her armies and air installations. But she could not move all her armies everywhere. She was limited by existing communications by road and rail; those in the Iberian and Balkan peninsulas were far below the standards of western and central Europe. But the Germans were subject to another limitation. From the end of July Hitler had in mind an invasion of Russia. As the year advanced this project grew upon him. Whatever date he finally fixed for its execution, Germany's main land and air forces must be ready by the spring of 1941. This fact must be remembered when we ask why Hitler did not exploit in this way or that his great preponderance of strength. Nevertheless there was plenty of time for secondary enterprises, and several were considered both before and after the abandonment of 'Sea Lion'.

The most obvious alternative—apart from the never-ceasing U-boat campaign—was to attack British interests in the Mediterranean. As early as July 1, when Hitler was concentrating his attention on disposing of Britain, he discussed possible operations by the Axis in the Mediterranean with Dino Alfieri, the Italian Ambassador, and it was suggested that Gibraltar and Suez must be attacked. At the end of the month the Army chiefs, not relishing either the proposed truncation of their invasion plan or their Führer's designs on Russia, toyed with the possibility of delivering the British a decisive blow in the Mediterranean, shouldering them away from Asia, helping the Italians to build up their Mediterranean Empire and, with the aid of Russia, consolidating the Reich they had created in western and northern Europe. 'That much accomplished we could face war with Britain for years.'

The Naval Staff, who had never liked 'Sea Lion', expressed similar views at the beginning of September. Control of the Mediterranean region was of vital importance for the Central Powers. The British should be excluded from this sea. For such a purpose the 'decisive strategic significance' of Gibraltar and Suez was recognised, and Hitler agreed that preparations for the capture of Gibraltar should be begun at once. The Naval Staff were sensitive to the inchoate co-operation between Great Britain and the United States symbolised by the recently announced exchange of destroyers for bases; they urged that these preparations should be completed before the United States played a more active part. Raeder also emphasised the danger of Britain or the United States occupying the Azores and Canary Islands should Portugal or Spain enter the war, and found that Hitler considered the occupation of the Canaries by the Luftwaffe 'both expedient and feasible'.[1] The idea of helping the Italians was to bear fruit later on. Hitler approved it, and on September 14 ordered that the preparation of a Panzer Corps for Libya should go forward. But for the present it was not acceptable to Mussolini. The plan of closing the western end of the Mediterranean by the capture of Gibraltar seemed more practicable, and it must now be mentioned.

For an expedition against Gibraltar the co-operation of the Spanish Government was highly desirable, perhaps essential. Hitler indeed seems hardly to have thought out the implications of marching through Spain without General Franco's good will. Communications were poor and it would have been very difficult to maintain a supply route from the French frontier to Algeciras with the population hostile. But such a question must have seemed academic, since Hitler always regarded his fellow-dictator as a potential ally and in 1940 counted on his soon becoming a belligerent. In August the German Ambassador in Madrid, in a memorandum to Berlin, referred to the Spanish promise, made in June, to enter the war on the side of the Axis, but only on the fulfilment of certain conditions. Spain must receive Gibraltar, French Morocco, Oran, and the enlargement of her existing possessions in Africa; she must also be provided with military and other assistance for the conduct of the war, in particular petrol and grain. At present, however, she was dependent for the necessary supplies on Britain and the United States. If Britain collapsed, or if the Axis could supply her needs, she would change her attitude. But the Axis countries could not supply her economic needs, and while Hitler had no objection to Spain eventually making large annexations in Africa—subject to certain pickings for Germany—he was not willing to antagonise Vichy, and indeed all Frenchmen everywhere, by handing over colonies to Spain before victory was assured. The Spaniards resented such a sacrifice of the interests of 'a friend of yesterday, tomorrow and forever'—so Franco's brother-in-law, Serrano Suñer, called them—to those of a beaten foe, and they were unwilling to divide

---

[1] *F.N.C.* pp. 134–135, 6 Sept. 1940.

the Moroccan lion's skin with Germany, still more to transfer to her any present Spanish territory. So matters reached a deadlock. Franco would not lower his terms and, though sedulously wooed by Hitler and constantly protesting his affection, he as constantly refused to name the day.

Hitler's reluctance to press too hard on Vichy was disappointing to the Italians also. They were anxious to realise their modest claims—Nice, Corsica, Tunis, French Somaliland—and more than once they brought forward the idea of a separate peace with France.[1] However, the determined resistance at Dakar at the end of September could only confirm the contrary view that it was worth while to play for Vichy's collaboration. Raeder was afraid that the British, with the help of the Gaullists and perhaps the United States, would make north-west Africa a centre of resistance; Germany should therefore work in concert with the French Government for its protection. At the same time he again urged on his master the need of taking Gibraltar and previously by air action securing the Canaries. The Führer was in general agreement with Raeder, but had not finally made up his mind whether it was more profitable to work with France or with Spain: 'probably with France, since Spain demands a great deal but offers little'. Nevertheless he had by no means given up hope of winning Spain.[2]

Strong diplomatic pressure had already been brought to bear on Franco and this was continued in October, notably on the 23rd, when Hitler came himself to meet the Caudillo at Hendaye on the Franco-Spanish frontier. It was after this meeting that Hitler is reported to have said that he would rather have three or four teeth extracted than undergo such an experience again;[3] but on November 4 he told his Service advisers that he was determined to occupy Gibraltar at the first opportunity and that Franco was 'obviously prepared to enter the war on Germany's side as soon as possible'.

The collapse of France had its immediate effects in the east of Europe also. A fatal blow was dealt to her traditional influence in the Balkan countries, and notably in Roumania and Yugoslavia, the survivors of the ill-starred Little Entente. The U.S.S.R. reacted promptly. Stalin, like Hitler, was taken by surprise by the speed and completeness of the German victory. Relations between the two Powers had hitherto been, if not cordial, correct, and their economic agreement was working reasonably well. But neither trusted the other, and the Soviet Government now thought it wise to foreclose on the interests it had acquired both in the north and in the

---

[1] Ciano, *Diplomatic Papers* 376, 397 (July 7, Oct. 4).
[2] *F.N.C.* pp. 141–143 (26 Sept.).
[3] Ciano, *Diplomatic Papers* p. 402.

Balkans. On June 17 a pro-Russian Government was established in Lithuania, after Russian troops had occupied the country. The same fate befell Latvia and Esthonia and in July all three were incorporated in the Soviet Union. Germany was bound by secret protocols of 23 August and 28 September 1939 to recognise these regions as within the Russian sphere of influence, and could not openly object,[1] but Hitler could only view with disgust the absorption in the new Soviet empire of lands so long associated with Germanism. Germany on the same occasion had declared that she had no political interests in south-eastern Europe, while Russia had asserted hers in Bessarabia. But Germany had reserved her economic interests in those parts, and her interest in Roumanian oil was very great.[2] So long as this was safeguarded she was well content with the *status quo* in the Balkans. But Italian designs on Yugoslavia and the Russian claim to Bessarabia, together with the long-standing Hungarian and Bulgarian hopes of recovering their former territories from Roumania, suggested in the spring of 1940 that Balkan peace might not last long.

Roumania, so fatally enlarged by the wars of 1913–18, was the first to suffer. On June 28, after presenting an ultimatum which Berlin advised Bucarest to accept, the Russians occupied Bessarabia and a considerable part of Bukovina besides, with its capital Czernowitz. This stirred up the Hungarians and the Bulgarians to press their own claims. The Roumanian Government, which on May 26 had concluded an oil pact with Germany, now repudiated the British guarantee of April 1939 and appealed to Germany for moral support against exorbitant demands by these new claimants; it was willing, however, to make reasonable concessions. For the next few weeks, until the end of August, there was constant interchange of views on this subject between the parties concerned, among whom Italy was now numbered. Roumania was eventually compelled to yield large slices of territory to both Hungary and Bulgaria, Germany and Italy guaranteeing the integrity of what remained.[3] The Russians, who had not been consulted, formally protested that Germany's action was a breach of the Non-Aggression Treaty of August 1939. The period of Nazi-Soviet concord had lasted exactly a year.

On September 5, a few days after the cession of the territory had been agreed to, the Roumanian Government fell. King Carol fled the country and General Antonescu, a friend of the Axis, made himself Prime Minister and Dictator. The fallen Government had some

---

[1] *Nazi-Soviet Relations* pp. 78, 167.

[2] See Ribbentrop's memorandum of 24 June 1940, *ibid.* p. 157.

[3] By the (2nd) Vienna Award, of 30 August 1940; territory in South Dobrudja had been ceded to Bulgaria a week earlier. Compare the two end-papers in this volume.

time previously petitioned the Germans to send a military mission to Roumania. Hitler had not then been prepared to comply, but now, when the request was repeated, after the settlement of the territorial claims, by a more congenial Government, he graciously consented. On September 20 a directive was issued by *OKW* accordingly.[1] The Führer had decided, on the request of the Roumanian Government for German instructors, to send Army and Air missions to that country. It must be made to appear that they were intended 'to aid Roumania, our friend, in organising and training her armed forces'. Their real objects, which must be kept secret, were to protect the oilfields; 'to enable the Roumanian armed forces to carry out certain tasks according to a definite plan drawn up in the interests of Germany'; and to prepare the ground for operations by German and Roumanian forces from Roumania 'in case we are forced into war with Soviet Russia'. The German 'demonstration troops' should consist at first of one motorised division reinforced by tanks.

Such was the beginning of the German move into the Balkans.

We must now turn to Italy. After the liquidation of Czechoslovakia in March 1939 Ciano had warned the German Ambassador in Rome that Italy could not disinterest herself from the future of Yugoslavia; he reminded him further that the Führer had 'always proclaimed Germany's lack of interest in the Mediterranean in general, and in particular the Adriatic which we intend in future to consider an Italian sea'.[2] Ribbentrop confirmed this statement of Germany's attitude and assured Ciano that she had no interest in the Croatian question. In May, after the Italians had occupied Albania, he informed Ciano that Germany recognised that, should the dissolution of Yugoslavia come about by an internal process, Italian policy must prevail.[3] A year later, in May 1940, there was a widespread belief that Italy intended shortly to attack Yugoslavia, and in addressing his Chiefs of Staff on the 29th Mussolini said that, while generally remaining on the defensive on land, 'we might undertake something in the east, possibly Yugoslavia'. But next day he assured Hitler that he would do his best to prevent the conflict from spreading to the Balkans and the Danube basin.

Early in July, shortly after Italy had entered the war, Mussolini was feeling more adventurous. He charged Ciano to impress on Hitler at their forthcoming meeting in Berlin that it was necessary to split up Yugoslavia, 'a typical Versailles creation, functioning against us'.[4] Hitler, however, insisted to Ciano on the importance of

---

[1] *Führer Directives* p. 115.
[2] Ciano, *Diplomatic Papers* pp. 276–280.
[3] *ibid.* p. 285.
[4] *Ciano Diaries* 5 July.

not stirring up trouble in the Balkans and provoking Russian intervention; but, should trouble break out of its own accord, Germany would welcome strong action on the part of Italy.[1] Mussolini acquiesced, and on July 11 directed that all resources should be sent to the Libyan theatre.

Discussion in Berlin also touched on Greece, Mussolini having instructed Ciano to tell Hitler of his intention to land on the Ionian Islands. Relations between Italy and Greece had long been difficult. The Greeks did not forget Mussolini's bombardment of Corfu in peacetime in 1923, while the Duce lived up to the classical principle of hating those whom one has wronged. He naturally coveted the Greek islands at the entrance to the Adriatic and was only too glad to accept unfounded reports that the Greeks were affording facilities to British warships. In the second week of August he expressed bellicose sentiments with regard to Greece, and, when on the 15th a Greek cruiser, the *Helle*, was sunk by an unidentified submarine, Italian treachery was suspected with good reason.[2] The Duce's designs on Greece were unwelcome to the Army high command, if only because up till now the bulk of the Italian forces in Albania were disposed for operations against Yugoslavia, the Greek frontier being very thinly held; so that the choice lay between attacking on a small scale only and losing the advantage of surprise.[3] On August 22, however, apparently under German pressure, Mussolini decided to take no immediate action against either Yugoslavia or Greece.[4]

In September Italian interest was focused on the abortive Libyan offensive, but by the middle of October the Duce was determined to attack the Greeks. Hitler had not consulted or informed him before occupying Roumania and he intended to pay his ally back in his own coin.[5] On the 15th he discussed the proposed campaign with selected officials, the Chiefs of Staff of the Navy and Air Force not being present. It was to commence with an offensive from Albania into Epirus, whence Corfu and other Ionian islands could be occupied and pressure exerted on Salonika; the second phase would include the occupation of Athens and the rest of the country. The overrunning of Epirus should not take more than ten to fifteen days, said General Visconti Prasca, commander of the Italian forces in Albania: 'this operation, which might lead to the liquidation of all the Greek forces, had been prepared down to the smallest detail, and was as perfect as was humanly possible'. Prolonged resistance from the Greeks was not expected; Turkey was thought unlikely

---

[1] Ciano, *Diplomatic Papers* p. 377.
[2] See *The Greek White Book* (1942) No. 129.
[3] See E. Canevari, *La Guerra Italiana* II (Rome 1949) 197.
[4] *Ciano Diaries*, Aug. 10, 11, 12, 15, 22.
[5] *ibid*. Oct. 12.

to intervene, and Bulgaria was 'a pawn in the Italian game'; as for the British, the Duce declared that it was out of the question for them to send land forces, while they had little to spare in the way of air resources. To minimise British aid, Mussolini wished Graziani to renew his offensive against Egypt a few days before the attack on Greece, and Ciano could imagine the Duce's indignation when the General reported that he would need another two months at least.[1] The three Chiefs of Staff, so Marshal Badoglio told Ciano on the 17th, were all opposed to the Greek project, and the whole impression given is one of a highly amateurish approach. Mussolini however insisted, and Ciano proceeded to concoct an ultimatum, in fact a declaration of war, to be presented to the Greeks at two o'clock on the morning of October 28. 'Naturally it is a document that allows no way out for Greece. Either she accepts occupation or she will be attacked.'[2]

[1] *Ciano Diaries* Oct. 16.
[2] *ibid.* Oct. 22.

CHAPTER XVI

THE MEDITERRANEAN AND MIDDLE EAST, NOVEMBER 1940–FEBRUARY 1941

THE SITUATION in the Mediterranean was transformed by the Italian invasion of Greece on October 28. In April 1939 the British Government, with the French, had given Greece a guarantee to come to her support with all the forces at their command should her independence be threatened and her Government decide to resist, and on 5 September 1940 the Foreign Secretary had reaffirmed the promise.[1] General John Metaxas, the Greek President of the Council, accordingly asked at once for British naval and air assistance for the protection of Corfu and of Athens. The Cabinet and the Defence Committee took his request into consideration the same day.

Since Graziani's offensive had halted short of Mersa Matruh on September 18 there had been no indication of its imminent resumption. But its resumption before long might be expected, especially if it were reinforced by German land or air units, in which case our troops in the Middle East might prove inadequate for the defence of Egypt. Hitler was in fact on September 14 thinking of sending armoured aid to Libya,[2] and the War Office, rightly divining his thought, urged that we should maintain a consistent policy of strengthening our forces in the Middle East; as an immediate measure, in spite of the weakness of the army at home in armoured fighting vehicles and the continuing threat of invasion, we should accept the risk of sending out a reinforcement of two cruiser and two light tank regiments. The Prime Minister agreed in principle; no one was more eager than he that the army of the Nile should be strong, for attack as well as for defence, but he was not convinced that either the General Staff or the Middle East Command were making the best use of the forces at their disposal.[3]

On October 15 the Defence Committee had before them a minute from the Prime Minister on 'The Mediterranean'. They agreed that the reinforcement of Malta was a matter of urgency and that, should

---

[1] *House of Lords Debates* vol. 117, col. 368.
[2] See above, p. 359.
[3] Churchill II 442.

October pass without invasion, we should set about the reinforcement of the army in the Middle East by the Cape route to the utmost limit of our merchant ships and escort vessels. The Admiralty were invited to submit a programme of naval requirements, and the Committee approved detailed proposals from the Air Staff for both accelerating the re-equipment with new aircraft of the existing units and expanding others with a lower establishment; this would amount to the equivalent of about six additional squadrons equipped with aircraft of superior fighting value. The Air Staff might find it possible to raise three new fighter squadrons in the near future, but this in any case must take time: the despatch of the necessary maintenance crews and equipment was a slow business, involving a time lag of about three months between the decision to send them out and their establishment in Egypt complete.

The need for air reinforcement as the pressing demand of the hour was reiterated in telegrams from Mr. Eden, the Secretary of State for War, who had been sent out to review the general situation in the Middle East and report to the Cabinet. General Maitland Wilson was confident, said Mr. Eden, of his ability to hold and defeat the Italians facing him, and hoped to be able to launch a small offensive himself in January. But success depended on air reinforcement.

It was generally agreed that reinforcement of the Middle East was urgent. Thus the appeal of the Greek Government on October 28 came at an inauspicious moment. We had for some time been receiving enquiries from Athens as to the help we could offer Greece if attacked, and had up to now been very guarded in our replies, since any forces sent to her would have to be diverted from other important tasks, such as the bombing of Germany. Moreover, quite apart from our own bareness, Greece was not an easy country to help. The northwest coast, including Corfu, was too close to Italian airfields to allow of any but intermittent protection by the Navy, while Greece herself was ill-found in airfields and the lie of most of the country did not favour their construction. On the other hand the use of Crete, and especially of the fine anchorage of Suda Bay, would be of great benefit to the Fleet. In the last days of Anglo-French co-operation a French force had been standing ready in Syria to occupy the island, but no action had followed. In any case much would have to be done before Crete could be regarded as an adequate naval or air base; the essential thing was to deny it to the Italians. In the circumstances it could be argued that any land or air reinforcements we could send to Greece would be too weak to have any decisive effect; the best way we could help her was by striking at our common enemy, and we could do that most effectively from regions where we had built up our strength and formed plans. It was somewhat the same argument that the Allies had used with reference to Poland. The Greeks themselves were reasonable, and General Papagos has stated that his countrymen expected no important assistance from us at this time.[1]

Nevertheless we were bound to do what we could, and the Defence Committee agreed in the first instance to authorise General Wavell to send up to one infantry brigade for the defence of Crete. The battalion which he was to have sent to Malta would now be found from the United Kingdom. Arrangements should be made for the bombing of Italy from Malta, and we would announce that if the Italians bombed Athens we should bomb Rome. The Prime Minister further commended Air Marshal Longmore's initiative in arranging to send to Greece at once a token force of one squadron.

On November 3 the Chiefs of Staff reported their considered proposals. They recognised the paramount importance of giving the greatest possible material and moral support in the shortest possible time. This must take the form of air assistance; but the size of the force to be sent must depend on the airfields available, and of these there appeared to be only two in southern Greece, capable of receiving not more than five squadrons between them; they would moreover need anti-aircraft equipment, of which the Greeks possessed very little. Prompt assistance could come only from Egypt, and our plan was to despatch thence to Greece three squadrons of Blenheim bombers, including that already on the way, and one of fighters (Gladiators), to be followed later by another, with one heavy and one light anti-aircraft battery. At the same time twelve Wellington bombers would be flown out from England to Malta to reinforce the twelve already there. It was proposed to compensate the Middle East by sending out thirty-four Hurricanes by the Takoradi route and thirty-two additional Wellingtons via Malta. The plan would admittedly leave Egypt 'very thin' for a period, but it was essential to help Greece, and the Cabinet approved it. Air Commodore J. H. D'Albiac was given command of the air units.

The Chiefs of Staff reported at the same time on the strategic implications. Our anti-aircraft resources in the Middle East were already inadequate, and we could ill spare the batteries now diverted to Crete and the Greek mainland. To provide the shipping required we must take two ships from a Middle East convoy. Both at home and in Egypt our fighter defences would for a period be perilously weak. On the naval side, four cruisers would have to be withdrawn from home waters, and the consequences at Gibraltar and in the eastern Atlantic might be grave. Mr. Eden, who was still in Egypt and in touch with the Middle East commanders, agreed that the hazards involved must and could be faced. But any increased commitment or

---

[1] *The Battle of Greece 1940–1941* (English translation, Athens 1949) p. 257.

attempt to hasten the rate of despatch to Greece would mean serious risk to our position in Egypt.

A staff appreciation, which they approved on November 5, shows how the Chiefs of Staff viewed the new situation in a wider context, and what were the principles which they wished to be followed in the employment of any forces we might send to the help of the Greeks. It was thought possible that Mussolini had acted independently for political reasons, but more likely that his move was part of an Axis design to divert our land and air forces from the defence of Egypt, to lure our fleet into dangerous waters, and to win air and naval bases in Greece from which the enemy could dispute our control of the Aegean. Perhaps a trap was being laid to tempt our forces into Greece only to be destroyed by a subsequent German advance through Bulgaria. Assuming that the Germans would eventually invade Turkey, they might try first to establish their position in Greece. It was doubtful if Turkey would come to the help of the Greeks against the Germans; she was only bound to help Greece in the event of an attack by Bulgaria. If on the other hand the Greeks could stem the Italian advance, we should be given the opportunity of extending our air offensive against Italy and establishing ourselves within range of the Roumanian oilfields. Given time, the Italians could no doubt defeat the Greeks, though the Greeks might hold out for a considerable period. But German intervention would be a very different matter, and no forces we could send in 1940 could long delay a German victory. It would therefore be wrong to lock up irrevocably in Greece forces which we might need for the defence of Egypt, for the threat to Egypt was not lessened by the Italian invasion of Greece. We might need them also for assistance to Turkey or for the control of the routes through Syria. The help we should offer to Greece should therefore be limited: at sea, to disputing Italian control of Greek waters and damaging the Albanian ports; in the air, to co-operating in the latter purpose; and on land, to the despatch of such technical units as could be spared from Egypt. Crete, moreover, must be denied to the enemy and kept as an advanced refuelling base for ourselves. The Chiefs of Staff noted that the plan already approved by the Prime Minister for assisting the Greeks was in general accordance with the conclusions of this appreciation.

The Italian offensive in Epirus was brought to an ignominous halt early in November. It had been envisaged as a mere promenade, but so stout was the Greek resistance that the Italians were forced back into Albania with heavy losses, and though the first crisis seemed to have passed by mid-December it was not for some months that they regained the initiative, after the arrival of large reinforcements. Hitler had been unofficially forewarned of the imminence of the October offensive, though the letter of October 19 which he received from Mussolini was but vaguely worded. He had not then raised any objection, and at his meeting with the Duce at Florence on the 28th he graciously offered his full co-operation for the Greek venture.[1] But as early as November 4 he spoke of it as 'a regrettable blunder'; on no occasion had he given 'authorisation for such an independent action' to the Duce.[2] Indeed it might queer his own pitch in the Balkans. Reports (in fact incorrect) of British landings in Lemnos as well as Crete suggested a bomber threat to the Roumanian oilfields, and on November 12 he ordered preparations for the invasion of northern Greece; a month later the order was expanded to provide, if necessary, for the occupation of the entire Greek mainland.[3]

On November 12 Mr. Eden gave the Cabinet an account of his recent visit to the Middle East. At Gibraltar, where the defences had been greatly strengthened in recent months, there were now four British battalions; at Malta, six, with a company of infantry tanks. We were poorly informed as to the enemy's communications with North Africa; this would be serious if German reinforcements were sent there. In the Western Desert there were no indications of an Italian advance on a large scale; the position here was far more favourable than had seemed possible a few months earlier. There was little doubt that we could hold an attack by Italian land forces. Our weakness was in the air: after the withdrawal of the five squadrons for Greece we should have only three fighter squadrons in Egypt, and we were still very short of anti-aircraft guns. At Khartoum it was thought that we had now ample forces to resist an Italian attack on the Sudan. General Smuts, whom Mr. Eden had met there, was anxious to remove any threat to Mombasa by an offensive against Italian Somaliland. The prospects of fomenting rebellion in Abyssinia had greatly improved; the Emperor had arrived in the Middle East in July and was waiting at Khartoum to re-enter his country at the first opportunity. General Wavell had summed up our strategy as, first, to defeat the Italian forces threatening Egypt; secondly, to liquidate the Italian forces in East Africa and so remove the threat to the Red Sea; thirdly, to build up forces to help Greece, Turkey and other countries in the Middle East.

Mr. Eden had also brought back very secret information as to Wavell's intentions, and the Defence Committee, meeting on November 13, encouraged the General, in the light of recent events, to execute them with all speed. It was unlikely that Germany would leave her flagging ally unsupported indefinitely. Consequently it seemed that now was the time to take risks and strike the Italians by

---

[1] Ciano, *Diplomatic Papers* p. 399.
[2] *F.N.C.* p. 146.
[3] *F.D.* pp. 121, 125.

land, sea and air. The Prime Minister had already assured him that the Government would sustain him in any well-considered, resolute operation, whatever its outcome might be.

'Recent events' did not refer only to the Italian *débâcle* in Epirus. The balance of naval power in the Mediterranean had been radically altered by a series of British successes.[1] These were usually connected with the sailings of the forces at Alexandria and Gibraltar to protect the passage of warships or convoys. The most dangerous section of the journey was the bottle-neck of the Sicilian Channel, ninety miles wide; but the destination of the convoys was often Malta, a perpetual focus of danger.

Mention was made earlier of the first (known as 'Hats') of these hazardous operations, which at the end of August passed a convoy to Malta from Alexandria and naval reinforcements to Alexandria from Gibraltar.[2] Their repetition, especially when the sailing of merchant ships from Gibraltar was concerned, always caused anxiety, for the result closely affected strategy in the Middle East. On November 11 a two-way passage through the Mediterranean was combined with a daring and brilliantly successful attack on the Italian fleet in Taranto harbour by naval aircraft flown from the carrier *Illustrious*. The immediate effect was to put out of action half of the Italian battlefleet —the three battleships *Conte di Cavour*, *Duilio*, *Littorio*—and so completely did the exploit change the respective surface strengths that the Admiralty soon found it possible to withdraw one battleship to home waters.[3] The remainder of the enemy fleet moved to the greater security of Naples.

It was about this time, during the month of November, that great interest was taken in Whitehall in a scheme, known as 'Workshop', for the capture of Pantelleria, the small Italian island in the Sicilian Narrows, about 120 miles north-west of Malta. It was first suggested to the Chiefs of Staff on October 30 by Sir Roger Keyes, the Director of Combined Operations, as within the scope of the troops which had been specially organised for offensive operations under his direction. He commended it as offering us a base for staging aircraft to the Middle East, for controlling the Sicilian Channel, and for attacking Italy and Sardinia by air. Pantelleria in British occupation would constitute a standing threat to Vichyite Tunis and a valuable

---

[1] See Playfair I, ch. xii, Roskill I, ch. xv.

[2] Above, p. 308.

[3] The *Malaya* and *Ramillies* left the Mediterranean before the end of 1940, the *Barham* replacing the latter.

alternative to Malta, with the advantage of providing an excellent airfield with underground hangars. Its capture should not require large land forces; a strength of four commandos was suggested. The Chiefs of Staff at first saw attractions in the idea, and its daring and aggressive nature made a special appeal to the Prime Minister. For the next two months it bulked large in our strategic thinking.

On closer inspection, however, the scheme came up against objections of various kinds. Our assault troops and still more our assault craft were very few, and there were competing demands for them. After the failure of the Dakar expedition small forces had been reconstituted and were still held ready for the capture, in certain circumstances, of the Portuguese Atlantic islands, while Admiral Cunningham had designs on the Dodecanese. But the Admiral felt other objections. Should we succeed in capturing Pantelleria, we should have to hold it, thereby imposing an additional, in his view an intolerable, strain on our existing resources and energies. Did we really wish to accept the responsibility of defending and supplying a second Malta? On November 16 the Chiefs of Staff were more sensitive to these objections, but three days later the view they expressed was that the operation seemed feasible and worth carrying out provided that the garrison was not larger than we supposed (one battalion) and that the expedition did not interfere with the more important project ('Brisk') for the possible occupation of the Azores. The Defence Committee accordingly approved 'Workshop' in principle—it should be carried out in the course of the passage of a convoy to Malta leaving the United Kingdom on December 15—but on the understanding that there must be no period during which it would be impossible to carry out 'Brisk'; this condition involved a nice calculation of the dates when the several assault ships would be available.

'Workshop' came again under frequent discussion in December. On the 9th, in spite of Cunningham's dislike and of the Chiefs of Staff's opinion that the chances against success were about three to one, the Defence Committee provisionally sanctioned the scheme. The Chiefs of Staff were now prepared to approve it in view of 'the ultimate possibility of being able to station two fighter squadrons there'. It seems clear however that they did not like it and, when the time came for the sailing of the convoy (code-name 'Excess'), apprehensions of a German move into Spain led the Defence Committee to retain the force detailed for 'Workshop' in the United Kingdom.

'Workshop' was still on the programme at the end of the year, though now postponed till mid-February. It was finally abandoned, to Admiral Cunningham's great relief, on January 20, by which time the arrival of German bombers in Sicily had immensely increased the danger from the air in the central Mediterranean.[1]

Another tempting combined operation, for which commandos could be based on Crete, was the capture of the twelve islands known as the Dodecanese. Their geographical position gave them obvious strategic importance and Rhodes and Leros had been fortified by the Italians. It was clearly desirable to deny them to the enemy, but there were political difficulties in respect of their eventual disposal. Before the Italians took them in 1912 they had been under Turkish sovereignty, and they lay close against the coast of Anatolia. But the great majority of their inhabitants were Greek, and their desire to be united to Greece was well known. The Chiefs of Staff noted also that hitherto the Italians had made little use of these islands, and it seemed possible that they might fall into our lap through starvation. Nevertheless the commanders in the Middle East were anxious for their early liquidation, emphasising that Italian naval and air forces could use them to threaten our main lines of supply to Greece or Turkey in the case of any major operations against an enemy in the Balkans, including air attacks on Roumanian oil. The present ineffective use of them by the Italians was mainly due to the fact that we had provided heavy escorts to our convoys at the expense of other tasks; should torpedo bombers start to operate from Rhodes they would be a serious menace to the fleet. The Chiefs of Staff accepted these arguments and instructed the Commanders-in-Chief to prepare provisional plans, to be executed either with or without elements of the force allotted to 'Workshop'.

This operation, which received the code-name of 'Mandibles', was naturally viewed as part of our plans for helping Turkey; the importance of her attitude was accentuated by our knowledge of the presence of German troops in Roumania and our concern for the continued resistance of the Greeks.

In a report of November 1 on a possible advance by the enemy through the Balkans and Syria to the Middle East the Chiefs of Staff had suggested that the Germans might intend, after the occupation of Bulgaria and Greece, to move next into Turkish Thrace and establish bridgeheads on the further side of the Straits; having achieved this purpose by the end of 1940, they might next consolidate their position in Anatolia and advance into Syria and perhaps into northern Iraq. An enemy advance by land through Syria would constitute a vital threat to our hold on Egypt; it would cut our

[1] *A Sailor's Odyssey* p. 291: for Mr. Churchill's views see his vol. II 552, 618, vol. III 51-53.

alternative line of supply via Iraq and Palestine and would force our small army in Egypt to fight on two fronts.

We know that the German army staff were interested in such a scheme: we are told of General Paulus' opinion, that the operation, carried out by two motorised corps, would only take three months. But Hitler rejected it, regarding it as a lengthy operation which would involve great difficulties.[1] It was in any case not calculated to appeal to a man contemplating a full-scale invasion of Russia in the spring. But it was a possibility, threatening disastrous consequences, which the British high command had to take into account; plainly the main bar to it was effective Turkish resistance. Consequently Turkey comes once more to figure largely in staff discussions, as she had in the spring of 1940.

The Defence Committee and Cabinet approved the general proposals of the Chiefs of Staff's report, namely that we should aim at having forces in the Middle East by the spring available for direct assistance to Turkey and for denying Syria and Iraq to the enemy and in the meantime prepare the necessary plans, including the formation of a military mission ready to move into Turkey as soon as she became involved in war, or earlier if her Government were willing.

It was not obvious, however, what course it was in our interest that Turkey should take in the immediate circumstances. The question was indeed an academic one, since the Turks had never suggested that they would abandon their neutrality unless Bulgaria attacked Greece or the Germans moved through Bulgaria against Greece. But our diplomatic representatives at Athens and Ankara took opposite views, and the Foreign Office asked the Chiefs of Staff for a military opinion.[2] They replied on November 17 that, while arguments on both sides were nicely balanced, they were in favour of doing all we could to bring Turkey in as a belligerent at once. If we knew for certain that she would ultimately join us, it would be better to wait until both she and we were stronger and better able to resist a German assault. But to allow an opportunity to pass, with the result that Turkey might fail to resist Axis pressure when turned on her, might be disastrous. Further, her entry at the present moment might have a decisive effect on Italian morale. They thought this outbalanced the risk of precipitating a German move against Turkey and Greece.

On November 17 King Boris of Bulgaria visited Hitler at Berchtesgaden. On the 20th Hungary, and on the 23rd Roumania, adhered to the Tripartite Pact.[3] It seemed that anything might happen

---

[1] *F.N.C.* p. 146.

[2] The two diplomats were Sir Michael Palairet and Sir Hugh Knatchbull-Hugessen; see the latter's *Diplomat in Peace and War* (1949).

[3] See p. 340.

in the Balkans. The Foreign Office did not agree with the Chiefs of Staff that we should put pressure on the Turks at the present time to enter the war, and the Cabinet decided that our immediate object should be to induce Turkey and Yugoslavia to join in a common front against German aggression; this done, they should be invited to seek Bulgaria's co-operation. After considerable discussion our Ambassador at Ankara was instructed that, while we wanted Turkey to come into the war as soon as possible, on the principle of a bird in the hand, we were not pressing her to take any special steps to help the Greeks except to make it clear to Bulgaria that any move by Germany through Bulgaria, or any movement by Bulgaria herself, against Greece, would bring about an immediate declaration of war. We should like Turkey and Yugoslavia to consult together at once and to be ready to warn Bulgaria and Germany at the first sign of a German movement towards Bulgaria. If Turkey did not immediately fight in the event of German troops crossing Bulgaria, she would find herself isolated and it would be beyond our power to help her. The Turks might be told that we hoped to have at least fifteen divisions in the Middle East by the summer of 1941, and nearly twenty-five by the end of the year.

In the Prime Minister's view such a move by the Germans was imminent; if Turkey were inclined to comply with our wishes that she should declare war, she would certainly make very heavy demands for help, in men and material. The importance of bringing her in, and perhaps Yugoslavia too, would far outweigh any Libyan operation, and Wavell would be reduced to the very minimum defensive role in Egypt. The sooner he could strike therefore the better.

Even before Graziani's offensive petered out in September, Wavell had had in mind the possibility of a counter-stroke designed to throw the Italians out of Egypt in the first instance and perhaps later to capture Tobruk. The halting of their offensive short of Mersa Matruh increased his own difficulties of transport and supply, apart from the fact that the Italian forces, on land and in the air—especially after the despatch of British help to Greece early in November—were much larger than his own. But he had formed a poor opinion of Italian enterprise and tactics, and with the full approval of the authorities at home he decided to attack at the earliest possible moment.[1]

Operations were designed to last for five days only, but Wavell always meant to exploit any success to the utmost; the whole campaign was a very daring one and depended for success on surprise as

---

[1] For the planning and execution of Operation 'Compass' see Playfair I ch. xiv.

well as on careful preparations for a long night approach march and the creation of forward supply depots. The detailed plan eventually adopted was that of Lieutenant-General R. O'Connor, commanding the force in the Western Desert. Complete success was achieved in three days by the efforts of all three Services, and when the battle ended on December 11 the Western Desert Force, consisting of one armoured and one Indian infantry division and one battalion of 'I' tanks, had defeated some seven infantry divisions, two of them native African. Success was largely due to elaborate measures of deception: Wavell had not worked under Allenby and studied his methods for nothing. Sidi Barrani was a miniature Megiddo. Indeed one might apply to it the words with which Wavell concluded his chapter in Allenby's biography on the preparations for that victory: 'This was to be no soldiers' battle, but the manœuvre of a great master of war.'[1]

The Prime Minister was jubilant and showered his congratulations on Wavell, Wilson and Longmore. The primary aim must now be 'to maul the Italian Army and rip them off the African shore to the utmost possible extent'. Action in the Sudan, important as it was, and in the Dodecanese was secondary.[2] This was Wavell's own feeling. The timing of his first battle made possible the relief of the 4th Indian division, whom he wished to employ in the Sudan, by the 6th Australian, now trained and concentrated. The advance continued, and on January 5 Bardia fell. The land attack was supported by naval fire from battleships as well as from the old monitor *Terror* and smaller ships, while fighter aircraft gave close support and bombers attacked airfields further west. Next came Tobruk with its valuable port; the garrison surrendered on January 22, and on the 27th the first ship was unloaded.

Meanwhile the Italians were being harassed much further south by the enterprise of a few experts in desert travel—the Long Range Desert Group (formerly Patrol) under Major R. A. Bagnold—who had learnt to operate in the Libyan sand-sea in small parties hundreds of miles from any base. In November the British force, in which New Zealanders were prominent, concerted measures with the Free French in the Chad province of French Equatorial Africa, and the capture of Kufra later on (March 1) by a small French force provided a base some 500 miles from the Mediterranean for further Allied enterprises.[3]

Early in January the Cabinet were again perturbed by the prospect

---

[1] *Allenby, Soldier and Statesmen* (1946 ed.) p. 229. The relevant part was first published in September 1940.

[2] Churchill II 542.

[3] See Playfair I ch. xv.

of an imminent German advance against Greece. They had information of German troops massing in Roumania and of German infiltration into Bulgaria. The Defence Committee accordingly decided on the 8th that it was of the first political importance to despatch at once to Greece the fullest support in our power; such action would have a good effect on Turkey and also on Russia. The Chiefs of Staff thought the most likely German move was to send a small armoured and motorised force, supported by dive-bombers, through western Bulgaria against Salonika. The exact form of our assistance could not be fixed without consultation with General Metaxas, but it should certainly include a high proportion of additional aircraft and anti-aircraft units, all types of artillery, tanks and engineers. Since the need might prove immediate—it was thought the Germans might move on January 20—this help could be supplied only by the Middle East, and the Chiefs of Staff suggested that the Commanders-in-Chief should be told that assistance to Greece must take priority over operations to the west of Tobruk and in the Sudan. This need not prevent an advance to Benghazi, 'if the going was good', nor need the projected operation to eject the Italians from Kassala in the Sudan be abandoned. Should the German advance not take place, part of the force proposed might render help to the Greeks in Albania, who were pressing a counter-offensive with the hope of securing the port of Valona. After approval by another meeting of the Defence Committee instructions on these lines were sent to the Middle East.

The proposed help included three Hurricane and two Blenheim IV squadrons, besides tanks and artillery, and the reaction of both Wavell and Longmore was one of dismay. But the policy of London was clear, and the two commanders proceeded to fly to Athens to discuss how help could best be rendered. They discovered at once that the official Greek point of view was entirely different from the British. What General Papagos, the Commander-in-Chief, wanted in Albania was in the first instance transport and clothing; he refused the artillery and tank units offered him. The President of the Council was convinced that on the Macedonian front the despatch of such troops as we could send would not suffice to ensure the safety of Salonika and would merely provoke a German attack. He had information that the Yugoslav Government took the same view. His own proposal was that we should consign stores and material to the Greeks for the purpose of preparing for the eventual landing of a strong British expeditionary force, capable of offensive as well as of defensive action. Once the Albanian situation was cleared up, large Greek forces would be available for the Salonika front, and he would then welcome assistance. In any case, should the Germans attack, the Greeks would fight to the last.[1]

---

[1] General Papagos' account is given in *The Battle of Greece 1940–41* pt. II, ch. vi.

It was the situation with which we were by now so familiar: the weak country wishing us well and eager for our help if that help would be effective; afraid, however, that it would not be effective but would merely convert a probability of aggression into a certainty. General Papagos complained afterwards that 'the idea of a unified plan did not dominate the general conduct of the allied struggle as a whole. This idea should have governed the choice of the front of the main allied effort and the order of priority of allied operations on the various fronts.' As it was, 'the commencement of British operations in Africa practically at the same time as the Greek operations in the Balkans . . . made any serious and timely strengthening of Greece impossible'.[1]

It is true that there had been no high-level consultations, though the Greeks had pressed for them; but the Greeks were not belligerents until the Italians attacked them, and the date of the attack was not foreseen by either the Greeks or the British. When it occurred a renewed Italian advance was threatening Egypt; to counter it Wavell was already preparing his tiny force, in deepest secrecy, for an offensive which was soon to cost the common enemy over a hundred thousand prisoners and hundreds of guns and tanks. It is unlikely that any comparable success could have been achieved in Epirus in view of the weather and the terrain. Moreover the expulsion of the enemy from the Libyan and Red Sea littorals was of the utmost importance for the protection of the sea communications of our forces fighting Italy—forces which at this time were far below requirements in men, equipment and means of transport by sea and land. It is difficult to see what practical ends would have been secured by such consultations as General Papagos desired.

On January 20 the Defence Committee considered at length a review by the Chiefs of Staff of our policy in the Mediterranean. We had to take account of two new factors: the Greek refusal of army reinforcements and the arrival of units of the German Air Force in Sicily. The basis of our strategy remained the security of Egypt and the control of sea communications. The two main threats were a German drive southwards through the Balkans—an attack against Turkey would be the form most dangerous for us—and German assistance to Italy in the central and western Mediterranean. After considering the present situation and future prospects in the different regions, the Chiefs of Staff concluded that our offensive in Libya should be continued as far as the capture of Benghazi, which would remove the air threat to Egypt. Subject to this primary purpose, we should continue such assistance to the Greeks as they were willing to receive, and should capture the Dodecanese at the first opportunity.

---

[1] *ibid.* p. 388.

The special troops and craft held ready for the projected operation against Pantelleria should be transferred to the eastern Mediterranean. Plans should however be prepared for the capture of Sicily. The Defence Committee agreed that Benghazi and the Dodecanese should be 'cleared up' as soon as possible and a mobile reserve, eventually of four divisions, constituted in Egypt for employment in Greece or Turkey within the next two months. The three assault ships of the Glen Line, with two commandos and landing craft, should sail at earliest for Suez round the Cape. Air dispositions must conform, but Longmore's first duty was the defence of Malta.

The Commanders-in-Chief were informed accordingly next day, January 21, and General Wavell could proceed with his plans for the capture of Benghazi, the central point of the Italian occupation of Cyrenaica. The masterly tactics, the speed, boldness and endurance, by which not only Benghazi was taken but practically the whole of the Italian Tenth Army cut off, are recounted elsewhere.[1] The manœuvre was the consummation of a series of brilliant victories and a revelation of the possibilities of desert warfare.

In accordance with his instructions, General Wavell did not attempt to advance into Tripolitania. After the victory of Beda Fomm British troops occupied El Agheila, the most southerly point on the Mediterranean coast, on February 8 and there halted; there were no enemy troops except stragglers within 150 miles of them. It was not found possible, however, to make use of Benghazi as an advanced supply base, as had been hoped; this was due mainly to the arrival of the Luftwaffe on the Mediterranean scene and our lack of air defence for the port.

Hitler had proposed to Mussolini on November 20 that German bombers should operate for a period from Italian bases against the Royal Navy. On December 10 he issued a directive to this effect (Operation '*Mittelmeer*'), and early in January *Fliegerkorps X*, from Norway, was establishing itself on Sicilian airfields.[2] The new formation announced its presence on January 10, when the aircraft-carrier *Illustrious*, taking part in one of the complicated operations concerned with the passage of convoys, was severely damaged west of Malta and put out of action for several months. The cruiser *Southampton*, too, was mortally wounded on January 12. The Luftwaffe possessed in their dive-bombers a weapon which made them far more formidable than the Italians and henceforward our commanders in the Mediterranean had to reckon with a new and very serious danger.

The order to prepare forces for Greece had come to General

---

[1] Playfair I ch. xix.
[2] *F.D.* p. 124, Dec. 10; see Playfair I ch. xv.

Wavell as an unpleasant shock; operations against Italian East Africa, on the other hand, had always formed part of his plans. He had told Mr. Eden at the end of October that the next object of our strategy, after securing Egypt in the west, was to liquidate the Italian forces in East Africa, and on the last night of the year the Prime Minister and the Chiefs of Staff agreed that operations to clean up Abyssinia should take priority next after those then in progress in the Western Desert.

The East African campaign, of which the main purpose was to remove the threat to our shipping in the Red Sea, is fully described by General Playfair.[1] Remarkable as it was, it can only be briefly referred to in this volume. It was remarkable for the vast extent and difficulty of the terrain, for the skilful co-ordination of forces attacking from bases many hundreds of miles apart, and for the combination of organised formations from the United Kingdom, India and South, East and West Africa with local bands of Patriots incited by British enterprise and inspired by the presence of their dethroned Emperor.

Early in July Italian columns had crossed the Sudanese frontier at Kassala and Gallabat, and had turned our garrison out of Moyale, just within the borders of Kenya; in August, after the capitulation of the French in Jibuti, they had overrun British Somaliland. Since then they had, on the whole, rested on their laurels. The Duke of Aosta, the Italian Viceroy and Commander-in-Chief, had larger forces than we could bring against him and large supplies of materials; but in view of the British command of the sea and Graziani's failure to conquer Egypt he had no prospect of receiving reinforcements and his troops resembled 'cut flowers in a vase'. Their defeat was therefore only a matter of time, or rather of timing, since on the one hand the rains would prevent operations during several months, while of the troops available to the British command some were inadequately trained and some would be required elsewhere in the spring. As it turned out, in Abyssinia as in Libya far more was achieved by our forces than had at first seemed possible.

Wavell's basic plan was that Lieutenant-General W. Platt, with two Indian divisions, should invade Eritrea by an eastward advance from Kassala and that Lieutenant-General A. G. Cunningham, with formations from South, West and East Africa, should move against the coast towns of Italian Somaliland (Kismayu and Mogadishu) from eastern Kenya, while Abyssinia should be attacked from the west by a guerrilla force organised in the first instance by Colonel D. A. Sandford and later by Major O. C. Wingate. Air support would be available from the Sudan, from Kenya and from Aden.

---

[1] Playfair I chaps. xxi–xxiii. See Map 16 (where Abyssinia is shown as Ethiopia).

General Platt's forces, which included the 4th Indian Division withdrawn from the Western Desert after Sidi Barrani, reoccupied Kassala, now abandoned by the Italians, on January 19 and proceeded to cross the Eritrean border. Also based on the Sudan, but further south, the Patriots were disorganising Italian movements in the mountainous regions of western Abyssinia, while at the beginning of February General Cunningham's force from Kenya entered Italian Somaliland, occupying Kismayu on February 14 and Mogadishu on the 25th.

At the Khartoum conference in October, at which General Smuts and Mr. Eden were present, it had been agreed that if administratively possible an offensive against Kismayu should be launched in January. In November General Cunningham, expecting increased opposition besides the administrative difficulties, proposed to postpone the main operation till May, after the rains. Both General Smuts and Mr. Churchill expressed disappointment, but Wavell accepted Cunningham's reasons. In January, however, after our successes in Libya, and after receiving welcome transport from South Africa, Cunningham felt it possible to make his effort in the following month, and Wavell at once agreed.

General Wavell had mentioned to the Secretary of State at the end of October as his third commitment—after the safeguarding of Egypt and the liquidation of Italian East Africa—the building up of forces to assist Greece, Turkey and the Middle East countries. Before considering further developments in this field of operations it may be well to say something of one perpetual theme of controversy beween London and Cairo.

We were still in the period of the war when, on the side of the Allies, there was simply not enough to go round; it was usually a case of doing what one could with admittedly inadequate resources. This meant that, while the Departments in England were straining every nerve to produce, or purchase, and transport overseas the precious equipment, commanders kept protesting that they were being called upon to make bricks without straw, and sometimes they must have thought bitterly of another text, that from him that hath not shall be taken away even that which he hath.

The Middle East was now the one theatre in which the Army, supported by the Royal Air Force, was making a great effort and incurring great dangers. It was natural that under the strain of war vehement and sometimes petulant messages should pass between Whitehall and Cairo—the latter insisting on their needs, their increasing commitments and the little they had received, the former stressing the efforts made to meet their needs and suggesting that the best advantage was not always taken of what it was possible to send. Two messages may be quoted.

From the Prime Minister to General Wavell, 7 January 1941, private and personal.

'I am sorry to jar the hour of your splendid victory by awkward matters of housekeeping. If your demands for non-fighting services are maintained on the present scale the whole scope and character of our effort in the Middle East will have to be reviewed. Shipping has now become the dominant factor and will remain so certainly for six months. Rations of heavy munition workers are being cut down to levels of which British armies except in actual operations have never dreamed. Severe stringency in human rations and slaughter of cattle through lack of feeding-stuffs lie before us. Transport of vital munitions, aeroplanes, trained pilots, raw materials for munition factories now offered from across the Atlantic are endangered. The main war effort of the nation may be compromised. The voyage round the Cape imposes an almost prohibitive burden. It is quite certain that all the convoys will have to be severely cut.

I think you will admit that I have done my utmost to reinforce and nourish the M.E. armies and we have not only made sacrifices but have run grave risks to do so. Therefore I feel I have a right to ask you to make sure that the rearward services do not trench too largely upon the effective fighting strength, that you have less fat and more muscle, that you have a smaller tail and larger teeth. You have well over 350,000 troops on your ration strength and the number of units which are fighting or capable of fighting appears to me disproportionately small. It is distressing to see convoys sent by the heart's blood of the nation's effort consisting so largely of rearward services of all kinds.

I am well aware of all the arguments which can be deployed in favour of every rearward establishment. I do not dispute their validity; the question is one of emphasis and proportion. This is no time for ideal establishments to be drawn up by staff officers and pushed out to us as essential minima. I beg you to convince me that you will continually comb, scrub and purge all rearward services in a hard, unrelenting manner as Kitchener did. This conviction will enable me to impose the severe sacrifices required upon the British Nation, and to secure for the campaign of 1941 in the Middle East the opportunities which may await it under your direction.'

Private for Prime Minister from General Wavell, 8 January, 1941.

'. . . I can assure you that I have always had question of rearward services constantly in mind, and have been as anxious as anyone to cut down non-fighting units. Except for anti-aircraft. Demands from subordinate commanders are nearly always for more administrative units than for more fighting troops, and I am

CC

continually being warned that I am working on a dangerously small administrative margin.

I will again carefully examine situation to see whether we are over-insured or over lavish in any direction, and I will make any possible reduction on demands for shippings. But the more I see of War, expecially present-day War, the more I am impressed by the part that administration plays.

I should like to thank you again for the support you have given us and risks you have taken to enable us to win successes here.'

Similar exchanges took place in connexion with Air resources; the Prime Minister could not understand why Longmore on various occasions did not have more aircraft available, while to the Air Marshal it seemed that Mr. Churchill failed to realise the difficulties of maintenance in a theatre where aircraft had to be flown across a continent to do battle in a world of dust and sand. There was controversy also with regard to the time required to bring new arrivals, both men and machines, to the state of fitness for action. Mechanised war, and particularly mechanised war in the desert, thousands of miles from home, was something new, which required fresh calculations of the proper ratio of forward and rearward services and of what could be expected of machines.

Bearing in mind these sharp differences of view, we may turn to the fresh demands occasioned by German activities in the Balkans.

On January 26, five days after conveying the decision of the Defence Committee that he was to advance to Benghazi and form a base there, the Prime Minister warned Wavell that he was convinced that the Germans were already making use of Bulgarian airfields and preparing for action against Greece. We must expect a series of very heavy disastrous blows in the Balkans, and the sooner Wavell could build up a strong reserve ready for employment there, the better.

The Commanders-in-Chief replied to the earlier telegram on January 27. They were agreed that the capture of Benghazi and of the Dodecanese was of urgent importance and noted the need for building up a strategic reserve. But 'hitherto the war [had] been conducted on an irreducible minimum of force, which [had] in fact been well over the danger line'. The risk might have been justifiable against Italians, but was no longer so in dealing with Germans. Prospects were especially bleak with regard to the Navy and Air Force. Our present naval forces could not guarantee the new long line of sea communication off the Libyan shore, and it would be some time before Benghazi could be used as a supply port. It was undesirable to postpone an attack on the Dodecanese until the arrival of the Glen ships made major operations (against Rhodes) possible, and permission was asked to nibble at the smaller islands of the group. The Chiefs of Staff on January 30 promised naval reinforcements and gave Longmore leave to raise as many new squadrons as his own resources allowed. They believed that the attack on Rhodes could be undertaken before mid-March and ruled that any smaller operations should be timed in relation to the larger and form part of one coherent plan.

For reasons which will appear later no attack on Rhodes or Leros was ever made at this period of the war. A minor operation staged in February against the island of Castelorizo was a failure.

By now the thoughts of the Prime Minister and the Chiefs of Staff were turning more and more to Turkey, regarded now as always as the pivot of our Balkan strategy. It was believed that some 4,000 of the Luftwaffe, some in uniform, most not, had infiltrated into Bulgaria and, apart from the actual damage which might be apprehended from bombers so situated, the moral effect on the Turks of a powerful German air force established on their borders might be disastrous; one result would be to deprive us of the chance of bombing the Roumanian oilfields. Sir Charles Portal urged that we should seek to persuade the Turks to accept British forces, particularly air forces, at once, and the Chiefs of Staff on 29 January made concrete recommendations for sending to Turkey as soon as possible, with her Government's approval, three fighter and seven bomber squadrons (exclusive of the five squadrons in Greece) and some hundred anti-aircraft guns, heavy and light, for the defence of Istanbul, Smyrna and the airfields. We should also make provision for sending considerable land forces to Turkey from the Middle East at the right moment. If these measures did not deter Germany from further aggression in the Balkans, we should at least be within striking distance of the oilfields, and the Straits would form a useful anti-tank ditch. The Chiefs of Staff recognised that if Turkey accepted this assistance we could offer little or no additional help to Greece, but they were clear that for the moment Turkey should have priority. It was most important, however, to hold Crete, and with the acquiescence of the Greek Government we should occupy Mytilene and Lemnos. This policy was approved at a meeting with the Prime Minister and Service Ministers that night, and telegrams were sent to Longmore and Wavell and, from the Prime Minister personally, to the President of the Turkish Republic; Mr. Churchill suggested to him that the two countries should repeat in defence of Turkey the same kind of measures which the Germans were taking on the Bulgarian airfields. The Cabinet gave their approval on February 3.

In neither case was the proposal well received. Longmore was 'astounded' at the suggestion of locking up squadrons in Turkey, perhaps for some time in idleness, while the Middle East was so short and active operations were still continuing. Later he reported that the three Commanders-in-Chief recognised the soundness of the 'high policy' of infiltrating air squadrons into Turkey, but thought the capture of the Dodecanese an essential preliminary. In any case local conditions made it impossible to release so large an air force in the near future. But the Turkish President's reply settled the matter. While pressing for the delivery of the equipment so long awaited, the need of which had been confirmed in recent Anglo-Turkish staff conversations at Ankara, he stood firm against the admission of British units in anticipation of a German advance. This would mean the entry of Turkey into the war.

Nor was information from Greece reassuring. The Greek advance in Albania was held up by weather and lack of transport. But this was not all. General Metaxas, the forceful President of the Council, had died on January 29, and his successor, M. Koryzis, told General Heywood, the head of the British Mission, that the situation seemed to him desperate. In two months there would be no artillery ammunition left. General Papagos said that if Germany attacked Greece— which he did not expect—Greece would resist, but in view of the slight prospect of timely help from outside her resistance would be little more than a protest and could not last long. A few days later M. Koryzis confirmed his predecessor's declaration that Greece would appeal for British help when the Germans crossed into Bulgaria, but left it to London to decide whether British reinforcements should then be sent to Greece and, if so, at what moment: the premature despatch of an insufficient force could only have disastrous results.

This depressing news from Greece synchronised with the capture of Benghazi, three weeks ahead of expectations, and the rounding up of the Italian Tenth Army. Wavell wired that a small force promptly despatched might be able to capture Tripoli; otherwise his reserves immediately available for Greece or Turkey were one armoured brigade group and the New Zealand Division (two brigades). By mid-March he could send a second armoured brigade group, the rest of the New Zealand Division and an Australian division (two brigades); this Australian division could probably be completed by mid-April and another Australian division sent by the end of April. He had not included the 6th British Division, earmarked for the Dodecanese. He reckoned that the factors limiting despatch would be shipping and escorts.

The Defence Committee met on February 10 and 11 to consider the new situation. The prospect of rounding off Wavell's victories by the capture of Tripoli and the expulsion of the Italians from North Africa was tempting. But the operation, even if successful, would not secure the Mediterranean supply route and would lay fresh responsibilities on the Navy. The critical theatre was now the Balkans. The key to the problem was still Turkey, but she had refused our help, while the gallant Greeks had asked for it. To support the Greeks in resisting the Germans might be the best way of bringing Turkey in. There was general agreement that we must not abandon the Greeks but that the effectiveness of our help would depend on the Greek plan of campaign, of which we had no knowledge. Obviously time was of great importance. The War Office estimated that the Germans, who were believed to be building up a force of thirty divisions, including five armoured, in Roumania, might, if they entered Bulgaria on February 17, arrive on the Greek frontier by 12 March with five divisions, including one armoured, and reach Salonika within a week; the country between Salonika and Athens was very difficult, but the Germans might eventually get ten divisions through.

Wavell was instructed that he should establish a secure flank at Benghazi and concentrate all available forces in the Delta in preparation for movement to Europe. Turkey having refused our assistance, our first thoughts must be for Greece, and we should offer to transfer to Greece the fighting portion of the army which had hitherto defended Egypt. This should not be less than four divisions, including one armoured, and whatever air reinforcements the Greek airfields could take. 'Mandibles' however was still regarded as urgent. In order to concert measures, both diplomatic and military, against the Germans, Mr. Eden, now Foreign Secretary, and Sir John Dill would leave forthwith for the Middle East, for consultations at Cairo, Athens and Ankara.[1]

Before closing the chapter we may look at the development of the German plans for the war in the Mediterranean during this period. The conduct of a consistent strategy was hampered by Hitler's long-standing concession to Italy of the leading role in this theatre, by the tergiversations of Franco, and by Hitler's own firm intention to make his great effort against Russia in the summer. We must consider Axis intentions in the Eastern Mediterranean, in the Western Mediterranean, and in the Balkans.

The German General Staff had from the end of July onwards considered the eventual despatch of an armoured formation to North Africa to support their ally. But at his meeting with Hitler on the Brenner on October 4 Mussolini had declined such help until the second stage of his advance had been completed by the capture of Mersa Matruh—a success first expected for that month but soon postponed to December. Just before the Italians attacked in Epirus

---

[1] Mr. Eden had succeeded Lord Halifax in January; see p. 421.

the Germans had received a discouraging report of conditions in Libya from General von Thoma. The Italians there did not seem to desire help, and the terrain was unpromising. On November 4 Hitler decided to postpone the despatch of armour to Africa indefinitely, and his directive of the 12th declared that the employment of German forces in support of the Italian offensive against Egypt would be considered, if at all, only when the Italians had reached Mersa Matruh. Even then it would be primarily a question of air assistance. An armoured formation, however, would be kept ready and shipping prepared to carry troops to Africa—either to Libya or to north-west Africa.[1] An advance against the Delta seemed unlikely before the summer, but he urged on the Duce the importance of taking Mersa Matruh as soon as possible, in order to secure an air base against Alexandria and the Canal. Even after the first defeats of his army in Libya Mussolini did not ask his ally for more than equipment or materials, and at the end of the year Hitler still saw no need to send him troops. But reports from his naval staff and from the Military Attaché in Rome impressed him with the gravity of the situation in North Africa; it seemed unlikely now that either the Italians or the Germans could re-open the offensive against Egypt with any success, at any rate until the end of 1942, but it was important to prevent the Italians from being turned out of North Africa. Accordingly on January 11 he issued another directive, declaring that 'for strategic, political and psychological reasons the Mediterranean situation, where Britain is employing superior forces against our ally, requires German assistance'. Help was to be given to Italy both in Albania and in Tripolitania; for the latter a blocking, or containing, formation (*Sperrverband*), capable of halting British armour, was to be made ready (operation '*Sonnenblume*').[2] On January 21 he ordered that the 5th Light (motorised) Division should start as soon as possible, about February 15. But as the news from Africa became worse and Italian intentions to attempt no more than to hold Tripoli itself transpired, the Führer decided that either more assistance should be offered or none at all.

On February 5 he wrote to Mussolini that a complete Panzer division would now be necessary as well as the Light Division, but this would only be sent on the understanding that a British advance from Cyrenaica would be resisted. The Duce agreed, and replaced Graziani by General Gariboldi, commanding the Fifth Army. The first German troops started on February 8; ten days later Hitler named the new force the 'German Africa Corps'; it would be under the command of General Erwin Rommel, who had led the 7th Panzer Division in France in 1940.

---

[1] *F.D.* No. 18, p. 120.
[2] *F.D.* No. 22, p. 132.

The mention of north-west Africa as an alternative objective was due to Hitler's eagerness in November to close the western end of the Mediterranean to the British. He was still hopeful of early Spanish intervention and he proposed after the capture of Gibraltar to move one or two divisions to Spanish Morocco 'to provide a guarantee against the possible defection of French Morocco or North Africa from France'.

At the same time (November 12) Hitler had ordered that preparations should be made for occupying continental Greece north of the Aegean, to enable German air units to attack targets in the eastern Mediterranean, especially British air bases threatening the Roumanian oilfields. In conversation with Ciano on November 18, and writing to Mussolini two days later, Hitler explained that his policy was to bring Spain into the war as soon as possible and to march on Greece through Bulgaria, but this move could not be made before the middle of March. He hoped to keep Turkey and Yugoslavia quiet, possibly to bribe the latter into co-operation; also to induce the Hungarians to allow large German troop movements through their country into Roumania, where the first echelon of the 'military mission' of about one division, had arrived by December 5. Negotiations with Bulgaria were rendered difficult by the simultaneous pressure to which she was subjected by the Russians, but Hitler was assured (23 November) that her sympathies were with Germany. Hitler had no success with Franco, but his plans against Greece were becoming definite. On December 13 he issued his directive for operation 'Marita'; he justified it by the importance, in view of the dangerous situation in Albania, of preventing the British from establishing, under the protection of a Balkan front, an air base which could threaten both Italy and the Roumanian oilfields. The plan was to build up a force in southern Roumania during the winter, with which, when the weather became suitable, probably in March, to occupy the northern Aegean coast and, if necessary, the entire Greek mainland. A total of up to twenty-four divisions was contemplated. The Bulgarian army would provide flank protection against Turkey, but the attitude of Yugoslavia could not be predicted. The Luftwaffe would support the army's advance, destroy the enemy's air force, and occupy British bases on Greek islands by airborne landings.[1] An army directive of December 9 had ordered that Twelfth Army should be ready to move into Bulgaria from February 7, so as to cross the Greco-Bulgarian frontier on March 22.

Early in January, with matters going badly for the Axis in Libya and none too well in Albania, Hitler decided to come to the rescue of his ally in both theatres. His decision to send a 'blocking formation'

---

[1] *F.D.* No. 20, p. 125.

to Africa has been mentioned above; but he also judged it important to contain the Greeks in Albania and prevent them from reinforcing their Salonika front. A German force must therefore be made ready for operations in Albania (Operation '*Alpenveilchen*'). A month later, however, he countermanded this order: the situation in Albania had improved, and was now neither alarming enough nor promising enough to justify the despatch of German troops.

Hitler's intentions in the Balkans cannot be considered without reference to his far-reaching designs against Russia. His comprehensive directive of November 12 ordered that preparations for the East which had been ordered by word of mouth should continue, regardless of the results of the negotiations with Molotov then in progress. His directive of December 13 for 'Marita' mentioned his intention to withdraw the force on its completion 'for new assignments', and on December 18 he issued his directive for 'Barbarossa': the German armed forces must be ready to crush Soviet Russia in a rapid campaign. This aspect of Hitler's grand strategy will be treated later.[1]

In the meantime political and military discussions were conducted with Bulgaria. Her compliance was assured. The commencement of operations against Greece was merely a question of convenience and of the weather. At the end of January Hitler envisaged the date for the attack on Greece as about April 1; German troops would not enter Bulgaria until the last possible moment. According to orders issued on February 19 and confirmed on the 25th the building of bridges across the Danube was to start on the 28th, and the actual crossing on March 2.

---

[1] See below, ch. xxiii.

CHAPTER XVII

THE WINTER OF 1940–41:
BLITZ AND BLOCKADE

URING the winter months those responsible in London for the higher conduct of the war passed through a time of extreme strain and difficulty. The great cities of the United Kingdom, and especially the capital, were being ruthlessly bombed, and no adequate system of protection had yet been made workable. The threat of invasion was not yet considered so remote that the forces assembled to counter it could be dispersed. In the Atlantic the menace from U-boats, long-range aircraft and surface raiders had by no means been mastered; we were fought by new methods to which, here again, we had as yet no adequate reply. If losses of merchant tonnage from U-boats declined sharply after October, losses from other sources brought up the monthly total of losses from all causes to figures far above any that we had suffered before the disastrous month of June.[1] At the same time the need for sending reinforcements and replacements overseas, especially to the Middle East, made increasing demands on what tonnage we had and threatened to restrict imports into the United Kingdom. In the Middle East and Mediterranean theatre, while we had for the moment secured the initiative, the despatch of German land and air forces could again put us on the defensive, either by threatening Gibraltar or by an offensive through the Balkans or by reinforcing the Italians in Libya. In the Far East, where the Japanese had entered into northern Indo-China, the consequences of the three-fold pact were unpredictable. The defences of Malaya were admittedly inadequate; in spite of heavy casualties inflicted on the German and Italian navies, the danger in the Atlantic still ruled out the possibility of sending the promised fleet to Singapore. American sympathy and material help were highly valued, but the Constitution and public opinion alike forbade any promise of armed assistance in the Pacific or elsewhere. As for the neutrals of the eastern hemisphere, Russia was still supplying raw materials to Germany and showed no friendliness to Britain. Turkey's neutrality was benevolent, and perhaps it was a mistake to expect more from her; she seemed less and less likely to take up arms against anything but a direct attack. In the case of France we were trying to ride two difficult horses at once: admiration for the Free

---

[1] See Appendix II.

French and satisfaction that considerable parts of the French empire had come over to them did not make it less desirable to obtain from Vichy, if not co-operation, at least the maximum of resistance to Germany. Somewhat similar considerations applied to Spain, except that there was no open Spanish opposition to Franco, and his sympathies, unlike Pétain's, were confessedly with the Axis. For the present, however, Spain depended economically on Britain and on America, and her actions were likely to follow the fortunes of the war.

In the present chapter it is proposed to return to the economic war, while noting that this was assuming also the character of a war against morale, in which, on both sides, attacks aimed directly and ostensibly at the enemy's economic life had the secondary but hardly unintended effect of striking at his will to resist by reducing the civilian population to misery. We shall consider the operations by sea and air carried on around, and over, and from bases in, the United Kingdom.

In a directive of November 1939 Hitler declared that the conquest of Britain was the prerequisite of final victory in the West, and that the most effective means to this end was to paralyse her economy.[1] As soon as the Army had defeated the French and British in the field and seized part of the coast facing England, the task of the Navy and Air Force would be of prime importance. By another directive, of 24 May 1940, the Air Force, independently of the operations proceeding in France, was to be given unlimited freedom of action against the British homeland as soon as sufficient forces were available. The Navy at the same time was authorised to conduct unrestricted warfare in the waters round the British Isles, against all ships except those of certain favoured neutrals.[2] Two days later, in a supplement to the November directive, Keitel briefly summed up the results of the economic war to date and sketched its aims under the new conditions. Attacks on ports and food stocks would help to break the British will to resist. The destruction of tonnage would not in itself have decisive consequences but, besides its immediate effect, it would increase the enemy's shipping difficulties by making necessary an extended use of convoys and more devious routes. Preparations should be made for interfering with public services; this might have decisive significance at the critical moment. And special stress was now laid on the destruction of the British aircraft industry.[3]

On August 1, in a directive already referred to, Hitler announced that 'in order to establish conditions favourable to the final conquest

---

[1] *F.D.* No. 9, p. 73.
[2] *F.D.* No. 13, p. 98.
[3] *F.D.* p. 98.

of Britain' he intended 'to continue the air and naval war against the British homeland more intensively than heretofore'. There followed the critical weeks of the Battle of Britain. On October 12 Hitler finally gave up the idea of bringing off 'Sea Lion' in 1940, but a week later Göring issued a comprehensive order for the continuation of air warfare against Britain: as targets he mentioned the aircraft industry, the fighter arm, London, the Birmingham-Coventry industrial area, and the principal south and west coast ports, including the mining of their approaches. Hitler himself appears to have issued no further directive for the air and sea war against Great Britain until February 6, when, while admitting that his efforts had not had the expected effect on the morale of the British people, he professed himself still hopeful of results from strictly economic warfare.[1]

The Blitz is usually taken as having been inaugurated by the attack on London on the night of 7 September 1940 and closed by that on Birmingham on the 16 May following.[2] There had been heavy attacks in the form of armed reconnaissance during the summer of 1940, from June onwards, and attacks did not cease after mid-May, 1941, but it was during those eight months that the enemy made his supreme attempt to paralyse the economic life of the country by bombardment and to break its determination to resist. Between the dates mentioned one can distinguish three phases of the offensive: the first, ending November 13, during which it was concentrated on London and in particular on its docks and railways; the second, from November 14 to February 15, directed mainly against provincial cities and ports, though London always remained a secondary target; and a third concerned chiefly with the western and south-western ports. From mid-May 1941 onwards the Luftwaffe in the West busied itself mainly with attacks on shipping and the laying of mines.

Both the inception and the termination of the Blitz argued a lack of consistent policy: its outbreak seemed due rather to the disappointing results of the daylight operations than to any mature purpose, and it was broken off in May not because it had succeeded or failed but because the main strength of the Luftwaffe was required against Russia. During this period the strength of the German long-range bomber force in the West had fallen from 1291 to 757 aircraft, but it was still perfectly capable of continuing the attack. On the other hand the defence was far more capable of resisting its onslaught in May 1941 than in September 1940.

---

[1] *F.D.* No. 23, p. 137.

[2] For this topic see Collier, *The Defence of the United Kingdom* ch. xvi, xvii.

In the Battle of Britain Fighter Command was matched against an enemy for whom it was well prepared; though overwhelming in numbers he used a strategy and tactics to which it was not too difficult to provide answers so long as our resources in pilots and aircraft held out. The Germans did more or less what was expected of them, and so did our fighters and anti-aircraft guns. But it was not so in the night battles. We were not prepared, either in resources or in training, to meet air attack in the dark, and for months we had no adequate counter to the skilled devices of the enemy. In the autumn our array of seaward-looking radar stations and of observers inland, our predictors and searchlights, our six specialised Blenheim night-fighter squadrons, were not capable of locating, tracking, fixing, engaging and hitting bombers flying at speed above 12,000 feet and guided to their targets by novel navigational aids.[1] It was only by slow and tentative steps, by trial and error, by scientific and mechanical ingenuity—this above all—working against time, by the redeployment of the anti-aircraft defences and frantic reallocation of priorities, that by the spring we were interfering successfully with the enemy's secret methods and equipping ourselves with devices by which we could fire accurately from the ground at unseen targets, or guide our own aircraft from below to within the range at which their radar sets would enable them to attack.

As a result of our failure to counter the massed night attacks of September an expert committee was set up with Marshal of the Royal Air Force Sir John Salmond as chairman; its findings led the Air Council to approve various changes in the organisation of control, training and research. The Prime Minister further convoked a Night Air Defence Committee, at which he took the chair himself. At its meetings, the first of which was held on October 7, progress or the reverse was reported, searching inquiries were conducted into the causes, remedies were prescribed and hastened forward. By mid-November the various methods of interception tried during the first phase of the Blitz had ended in failure, but the essentials of future success were now recognised. All depended on the development of radar: guns were using Gun Laying (G.L.) sets to direct fire at invisible targets, Ground Controlled Interception (G.C.I.) sets were being installed to track bombers inland and relay the information to aircraft, and an improved model of Air Interception (A.I. Mark IV) sets was being produced for use in the air. It was the two last inventions, with the provision of suitable aircraft (Beaufighter) and skilled men to exploit them, which proved the key to success.

On December 8 Air Marshal W. S. Douglas, who had succeeded Sir Hugh Dowding at Fighter Command, urged that the number of

---

[1] See Collier ch. ix, sect. iv; Churchill II 338–346 on 'bending the beam'.

specialised night-fighter squadrons should be increased and that more of these should be twin-engined aircraft fitted with A.I. sets. This programme could not be wholly completed before the summer of 1941, but by May 11 Air Marshal Douglas could claim increasing success both for the twin-engined aircraft using the latest scientific aids and for the 'cat's eye' fighters relying on visual contact on moon-lit nights. An important part in the defence was played by gunners on the ground. General Pile, of Anti-Aircraft Command, referred to the whole period as essentially a gun battle. Even when they did not hit, the 'barrages' were valuable as deterrents to keep bombers at a respectful height as well as in maintaining the spirits of the people. All through the winter and spring, however, Anti-Aircraft Command had many less guns than the number approved at the outbreak of war.

The effects of the Blitz were of course spectacular to the last degree: it destroyed many famous and historic buildings, including the Commons' chamber at Westminster, and innumerable homes. It killed and maimed indiscriminately large numbers of men, women and children. It also caused damage, deplorable in the particular case, to the national war effort, setting alight oil works, cutting communications and blocking ports at a time when their full functioning was of the utmost importance. It did not however break or shake the national will to continue the fight—indeed it strengthened and hardened it, and sympathy due to common misfortune worked to unite all sections of the people in the battered regions; in the expression of this sympathy the visits of the King and Queen, who had seen the Blitz strike their own London home, and of the ubiquitous Prime Minister, played an inspiring part. Practical comfort and support were further provided by the efficient ministrations of the national and local organisations grouped under the head of Civil Defence, now proving its claim to rank as a fourth war Service. Even on the material side the Ministry of Home Security, in its survey of the harm done, concluded that 'effective damage has not been serious in relation to the national war effort'. The reasons given were 'firstly the policy of placing new factories outside major town areas and, secondly, the general dispersal of the key industries by splitting up their shops and locating them in isolated positions in various outlying districts'. Even at Coventry, so ferociously assailed on November 14, the Ministry declared that there had been 'no case of damage which could be interpreted as catastrophic to the aircraft and also aero-engine industry', since the enemy had not repeated his attack. Speaking of the railways, the Ministry asserted that there was in 1940 no wholesale or lengthy interruption of the main arteries of traffic, and no serious interference with the war effort was held to have been caused by dislocation of the railway system; the ability of the Port of

London, too, to handle imports and exports was little interfered with by the onslaught on the docks on September 7.[1]

The scale of the attack was indeed slight compared with the tremendous mass of explosives dropped by the Allies upon Germany in the later years of the war. A 'major raid' at this time was one in which 100 or more tons of high explosive fell; in the first phase of the Blitz fifty-seven major raids were launched against London and during them 13,651 tons were dropped; in the epoch-making attack of September 7 the Germans stated that they dropped 335 tons, and in the heaviest of all, on 19th April, 1,026 tons, with 4,252 incendiary containers. This was nothing to what the Germans endured in 1943–1945.[2]

The German blockade was not so dramatic as the Blitz and its danger was not so evident to the British people, but it was a formidable threat to our power to carry on the war. In none of the nine months between June 1940 and April 1941 did the total losses of British, Allied and neutral merchant ships amount to less than 320,000 tons, and in April this figure was more than doubled.[3] After August 1940 the vast majority of these losses occurred in the North Atlantic, the area of greatest danger shifting further and further out. Taken in the large it was a war of attrition, a dogged struggle in which efficient organisation of the control and protection of our shipping finally defeated the attackers. But this was not until increased resources enabled us to provide the convoys in the Atlantic with continuous air and surface escort. Seen more closely the struggle was a succession of thrilling incidents requiring the highest degree of alertness, skill and endurance both in attackers and in attacked and not least in the merchant seamen who put to sea time and again after extreme hardship and the narrowest escapes. Like the night warfare in the skies over England it was a contest of scientists no less than of fighting men, and the date by which an invention could be made practically effective might be of supreme importance.

The capture of their records has shown us how the German naval staff viewed the progress of the struggle and planned for the future. On both sides, of course, there were competing demands for limited resources, but in one respect the island Power inevitably had the advantage. No British statesman or commander could forget the pre-eminent need to secure our vital imports: the knowledge was inbred

---

[1] For a diagram showing the principal targets, see Map 17; also C. B. A. Behrens *op. cit.* ch. vi for the general failure of the attack on the ports.

[2] E.g. on the night of the 14/15 Oct. 1944 Duisburg received 4,547 tons of bombs; 1,600 tons was a typical bomb load.

[3] See Appendix II for the losses of British, Allied and neutral merchant ships September 1939–June 1941.

in him. Only for a few months, from June to September 1940, could any other danger be rated higher. On the enemy side values were different. Many Germans knew how near they had come to starving us in 1917, and Hitler had remarked in October 1939 that Germany's weapons in a long war, so far as her principal enemy was concerned, were the Air Force and the submarine.[1] But owing mainly to his own peculiar position and peculiar mentality there was no consistency of aim. Raeder, and of course Dönitz, Flag Officer, U-boats, constantly urged that the way to bring England to terms was to cut off her supplies by unrestricted warfare by sea and air directed at her ships and her ports. They regarded both 'Sea Lion' and 'Barbarossa' as regrettable distractions from the main objective. The Führer agreed with Raeder's thesis in principle but hoped for a short cut. He trusted at first that the conquest of Poland, still more the conquest of France, would finish the war in a few weeks. It was not till 10 July 1940 that he authorised immediate measures for the completion of the U-boat programme of 30 December 1939—itself only a 'modified programme', since it fell short of the plan put forward by Raeder in the previous October for a monthly output of rather more than twenty-nine U-boats; it was not till July 31 that he cancelled all restrictions on materials for submarine construction, allowing also for the completion by the end of 1942 of an additional 120 boats over and above the 'modified programme'.[2] But before the end of 1940 and again in March 1941 Raeder was complaining that submarine construction was being neglected and that unless more workers were allotted to it the current rate of production must remain inadequate.[3] In December 1940 Hitler had characteristically given precedence to the needs of the Army for the Russian compaign before the demands of the Navy and Air Force.

There was another respect in which Germany's enemy had the advantage, namely in the capacity of the Service chiefs to work together in harmony. This point has been mentioned already; it is notably illustrated in the campaign of this winter. The agreement reached between the British Admiralty and Air Ministry in December 1940 over the operational control of Coastal Command stands in bright contrast to the temporary compromise which was all the German Naval Command and Luftwaffe could come to in February 1941.[4]

As protagonists on the German side we think chiefly of the U-boats; but other combatants—the minelayers, the surface raiders, the

---

[1] F.D. p. 61.

[2] The 'modified programme' was intended to produce a total of 372 U-boats by the end of 1941.

[3] F.N.C. pp. 119, 130, 138.

[4] F.D. p. 143. See below, p. 402.

E-boats (motor torpedo boats), and in particular the Luftwaffe—also took their toll.

On August 17 the Germans declared a total blockade of the British Isles; within the danger-zone U-boats were authorised to attack, without warning, all vessels including liners (which had hitherto been privileged) with the sole exception of a few specified ships belonging to Eire. A few Italian submarines also took part in the Atlantic war. As the range and effectiveness of our escorts was extended, the enemy likewise was impelled to seek for his successes further from the United Kingdom, and by the middle of November his main area of operation had moved to over 200 miles from the Irish coast. While this made it harder for him to mark down his prey in the ocean spaces it also extended the dangerous area for convoys. This area had now to be taken as including West African waters, since, although large-scale operations did not begin here until March 1941, single U-boats were active in July 1940 and again towards the end of the year.

Granted a sufficiency of escort vessels, the Royal Navy had been confident that the asdic and the adoption of the convoy system would defeat the U-boat. The asdic was unfortunately no longer a secret weapon, since the French had not kept the knowledge of it from the Germans, but it was a valuable means of directing an attack under water within a range of 1,500 yards or so. It was useless, however, against a vessel on the surface, and from August onwards U-boats adopted the tactics of shadowing a convoy by day and closing up at night to attack it on the surface. Later on, the co-operation of the Luftwaffe with the U-boats was to achieve successes, but in the opinion of Admiral Dönitz German air reconnaissance was negligible until the end of 1940: usually one aircraft was available daily, never more than three, and the Navy had not complete control of them. At length in January Hitler decided, against Göring's wish, to subordinate to the Navy for tactical reconnaissance a unit of Kondors (Focke-Wulf 200) capable of searching as far out as 20° West.

The enemy's most serious weakness was the continuing deficiency of U-boats. During the first year of war new construction only just kept up with losses, and the average number of operational boats was as low as thirty-three, of which fourteen were normally at sea in the North Sea and Atlantic.[1] By September 1940 only twenty-seven boats, as compared with thirty-nine a year before, were ready for operations, and in February the number reached nadir at twenty-one. After that conditions improved (the operational strength rising in June to seventy-seven) and over the whole year from August 1940 to July 1941 the number actually working in the operational area was increased by more than 25 per cent over that of the first year.

---

[1] For particulars of the sinkings of German and Italian U-boats see Roskill I App. K.

Small as their numbers were, the U-boats achieved startling results, particularly against unescorted shipping; in the second half of October they played havoc with two homeward bound Atlantic convoys, sinking twenty ships of the one and twelve of the other.[1] In the three following months their toll was distinctly less; but in one operation at the end of February four U-boats sank nine ships of an unescorted group.

Meanwhile the Germans had taken advantage of the inadequacy of our reconnaissance and patrol forces to pass surface ships into the Atlantic and beyond: one ship, the *Komet*, actually found her way from Norway north of Siberia into the Pacific. Between mid-July and the end of the year six armed merchant-ships were at large, preying on our commerce—mostly on ships sailing independently—and maintaining themselves by rendezvous with supply ships sent out for the purpose.[2] Only one of these raiders was sunk in the period covered by this volume.

More dangerous than these converted merchantmen were the warships. The pocket-battleship *Admiral Scheer* announced her presence in the Atlantic by sinking on November 5 the armed merchant cruiser *Jervis Bay*, who most gallantly sacrificed herself for the sake of her convoy. The *Scheer* remained at large, disorganising shipping and eluding search, for several months and penetrated to the Indian Ocean. In December the cruiser *Admiral Hipper* sailed out for a short foray, before putting into Brest for a longish sojourn; she was attacked there by British bombers but suffered no hurt. In February she made a second sortie, and she eventually regained Germany on March 28. In January the *Scharnhorst* and *Gneisenau*, now recovered from the damage received in the summer, left Kiel and after a profitable foray likewise took shelter at Brest; in a cruise of two months they not only sank or captured 22 ships of 115,622 tons but also caused, for a short time, the complete dislocation of our Atlantic convoy cycles with serious consequences to our vital imports.[3] Such marauding outbreaks as these compelled the Admiralty, even before the commissioning of the *Bismarck* and *Tirpitz*, to keep a disproportionate number of heavy ships in home waters or at Gibraltar; it was always possible that complicated operations in the Mediterranean might be held up because Force H was required for service in the Atlantic.

The tabulation of figures of shipping losses is impressive but not necessarily illuminating. The historian of Merchant Shipping has been quoted in an earlier chapter for the conclusion that 'it was the

---

[1] Roskill I 348.
[2] For the exploits of the surface raiders see Roskill I chaps. xiv, xviii.
[3] Roskill I 377.

loss of carrying capacity in the second year of war that was the principal cause of the shipping shortage, not the loss of ships or the rise in the demands of the Services'.[1] The effective use of the ships disposable was restricted by many factors, such as the need to wait for escorts or to sail by longer routes; much delay was also suffered after the ship reached port; in fact it was doubtful in the summer of 1940 whether ships or port capacity would prove the limiting factor. As a result of the attacks in the North Sea and Channel, and notably of the bombing of London in September, large ships were forbidden to use the Thames or east coast ports, while machinery did not exist for enabling ports on the west coast to fill the gap. For some weeks the crisis was acute, but it was surmounted by tremendous feats of organisation. 'One or two months', says Miss Behrens, 'of intensive effort, applied both locally and at the centre, had been enough to dispel, without any increase in facilities, the danger that the cause of the free peoples would come to disaster in this country's ports . . . It was fortunate that the crisis in the ports in the winter of 1940 to 1941 was tackled when it was, for it had no sooner been disposed of than the heavy bombing started.'[2]

If the crisis in the ports had been surmounted by March 1941, the crisis caused by congestion in the repair yards had not. In January of that year some 2·8 million tons deadweight of ocean-going dry cargo shipping—nearly 13 per cent of the total fleet under British control—lay 'immobilised under repair', and it was months before the total was effectively reduced.[3]

The question how far the shipping stringency influenced our military strategy apart from its effect on the importation of food and other necessaries is not easy to answer. It is obvious that, from the time when it was decided to build up a great army and a great base in the Middle East out of resources many thousands of miles away, shipping must have been recognised as, in theory at least, a limiting factor. On the other hand, if the available shipping was limited, so too were the quantities of men and munitions ready for despatch, and so were the warships needed to escort them.

For a fuller treatment of this complicated subject the reader must be referred again to Miss Behrens:

'In general the demands of the Services at this time had an over-riding priority. They were growing, slowly but continuously: it was doubtful if they could be met; but the doubts arose not from fear that, in the immediate present at any rate, there would not be enough tonnage, but because of lack of ships of the right type—

---

[1] Above, p. 238.
[2] C. B. A. Behrens, *op. cit.* p. 138.
[3] *ibid.* p. 143.

of enough troopships with the necessary qualifications, of enough cargo-ships with a speed sufficient to keep up with the military convoys, with enough height in the 'tween decks to accommodate the military lorries, with enough endurance to sail, from this country and North America, to Freetown without a stop.

These requirements gave rise to a great many difficulties. Nevertheless, in 1941—and, for that matter, in 1942—the War Cabinet never questioned the right of the Services to determine how many men and how much supplies and equipment were needed in the theatres of war, nor their right to the tonnage necessary to transport them provided that ships of the right type were available and provided that they were not wastefully used.'[1]

It was in June 1940 that the first troops sailed from this country round the Cape; they were followed by a series of convoys, carrying troops mainly for Egypt, which sailed on an average once a month. 'The problem in the autumn of 1940', says Miss Behrens, 'appeared to be whether or not we could endure the loss of imports into this country that must result if more passenger-cargo liners were withdrawn from the trade-routes and converted to trooping, and if more cargo-ships were taken at the same time to supply the troops they carried,' and she quotes a warning of the end of September from the Minister of Shipping to the effect that if operations in the Middle East were to be on a large scale the whole question of their practicability might have to be reviewed.[2] None the less, the reinforcement of the Middle East continued on an ever-increasing scale.

This does not mean, of course, that commanders overseas received all that they desired or all that their Departments at home would have liked to send them. The decision what reinforcements to pass through the Mediterranean to Malta or Egypt depended on a nice calculation of what could be stowed into the particular ships available, while in February 1941 Wavell had to choose between a complete fresh division and the units required to make his existing formations effective. It seems true, however, that no important strategical move, on other grounds desirable, was prevented during this period by shortage of shipping.

Miss Behrens points out that it was long before the demands of the Services were put forward 'within the framework of a general plan agreed beforehand with the shipping authorities'. In the autumn of 1940 the uncertain factors were too many to allow of long-term planning, and the broad lines of military strategy had to be drawn

---

[1] *ibid.* pp. 183–189. Miss Behrens is referring specifically to the spring and early summer of 1941, but what she says applies *a fortiori* to the winter of 1940–41.

[2] *ibid.* pp. 218, 220.

without the means of estimating whether or not the necessary ships were likely to be available. But until the summer of 1941 practical requirements could usually be met by *ad hoc* agreements reached after argument and compromise.[1]

Enough has been said to show that it was not only by the destruction of our ships and crews that the Germans imperilled our sea communications.

The danger to our shipping was considered at many meetings of the Defence Committee. The shortage of escort craft was deplorable. Special protection could always be found for troopships, but escorts for ordinary cargo vessels were for long too few and could only afford protection for a few hundred miles into the Atlantic. Only nine of the American destroyers were in service before the end of the year, and our own corvettes were still comparatively few. For long the Admiralty had difficulty in obtaining the release of destroyers and trawlers from anti-invasion to trade-escort duties. At the beginning of October the Defence Committee held that invasion was still the greater danger: whereas we could afford for some time to come to sustain a heavy rate of sinkings, we could not afford to give the enemy an opening to launch his attack. But, as the month wore on, the extreme gravity of the shipping situation was realised; the new German tactics and possible counter-measures were discussed. Among the latter the use of the air weapon, to search and strike, of course ranked high, but the existing resources of Coastal Command were quite inadequate.

Sir Frederick Bowhill's strength on November 1 was seven flying-boat and twenty-two general reconnaissance and fighter squadrons, exclusive of a squadron and a flight lent from the Navy; but the number of aircraft available fell far below the establishment by reason of the shortage of trained crews. The Defence Committee on October 31 took note that, in the formation of new squadrons, the Air Ministry would give priority during the next few months to fighter squadrons, with the object of building up the Metropolitan Fighter Force to meet a sustained enemy offensive next spring, but agreed that the reconnaissance aircraft (Whitley bombers) fitted with long-range A.S.V. at the disposal of Coastal Command should be increased to a total of three squadrons as soon as was practicable.[2]

The question of the employment of aircraft for the defence of trade

---

[1] C. B. A. Behrens, *op. cit.* pp. 219–222.

[2] A.S.V. (Air to Surface Vessel) was the abbreviation used for airborne radio-location of ships.

was not allowed to rest here. The Admiralty were not content with so meagre a strengthening of Coastal Command: at the next meeting of the Defence Committee they proposed, for immediate needs, that new aircraft should be used to form fresh squadrons rather than to re-equip existing ones and, on a longer view, that in the planned expansion of the Royal Air Force fifteen out of the hundred new squadrons should be assigned to Coastal Command, which, so they said, had always been the Cinderella of the Service. One of the Ministers present then revived a proposal of former days, namely that the Navy should take over Coastal Command and run it themselves. The Air Staff objected that, in principle, all our efforts ought to go towards hitting the enemy (meaning the bombing of Germany) and only the bare minimum to merely protective duties; moreover the transfer of Coastal Command alone to the Navy would not give that Service control of all air forces concerned in the defence of trade, since one of the duties of Fighter Command was to protect convoys when within range of shore stations. It was decided to refer particular points to the Ministers concerned, and the matter was discussed further a month later, on December 4.

A joint proposal had now been presented by the naval and air staffs. The Air Ministry had promised to strengthen Coastal Command as an immediate measure by the equivalent of some four-and-a-half squadrons, and flying-boats also, and by June 1941 to allot to it, as requested, fifteen out of the planned hundred squadrons. The Admiralty, though they had not initiated the suggestion for the transference of Coastal Command, were in favour of it in principle: they held that they should have 'full control of all aircraft whose normal function is to fly over the sea'. Their urgent need, however, was to secure a rapid expansion now, and they left it to the Cabinet to decide whether an immediate transfer could be brought about without undue dislocation and therefore without a period of reduced efficiency. The Air Ministry were convinced that it could not, and used further arguments. While Germany maintained her present superiority in air strength, it would never do to allot more than the minimum of our resources to defence; we must preserve flexibility. The only serious objection to the present system, they held, was the numerical weakness of Coastal Command, which they were doing all they could to remedy. A mere change of allegiance would gain nothing in operational or in training efficiency. To split the Royal Air Force would be a retrograde step; it would not produce a single additional aircraft for the defence of trade but would shatter mutual confidence and the *esprit de corps* of the Service. The Air Staff were prepared however to see the Navy take operational control of Coastal Command, and on this basis agreement was reached. In the event of difference of opinion between the two Departments as to the number and type of aircraft to be assigned to Coastal Command the Defence Committee would pronounce.[1]

The implications of this scheme were worked out by a small committee, who reported on March 19.

The operational control of Coastal Command would be exercised by the Admiralty through the Air Officer Commanding-in-Chief, who would normally delegate the day-to-day detailed conduct of operations to the Coastal Command Group headquarters; they would be responsible to him for meeting the air requirements of naval commanders-in-chiefs. The resources of Coastal Command would not be diverted to other purposes without the express concurrence of the Admiralty or a decision of the Defence Committee. The new arrangement, on the lines proposed, came into force on April 15.

Meanwhile the seat of the naval Western Approaches Command had been moved from Plymouth to Liverpool, where it worked in concert with No. 15 Group, Royal Air Force, in an Area Combined Headquarters. Another development was the establishment of a naval fuelling and repair base at Hvalfiord in Iceland. Aircraft had first been based there in August for local defence, and it was only later that they came to be used for maritime tasks. Approval for a Wing headquarters under Coastal Command to be set up there was given in January, but operations did not begin until April. The loss of bases in Eire, especially the airfield at Foynes, was bitterly felt.

On 8 November 1940 the Minister of Shipping warned the Cabinet that on the current rate of sinkings our imports in the third year of the war might well fall to 32 million tons as against 43·5 millions actually imported in the first year; these figures made no allowance for increased military demands. The possibility of further American help, involving the amendment of the Neutrality Acts, was considered, and the Prime Minister told President Roosevelt that shipping, not men, was now the limiting factor.

At the end of February 1941, at a meeting of the Chiefs of Staff, the Prime Minister gave his opinion that the protection of our shipping in the North-Western Approaches must now take absolute priority. Various measures were agreed to, such as the provision by the War Office of light anti-aircraft guns and machine guns, with crews, for use in ships. East-coast naval convoy-escorts were to be reduced for the benefit of North-Western Approaches, Bomber Command was to relieve Coastal of certain duties in the North Sea and Channel, and six squadrons of Coastal Command were to be sent to the north of Ireland and the north of Scotland. The provision of airfields in north Ireland and the Hebrides was to be extended. A

---

[1] See *House of Commons Debates* 10 Dec. 1940, vol. 367, cols. 787–788.

few days later, on March 6, the Minister of Defence issued a comprehensive directive on the Battle of the Atlantic, which, he said, from various German statements we must now assume to have begun.[1]

So far we have been concerned with the German offensive by air and sea; it is time to turn to the British. The Government's intention was both to prevent supplies reaching the Axis countries and to destroy the supplies, along with the means of production and distribution, which they already possessed. The first was the task of diplomacy and sea-power, the second of the bomber and, in lesser degree, of the saboteur. Before considering the endeavours made in this period, it will be convenient to see how the problem and the prospects presented themselves.

The Prime Minister, in a minute of September 3, expressed the natural view that the weapon of blockade had become blunted and rendered, so far as Germany was concerned, less effectual on account of her land conquests and power to rob captive or intimidated peoples for her own benefit. There remained, he thought, no very important special commodities the denial of which would hamper her war effort.[2] From this gloomy reflection he deduced that we must concentrate on our bomber force. But the Chiefs of Staff, briefed by economic authorities, took as we have seen, a more cheerful view. They calculated, with regard to oil alone, that Germany's position would become precarious after June 1941 and perhaps by the end of the year disastrous.[3]

Apart from food, the most important commodities for which Germany at the outbreak of war relied on imports were iron and oil. Shortage of food supplies does not appear to have seriously affected her war effort during the period of this volume. In bread-grains she was nearly self-sufficient and harvests were good. The principal reductions were in meat and fat rations; towards the end of the war these were causing hardship.

In iron and steel Germany started with stocks sufficient to see her through a short war; anxieties as regards a prolonged war were relieved by the capture of the Lorraine and other West European orefields as well as production plants. Germany also succeeded, by stringent economy, by scientific ingenuity and by the exploitation of occupied countries, in meeting her minimum requirements for light and non-ferrous metals and for ferro-alloys.[4]

---

[1] See below, p. 465.

[2] Cf. Jodl's assumption, in a memo. of 30 June, that the Royal Navy could not carry out an effective blockade. *N.D.* 1776–PS.

[3] Above, pp. 214, 234, 342.

[4] See W. S. Medlicott, *The Economic Blockade* (1952) I 32.

The question of oil remains. Any assessment of Germany's oil position had to take account, on the asset side, of stocks, of domestic production, and of imports. On the liability side were the needs of the armed Services, of German civil consumption and of occupied Europe. From a calculation of these it was possible to form some sort of estimate of Germany's monthly balance or deficit, and so of her prospects for continuing the war.

The British Cabinet, and in the first instance Lord Hankey's Committee on preventing oil from reaching Germany, were advised on these matters by Mr. Geoffrey Lloyd's expert committee on the German oil position. Two reports from this committee, of July 14 and December 16, were presented during the second half of 1940.

The committee had earlier estimated Germany's pre-war stocks at three million tons; in July, taking into account stocks in Italy, France and other occupied countries, they put the present total at 7·5 millions; but of this they considered that about 2·5 millions must be held as a reserve to make internal distribution possible, so that only five million tons would be freely disposable.

The amount available from production (natural and artificial) in countries under Axis control they put at five million tons, of which three millions would be synthetic oil. With regard to supplies from without, they calculated the Russian contribution as 500,000 tons, but imports from Roumania were harder to estimate: the limiting factor would be transport, whether by rail, by the Danube, or by the Black Sea and Mediterranean, and the year's supply might range from 2·1 to 4·2 million tons. This made a total yearly income of between 7·6 and 9·7 million tons, in addition to stocks of five millions. On the expenditure side, they put the wartime requirements of Germany and Italy for all purposes at 8·5 millions, and noted that the 1938 consumption of the other countries for whose maintenance the Axis were now responsible had been 13 millions; this left a wide gap, which could only be filled by a drastic reduction of consumption in Europe.

The moral drawn by the committee was that we should try to prevent the transport of Roumanian oil to Mediterranean ports by sea and to destroy German hydrogenation and synthetic plants; also to destroy refineries and adjacent stocks in Italy and France and to interfere with communications into Germany by the Danube and by rail.

The December report raised the estimates of initial German stocks, of German production, and of imports from Russia. Imports from Roumania would be much greater in the six months April–September 1941 than in the previous six months. Stocks freely available on 1 October 1940 were put at 3·3 millions. On the expenditure side, German and Italian consumption was now taken as 10 millions, and our bombers were credited with reducing the output of German synthetic oil by 15 per cent—this by the dropping of 539 tons of bombs.

The conclusions drawn were that Axis oil stocks would fall substantially during the winter, but that greatly increased imports from Roumania would improve the situation during the spring and summer. Attacks on German synthetic plants should be pressed without intermission, and also on nitrogen plants, and all possible action should be taken against Roumanian oil supplies. 'British control of the Eastern Mediterranean remains of paramount importance.' We shall see shortly how these views influenced strategy.

The confidence in the efficacy of our bombing at this time was altogether misplaced; but in many respects the factual estimates of the committee were not unreasonable, and when they erred they erred in both directions: if they over-estimated the reserves the enemy must keep for distribution, they also over-estimated his imports from Roumania. We know from a German document of July 1939 that stocks were little over two million tons—quite insufficient for a long war;[1] domestic production was about 3·3 millions, while peacetime imports from Russia and Roumania were a little over two millions. Germany's own needs were put, in this document, at between 8 and 8·5 million tons a year. Thus her position was highly precarious; it was saved by the unexpected speed and economy of the early campaigns and the rich booty which they provided, beginning with the oilfields and refineries of western Poland. The vast territorial acquisitions of Norway, Denmark, the Low Countries and France were made at the cost of a total oil consumption of under 500,000 tons, or an additional consumption over 'normal' of under 300,000 tons. To these territorial gains must be added the captured oil stocks, amounting to between 1·5 and 2 million tons. It is not possible to account for the disposal of all this loot, but a rough German balance sheet for the year 1940, covering aviation spirit, motor gasolene and Diesel oil alone, indicates that at least half a million tons of the spoil were required to keep the position in equilibrium. However, in spite of the expenditure on the Battle of Britain and other operations, aviation spirit stocks at the end of 1940 were over 100,000 tons higher than at the outbreak of war.

A German summary of the position in 1941, presented in the following year, estimated the supplies available to Germany and her dependencies (including from 1·2 to 1·5 millions drawn from stocks) at 12·7 million tons; consumption it estimated at slightly more—12·8 millions, of which 4·8 went to the armed forces and the remainder to civilian economy, including two millions to Italy. Germany was

---

[1] Great Britain's stocks were 6·7 millions.

living on her stocks and gradually reducing them. The position was never again so secure as at the end of 1940.

Germany was still to an unsatisfactory extent dependent on imports, and Hitler felt great anxiety for the integrity of the Roumanian oilfields, as the last chapter showed. His fears in this respect, however, were in fact unfounded; though Roumanian production was falling throughout the period, Germany steadily increased her imports of Roumanian oil from just under a million tons in 1938 to 1·4 millions in 1940 and more than double that amount in 1941; in that year the Axis were taking 78 per cent of Roumania's total oil exports. As regards Russia, hopes of acquiring the Caucasian oilfields undoubtedly reinforced Hitler's other motives for invading the country.

The difficulties created for the Royal Navy in its enforcement of the blockade by the events of the summer of 1940 have been mentioned earlier.[1] Its task was now to prevent all exports from Germany and Italy, and such imports to those countries as contrived to elude the Ministry of Economic Warfare's system of controlling contraband at source. The enemy on the other hand was encouraged to dispute our blockade by the extension of German-controlled coast-line and by the strain on our warships due to the German war on trade. We find Raeder telling Hitler in November that preparations were being made for the return of German merchant ships from abroad and for outward-bound blockade-running.[2]

The leaks in the naval blockade were three.[3] Obviously the Navy could do nothing—and in fact diplomacy could do nothing—to stop the important traffic over Germany's long eastern frontier. But it was theoretically possible to prevent importation of rubber and non-ferrous metals into Germany across Siberia through the ports of Dairen and Vladivostok. Interception north of Hong Kong, however, was hardly possible in practice owing to our naval weakness in the Far East, and there were diplomatic difficulties also.

The second leak was the eastern Mediterranean. With Turkey neutral we could not send ships into the Black Sea. With Turkey and Greece neutral we could not set up control bases in the Aegean, and after Greece became our ally the many demands on Admiral Cunningham's forces left little margin of effort for the control of contraband.

The third leak—which caused the most trouble—was the traffic to

---

[1] Above, p. 233.
[2] *F.N.C.* p. 152 (14 Nov. 1940).
[3] See Medlicott *op. cit.* I ix, xi (v), xx (ii).

French Mediterranean ports from French West Africa. The passage of relief ships from America was a matter for the Foreign Office, not for the Admiralty; but the passage of ordinary commercial vessels closely affected the Navy and led to some controversy in Whitehall.[1]

The Cabinet had decided that contraband control should apply to imports for the whole of France, occupied and unoccupied, and also for French North Africa, and the Prime Minister explained and justified our policy in the House of Commons on August 20. But this policy was never fully carried out. Indeed, ever since July 11 we had agreed not to interfere with French ships, if escorted, passing to Mediterranean ports. Professor Medlicott speaks of the concern of the Ministry of Economic Warfare at 'the fact that the blockade had almost completely broken down—and had indeed never really been established—in relation to merchant shipping passing to and from ports in unoccupied metropolitan France'.[2] This was due partly to diplomatic and partly to naval considerations. Our relations with Vichy were of a slippery and inconclusive nature, if only because different members of Pétain's team pulled in different ways and because Germany in the last resort had the whip hand. M. Baudouin, who was Minister of Foreign Affairs until the end of October, when Laval succeeded him, was in favour of an economic understanding with Britain allowing for limited trade between unoccupied France and North Africa, under guarantees against the goods falling into German hands, and of a *modus vivendi* of some sort with regard to the French colonies generally. The British Government were not averse in principle to negotiations with Vichy, hoping to encourage a spirit of resistance to the common enemy. The Foreign Office opinion was that, if only the French colonies would act in a healthily anti-German and anti-Italian spirit, it was immaterial to us by whom they were ruled.

A suggestion for a review of our relations with Vichy put forward by the Foreign Office after our failure at Dakar was strongly supported by the Admiralty. Concerned at the Navy's heavy commitments in home waters, in the Mediterranean and for the protection of trade, the Admiralty were alarmed by the naval implications, especially with regard to Gibraltar, of hostilities with Vichy; should we lose the use of Gibraltar, not only would French West African produce pass through the Straits, but our naval blockade of Italy, and hence of Germany, would become 'almost completely ineffective'; no patrol based on the Azores could be one-quarter as effective as interception at the bottleneck of the Straits. The Cabinet decided to let Baudouin know that they could contemplate a relaxation of the

---

[1] For the relief-ship controversy see below, ch. xviii.
[2] *op. cit.* p. 558. See his chapter xvii (ii) generally.

blockade only if satisfied that the French Government would adopt a more co-operative attitude towards ourselves and were able and willing to act independently of enemy dictation in the matter of their overseas territories. Nothing came of the *démarche* to Vichy, and the Cabinet, taking a middle line between the demands of the Ministry of Economic Warfare that the considerable traffic from West Africa (mainly in ground-nuts) to Marseilles should be stopped and the repeated objections of the Admiralty, decided on October 18 that the Admiralty should no longer be debarred from applying contraband control measures to escorted French convoys passing through the Straits, but that this authority must be used with discretion.

A month later the Committee on Foreign (Allied) Resistance called attention to the magnitude of this continuing leak in the blockade: since the middle of September, they said, at least fifty French ships had passed unchallenged through the Straits, all but four eastwards, and a transatlantic trade was developing from Martinique to Dakar and thence up the West African coast. The Ministry of Shipping agreed, and the Foreign Office were now convinced that the present abuse must be stopped. The Admiralty admitted that since June, owing to the number of our warships undergoing repair, our blockade had been largely a matter of bluff, but they were still most anxious to avoid a clash with the French Fleet. The Cabinet decided that action should be taken, on the first convenient opportunity, on the lines they had approved in October. But it was not till the end of the year, when the Committee on Foreign (Allied) Resistance were again protesting, that an eastbound convoy of four French merchantmen was stopped and detained at Gibraltar. The Admiralty a few days later explained to the Fleet the Government's policy with regard to Vichyite ships; the consequent operations would be known under the collective code-name 'Ration'.

No appreciable change in the situation occurred in the next few months. Our policy remained the same, but the Navy had not the ships available to render interception regularly effective. They were also hampered by the use made of territorial waters by the French ships, and in April the Cabinet decided that all French territorial waters, except on the China station and in the American sphere, might be entered in order to intercept French merchantmen.

'The Navy can lose us the war', wrote the Prime Minister on September 3, 'but only the Air Force can win it. Therefore our supreme effort must be to gain overwhelming mastery in the air. The Fighters are our salvation, but the Bombers alone provide the means of victory. We must therefore develop the power to carry an ever-increasing volume of explosives to Germany, so as to pulverise the entire industry and scientific structure on which the war effort and economic life of the enemy depend.'[1]

Such was the aim and eventually, in large measure, the achievement of the Strategic Air Offensive of the Allies, but it was long before the aim was achieved.[2] The strategic bombing of Germany was first authorised, it may be remembered, on 15 May 1940, a few days after the Germans invaded the Low Countries.[3] Calls for support, however, from the retreating armies prevented any continuous or concentrated action against targets in Germany at that time. Later in the summer the weight of our bomber effort had again been diverted, this time to anti-invasion targets and especially to the craft assembling in the ports. Operations against German air industries, oil plants and communications were carried on intermittently, but it was not until the Battle of Britain had petered out that new directives were issued for intensifying and concentrating the offensive against German industry.

Even in the first half of October there were rival claimants for the bombers. Home Forces urged that, as preparations for 'Sea Lion' were still being maintained in an advanced state, the attacks on the Channel ports should be continued. The Admiralty asked for the full weight of our bombers to be thrown against the German heavy ships in their northern bases, since the need of keeping a large fleet to watch them was prejudicial to our naval strength elsewhere, and thus to the economic war; hence to attack the German ships would not be a diversion from the bombers' main purpose. The Air Staff in reply explained the technical difficulty of hitting such targets, but promised that from ·fifty to a hundred bombers should attack the German capital ships on three occasions, weather permitting, during the next periods of bright moonlight; such a scale of attack should damage the ships sufficiently to immobilise them for some months. The Defence Committee approving, on October 15 and 16 some forty Wellingtons were ordered to strike at the *Scharnhorst* and *Gneisenau* at Kiel, but they failed to secure a hit. Similar requests were made and complied with in the following months.

Another activity in which the Admiralty constantly pressed for assistance from the air was that known as 'Gardening', the 'planting' of mines in the coastal waters of countries under enemy control. The mines were mostly of the magnetic type; they were first laid by the British in April, just after the German invasion of Norway and Denmark, though plans had long been under consideration. It was an activity in which Coastal Command was primarily interested, but in

---

[1] See above, p. 349.

[2] This subject is treated at length by Sir Charles Webster and Dr. N. Frankland in volumes in this series (now in preparation).

[3] Above, p. 182.

fact the larger part was soon played by Bomber Command with its more distant range. The strategic purpose was first defined as 'to menace enemy shipping passing in and out of their base ports', including both warships and trading vessels. Mines were laid in the summer as a measure against invasion, and later to immobilise the battle-cruisers using Biscay ports. By the end of February 1941 seventy-five enemy ships, of over 65,000 tons, are reckoned to have been sunk by this means, nearly all of them in the Western Baltic, round Denmark, or off the German and Dutch North Sea coasts.[1] The nuisance thus caused to the enemy was of course much greater than the mere figures of shipping sunk would indicate.

As the bombing of British towns proceeded, it provoked a political demand for retaliation. To anyone who has viewed the devastated areas in London and elsewhere it must seem of small consequence whether attacks were directed on non-military targets as such. But the matter is of some historical interest. In his directive of August 1 Hitler reserved for himself 'the decision of retaliatory terror attacks', and the dropping of bombs on London on August 24 was unintentional.[2] It was in reprisal for this that a few British bombers were sent to Berlin the following night. The Cabinet took credit for an intention to bomb military targets only (though in such a case the distinction could not possibly be observed), but it was remarked at the meeting that in view of the indiscriminate bombing practised by the Germans we might in the near future have to consider making a temporary but marked departure from this policy. A few days later the Luftwaffe increased the scale of their attacks on towns, and on September 5 Hitler ordered them to make day and night attacks on large cities, particularly London; Göring in a broadcast referred to attacks on London as reprisals taken on the Führer's orders. On September 19, after a heavy raid on London, in which the powerful bombs known as land-mines were dropped, the Cabinet agreed that we should reply by bombing Berlin: the enemy must now be taken, it was claimed, to have abandoned all pretence of aiming at military objectives. Accordingly Berlin was bombed by 119 of our aircraft on September 23. Berlin, however, was too far away to make a satisfactory target, and Sir Charles Portal, Air Officer Commanding-in-Chief, Bomber Command, argued convincingly that mere sporadic bombing would be an uneconomical use of our small force; nor did he favour the suggestion that we should make use for such purposes of a second-line bomber force manned by crews drawn largely from instructional units. The Air Staff, too, favoured a policy of concentrated attack on selected industrial targets.

---

[1] See Roskill I, 123, 335–336.
[2] *F.D.* No. 17; Collier, *op. cit.* pp. 322, 361.

This policy was only gradually abandoned or modified, and it is hardly possible to fix on a definite date for the adoption of 'area bombing'. It was largely a matter of experience. There was certainly in some quarters a desire to make the German people suffer what British cities had suffered and thereby to break down their morale; on the other side was the belief that industrial targets, and oil in particular, were the most remunerative and that it was possible to hit them. The result was something of a compromise.

On October 15 the Defence Committee put on record that it was desirable to deliver on Germany the maximum load of bombs and that some of these should be of the heaviest type (1,000 lb.).[1] A week later, on October 23, Sir Charles Portal, who was on the point of succeeding Sir Cyril Newall as Chief of the Air Staff, proposed 'that a primary target should be selected in a large populous area, and that a heavy concentrated attack should be delivered upon it. This would probably ensure the destruction of the target, e.g. a power station or gas works, and this in itself would have a considerable effect on those living near it as well as on the industries situated in the town by depriving them of power and demoralising their workpeople. There would also be considerable secondary effects from bombs dropping on the area round the target damaging houses, water-mains, etc. He thought that a heavy attack should be delivered on a target of this sort in a selected town as often as possible during dark periods when precise bombing of small military objectives was difficult.' 'This proposal amounted to following the example of the German bombing of Rotterdam,' and should be most effective against the Germans. On October 30 the Cabinet approved the proposal that 'whilst we should adhere to the rule that our objectives should be military targets, at the same time the civilian population around the target areas must be made to feel the weight of the war'; and on the same day the Air Ministry issued a directive to that effect. Oil installations were still to be the primary objective when conditions of weather and moon were favourable. But, in second place, 'regular concentrated attacks should be made on objectives in large towns and centres of industry, with the primary aim of causing very heavy material destruction which will demonstrate to the enemy the power and severity of air bombardment and the hardship and dislocation which will result from it'.

The Cabinet had been invited to regard the new proposal as a somewhat broader interpretation of our present policy, rather than as any fundamental change. But their decision was an important step in the transition to the policy of area bombing, as it came to be known, which certainly in practice meant the extension of the air war to the civilian population.

---

[1] 2,000-lb. bombs were in production, but were not available for operations.

Six weeks later, after the devastation of Coventry, Birmingham and Bristol, the Cabinet were invited to take a further step and to sanction a 'crash concentration' against a single German city. Hitherto, they were told, we had never sent more than eighty bombers to attack one town, and we had been faithful to our policy of picking out military targets. Should we now, in view of current German action, seek to cause the greatest possible havoc in a built-up area? The Cabinet, after considerable discussion, 'while confirming our existing air policy, agreed that the maximum scale of attack should, by way of experiment, be concentrated, on one night in the near future, against a single objective'. So on the night of 16 December 134 bombers were sent to attack the large industrial city of Mannheim, no specific target being indicated; other heavy attacks followed in the new year, the chief victims being Bremen, Gelsenkirchen, Hanover, Cologne and Wilhelmshaven, where many fruitless attempts were made to disable the new battleship *Tirpitz*.

The German bombing of the large city of Rotterdam in May 1940, not to mention Warsaw in the previous autumn, opened a further chapter in the tale of the horrors of war.[1] By the winter of 1940–41 both sides were practising the new technique. The gloves were off, and the British Government had proceeded beyond the point which the Chiefs of Staff had assumed in September 1939 that they would never pass.[2] With the legal aspect the present writer is not qualified to deal. It would seem, however, apart from the question of the legitimacy of reprisals, that the advent of 'total war' has rendered inapplicable many of the accepted rules, to say nothing of the fact that some of the most important conventions—such as the Hague Rules of Aerial Warfare of 1923—were never ratified. This process began long before 1939. 'In fact,' a distinguished international lawyer has written, 'it is probable that the rules of warfare as applied in the First and Second World Wars cannot be related to any over-riding legal principle or principles other than those which are of a humanitarian origin or complexion. In any event, apart from them, there are probably at present no over-riding, universally or generally agreed, juridical principles of the law of war.' He proceeds to instance the fading out of the formerly fundamental distinction between combatants and non-combatants.[3]

At the end of the year the Chief of the Air Staff presented a paper on bombing strategy suggested by the recent report of the Lloyd Committee on German Oil.[4] It appeared that the next six months

---

[1] See Appendix I (b).

[2] Above, p. 20.

[3] H. Lauterpacht, The Problem of the Revision of the Laws of War, in *British Year Book of International Law, 1952*. See also Oppenheim, *International Law* vol. II (1952) pp. 517–530.

[4] See above, p. 404.

offered a unique opportunity of striking at Germany's supply, and he urged a combination of a concentrated air offensive against her synthetic plants with all possible means—at present probably mainly sabotage—of reducing her supplies from Roumania. To eliminate all her seventeen synthetic plants at least 3,400 bomber sorties would be required every four months.

The Chiefs of Staff approved on January 7 a report in which Sir Charles Portal's proposal of October was weighed against alternative primary aims for the bomber force, including civilian morale and naval targets, such as ships in harbour and U-boat construction pens.[1] Having stated the advantages and disadvantages of each the report pronounced, *assuming that the figures of the Lloyd Committee were approximately correct*, in favour of bombing the synthetic oil plants. These were comparatively large targets, few in number, and mostly in areas not so heavily defended as others. As the secondary object, to be pursued when the primary aim was not attainable, they recommended the lowering of enemy morale, particularly in industrial areas. Diversions from these two objectives should be allowed in two cases only: against assembly ports when invasion was believed imminent or against warships when specially favourable opportunity offered. The Defence Committee, after a discussion in which some misgivings were expressed whether too great hopes were not laid on the Oil Committee's calculations, were strongly attracted by the principle of concentrating our forces and pronounced in favour of the Portal plan; they also gave provisional approval for sabotage operations in Roumania.

So a new directive went out to Bomber Command on January 15. Their sole primary aim till further notice was to be the German synthetic oil plants; the complete destruction of the nine largest would reduce Germany's internal production of oil by about 80 per cent. So greatly, however, did operations depend on the weather, and so uncertain was the weather of that hard winter, that what actually happened from January 1 to February 27, so the Commander-in-Chief told the Chief of the Air Staff, was that on nineteen nights naval targets were attacked, on six nights industrial towns, on five the Channel ports, and oil targets exclusively on only three. In March the main energies of Bomber Command were diverted to the Battle of the Atlantic.

The oil directive had little prospect of attaining its object. It had long been accepted that the casualties incurred in daylight bombing were prohibitive: it had not been realised that in the absence of scientific navigational aids night bombing could make no pretence to accuracy even when weather allowed an attack on the designed

---

[1] There was no suggestion that more bomber units might be sent overseas.

E E

targets. It was now coming to be understood, from photographic evidence, that our efforts to paralyse German industry had so far been quite ineffective, and the German records have since confirmed the failure. It seems clear that no mere increase in the quantitative delivery of bombs, such as the Prime Minister pressed for with the Air Ministry, would have made any difference at this time.

In any case Bomber Command was lamentably weak for all the demands made on it. In mid-November its five Groups comprised twenty-nine operational squadrons; fifteen others were re-equipping —one with the new four-engined Halifax, one with Stirlings, and one with Manchesters. There was a shortage of crews also. On March 1 the proportion of crews fit, operationally, was only 57 per cent of establishment, and even those nominally available were continually being drawn upon for various duties, such as ferrying aircraft to the Middle East, whence they were not sent back.

The Prime Minister was gravely perturbed by the slow rate of expansion of Bomber Command, and at the end of the year complained of its stagnant condition, whereas the fighters were going ahead well. The Chief of the Air Staff agreed as to both the present weakness of the bomber force and the supreme importance of a rapid increase. He reminded the Prime Minister that the present state of affairs was the price we were paying for the rapid development of Fighter and Coastal Commands, for resources diverted to the Middle East, and for the large-scale expansion of the training organisation. A great development in bomber strength was planned for 1941, but most of the new squadrons would not come into the line until the second half of the year. Under present plans there should be twenty-seven heavy bomber squadrons in the Metropolitan Air Force fit for operations by April 1, and it was proposed to add as early as possible a minimum of six heavy bomber squadrons by forming at least three new squadrons and by re-arming three medium bomber squadrons as heavy bombers. The necessary aircraft were available. The bottle-neck at present was trained crews, particularly pilots, and Portal was strongly opposed to any general reduction of the period of training given to night-bombing crews. He was also unwilling to interrupt the development of Fighter and Coastal Commands, but he proposed to draw on army co-operation squadrons and to some extent on the Middle East: Longmore would be asked to return crews surplus to the new re-equipment programme, and the tentative suggestion for a further reinforcement of the Middle East by six fighter and six medium bomber squadrons would be modified.[1] He hoped further to minimise wastage at home by reducing the scale of operations in bad weather. The Prime Minister approved these proposals.

---

[1] See p. 351, above.

By the end of March the Command comprised thirty-nine operational squadrons—three of them armed with the new heavy types—with 624 aircraft. The programme to which they were working called for a total force of seventy-five heavy and twenty medium squadrons by the end of 1941 (Target Force A), and it was proposed ultimately to raise the initial establishment of all squadrons from sixteen to twenty-four aircraft.

It may be added that relations between the Air Ministry and the Ministry of Aircraft Production were no more harmonious than in the summer, but the Prime Minister thought that this had its compensations. 'I am definitely of the opinion', he wrote in a private minute, 'that it is more in the public interest that there should be sharp criticism and counter-criticism between the two Departments than that they should be handing each other out ceremonious bouquets. One must therefore accept the stimulating but disagreeable conditions of war.'[1]

---

[1] Churchill II 623.

CHAPTER XVIII

NEUTRALS FRIENDLY AND UNFRIENDLY; NOVEMBER 1940 – MAY 1941

NO FACTOR in the Prime Minister's policy was more constant than his determination to do or say nothing which might prevent or delay the entry of the United States into the war on the British side. He had no patience with suggestions that this might be a doubtful benefit. A certain ambassador 'should surely be told forthwith', he minuted on October 4, 'that the entry of the United States into war either with Germany and Italy or with Japan is fully conformable with British interests'. He added that 'nothing in the munitions sphere can compare with the importance of the British Empire and the United States being co-belligerent', and that 'if Japan attacked the United States without declaring war on us we should at once range ourselves at the side of the United States and declare war upon Japan'.[1] It is not the least part of his statesmanship that he realised from the very outset the supreme importance of American good will and set himself, as the 'Naval Person' and 'Former Naval Person', to win President Roosevelt's confidence by keeping him fully informed of our intentions, our motives, our difficulties and our needs. Mr. Churchill may have at one time exaggerated the President's influence and so cherished false hopes in June 1940, but he was justified in pinning his faith to Mr. Roosevelt's democratic sympathies and political skill, and it was natural that he should hope and pray for his re-election for a third term in November.[2] Both the Democratic and Republican candidates, it is true, though eager to help Britain to resist Hitler, paid lip-service in the last weeks of the campaign to the American people's horror of being involved in war; but there was a great deal, as the event showed, which a country and a President so benevolently neutral could do before that final decision has to be faced.[3] The world now knows to what extraordinary lengths, inconceivable from the standpoint of the traditional law of nations, President Roosevelt could stretch assistance

---

[1] Churchill II 599.

[2] ibid. p. 489.

[3] See R. E. Sherwood, *The White House Papers of Harry L. Hopkins* I 187–189. See also W. L. Langer and S. E. Gleason, *The Challenge to Isolation* esp. ch. xx, and *The Undeclared War* esp. ch. vii.

to one belligerent without provoking the active hostility of the other.

This assistance had been very notably stretched in the course of the late summer. In August staff 'exploratory' conversations had been held in London, and in September agreement had been reached in principle and publicly announced on the transfer to Britain of American destroyers and the lease to the United States of British bases in the Caribbean and western Atlantic.[1] In the negotiations leading to the latter an indispensable part had been played by Lord Lothian; the final lap of the presidential election campaign offered a suitable opportunity for the Ambassador to come home on leave, and he was present at several important conversations in England.

On November 8, three days after Mr. Roosevelt's re-election, Lord Lothian met the Chiefs of Staff. The Americans, he said, realising the danger to themselves of a German control of the oceans, had already accepted the slogan 'Save America by helping Britain', and it was now vitally important for us to formulate our requirements and present them, whether or not we expected them to be met at once or *in toto*. We should strike while the iron was hot. He summed up our requirements under four heads: financial, naval and mercantile, West Africa, and Far East. All of these raised problems which neither we nor the Americans could solve independently. We must have their co-operation. What did we want them to do? It was agreed in discussion that without financial assistance other forms of aid would come to nothing, but this was hardly a matter for the Chiefs of Staff; the points which they asked him to raise with the United States Government were the following: first, the issue of instructions to Admiral Ghormley with regard to the scope of the more comprehensive naval discussions which Lothian knew the President to desire, provided that they could be conducted without publicity; secondly, the advantages of basing the United States Pacific Fleet at Singapore; thirdly, our urgent need of naval and air bases in Ireland; and, lastly, 'the paramount importance of providing us, as rapidly as possible, with supplies and equipment with which to continue to fight the war'.

Lord Lothian also, of course, discussed matters with the Prime Minister, and Mr. Churchill has told how, on the Ambassador's prompting and after consultation with the Departments, he wrote to the President 'a very long letter on the outlook for 1941', in which he laid our cards on the table. In this letter, finally dated December 8 and now published in Mr. Churchill's book, after arguing that it was in the common interest of both countries that Great Britain should

---

[1] See above, chaps. x, xi.

hold the front against Nazi aggression for the two years at least which the United States would need for the completion of her vast defence programme, he proceeded to explain our urgent needs.[1]

> 'The danger of Great Britain being destroyed by a swift, over-whelming blow has for the time being very greatly receded. In its place there is a long, gradually-maturing danger, less sudden and less spectacular, but equally deadly. This mortal danger is the steady and increasing diminution of sea tonnage. . . . It is therefore in shipping and in the power to transport across the oceans, particularly the Atlantic Ocean, that in 1941 the crunch of the whole war will be found.'

He appended a statement of our shipping losses. Whereas we estimated that we ought to import 43 million tons of supplies yearly to maintain our effort at full strength, the tonnage entering our ports in September and October had been only at the rate of 37 and 38 millions.

He then pointed out the narrow margin in battleship superiority which we must expect in the next six or seven months, and the possible dangers from Vichy France and Japan.

> 'In the face of these dangers we must try to use the year 1941 to build up such a supply of weapons, particularly of aircraft, both by increased output at home in spite of bombardment and through ocean-borne supplies, as will lay the foundations of victory.'

He then set forth the various ways in which America could help us. The prime need being to reduce the loss of tonnage, the United States could help us by reasserting the doctrine of the freedom of the seas from illegal and barbarous methods of warfare, in accordance with the principles accepted after the former war, and allowing her ships to trade with countries not subject to an effective legal blockade; she might protect such trade by armed escort, which would be far more effective if her ships could use bases in Eire. Such a policy 'would constitute a decisive act of constructive non-belligerency by the United States and, more than any other measure, would make it certain that British resistance could be effectively prolonged for the desired period and victory gained'. Other suggestions were 'the gift, loan or supply' of American warships, especially destroyers, already in the Atlantic; the extension of American maritime control to a line covering the new American bases on British islands; American diplomatic support in pressing for the use of naval and air bases in Eire. Further we should require for victory at least 3 million tons of merchant ship-building capacity, additional to the $1\frac{1}{4}$ millions

---

[1] See Churchill II 493–501.

which we could build yearly ourselves, and in the meantime, for 1941, every ton of merchant shipping which the United States could spare. Help on a comparable scale was needed in the air. Our present programme of 7,000 first-line aircraft by the spring of 1942 would not suffice, and the President was invited 'to give earnest consideration to an immediate order on joint account for a further 2,000 combat aircraft a month', of which the highest possible proportion should be heavy bombers. With regard to land forces, while expressing gratitude for the substantial help already promised, he urged the importance of expanding to the utmost America's productive capacity for small arms, artillery and tanks.

Having thus prepared the ground, Mr. Churchill proceeded to the delicate subject of finance, an issue long charged with disagreeable emotions on both sides of the Atlantic. Under existing legislation loans to Great Britain were prohibited. 'Cash and carry' was still our rule, and despite all the efforts of the Treasury to mobilise the resources our cash was running out. 'By the end of 1940 British commitments in the United States for initial orders and capital development . . . amounted to nearly $10,000 millions'; this was 'far in excess of total British assets in the United States of America', and there was 'not the slightest hope that Britain could raise the dollars to finance the necessary production' in America of the munitions we needed.[1] The United States Treasury had been warned of our impending lack of dollars in May and again in July, but were anxious not to have to decide how to meet the difficulty until after the presidential election.

The position was eloquently summarised by the Prime Minister.

> 'While we will do our utmost, and shrink from no proper sacrifice to make payments across the exchange, I believe you will agree that it would be wrong in principle and mutually disadvantageous in effect if at the height of this struggle Great Britain were to be divested of all saleable assets, so that after victory was won with our blood, civilisation saved, and the time gained for the United States to be fully armed against all eventualities, we should stand stripped to the bone . . . If, as I believe, you are convinced, Mr. President, that the defeat of the Nazi and Fascist tyranny is a matter of high consequence to the people of the United States and to the Western Hemisphere, you will regard this letter not as an appeal for aid, but as a statement of the minimum action necessary to achieve our common purpose.'

This letter, which the President received at sea on December 9, had, we are told, 'a profound effect' on him, and on the 17th at a press conference he launched the idea, symbolised by the 'elimination

---

[1] Hancock and Gowing, *British War Economy*, p. 232.

of the dollar sign' and the parable of the garden hose, which took shape in Lend-Lease.[1] On December 29, in his Fireside Chat he came out with the defiant assertion that 'a nation can have peace with the Nazis only at the price of total surrender' and declared that America must be made 'the great arsenal of democracy'.[2]

Mr. Sherwood believes that it was the garden hose analogy which won the fight for Lend-Lease. It was with a similar desire to appeal to the imagination of the American people and arouse them to the imminence of the common danger that Lord Lothian, speaking to pressmen on his return to America, had used with regard to the financial crisis language which the Treasury and the Prime Minister considered indiscreetly forthright. He developed his theme in the last of his speeches, read for him by his second-in-command on the night of his untimely death.[3] Exactly a year was to pass before the United States entered the war, but she was already 'in effect a non-belligerent ally'; [4] and perhaps no one except the President, the Prime Minister—and Hitler, had contributed more to this result than the man who, as Philip Kerr, had long shown an instinctive understanding of the American outlook.

To replace Lothian the Prime Minister decided to invite no less authoritative an interpreter of the Government's policy than the Foreign Secretary himself, and Lord Halifax sailed for Washington in the newly commissioned battleship *King George V*. Even more important was the arrival in England on January 9 of Mr. Harry Hopkins, the President's 'close friend and confidant', who on his return to America some five weeks later was to act as the '*de facto* Deputy President' in matters concerning Lend-Lease.[5] Shortly afterwards, on March 1, Mr. John G. Winant arrived as United States Ambassador, and Mr. Averell Harriman, with the rank of Minister, was appointed to act as Hopkins' representative in London. In Winant, Hopkins and Harriman Mr. Churchill was now in touch with three Americans of whose devotion to the common cause there could be no doubt and with whom matters of the highest secrecy and importance could be discussed with the utmost confidence. Mr. Wendell Wilkie, the unsuccessful Republican candidate for the Presidency, also visited London at this time, as though to prove that good will to this country and interest in its war effort were by no means the monopoly of one American party.

---

[1] If one's neighbour's house was on fire and one had a hose, one did not bargain about the selling-price; one lent the hose.

[2] Sherwood, *White House Papers* I 222–225.

[3] Read at Baltimore, Dec. 11, by Mr. Nevile Butler; *The American Speeches of Lord Lothian*, 1941; printed also in the *Annual Register 1940*, p. 385.

[4] *The Roosevelt Letters*, ed. Elliott Roosevelt III (1952) 346 n.

[5] See *White House Papers* I ch. xi, p. 267.

The Lend-Lease Bill was introduced into Congress on January 10 and became law on March 11. Until this date the Prime Minister was particularly careful to allow no act or word which might imperil its passage; his public appeal on February 9, including the famous 'Give us the tools and we will finish the job', on which Hopkins had been consulted, was meant to still American fears of being asked to send an expeditionary force to Europe. The essence of the bill was to authorise the President to 'sell, transfer title to, exchange, lease, lend or otherwise dispose of . . . any defense article' to any nation whose defence he deemed vital to that of the United States. He was also given power to decide what form of repayment should be made to the United States by the recipients, the definition being left purposely vague since future events alone could determine the form of recompense most beneficial to America. Congress reserved the right of appropriating funds for the Lend-Lease programme, and the Act did not otherwise alter the existing neutrality legislation.

The President lost no time in making the Act applicable to Great Britain and to Greece, nor did he delay in presenting to Congress his first Appropriation Bill for seven billion dollars. By the end of June four billion of these had been allocated to procurement agencies: nearly two billion for aircraft, over a billion for ordnance and over half a billion for the increase of merchant tonnage. It naturally took time for such allocations to be turned into deliveries, time during which American industry had to be vastly expanded, and in the meantime supplies had been ordered and received by us under earlier contracts; we were still paying dollars for the greater part of our supplies from America until the day when she actually became a belligerent. The President had in fact speeded up the tempo of assistance within a few days of his re-election, announcing that henceforth half of all the aircraft and other implements of war produced in the United States would go to Britain and approving a British order for 12,000 more planes beyond the 11,000 already on order.

To make the most of the swelling tide of American help no small organisation on the British side was required; an account of the development of this organisation, and of the numerous bodies set up in America for the purpose of presenting and co-ordinating our demands, will be found in the series of Civil Histories.[1] Separate mention should perhaps be made of the special arrangements for the exchange of secret scientific and technical information. When this subject first came before the Cabinet in December 1939, the Admiralty had been reluctant to agree except on a basis of strict

---

[1] See in particular Hancock and Gowing, *British War Economy*, and H. Duncan Hall, *North American Supply*.

reciprocity—an asdic for a bomber sight—as to which for some time there were difficulties on both sides. However, in the summer of 1940 both the Admiralty and the Air Ministry were eager to exchange secrets with the Americans, and at the beginning of July Lothian was told that the Government approved in principle. A fortnight later the President declared his willingness to receive a special mission from the United Kingdom. The mission consisted of representatives of the three Services and the Ministry of Supply, with Sir Henry Tizard as its chairman. Its report was considered by the Cabinet in November, and in January 1941, after the introduction of the Lend-Lease Bill into Congress, a British ministerial committee recommended that, while no information connected with forthcoming operations should be imparted, information should otherwise be given, subject to proper precautions, whenever we ourselves were interested in the manufacture of the articles concerned; in other cases requests should normally be granted except for very special reasons. In February, as a result of Hopkins' visit, arrangements were made for yet closer collaboration.

During these early months of 1941 staff discussions of the highest importance on matters of grand strategy were proceeding in Washington. On 12 November, after the return of the 'special observers' from their exploratory discussions in London, and after receiving more detailed information from Admiral Ghormley of his conversations with the Bailey committee, Admiral Stark, the American Chief of Naval Operations, had with the concurrence of General Marshall, Chief of Staff of the Army, submitted to the President a memorandum on 'National Defense Policy'.[1] He wrote:

> 'I believe that the continued existence of the British Empire, combined with building up a strong protection in our home areas, will do most to assure the *status quo* in the Western Hemisphere, and to promote our principal national interests . . . I also believe that Great Britain requires from us very great help in the Atlantic, and possibly even on the Continents of Europe and of Africa, if she is to be enabled to survive.'[2]

His plan (known as 'Plan Dog') envisaged full military co-operation with the British against Germany and Italy, should the United States be drawn into war, while every effort would be made to avoid war with Japan. The Admiral accordingly advised the President to authorise secret and formal conversations with the British. Further,

---

[1] For Admiral Bailey's committee see above, p. 243.

[2] Cited in *The Undeclared War* p. 222; see also Matloff and Snell, *op. cit.* pp. 25–28.

on January 16, the President, as reported by General Marshall, issued a directive in the following sense:

> 'That we would stand on the defensive in the Pacific, with the fleet based on Hawaii; that the Commander of the Asiatic Fleet would have discretionary authority as to how long he could remain based in the Philippines and as to his direction of withdrawal—to the East or to Singapore . . .
>
> That the Navy should be prepared to convoy shipping in the Atlantic to England, and to maintain a patrol off-shore from Maine to the Virginia Capes.
>
> That the Army should not be committed to any aggressive action until it was fully prepared to undertake it; that our military course must be very conservative until our strength had developed . . .
>
> That we should make every effort to go on the basis of continuing the supply of material to Great Britain, primarily in order to disappoint what he thought would be Hitler's principal objective in involving us in war at this particular time, and also to buck up England.'[1]

These conclusions, that the main American effort, in case of war, should be made in the east, and that formal conversations, looking to armed co-operation in that case, should be opened with the British, mark an epoch in American policy.

On the British side it was learnt on November 30 that the President had agreed to secret staff talks being held in Washington. The Chiefs of Staff met the British delegation on December 15 and discussed with them their instructions, which were finally approved by the Defence Committee. Conversations should be conducted in a spirit of complete frankness, only details of impending operations being withheld. The policy advocated by His Majesty's Government was (a) the acceptance of the European theatre as the vital one, where a decision must first be sought; (b) to aim at defeating Germany and Italy first and then deal with Japan; (c) the security of the Far East, including Australia and New Zealand, which involved the retention of Singapore as the key to these interests.

As regards specific assistance from the United States, their navy, after providing for home security, could best help the common cause by supplying reinforcements of cruisers, destroyers, submarines, reconnaissance aircraft and a few older battleships in the European theatre, and in the Far East a fleet strong enough to secure Allied interests. In our view the proper strategical base for the Eastern Fleet was Singapore, whereas it was clear that the Americans favoured basing it initially at Hawaii, 'with a limited offensive role'.

---

[1] See Mark S. Watson, *Chief of Staff: Pre-war Plans and Preparations* (Washington 1950) p. 124.

We believed that a fleet so based with such a role would be unlikely to prevent a Japanese southward move; such a move might well be directed against the Netherlands East Indies, on which the United States would for some months depend for raw materials. With regard to help in the air, four principles were to be considered: (i) any demands we made must not interfere with our own programme of expansion and purchase in America; (ii) we should ask the United States to take responsibility for the defence of West Africa and help in the Middle East; (iii) for administrative reasons United States units should as far as possible be armed with aircraft of the same type as our own in any particular area of co-operation; (iv) while at first we should get all the help we could in building up our own resources, later we would rather the Americans concentrated on their own.

While approving these instructions the Defence Committee emphasised that in discussions on naval strategy we should show deference to United States views in all matters concerning the Pacific theatre. We should not ask the Americans to come and defend Singapore, Australia and India, but rather offer them the use of Singapore if they required it.

The Committee also approved the answers to certain questions asked by Admiral Ghormley and Brigadier-General Lee, Military Attaché in London. To the inquiry what were the major features of our strategical plans for the next two years, we should reply that our eventual aim was the creation of such intolerable conditions in Germany by an ever-increasing force of bombers that the German armies would be forced to return and the Nazi régime be overthrown.

Our representatives sailed on January 12 and conversations began on the 29th. On February 17 they reported progress, with proposals which were welcomed by the Chiefs of Staff, and at the end of March the British and American delegations issued a Joint Report, commonly known as the ABC-1 Report.[1]

The report came before the British Chiefs of Staff on May 1; the British members had added a commentary summarising the chief points calling for consideration and decision.

The Joint Report was of course concerned only with a hypothetical situation, that of the United States being 'compelled' to resort to war, though with regard to organisation it contained proposals to take immediate effect. The long-term proposals came to be superseded in due time and will be more properly mentioned in Volume III; they envisaged a Supreme War Council for the higher direction

---

[1] The British delegation consisted of Rear-Admiral R. M. Bellairs, Rear-Admiral V. H. Danckwerts, Major-General E. L. Morris, Air Chief Marshal C. E. H. Medhurst. The chief American representatives were Lieutenant-General Stanley D. Embick, Vice-Admiral Robert L. Ghormley and Colonel Joseph T. McNarney.

of the war advised by the Chiefs of Staff of the two countries, while the strategic recommendations included military, diplomatic, economic and financial pressure, a sustained air offensive, and 'the building up of the necessary forces for an eventual offensive against Germany'. It was agreed that, since Germany was the predominant Axis Power, the Atlantic and European area would be the decisive theatre; the principal United States military effort would be exerted in that theatre, and the operations of United States forces in other theatres would be conducted in such a manner as to facilitate that effort. Should Japan enter the war, the military strategy in the Far East would be defensive.

As immediate measures the Report recommended the setting up in Washington and London of nucleus organisations of military missions, the convening of a conference of commanders in the Far East, including the Dutch, to prepare plans, and an agreed procedure for the allocation of military material both before and after the entry of the United States into the war. The United States consented also to exchange liaison officers with Canada, Australia and New Zealand.

This report received the tentative approval of the United States Chief of Naval Operations and Chief of Staff of the Army, and they promised to recommend it to the President. The British Chiefs of Staff, for their part, after discussion with the delegates on their return from Washington, expressed their provisional agreement and recommended that the approval of the United Kingdom and Dominion Governments should be obtained as soon as possible. On May 15 the Defence Committee gave their approval so far as the United Kingdom was concerned; they agreed also to the suggestion, to which they understood that the American representatives attached importance, that the two countries should exchange full texts and particulars of any treaties or other commitments which might affect the proposed military action or peace terms. On learning that the President, while not at this time giving formal approval, in case of war would 'expect to take appropriate action', the British Government hastened to inform Washington that they themselves approved it.

The Chiefs of Staff now issued a directive for their permanent representatives in Washington (to be known in their corporate capacity as the Joint Staff Mission) who in accordance with the Joint Report were to maintain the contact thus happily begun. Until such time as the United States Government was ready to recognise them as such, they would be known as 'Advisers to the British Supply Council in North America'. Such were the origins of the organisation which was to develop into that great engine of victory, the Combined Chiefs of Staff.

A few days later the Chiefs of Staff in London welcomed Major-

General J. E. Chaney, Special Observer, United States Army, whose instructions explained that he might in the future be appointed Army Member of a United States military mission; the methods by which the military chiefs of the two nations might best communicate with one another were discussed.

The results of the conversations, as they affected British strategy in the Battle of the Atlantic and in the Far East, will be considered later.[1]

American co-operation was also of great importance in the conduct of our relations with Vichy France and Spain. At the end of September both the Foreign Office and the Admiralty were in favour of reaching a *modus vivendi* with Vichy, and such in general was the trend of United States policy. But, apart from arguments based on the need of maintaining the blockade, strong objections might be urged against any advances to the Pétain Government; there was the distrust of the whole régime, and especially of some of its powerful personalities, engendered by events since M. Reynaud's fall, and there were our obligations to de Gaulle, whose forces had recently been fighting alongside ours at Dakar.

The period from October 20 to November 12 was one of great anxiety in Downing Street. We had reports, without definite information, that the Germans were pressing Vichy, as part of a bargain, to allow Germany the use of the French fleet and bases in Africa, and that Darlan and Laval were using their influence on Pétain in this sense. Vigorous appeals to resist were made to Pétain directly from London and, even before a British request reached him, by Mr. Roosevelt.[2] The thought that the new battleships (*Jean Bart* and *Richelieu*) might move from Casablanca and Dakar to ports within German control was especially alarming, and the Cabinet decided on November 8 that this must be prevented, if necessary by submarine action. The reply of the Vichy Government to a warning which we had conveyed to them was that they had no intention of moving either ship, but would not be deterred from doing so, if they wished, by any influence on our part.

The Foreign Office, from their desire to win over French North Africa, and the Admiralty, from regard to the balance of naval strength, were still most unwilling to see French and British ships fighting one another; but the Prime Minister felt strongly that we must not become obsessed with the idea that we should never in any circumstances offer provocation to Vichy. As a matter of fact,

---

[1] See chaps. xx and xxi.
[2] *The Undeclared War* p. 86.

although he allowed Laval to succeed Baudouin as Foreign Minister on October 28, Pétain had no intention of permitting the Germans the use of French ships or bases, nor were the Germans prepared to use force to secure them; that would not have been in accordance with Hitler's ideas at this time. Pétain gave the President a solemn promise that the ships should not fall into enemy hands, and we were assured through Madrid that Vichy did not mean to allow the Axis the use of French bases either. The Germans realised that things were not going well for them, and on December 10 Hitler went so far as to issue a directive for the preventive measures to be taken (Operation 'Attila') in case a secession movement should occur in the parts of the French colonial empire under General Weygand's control. It would be necessary to occupy the whole of continental France and seize the French home fleet.[1]

Weygand had since early in October been at Algiers as Delegate-General and Commander-in-Chief in French Africa. His intention, he has recorded, was to nurse the French forces until they were in a position to take the field against Germany. In the meantime he would resist any German attempt to exceed the terms of the armistice and would allow no German forces into his command; but he would at the same time resist any British aggression, since it could only have the effect of aggravating German pressure on France. Hence his *mot*: 'If the English come with four divisions, I shall fire on them; if they come with twenty, I shall embrace them.'[2]

The British Government were at the end of October supplying information to General Weygand through our consulate-general at Tangier, and had considered appealing to him personally in order to stiffen his reported opposition to German demands for a transfer of the French fleet and bases. They took several opportunities of assuring him of our determination to carry on the war, and at the end of the year allowed him to be told that we would send six divisions to North Africa to support him if he himself raised the standard of resistance. The same information was conveyed to Marshal Pétain. This was a bold offer, but the Chiefs of Staff had thought its fulfilment not beyond our powers, though of course it would reduce by so much the forces we could send to the Middle East. They considered on various occasions how we could render assistance to a French rising, but nothing came of the idea. Nor, naturally, did anything come of the schemes to land a small force to support Spanish resistance, should the Germans, as was at this time thought likely, attempt to march through Spain against Gibraltar.

---

[1] *F.D.* No. 19, p. 123.
[2] See M. Weygand, *Rappelé au Service* pp. 347 ff., 470.

In General Weygand's view not only her weakness told against co-operation with Britain, but also her support of de Gaulle. To him, as to Vichy, de Gaulle appeared as a mutineer and a rebel, and the form of a letter which he received at this time from the junior officer was not such as to dispel his prejudice.[1]

To Vichy, of course, de Gaulle was a red rag. Suggestions of the acceptance of the colonial *status quo* as a basis for improved Franco-British relations were frustrated on the Vichy side by governmental prestige, and on the British by the fact that during the autumn of 1940 de Gaulle was conducting successful operations in Equatorial Africa; on November 13 the Free French forces entered Libreville in Gabon.[2] For military operations their chief was dependent on British assistance, but he was by no means always willing to conform to British policy and his separate action often caused embarrassment in London. This was particularly so when, as now, we were contemplating improved relations with Vichy: on 27 October the General unexpectedly announced from Brazzaville in French Congo the establishment of a Council of Defence to exercise the powers of a war Government in the name of France and of all French territories which were, or might in future be, fighting for Free France; the powers formerly exercised by the Chief of State and Council of Ministers would for the present be exercised by the leader of the Free French forces assisted by the Council of Defence. He denied the legitimacy of the Government at Vichy. The General on his side was not unnaturally perturbed by the British Government's attitude towards Vichy, and after his success at Libreville he came to London for consultation. Asked by the Foreign Secretary whether he thought us wrong in trying to establish a *modus vivendi* with Vichy, he answered that on a short view indeed we might not be wrong; but on a longer view the essential fact was that the small concessions, which were all that we could offer, could only postpone the decisions which Vichy was bound to take, whereas by such a policy we might offend the majority of Frenchmen, who were now coming to realise that the Vichy Government was wholly bad and entirely under German orders. Relations were made still more difficult by the fact that, as Mr. Churchill puts it, the General felt that he had to be rude to the British to prove in French eyes that he was not a British puppet. 'He certainly carried out this policy with perseverance.'[3] A further annoyance was the frequent friction between leading members of the Free French movement.

For the near future General de Gaulle had in mind an expedition

---

[1] *ibid.* p. 549.
[2] See Map 12.
[3] Churchill II 451.

F F

for the recapture of French Somaliland (Jibuti) which had gone over to Vichy in July; it was to be executed by the Free French forces now in Equatorial Africa. This proposal (Operation 'Marie') found favour in principle with the Chiefs of Staff, subject to Wavell's approval, but after a great deal of discussion and planning it was eventually cancelled in March 1941, on the decision of the local French commanders. By this time, however, Free French forces had been taking part in the campaign in the Western Desert and had started to raid Italian bases in Libya from the Chad province.[1]

The Germans had for some time been desirous of improving their relations with Vichy. Encouraged by the stubborn resistance of the garrison at Dakar, Hitler told Mussolini, at their Brenner meeting on October 4, that he did not exclude the possibility of having the French forces on the Axis side in a continental coalition against Britain.[2] In conversations with Laval and Pétain at Montoire on October 22 and 24 respectively he angled for such support, but obtained, at any rate from the Marshal, nothing but vague promises of collaboration.[3] In his rough wooing of Vichy Hitler had a difficult game to play. Both the Axis powers, to say nothing of the incompatible desires of Spain, had designs on French African territory, and knowledge of these might well stimulate resistance in Africa and play into the hands of the British. From reports of his talks with Mussolini and Raeder soon afterwards (October 28 and November 4) it seems that Hitler held to the opinion that it was in the interests of the Axis that the French should for the present retain control of their empire in North Africa and, while disarmed at home, be allowed the strength to defend their colonies against de Gaulle and the British.[4] For the time being, he announced in his directive of November 12, France would play the part of a non-belligerent Power which was required to allow German war measures to be taken in the territories under its sovereignty—especially in the African colonies—and, if necessary, must even support these measures by the use of its own means of defence.[5]

There was also the Spanish question: the continued non-belligerency of Spain became more likely with every Axis disappointment, but it could not be taken for granted. General Franco replaced Señor Beigbeder as Foreign Minister by the Falangist Serrano Suñer on October 17, and at his meeting with Hitler at Hendaye on the

---

[1] See above, p. 375.

[2] Ciano, *Diplomatic Papers* p. 396.

[3] P. Baudouin, *Private Diaries* pp. 260–271.

[4] Ciano, *op. cit.* p. 400; *F.N.C.* p. 148.

[5] *F.D.* p. 118.

23rd gave a vague assurance of Spain's eventual entry into the war.[1] On November 4 the Spaniards, in disregard of British rights, assumed administrative control of the international zone of Tangier; on December 1 they incorporated Tangier in the Spanish Zone of Morocco and dismissed British officials. However, they went no further. Our possession of Gibraltar was a thorn in Franco's side, but Spanish war-weariness and economic weakness were decisive.

Hitler, however, as we have seen,[2] was determined at the beginning of November to occupy Gibraltar at the first opportunity, and in his directive of the 12th he outlined a scheme for driving the British from the Western Mediterranean. For this purpose it was necessary to take Gibraltar and close the Straits, and to prevent the British from obtaining a foothold anywhere else in the Iberian peninsula or the islands in the Atlantic.

Operation 'Felix' in its original form envisaged action by all three Services.[3] The Army units must be strong enough to capture the Rock from the land side even without Spanish assistance; one corps was the force later assigned. A smaller force would stand ready to help the Spaniards to repel a British landing elsewhere, and a third, motorised, force would follow in order to occupy Portugal if necessary. The Air Force would begin by attacking British warships at Gibraltar and would consist largely of dive-bombers, while the Navy would supply submarines. Since this operation would increase the strategic importance of the Canary and Cape Verde Islands, the German naval and air chiefs were to examine the problems of helping the Spaniards to defend the former and of occupying the latter, a Portuguese possession. The possible occupation of the other Portuguese islands, Madeira and the Azores, was also to be studied and an early report was demanded.

Hitler told Suñer, now Foreign Minister, shortly after this that the best time for the German soldiers to fight in Spain would be December and the two following months; in March or April they might be required for other tasks. But 'Felix' was never put to the proof. Hitler countermanded the operation on December 11 on the ground that the required political condition did not obtain, and confirmed his decision on January 10.[4] Any desire which Franco may have cherished to join his fellow-dictators in arms was quenched by the German refusal to grant his terms and by the economic aid of Britain and the United States; the failure of the Axis in September over England and in North Africa may well have convinced him that

---

[1] See Ciano, *Diplomatic Papers* p. 401; for a personal appreciation of Suñer see Templewood, *Ambassador on Special Mission* p. 56.

[2] Above, p. 360.

[3] *F.D.* p. 119.

[4] *F.D.* pp. 125, 131.

the war would be prolonged and that he could bide his time. Nevertheless the possibility of a German thrust against Gibraltar or the Atlantic islands long caused anxiety to the British high command and valuable troops and ships were held ready to parry it.

The Chiefs of Staff considered in October and November the requirements of the fortress for sustaining a long siege and approved the estimate of the Governor (Lieutenant-General Sir Clive Liddell) that supplies for six months should be held. Discussions took place with him in London in January; it was clearly understood that in the event of a land attack the use of the naval base would have to be given up. The Governor also pointed out the inadequacy of Gibraltar as a base for contraband control.

The need for an alternative to Gibraltar was always in the British Government's mind, and forces were kept in being for the occupation of some of the Atlantic islands should the Germans invade the Iberian peninsula with or without the consent of their Governments. The forces had been re-constituted after the Dakar expedition, and various projects, with a bewildering series of code names, were discussed at all levels right through the winter and spring. There was of course the danger of the Germans again forestalling us as in Norway, and at the end of November it seemed that this danger might be imminent. The Defence Committee, however, stood by the Government's earlier decision (of 22 July) that we should not take the first step.

Staff papers of this period illustrate the extreme complexity of the practical implications of such amphibious projects; apart from that of finding troops suitably trained and equipped, they involved difficult problems of logistics, such as the time required to load and unload ships of different kinds in different ports and the interference so caused both with other military movements and with hardly less important commercial sailings. It is perhaps as well that General Weygand did not accept our offer to despatch six divisions to North Africa at this time.

Addressing the Chiefs of Staff early in January 1941 on the subject of future strategy, the Prime Minister said that he regarded a German invasion of Spain in order to force a way through Gibraltar as unlikely. Attempted against the will of the Spanish Government, especially in winter, it would be a most dangerous and questionable enterprise. With the permission of the Spanish Government it would of course be a short and easy matter for the Germans to gain control of Lisbon and of the Algeciras and Ceuta batteries, together with the airfields desired. But it was becoming increasingly unlikely that the Spanish Government would give them passage, and it was most improbable that they would try to force their way through before April. If matters hung fire in Spain until the spring, it was possible that Vichy might by then have been provoked by the Germans to undertake or allow the resumption of war in North Africa, in which case the whole situation in the Mediterranean would be transformed in our favour. From every point of view the delay was helpful to us, and we must be most careful not to precipitate matters in Spain. Since the expeditions against the Atlantic islands could not be contemplated unless or until Spain offered passage to the Germans or Germany began to force one, it would seem that they need no longer be kept ready at 48 hours' notice.

This settled the matter for the present, but the reversal of fortune in the Near East in the spring revived our apprehensions. Towards the end of April the Chiefs of Staff presented a report expressing the opinion that Germany's position was now so strong that within a few weeks she could bring irresistible pressure on Spain and deprive us of the use of Gibraltar. It had always been recognised, they said, that the only substitute for Gibraltar as a base for big ships was the Canary Islands, but not until recently had we available the assault craft for capturing them and the fighters for defending them. They recommended that a force should be assembled at once for this operation (code name 'Puma') in addition to those prepared for the Cape Verde and Azores groups. The proposal was approved at a meeting at which the Prime Minister and the Foreign Secretary were present, but the decision to launch the expeditions was to remain with the Government. Discussions about 'Puma' were in fact still continuing in July.

Some embarrassment was caused in London by the fact that early in March a Portuguese staff mission had visited England to discuss how Portugal could best resist a German invasion through Spain and what help her ancient ally could provide. The Portuguese believed that the Spaniards would offer but slight opposition, and they were disappointed to find how little we could do for the defence of the Portuguese mainland. Indeed, when the matter was under consideration at the end of May the Defence Committee took the view that their Government's best policy, in the event of invasion, would be to abandon Portugal for the Azores. For this we could offer naval co-operation and a certain amount of anti-aircraft and other equipment. Dr. Salazar had been unwilling to allow the presence of British technicians in the Azores. In the year 1807, in not dissimilar circumstances, a Portuguese Government had sailed from Lisbon with the assistance of the Royal Navy for a refuge overseas; but Dr. Salazar had no wish, one may suppose, to provoke another Peninsular War. And indeed it was no part of our policy to give the Germans an excuse for a descent on the Atlantic islands.

Possession of the Azores brings a European Power a thousand miles nearer to America, and the United States could not fail to be interested in their future. The Prime Minister kept the President informed of what we had in mind and assured him that co-operation of any sort would be welcome. Mr. Roosevelt had at the end of March, in response to a British suggestion, proposed the visit of an American squadron to Portuguese waters, and in May he did in fact order plans to be drawn up for an occupation of the Azores by United States forces. But the Portuguese Government objected even to the former proposal, and nothing came of either project, so that in this matter American help was of no immediate advantage to us.[1]

Hitler had earlier, in November, ordered his staff to study the possibilities of occupying the Atlantic islands;[2] but Admiral Raeder reported that the occupation and defence of the Cape Verdes and Canaries would hardly be possible while the British had command of the sea, and no serious plans were made. We have seen too that preparations for Operation 'Felix' for the capture of Gibraltar were called off on January 10: Hitler told his staff that there was, for the time being, no prospect of Spain becoming Germany's ally. But the idea of an attack on Gibraltar with Spanish help was never given up; even after the invasion of Russia had become the main concern the German staff contemplated launching one in the course of the summer, possibly before operations against Russia had ended. Early in May Hitler thought it possible that the British might forestall him in Spain, and a plan ('Isabella') was produced for the expulsion of the British force and the occupation of the chief Spanish ports.

Sir Samuel Hoare, our Ambassador in Madrid, laid great stress on the way in which American moral support could help us in Spain.[3] He appreciated the visit of Colonel Donovan, the President's emissary to Madrid and Lisbon in February 1941, at a time when German propaganda was particularly active. Our Ambassador expected soon after this that the crisis over the German demands would occur in two or three months; but on May 8 the Foreign Office were informed on good authority that as long as we held the Suez Canal Franco would be able to resist German requests for through passage to Gibraltar.

Much more important was the President's diplomatic support in our relations with Vichy. It is true that the standpoints were not the same. The American aim was identical with ours, to uphold the cause of freedom against dictatorship and help to restore an independent France, but our opinions differed as to the best means of bringing about this result. The United States had not suffered injury at the hands of the Pétain Government as had Britain, and consequently

---

[1] *White House Papers* I 296; *The Undeclared War*, pp. 366–369. S. E. Morison, *The Battle of the Atlantic* p. 66.

[2] *F.D.* 18, p. 120.

[3] *Ambassador on Special Mission* p. 105.

had less cause to distrust them; nor was Washington bound by commitments to the Free French. The British Government could not regard Pétain and his colleages as the true Government of France; they were mere puppets of Germany, and our policy was to maintain the blockade of France without relaxation as the best means of dissuading them from collaboration with the enemy. The President preferred a gentler policy. He recognised the Vichy Government and at the end of the year sent his close friend, Admiral Leahy, as ambassador, with instructions to use his personal influence to keep the Marshal in the right way. There was a good case to be made out on either side.[1]

The most obvious point at which the two policies clashed was whether, on humanitarian grounds, relief ships from America should be allowed to pass the blockade for the benefit of the civilian population of unoccupied France and North Africa. The British Government argued that under international law the Germans were responsible for feeding and clothing the peoples under their control and that, even if they did not actually secure for themselves a large part of the contents of the relief ships, they would indirectly benefit by being enabled to keep back so much more for themselves; the Ministry of Economic Warfare moreover did not believe that the peoples of Europe need be in any danger of starvation while the 1940 harvests lasted. The British were reluctant to abandon this position, but there was strong humanitarian pressure the other way in America, and when the President asked for a relaxation they felt they must go some way to meet his wishes. In any case, as we have seen, there were naval difficulties in the way of a watertight blockade.[2]

British distrust of Vichy increased in February when Admiral Darlan, who was bitterly hostile to us, had become not only Foreign Minister but Vice-President of the Council and successor-designate to Pétain. But in one or two cases concessions were made, at the President's request, for the passage of individual relief ships to unoccupied France. As regards North Africa, Washington and Vichy came to an arrangement in March providing for the shipping of supplies thither against payment, on condition that the distribution should be supervised by American officials.[3]

There was much less difference of opinion between the British and American Governments on other matters. Early in 1941 it appeared that Vichy was moving towards collaboration with the Germans, in the hope of securing in exchange some alleviation of treatment.

---

[1] For the American attitude, see W. L. Langer, *Our Vichy Gamble* (New York 1947); also *The Undeclared War* chaps. iii, xii; also Fleet Admiral W. D. Leahy, '*I was there*' (London 1950).

[2] See above, p. 408. For a short treatment of the long negotiations see Medlicott *op. cit.* ch. xvi.

[3] For the 'Murphy-Weygand Agreement' see *The Undeclared War* pp. 378–381.

Germans were allowed to infiltrate into North Africa, and proceeded to join or replace the Italian members of the Armistice Commission.[1] On April 18 President Roosevelt warned Pétain that his behaviour might forfeit American relief supplies. The President's diplomatic action was further of assistance in April in preventing the move of the battleship *Dunkerque* from Oran to Toulon, which we had learnt to be Darlan's intention. There was discussion in the Defence Committee whether, should diplomacy fail, we should attempt to sink the ship. The representatives of the Foreign Office and Admiralty again felt misgivings, as in the earlier case of the *Jean Bart* and *Richelieu*, but the Committee decided for the bolder course. The necessity did not arise, however, since Pétain agreed to do nothing without American consent.

Matters came to a head in May, when British anxieties in the Near East, and not there only, were increasing. The Foreign Office feared that German troops might land in Syria, that they might occupy Morocco, and that they might pass through Unoccupied France. The Cabinet decided that extreme pressure must be exerted on Pétain, and the United States were asked to transmit a strongly worded warning to Vichy, with their own support; we suggested a visit of American warships to Dakar and Casablanca. At the same time we offered the French all the assistance in our power if they stood firm against German demands. The United States however preferred less drastic methods, merely informing Vichy that if they acquiesced in demands exceeding the terms of the armistice American economic help would cease. Pétain assured Admiral Leahy that he had no such intention: there had as yet been no German pressure to allow more Germans in North Africa or a passage through Unoccupied France into Spain, and no demand had been made for French assistance against Great Britain. He expected further demands for collaboration but would not go beyond the terms of the armistice. He refused to comment on the offer of British help in resisting such demands, since the armistice bound him not to allow the use of the French Fleet against the Axis. Admiral Leahy thought there was no hope of French resistance until a British victory had shown that the Germans could yet be defeated; events in Greece and Libya had seriously damaged British prestige at Vichy and disheartened the pro-British minority.

So true was this that it was not many days before the Marshal began to yield to pressure from the other side. In the first half of May Darlan was negotiating with the Germans, offering a considerable degree of collaboration in return for a less harsh treatment of France by Germany; the Germans secured not only the despatch of French

---

[1] See Weygand, *Rappelé au Service*, pt iv, chap. iv.

lorries from Tunisia to Rommel, but the use of French war material and airfields in Syria with a view to operations in Iraq.[1] On May 12 Pétain merely promised Admiral Leahy that he would not give the Germans 'voluntary active military aid', and in a broadcast on the 15th he spoke with approval of 'the present conversations with the German Government', appearing to suggest that in such relations lay France's only hope for the future. At the end of the month collaboration reached its furthest limits, on paper at any rate, with the conclusion of the Paris agreements of May 27 and 28.[2] These granted the Germans facilities in Syria (for Iraq), in North Africa and at Dakar; but their actual importance was slight, not only because the emergency in Iraq was past but because the French succeeded by protracted negotiations in delaying their execution. In this obstructive process an honourable part was played by General Weygand, who was determined that French Africa, at least, should not benefit the Germans.[3]

---

[1] See below, chaps. xix, xxii.

[2] Texts in A. Kammerer, *La Vérité sur l'Armistice* (Paris 1945) pp. 505–512.

[3] See *The Undeclared War* pp. 386–390, 497–501; Weygand, *Rappelé au Service* pp. 418–441.

CHAPTER XIX

THE MEDITERRANEAN AND MIDDLE EAST, FEBRUARY – MAY 1941

ON February 11 the Defence Committee had taken important decisions. The advance in Libya was to be halted at Benghazi and our efforts there limited to the creation of a secure flank for Egypt. All of Wavell's forces that could be spared would be transferred to Europe, and to Greece rather than to Turkey. The capture of Rhodes ('Mandibles') was regarded as no less urgent than before.[1]

It was still our policy to build up a Balkan front against Germany, and a further reason for sending reinforcements to Greece, apart from our alliance and her recent appeal, was that by doing so we might induce Turkey and perhaps Yugoslavia to join with us—of which there seemed otherwise little prospect. But we did not know the Greek plans for meeting a German attack, and it was decided that Mr. Eden and Sir John Dill should go out at once to deal with the situation.

A note containing instructions from Mr. Churchill stated that the Foreign Secretary would represent His Majesty's Government in all matters diplomatic and military, reporting whenever necessary to the War Cabinet through the Prime Minister. The Chief of the Imperial General Staff would advise on the military aspect and Mr. Eden would make sure that in case of any difference his views also were placed before the Government; the same applied to those of Air Marshal Longmore. The principal object of the mission was the despatch of speedy succour to Greece; 'Mandibles' was to be executed at the earliest possible moment, provided that it did not become an impediment to this main issue. The completion of the campaign in Eritrea was urgent; the reduction of the Italian forces in Abyssinia mattered less. But the mission was not concerned with grand strategy only. 'The great mass of troops, over 70,000, now engaged in the Kenya theatre must be severely scrutinised in order particularly to liberate South African divisions for service in Egypt.' Similarly Mr. Eden would 'address himself to the problem of securing the highest form of war economy in the armies and Air Forces of the Middle

---

[1] See above, p. 385. For a fuller account of the events described in the next few pages see Playfair I ch. xx.

East for all the above purposes, and to making sure that the many valuable military units in that theatre all fit into a coherent scheme and are immediately pulling their weight'. He would also advise upon the selection of commanders, consulting with 'General Wavell who enjoys so large a measure of the confidence of His Majesty's Government'. The selection of the general to command in Greece was of the highest consequence. In short, the Foreign Secretary was to 'gather together all the threads, and propose continuously the best solutions for our difficulties, and not be deterred from acting upon his own authority if the urgency is too great to allow reference home'.[1] No doubt for reasons of security, the terms of the directive were not communicated to the whole War Cabinet for their approval until February 20.

The directive was dated 12 February, and that evening the party set out. Weather was bad for flying and they did not reach Cairo till the 19th—an unfortunate delay when time was of such moment: the War Office thought the Germans might reach the Bulgarian-Greek frontier on March 12.[2]

As a result of their first discussions in Cairo, in which the heads of our military mission in Greece (Major-General Heywood) and of our liaison delegation just returned from Ankara (Lieutenant-General Sir J. Marshall-Cornwall) were included, the Cabinet's emissaries were convinced, on February 21, that we should do everything in our power to bring the fullest measure of help to the Greeks at the earliest possible moment. But it would not be possible to send help to Turkey at the same time. It is interesting to note that General Dill in a signal of the same day admitted that he had come out with the idea that any forces sent to Greece would certainly be lost and that we should concentrate on helping Turkey; but he was now converted to the view that we must help Greece. This was 'our only chance of preventing the Balkans being devoured piecemeal'. The risks were admittedly considerable but inaction would in his view be fatal. He was satisfied that 'there is a fair military chance of successfully holding a line in Northern Greece if we act at once'. Mr. Eden pointed out our air weakness, which was greater than had been estimated in London. Mines had already been laid in the Canal by German aircraft, and there was a risk that it might be closed for from five to seven days. This was the more serious in that over fifty ships would be needed to transport the expedition to Greece, and they could only be found by drawing on convoys arriving.

The Prime Minister thought well to warn his emissaries not to consider themselves obligated to a Greek enterprise if in their hearts they

---

[1] See Appendix III for Mr. Eden's instructions; they are also printed in full in Churchill III 60–62, along with the Prime Minister's telegram of the same date to General Wavell.

[2] See above, p. 385.

felt it would merely be another Norwegian fiasco. But they had already decided for it in principle, and Eden replied that, as regards the general prospects of a Greek campaign, 'it is, of course, a gamble to send forces to the mainland of Europe to fight Germans at this time. No one can give a guarantee of success, but when we discussed this matter in London we were prepared to run the risk of failure, thinking it better to suffer with the Greeks than to make no attempt to help them. That is the conviction we all hold here . . .' But the hope of stopping the Germans did not seem a forlorn one, whereas if we failed to help the Greeks there was no hope of action by Yugoslavia, and Turkey might be permanently lost to us. 'It is of course quite possible that when we see the Greeks tomorrow they may not wish us to come. But all my efforts will be concentrated on trying to induce the Greeks to accept our help now.' If they did, he and his military advisers were agreed that General Wilson was the right commander; 'his appointment to lead the forces in Greece will be a guarantee to the Greeks that we are giving of our best'.[1]

The Cabinet met on the afternoon of February 24 to take further important decisions. They had before them, besides the telegrams referred to above, one from Athens from the Foreign Secretary summarising discussions held during the evening of the 22nd. These had been both political and purely military, King George and the President of the Council being present at the former. M. Koryzis had begun by repeating his declaration of his country's unshakable resolve to fight on by the side of her ally till final victory against Germany, should the case occur, as well as against Italy; but in eastern Macedonia, facing Bulgaria, Greece had only three divisions, and the question arose what Allied reinforcements were needed to make effective resistance possible. It was highly important to know the intentions of Turkey and Yugoslavia.[2]

There had followed an expert discussion between Dill, Wavell, Longmore and General Papagos, from which it emerged that in view of the doubtful attitude of Yugoslavia the only line that could be held and would give time for withdrawal of troops from Albania was the so-called Aliakmon position, running north-west for some seventy miles to the Yugoslav frontier from the sea west of the River Vardar, and therefore sacrificing Salonika.[3] It would be impossible to hold a line covering Salonika unless Yugoslavia came in, so protecting the Allies' left flank. Conversely, it might have been added, since the

---

[1] Sir Henry Maitland Wilson had recently relinquished the command of British Troops in Egypt to become Military Governor and General Officer Commanding-in-Chief, Cyrenaica.

[2] A translation of the Greek declaration is printed in Playfair I App. 6.

[3] The Aliakmon position was also known as the position Mt. Olympus-Veria-Edessa-Kajmakcalan; see map 18. The river Aliakmon also appears as Haliakmon, Bistritza or Vistritza.

Yugoslav forces could only be supplied through Salonika, Yugoslavia would be unable to resist for long unless that port were held.

It had therefore been decided, said Mr. Eden, that in view of the strategic importance of the Yugoslavs' attitude he should make a further effort to bring them in; but that the Greeks should at once make, and start to carry out, preparations to withdraw the advanced troops to the position which we should have to hold if the Yugoslavs would not come in; that work should immediately begin on improving communications in Greece to facilitate the occupation of this position; and that the movement of British troops should commence forthwith. The Greeks 'very warmly received' the suggestion that General Wilson should command the British troops, and it was agreed that he should come under the direct orders of General Papagos, with the right to refer to the Commander-in-Chief, Middle East, and through him to the Government in London. Particulars of the forces we could send had been explained to the Greeks, and M. Koryzis had formally accepted our offer with gratitude and approved the detailed arrangements reached between the two staffs.

Mr. Eden concluded his report by saying that he was quite sure the Government had no alternative but to back the Greeks whatever the ultimate consequences.

The Cabinet had also before them a report of the Chiefs of Staff, who had prepared a balance sheet of advantages and disadvantages.[1] By going to Greece we took the only remaining chance of forming a Balkan front; success in this would force Germany to fight at the end of a long line of communication, interfere with her oil traffic from the Black Sea to the Adriatic, and give us a platform from which to bomb Italy and the Roumanian oilfields. If the Germans gained control of the Balkans, they would acquire naval and air bases from which to threaten our position in the Eastern Mediterranean, and would have paved the way for a drive through Asia Minor and beyond; they would also secure their oil traffic.

On the other hand, by embarking on the Greek adventure we should be undertaking a commitment of which we could not see the end; we should have to divert to it an immense quantity of shipping and perhaps forgo a million tons of imports a year. We should have thrown in our strategic reserve in the Middle East 'at the outset of the battle', with unhappy consequences, perhaps, for Turkey or for Egypt. Nevertheless the Chiefs of Staff were in favour of taking the risk. 'Our considered opinion', they said, 'is as follows: The possible military advantages . . . are considerable, though their achievement is doubtful and the risks of failure are serious. The disadvantages of

---

[1] Lieutenant-General Sir R. H. Haining, V.C.I.G.S., was acting in place of Sir John Dill.

leaving Greece to her fate will be certain and far reaching. Even the complete failure of an honourable attempt to help Greece need not be disastrous to our future ability to defeat Germany. A weighty consideration in favour of going to Greece is to make the Germans fight for what they want instead of obtaining it by default. On balance we think the enterprise should go forward.' But they wished 'to emphasise that, if we are to undertake this commitment, every possible effort should be made to get the Turks and the Yugoslavs to join in the struggle on our side. Without the support of one or other our help to Greece is unlikely in the long run to have a favourable effect on the war situation as a whole.'

The unanimity and weight of the recommendations to go forward were impressive, and the Cabinet were convinced. There were present on this occasion a number of other Ministers, and the views expressed by all of them were favourable. Also present, as it happened, was the Prime Minister of the Commonwealth of Australia, Mr. R. G. Menzies, then visiting the United Kingdom. This was particularly appropriate, since two of the divisions which it was proposed to send to Greece were Australian. Another was the New Zealand Division, and the Cabinet made their authorisation of the expedition as proposed dependent on the consent of these two Dominions. Mr. Churchill expected no difficulties in either quarter, and sent Eden the message: 'Full-steam ahead.'

Canberra and Wellington had come to an agreement with the War Office many months before on the terms of their troops' co-operation in the Empire's war; they should be under the operational control of the Commander-in-Chief of the theatre, but should serve as separate formations under their own commanders. Both Governments now gave their consent to the participation of their divisions in the Greek expedition, but they expressed certain apprehensions as to the adequacy of the proposed force, with suggestions as to how their troops might fight in the best possible conditions.[1] The United Kingdom Cabinet on the 27th recorded their high appreciation of these answers and confirmed their decision of the 24th. The difficulties inseparable from the long sea-route were noted, and it was also noted that there were no indications that the Germans were preparing to attempt the considerable operation of an advance across the Western Desert. On the 28th the Prime Minister signalled to General Smuts that we had taken the grave and hazardous decision to sustain the Greeks and try to make a Balkan front.

The first part of their mission thus accomplished, the emissaries proceeded for further high-level discussions to Ankara. The Turks approved our decision, Mr. Eden reported, to send all the help we

---

[1] See *Official History of New Zealand in the Second World War 1939–1946, Documents,* I pp. 239–243.

could to Greece but pressed, not for the first time, their own urgent need for equipment. They were ready to concert action with the Yugoslav Government, but had only received an evasive reply to a recent approach. Further they felt concerned lest they should be attacked by Russia if they became involved in war with Germany. The upshot was that Turkey undertook to enter the war at some stage, and would do so at once if directly attacked, but would prefer to delay her entry till she could make it with greater effect.

While at Ankara, Mr. Eden received on February 27 an even less satisfactory reply from Belgrade. Before leaving Athens he had sent a message to the Prince Regent of Yugoslavia asking what was the attitude of his country with regard to the defence of Salonika. The answer was non-committal. Yugoslavia would defend her territory and would not allow foreign troops passage, but she could not say what line she would take if the Germans moved through Bulgaria.

She was not given long to make up her mind. On March 1 Bulgaria publicly adhered to the Axis, and on the following day, with Bulgaria's connivance, elements of the German Twelfth Army began to cross the frozen Danube. To the Cabinet it seemed, on March 4, that Greece would now have to fight for her life and that Yugoslavia would take no action till she herself had been surrounded.

Next day there was still worse news. On returning to Athens on March 2 our envoys had found a change of atmosphere. The Greeks were much disappointed by the attitude of Turkey and Yugoslavia, but were still determined to resist the Germans, while continuing to fight the Italians. The disturbing fact was that General Papagos had not, as they believed had been arranged on their previous visit, begun to withdraw his troops on the Salonika front to the Aliakmon position; further, he was no longer prepared to order such a withdrawal, since the political effect would be disastrous and the troops would now be caught on the march by the Germans. Nor could he transfer any of his exhausted and outnumbered troops from Albania. His excuse was that this movement had all along been dependent on the receipt of an answer from Belgrade.

The result was deplorable. The British parties to the earlier discussions were emphatic that it had been well understood that the withdrawal of the troops from Macedonia and Albania was to take place immediately, since otherwise it would be too late. General Papagos however asserted the contrary, and his book repeats his contention.[1] What he now advocated was to leave the four divisions in eastern Macedonia and Thrace in position on the Bulgarian frontier and send up the British troops piecemeal on their arrival to join them—a thoroughly unsound proposal.

---

[1] *The Battle of Greece* pp. 322–327.

Eden and Dill sent for Wavell, and eventually reached a compromise with Papagos. Three Greek divisions would remain to delay the enemy on the frontier, while the Aliakmon line would be held as the main position by the British troops along with three Greek divisions and with some battalions from western Thrace—twenty-three battalions at most instead of the thirty-five previously offered. The agreement was signed by Dill and Papagos, and Eden and Dill returned to Cairo.

The British representatives, so they reported on the 5th, considered that the alternative of withdrawing our offer of military support would have a disastrous effect, as leading both to the rapid elimination of Greece from the war and to unfortunate political reactions in the Near and Middle East, and in America too. Moreover, it would not be easy to withdraw our Air and other troops already in Greece. They had therefore agreed 'after some misgivings' to the compromise scheme, but on the condition, which was accepted, that General Wilson should assume command of all troops in the Aliakmon position. From the military aspect it did not seem a hopeless proposition to check and hold the German advance on this line; at worst a fighting withdrawal should be possible through country eminently suitable for rearguard action. Eden, Dill and Wavell were all sure that they had in a very difficult situation arrived at the correct decision; the depressing atmosphere among the Greeks had already improved. But 'the hard fact remains that our forces, including Dominion contingents, will be engaged in an operation more hazardous than it seemed a week ago'.

A later telegram gave details of the probable time the enemy and Allied forces would take to reach the Aliakmon line. The first British troops should take up positions between March 16 and 19. The first flight had in fact sailed from Egypt on the 4th (Operation 'Lustre').

In the meantime the Foreign Secretary had determined to make a fresh approach to Belgrade but this also was to lead to nothing effective.

The result of the *démarche* to Yugoslavia was not known when the Cabinet met on the afternoon of March 5, with Mr. Menzies again present, but the change in the situation was disturbing enough. They had now learnt from Egypt that the Canal had been again mined and might not be passable for a week and that the operation against Rhodes could not be attempted until after the movement of forces to Greece, in fact until April. The Chiefs of Staff had pointed out that these two factors would not only affect our time-table but compel the division of part of our air forces to neutralise enemy air action from the Dodecanese. The Cabinet were evidently surprised that Eden and Dill should still think success possible and felt that the whole

G G

question must be reconsidered: it would be wrong to urge the Greeks against their better judgement to fight Germany now that the prospects of a Balkan combination were so slight. A draft telegram from the Prime Minister to Mr. Eden on these lines was approved at a meeting of the Defence Committee that night, containing the warning: 'Grave Imperial issues are raised by committing New Zealand and Australian troops to an enterprise which, as you say, has become even more hazardous. We are bound to lay before the Dominion Governments your [telegram of March 5] and Chiefs of Staff appreciation. Cannot forecast their assent to operation. We do not see any reason for expecting success except that, of course, we attach great weight to opinions of Dill and Wavell.' Mr. Eden must understand that the Cabinet next day would probably decide to call off the whole affair.[1]

But matters turned out otherwise. Telegrams from our Minister at Athens insisting that the Greeks would fight in any case and that it was 'unthinkable' that we could go back on the signed agreement began to swing opinion over, but the Cabinet agreed on the 6th that a decision must wait on further information. On the same day important signals were sent from Egypt. Eden and Dill and the three Commanders-in-Chief had not yet received the Prime Minister's telegram of the night of March 5, but after re-examining the question they were unanimous that in spite of everything the decision taken at Athens had been right. Dill signalled that Wavell had explained the additional risks to the commanders of the Dominion forces, Generals Blamey and Freyberg, and both had 'expressed their willingness' to incur them.[2] Moreover Headquarters, Middle East, considered that the Chiefs of Staff had underestimated the time which the Germans would need to reach the Aliakmon position in force.

With these telegrams before them, and influenced by the Chiefs of Staff's opinion in favour of accepting the judgement of our advisers on the spot that the campaign would not be a hopeless venture, and of proceeding accordingly, the Cabinet on March 7 confirmed their previous decision to give the agreed assistance to the Greeks. The Prime Minister so informed Mr. Eden, saying that the Cabinet accepted fullest responsibility. The same day came supporting telegrams from Cairo, where after the receipt of Mr. Churchill's signal of the night of the 5th the position had again been reviewed with the Commanders-in-Chief and General Smuts. It was true that Longmore was very short of aircraft, particularly fighters, and was by no

---

[1] Churchill III 90.

[2] The Dominion Governments were of opinion afterwards that the views of their commanders on the feasibility of the proposal had not been properly ascertained or reported; but the commanders themselves seem to have been uncertain what their responsibilities were in such a case.

means confident that he could give adequate air support; it was true that the naval situation had worsened, and that Cunningham could not guarantee to clear the Greek ports of air-sown mines; but Wavell considered that, if his forces could be once concentrated on the Aliakmon position, there was 'a good chance of holding the enemy advance'. However that might be, all were agreed that we should help the Greeks.[1]

It is often difficult to disengage purely military from political motives; grand strategy must give weight to both. In this case it would seem that the dominant feeling at Cairo was that the 'collapse of Greece without further effort on our part to save her by intervention on land, after the Libyan victories had, as all the world knows, made forces available, would be the greatest calamity'. The effect on Balkan resistance would be deplorable. 'No doubt our prestige will suffer if we are ignominiously ejected, but we should presumably escape the ignominy [*sic*], and in any event to have fought and suffered in Greece would be less damaging to us than to have left Greece to her fate'. It is often difficult also to disengage motives of honour from motives of policy. The decision in London appears to have been made on much the same grounds as these, with the exception that the military arguments had to be taken at second hand—or indeed at third hand, since Dill and Wavell had not reconnoitred the terrain.[2] It is remarkable that no 'precise military appreciation', such as Mr. Churchill asked for, was ever received from Cairo; nor does account seem to have been taken in London of the drain on our resources in Egypt which a prolonged campaign in Greece would imply; in fact, no considered estimate was made of how much we were prepared to lose.

The difficult decision was rendered more delicate by the fact that so large a part had to be assigned to troops from outside the United Kingdom—two Australian divisions, and the New Zealand and Polish formations which composed so high and precious a proportion of their countries' fighting strength.[3] The Prime Minister confessed that he much regretted that we were not using a single United Kingdom division—though a very large percentage of the total force came in fact from the British Isles.

Mr. Menzies was present at the Cabinet on the 7th and concurred in its decisions, to which the assent of the two Dominions was to be asked. But at the meeting on the previous day he pointed out that these Governments could not feel bound by an agreement signed by a British general at Athens without their approval, especially when the enterprise, always hazardous, was now admitted to have become

---

[1] Important telegrams are printed in Churchill III 90–94.

[2] See Lord Wilson of Libya, *Eight years Overseas 1939–1947* (1948) p. 100.

[3] General Sikorski agreed on 14 March to the despatch of the Polish brigade.

even more so. Mr. Eden's instructions, Mr. Menzies might have said, had authorised him to act on his own authority if the urgency was too great to permit reference home, but these instructions had never received the sanction of the Dominion Governments. Mr. Menzies argued that their approval should be asked for on the ground, not that we were committed by an agreement signed by a United Kingdom general at Athens, but that we could not leave the Greeks in the lurch when they were determined to fight on, and that our military advisers on the spot thought we had a fair chance. Mr. Churchill expressed this point of view in a signal of the 7th to Eden.

The New Zealand Government in fact replied promptly, underlining the fact that the operation had become much more hazardous, urging immediate consideration of the means of withdrawal, should that become necessary, but agreeing that we could not possibly abandon the Greeks and therefore accepting the United Kingdom proposal. 'In this dangerous enterprise they are confident that the New Zealand troops will worthily uphold their traditions and indeed would be the first to approve the decision now taken.'[1]

The reaction of the Australian Government was similar: they regarded the project as 'a desperate venture' and asked Mr. Menzies for a further statement of the grounds for arguing a reasonable chance of success: they protested moreover against the action of a British Minister in entering into an agreement affecting Dominion troops without prior consultation. The 'repetition of such an action might well have far-reaching and unfortunate Imperial repercussions'. Nevertheless they gave their consent. A feeling, however, remained that before committing themselves to important changes of policy, such as the despatch of large forces to Greece, which closely affected the Dominions, London ought to consult their Governments at an earlier stage, and that machinery should be devised for this purpose.[2]

Hopes of building up some sort of combined Balkan resistance to German aggression died hard. The action of Yugoslavia was crucial. If she could be induced to regard a German advance on Salonika as a *casus belli* she should be able to strike with effect at the flank of such an advance;[3] she could also put the Italian army in Albania in extreme peril. Should she on the other hand allow passage to German troops, they could turn the Greek positions, both east and west, by an offensive through the undefended Monastir Gap into northern Greece.[4]

---

[1] See N.Z. *Official History, Documents* I 246–263.

[2] See below, ch. xxiv. For the Australian view see Gavin Long, *Greece, Crete and Syria* (Canberra 1953); P. Hasluck, *The Government and the People* (1952) pp. 334–338, both in the series '*Australia in the War of 1939–1945*'; the New Zealand view was stated by Mr. Fraser when he visited London in June.

[3] For Hitler's apprehensions see Ciano, *Diplomatic Papers* p. 432 (25 March).

[4] See Map 18.

In the hope that Yugoslavia might be induced to take the line we desired by a promise of support from Turkey, Mr. Eden arranged a meeting with the Turkish Foreign Minister in Cyprus on March 18 and 19. Nothing, however, came of this. Hitler had on March 4, when entering Bulgaria, assured the Turkish President that he had no intention of approaching the frontiers of Turkey; to which the Turks had replied that neither would they take the initiative in military action against Germany. The Chiefs of Staff did not at this time expect Turkey to take offensive action, but her refusal to make the desired approach to Yugoslavia was disappointing.

The attitude of Yugoslavia herself was more disappointing still. Her Government would not accept a visit from Mr. Eden or the Chief of the Imperial General Staff, and, in spite of strong diplomatic pressure from the British side, were induced at length, on March 25, to sign the Tripartite Pact at Vienna. Rumours that such a capitulation was on foot, however, aroused popular indignation in the country and, with the encouragement of British elements, a *coup d'état* took place in Belgrade on the morning of March 27; the pro-Axis Government was overthrown and General Simovitch became President of the Council. Thereupon Mr. Eden and Sir John Dill, who had reached Malta on their return flight from Cairo, returned to Athens forthwith.

For a few days prospects looked bright. It seemed that Hitler had overreached himself—as indeed he had, but not to the immediate benefit of Greece and the British Empire.[1] The Prime Minister saw a golden chance of at last uniting the three Balkan States with ourselves in a coalition which might deter the Germans from attacking; they might even 'think it better business to take it out of Russia'. Events at Belgrade had put 'Lustre' in its true setting, 'not as an isolated military act, but as a prime mover in a large design'; the decision was already justified.[2] Papagos for his part was eager to push troops forward to defend Salonika, but it was agreed that we must first make sure of Yugoslavia.

General Simovitch, as it happened, was willing to receive Sir John Dill, though not Mr. Eden: the new Government were most anxious not to provoke war with Germany. Nothing resulted, however, from the visit except an abortive meeting between British, Greek and Yugoslav generals near Florina, close to the Yugoslav frontier, on April 3. Three days later the Germans attacked both Greece and Yugoslavia.

In East Africa we were gaining more permanent successes.[3] Both

---

[1] See below, ch. xxiii.
[2] Churchill III 151–152.
[3] See Map 16.

in the north and in the south the forces of the Commonwealth were making notable progress. General Platt in Eritrea, having been held up for some weeks by the mountain defences of Keren, broke his way through on March 27 and on April 8 reached Massawa on the Red Sea coast; this had the desired effect of enabling President Roosevelt to allow United States vessels to enter the Red Sea and so relieving the strain on British shipping. General Cunningham, after driving the Italians out of Somalia—we seemed, as the Prime Minister pleasantly said, 'to have swopped Somalilands with the enemy'—had struck into Abyssinia; on March 26 he had occupied Harar, and on April 6 his forces entered Addis Ababa. On May 5 the Emperor re-entered his capital, and a fortnight later the Duke of Aosta himself surrendered at Amba Alagi. Considerable enemy forces remained under arms, and fighting went on until the capture of Gondar at the end of November, but the back of Italian resistance was broken, and the Indian and South African divisions could be transferred to Egypt.

The whole campaign was a masterpiece of administrative planning and of economising force. Such economy was most necessary, since though the campaign destroyed an empire it was always a side-show. Commanders knew that even when the richest prizes were within their reach they might have to surrender the means of securing them in order to serve some distant end judged more important by Cairo or London. From Wavell's point of view it was a question of precisely how soon he could switch a formation to another region where it could be still more useful. He was complimented by the Prime Minister on his 'exact measurements'.

Hard on the land successes at Harar and Keren followed a brilliant naval victory; the Italian battleship *Vittorio Veneto* was damaged and three 8-inch cruisers destroyed in a fleet action off Cape Matapan on the night of March 28.[1] This reward to the long and tedious labours of Admiral Cunningham's force was immensely heartening at a time when the Greek expedition was making new and exacting demands on it. As the Admiral had pointed out on March 4, when the first convoy was about to start, the transport of 'Lustre' force would absorb the whole activity of the Fleet for two months and would rule out the possibility of 'Mandibles' and other offensive operations for the time being. His resources for the next two months would be 'taxed to the limit'; indeed 'by normal security standards' his commitments exceeded his resources. Fortunately the disabled carrier *Illustrious* had been replaced by the *Formidable* and Cunningham had again felt justified in escorting a convoy to Malta; but on

---

[1] See Playfair II, ch. iv; Roskill I, ch. xx.

the 26th the 8-inch cruiser *York* fell a victim to motor-torpedo-boat attack in Suda Bay, and on the 31st the cruiser *Bonaventure* was torpedoed and sunk south of Crete.

Throughout the month of March the building up of 'Lustre' force in Greece proceeded steadily; the job was carried out by the Navy without a single casualty to the expedition, though at some loss to ships which had disposed of their cargoes. But a few days before the Germans crossed the Greek frontier events occurred in Libya which gravely affected Wavell's dispositions.

General Wavell's original approval of the Greek project had been given on two suppositions: that the Greeks would supply such a force at the right place as would afford a reasonable hope of defending their country, and that adequate forces would be left in Egypt to safeguard its western flank. We have seen how the prospect in Greece was darkened by General Papagos's failure to move the expected divisions to the Aliakmon position directly after the first conversations with the British; we have now to see how the other supposition also proved to be ill-founded.

On February 27 the War Office asked Wavell for an appreciation of the position in Egypt and Cyrenaica in view of the arrival of German armoured formations in Tripolitania. He replied on March 2 that there was no evidence that the Germans had landed more than one armoured brigade group at Tripoli.[1] The distance thence to Benghazi and the poverty of communications and water supply made it unlikely that they could maintain a large enough force to advance against Benghazi in the near future; nor could a larger offensive— three or four divisions was the most that could be maintained from Tripoli—well develop before the end of the summer. The garrison of Cyrenaica would soon consist of the 3rd Armoured Brigade (of the 2nd Armoured Division, the other brigade of which was destined for Greece), the 9th Australian Division, and the 3rd Indian Motor Brigade. The two last were incompletely trained and equipped, and more anti-tank units were urgently required. It was in the air that we were perilously weak, now that German bombers were troubling us from Tripoli, Sicily and the Dodecanese.

During March evidence accumulated of the presence of German armour in Libya and Wavell reported on the 20th that the situation on the Cyrenaican frontier was 'causing some anxiety'. But he thought administrative problems should preclude anything but a limited advance by the enemy. On the 26th the Prime Minister

---

[1] The greater part of this telegram is printed in Churchill III 174. Owing to the Government's anxiety not to provoke Italy, we had been able to procure very little information from Libya in the months preceding her entry into the war.

expressed concern at the rapid German advance to El Agheila on the frontier, and next day Wavell admitted that he had taken considerable risks in Cyrenaica after the capture of Benghazi, in order to provide the greatest possible support for Greece. He was now weak in Cyrenaica and no armoured reinforcements were available, since the 7th Armoured Division was refitting after its great exploits. The next month or two would be anxious.

We now know that when the *Afrika Corps*, which then consisted of one Light (motorised) division, landed at Tripoli in mid-February the sole intention of the high command was to use it for defence against a British advance into Tripolitania, then considered a serious danger. By the beginning of March Rommel was satisfied that this task had been accomplished, and he suggested to *OKH* that he should go over to the offensive before the hot weather began. His proposal was not sanctioned, and it seems probable that when he returned to his command on March 23 from a visit to Berlin and Rome he had no immediate intention of launching an attack. He decided, however, to exploit the defeat of the British detachment at El Agheila on the 24th, and one success against weak opposition followed another until Wavell's territorial gains of the winter had been wiped out. 'There'll be consternation amongst our masters in Tripoli and Rome, and perhaps in Berlin too', wrote Rommel on April 3; 'I took the risk against all orders and instructions because the opportunity seemed favourable . . .'[1]

The British force evacuated Benghazi that day, and by April 11 or thereabouts was back on the Egyptian frontier, except for a garrison, composed mostly of Australians, left invested in Tobruk. Little of the 2nd Armoured Division escaped destruction or capture. In the confusion of the retreat both General O'Connor, commanding British troops in Egypt, and General Neame, commanding in Cyrenaica, were taken prisoner. To command in the Western Desert Wavell now appointed Major-General N. M. Beresford Peirse, who had shown himself at Sidi Barrani and in Eritrea a 'fine fighting commander'.

The story of this disaster and its causes are told elsewhere.[2] The disorganisation of our plans was serious. Wavell was not sure, on the 10th and 13th, of his ability to hold even Tobruk indefinitely, and he had practically no reserves in hand except the British 6th Infantry Division, earmarked for 'Mandibles', and detachments of Australian and New Zealand troops arriving as reinforcements for Greece. Cunningham was considering the possibility of having to move the fleet to Port Said or Haifa, using Alexandria only as an advanced base, and Wavell retained the Polish brigade for the port's defence.

---

[1] *The Rommel Papers* (ed. B. H. Liddell Hart, 1953) p. 111.
[2] See Playfair II ch. ii.

On the 17th Wavell signalled that he had decided to suspend all further reinforcement of 'Lustre'.

The Chiefs of Staff, with the Prime Minister presiding, ruled on April 3 that 'the re-establishment of a front in Cyrenaica should have priority in the resources of all three Services in the Middle East' and approved Wavell's proposal that 'Mandibles' should be postponed, despite the consequences, and that the 7th Australian Division should not move to Greece for the present. The Chief of the Air Staff was now of opinion that the need for fighters was greater in the Middle East than at home, and it was agreed on the 7th to send out six complete Hurricane squadrons. Hurricanes and Blenheims were also coming in well via Takoradi, so Longmore reported. On land Wavell was very short of armour; the Prime Minister was determined that he must be reinforced with tanks with all speed and at all costs, and on the 21st it was decided that a convoy of fast merchant ships should be sailed through the Mediterranean (operation 'Tiger'), leaving the United Kingdom on the 26th; Force H would be strengthened by the battleship *Queen Elizabeth* for this occasion.[1] The Commander-in-Chief, Home Forces, had recently expressed concern at the reduction of our armoured strength in Great Britain, and Sir John Dill was opposed to the despatch of as many cruiser tanks as the Prime Minister demanded; naval objections too might be raised to the running of such risks on the passage; but the convoy with additional cruiser tanks duly arrived in Egypt on May 12, after losing one ship to a mine. 'Tiger' brought in 43 Hurricanes and 238 tanks, but less than half the latter were cruisers, the type most in demand for operations in the desert.

It was no less important to prevent the enemy from reinforcing Rommel, and the Prime Minister and the Admiralty urged on Cunningham the need of cutting the vital thread in his supply line. On April 16 the Chiefs of Staff despatched to the Middle East a directive on the War in the Mediterranean by the Prime Minister and Minister of Defence, stating that it became the prime duty of the Mediterranean fleet to stop all sea-borne traffic between Italy and Africa by the fullest use of surface craft, aided so far as possible by aircraft and submarines. 'Heavy losses in battleships, cruisers and destroyers must if necessary be accepted. The harbour at Tripoli must be rendered unusable by recurrent bombardment, and/or by blocking and mining.' The reputation of the Navy was engaged in stopping this traffic. Tactical directions for operations by land and sea were included.[2]

The importance of cutting Rommel's sea communications was of

---

[1] See Churchill III 216–220.
[2] *ibid.* 186–188.

course realised by Admiral Cunningham, but the vulnerable part of
the enemy's convoy route was short. Much of it passed along the
Sicilian and African coasts, and the only section in open sea was
between Sicily and Cape Bon in Tunisia. It was not yet possible to
station the fleet at Malta, but on April 16 four destroyers from the
island, under Captain P. J. Mack, succeeded, at the cost of one of
their number, in sinking an entire convoy of five enemy ships with
their three escorts. However, the activity of the Luftwaffe made
action by surface ships difficult and dangerous, and most of our
successes in this work fell to the submarines.

The Admiralty and Defence Committee had for some days been
considering how the port of Tripoli might be bottled up by bombing
or blocking. 'The effectual blocking of Tripoli harbour would be well
worth a battleship upon the active list,' said the Prime Minister in
the directive quoted: he thought that bold action was justified by the
present attitude of President Roosevelt, and that there was little
chance of Japan coming in against us at the moment. Admiral
Cunningham's views as to how the desired end could best be
achieved differed sharply from those of the authorities at home, but
eventually on April 21 the battle fleet bombarded the harbour at
close range. The results were small and, contrary to the Admiral's
expectation, were achieved without loss; but in his view it had been
an unjustifiable gamble. It appeared to him that Whitehall did not
realise under what a strain the fleet was working or the impossibility
of its meeting its numerous commitments without a great increase in
air strength at Malta and elsewhere.[1]

The set-back in Cyrenaica was troublesome enough, especially in
view of bad news from Greece and Iraq. But the immediate threat to
Egypt did not develop. We now know that Rommel was even more
surprised by his initial success than Wavell had been by his own in
December, and though he was quick to exploit he was not ready for
any far-reaching operations. He knew also that Hitler did not think
it would be possible to renew the offensive against Egypt before next
October.

Wavell was of opinion by the end of April that the enemy had shot
his bolt for the present and, while admitting that German performance often surpassed expectations, calculated that a force composed
of two German divisions (one Light and one Armoured) supported
by two Italian would not be ready for a forward move till mid-June.
The Prime Minister was accordingly eager that Wavell should resume
the offensive as soon as possible. On April 14 Mr. Churchill had
urged that Tobruk, now cut off by the enemy, should be regarded as

---

[1] See Playfair II ch. xxix, Roskill I ch. xx; the views of the Prime Minister and the
Admiral are stated in Churchill III 211–216 and *A Sailor's Odyssey* pp. 340–351.

a sally-port or bridgehead; on the 28th, when disaster in Greece had brought our fortunes low, he not only stressed the need for fighting every inch of the way in Egypt but thought Sir John Dill should impress on Wavell the need for hard fighting and bold action. Dill replied that our troops were inferior to the Germans in nothing but equipment; in desert fighting everything depended on tanks; he was sure that when the tank situation improved the Commander-in-Chief would not be lacking in action.

The need for air reinforcements was constantly being urged by the commanders in the Middle East and constantly engaged the attention of the Departments at home. Takoradi was now in full use for conveyance of aircraft to Egypt, but there was also strong pressure for the strengthening of Malta. On occasion fighters could be flown in from a carrier sailing from Gibraltar, but the Admiralty warned Longmore that this could not be a routine matter, especially when the presence of German heavy ships in the Atlantic or at Brest required the use of our own battleships for escorting ocean convoys. Controversy also arose from discrepancies between numbers of aircraft sent from England and received in Egypt, due partly to the time-lag occurring on the Takoradi route.

The German offensive in the Balkans began on April 6. Its shape had been recast after the Yugoslav *coup d'état*. The original plan of 'Marita' had not implied violation of Yugoslav territory, but Hitler now declared that Yugoslavia was to be regarded as an enemy and destroyed as quickly as possible, even if she proclaimed her loyalty to Germany. His intention was to break into the country by converging attacks from Styria in the north-west and Sofia in the south-east; at the same time, by a westerly attack from Kustendil in Bulgaria, he would cut off southern Serbia, which would serve as a base for Italo-German operations against Greece. He hoped to bribe Hungary and Bulgaria to join in this offensive by increase of territory and to foment internal Yugoslav discord by promises to the Croats. The Luftwaffe was to destroy the city of Belgrade as soon as its strength and the weather allowed, and about the same time, not earlier, 'Marita' was to be launched with the initial objective of seizing the Salonika basin and a foothold on 'the heights of Edessa'; for this purpose one of the corps of Twelfth Army might move into position in Yugoslav territory.[1]

The course of the campaign will be only briefly summarised. Approximately ten divisions of the German Twelfth Army fought in Greece, and five, including three Armoured, were in action against

---

[1] *F.D.* No. 25 p. 161, 27 March 1941.

the British. The attack was directed against both Greece and Yugo-slavia. In Thrace and East Macedonia the invaders struck south from Bulgaria at four points, in greatest force at the westernmost, down the Struma Valley. These thrusts in a few days effectively overpowered Salonika and the region east of it. More dangerous to the Allied cause was the westerly drive into southern Serbia, overwhelming the Yugoslav forces and intended both to join up with the Italians in Albania and to turn the inner flanks of the Greek army in that region and General Wilson's forces in the east.

As agreed with Papagos on March 4, General Wilson was to hold the Aliakmon position, but when the offensive opened none of the troops had had time to settle in. Resistance in southern Serbia col-lapsed on April 8 before any common plan had been concerted by the Allies, and in view of the strategical situation on his left Wilson on the 9th ordered a first withdrawal, to begin on the night of the 11th/12th, by which time the detachment guarding the road from Monastir to the south was heavily engaged with the Germans. It was clear that the Allied line was strung out too thin to prevent penetra-tion of the long front, and the left was still in danger, particularly in view of the unwillingness of the Greek Government to sanction a withdrawal of their victorious but exhausted army in Albania. Accordingly, late on the 14th Wilson ordered a further retirement to the shorter Thermopylae position. There was hard fighting here as there had been further north, but the uncovering of the Epirus front, where the Greek forces had come to the end of their tether, made prolonged resistance anywhere impossible. Papagos first on 16 April suggested the departure of the British Empire contingent, and the final decision to evacuate was taken in Athens on the 21st with the full approval of the Greek Government; by this time resistance in Epirus had collapsed. General Blamey, commanding the Australians and New Zealanders, now reunited in an Anzac Corps, agreed that re-embarkation was necessary, and the British Cabinet endorsed the decision that afternoon.

Hitler had achieved most of the aims of his Directive No. 27 of April 14:[1] the break-up of the Greco-British forces and the ejection of the British from the Balkans, a break-through in Albania and a southward advance to the Gulf of Corinth, and he was soon in occupation of the whole of the peninsula. But he did not 'envelop' his enemy by a break through towards Larissa, nor did he prevent the evacuation of the bulk of the British force.

Longmore had asked the Air Ministry for a general air directive on the 17th which should indicate 'relative priorities' to govern the use of his inadequate force in the predicament seen to be impending. On

---

[1] *F.D.* No. 27, p. 166.

the 18th a reply came in the form of a directive from the Prime Minister issued by the Chiefs of Staff to the Commanders-in-Chief. It pointed out that no 'precise sequence and priority' could be laid down between interests none of which could be wholly ignored. 'The extrication of the New Zealand, Australian and British troops from Greece affects the whole Empire,' but the general principle to be observed was that 'victory in Libya counts first, evacuation of troops from Greece second'.[1] The evacuation—operation 'Demon', a second and perhaps more difficult 'Dynamo'—was an exceedingly hazardous affair which tried the capacity of the Navy to the utmost. The Luftwaffe had at the outset of the campaign rendered the Piraeus almost unusable as a port by a devastating raid, and throughout, except when weather forbade, they enjoyed a superiority in the air which by the time of the evacuation had become supremacy. On April 6, when the Germans invaded Greece, we had only the equivalent of eight squadrons—say 80 serviceable aircraft—against an enemy force at least ten times as powerful. Wavell claimed that only in numerical superiority in aircraft and armoured fighting vehicles had the enemy the advantage of our forces; but that was enough. Embarkation began on the 24th and continued from various beaches until the night of the 28th/29th. About 62,000 British Service personnel had been transported to Greece (some 58,000 of them in the 'Lustre' convoys); the number of Allied personnel embarked from the beaches was rather over 50,000. But the losses in equipment, including artillery and transport, were crippling.[2]

It followed that the Germans now secured control of the Aegean Sea and the Greek islands, with the exception—for the present—of Crete, where the King of the Hellenes and his new Prime Minister, M. Tsouderos, proposed to establish the Government. Yugoslavia had capitulated on the 17th, but not till she had imposed a delay on Hitler's plans which was to prove of immense importance.

The motives which induced the three Governments of the British Commonwealth to sanction so risky an enterprise have been discussed already: honour, prestige and the hope of upsetting the German plans in the Balkans. Wavell was convinced that there was a fair chance of holding the enemy, and Sir John Dill did not dissent. It was possible that we might achieve a great success, and even total failure would hardly endanger our chances of winning the war. We took a risk on a stake we thought we could afford. Does the result of the venture throw any further light on the question whether it was justifiable?

---

[1] Churchill III 201.

[2] For the numbers see Playfair II ch. v; many telegrams are printed in *N.Z. Official History, Documents* I 265–278.

Sir John Dill, arriving home on April 10, was anxious about the defence of Egypt and already feared a bad mistake had been made. General Maitland Wilson, writing eight years later, says that at the time he thought the venture 'politically and morally right', but from the strictly military aspect a gamble; how much of a gamble he did not realise until he arrived in the country and experienced for himself the difficulties both of the terrain and of working or planning with the Greek and Yugoslav armies; he considers that we suffered from an inadequate intelligence service in the Balkans.[1] General de Guingand, writing in 1946, records how his misgivings as a junior staff officer appreciating the prospects of the expedition on paper were confirmed by a reconnaissance of the ground at the end of February—the width of the front and the wretchedness of the communications.[2] The roads were unsuitable for heavy traffic, particularly after rain, and the few airfields made the dispersion of aircraft difficult.

The Greeks had fought heroically against the Italians, but the after-effects of the rigorous winter and shortage of arms and equipment made them no match for the Germans. From the outset uncertainty as to the reliance which could be placed on Yugoslavia bedevilled the strategy of the campaign. Mr. Churchill wrote after its failure that personally he had never expected the Greek venture to succeed unless Turkey and Yugoslavia both came in. One must be chary in accepting at face value any man's *obiter dictum* as to his thoughts several weeks previously, but it would seem that only a very sanguine nature could, after our many rebuffs, have expected Turkish intervention; while the hope of Yugoslav belligerency, though actually fulfilled, was founded on no firm knowledge of the country's military strength.

In the appreciation of possible action by Yugoslavia, which they produced on March 28, the day after the *coup d'état*, the Joint Intelligence Committee expressed the view that the new Simovitch Government should, despite the existence of disintegrating elements, be able to maintain the unity of the country, at any rate in the south. The morale of the army, of which four-fifths (800,000 men) was mobilised, was high; the twenty-four infantry divisions were strong in manpower but weak in artillery and especially, like most armies, in anti-aircraft and anti-tank guns. Yugoslavia had the best equipped and trained air force of the Balkan countries—about 170 bombers and 120 fighters of modern types—but spares were short, and there was only enough aviation spirit for one month's intensive operations. It was hoped, as we have seen, that the Yugoslavs would attack the

---

[1] Lord Wilson of Libya, *Eight Years Overseas 1939–1947* pp. 70, 74.
[2] Sir F. de Guingand, *Operation Victory* (1946) ch. iii.

Italians in Albania and, in co-operation with the Greeks, dispose of them in two to three weeks; also that the difficulty of the ground and communications on the Bulgarian frontier would hold up a German attack from that quarter.

The Joint Planning Staff, however, appreciating the situation on April 8, two days after the German aggression but before the news of operations had come through, while wrong in supposing that the offensives in the Balkans and in Libya were part of a co-ordinated plan, took a more realistic view of what might be expected in the north. They thought that Yugoslavia's resistance was not likely to be prolonged and that her collapse would enable the enemy to widen his front against Greece. It is indeed surprising that in view of Germany's military record, her vastly superior armaments and her proximity we should have expected the Balkan countries to join in the war against her or, if they did, to withstand her. It would appear that in such matters the Norwegian campaign had taught us little. The New Zealand Government had seen matters from a distance in clearer perspective; they advised on March 9 that there seemed small prospect of Yugoslav or Turkish assistance, and consequently the possibility of such assistance should be entirely disregarded. Had we taken this advice and been able to persuade our Greek allies to take it, more would have been done to prepare the Aliakmon position and the danger from the direction of Monastir could not have been neglected. That is not to say that we should have stopped the Germans. But even as it was they were made to fight hard for their gains.

The story illustrates, as has been said above, the difficulty of disentangling military and political motives. To form a Balkan front, which would deny Greek bases and airfields to Germany while enabling Allied bombers to attack the Roumanian oilfields, was a military object of the first importance; it was also closely entwined with the sense of obligation to continue our pledged assistance to the Greeks. To what extent the desire to achieve these objects may have persuaded the military advisers of the Government that the achievement was possible can only be guessed; all were convinced that the attempt must be made.

Our defeats in Cyrenaica and Greece naturally caused great dissatisfaction at home. The Government thought it well to ask for a vote of confidence specifically approving the decision to send help to Greece. The debate took place on May 6 and 7, almost exactly a year since the fateful debate on the Norway campaign which had brought Mr. Churchill into power. But the tone was as different as the result —a majority of 447 to 3. There was no suggestion of a change of

Government and indeed no one challenged the decision to send help to the Greeks—honour was held to have demanded it; but our diplomacy, our intelligence service, the reticence of our communiqués and, to a lesser degree, our organisation for war come in for a good deal of criticism. The Prime Minister defended the demand for a vote of confidence above all as an assurance to foreign countries that the national purpose had not weakened. He doubted whether Italy and Germany would gain in the long run by their aggressions in the Balkans. He asserted our determination to fight for the Nile Valley and the Suez Canal and Malta and our position in the Mediterranean with all the resources of the British Empire, and he declared that we intended to defend 'to the death and without thought of retirement the valuable and highly offensive outposts of Crete and Tobruk'.[1]

It was said above that bad news had been received from Iraq. This requires explanation.

Iraq was bound by a treaty of 1930 to give Great Britain aid in war and to allow the full use of her communications for the passage of troops. There was a British mission with the Iraqi army, and the Royal Air Force had stations at Habbaniya some forty miles west of Baghdad and at Shaiba near Basra.[2] The Iraqi Government had broken off diplomatic relations with Germany, but not with Italy when she declared war on Britain; the anti-British Rashid Ali was then in power, supported by a clique of high army officers known as the Golden Square. Rashid Ali resigned in January 1941, but relations had still not been broken off with Italy when, at the beginning of April, he regained power by a *coup d'état*. This involved the flight of the Regent, who was friendly inclined to Great Britain, and the British Government refused to recognise the new régime.

Iraq was of great strategic importance. Through it passed not only the pipe-lines carrying oil to Haifa and Lebanese Tripoli but the land route to the Persian Gulf. Towards the end of March 1941 Basra acquired special interest as a possible port for the trans-shipment of American supplies for the Middle East, particularly aircraft. On April 8 the Joint Planning Staff, in a report on military policy in the Middle East, recommended that all possible steps should be taken to overthrow Rashid Ali's Government and that India should be asked to send a small force at once to Basra. (Since the middle of 1940 it had been the British Government's intention to send a division from India to Basra to counteract hostile influences, but the troops had been despatched to Egypt instead.) Action was taken at once: the Viceroy

---

[1] *House of Commons Debates* vol. 371, cols. 727–826, 867–946.
[2] See Map 19.

agreed to divert to Basra a brigade already embarked for Malaya, with two further brigades to follow, and London accepted the offer in view of the slackening of tension in the Far East. It was decided also to send troops by air from India to Shaiba, to arrive at the same time as the convoy.

The troops were being sent, said the Chiefs of Staff, in order to stabilise the situation in Iraq and keep out Axis influence; they would also add security to our oil interests and the air reinforcement route. Although the treaty provided that Iraq should help Great Britain in war, Rashid Ali objected to the stationing of British troops in the country and there were long discussions as to the best means of overcoming his reluctance to allow our forces to land. Eventually hostilities broke out. On the night of April 29/30 Iraqi troops surrounded the British air base at Habbaniya; in Baghdad the recently arrived Ambassador, Sir Kinahan Cornwallis, and the British community were prevented from leaving the Embassy. By the evening of May 1st the force threatening Habbaniya amounted to some 9,000 men with artillery, and the flood season made ground movement from Basra difficult. Habbaniya was merely a training base, which had in the last few days been reinforced by a few aircraft from the Middle East and some British infantry flown from Basra. After desultory fighting the British aircraft on the 7th dispersed the besieging forces, and on the same day the garrison made a successful sortie which removed the immediate threat to Habbaniya; Iraqi forces continued, however, to block the road to Baghdad.

Iraq had from the beginning of the war fallen within Middle East command, but had recently, at the time of the landing of the Indian brigade at Basra on April 18, been transferred to Commander-in-Chief, India. On May 2, however, in view of the trouble at Habbaniya, the Defence Committee decided to hand the responsibility back, temporarily, to Middle East, and Wavell was invited to send all possible help to Air Officer Commanding, Iraq (Air Vice-Marshal Smart). Wavell was thus faced with fresh demands just when, as he replied to the War Office, his forces were 'stretched to limit everywhere' with preparations for recovery in the Western Desert and for the defence of Crete. His first response was to protest against accepting responsibility for a force at Basra of whose dispositions and strength he was ignorant; nothing short of a brigade group with strong support of artillery and tanks could restore the situation in Iraq, and to send weak forces of cavalry or infantry, which was all he had in Palestine, seemed merely asking for trouble. He and Longmore could only advise negotiation with the Iraqis, with the threat of blockade and air bombardment as the alternative to a settlement by consent. But in a later signal on the same day he calculated that, at the risk of leaving Palestine 'most dangerously weak', he could

HH

scrape together one mechanised brigade, one infantry battalion and the greater part of a field artillery regiment. These, with an Arab contingent, were the elements out of which 'Habforce' was improvised.

Wavell was not convinced by an assurance from the Chiefs of Staff that the commitment in Iraq was inevitable owing to the country's military importance and that we could make no concessions to Rashid Ali. But the Defence Committee, with Air Chief Marshal Longmore present, refused to accept Wavell's gloomy view of the situation; the Iraqis, they thought, had taken action before their German friends were ready, and should not be regarded as formidable. The force as proposed by Wavell, strengthened if possible by a few light tanks, should start without delay. 'Habforce' in fact reached Habbaniya on May 18 and, after some fighting, the outskirts of Baghdad on the 30th. This was the end of an episode which, had Rashid Ali and his party shown more determination and the Axis been able to provide adequate support, might have had serious consequences for the British.

We now know that, although the Germans had long planned to stir up trouble for the British in Arab lands, they had made no effective arrangements for the supply of war material to the insurgents before the *coup d'état*. Not till the middle of May were arms and supplies beginning to trickle through from Syria, after negotiations with Vichy and with the Italian Armistice Commission. It was then too late. Nevertheless on May 23, after the arrival of 'Habforce' at Habbaniya, Hitler issued a directive on the Middle East, announcing that he had decided to speed developments in that region by supporting Iraq, but that nothing more ambitious could be taken in hand till after the invasion of Russia. The Arab liberation movement, he said, was Germany's natural ally against Britain, and the Iraq rebellion was of special importance. Support should be rendered by the despatch of a military mission, by air reinforcement and by the delivery of munitions. The air force sent was to be of limited strength; arms were to be despatched from Germany and from Syria 'on the basis of the agreement concluded with the French'. In fact, only a small air detachment arrived, making use of Syrian landing grounds.[1] The prompt action of the British Government had nipped the troublesome affair in the bud and justified the risk taken in sending so small a column to face far superior forces.

The Prime Minister told the Chiefs of Staff that he was deeply disturbed by Wavell's response to the challenge. It was extraordinary that he had never organised a mobile column out of the cavalry units in Palestine. He seemed to have been taken as much by surprise on

[1] See pp 437, 517.

his eastern as he had been on his western flank. 'He gives me the impression of being tired out.'[1]

Wavell was not the only member of the Middle East triumvirate to incur the Prime Minister's displeasure. The three commanders had during this difficult time worked together in notable harmony, but the team was now to be broken up. Air Chief Marshal Longmore was the first to go. It had for some time seemed to the Prime Minister that he complained too much of his shortages, not appreciating the stupendous efforts made at home on his behalf, and failed to make full operational use of what he had. The Chief of the Air Staff defended Longmore on these points, and on April 15 the Prime Minister expressed pleasure at all his 'vigorous reactions'. A fortnight after this he was recalled to England 'for discussion on all aspects of air operations', but on May 18, while he was still at home, it was decided that 'after his most distinguished services in the Middle East' he should now be replaced by his deputy, Air Marshal A. W. Tedder, whose recent appreciation of the situation in that theatre had made a particularly good impression in London.[2] Longmore's task had been an exceedingly difficult one; as his successor put it, 'the main recurring problem in this command is how to apportion the limited air forces immediately available to meet concurrent and often conflicting demands'. Longmore had never had anything approaching the resources required for these demands, and much of what he had was of little fighting value. Maintenance too was a grave problem, by reason not only of the climate but of the absence of well-established Service and civilian repair facilities. He was unfortunate in being relieved of his command just when the days of acute shortage were drawing to a close.

At the same time a mission was sent out from the Ministry of Aircraft Production, under Air Vice-Marshal G. G. Dawson; he was to study the organisation for aircraft maintenance and to become Chief Maintenance Officer at Air Headquarters, Middle East. The subsequent development carried out by Tedder, who had known Dawson at the Ministry of Air Production and welcomed his appointment, was to prove of immense value in the build-up of air strength in the theatre.

---

[1] Printed in Churchill III 228. Iraq was not within Wavell's sphere of responsibility when the threat to Habbaniya developed.

[2] See Sir A. Longmore, *From Sea to Sky* (1946) pp. 282, 285.

CHAPTER XX

THE BATTLE OF THE ATLANTIC.
THE SERVICE PROGRAMMES,
MARCH – JUNE 1941

THE PROGRESS of the economic war in the winter of 1940–41 was sketched in chapter XVII. We must now turn to its development in the spring and early summer of 1941. No sharp break divides the two periods, but there was an intensification of anxiety and effort which won for the latter phase, in particular, the name of the Battle of the Atlantic. The issue at stake in this recurrent struggle was the ability of an island people, self-sufficient in no material respect, to support themselves and to carry on the war. No offensive operations by land or air, in Europe or elsewhere, could save us from defeat if we lost, even for a few weeks, the power to bring in the food and raw materials and armaments without which we could not fight or live.

In the last week of February 1941 the Prime Minister was concerned at the shrinkage of our imports, and the Chiefs of Staff were instructed that the protection of shipping in the North-Western Approaches must now be given an absolute priority. On March 6, as Minister of Defence, he issued a rousing directive.[1]

> 'In view of various German statements, we must assume that the Battle of the Atlantic has begun.
>
> The next four months should enable us to defeat the attempt to strangle our food supplies and our connection with the United States. For this purpose—
>
> 1. We must take the offensive against the U-boat and the Focke-Wulf wherever we can and whenever we can. The U-boat at sea must be hunted, the U-boat in the building yard or in dock must be bombed. The Focke-Wulf and other bombers employed against our shipping must be attacked in the air and in their nests.
>
> 2. Extreme priority will be given to fitting out ships to catapult or otherwise launch fighter aircraft against bombers attacking our shipping. Proposals should be made within a week.
>
> 3. All the measures approved and now in train for the concentration of the main strength of the Coastal Command upon the North-Western Approaches, and their assistance on the East

---

[1] Printed in full in Churchill III 106.

coast by Fighter and Bomber Commands, will be pressed forward. It may be hoped that with the growing daylight and the new routes to be followed, the U-boat menace will soon be reduced. All the more important is it that the Focke-Wulf, and, if it comes, the Junkers 88, should be effectively grappled with.'

In later paragraphs he dealt with such points as the provision of guns, the repair of shipping, the mobility of labour and congestion in the ports. A standing committee of representatives of the Admiralty and the Ministries of Shipping and Transport were to meet daily and report any hitches to Sir Andrew Duncan, the chairman of the recently formed Imports Executive. Besides and above this group of experts a special ministerial body, known as the Battle of the Atlantic Committee, with the Prime Minister himself in the chair, and with power to take emergency decisions, met weekly until the beginning of May.

As we now know, Admiral Raeder was constantly impressing on his master that the economic weapon was the only sure one for bringing Britain to her knees, but that the Navy alone could not command success. 'Working in close co-operation, our planes and submarines are capable of exerting a decisive influence in the struggle against Britain and America. To this end, however, co-ordinated well-directed operations against enemy shipping are essential. Ships afloat must be the target of the submarines; ships in harbours and shipyards must be the target of the Air Force.' The naval staff noted that 'the Führer agrees; he is of precisely the same opinion'. But that did not settle the matter.[1]

It was immediately after this, on February 6, that Hitler issued his Directive No. 23, for the war against the British war economy.[2]

> 'The aim of further operations against the British homeland must be to concentrate all means of naval and air warfare against the enemy's supplies, to slow down the British aircraft industry and, if possible to cause further damage to it. For this purpose it will be necessary: (a) to destroy the most vital British import harbours, especially harbour works and ships at anchor or under construction; (b) to fight shipping with all means at our disposal, especially inbound traffic; (c) to destroy systematically the nerve centres of aircraft production, also the anti-aircraft industry and industries producing powder and explosives. These missions must be carried out by the forces remaining in this area even if strong units of the Air Force are withdrawn to other theatres of operations during the course of the year.'

---

[1] *F.N.C.* p. 178, 4th Feb. 1941.

[2] *F.D.* no. 23, p. 137; this directive was based on an appreciation of January 13 by Jodl.

Plate 2: Mr. Churchill's War Cabinet, 1941.

Back row: Mr. Greenwood, Mr. Bevin, Lord Beaverbrook, Sir Kingsley Wood.
Front row: Sir John Anderson, Mr. Churchill, Mr. Attlee, Mr. Eden.

He added that sinking merchantmen was more important than fighting warships, and concluded by saying that separate orders would be issued for reconnaissance at sea, to provide the necessary co-ordination between sea and air warfare.

Accordingly on February 28 Hitler produced a further directive stating the difference of opinion between the Navy and Air Force with regard to the organisation of coast and sea reconnaissance and defining their respective responsibilities.[1] The main pronouncement affecting the Battle of the Atlantic was that Commander-in-Chief, Air, would be in charge of air reconnaissance and air protection in the Atlantic and would appoint an Air Commander, Atlantic, with headquarters at Lorient. Other paragraphs defined the functions of the two Services in the North Sea and English Channel on a geographical basis. This arrangement would come into force on March 15; it was merely temporary, to meet the emergency period of the coming spring, during which only small air forces could be used against the British Isles.

On March 6, in his Directive No. 1 for the attack on Russia, Hitler stated that the principal target for the Navy remained Britain, and that its duty was to maintain and if possible aggravate the pressure against this main enemy, especially in the Atlantic. The Air Force also would continue the raids against Britain, particularly with a view to cutting off her imports.[2]

As previously, the attempt to disrupt our supply lines took four principal forms: U-boat warfare, air attack, mining and surface raiding.[3] In studying the figures of sinkings, with their differences from month to month, it should be remembered that they represent the totals as known to us now, not as estimated at the time; that there was always a timelag before losses could be reported or assessed; and that classification by months is purely arbitrary. Nevertheless, the increase in our losses after January is striking; the next volume will show how striking also is the decline after June, and to what measures the decline was due. It will be noted that the catastrophic figures for April are swollen by the loss of over 100 ships in the Mediterranean.

The U-boats available for operations numbered at the beginning of February only twenty-one, the lowest figure since the war began; this was partly owing to Admiral Dönitz's insistence on retaining a due proportion for training. From February on, the number rose, but not till July did it equal the initial figure (forty-six) of September 1939. Between August 1940 and July 1941 the number averaged about thirty, of which some sixteen were at sea at any one time.

From February the boats were shifting their scene of operations,

---

[1] *F.D.* p. 143.

[2] *F.D.* p. 150.

[3] See Roskill I, esp. ch. xxi; for figures see below, App. II.

under the pressure of our counter-measures, further out into the Atlantic. From April 1 the blockade zone was extended to include Iceland, and early in May a further westward move (to about 35° West) was ordered. By the spring, with the number of boats rising, the enemy finally adopted the method of attacking in packs, constrained thereto by the growing efficiency of our convoy system. Nevertheless, while in November eight merchantmen were sunk for every U-boat at sea, in the spring the ratio had dropped to two. In March three of the most skilful U-boat commanders were disposed of.

Finding convoys in northern waters harder to locate and attack, U-boats became active again in the central Atlantic in March and enjoyed some successes in the area of Freetown against shipping routed independently. Until July they were able to refuel at night in the Canaries, but Vichy refused them the use of Dakar. Neither Raeder nor Hitler was willing to send German submarines into the Mediterranean at present.[1]

British losses due to sinkings by aircraft rose sharply in March, those in April being inordinately high. The figures cover merchant-ship losses in all waters, off the coasts and in the ports and estuaries of the United Kingdom as well as in the Atlantic. Liverpool and the Clyde, the principal ports for ocean shipping, were heavily raided as part of the Blitz; otherwise the enemy used his aircraft mainly for minelaying, and only to a lesser extent for co-operation with the U-boats in the Atlantic. In May the new routeing of our convoys and more effective protection eventually made these combined attacks impossible, and the last successes of German aircraft in the North-Western Approaches were achieved in early June.

In minelaying round our coasts, for which they employed both aircraft and E-boats, the Germans did not in the present period equal their successes of the last quarter of 1940, still less those of the previous winter; but in the three months March–May 1941 they improved on the results of January and February. Against this form of attack also convoy proved a valuable protection by reason of the closer control which could be exerted over ships in danger.[2]

Of the merchant raiders mentioned earlier, four were on the prowl by the end of June; the actual damage done by them was far exceeded by the trouble they caused; their known or suspected presence entailed prodigious effort to our warships and caused continual anxiety to unescorted merchantmen. The German warships were of course an even greater nuisance. No merchant ships were actually sunk by them between March and September, but the need of using

---

[1] *F.N.C.* p. 191, 20 April.
[2] See Roskill I 328, 498.

capital ships as escorts in case they might appear forced the Admiralty to maintain a number of such ships in western waters far out of proportion to the relative strengths of the two navies. How completely our dispositions might have to be recast and how easily a standing menace to our economy might have been created was shown by the brief but dramatic episode of the *Bismarck* and *Prinz Eugen* in the last days of May.

In seeking to defeat the enemy's attempt to cut off our supplies the British Government had four main tasks: to reduce losses by defence measures, to increase the provision of ships, to reduce delays at sea and in port, and to make the most profitable use of the shipping available by careful allocation between the various competing demands, military and civil.

As in the former war, far the most effective method of defence proved to be the convoy system, and such defence was by no means passive, since it was in the neighbourhood of the convoys that there was the best opportunity of sinking U-boats. But it was some time before the system became adequate to foil the improving tactics of the enemy. Only gradually were more escort vessels brought into service, so that convoys were less often dependent on a single ship for their protection, and only gradually were anti-submarine and reconnaissance aircraft provided. From January onwards really reliable radar was beginning to be fitted in both ships and aircraft. More anti-aircraft guns and machine guns were supplied for merchant ships. Airfields were prepared in Northern Ireland, in the Hebrides, and in Iceland from which the aircraft could work. By mid-April escorts could provide protection as far as 30° West, and eventually in June 'end-to-end' surface escorts were introduced with the help of the Royal Canadian Navy, an advanced escort base having been established at St. John's, Newfoundland.

Within a few days of the issue of the Prime Minister's directive of March 6 a considerable redeployment of our Air power had been effected. The strength of Coastal Command in Northern Ireland had been increased. Fighter Command was taking over further responsibility for the protection of east coast convoys, and anti-aircraft guns were being redistributed for the benefit of ports on the west coast; these, not aircraft factories, were now to be Fighter Command's primary charge. In April Hudsons and Sunderlands, with an Area Combined Headquarters, were established in Iceland.

On May 22 Hitler instructed Raeder that the Navy's main task in the summer of 1941 must be the disruption of British supply lines; [1]

---

[1] *F.N.C.* p. 199.

but none the less June 1941, with the introduction of end-to-end anti-submarine escorts, marks a turning-point in the war against the U-boats. Experience had now secured agreement on the technical developments to be exploited. A joint committee of the Navy and Coastal Command, which reported in May, stressed the need for long-range aircraft within the Command, for long-range A.S.V. radar in aircraft, and for the use of high-frequency direction-finding apparatus as well as radar in escort vessels. Further requirements which the future was to supply were more effective depth-charges and searchlights. Before the end of June a few merchant ships had been provided with high-performance fighters to be released by catapult, but no escort carriers were ready yet.

The peculiar problems of Fighter Command were touched upon in an earlier chapter.[1] It was mentioned that as early as February 1941 Hitler envisaged the scaling down of the air offensive against Great Britain in view of the need to transfer formations elsewhere, and in effect Fighter as well as Coastal Command had much fewer German aircraft to contend with from May onwards. Between May 11 and the end of June only two 'major' raids were launched against our cities—against Birmingham on the night of June 4, and against Southampton on that of June 12—but neither was near the standard of the great raids of the earlier period.

The strategy prescribed for Bomber Command will be dealt with later in this chapter, but its part in the Battle of the Atlantic must be mentioned here. The Chiefs of Staff's meeting on 27 February, at which the Prime Minister presided, 'invited the Chief of the Air Staff to examine the practicability of developing a heavy scale of bombing attack on the Focke-Wulf base at Bordeaux'. From the time of the arrival of German submarines and aircraft in the Biscay bases, attacks at source had been conducted mainly by Coastal Command; but Bomber Command gave increasing assistance. On March 9, as the result of the Prime Minister's directive, they were instructed to make the defeat of the enemy's offensive against our shipping their prime object, and to attack targets connected with his submarines and long-range aircraft. Bomber Command were also directed to continue their attacks on German warships, particularly in the French west coast ports, as weather and opportunities (revealed by photographic reconnaissance) might serve.

Pleas put forward on behalf of Coastal Command in March for priority in the allocation of the new four-engined aircraft, for the purpose of protecting convoys against U-boats in the North-Western Approaches, were opposed by Bomber Command and rejected by the Air Staff, who thought it more profitable to attack the U-boats

---

[1] Chapter xvii.

in their pens. The Air Staff were also convinced that the use of shore-based aircraft for countering Focke-Wulf heavy bombers far out in the Atlantic was uneconomical, and that 'it would be wasteful in the highest degree to divert still more of our scanty bomber force from the task of attacking targets which we know they can hit to the task of patrolling the ocean in the remote hope of intercepting a Focke-Wulf'. Later evidence shows that the figures of U-boats destroyed in Biscay bases were in fact incorrect, whether or not the argument they were used to support was sound, and whether or not 'the remote hope of intercepting a Focke-Wulf' was a fair description of their purpose. But Coastal Command had at present to rest content with a few American P.B.Y. flying-boats (Catalinas) and the promise of Flying Fortresses or Liberators. Effective escort by shipborne aircraft was still to come.

The task set to the bombers was an extremely difficult one, and the forces available were inadequate. It appears that no U-boat was ever destroyed by the bombing of the French bases and only one damaged (in December 1940), and that not seriously. It would seem further that this was the only U-boat prevented from putting to sea from the west coast of France as the direct result of an air raid, and the maintenance of the U-boats was not noticeably interfered with either. Nor does it appear that much damage was done during this period of the war to submarine building-yards or to the submarine industry in general. On the other hand our losses in aircraft in the period July 1940–June 1941 were considerable: 26 lost in bombing U-boat bases, 129 lost in bombing building-yards in German ports.

Attacks on surface ships in the Biscay ports were more successful. The *Gneisenau* was seriously damaged in Brest on April 6 by a torpedo of Coastal Command, and again on the night of April 10 by Bomber Command, with the result that she was unable to join the *Bismarck* in her fateful sortie next month, and that both she and the *Scharnhorst* were immured in the Bay of Biscay for the rest of the year. This does not mean that their presence there was not a great nuisance until they eventually made their celebrated break-back to Germany. Much effort was devoted to 'sewing them in' by mines, and important ships were kept occupied in watching for them.

Great efforts were still required from civil Departments.

> 'As the spring wore into summer in 1941 each of the various crises was brought under control, new techniques were developed for dealing with the unprecedented situations, and ways of proceeding began gradually to settle into routines; but before the crises were overcome the situation was obscured by many uncertainties and nothing could be clearly discerned except that the volume of imports that reached this country was diminishing month by month. It was the most anxious moment of the war,

for though, later, ships were to be fewer, sinkings heavier and military commitments larger, the future was never again to seem so much in doubt.'[1]

Miss Behrens' finding as to the direct influence of the shipping shortage on our strategy has been quoted in a previous chapter.[2] It may be noted that, when, in a report of March 1, the Chiefs of Staff estimated that the despatch and maintenance of an expeditionary force to Greece on the scale proposed would entail a total loss of 910,000 tons of imports over a period of twelve months, the Prime Minister commented that the shipping must be found from the pool of over two million tons lying idle under repair. Later on, on June 11, the Chief of the Imperial General Staff remarked that 'the limiting factor in completing General Wavell's reinforcement demand' was shipping space, and that 'he himself viewed the shipping situation with grave concern'.

It will be relevant before leaving the Battle of the Atlantic to say something on how our supplies were actually affected.

In January 1941 total imports into the United Kingdom were at the rate of 35 million tons a year, of which the Import Executive agreed that 15·42 millions should be allotted to food. But by mid-March the prospective total for the second year of war was down to 30 millions, of which 13·2 millions would be food's share. On March 31 the Cabinet had before them a memorandum by the Prime Minister recommending that an import total of not less than 31 million tons in 1941 should be assumed; of this total, 15 millions should be assigned to food and one million to the requirements of the Board of Trade, leaving 15 millions for the Ministry of Supply. This Ministry had been previously working to a figure of 19 millions out of an estimated total of 35, and they would therefore have to accept a cut of four millions. Should our total imports in fact exceed or fall below the estimated 31 millions, the difference should be shared by Food and Supply in the proportion of 1 to 2. The Cabinet approved these proposals.

As it turned out, total imports for 1941 were 30·5 million tons, of which Food took 14·7 and Raw Materials 15 millions. But so far were we from approaching starvation or effective shortages of raw materials that stocks of the latter, as well as of food, rose considerably between June 1940 and the end of 1941. Estimates of minimum requirements had been too high. But this stockbuilding was 'paid for largely by adjustments in British industry and agriculture, by a

---

[1] Behrens, *op. cit.* p. 188.
[2] Above, p. 398.

rigorous reduction of exports, of capital equipment and of the civilian standard of living'.[1]

During these anxious months the movement of opinion in the United States brought us help and encouragement on an ever increasing scale. More and more Americans were coming to believe that Hitler was a growing danger to the Western Hemisphere, and that to uphold Britain's fighting power was both possible and worth while and necessary. But the President had to take account of Congress as well as of outside opinion, and it still had to be assumed that America might be able to keep out of war. In the meantime she had adopted the formula of 'all aid short of war', and proceeded to interpret it in a large-minded American way. The passing of the Lend-Lease Act early in March 1941 was an immense relief: by the end of June four billion dollars had been allocated to procurement agencies for our benefit.

So too was the knowledge in high places that the staff talks at Washington were disclosing a broad agreement between British and American strategic thought, until at the end of March the representatives of the two countries were able to sign their joint reports on future co-operation.[2] But the emergency of the spring and early summer called for immediate practical help, and by the first week of May only thirty of the old American destroyers were in use. However, there were many other ways in which America could help us.[3]

On March 23 the Prime Minister passed to the Chiefs of Staff a note from Mr. Harriman distinguishing between the direct and indirect aid which the United States could furnish. On the one side she could transfer certain naval and merchant ships and suitable aircraft; the President in this way promised us ten Coast Guard cutters for use as escort vessels, and in June Congress gave him authority to requisition foreign ships lying idle in American ports, whereupon forty Danish vessels were taken and put to work.[4] The President also allowed the *Malaya* and other damaged vessels to be repaired in American yards. Indirectly, the United States could help us by arranging for American merchant ships to take over the tasks of ours in certain areas and under certain conditions, and so free both them and their escorts for other duties. Soon afterwards, on April 10, after the collapse of Italian resistance in Eritrea, the

---

[1] See Hancock and Gowing, pp. 264–268.

[2] See above, ch. xviii.

[3] A useful account of developments in America is given in *The Undeclared War 1940–1941*, esp. chapter xiv.

[4] *See the Memoirs of Cordell Hull*, pp. 942–943.

President allowed American merchantmen to enter the Red Sea, as no longer a combat area.

Next day (April 11) the President took what Mr. Churchill described as a long step towards our salvation, by secretly extending the patrol areas of the United States Fleet to cover all North Atlantic waters up to 25° West.[1] It was suggested that British merchant ships should take advantage of this patrolled area as far as possible, the United States being informed of the routes proposed for convoys. Then on April 24 came notification from the President of 'Navy Western Hemisphere Defence plan No. 2', which authorised United States ships to report movements of German vessels west of Iceland, but not to fire on them. The original plan authorised shooting too, but the news of the Soviet-Japanese neutrality pact, so Mr. Sherwood tells us, caused such alarm with regard to the Pacific that it had to be modified.[2] This promise of American help supplies the background to the Prime Minister's willingness to release capital ships to the Mediterranean (as he explained to Admiral Cunningham) and also, somewhat later, to welcome the diversion of a substantial part of the United States Pacific fleet to the Atlantic.[3]

The idea of American troops using Iceland as a base whenever the United States entered the war had for some time been under consideration.[4] The possibility of earlier action was taken up with the Icelandic authorities in April, and on 19 June the Prime Minister told the Cabinet that the United States were sending a force of Marines to the island to reinforce the British garrison; later on American troops would take over responsibility for its defence and free the British force for service elsewhere. At the same time the President informed us that he had frozen German and Italian assets and closed German consulates in the United States.

On May 27, after the sinking of the *Hood*, President Roosevelt spoke to the people of America and of the world, announcing that he had proclaimed a state of 'unlimited national emergency'.

> 'From the point of view of strict naval and military necessity we shall give every possible assistance to Britain and to all who, with Britain, are resisting Hitlerism or its equivalent with force of arms. Our patrols are helping now to insure delivery of the needed supplies to Britain. All additional measures necessary to deliver the goods will be taken.'[5]

'The entry of the United States into the war against Germany',

---

[1] Soon altered to 26° West.

[2] *White House Papers* I 291; *The Undeclared War* p. 445.

[3] See chapter xxi below and S. E. Morison, *The History of United States Naval Operations, in World War II* (Boston 1950) III 56–58.

[4] *White House Papers* I 290; *The Undeclared War* p. 452.

[5] *White House Papers* I 298; *The Undeclared War* p. 457.

says Mr. Sherwood, 'was now considered inevitable and even imminent.' Even if, as he goes on to tell us, at a Press conference next day the President seemed resolved to diminish the effect of such language, his words were on record; and one may ask how Germany, in other words the Führer, reacted to such words and to all the actions which had preceded them.

On 14 November 1940 Raeder complained to Hitler that the Pan-American safety-zone was harmful to cruiser warfare, and made the proposal to 'change the regulations governing conduct in this zone as soon as the attitude of the United States becomes more unfriendly, particularly since the British have violated the regulations on numerous occasions'.[1] On December 27, reviewing the course of the war against British economy, he pointed out that while British shipping losses could not at present be replaced by British shipyards they might be made good by developing construction in the United States, which was already supplying Great Britain with 350–400 operational aircraft monthly and seemed determined to give more help. The Naval Staff expected the transfer of more destroyers and auxiliary vessels; the 'assumption of British patrol duties as in American coastal waters'; and later, possibly, the assumption of escort duties in American coastal waters. But very strong support would not be forthcoming before the end of 1941.[2] Raeder showed remarkable prescience.

On neither of these occasions is the Führer reported as making any comment. On January 8 or 9 he spoke slightingly of the economic potential of Great Britain and America compared with that of Europe, but admitted that 'if the United States of America and Russia should enter the war against Germany, the situation would become very complicated. Hence any possibility for such a threat to develop must be eliminated at the very beginning'. The collapse of Russia would increase the danger to the United States from Japan.[3]

On March 18, after the passing of Lend-Lease, Raeder reported that the Navy had information that American convoys, probably with United States escorts, called at Iceland, which was outside the Western Hemisphere, and suggested, first, that the 'closed area' should be extended to cover Iceland and the Denmark Strait and that in this area American ships should be attacked without warning; secondly, that Germany should refuse to recognise the Pan-American safety zone, at any rate beyond 300 miles from the coast. Hitler was

---

[1] *F.N.C.* p. 151.
[2] *ibid.* p. 161.
[3] *ibid.* p. 171.

generally favourable and said that, if it turned out to be true that British naval vessels were being repaired in American yards, he would try to arrange for German warships to be repaired in Japan. Raeder recommended further that Japan should be urged to seize the present favourable opportunity to capture Singapore.[1]

Nevertheless, Hitler was chary of risking full American intervention at a critical period. On April 20 he announced his decision, 'in view of America's undecided attitude resulting from events in the Balkans', to recognise henceforth the whole extent of the Pan-American zone north of 20° North (viz. off the coast of the United States), but further south only so far as the 300-mile limit.[2] Iceland and its waters had since April been included in the German blockade area, but American merchant ships were not to be attacked there for the present. On June 6th he was still unwilling to give leave for warfare to be waged against such ships even in accordance with accepted prize regulations;[3] and on the 21st, after an encounter in the blockade area between a U-boat and the American battleship *Texas* and an American destroyer, he explained that until the campaign against Russia was well under way he was anxious to avoid any incident with the United States. In the next weeks, therefore, all attacks on naval vessels in the closed area must cease, unless these were large ships clearly recognised as enemy. Even after American troops had landed in Iceland he held to his desire to postpone the entry of the United States into the war for another month or two.[4]

Evidently the German high command were under no illusions as to either the help which the United States was already giving to Britain, or the importance of this help, or the likelihood of its developing into full-blooded belligerency before long. But they believed that it could not be really effective before 1942 at earliest; and hoping, as certainly Hitler did, that the war would be ended, or at any rate that overwhelming successes would be gained in Europe, before that date, they wisely decided to put up with American provocation for the present. If in the meantime Japan could be induced to take action weakening America's position in the Far East, so much the better.

The day of the President's forthright speech, May 27, was also the day of the sinking of the *Bismarck*, an achievement which did much to revive British hearts heavy with the loss of the *Hood* three days

---

[1] *F.N.C.* pp. 183–187.
[2] *ibid.* p. 192.
[3] *ibid.* p. 198.
[4] *ibid.* pp. 219–221.

before and with bad news from Crete. We now know that the purpose of the German venture was to wage war on merchant shipping in the north and central Atlantic.[1] It has since been remarked that, had Hitler waited to send the *Bismarck* out until her sister-ship, the *Tirpitz*, was ready, the combined threat of the two monsters, so much more powerful than any British ship, would have been serious indeed. The story of the long eventful hunt is fully told by Captain Roskill.[2] He brings out the immense concentration of ships and aircraft needed to dispose of the great 41,000-ton battleship and how easily, but for the leak of fuel-oil and the damage to her steering-gear, she might have made her way to comparative safety in a French port. As it was, her destruction vindicated the Admiralty's far-spread control, while illustrating the possibilities of skilful co-operation between surface vessels and aircraft.

The Battle of the Atlantic naturally affected the programme of the Fighting Services. On March 31 the Cabinet discussed and approved further directives by the Prime Minister, as Minister of Defence, concerning the expansion of the Navy and Army with special reference to the import programmes.[3]

The new naval construction programme, drawn up in accordance with the Minister of Defence's directive, was presented to the Cabinet by the First Lord on April 24 and approved. He explained that the Admiralty's general policy was to concentrate on the lighter craft, since it was in these that the greatest expansion was needed and the heaviest losses had been sustained. He mentioned in addition the large numbers of light craft which he hoped to obtain from America. As for larger ships, Mr. Churchill had said that we could not at present contemplate the building of heavy ships which could not be completed in 1942. Work would therefore be limited to completing the three remaining battleships of the King George V class (*Prince of Wales, Howe,* and *Anson*) and to building three medium cruisers (6-inch) and one Monitor (to replace the *Terror* destroyed in the Mediterranean). It was proposed also to press on with the *Vanguard*, steel permitting. Important though it was to have more fleet aircraft-carriers, particularly in view of the loss of the *Courageous* and *Glorious*, no new construction was included in the 1941 programme, but it was intended to complete the *Victorious, Indomitable* and *Indefatigable*.

The limiting factors were the demand for steel and for tanks, the necessity for concentrating the available labour on repairs, and the

---

[1] *ibid.* p. 197, 22 May.
[2] *The War at Sea* I ch. xix.
[3] Churchill III 111 ff.

need of merchant ships. In view of the urgency of repairs Mr. Churchill had directed that the present target of 1¼ million tons annually might be reduced to 1,100,000 for 1942, and we should not at the present time proceed with any merchant vessels which could not be completed by the end of 1941. It was to American building that we must look for relief in 1942.[1]

It was decided that policy with regard to heavy ships should be reviewed in September. The Admiralty were anxious that long-term as well as emergency needs should then be taken into account.

In the case of the Army limits were imposed by factors of man-power as well as of importing capacity.

At the same time as his directive on the Battle of the Atlantic the Minister of Defence submitted another on Army Scales.[2] It was the result of long discussions with the War Office, whom he was continually urging to cut down overheads and troops not destined for combatant roles. He would always sustain the Army, he assured Captain Margesson, the Secretary of State, in every possible way, if he were convinced that it would comb itself. The War Office, on their defence, explained the complexities of organisation made necessary by modern methods of fighting and the peculiar conditions of the different theatres.

Mr. Churchill agreed that, as the bulk of the Army now had to defend the island against invasion, and as the shipping stringency made it impossible to transport and maintain very large forces over-seas, and as we had heavy eastern commitments, there could be no question of an advance in force against the German armies on the mainland of Europe. 'An amphibious striking force of eight to ten divisions, mostly armoured, is the utmost that need be envisaged in the west.' It was thus impossible for the Army, except in resisting an invasion, 'to play a primary role in the defeat of the enemy. That task can only be done by the staying power of the Navy, and above all by the effect of Air predominance.' The organisation and character of the Army should therefore be adapted to 'operations of a secondary order'. As regards man-power, the present ration strength of the British Army at home was 1,800,000 men, of whom 735,000 were in 'tactical formations'. The remainder formed the pool on which, apart from the annual intake of recruits, the Army must live, and they would be judged by the effective fighting use they made of it. At the same time it would be well to plan an eventual increase of armoured formations to the equivalent of fourteen or fifteen armoured divisions.

The General Staff commented at length on this directive on

---

[1] Churchill III 779 ff.
[2] Printed in Churchill III 705 ff.

March 23. Granting that the primary present task of the Army was to ensure the safety of the United Kingdom and the territories and key positions, such as Egypt and Iceland, overseas, they would not admit that the role of the Army must always be secondary. For the immediate future they thought that Mr. Churchill's striking force of eight to ten divisions was more than could be spared until the danger of invasion was past, and this was not likely to be before the end of the summer of 1942.

They proceeded to assess the requirements of the several theatres, and first the United Kingdom. They considered that in view of the demands made on the Navy in present circumstances by the attack on our trade the Army might be required to defend the island for five to seven days, before our naval forces would be fully concentrated. There was also the long and vulnerable coastline for which infantry were required, and there was the danger of large scale parachute raids. All things considered, the Chiefs of Staff had reached the conclusion that not more than two infantry divisions, including one earmarked for Northern Ireland, could be moved from Great Britain until the autumn.

In the Middle East the forces required would depend largely on the result of the campaign in Greece. We might have to fight in Cyrenaica, or go to the help of the Turks, or hold Palestine and Syria against a German invasion. Our present strength there (assuming the intended conversion of the Cavalry division to armour) was three armoured and five infantry divisions. By the spring of 1942 we might expect reinforcements of one armoured division (British) and eleven infantry (two South African, six Indian and three British).

In the Far East, in order to raise the garrison to four infantry divisions plus an army tank brigade, which was considered adequate in present circumstances, it would be necessary to send out two more infantry brigades and the army tank brigade. For these we should look to Australia.

Summing up, they proposed that until the autumn no divisions beyond the 5th (for Northern Ireland) and 50th (for the Middle East) should leave Great Britain, and stated further that, unless the naval and air situations improved considerably, forces at home would be below the strength in infantry which the Commander-in-Chief, Home Forces, thought necessary to face a full-scale attempt at invasion. We might find ourselves with insufficient forces in the Middle East, and it might be impossible to find troops for operations in the Western Mediterranean or North Africa. The land forces available for the Far East now or at short notice in emergency appeared 'reasonably adequate'.

Such was their comment from the general strategic point of view. On the side of organisation and equipment, they pointed out various difficulties involved in the directive; in order to maintain the strength of the British Army at the figure of 2,195,000 as estimated for 1 October 1941, a yearly intake of more than the 19-year-old class would be required; further, no allowance had been made for battle casualties.

To secure the full requirement of fifteen armoured divisions (or their equivalent), of which it was hoped that Australia would eventually provide one, they suggested that the total should be made up of twelve armoured divisions proper and nine army tank brigades; it would be necessary to convert infantry formations for this purpose, and their value as infantry would be lost during the process. From the point of view of equipment, the first new armoured division could not receive its tanks until November 1941, and would not be ready for operations for another six months.

Whatever force we might find it possible to send abroad, they pressed that equipment should be planned for on the basis of the ten divisions suggested in the Prime Minister's directive. Otherwise sufficient reserves and manufacturing capacity would not exist when the time came to send further forces overseas. Further it was desirable to provide additional 'reserves of artillery and other equipment which takes a long time to produce', not only to cover unforeseen contingencies but also to meet the needs of possible allies.

The proposed reorganisation implied a grand total of the 'equivalent of $59\frac{1}{3}$ divisions', of which $38\frac{2}{3}$ would come from the United Kingdom; these last would include ten armoured divisions and seven army tank brigades, three army tank brigades being taken as the equivalent of an armoured division. The balance would be made up by $4\frac{1}{3}$ Canadian divisions ($1\frac{1}{3}$ armoured), $5\frac{1}{3}$ Australian ($1\frac{1}{3}$ armoured), 1 New Zealand, 2 South African, and 8 Indian.[1]

Mr. Churchill replied in a minute of 25 March to the Secretary of State. He accepted the 'target figure' of $59\frac{1}{3}$ divisions for the 'Imperial Army' in March 1942, and agreed that the total manpower figure to be maintained by the United Kingdom might be taken as 2,195,000. If the annual intake of 19-year-olds was not sufficient to keep up this number, then wastage and battle casualties must be met by the lifting of additional reservations.

He did not agree that only two divisions could be spared from the very large forces gathered at home. We must not get too invasion minded. However, he was confident that, when real needs arose in other quarters, risks would be run with courage here, with the full assent of Commander-in-Chief, Home Forces—as had been the case in August 1940.

---

[1] Compare p. 347. The East and West African formations were not now included, nor the garrison of Iceland.

This interchange of views did not lead to any modification of the Prime Minister's directive, which was approved by the Cabinet on March 31.

The growing insistence on armoured formations, stimulated no doubt by the demands of desert warfare and appeals from the Middle East for more and better tanks, naturally drew increased attention to the production of tanks at home. Something was said earlier of the efforts made in this matter in the summer of 1940.[1] In November it was again discussed by the Defence Committee (Supply), the Prime Minister expressing extreme concern to find so great a failure to attain forecasts in the total of infantry and cruiser tanks. It appeared that the most serious deficiency was in the Mark V and VI cruisers, which had been designed to give better protection than Mark IV but were in fact suffering from teething troubles. The Prime Minister complained that it was the continual introduction of fresh ideas into established programmes which was one of the main causes of our present deplorable situation. We had suffered too much in the past from continual changes of ideas, and attempts to reach perfection. Everything should now be concentrated on getting the maximum production of approved types.

The Minister of Supply declared that our tank production as a whole suffered from the fact that there had been a gap in design and development between the wars: no organisation existed for creating new tanks, and we had been attempting to produce and redesign at the same time. Professor Postan supports this complaint. He points out the grave handicaps which resulted from the 'desuetude' in the manufacture of armoured fighting vehicles in that period, only one firm retaining the necessary plant and skill. 'New capacity had therefore to be created and educated', and 'the production of tanks in quantity did not begin until several months after the outbreak of the war'. Even then, and even after the French collapse, it was not given the highest priority.[2]

At the end of November 1940 reports were rather more satisfactory for the future, but the present lack of cruiser tanks was lamentable. The Prime Minister again urged the need of pressing on with production. In our present situation it was numbers that mattered; the results of our existing programmes might not be ideal, but we should have to adapt tactics to suit the tanks we should possess, rather than try to change the programme. At a meeting of the Defence Committee (Supply) on February 26 the Prime Minister said that the output of infantry tanks had been coming well up to forecast. But the trouble was that this was not the kind now in chief

---

[1] p. 346.
[2] See M. M. Postan, *British War Production* pp. 183–193, with Tables 22 and 25.

demand. It was cruisers for which Wavell was crying out, or would soon be crying out, the Matilda infantry tank being greatly inferior in speed, mobility and radius of action. The need for more cruisers had been recognised after Dunkirk, and in July the War Office had asked that 45 per cent of the tanks supplied should be cruisers; in December the proportion was raised to 78 per cent. 'A radical change of this nature', however, 'was impossible without unsettling the entire scheme of production. It was therefore agreed that in practice no immediate alteration should be made to capacity which would involve any loss in gross production, and that until an adequate supply of cruisers could be produced a certain number of armoured divisions would be equipped with I tanks.' [1] The design of the A.22 (Mark IV) I tank (afterwards known as the Churchill) had been approved and 1,500 had been ordered; some would certainly be produced by May. But the 6-pounder gun, with which it was proposed to arm it, would not be available till October.

This was in February; but it was in April, after our unexpected set-back in the Western Desert attributable to the weakness of our armoured force, that tank production assumed the foremost place in the British public's mind. It was then that the Prime Minister summoned his Tank Parliament, to which commanders of armoured divisions were to be invited as well as representatives of the Ministry of Supply. At the end of June he was taking up tank production as an urgent matter with the Americans.

Until the 6-pounder tank gun was available, our tanks were armed with a 2-pounder. This weapon was also that provided for our anti-tank units, but the output was not sufficient to meet both needs. Moreover, while about as good as the corresponding German 50-mm. tank gun, it was markedly inferior to the German anti-tank gun of the same calibre. [2] The Defence Committee (Supply) were also concerned during the winter and spring with artillery of all kinds and mortars and rifles, including the appropriate ammunition. The bottleneck in the provision of gun ammunition was the difficulty in procuring labour for the filling factories, a difficulty which it was hoped to surmount by improving the conditions of work.

The Army requirements of gun and mortar ammunition always seemed enormous. The Prime Minister remarked in February that both strategy and shipping shortage might impose a still larger proportion of armoured divisions to infantry, and that this might affect the ammunition question.

At the end of May the General Staff put in a plea for the provision of an organisation for air support to the army on a greatly extended

---

[1] Postan p. 191.
[2] See Playfair II App. 4.

scale—in fact for 109 squadrons primarily devoted to army co-operation. The Air Staff responded with a more limited but in their view practicable proposal, and the Chiefs of Staff at the end of June left the matter for discussion between the two Chiefs concerned.

The Air Force programme, due for completion in the spring of 1942, was still that of September: it aimed at producing, for the Metropolitan force, 100 heavy bomber squadrons, 25 medium bomber, 93 fighter, 32 general reconnaissance (17 armed with land planes and 15 with flying-boats), and 20 army reconnaissance—270 squadrons in all, with 4,295 first-line aircraft. For overseas we should have 3 heavy bomber squadrons, 26 medium bomber, 23 fighter, 26 general reconnaissance and 12 army co-operation, totalling 90 squadrons, with 1,328 first-line aircraft. The Dominions would take 60 squadrons, with 736 aircraft, making a grand total of 420 squadrons with 6,359 first-line aircraft. This programme was based on the production programme of the United Kingdom, supplemented by the production potential of the United States of America.[1]

If this expansion was not interrupted, the Air Ministry hoped by the end of 1941 to be able to deliver a weight of bombs on Germany comparable to what the Germans had been able in the spring to drop on us, and they hoped by further expansion (Target E) to reach the figure of 4,000 heavy bombers (250 squadrons) by the spring of 1943, as compared with 1,648 under the existing programme.

Our present strength, however, was very far short of this. At the beginning of June Bomber Command consisted of forty-five squadrons which could be described as operational—768 aircraft on initial establishment—and of these only four were of the 'new heavy' types. The delays in bringing these types into service were disappointing: in April and May the aircraft produced had shown mechanical defects, and over the period March–June only 54 per cent of the expected total had been produced. The great majority of the bombers in use at this time were 'mediums', of which there were thirty-three operational squadrons (576 aircraft I.E.), and the mainstay was the Wellingtons. This was the 'paper strength', but in fact, even during the latter part of 1941, not more than an average of 380 mediums and 40 heavies were available for operations at any one time.

On March 9 Bomber Command were directed to give priority to operations designed to defeat the enemy's attack on our shipping,[2] and they carried out their orders where opportunity offered. But on April 15 Air Marshal Peirse protested against the uneconomical use

---

[1] The document containing this programme does not mention Dominion production. Hurricanes were in fact being produced in Canada in 1940.

[2] See above, p. 470.

of bombers against the German heavy ships at Brest, where results seemed disproportionate to the effort. Mr. Churchill expressed disappointment at the failure of our bombers to hit these vitally important ships—the *Gneisenau* had in fact been hit twice; he thought the policy of the Air Ministry in neglecting the dive-bomber to have been a 'very grievous error', and urged that efforts should be made to overcome the causes of failure, by daylight attacks if possible, with fighter cover. He agreed however with the Chief of the Air Staff's proposal that the bulk of Bomber Command should be used against German targets, but photographic reconnaissance of the battle-cruisers should take place every day, and frequent attacks be made on them at night, when weather was suitable, in moderate force, but by larger forces when any movement was observable. In fact, however, co-operation in the Battle of the Atlantic remained the primary task of the bombers for some time yet, and at the end of May the Air Staff once more pressed for a return to the long-term policy of strategic bombing.

Even as it was, though almost negligible in comparison with the devastating onslaughts of 1944 and 1945, the scale of attack on German cities was mounting. On 8 May 184 sorties were flown against Hamburg and 133 against Bremen—far the largest operations so far planned. The proportion of new heavy bombers was gradually increasing, and so was the size of their bombs: a 4,000-lb. bomb was dropped for the first time on the night of March 31.

Air strategy was discussed again in June. Lord Trenchard, the father of strategic bombing, had urged that 'absolute priority' should be given to the long-range bombers for the purpose of striking at military targets in Germany, with consequent devastating effects on the civil population. The tasks of hitting at the oil in Rotterdam, the shipping off the coasts, the invasion ports, the empty barges, the ships in Brest and other such targets should be left to bombers of shorter range. This policy should be relentlessly pursued on every single night and most days, despite the heavy casualties that might be incurred.

The Chiefs of Staff agreed broadly with the thesis that 'the most vulnerable point in the German nation at war is the morale of her civilian population under air attack, and that until this morale has been broken it will not be possible to launch an army on the mainland of Europe with any prospect of success'. They could not agree however that 'absolute priority' ought to be given in present circumstances to the carrying out of such attacks by heavy bombers, and recommended that 'subject to the requirements of security (including of course the Battle of the Atlantic)' we should recognise a distinction in our offensive bombing between immediate and eventual objectives. As a short-term policy 'we should attack transportation targets so as to achieve dislocation, coupled with the maximum direct effect on morale', since the best railway targets generally lay in congested industrial districts; as a long-term policy we should, when we had a sufficient force, 'undertake the direct attack of the morale of the German people'.

Answering some criticisms from the Prime Minister to whom this short-term policy seemed very bleak and restricted and less attractive than a flexible monthly programme, the Chiefs of Staff insisted that if the best results were to be obtained from the Bomber Force its operations must be conducted on a definite strategic plan rather than in a hand-to-mouth manner. They urged the importance of the communications traversing and radiating from the Ruhr-Rhineland area and emphasised that the kind of attack on railway centres which they now had in mind was something quite different from 'the series of harassing attacks which were delivered against marshalling yards, such as Hamm, earlier in the war, when our Bomber Force was insignificant and our primary objective was German oil'.

The Defence Committee on June 25 approved the Chiefs of Staff's comments on Lord Trenchard's paper, and also their recommendations, and a directive embodying the decision was issued by the Air Staff on July 9.

But though the Bomber Force was no longer 'insignificant' it was still far from possessing the power of seriously damaging German economy. Even after May not more than 67 tons of bombs, on an average, fell on Germany in twenty-four hours, and there was no certainty that of the bombs which fell more than a small proportion fell on or near the target. The optimism of earlier months was belied by the photographic test now coming into regular use. The first inquiry of this nature, based on some 650 photographs obtained from about 10 per cent of the sorties on a hundred separate raids, showed that only one sortie in five arrived within five miles of the target. Over the Ruhr, only one in ten arrived within five miles. 'It was obvious that crews were being gravely misled and mistaken in their target identification.' It was only after the period covered by this volume that the difficulties due to weather and the dark were surmounted by scientific devices and improved tactics; the Air Ministry were still not convinced of the possibility of building long-range fighters of sufficiently high performance to escort the bombers by day.

It was accepted that we could not launch an army on the Continent until German morale had been broken by bombing, but that did not prevent other forms of aggressive action. It was largely for such purposes that the Directorate of Combined Operations had been formed. We have seen how in September the troops assigned to it were placed under the command of Home Forces, but that after the Dakar fiasco men and craft were held ready for various projects for the capture of the Atlantic islands. In January the Defence Committee sanctioned the diversion of three Glen-type infantry assault ships, complete with landing craft, and two commandos to the Middle East, where a combined training centre had already been started. These troops were intended for the capture of the Dodecanese, and did in fact prove their value in the operations in Greece and Crete. It was decided that the commando force remaining at home should at once be brought up to the full strength of 5,000 and be fully equipped. Shortly afterwards approval was given for an operation (known as 'Claymore') intended to destroy the fish-oil plants under German control in the Lofoten islands off the coast of Norway. It was to be carried out under the auspices of the Director of Combined Operations (Sir Roger Keyes) in consultation with Admiral J. C. Tovey, Commander-in-Chief, Home Fleet, and the Special Operations Executive.[1] This raid was successfully executed on March 4; the small force was escorted by destroyers and covered by larger ships, admirable co-operation between the two Services being achieved. Thus at length, after many disappointments and delays, was proof given of our capacity to fulfil the hope expressed by the Prime Minister at the time of the Dunkirk evacuation that we should use our maritime power to harass the enemy at one unexpected point after another.

---

[1] Admiral Tovey had succeeded Sir Charles Forbes in December 1940.

CHAPTER XXI

THE FAR EAST,
OCTOBER 1940–JUNE 1941

THE STATE of affairs in the Far East at the beginning of October 1940 was that Japan had recently joined in a tripartite pact with Germany and Italy and had forced an agreement on the Vichyite Government of Indo-China giving her facilities for bases in her war against China. The British Government on the other hand had announced that the closure of the Burma Road would not be continued after the expiry of the current agreement on October 17, and no reprisals on the part of Japan had followed. The Chiefs of Staff had presented to the Cabinet an elaborate appreciation of the situation in the Far East, which stated the necessity in present circumstances of holding the whole of Malaya rather than concentrating on the defence of Singapore Island. They had been informed that, while the Cabinet had deferred decision on the strategic issues, the Prime Minister had authorised action in accordance with their main recommendations.

The principal features of the months following were the consolidation of the occupation of northern Indo-China by the Japanese, with every prospect of their encroachment into Siam (Thailand), and the efforts of British and American diplomacy to halt this advance; also a long succession of appreciations and conferences, on national, imperial, and international levels, attempting to define and meet the strategic and tactical needs of the powers threatened by Japan. Unfortunately the practical result was slight. Considerable reinforcements were sent, but the event proved that, particularly in the air, they were quite inadequate. The fact was that British resources were stretched by the demands of current operations in the Atlantic and the Mediterranean as well as of Home Defence, while the Prime Minister thought it unlikely that Japan would risk war against both Britain and the United States.[1]

It was proposed, as one of the results of the Chiefs of Staff's Far Eastern Appreciation, that a conference should be held at Singapore to discuss defence questions concerning the Far East, at which India and Burma, as well as Australia and New Zealand, should be represented. Before this conference met, a tactical appreciation was to

---

[1] The matter of this chapter is more fully treated in Kirby, *The War against Japan* vol. I, ch. iii.

be prepared by the British commanders in the Far East, and the conference should also, so the Chiefs of Staff suggested, consider the problem of Anglo-Dutch defence plans, with a view to discussion with the Dutch later in October, when the British reinforcements recently authorised had arrived in Malaya. The Chiefs of Staff considered that the Singapore Conference between representatives of the United Kingdom, Australia and New Zealand should be held as soon as possible and independently of the Anglo-American staff talks in Washington, which the President was known to have suggested, though they welcomed the suggestion and thought that the way might profitably be prepared for them by preliminary discussions in London. Later on, further conversations with American and Dutch representatives might be held at Singapore. But on October 14 it was learnt that the State Department were now opposed to any conference which might attract publicity before the presidential election, so it was agreed that conversations should be secret and on technical matters only; a few days later it was learnt that the Dutch in their turn were reluctant to go so far as to send representatives to Singapore, but arrangements would be made for the exchange of information in London.[1]

Shortly before this the United States Navy Department had asked to what extent base facilities at Singapore could be placed at the disposal of the United States Fleet in the event of trouble in the Far East. The reply was that they would be welcome to the whole of these facilities except in so far as we needed them for our own warships. The Prime Minister considered this inquiry to be of the highest importance. The Americans had refused, however, to send a squadron to visit Singapore as an insurance against Japanese reactions to the re-opening of the Burma Road.

On October 12 the Chiefs of Staff discussed and approved a proposal to establish a system of unified command for British forces in the Far East. The Prime Minister gave his sanction, and Air Chief Marshal Sir Robert Brooke-Popham was appointed Commander-in-Chief. As his mandate was eventually redefined, he was to be responsible to the Chiefs of Staff for the strategic control of all British land and air forces in Malaya, British Borneo, Burma and Hong Kong and for the co-ordination of plans for their defence. He was to deal primarily with matters of major military policy and strategy, and was not to be burdened with administrative or financial responsibilities.

This appointment is of special interest as the first attempt to unify

---

[1] See Feis, *The Road to Pearl Harbour* ch. xvi.

command of the Services at a high level, but it did not include the Navy; nor did it provide for co-ordination with the civil authorities. Brooke-Popham was to consult and, when appropriate, co-operate with the naval Commanders-in-Chief, China and East Indies, as well as with the Commander-in-Chief of the Army in India. The extension of his sphere to Burma was in accordance with a decision of the Chiefs of Staff early in September, when they rejected a suggestion that, since the Bay of Bengal and the surrounding lands constituted a single strategical area, they should be placed under the general control of the Government of India; the Chiefs of Staff took the contrary view that defence of the Bay of Bengal area formed part of the general problem of the defence of the Far East, of which Malaya was the focus, whereas India's primary interest was her North-West frontier. India was however closely concerned in Far Eastern matters, and it was arranged that Brooke-Popham should spend a few days at Delhi on his way out.

Before leaving England the new Commander-in-Chief submitted to the Chiefs of Staff certain reflections on the task facing him and the resources available; they had this paper before them on November 5 along with a draft appreciation from the delegation designated to discuss Far Eastern questions with the Americans at Washington.

The Air Marshal pointed out in picturesque language that, since the defence of Singapore was 'not a question of holding on to an isolated fortress, which is only of value in itself, but of ensuring that a naval base can be used by His Majesty's ships', an extended defence was necessary and 'we must combine the resisting power of an army with the striking power of an Air Force'; also that, although the requirements of Singapore were not of immediate urgency today, the situation might change at any moment and it was desirable to get the essentials delivered before the outbreak of war with Japan and not after. Among essential requirements, on the basis of the Chiefs of Staff's Far Eastern Appreciation, he noted that as against 336 first-line aircraft therein mentioned as the minimum we had at present only forty-eight modern ones, plus thirteen in reserve, and no fighters at all; he referred also to the deficiencies in anti-aircraft and field artillery and in signal equipment.

The memorandum submitted by Admiral Bellairs, the chairman of the delegation for Washington, argued that of the two possible main bases for an Allied Fleet, Singapore and Pearl Harbour in Hawaii, the former was strategically preferable, but noted the deficiencies in Malaya below the approved scale and pointed out the unfortunate effect which their disclosure might have on the Americans and the Dutch. 'On the one hand we shall say to the Americans that the whole safety of the Far East depends on the arrival of their battle fleet at Singapore. On the other hand we shall also have to say that we have not placed a garrison in Malaya sufficiently powerful to ensure that the base at Singapore will be intact when the United States fleet arrives. . . . The position might be considerably improved if we could give the Americans a firm promise that reinforcements to bring the garrison of Malaya to full strength would be sent by a certain date, say 31 March 1941.'

The Chiefs of Staff however held that 'there were no real grounds for the view that our garrison in Malaya was not sufficiently strong to ensure that the base in Singapore would be intact when the American fleet arrived'. It was not thought that a Japanese threat to Singapore could develop suddenly. The enemy would need time to establish airfields in north-east Malaya, while an overland advance down the Isthmus of Kra and across Malaya was fraught with difficulty and should be particularly vulnerable to air attack. The memorandum was amended accordingly in a more optimistic sense, and the Service Departments were invited to circulate a programme of reinforcements likely to reach Malaya in the course of the next six months. The reply of the General Staff was that with the exception of one field artillery regiment and a small monthly quota of anti-aircraft equipment nothing could be sent from the United Kingdom or from India; the reason in the former case was lack of shipping, in the latter lack of trained troops and equipment. The only hope seemed to be Australia.

By this time (9 November) telegraphic summaries had reached London of the Tactical Appreciation (dated October 16) of the defence situation in Malaya by the three local commanders, and also of the report of the Singapore Defence Conference; at the latter, Service representatives of Australia, New Zealand, India and Burma were present, with an officer of the East Indies naval station, as well as a United States naval officer as an 'observer' only.[1] The full texts were not available till December, when the Chiefs of Staff had also before them a report on staff conversations held with the Dutch at Singapore in November and a summarised appreciation by the new Commander-in-Chief.

The Tactical Appreciation was founded on the Chiefs of Staff's Far Eastern Appreciation; it accepted the principles that the cornerstone of our strategy was still to base a powerful fleet at Singapore, but that its arrival would only partially guard against a Japanese overland threat; that the problem, in the absence of a capital-ship fleet, was to make the best dispositions possible to secure the most important of our interests in the Far East without the cover which a

---

[1] The local commanders were Vice-Admiral Layton, Lieutenant-General Bond and Air Vice-Marshal Babington.

Plate 3: The Defence Committee (Operations), 1941.

Back row: Sir Charles Portal, Sir Dudley Pound, Sir Archibald Sinclair, Captain Margesson, Sir John Dill, Sir Hastings Ismay, Colonel L. C. Hollis.

Front row: Lord Beaverbrook, Mr. Attlee, Mr. Churchill, Mr. Eden, Mr. A. V. Alexander.

capital-ship fleet would provide, and that our policy was to rely primarily on air power; also that it was necessary to hold all Malaya rather than concentrate on the defence of Singapore Island.

The appreciation went into much detail; its general conclusion was that for the defence of the Far East (including Burma) a strength of 566 first-line aircraft, rather than the 336 of the Chiefs of Staff's appreciation, would be necessary, and an army strength of twenty-three battalions in Malaya, and three for Borneo, all over and above the local and volunteer forces. They recommended that the protection of trade in the Indian Ocean, including the Bay of Bengal, should remain the responsibility of the Commander-in-Chief, East Indies. As for co-operation with the Dutch, they considered that at present the primary object of our mutual defence plans must be to deny to the Japanese the use of naval and air bases; mutual reinforcement could be supplied only by air.

The report of the Singapore Defence Conference (dated October 31) was divided into three parts. Part I was a survey of the defence problem in the Far East supplementary to the Tactical Appreciation; Part II was a report on the defence of India and Burma against Japanese attack; Part III stated our deficiencies and suggested how far they might be met from India, Australia and New Zealand. Subjects for discussion with the Dutch and Americans respectively were also proposed.

Part I accepted the defence of Malaya against direct attack as the first and immediate consideration; it accepted also the view of the Tactical Appreciation that the army and air forces there, including 'the reinforcements now being provided', were in numbers and equipment far below what was required. Indeed they added another sixteen aircraft (a fighter squadron for Burma) to the previous estimated minimum of 566 for Burma and Malaya. Ground facilities should be prepared throughout the Far Eastern area forthwith without waiting for the aircraft to arrive. They noted that troop convoys in the Indian Ocean would require a capital-ship escort (assuming that 'in accordance with the Prime Minister's telegram' a battle-cruiser and an aircraft-carrier would proceed thither) and that Australian and New Zealand forces would return to their home waters, on the outbreak of war with Japan.[1]

Part II pointed out the imperial importance of Burma, due to its oil and minerals, its communications with Singapore and China, and its position as an outpost of India. The occupation of Siam by Japan would expose Burma to invasion by land as by sea and air. Burma should receive in addition to her existing land force two brigades and one battalion of infantry, one field regiment, and one

---

[1] The 'Prime Minister's telegram' is presumably that of 11 August 1940 to the Prime Ministers of Australia and New Zealand; printed in Churchill II 385; see above, p. 333.

heavy and one light anti-aircraft regiment along with minor reinforcements. With the forces at present available the most that could
be done was to hold Rangoon and the northern part of Tenasserim
in the Malayan isthmus.

Part III summed up the deficiencies: they included 19 infantry
battalions for Malaya and Burma, 144 heavy anti-aircraft guns and
166 light, 138 searchlights, and 534 modern aircraft, plus 270 modern
aircraft for Australia. It was noted that India had been asked to
provide four divisions for service overseas by December 1941, but
that their present allocation was to the Middle East. Australia should
be able to provide one strong brigade group by the end of 1940, but
it would only be equipped on a modified scale; as regards aircraft,
she hoped to provide 180 Beauforts in 1941, of which she needed 90
for herself.

In the meantime decisions had been taken on the telegraphed
summaries. On the basis of papers produced by the General Staff
and the Air Staff the Chiefs of Staff Committee on 19 November
submitted to the Prime Minister a memorandum noting that it was
no longer possible to secure the naval base at Singapore by merely
holding the island, and that the three local commanders had recommended a total garrison of twenty-six battalions, involving an
addition of nine to the seventeen already provided for: they noted
also that it might be impossible to reinforce Malaya once war with
Japan had broken out; that shortage of shipping forebade the despatch of reinforcements now from the United Kingdom; and that
India could send none until May 1941. They advised therefore that
Australia should be asked to send to Malaya a brigade or as much
of the 8th Australian Division as she could equip to the required
limited scale. In May this force should be relieved by an Indian
division and proceed to join the Australian corps in the Middle
East. We should also hasten to despatch some of the air reinforcements already proposed, namely two fighter squadrons as soon as
possible, and aircraft to re-equip two bomber squadrons (by June)
and a flying-boat and a torpedo squadron.[1]

On December 2 the Chiefs of Staff had before them a memorandum from Mr. R. A. Butler, the chairman of the inter-departmental Far Eastern Committee, calling attention to Japanese
activities in south-east Asia and asking whether the recent mauling
of the Italian fleet at Taranto might not justify the despatch of, say,
a battle-cruiser and an aircraft-carrier to Ceylon, where they would
be well placed to reinforce the Far East if occasion arose. The First
Lord had replied that any capital ship which our recent success
might allow us to withdraw from the Mediterranean would be

---

[1] See above, p. 336.

needed on the Atlantic convoy route; surely the real deterrent to Japanese aggression in the Far East could only be found in the willing and open co-operation of the United States.

The Australian Government also were 'gravely concerned at the most serious position' revealed by the report of the Singapore Defence Conference. They referred to expectations held out in 1937 that Singapore would be enabled to resist and they repeated the argument that we could hardly expect the United States to base strong naval forces in that region until this object had been secured. They now expressed their readiness to send a brigade group to Malaya until such time as the 8th Australian Division, of which it formed part, could be concentrated in the Middle East, and they made further offers of assistance.

These offers were gratefully received, and replies were drafted early in December, by the Prime Minister expressing an optimistic view of the general situation as regards Japan, and by the Dominions Office announcing the air reinforcements we proposed to send. But the Prime Minister, who had never given his approval to the Chiefs of Staff's memorandum of November 19, was unwilling to divert so many aircraft, especially the flying-boats, to what was at present an inactive theatre, and the British reply to Australia eventually took the form of the telegram of 23 December to Mr. Menzies which Mr. Churchill has printed.[1] He regarded the danger of Japan making war on us as definitely less than it had been in June. Our growing advantage in the Mediterranean, where we had occupied Crete and were 'making at Suda Bay a second Scapa', would not be lost on Japan; but we could not withdraw our fleet from the Mediterranean without sacrificing all our gains and ruining our prospects for the future. When we had broken Italy as a combatant we could send strong naval forces to Singapore. At present we were at 'the fullest naval strain' Mr. Churchill had seen in either this or the former war, but he was convinced that, if Japan entered the arena, the United States would come in too, and that would 'put the naval boot very much on the other leg'. In the meantime we must try to bear our Eastern anxieties patiently and doggedly, 'it always being understood that if Australia is seriously threatened by invasion we shall not hesitate to compromise or sacrifice the Mediterranean position for the sake of our kith and kin'. As for air reinforcements, with the ever-changing situation it was 'difficult to commit ourselves to the precise number of aircraft' which we could make available for Singapore. Broadly speaking, our policy was to build up as large as possible a fleet, army and air force in the Middle East, and keep this in a fluid condition, either to prosecute war in Libya,

---

[1] Churchill II 628.

KK

Greece and presently Thrace, or to reinforce Singapore should the Japanese attitude change for the worse.

Before the end of the year the Australian Government had arranged to despatch a brigade group to Malaya as soon as shipping could be found, and the Commander-in-Chief, Far East, was instructed to prepare for it.

Meanwhile conversations with Netherlands officers had taken place at Singapore at the end of November. It was agreed that the primary naval role of the Dutch would be to provide local defence in the East Indies and hold the gateways into the Indian Ocean in co-operation with other Allied forces. Dutch resistance would be dependent however on the supply of munitions from Great Britain and the United States. It was only in the air that a redistribution of existing forces could usefully be effected: three Dutch squadrons might be transferred to Malaya, and four British squadrons to Sumatra.

The Chiefs of Staff had also received a summarised appreciation from the newly arrived Commander-in-Chief, sent on 7 December, with the naval Commander-in-Chief's concurrence. The two commanders thought that in certain circumstances Japan might act suddenly and take a decisive step which would force us either to go to war or to surrender important strategic advantages. To prevent war our policy must be firmness, not appeasement. We should encourage the Chinese in their resistance and seek to convince Japan that an attack on either British interests or the Netherlands East Indies would mean war with both Powers. Brooke-Popham was considering the possibility of occupying the Siamese part of the Isthmus of Kra should the Japanese penetrate Siam. Although 'convinced that in the event of war Japan would even now be up against a tough proposition before security of Singapore would be seriously jeopardised', he urged that in view of the possibility of a sudden move everything possible should be done to strengthen ourselves in the immediate future. He made concrete suggestions for doing so from both internal and external resources.

The Chiefs of Staff on December 21 gave general approval to the commanders' proposals, and on January 8 discussed at length the recommendations contained in the Tactical Appreciation and report of the Singapore Defence Conference, of which they had now received the full texts. They informed the Commander-in-Chief that they had noted that the recommendations agreed generally with their own expressed major defence policy; they were fully alive to the weaknesses in land and air forces, particularly the latter, and were doing all they could, having regard to theatres which were already the scene of war.

The Singapore Defence Conference had asked for 582 aircraft for

Malaya and Burma; the Chiefs of Staff agreed that this was an ideal, but thought that their own figure of 336 should give a 'very fair degree of security', taking into account the experience of the Middle East, Malta and the Air Defence of Great Britain. The Japanese should not be overestimated. In any case the target figure of 336 aircraft could not be increased before the end of 1941 and it remained subject to the general situation and the supply of aircraft. They would try to provide five fighter squadrons during 1941 (as against four in their own Far Eastern Appreciation), and they sanctioned the construction of more airfields. They regarded the threat of air attack on India in present circumstances as 'virtually negligible', and thought that only a light attack could be made on Burma.

Regarding land forces, they agreed that their previous estimate for the final strength of the garrison was too low, and now accepted the figure of twenty-six battalions for Malaya, including three for Borneo; this figure should be reached by June 1941, when a second infantry division was due to arrive from India. They could not agree however to provide immediately the seven battalions demanded for Burma, but would ask India to earmark a brigade group for despatch in an emergency. They could not meet the demand for field or anti-tank artillery, or for tanks.

A telegram was sent to this effect to Brooke-Popham. The Prime Minister however objected to such large diversions of force, which did not seem required by the political situation in the Far East or warranted by the strength of our Air Force. He did not take an alarmist view about the defence of Singapore at the present time, whereas the need for flying-boats for the North-Western Approaches was urgent. But the Chiefs of Staff justified their recommendations, pointing out that it was essential to make a start on our long-term reinforcement programme for the Far East; that at present we had no fighters there, and that the provision of a few modern flying-boats was required to locate raiders in the Indian Ocean.

At the same time the Chiefs of Staff agreed with the Prime Minister that a proposal of the Commander-in-Chief to increase the garrison of Hong Kong from four to six battalions was unsound. Hong Kong could be held only as an outpost. They considered it an undesirable military commitment, which we could not now disclaim. Prestige demanded that we should defend the Colony as long as possible with its present garrison, and reserves of all kinds should be held for a 'period before relief' of 130 days.[1]

In all these discussions the attitude of the United States was

---

[1] Two Canadian battalions were eventually, in the autumn of 1941, sent to reinforce Hong Kong.

recognised as being the decisive factor, and it is time to discover how American strategists viewed the situation in the Far East.

Until the rise of Hitler America's only potential enemy was Japan, and her navy expected to have to fight in one ocean only, the Pacific. From 1922 onwards the United States Fleet was mainly concentrated in the Pacific, using west coast bases; the detachment known as the Asiatic Fleet was stationed in Chinese and Philippine waters. Events in Europe brought changes of profound importance. Strategical plans (the 'Rainbow' series) envisaging the possibility of war against several Powers at once were initiated in the spring of 1939. In the autumn naval expansion was under discussion; and on 17 June 1940, the day after the fall of the Reynaud Cabinet, Admiral Stark asked Congress to authorise the building of a two-ocean navy.[1] The interval that must elapse before the expansion was completed would be a dangerous one; during it America would be particularly anxious not to provoke war, and she would be glad to enjoy the assistance of the British Fleet. Nevertheless, for all his unwillingness to risk war with Japan, President Roosevelt was not prepared to remain inactive in face of her insults and aggressions, and in May 1940 the United States Fleet, then concentrated at Hawaii at the end of an exercise, received orders to remain there; the westward shift was intended as a warning to Japan.[2]

The next crucial decision has been mentioned already: the recommendation made in November 1940 by the Chiefs of the Naval and Army Staffs, and approved by the President, that should America become involved in war against the Axis and Japan the European theatre must be regarded as the decisive one and a strategic defensive adopted in the Pacific.

On this fundamental principle the naval strategists of Britain and America were at one, but their views were irreconcilable on the subject of Singapore. To the British, apart from its political importance, this 'vital base' was 'the key position in the East' and was clearly marked out as the correct point of concentration for the main Allied fleet, which should use Manila as an advanced base. Pearl Harbour, though advantageously placed on the flank of the Japanese southward communications, was nearly twice as far from Japanese home waters; moreover, as the Japanese moved south they would be nearer to Singapore but further from Hawaii. Plans should therefore be laid for the United States Main Fleet to move to Singapore—some 5,800 miles—as soon as possible after the outbreak of war. But the Americans were not to be persuaded. Politically it would have been hard for any nation at war to send its main fleet to a foreign

---

[1] See S. E. Morison, *United States Naval Operations in World War II* I 27.
[2] See Morison III 43.

base, thereby uncovering to the enemy the direct route to its shores. But strategically even the detachment of a considerable force to Singapore—whose retention they did not think necessary for the defence of the Malay Barrier and whose defences seemed none too secure—appeared altogether unsound.[1]

The disagreement was accepted with philosophy in London. The Prime Minister had learnt with pleasure that it was Admiral Stark's view that if the United States entered the war all possible naval and military aid should be concentrated in the European theatre and a defensive attitude maintained in the Pacific. He felt sure that there would be ample naval forces to contain Japan by long-range controls in that region; the Japanese Navy was not likely to venture far from its home bases so long as a superior battle fleet was maintained at Singapore or at Honolulu. The Japanese would never attempt a siege of Singapore with a hostile, superior American fleet in the Pacific. Consequently he was not perturbed by the American admiral's unwillingness to conform to what could be represented as a purely British interest by sending the whole American Fleet to Singapore. There was no use in proposing to the Americans a naval policy which would be distasteful to them and increase their reluctance to come into the war. If they preferred Hawaii to Singapore, their decision must be accepted.[2]

To us, with our after-knowledge, the Prime Minister's grounds for confidence may recall those which the weird sisters gave Macbeth. But in those days a disaster like Pearl Harbour was just as unthinkable as that of the Meuse had been before May 1940.

At the end of January there was evidence that a southward move by the Japanese was imminent. The collapse of France had encouraged the Siamese Government to put forward claims against French Indo-China, and local fighting had broken out on the 15th. The Japanese seized the opportunity to come forward as mediators; it seemed likely that they would not only secure as their commission a naval base at Camranh and air bases in Cochin-China but conclude a military agreement with Bangkok for action against Dutch or British possessions. In fact, a truce was negotiated between Indo-China and Siam under Japanese auspices on January 31; to enforce the truce and also as a demonstration of strength the Japanese disposed a considerable naval force along the coasts of these two countries. On February 5 the Joint Intelligence Sub-Committee gave warning that a move against the Netherlands East Indies was probable in the near

---

[1] Morison III 50; see also Feis, *The Road to Pearl Harbour* ch. xvii.
[2] See Churchill II 614; *The Undeclared War* pp. 285 ff.

future, but they would not affirm that the Japanese were prepared as yet for a final rupture with the British, the Dutch and the Americans. The Chiefs of Staff accepted this report, which seemed confirmed by further information; they agreed that there was no military action which we could take beyond the moves of army reinforcements already approved, and urged that the only course was for both the United States and ourselves to adopt a firm diplomatic line with Japan. The matter was discussed that night (February 6) with the Prime Minister and on the following night with the Foreign Secretary, who had seen the Japanese Ambassador that morning. The question whether we should make aggression against the Dutch islands a *casus belli* with Japan and give the Dutch a guarantee was brought forward but left open; it was to lead to much argumentation in the next few months. On the 10th the Chiefs of Staff approved a warning telegram to Commanders-in-Chief abroad and on the 11th they agreed that for the present Malaya should have priority over the Middle East for shipment of troops and stores from India. They had already decided, on the 7th, to accept an offer from India to accelerate the despatch of the promised division (9th Indian) and to send also some 300 artillerymen and four Indian States battalions, for internal security, to Malaya; the proposed brigade, with some artillery, should forthwith be earmarked for Burma and despatched as soon as possible. India should also release for Malaya one bomber and one fighter squadron—to be replaced as soon as possible from the United Kingdom. The Dominion Governments were informed of these steps.

The Chiefs of Staff proceeded to consider the implications of a southward move by Japan and informed the Cabinet of their conclusion that Japanese control over Indo-China alone would indeed bring the threat of attack on British possessions nearer, but would not in itself directly affect our vital interests. On the other hand, a Japanese penetration of Siam would threaten Singapore and make the defence of Burma and Malaya far more difficult. It would be an added threat to our communications in the Indian Ocean.

Representations were also being made in Washington.[1] The President's information about Japanese intentions agreed with ours, but he did not think American public opinion would approve a declaration of war if Japan attacked only British or Dutch possessions; in any case, in view of trends in the Atlantic, the United States would have to limit operations in the Pacific to a holding war. Lord Halifax, however, was instructed to point out to the Secretary of State, on the lines of an *aide-mémoire* from the Chiefs of Staff, how war with Japan would 'inevitably lengthen war with Germany and

---

[1] For the American attitude see *The Undeclared War* ch. x, sect. 6; also H. Feis, *op. cit.* ch. xx.

would make ultimate success improbable without the full participation of the United States of America'. And on February 15 the Prime Minister told the President that, while he was not convinced that this was not just a war of nerves designed to cover encroachments in Siam and Indo-China, 'the weight of the Japanese Navy, if thrown against us, would confront us with situations beyond the scope of our naval resources'. What he most feared was the possible raiding of our trade routes and ocean communications, which would upset our whole reinforcement system; while 'any threat of a major invasion of Australia or New Zealand would, of course, force us to withdraw our fleet from the Eastern Mediterranean'.[1] The President had in fact already warned the new Japanese Ambassador that another Japanese move might lead to war with the United States.

This was precisely the time when the Defence Committee had to take the decision whether General Wavell should advance to Tripoli or transfer his surplus forces to Greece and when it was decided that the Foreign Secretary should fly to the Middle East. It may be noted that in the telegram sent to Wavell on the 11th the plain possibility that Japan might attack us in the near future was mentioned as one of the features in the situation.

By February 17 it seemed to the Cabinet that, for whatever reason, the tension in the Far East had relaxed. This disquieting fortnight might, however, have served as a warning of how quickly a crisis might occur in our relations with Japan. The Japanese did moreover bring off a considerable success; at length on March 11 they induced the Vichy Government to undertake to accept Japanese mediation in any future dispute between Indo-China and Siam, and not to enter into any agreement prejudicial to Japan.

The view held in London at the end of February that Japan no longer intended a southward venture in the immediate future was confirmed by the news that her Foreign Minister, M. Matsuoka, was soon to pay visits to Berlin, Rome and Moscow. Though ominous for the future, this information suggested that nothing desperate was imminent, and in fact the Minister was not authorised by his Government to enter into any commitments during his tour regarding Japan's participation in the war; his main object was to secure Japan against attack from the north in the event of a further move southward. Matsuoka left Tokyo on March 12. On April 2 Mr. Churchill sent him a friendly message—similar to that which he had addressed to Mussolini in May 1940—which was in fact a warning to Japan to think twice before provoking a war against Britain and America.[2] Matsuoka was successful in his main object: on April 13 a neutrality

---

[1] Printed in Churchill III 157.
[2] Printed in Churchill III 117–118.

pact was signed between the U.S.S.R. and Japan. Hitler was bound to regard this agreement with different feelings according as he was thinking chiefly of Russia or Britain as the enemy: as freeing Russia from the danger of a war on two fronts, it could not be welcome to him, and it is clear that he had discouraged it; on the other hand, he had no doubts of Germany's ability to defeat Russia single-handed, whereas he was anxious to set Japan free to make war on Britain.[1]

The presence of Mr. Menzies, the Prime Minister of Australia, in London at the end of February was particularly convenient in view of the part to be played by his countrymen in the expedition to Greece. His visit was no less timely with regard to the Far East. Doubts about this theatre were indeed the cause of his journey, since there was undoubtedly no small anxiety in Australia due to the weakness of our resources in that part of the world.[2] On the 27th Mr. Menzies met the ministerial heads of the Service Departments and the Chiefs of Staff. They gave him an account of the progress of discussions with the Americans and the Dutch and also of the current military situation and of our plans in the Far and Middle East. They admitted that in a war in the Far East we should incur great danger without American support. When Mr. Menzies stressed the need for fighter aircraft at Singapore and said that he thought the deficiency there was proportionately greater than in this country, the Chief of the Air Staff explained that forty-eight Brewster aircraft—a type which should be adequate for their task—ought by now to have arrived from America; to send Hurricanes from the United Kingdom would take three months.

A month later Mr. Menzies, who was clearly not wholly satisfied with what was being done, presented a memorandum asking for precise information as to how the report of the Singapore Defence Conference was being implemented; he referred particularly to the finding of the Australian delegates that 'in the absence of a main fleet in the Far East the forces and equipment available for the defence of Malaya were totally inadequate to meet a major attack by Japan'.

The Defence Committee on April 9 gave general approval to a reply drawn up by the Chiefs of Staff. They appreciated Mr. Menzies' desire to be in a position to give definite assurances to the Australian people that adequate provision had been made for their defence. But they were of opinion that, in view of the slackening

---

[1] See *N.D.* 75–C, 170–C; *Nazi Soviet Relations* 289–316, 321–324.
[2] See Hasluck, *The Government and the People* p. 296.

tension in the Far East and the more urgent need in the Mediterranean, it would be a mistake to send further reinforcements to
Malaya in the near future. Nor was it possible now to draw up a
timed programme for the eventual move of particular ships to the
Far East in the event of war with Japan: there were too many unknown factors. We stood by our promise to cut our losses in the
Mediterranean, if necessary, should Australia's vital interests be
threatened. Our intention was to send a battle-cruiser and a carrier
to the Indian Ocean at the outbreak of war with Japan, but the
despatch of further heavy ships must depend on the strength and
disposition of the German Fleet, on the course of events in the Eastern
Mediterranean, on our own capital-ship strength and on the likelihood of an invasion of the United Kingdom. On a broad view, the
security of Australia had been immensely strengthened by the
changing attitude of the United States. Though nominally neutral,
it was said, she was now so closely identified with our cause that the
potential threat of her Pacific Fleet (so named since February 1st)
at Hawaii must alone impose a most powerful restraining influence
on Japanese freedom of action to move southwards.

On April 24, when things were going badly in Greece, the Commonwealth Government asked for a candid and outspoken appreciation of the new situation, with an 'accurate statement of assistance
we could definitely rely on rather than hope for in the circumstances
outlined'. In their view the Empire, and in particular Australia,
should now have plans in train 'to meet the contingencies which may
be regarded as reasonably proximate'. Among such contingencies
they reckoned the control of Turkey and perhaps Persia by Germany,
the closing of the Suez Canal and straits of Gibraltar, and a struggle
on the part of the Fleet to fight its way out of the Mediterranean,
which might lead to Japanese attacks on Singapore, the Dutch East
Indies and Australia. They did not think it prudent to assume that
the United States would enter the war on our side, at any rate
immediately. Replying on the 29th, the Chiefs of Staff refused to
accept such contingencies as 'reasonably proximate' and declared
their inability to answer 'in isolation' the hypothetical questions put
to them. They supplied Mr. Menzies, however, with a brief appreciation of the difficult situation in the Middle East, where we were so
short of our requirements; they concluded with the reminder that
the war could only be won or lost in and around the United Kingdom.
While we were building up our resources for winning the war, we
must not lose it at home by taking too great risks in strengthening our
forces overseas. At a meeting of the Defence Committee that day,
April 29, at which Mr. Menzies was present, Mr. Churchill reiterated his firm opinion that the Japanese would not enter the war
unless a successful invasion of this country took place; they would be

most unlikely to do so if they thought that they would thereby bring in the United States; and that if they did declare war the United States would certainly do so too. Mr. Menzies did not press for a written statement of our strategic intentions in certain eventualities, but it was arranged that he should have a further discussion with the Chiefs of Staff.

This took place on May 1. A complication had then been introduced by a suggestion made to Admiral Danckwerts in Washington on April 29 by Colonel Knox, the Secretary of the Navy. 'What did we think would be the result if the United States now moved almost the whole of their Pacific Fleet into the Atlantic, leaving Hawaii to defend itself against any attack?' Three weeks previously the President had authorised Admiral Stark to give orders for three battleships and a carrier, with attendant vessels, to be so transferred, but he had since cancelled the authorisation. Some of his advisers were now urging him to allow a more far-reaching measure.[1] The British Defence Committee, on the night of April 30, had welcomed it on political grounds, contrary to the advice of the Naval Staff; it was to be suggested however to the Americans that whatever force was left behind at Hawaii should be such as would prove the most effective deterrent to Japan, and that aircraft-carriers were especially important for this purpose.[2]

Mr. Menzies had not been present at this meeting and protested that the matter was one which vitally affected the defence of Australia. A special meeting of the Defence Committee was accordingly held in the afternoon of May 1, at which Mr. Menzies expressed his opinion that, while he was personally disposed to think that the decision of the Defence Committee had been right, the Dominion Governments ought to have been consulted. His view was accepted and the Delegation in Washington were instructed to hold their hand. The reason for the Committee's hasty action had been that our naval delegates had on strategical grounds discouraged the American offer without reference home.

The British reply was eventually sent on May 8, after the Dominion Governments had expressed their views. It was to inform the United States that in the opinion of the Government of the United Kingdom, which was generally concurred in by those of Australia and New Zealand, any marked advance by the United States Navy into the Atlantic was more likely to deter the Japanese than the maintenance of the present very large American fleet at Hawaii, and that we should therefore welcome it. We hoped however that at least six capital ships and two carriers would be left in the Pacific.

---

[1] *The Undeclared War* pp. 446–451.

[2] Under this scheme, the forces left in the Pacific would be of the order of three or four battleships, four 6-inch cruisers etc.

Both the Dominion Governments had pressed strongly that some representation in the sense of the last sentence should be included. While appreciating the importance of the American gesture and acquiescing in the proposed reply, they feared—and Sir Robert Craigie, our Ambassador in Tokyo, agreed with them—that the Japanese might seize the opportunity presented by the temporary weakening of their opponents' naval force in the Far East to take some aggressive step, and as a counter-measure they urged the immediate naval reinforcement of Singapore. The Defence Committee considered these arguments on May 19, but held to their opinion that no plea should weigh against the importance of the entry of the United States into the war, and that the presence of these American ships in the Atlantic would tend towards that result; if the United States did not enter the war, their presence in the Pacific would not help the Dominions. This argument did not meet the point that the reduction of American strength in the Pacific might itself encourage the Japanese to aggression.

Concerning our own action, the Admiralty pointed out that, once the American fleet in the Atlantic was at war, we might hope to send capital ships of our own to the Far East; but until then we could only find ships for the Far East by withdrawing them either from convoy escort or from Force H at Gibraltar.

Eventually three American battleships and a carrier—the force originally projected—passed into the Atlantic in June, leaving nine battleships and three carriers in the Pacific Fleet.[1]

On the international plane, co-operation with the Dutch had been carried a stage further by an Anglo-Dutch-Australian conference held at Singapore in February, at which the Australians represented New Zealand also and Americans were present again as observers only. The Chiefs of Staff had a summarised report before them on March 12; they found it encouraging, as showing that the Netherlands authorities were 'co-operating in a realistic spirit'. The report's basic assumptions were that United States intervention could not be relied on, and that it was unlikely that Japan could launch simultaneous major attacks on Malaya and the Netherlands East Indies. The Chiefs of Staff expressed their general agreement with the report, and noted that the desire of the participants that all the Governments concerned should undertake now to co-operate fully, should any one of them have to take up arms against Japanese aggression, could not be complied with, since the Cabinet had decided on February 20 that a decision on this point must await

[1] Morison III 58.

the passing of Lend-Lease; the question what would constitute an act of war, such as to justify immediate counter-measures, was also reserved for the Government to decide at the time. The first of these two points was discussed by the Defence Committee on April 9; opinion was divided, the opponents of automatic participation in the war if the Dutch were attacked arguing that there was little help we could give them unless the United States joined in, and that the essential thing was to win the war against Germany. The Prime Minister was prepared to enter into any declaration, or any commitment, provided the Americans joined in it.

The defence of Malaya was still under consideration; on April 7 the Chiefs of Staff approved a proposal by the Commander-in-Chief, Far East, that, in the event of a Japanese threat to Malaya through southern Siam appearing imminent, British troops should advance into the Siamese part of the isthmus north of Singora. It would be necessary to act very promptly, but not too precipitately, in view of our treaty of non-aggression with Siam. A rapid decision by His Majesty's Government would probably be required. On this the Prime Minister minuted that there was no objection in principle, but that it would be wrong to lock up a large force in an area which we could readily reinforce from India. He viewed with great reluctance the continued diversion of troops, aircraft and supplies to a theatre which was unlikely to become active unless we were heavily beaten elsewhere.

The report of the negotiations at Washington (ABC–1), as has been mentioned, was in the hands of the Chiefs of Staff by May 1. It was concerned, of course, only with the situation after the United States of America had been forced to make war. Even so, should Japan enter the war, the military strategy in the Far East would be defensive.

> 'The United States does not intend to add to its present military strength in the Far East, but will employ the United States Pacific Fleet offensively in the manner best calculated to weaken Japanese economic power, and to support the defence of the Malay barrier by diverting Japanese strength away from Malaysia. The United States intends so to augment its forces in the Atlantic and Mediterranean areas that the British Commonwealth will be in a position to release the necessary forces for the Far East.'

By this time an American-Dutch-British conference had met at Singapore and a summary of its report had arrived in London.[1] Its object had been to prepare plans for the conduct of military operations in the Far East on the basis of the Washington Conference, on

---

[1] Australia, New Zealand and India were all represented.

the hypothesis of war between Germany, Italy and Japan on the one side and the British Empire with its present allies and the United States on the other. It is unnecessary to enter into the recommendations of the report if only because it never won American approval.[1] The British Chiefs of Staff were in general agreement with its findings, and pending ratification by the Government, which must await the full report, issued instructions that action, where required, should be taken as proposed.

The question whether we should announce that in the event of an attack by the Japanese on the Netherlands East Indies we should go to the assistance of the Dutch came up again before the Defence Committee on May 15. In carrying out such an obligation we must expect losses to our merchant ships in view of our naval weakness in the Far East. But the Committee decided in a sense contrary to such considerations, subject to the concurrence of the Dominions. It was argued that not only should we be morally bound to come to the assistance of the Dutch, as our allies, but our interest in the security of the line of communication running from Malaya through the Dutch islands to New Zealand would virtually compel us to do so. We should not consult the United States further before making the announcement, but should inform them beforehand of our intention.

Both in the sphere of grand strategy, as represented by the Washington conversations, and in the local strategy of the Far East agreement on the general lines of eventual co-operation had now been reached between the representatives of the United States and the United Kingdom, in consultation with those of the Dominions concerned; if each Government could not induce the others to act exactly as it would wish, it at least knew the others' point of view. This was a considerable advance. But little had been done to add to the prospective material strength of the countries which Japan might attack.

The importance of Singapore was of course common ground in high circles in London, but there were differences of opinion as to the urgency of its needs and the priority which should be accorded to them. This difference had shown itself in September 1940 when the War Office could not accept the view that the Japanese threat in Malaya was not serious. It appeared again in April 1941. The Prime Minister, in a directive of the 28th, had repeated his belief that the likelihood of Japan entering the war was remote and that, if she did, the United States would almost certainly enter it on our

---

[1] See Feis, *op. cit.* p. 170.

side. Should these conditions cease to hold good, it would be the responsibility of Ministers to notify the Service staffs in good time. Meanwhile there was no need to make any further dispositions for the defence of Malaya and Singapore, beyond the 'modest arrangements' already in progress. He had gone on to say that the loss of Egypt and the Middle East would be a disaster of the first magnitude to Great Britain, second only to successful invasion and final conquest.

The three Chiefs of Staff were not altogether happy about this directive. They thought it their duty to emphasise that in the case of the Far East 'good time' meant at least three months, since that was the minimum period within which reinforcements and equipment could reach Malaya. Sir John Dill in a separate memorandum, of May 6, while agreeing that the loss of Egypt would be a terrible calamity, maintained that a successful invasion of the United Kingdom would alone be a mortal blow to us; Egypt was 'not even second in order of priority', for it had been an accepted principle in our strategy that in the last resort the security of Singapore came before that of Egypt.[1] Yet the defences of Singapore were still considerably below standard, though, as he added later, 'quite a small addition' of force there 'would make all the difference between running a serious risk and achieving full security'.[2]

In an elaborate paper on Future Strategy drawn up by the Future Operational Planning Section and presented to the Defence Committee in June the importance of the Far East was insisted upon. 'The threat in this area is only potential; consequently it tends to become obscured by other threats which are more grimly real. But, should it develop, this threat may bring even greater dangers than those we now face. Singapore, is of course, the key . . . It is vital to take, as soon as possible, the necessary measures to secure the defence of Singapore.'

The forces required to defend the Far East, they said, had been estimated at 'two equivalent divisions from the Field Force', plus local forces, giving a total of about four divisions, and 22 squadrons of aircraft (336 aircraft). 'The army garrison, though nearly up to strength, is seriously deficient in important items of equipment, notably anti-tank, anti-aircraft, and field guns. The present Air Forces comprise $12\frac{1}{3}$ squadrons (150 aircraft).'

The Middle East, the Planners proceeded, came in a different category. 'With the Mediterranean already closed to our shipping, the direct effect of its loss on our sea communications would not be vital, so long as enemy naval egress to the Red Sea and Indian Ocean was barred.' However, 'the loss of Egypt would be a disaster of the

---

[1] See above, p. 324.

[2] See the documents printed in Appendix IV and in Churchill III 373–377.

first magnitude. No sacrifice is too great in order to avoid it, except the sacrifice of the United Kingdom, our vital sea communications, or of Singapore.'

No further reinforcement of Malaya was carried out during the period covered by this volume. The obligation to send a fleet to the Far East, sacrificing if necessary our position in the Middle East, should the vital interests of Australia and New Zealand be threatened was always admitted; but the resources to meet the obligation did not exist. In the meantime our commitments in the Middle East continually increased.

It will be convenient to bring the naval story up to date. The scheme accepted in the Anglo-American conversations of the winter was based on the principle that the Americans, while leaving a sufficient fleet in the Pacific to deter Japan from aggression, would from there reinforce their Atlantic fleet in such a way as to permit the British to send a fleet to the Far East on the outbreak of war in that region.[1] It was proposed that the British should then send out a battle-cruiser and an aircraft-carrier (from Force H) as immediate reinforcements, to be followed eventually by five battleships. On June 10, when the American detachment of three battleships and an aircraft-carrier had just completed their move into the Atlantic, the British Defence Committee discussed an American proposal that three more battleships should follow: the proposal was not supported by the United States Naval Staff, and the Defence Committee advised against the move taking place at the present time, when six of our own capital ships were out of action; by August it should be acceptable. Sir Dudley Pound, however, wrote on July 16 that until the Americans came in we could not 'collect a fleet to proceed to the Far East', and it is of interest that Vice-Admiral Sir Tom Phillips, the Commander-in-Chief designate of such a fleet, is reported as saying on August 8 that our strategy should be to avoid war with Japan and give way as long as we could afford to, until America was ready and willing to support us. The Government saw no less clearly that our strategy must depend on the attitude of America, but they refused to believe that Japan would risk war with an undefeated Britain and the United States, or that if she did we should not be warned in time to send reinforcements. The next volume will show that this confidence was misplaced.

---

[1] Above, p. 504.

CHAPTER XXII

THE MEDITERRANEAN AND
MIDDLE EAST,
MAY–JUNE 1941

ROMMEL'S halt on the frontier of Egypt and the with-drawal of our forces from Greece afforded an opportunity for a review of our strategy. The enemy had regained the initiative, and we could only guess at his intentions. The point of greatest danger at the moment was thought to be Egypt, and at a meeting of the Defence Committee on April 28 the Prime Minister insisted on the need of fighting every inch of the way on this front. His directive of the same day, already referred to, demanded that this should be impressed on all ranks of the Army of the Nile; he was alarmed lest the fact that the possible evacuation of the country had been secretly considered should become known. The Chiefs of Staff, while of course at one with the Prime Minister as to the need to defend Egypt resolutely, considered that he was in fact overstating the comparative importance of possessing it. It was essential that sufficient forces should be kept in the United Kingdom as a defence against invasion: the enemy on interior lines could change front overland far more quickly than we could by sea; and, though at the moment shipping, as the Prime Minister had said, would limit the amount of troops which could be sent from Britain, this need not always be so, since American assistance might make it possible to convey reinforcements to the Middle East so large that their departure would jeopardise the safety of the United Kingdom.[1]

Sir John Dill agreed with the Commander-in-Chief, Home Forces, that we ought to keep at home six armoured divisions and four army tank brigades (some 2,600 tanks). We expected to have by June 1941 but five armoured divisions and three army tank brigades, which owing to deficiencies of training or equipment would be equivalent only to three fully effective armoured divisions, against the six Panzer divisions (some 2,400 tanks) which the enemy might hope to land. Unrealistic as such an estimate must appear in the light of our present knowledge of Hitler's plans for 1941 and of the difficulties of a large-scale opposed landing, it illustrates the anxiety which still beset the Army in the spring of that year.

---

[1] See Appendix IV; also Churchill III 373–377.

To return to London's appreciation of the enemy's intentions, it was thought that he might cherish designs on Syria or on Morocco, and the Cabinet decided to put such pressure as they could on Vichy, through the United States Government, to resist demands for collaboration.[1] There were no signs however of extensive troop movement through France towards the Spanish frontier, whereas in the view of the Foreign Office Germany might well attack Russia as soon as the Greek war was over. But as early as 22 April reports of German activity indicated that an attack on Crete was being prepared, possibly as cover for a descent on Cyprus as a stepping-stone toward Syria. On the 27th our Intelligence appreciated that a combined sea and air attack on Crete was to be expected very soon, and the Defence Committee considered the matter next day. It was assumed that the island must be defended. The First Sea Lord pointed out that it was the same distance as Rhodes from Alexandria, and that German aircraft operating from Crete would enjoy improved opportunities of causing trouble to the Fleet. Sir Charles Portal thought that, subject to the Navy's requirements, we should do well to concentrate our fighters in Egypt.

Interest was now focused on Crete. This island, the ancient cradle of sea-power, a stronghold of patriots resisting oppression, had now to face a challenge of a novel kind which it was ill prepared to meet.

It was to the Navy that it had been of especial value, as offering a fuelling base 400 miles out from Alexandria; any danger from the Italians had been considered acceptable. But the centre of the island was only 150 miles distant from Rhodes and Cos in the Dodecanese, only 200 miles from Athens, and about as far from the Libyan coast, from all which directions the German bombers might now operate. On the other hand, the distance between Crete and the African coast ruled out any hope of effective fighter protection from Egypt. Thus it would be much easier for the enemy to attack Crete than for us to defend it. Suda Bay was certainly not a second Scapa; the Mobile Naval Base Defence Organisation sent to the Middle East some time before had not yet arrived in the island. There were only two airfields, at Heraklion (Candia) and Maleme, and one landing-strip, at Retimo, and there were very few aircraft, while the anti-aircraft artillery consisted of two heavy and three light batteries only. The permanent garrison of three British battalions (without field artillery), exclusive of Greek units only partially trained and equipped, was now being reinforced by troops evacuated from Greece.

The long, mountainous island was traversed by only one good

---

[1] Above, p. 436.

road, running along the north coast, and central control would evidently be very difficult. Whatever might and should have been done in the six months of the British occupation to improve its defences in view of its strategic importance, very little had been done in fact. An inter-Service Middle East committee appointed in June 1941 found that 'with notable exceptions' the period of comparative peace was 'marked by inertia, for which ambiguity as to the role of the garrison was in large measure responsible'. Was it to defend the base at Suda Bay or to prevent invasion? They commented also that there had been a succession of five commanders in six months. Wavell in his despatch excused the failure to do more by 'the constant shortage of men and materials in the Middle East and the lack of available labour'. Shipping too was short, and a good deal of the material actually sent was sunk. 'It had always been intended', he said, 'to develop landing-places on the south of the island and roads from them to the north, in order to avoid the exposed sea passage to them round the north of the island, but there had never been . . . sufficient means to carry this out.'[1] In other words, other needs had always seemed more pressing.

After visiting Crete on April 30 Wavell spoke of its defence as at present 'a difficult and dangerous commitment'. At the suggestion of the Prime Minister he had entrusted the command of the forces in the island—including, at their Government's request, the Greek troops—to Major-General B. C. Freyberg, V.C., commander of the New Zealand Division, who with the greater part of his two brigades had just arrived from the mainland. Next day, May 1st, General Freyberg sent a report to the New Zealand Government which moved them to suggest to London that either their troops should be supplied with sufficient means to defend the island or the decision to hold Crete at all costs should be reviewed. The General explained that it was the seaborne, not the airborne, attack which troubled him. As to the latter, both he and Mr. Churchill felt confident.

On April 25, the day after the evacuation from Greece began, Hitler ordered that a plan (known as 'Merkur') should be prepared for the capture of Crete; he proposed to use the island as a base for attacks against the British. Air forces primarily would be employed, and the Commander-in-Chief, Air, was to be in command. Transport arrangements, however, were not to delay the assembly of forces for the invasion of Russia, and after the island had been occupied the Army would relieve all or part of the airborne corps for new tasks.[2]

The attack began on May 20 and continued with undiminished intensity during the following week. Bombing and machine-gunning from the air covered the arrival of parachute troops, gliders, and

---

[1] Cf. F. de Guingand, *Operation Victory* pp. 82–86.

[2] *F.D.* No. 28.

troop-carrying aircraft. The plan was to execute seaborne landings also, but these were foiled by the Royal Navy.

The story of the gallant defence of Crete and of the great part played by the Navy is told elsewhere.[1] Wavell had intended to reorganise in Egypt the Australian and New Zealand troops evacuated from Greece to Crete, and to relieve them by the 6th British Division hitherto earmarked for the Dodecanese, but both time and shipping were lacking. When the attack came it had to be met mainly by the troops from Greece plus the former garrison and one commando from Egypt, strengthened by a few battalions which arrived at the last moment and a portion of the Mobile Base Defence Organisation. Forty-six field-guns had also been received, and thirty-two heavy anti-aircraft guns out of fifty-six agreed to be the minimum required. Most of the few aircraft available were obsolete, and after heavy fighting orders were given on May 19 before the enemy's main attack to withdraw the remaining seven from the island.

When the Defence Committee discussed the happenings in Crete on the second day, May 21, they thought that, if Wavell could land reinforcements on the south coast and if the Navy could prevent a seaborne landing by the enemy, it should be possible to hold this 'key position in the Mediterranean' against attack from the air; but next day the First Sea Lord warned the other Chiefs of Staff that if the Mediterranean Fleet continued to sustain heavy losses it would be unable to prevent a landing, in view of attack by dive-bombers and the lack of fighter cover. On the 23rd Tedder explained to the Chief of the Air Staff that the events of the past day-and-a-half at sea had shown that it was no longer possible for our ships to operate in the Aegean or the vicinity of Crete by daylight, whereas our Blenheims from the Western Desert could not hope to stop German convoys to Crete escorted by Messerschmitt 110's.

On the same day Admiral Cunningham, who on the 22nd had signalled to the Fleet that they must 'stick it out' and 'not let the Army down', told the Admiralty that he was forced to the 'melancholy conclusion' that owing to our weakness in the air we must admit defeat in the coastal area and accept the fact that at the cost of such losses we were not justified in trying to prevent landings from the sea. On the 25th the position was not judged hopeless by Wavell, since the enemy had only established himself in strength in one part of the island and appeared to be stretched to the limit; but reinforcements and supplies could now be brought only by fast ships at night.

The Chiefs of Staff, meeting on the afternoon of the 25th, felt

---

[1] Playfair II ch. vii; Roskill I ch. xx; see also the volume *Crete* by D. M. Davin (Wellington 1953) and the volume *Greece, Crete and Syria* by Gavin Long (Canberra 1953) in the New Zealand and Australian official histories.

that, if a great effort were made by all three Services during the next three days, the battle might yet be won, and they despatched with the Prime Minister's approval the following signal:

1. If the situation is allowed to drag on, the enemy will have the advantage because, unless more drastic naval action is taken than is suggested in your appreciation, the enemy will be able to reinforce the island to a considerable extent with men and stores.

2. It is essential therefore that Commanders-in-Chief should concert measures for clearing up the situation without delay. In so doing the Fleet and the Royal Air Force must accept whatever risk is entailed in preventing any considerable reinforcement of men and material from reaching the island either by night or by day.

3. Should air reconnaissance show any movement by sea or any collection of craft at Melo, it will be essential for the Fleet to operate north of the island by day. It is probable that the losses incurred in doing so will be considerable, and only experience will show for how many days this situation can be maintained. This confirms that time is the dominating factor.

To the men on the spot the message seemed unrealistic and it was deeply resented, so he has told us, by Admiral Cunningham. The Lords of the Admiralty might rest assured, he replied, that the determining factor in operating in the Aegean was not the fear of sustaining losses, but the need to avoid loss which, without commensurate advantage to ourselves, would cripple the fleet under his command. It was unnecessary to wait for further 'experience' of losses in order to know how long the situation could be maintained. In three days two cruisers and four destroyers had been sunk, and one battleship would be out of action for several months; two other cruisers and four destroyers had suffered considerable damage. 'I feel that their Lordships should know', he continued, 'that effect of recent operations on personnel is cumulative. Our light craft officers, men and machinery alike are nearing exhaustion. Since "Lustre" started, at the end of February, they have been kept running almost to limit of endurance, and now, when work is redoubled, they are faced with an air concentration beside which, I am assured, that in Norway was child's play. It is inadvisable to drive men beyond a certain point.'[1] On May 30, in a personal letter to the First Sea Lord, Admiral Cunningham said that if the Prime Minister or the Admiralty would like a change of command he would not feel in any way annoyed, more especially as the happenings of the last few days might have shaken the Fleet's faith in his handling of the affair. Admiral Pound's

---

[1] Printed in Churchill III 260, where several of the other signals are quoted.

reply ignored the suggestion of a change of command; he had not the slightest fear that the Fleet's confidence in their commander had been shaken.[1]

The tired troops too were finding conditions intolerable. Our Intelligence had been remarkably accurate and precise, and the Germans met with much stiffer resistance than they expected; their losses in men and aircraft were serious, but they were bold and persistent and their air power was crushing. On the 27th Wavell reported that Freyberg had decided that evacuation was necessary, and that he himself had sanctioned it. His signal crossed with one from the Chief of the Imperial General Staff to the same effect, and the Prime Minister that night informed the Defence Committee of the decision. It was a sad set-off to the sinking of the *Bismarck* that morning.

Wavell explained in a later signal on the 27th that it had become quite obvious that the attempt to prolong the defence would be not only useless but likely so to exhaust the resources of all the Services as to compromise the position in the Middle East even more gravely than would the loss of Crete. The enemy's overwhelming air superiority had made reinforcement impossible, while the Royal Air Force, not having bases within fighter range, had been unable to prevent him from landing fresh troops of his own by air.

The decision to evacuate meant a further series of operations, ending on the night of May 31, of extreme difficulty, danger and strain for troops and Navy alike. The evacuations from both the mainland of Greece and from Crete tried the Navy to the utmost; in both cases most of the embarkations had to be effected from open beaches and there was no air cover. In spite of heavy casualties, including the loss of three cruisers and six destroyers and serious damage to two battleships and a carrier, sustained before the evacuation and in the course of it, some 18,000 United Kingdom, Australian and New Zealand troops were conveyed safely to Egypt out of some 32,000 in the island.[2]

British casualties in Crete included nearly 1,800 killed and nearly 12,000 prisoners, of whom many were wounded. The casualties in the Royal Navy were over 1,800 killed. The Royal Air Force lost seven Wellingtons, sixteen medium bombers and twenty-three fighters—mostly over Crete—in the period from a week before the battle began until the end of the evacuation.

The Germans' losses in aircraft during the same period were 220 destroyed and 144 damaged—not all from enemy action. Their losses

---

[1] See *A Sailor's Odyssey* pp. 375, 390.

[2] Playfair II 215. The cruisers lost were the *Calcutta, Fiji, Gloucester*; the two damaged battleships were the *Warspite* and *Barham*; the carrier was the *Formidable*.

in men were a little over 6,000, of whom nearly 4,000 were killed or missing.[1]

The capture of Crete was a landmark in the history of war. Never before had a country only accessible by sea been overrun by a Power not possessing even local naval superiority. Göring might well boast that there were 'no impregnable islands'. The lesson was not lost on those responsible for the defence of Great Britain. The protection of aerodromes against airborne attack seemed the most urgent problem and on May 28 the Chiefs of Staff appointed a special sub-committee, with Sir Findlater Stewart as chairman, to report on the measures to be taken to guard against this danger in the next two months. The Chiefs of Staff considered and in general approved the interim recommendations of the sub-committee on June 9. They agreed that no basic reorganisation was practicable as an emergency measure, but various other proposals were accepted, including the principle that Field Force troops should be disposed within a mile or so of the twenty-nine fighter airfields considered of vital importance. The Defence Committee next day asked that a full report should be furnished by the Commander-in-Chief, Home Forces, on the measures which he intended to take.

On the same day, June 10, a debate took place in the House of Commons;[2] it was comparable to that occasioned by our failure in Norway, with the important exceptions that no one now desired a change of leadership and that no division followed. But it was asserted that our strategy lagged far behind the enemy's 'in tempo and resourcefulness', that co-operation between the three Services was defective and that the enthusiasm of the people had faltered. More particularly it was asked who was responsible for withdrawing our aircraft from Crete during the battle (withdrawal was in fact ordered before the battle and there were only seven of them), why we had not in six months provided more and safer airfields, and whether the Army and Navy should not have more effective control of the air forces working with them. The Prime Minister, replying, pointed out the dangers which might arise from ministerial explanations in public. He emphasised our all-round shortage in the essential anti-aircraft artillery and the difficulties and delays in transporting aeroplanes to distant theatres. He did not apologise for the decision to defend Crete.

'The choice was: should Crete be defended without effective air support or should the Germans be permitted to occupy it without

---

[1] Figures from Playfair II ch. vii.
[2] *House of Commons Debates* vol. 372, cols. 63–155.

opposition?' It was absurd to suggest that one should not attempt to defend any place that one was not sure of holding. 'Crete was an extremely important salient in our line of defence. It was like Fort Douaumont at Verdun in 1916; it was like Kemmel Hill in 1918.' The Germans took both, but they lost the war; 'who could say what the results would have been if they had not been fought for?' Mr. Churchill could not know that the German airborne forces had received such a hammering in Crete that never again would Hitler attempt to launch an airborne attack on the grand scale. Crete, said General Student, commander of the XI Air Corps, was the grave of German parachutists.[1]

But though the Prime Minister defended our strategy in public he was far from satisfied with its execution. He could not feel that Middle East Headquarters had shown any real grip on this operation. While admitting the strategic importance of the island they had treated its defence as a troublesome necessity. He informed the Chiefs of Staff that there would have to be a detailed inquiry into the defence of Crete, and later on issued an elaborate questionnaire for Middle East Command to answer.

The two Dominion Governments concerned were naturally perturbed at the inauspicious opening to the return of their troops to a European theatre. They felt that they had not been consulted fully and promptly enough and perhaps that they had been misled by too sanguine estimates. It was difficult to explain to their peoples why things had gone so badly; confidence in the capacity of the United Kingdom authorities must be shaken. The Australians had wished General Blamey to command 'Lustre' force; he was, in fact, on his return from Greece, appointed Wavell's Deputy in the Middle East.[2]

Besides Crete, Cairo was concerned with two other fronts during the month of May—Syria and the Western Desert.

The campaign in Syria comes into our story in a twofold connexion, as an episode in the war in the Middle East and as an episode in our relations with the French. Ever since June 1940 the French authorities in the mandated territories of Syria and the Lebanon had taken their orders from Vichy; the High Commissioner was now General Dentz. At the end of March 1941 reports that Syria was seething with unrest raised hopes that before long the country might

---

[1] Under interrogation in September 1945.

[2] G. Long, *Greece, Crete and Syria* pp. 151, 194, 318; New Zealand *Documents* I 322. Mr. Fraser, Prime Minister of New Zealand, was in Egypt for some weeks from May 15.

be won to our side, but the Prime Minister and Chiefs of Staff decided that no action was called for at present. Syria could be left to simmer. But some three weeks later, while the evacuation from Greece was in progress, the Foreign Office and the War Office had in mind the danger of an airborne German descent on Syria, and the War Office asked Wavell what force he could spare to help General Dentz to resist. The help of Free French troops was not at this time contemplated, at least in the first instance. This was a few days before Rashid Ali's *coup d'état* at Baghdad and the demand on Wavell for a force to relieve Habbaniya.[1] At the same time Vichy were warned through the United States Government that we were deeply concerned in their attitude towards a German or Italian landing, and aid was promised them in the event of their resistance. Marshal Pétain, however, merely stated that he would not agree to any form of collaboration with Germany which exceeded the armistice terms, and would render her no 'voluntary active military aid'.[2]

Early in May there were reports that the arrival of German troops in Syria was imminent, and the Defence Committee discussed the position on the 8th. Syria might be a stepping-stone towards either Iraq or Egypt, and it was thought unlikely that Dentz would resist. Air Marshal Longmore, who was present, told the Committee that when he left Egypt twelve Blenheims were standing by in Palestine to deal with German transport aircraft. The only British mobile land force in Palestine was starting for Habbaniya. There was however a Free French force of six battalions with some artillery and tanks, and their commander, General Catroux, had for some time been seeking to win over the French in Syria by propaganda. The Defence Committee decided that the best course was to give Catroux what help we could and encourage him to enter Syria as soon as the Germans arrived; it was thought that he was unlikely to gain much support if he went in earlier.

On May 12 it was known that Axis aircraft had alighted at Damascus; General Dentz had said that his present instructions did not provide for a German occupation of Syria, but if such orders came from Vichy he would obey them. The Defence Committee on the 14th authorised Air headquarters to bomb German aircraft in Syria irrespective of the effect of such action on our relations with the French; they should realise that it was they who were drawing the war to their country by conniving at and indeed assisting German penetration. These landings, which were on a very small scale, anticipated by some days Hitler's directive of May 23 for the Middle East, already referred to, which ordered an air force of limited size

[1] See above, 460.
[2] See above, 437.

to support the Arab liberation movement in Iraq; but by this time the most critical period was passing. The Defence Committee agreed that we must do everything possible to organise a force for Syria. Unfortunately the Free French lacked transport and we had little to supply them with, while Wavell discouraged hasty action with weak forces; he considered that the attitude of Turkey was what mattered. Politics also were involved in the form of the manifesto which General Catroux should issue.

The Chiefs of Staff were anxious not to lose the opportunity of Turkish co-operation and on May 19 told Wavell that they saw no option but to improvise the largest force that could be made available without leaving the Western Desert too bare. The General promptly made provisional arrangements for the 7th Australian Division to move to Palestine, though this meant weakening the defences of Egypt and using up two Polish and South African brigades kept as reserves for Crete. General Maitland Wilson, who on his return from Greece had been given the command of British troops in Palestine and Transjordan, was warned to prepare for an advance into Syria. Wavell considered that the force must be composed of both British and Free French troops, the British leading, and he did not approve General Catroux's plan to advance on Damascus rather than along the coast.[1] But on the 20th the Defence Committee authorised the movement of the Free French force to the Syrian frontier, and beyond it should their General think the situation favourable. It was worth taking a chance which might come off, rather than watch the Germans establishing themselves.

The Commander-in-Chief was disquieted. The Defence Committee on the 20th had not followed his advice, and it seemed to him that too much weight was being attached to opinions emanating from the Free French, whose sources of information he distrusted. One of the arguments used for prompt action had been reports that General Dentz's troops were withdrawing to the Lebanon, presumably to leave Syria free for the Germans; but it now appeared that on the contrary they would defend all approaches to Syria. A disgruntled signal from Wavell on the 21st drew from the Defence Committee a reply with a sting in the tail. He was making preparation, he said, for a combined British and French operation if the situation was favourable, but the Government must trust his judgement in the matter or relieve him of his command. It was unacceptable that the Free French should dictate action that was bound seriously to affect the military situation in the Middle East. Sir John Dill, while repudiating the suggestion that anyone but His Majesty's Government was dictating action, advised that nevertheless

---

[1] See Map 19.

Wavell should either be allowed to carry out the policy he believed to be sound or be relieved of his command. But the Defence Committee took a firmer line:

'. . . There is no objection to your mingling British troops with the Free French who are to enter Syria; but, as you have clearly shown, you have not the means to mount a regular military operation, and as you were instructed yesterday, all that can be done at present is to give the best possible chance to the kind of armed political inroad described in [a Chiefs of Staff signal of May 20].

You are wrong in supposing that policy described in [that signal] arose out of any representations made by the Free French Leaders or General Spears. It arose entirely from the view taken here by those who have the supreme direction of war and policy in all theatres. Our view is that if the Germans can pick up Syria and Iraq with petty air forces, tourists and local revolts we must not shrink from running equal small-scale military risks, and facing the possible aggravation of political dangers from failure. For this decision we, of course, take full responsibility, and should you find yourself unwilling to give effect to it, arrangements will be made to meet any wish you may express to be relieved of your Command.'[1]

It was a day of severe strain—the second day of the assault on Crete. But Wavell was not lacking in toughness, the quality he had declared the most necessary in a general, and, though he thought these 'political adventures and Jameson raids' were dangerous, he was already proceeding to 'consider in a calmer atmosphere' than that of the recent rumours how best to prevent the Germans from establishing themselves in Syria; and he was promptly assured by the Prime Minister that it was his views which weighed with the Government and not those of the Free French. General Catroux himself now recognised that any attempt to advance on Damascus with the resources at his disposal was out of the question.

But preparations for a better-found expedition went forward. Wavell on the 25th proposed a plan (to be known as 'Exporter'); he could not move before the first week of June, and both he and General de Gaulle agreed that the force available—7th Australian Division (less one brigade), six Free French battalions with a few guns and light tanks, part of 1st (British) Cavalry Division and certain other units—was inadequate, but it was all that could be scraped together. The Defence Committee on the night of May 27—it was the meeting which sanctioned the evacuation of Crete—approved Wavell's proposals. Our prime object was to destroy the enemy forces in the Western Desert, and the apportionment of aircraft

---

[1] Printed with other telegrams in Churchill III 290.

between the two fronts would be difficult. But it was important to strike in Syria before the Germans recovered from the drain which Crete must have occasioned to the Luftwaffe. It was decided also to ask the Turks to occupy airfields in northern Syria, particularly at Aleppo, and that no attempt should be made to reinforce Cyprus at present.

Planning for the Syrian expedition had been affected by wider differences with the Free French. General de Gaulle, who after a visit to Cairo in April had returned to Brazzaville, had been at variance with Middle East Command over the question of the blockade measures to be applied to French Somaliland. He had found the British attitude with regard to Free French interests in the Middle East sadly negative. Wavell had not previously been in favour of the General coming to Cairo, but on May 16 he urged that he should now be invited; the Prime Minister had in fact already sent an invitation, and de Gaulle accepted it. On the 25th he discussed the situation with Wavell.[1] For the leader of the Free French the expedition to Syria was much more than a military question. He was bound to take into account the interests of a restored and sovereign France, and this would naturally influence his views on the subject of Turkish co-operation. In the event, the Turks took no further action than to send troops to the Syrian frontier.

'Exporter' was launched on June 8.[2] General Maitland Wilson had an Indian brigade group (from Eritrea) and a commando battalion in addition to the units previously mentioned, but no medium or heavy tanks. A naval force of two cruisers and several destroyers supported his left flank. Our weakness was as usual in the air; only four squadrons—one bomber, two fighter, one army-co-operation— could be allotted him, and the deficiency made itself felt, at sea as well as on land.

It was hoped to reach Damascus and Beirut on the first day and after seizing Rayak to press on, if possible, to Tripoli, all with as little fighting as possible. The force would represent itself as having come to fight the Germans, not the French: it was recognised that success would depend largely on the attitude of the French garrison and the local population. The garrison, as it turned out, put up a stout resistance; they had eighteen regular battalions and ninety tanks, though without much hope of reinforcement, and after the first few days Allied progress was disappointingly slow. The prisoners taken in these days were mostly loyal to Pétain; they denied that there were any German troops, except airmen, in Syria. At length

---

[1] See Charles de Gaulle, *Mémoires de Guerre, l'Appel, 1940–1942* (Paris 1954) p. 155; the book contains over 400 pages of documents.

[2] An account of the campaign will be found in Playfair II ch. x. See also Lord Wilson of Libya, *Eight Years Overseas*, ch. iv, and G. Long, *Greece, Crete and Syria* in the Australian Official History; also Catroux, *Dans la bataille de Méditerranée* (Paris, 1949).

on June 21 the Allies entered Damascus, but the Vichy forces continued to fight skilfully, and it was not till July 11 that General Dentz asked for terms and the cease-fire was ordered. By then forces from Iraq were harassing his eastern flank. On July 3 a column ('Habforce') including troops of the Arab Legion, under Major-General J. G. W. Clark, advancing from east and south-east had occupied Palmyra after unexpected delays due to the enemy's local air superiority. A larger force, 10th Indian Division, under Major-General W. J. Slim, moving up the Euphrates with Aleppo as its ultimate objective, had occupied Raqqa, 220 miles north-east of Damascus, with its important airfield, on July 5. Two further British brigades and one Australian, with some artillery, had reinforced General Wilson before the end of June, and Wellington bombers from Egypt had joined in.

The negotiations between the commanders, for which the way had been prepared earlier by inquiries from Vichy through American channels, brought out the different points of view of the British Empire and the Free French. De Gaulle, while respecting the supreme military authority of the British commander, held that political authority in Syria and the Lebanon should naturally revert to him as the proper representative of the Mandatory Power. Being most jealous of any British interference in political matters, he had resented the insistence of the British Government on publicly associating themselves with the promise of independence for the two mandated territories proclaimed by Catroux on behalf of de Gaulle when crossing the frontier on June 8. The British, as the Prime Minister had declared two days later, had no territorial designs in Syria or anywhere else in French territory. On the contrary we should 'do all in our power to restore the freedom, independence and rights of France'.[1] But our main concern was to win the war, and hence to ensure that so long as the war lasted Syria should cause us as little trouble as possible. It was important therefore to preserve the good will of the Arab peoples of the two countries, and British observers were clear that the Arabs would not willingly accept a mere transfer from one French authority to another as the result of the Syrian campaign. We believed that the Arabs regarded us as more disinterested than the French, and we could not disclaim all responsibility for their government in the immediate future. The British therefore continued to press, after as well as before the signature of the armistice convention on July 14, for the early fulfilment of the promise of independence.

There was difference of opinion too over the treatment of the enemy forces after surrender. The British object was to wind up the Syrian affair without delay and without unnecessary provocation to

---

[1] *House of Commons Debates*, vol. 372, col. 157.

Vichy. Doubts as to the probable reaction of the French naval crews at Alexandria had been resolved by Admiral Godfroy's willingness to respect the *status quo*, and no trouble had resulted. With regard to the land forces in Syria, the British view was that they should be given the option of joining the Free French or of being repatriated to France in Vichy ships, and these were the terms eventually agreed on. But de Gaulle protested against the notion of sending home men who had fought for Vichy: not only would the incentive to join his own forces be greatly diminished, but seasoned troops would be available to fight another day against the Allies. De Gaulle had himself left Syria for Brazzaville before the convention was signed, and though Catroux approved it his chief telegraphed vehement dissent. But a pledge had been given which the British authorities felt unable to disregard. In fact, less than 6,000 men opted to join the Free French, while 37,500 perferred repatriation to North Africa. Moreover, commenting on the Syrian campaign in the House of Commons on July 15, the Prime Minister referred respectfully to the fighting qualities of the enemy and claimed that our relations with Marshal Pétain's Government, 'such as they are', had not worsened 'during these weeks of distressing fighting'.[1] These remarks cannot have been pleasing to General de Gaulle.

Hence the Syrian campaign, won by joint effort, resulted in very strained relations between the Free French leader and the British Government, and the strain lasted even after the agreements come to between de Gaulle and the British Minister of State at the end of July and beginning of August. The agreements concerned the interpretation of the armistice convention and future collaboration between the British and Free French authorities in the Middle East. Great Britain repeated that she had no interest in Syria or the Lebanon except to win the war, and she 'freely admitted' that after their independence had been secured France should have 'the dominant privileged position in the Levant among European nations'. But the Middle East constituted a single theatre of operations, and, 'in view of the large preponderance at the present time of the British forces in comparison with the French forces in the Middle East, it is for the British command in the Middle East theatre of operations to draw up plans and fix the role to be played by the French forces in the joint operations'. An ultimate appeal to His Majesty's Government in the United Kingdom and General de Gaulle was provided for.[2]

The British Government's intention in urging an advance into Syria with so improvised a force had been to forestall a German occupation, believed imminent. As it turned out, French resistance

---

[1] *House of Commons Debates*, vol. 373, col. 464.

[2] General de Gaulle's point of view is stated in his *Mémoires de Guerre*; the book illustrates his deep suspicion of British motives. See also Catroux, *op. cit.* chaps xx, xxi.

was more stubborn than they had expected and the danger less pressing than they supposed. Hitler had by the end of May written off the insurrection in Iraq as a failure, and his immediate purpose was to give the British no excuse for intervention in Syria; he had no thought now of occupying the country himself until he had settled accounts with Russia. Thus there would have been time for Middle East headquarters to prepare at leisure for an advance in greater strength. But the British Government preferred the risks of action to the risks of delay. Once the unsatisfactory campaign was won, it was a relief to have kept the Germans out of a region whence they could have threatened to take the Turks in reverse and made ready to strike at Egypt or Iraq; a descent on Cyprus, hitherto almost defenceless, was now unlikely; and on the positive side it was something to have secured a land connexion with Turkey and ports which might be useful to the Navy.

Success in another minor campaign, which had been assured by the surrender of the Duke of Aosta at Amba Alagi on May 18, was clinched by the capture on June 11, by a mixed British and Indian force from Aden, of Assab in the extreme south of Eritrea. This was the last port remaining in Italian hands, and the Red Sea was now under unchallenged Allied control. Early in July Italian resistance in south-west Abyssinia collapsed. On July 13 the Army Council congratulated Generals Cunningham and Platt on the conclusion of their victorious operations. The one remaining Italian stronghold in East Africa, at Gondar in the mountainous region of northern Abyssinia, was now isolated, and, though it was not reduced till November, after the summer rains, operations in this part of Africa were no longer a serious distraction to Middle East Command. Nor were we perturbed by the fact that French Somaliland was still under the control of Vichy. Our blockade of the country continued, but we had no intention of undertaking military operations against the garrison.

The Cabinet had decided in February that the administration of the territories in Africa overrun by Wavell's offensive should be undertaken by the War Office, 'with the active support and co-operation of other Government Departments'. The same principle was applied to the Italian colonies further south.[1]

Neither in Crete nor in Syria, important as were both strategically,

---

[1] The military administration of Italian East Africa under British control is described in the monograph by Lord Rennell of Rodd, *British Military Administration in Africa 1941–47* (H.M.S.O. 1948).

were our interests so deeply engaged as in the Western Desert. It was not that, for the present, an advance by land against the Delta was threatened by Rommel's small army, but the area west of Sollum offered almost unlimited sites for aircraft bases, and from it the enemy could develop a heavy scale of attack not only against our land line of communications and Egypt but against the fleet at Alexandria and our communications by sea. The acquisition of Crete by the enemy increased this last disadvantage, and for the time being it was hardly possible for any surface craft to ply between Alexandria and Malta. 'This campaign', said Air Marshal Tedder, 'is a battle for aerodromes.' To the fleet the task of supplying the beleaguered garrison of Tobruk was an expensive commitment, and the importance of pushing back the Germans in Cyrenaica was generally accepted. It was also desirable to strike as soon as possible, before Rommel had been reinforced.

The Prime Minister was not satisfied at the end of April that the commanders in the Middle East were showing the necessary energy. Our increased strength in tanks ought to make some action possible, and the repair organisation for aircraft seemed to call for improvement. Wavell replied on May 2 that he had ordered plans to be prepared for offensive action at the earliest possible moment, but this would depend on the arrival of strong reinforcements of aircraft, tanks and transport. He saw no prospect of taking the offensive during the present month (May), and his ability to do so early in June depended on a 'variety of uncertain factors'. This was not the sort of answer to please the Prime Minister, who refused to accept his plea, sent next day, that he was incapable of despatching an effective force to Iraq. On the 4th the Prime Minister applied a further prod in view of reliable information just received of Rommel's weakness; he remarked that Wavell appeared to have close on half a million men under his command, whereas he did not believe there were more than 25,000 Germans in Africa. Wavell replied that the possibility of taking the offensive depended largely on the air support available; his numbers might be impressive on paper, but he was still very short of equipment, particularly tanks, anti-aircraft guns and transport.

The air reinforcement of the Middle East had not been neglected at home. For some time fighters had been sent out through the Mediterranean, by combined naval and air operations to Malta, as well as in the 'Tiger' convoy to Egypt. They were also being sent across Africa from Takoradi. On May 15 the Defence Committee discussed and approved a comprehensive scheme of the Air Staff aiming at the provision in the Middle East by the middle of July of $40\frac{1}{2}$ squadrons, including five of Wellington heavy bombers; these would comprise a serviceable strength of 520 aircraft (an increase of about 220) which would enable us, by virtue of our superior maintenance organisation, to meet a German total of 650. To achieve this object, allowing for wastage, would not be easy: it would mean moving 862 aircraft to the Middle East by the date mentioned, and crews would have to be taken from Bomber and Fighter Commands at home.

A minor British attack on May 15 in the Sollum area (operation 'Brevity'), supported by action from Tobruk, gained some ground, but resulted in stalemate, and on the 27th the enemy scored an important point in recapturing Halfaya Pass. The 'Tiger' convoy had by now arrived, but the tanks were not ready to take part in this operation. On the 20th the attack on Crete began; its success, by enabling the Germans to establish a direct line of communication to Cyrenaica via the west coast of Greece and Suda Bay, made British advance in the Western Desert all the more desirable.

General Wavell told the Chief of the Imperial General Staff on the 15th that he assumed that the enemy intended an early attack on Crete, as preliminary to an attack on Egypt from the west through Libya and from the north through Syria. Sir John Dill similarly ascribed to the Germans more ambitious designs in the Middle East than they at that time cherished.[1] He thought they would consider that without capturing Malta they could build up a strong enough force in Cyrenaica for an advance on Egypt; but he did not think they would attempt a serious move in Libya until they could threaten our northern flank in Syria; for an attack from the north they would find Cyprus of great value, but they would also need land communications through Turkey. To parry so many threats, said General Dill, called for 'the highest degree of generalship'; such generalship could only be exercised in the Middle East and 'we must avoid undue interference with the conduct of operations'. In the west, the moment for action should be chosen by Wavell, and the extent of the advance must be regulated by him.

The Prime Minister was in general agreement with Dill's views, but insisted that the priority and emphasis of the operations must be prescribed from London. After discussion in the Defence Committee, a directive was sent to Wavell by the Chiefs of Staff, on the general lines of a minute by the Prime Minister, on May 28. In view of the danger to our communications entailed by the enemy's possession of Crete and the impossibility of a strong enemy land attack from the north developing for a good many weeks, 'our first object must be to gain a decisive military success in the Western Desert and to destroy the enemy armed forces in a battle fought with our whole available

---

[1] High German authorities did however at different times consider seriously the possibility of attacking Egypt from the east as well as from the west at a favourable moment. See *Halder Diary*, 27 and 28 October, 1940, and *F.D.* (draft) No. 32 of 11 June 1941.

M M

strength'. The Prime Minister added a private signal, which Sir John Dill thought unnecessary. It seemed to Mr. Churchill that now for the first time Wavell had a definite superiority in numbers of armoured fighting vehicles, especially the heavier types, as well as in mechanised infantry, artillery and supplies. The Tobruk sallyport also presented strategic opportunities of the highest order. Now, before the enemy had recovered from his heavy losses in Crete, was the time to fight a decisive battle in Libya and go on day after day facing all necessary losses until Wavell had beaten the life out of General Rommel's army. In this way the loss of Crete would be more than repaired, and the future of the whole campaign in the Middle East would be opened out. The Prime Minister also asked if it was not possible for General Wilson even now to be given the command in the desert. Wavell replied that all available armoured strength, which would be the deciding factor, was being put into the projected operation. But various difficulties were delaying the reconstitution of 7th Armoured Division, and he stated fairly that he was doubtful of the measure of success which would be attained. He was not happy about the capacity of our armoured cars or tanks to stand up to the German weapons, and he pressed for an 'adequate flow of armoured reinforcements and reserves'. He was not in favour of making a change in the command just when the planning for both the Syrian and Libyan operations was in its final stages. On the 30th he reported that a large number of the tanks received from the 'Tiger' convoy would require heavy repairs. Next day he told Dill that mainly on account of technical delays he had postponed the operation until June 15.

On June 6 Wavell sent home his appreciation of the coming offensive, now named 'Battle-axe'. It would be carried out in three stages: first, attack on enemy forces in the Sollum–Capuzzo area; second, advance to the Tobruk area, in conjunction with the garrison of Tobruk, and defeat of the enemy there; third, exploitation. He said, with characteristic caution, that, while he did not anticipate complete failure in the first stage, our strength at the end of it might not enable us to carry out the second stage and reach Tobruk. We were operating far from railhead; the mechanical state of our tanks was not good, and our recovery system was nothing like as efficient as that of the Germans.

'Battle-axe' was duly launched on June 15, but two days later Wavell reported that it had failed: after initial success our troops had been driven back by counter-attack practically to their starting positions, with heavy loss of tanks.[1] Not even the projected first stage had been accomplished. On the following day he reported that no

---

[1] An account of the battle is given in Playfair II ch. viii. 'The real root of the whole trouble', wrote Wavell, 'is lack of training.'

offensive in the Western Desert would be possible for at least three months. He proposed, as in the previous year, to maintain light covering forces near the frontier and await the enemy at Mersa Matruh. He and his colleagues were at first uncertain whether to hold Tobruk, but after some days decided to do so until supply difficulties or the imminence of an overwhelming attack made evacuation desirable.

Our defeat was a bitter disappointment. The setback did not imply any immediate danger to Egypt, but it meant the loss of what had seemed in London a priceless opportunity to avert a future danger while the enemy was still weak. The authorities at home had lost no opportunity of impressing on the commanders the 'supreme and possibly decisive strategic importance' of the impending battle. It might be 'the turning-point of the whole campaign'. We had hoped to clear Cyrenaica of the enemy, to recover the airfields there, so valuable for both defence and offence, and to release our forces for more positive tasks. As it was, Tobruk remained an expensive 'commitment' and we had to keep land and air forces on guard in the west.

The Prime Minister was deeply chagrined. He had taken a close personal interest in the 'tiger-cubs' and had hoped much from them. Now it seemed that all our plans had failed and the enemy had secured control of the Central Mediterranean. It looked as if in face of the Luftwaffe our surface ships could not enforce a blockade anywhere in those waters nor our aircraft prevent the reinforcement of North Africa. Must we tamely submit to such frustration? Impatient as ever of the defensive, the Prime Minister revolted from Wavell's acceptance of a three months' pause, which seemed to imply the early evacuation of Tobruk; on the contrary he suggested to the Chiefs of Staff a renewed attempt to regain the initiative in Libya and disengage Tobruk. Could not 100 cruiser tanks be passed through the Mediterranean, if and when the enemy was engaged against Russia? Plans were already in preparation for sailing a convoy to Malta from the west, but the Naval Staff were unwilling to risk the further voyage, now that we had only two battleships in the Eastern Mediterranean, and Dill was reluctant to send so much armour out of the country until the invasion season was past. Three days before this the German hosts had moved against Russia and so, as time was to show, not only freed the British Isles from any possibility of invasion but also immensely eased the pressure in the Middle East.

The failure of 'Battle-axe' shattered what remained of such confidence as the Prime Minister had felt in General Wavell. For some time he had not been happy about the Commander-in-Chief's conduct of affairs. He recognised his splendid services in liquidating the Italian army and the Italian empire in East Africa, but he regarded him, certainly from the beginning of May, as having lost his resiliency and drive and as unable to inject these qualities into his staff. Wavell had shown, he thought, undue reluctance to face necessary risks in Iraq and Syria, and surely more could have been done to make Crete defensible: our Intelligence on that occasion had been remarkably accurate, but Middle East headquarters had been slow to act upon it and had in general shown a lack of drive. He was convinced that very far-reaching steps would have to be taken. Nor could he understand how with such an immense ration strength in the Middle East Wavell could not put larger forces into the field.[1]

Looking back on past disappointments and forward to the fifteen divisions which he hoped would be available in the Middle East in the autumn, he proposed early in June to strengthen the command on the administrative side by sending out Lieutenant-General Sir R. H. Haining, the Vice-Chief of the Imperial General Staff, as 'Intendant General of the Army of the Middle East', along with Mr. T. C. L. Westbrook of the Ministry of Aircraft Production. The General would discharge for Wavell many of the services rendered by the War Office and Ministry of Supply to the Commander-in-Chief, Home Forces; his duties would include the supervision and control of rearward administrative services, including the military manpower not embodied in the tactical units or employed in the active military zone. Mr. Westbrook would be concerned with ports and transportation and with the care of armoured vehicles and mechanical transport. President Roosevelt had been asked to allow Mr. Harriman to accompany the mission.

Wavell welcomed the imposed assistance, but loyally claimed that his Deputy Quartermaster-General, General Hutchison, had shown remarkable ability in coping with these complex problems. He pointed out further that the Prime Minister's figure of 530,000 men, which included 132,000 Africans and Sudanese who were not available for Egypt and Palestine, and some 20,000 men of labour units, perhaps gave a wrong impression of his fighting strength in those two countries. He emphasised also his weakness in artillery and transport; he was deficient, in particular, of anti-aircraft and anti-tank guns; 8,800 vehicles had been lost in Greece and Crete. He was well aware, he ended, of the great difficulty still prevailing as regards equipment and the efforts being made to supply his needs, but this war was 'so much a matter of equipment' that he thought it right to give the figures to the Prime Minister.

---

[1] The topics of the reinforcement of the Middle East and the changes of organisation proposed and put in force are fully discussed in Playfair II chs. xi and xii.

Just at this time, the first week in June, Wavell let it be known privately that after nearly two years' heavy responsibility he was feeling the strain and would like a month's rest. If 'Exporter' and 'Battle-Axe' went well there might be something of a lull until the autumn. He and his staff had indeed borne a colossal burden, greater perhaps than any British commander in the past: the control of active operations in Libya, Kenya, the Sudan, Somaliland, Abyssinia, Greece, Crete, Syria and Iraq; the taking of precautions against internal trouble in Egypt and Palestine; diplomatic relations with an Ethiopian emperor, a Greek king, a Turkish president, and a Free French leader; and the ceaseless stream of correspondence with the War Office and the Minister of Defence, whose inquiries, exhortations and admonitions sometimes seemed excessive. In saying this, it is fair to say also that Wavell's caution in forecast, his quite individual taciturnity and his extreme loyalty to his subordinates were no doubt trying to an impatient and adventurous Minister.

On April 18 the Commanders-in-Chief in the Middle East had represented to the Chiefs of Staff the disadvantage from which they suffered, compared with the Germans, in needing to consult the local representatives of so many Departments of the British Government—who in turn had to refer to their chiefs at home—on political and financial matters. Mr. Eden's recent visit had shown the benefit of having a Minister on the spot capable of taking decisions, and they suggested the permanent appointment of some such local representative of His Majesty's Government, directly responsible to the War Cabinet. It may be remembered that in June 1940 Wavell had himself suggested that some delegation of central authority was desirable, but that his actual proposal was not considered practicable.[1]

At the end of June the Prime Minister informed Wavell that Captain Oliver Lyttelton, formerly President of the Board of Trade, was being sent out forthwith as Minister of State to represent the War Cabinet in the Middle East. This was largely in accordance with the Commanders-in-Chief's suggestion in April but went a good deal further. The Minister's function was not precisely defined, but his principal task would be to relieve the Commanders-in-Chief as far as possible of those extraneous responsibilities with which they had hitherto been burdened; to give them political guidance, and to settle promptly matters within the settled policy of the Government but involving several local authorities. To enable him to discharge his second function he would preside over meetings of the Commanders-in-Chief whenever they so desired or he had any point to raise. The Cabinet were informed of the new arrangement and approved it next day.

---

[1] See above, p. 302.

But it would not be General Wavell who would benefit from this relief. On June 21, after the news of the failure of 'Battle-Axe', the Minister of Defence informed him that he had come to the conclusion that the public interest would best be served by his relinquishment of the command in the Middle East. Mr. Churchill felt that, after the long strain Wavell had borne, a new eye and a new hand were required in this most seriously menaced theatre. Wavell would be replaced by General Auchinleck, whom he would succeed as Commander-in-Chief in India.[1]

Sir John Dill had agreed that Wavell needed a rest of several weeks, but did not for that reason think it necessary to relieve him permanently of his command. He believed that Wavell had the confidence of his troops, unless events in Crete and the Western Desert, not to mention Syria, had shaken it. But he had no doubt that, since Wavell clearly did not possess the confidence of the Prime Minister and of other members of the Cabinet, it was best that he should go. Wavell had been prepared for such a decision for some weeks, and characteristically did not dispute its rightness now. The Prime Minister, he said, bore the supreme responsibility and, since he had obviously lost confidence in him, was right to make a change of bowling; he had had several sixes hit off him, some perhaps through bowling to orders; anyway he had had a long spell, got some wickets, and had no grouse at being taken off.

Rommel, as is well known, wrote of Wavell as the one commander he met in Africa who showed a touch of genius. He possessed to the full the respect and confidence of his colleagues and subordinates. Great tasks still awaited him as soldier and as statesman in the East; but the historian must regret that a general of such quality was never given the opportunity of facing a first-class enemy in the field with an army properly trained and properly equipped. 'It's all a matter of equipment', Wavell wrote to a friend on June 5, 'and that is still desperately slow to come out.'

General Auchinleck arrived in Cairo on June 30. A few days previously Sir John Dill, in consultation with the Director of Military Operations, Major-General J. N. Kennedy, had written him the following 'personal and secret' letter, dated 26 June, 1941.[2]

> 'On your taking over command in the Middle East, may I add to my congratulations, which I have sent you by telegram, a few words on the situation and perhaps of advice?
>
> After Wavell had captured Benghazi, there was a possibility that he might have pressed on to Tripoli. He could only have done this with very small forces (as the so-called 7th Armoured

---

[1] See Churchill III 308–314, where the signal of 21 June is printed.

[2] For permission to print this letter I have to thank Lady Dill and F.M. Sir Claude Auchinleck.

Division was worn out) in the hope that the Italians were so demoralised that they could offer no effective resistance. But any hope there was of such a venture was ruled out by the decision of H.M.G. to support the Greeks. It then became a case of sending the maximum strength to Greece and leaving the minimum to hold Cyrenaica.

The result you know. We did not leave enough to secure Cyrenaica and the forces we sent to Greece and subsequently to Crete suffered heavily and lost much precious material— material which, as you will realise from your experience in England, is desperately difficult to replace. To right the situation, we did our best to send equipment at express rate and some 295 tanks were sent through the Mediterranean at great risk, and, with great luck and good management on the part of the Navy, 238 arrived, only one ship containing 57 was sunk. Then came a very difficult period. It was most desirable to clear the Germans back in Libya at the earliest possible moment, so that the Navy might be able to get the air protection necessary to enable it to attack the enemy's communications with Tripoli and also maintain Malta.

It was also highly desirable to act rapidly in Syria to forestall the Germans.

From Whitehall great pressure was applied to Wavell to induce him to act rapidly, and, under this pressure, he advanced into Syria with much less strength than was desirable and in the Western Desert he attacked before in fact he was fully prepared. The fault was not Wavell's, except in so far as he did not resist the pressure from Whitehall with sufficient vigour.

You may say that I should have minimised this pressure or, better still, that I should have seen that, having been given his task in broad outline, he was left to carry it out in his own way and in his own time. I might possibly have done more to help Wavell than I did, but I doubt it. The fact is that the Commander in the field will always be subject to great and often undue pressure from his Government. Wellington suffered from it: Haig suffered from it: Wavell suffered from it. Nothing will stop it. In fact, pressure from those who alone see the picture as a whole and carry the main responsibility may be necessary. It was, I think, right to press Wavell against his will to send a force to Baghdad, but in other directions he was, I feel, over-pressed.

It is about this question of pressure which I particularly want to speak. You may be quite sure that I will back your military opinion in your local problems, but here the pressure often comes from very broad political considerations; these are sometimes so powerful as to make it necessary to take risks which from the purely military point of view, may seem inadvisable. The main point of view, is that *you* should make it quite clear what risks are involved if a course of action is forced upon you which, from the military point of view, is undesirable. You may even find it necessary, in the extreme case, to disassociate yourself from the consequences.

Further, it is necessary that such a Commander should not wait for pressure and suggestions or even orders. He should anticipate these things and put clearly before his Government in the most secret manner how he views the situation and the action he proposes to meet it. He should point clearly to the risks he is prepared to accept and those which he considered too great. He should demand the resources he considers strictly necessary to carry out any projects and he should make it clear what he can and cannot do in their absence.

You, in your responsible Command, will never have in the near future all the resources which you would like to have to carry out your great task. You, having served here, know something of the situation and the immediate paucity of our resources. You know too what the essentials are in our great picture—to hold England, retain a position in the Middle East, maintain a firm hold in Malaya and keep open our sea communications, which last-named involves such things as continuing to be able to use West Africa. The time will come when we can strike out with effect and there is hardly a soul in the world outside Germany who will not rejoice at our success and join in our final victory. But in the meantime we have a grim fight to fight and we cannot afford hazardous adventures. So do not be afraid to state boldly the facts as you see them.

The second, and last point upon which I would like to touch concerns "air co-operation". Nowhere is it good. Nowhere have we had sufficient training. You will find the "Air" out to help but they have no complete understanding of what is required of them from the purely Army point of view and how necessary training is. Also, to ensure that our military and air strategy works in complete harmony is uncommonly difficult. It is quite clear that Tedder has to serve the Navy as well as the Army, but his main mission in life is to support the Army to the nth degree in any operation it has to undertake and to support it in the manner most acceptable to the Army Commander concerned. When you have had time to look round, you may be able to let me know how you view the problem and whether I can do anything to help.'

CHAPTER XXIII

THE RUSSIAN FACTOR

APART from the continuing anxiety over our shipping losses and the possibilities of invasion the British high command at the beginning of June 1941 were mainly concerned with the Middle East. But the German high command were not primarily interested in Tobruk, or Syria, or Malta, or the Battle of the Atlantic, and certainly not in 'Sea Lion'. They had other, larger, fish to fry. Indeed it is rather ironical to turn from the interchange of signals between Cairo and Whitehall about the possibilities of finding a brigade group for some important operation to German directives for the employment of a hundred or more divisions on the eastern front.

The plans and the building up of the forces for 'Barbarossa', as well as its launching and its outcome, will be recounted in the following volume. The present volume is concerned with them only in so far as they affected theatres in which we ourselves were engaged or threatened. It affected them directly by the withdrawal of German troops and especially air formations. A number of bomber units had been recalled from the West in April for the Balkan campaign, and at the end of May Field-Marshal Kesselring, with the whole of *Luftflotte* 2, moved to the east in readiness for 'Barbarossa'. Units were withdrawn also from North Africa and Greece for the Russian campaign; they were replaced by units from Sicily, to the great benefit of Malta.[1] More generally, Hitler's Russian pre-occupations afforded us a welcome respite in the Mediterranean theatre and elsewhere.

British relations with the Soviet Union, after the close of the Winter War with Finland (December 1939–March 1940), were on the diplomatic plane and hardly fall within the scope of a military history except in so far as we were concerned, for military reasons, that Russia should be as little useful to Germany as possible and should not influence Turkey in a way harmful to ourselves; it was against our interests that Turkey should be distracted by increasing distrust of Russia from putting all her strength into resisting a German drive through Bulgaria, or, still worse, should feel obliged to look to Germany for protection. Russian aggression against Persia or on the north-west frontier of India was not seriously apprehended.

In June 1940 Sir Stafford Cripps was sent as ambassador to Moscow with the purpose of negotiating a trade agreement with the

---

[1] See Playfair II ch. iii.

U.S.S.R. and generally improving our relations. On July 1 he presented to Stalin the Prime Minister's message suggesting that a German hegemony in Europe might not be in Russia's interests. But after that he was rarely given an opportunity of meeting any Soviet personage of importance. His thankless mission was comparable to that of Sir Samuel Hoare at the other end of Europe, but there were two main differences. Spain needed our economic assistance, while Russia did not, and Franco was sympathetic to Hitler's ambitions, which could not be said of Stalin. For the first reason, our attempts to secure a barter agreement failed; the ostensible obstacles were our refusal to recognise *de jure* the Soviet incorporation of the Baltic States and our unwillingness to export to Russia raw materials, such as non-ferrous metals, which might be re-exported into Germany. But the real obstacle, apart from traditional suspicion, was no doubt Russian fear of provoking German hostility. Efforts to find a common interest in improving Russian relations with Turkey foundered on the evident desire of Moscow to obtain a foothold in the region of the Straits. What worked in our favour on the other hand was the clash of Russian and German ambitions in the Balkans, first in Roumania, later in Bulgaria and finally in Yugoslavia.

We have seen how at the end of June 1940 Russia decided to cash in on her expectations under the Russo-German secret protocol of the previous August and annexed Bessarabia and northern Bukovina; and how Roumania, feeling the pressure of the nether millstone, had to consent to large territorial losses in Transylvania and the Dobrudja, while accepting an Axis guarantee for the rest of her territory. Roumania rapidly became a satellite Axis State, and, under the guise of a military mission, German land and air formations moved in in increasing numbers.[1] A German occupation of Roumania was bound to raise doubts as to the future of its neighbour, Bulgaria, a country in which Russia had long taken a special interest by reason both of its Slav population and of its proximity to the Straits.

On November 12, in response to an invitation extended on October 13, the Soviet Foreign Minister, Molotov, paid a visit to Berlin and discussed high policy with Hitler and Ribbentrop. The Tripartite Pact between Germany, Italy and Japan had been signed some weeks before, but Ribbentrop explained that there was no reason why this should disturb the relationship of the three Powers with Russia; Japan was now oriented towards the south, not the north. Hitler said further that Germany had no political interests in the Balkans; she was active in Roumania purely for temporary

[1] Above, p. 362.

military reasons, while she must prevent England from establishing air and naval bases in Greece, mentioning especially Salonika. It soon appeared that the two participants were at cross-purposes. The Germans wished to obtain Russian consent to large airy schemes for the partition of the bankrupt estate of the British Empire into spheres of influence. The German sphere would lie in Central Africa, the Italian in North and East Africa, the Japanese in Greater East Asia, while Russia was invited to claim hers in the regions of the Persian Gulf and Arabian Sea. Russia was further entitled to a privileged position in the Straits of Constantinople, and was encouraged to enter into a non-aggression pact with Japan. But Molotov cared for none of these things. He wanted to know when the Germans would stop passing troops to Norway through Finland; whether they would object to Russia giving to Bulgaria a guarantee similar to that which Germany and Italy had given to Roumania; what were the Axis intentions with regard to Yugoslavia and Greece; what was meant by the Greater East Asian sphere; while, as for the Straits, Russia required not rights on paper but effective guarantees. Molotov was also unkind enough to remark that it was difficult to reconcile the Führer's claim that the war against England was already won with his plea that Germany was engaged in a 'life-and-death struggle' against her. He could only conclude that Germany was fighting for life and England for death.[1]

It is of interest that on the very day of his first conversation with Molotov (November 12) Hitler included in his omnibus directive of that date a paragraph on Russia, to the effect that 'political discussions have been initiated to sound out Russia's attitude for the near future. Regardless of the results of these discussions, all preparations for the East which have been ordered verbally are to be continued. Directives will follow as soon as the Army's basic operational plan has been reported to and approved by me.' The directive for 'Marita' followed on December 13, and that for 'Barbarossa' on December 18: 'The German Armed Forces must be ready to crush Soviet Russia in a rapid campaign, even before the termination of the war with Britain.' On the flanks of their operations they could count on the active participation of Roumania and Finland.[2]

In view of Hitler's lust for Russian grain and oil and land, his contempt for the Slav race, and his detestation of Bolshevism, the question to be answered is not, why did he decide to attack Russia, but why did he decide to do so when he did? Sooner or later he was bound to seek to realise the dreams declared in *Mein Kampf*.[3]

---

[1] See *Nazi-Soviet Relations 1939–41* pp. 217–254.

[2] *Führer Directives* Nos. 18, 20, 21.

[3] This chapter is greatly indebted to an unpublished monograph by Mr. E. M. Robertson, of the Enemy Documents Section; *Barbarossa; the origins and development of Hitler's plan to attack Russia.*

In November 1939, in an address to his Commanders-in-Chief, he said that Russia was not dangerous. She was weakened by too many recent happenings. 'Moreover we have a pact with Russia. Pacts, however, are not everything and hold only so long as they serve their purpose. Russia will abide by it only as long as she considers it to her benefit. Let us regard the pact as a security for our back. . . . Now Russia has far-reaching goals, above all in strengthening her position in the Baltic. We can only oppose her there when we are free in the West.'[1] For the first months of the war, therefore, his underlying intention to destroy the Soviet Union was in abeyance.

Until the French armistice Hitler had his hands full in the West, and after that he was concerned with Britain, on the one hand hoping that she would make peace, on the other turning over thoughts of an air assault and invasion. On 16 July 1940 he issued his Directive No. 16 stating that he had decided to prepare an invasion, and if necessary to carry it out. Preparations were to be completed by mid-August. But three days later he made his final appeal for a peaceful settlement. On the 22nd Raeder told him that the date set for the completion of preparations was impracticable, and he must have realised that his peace offensive had failed.[2] It is interesting to find in Halder's diary under July 13 the remark: 'The Führer is most strongly pre-occupied with the question why England does not wish to follow the road to peace. He sees the answer, like us, in Britain's hope in Russia.' Some support for this absurd theory could be found in reports which reached Berlin in July of intercepted conversations in Moscow suggesting that Stalin was coquetting with Sir Stafford Cripps and otherwise playing false to Germany.

There were more substantial grounds than this for Hitler's suspicions of Russia. At the end of June Russian troops had marched not only into Bessarabia, which was assigned to her by the agreement of August 1939, but into northern Bukovina, which was not, and in Bessarabia Russia now had a frontier on the Danube, only some hundred miles distant from the precious Roumanian oilfields.

On July 21 Hitler told Brauchitsch that Britain was continuing the war because she looked for a more favourable attitude on the part of the United States and because she pinned her hopes on Russia. 'Our attention must be turned to tackle the Russian problem.'[3] Preliminary studies should be made for an invasion of Russia. But it was not till the last three days of July that the Führer seriously discussed this matter with his subordinates. On the 31st, again mentioning the need of eliminating all political factors which offered England any hope, he announced his momentous decision: Russia must be

[1] *N.D.* 789–PS, *N.C.A.* III 575 (wording slightly altered).
[2] *F.N.C.* p. 120.
[3] *Halder's Diary*, 22 July 1940.

liquidated in the spring of 1941. The Soviet State must be shattered in one blow. Five months from May 1941 should complete the work. It would have been best to carry it through in 1940, but that was not feasible. It seems probable that the Army chiefs disliked the proposal, but Hitler's prestige was at its zenith and there is no evidence that they made any concerted attempt to dissuade him at this time.

Fantastic as were many of his ideas, it is not to be supposed that Hitler seriously decided to invade Russia simply as a move in the war against Britain. But it does not seem unlikely that one of the influences which brought his latent intention of invading her to the surface at this time, when he was preoccupied with 'Sea Lion', was the feeling that British stubbornness was being encouraged by intrigues with Russia. If this is so, British attempts to improve relations with the Soviets may, indirectly, have had more far-reaching consequences than appeared at the time.

In any case Hitler's decision was not irrevocable and, as we have seen, it was not till December that the directive for 'Barbarossa' was issued, the name recalling the most romantic of German adventurers in the East. But planning and preparations continued, while relations with Russia grew worse. Early in September, for instance, the Soviet Government protested against the further partition of Roumania without their assent or previous knowledge, claiming that it violated the Pact of the previous August. The Tripartite Pact with Italy and Japan later in the month was also concluded without Russia's knowledge. Moreover in the economic sphere, in which the most tangible fruits of the Russo-German entente had been gathered, trade was now declining. Deliveries from Germany in August stood far below their Russian counterpart.

An account of the preparations made during the autumn will be found in Volume III. Here it is enough to say that planning had by the beginning of October 1940 developed on three lines: actual plans for invading Russia had been drawn up, the strength of the forces in the adjacent districts had been increased, and information about Russian forces was being collected. Early in September orders had been issued for raising the German Field Army to a new total of 180 divisions by 1st May 1941; twenty of these would be armoured divisions and ten motorised. On October 12 'Sea Lion' was called off so far as 1940 was concerned, preparations for a landing being kept up during the winter merely as a measure of deception.[1]

The outbreak of war in the Balkans at the end of October 1940 and the arrival of British Air squadrons in Greece was bound to quicken Germany's interest in those regions. On November 4 in conference with his Commanders-in-Chief Hitler discussed the possibility of

---

[1] See above, p. 290; later chapters have shown how until the end of our period the possibility of a renewed attempt at invasion was taken seriously in London.

attacking Greece and a few days later his officers spoke of sending an anti-aircraft unit to Bulgaria. It was desirable to discover Russia's intentions as regards Bulgaria and Turkey, and this, besides keeping her quiet for the present, would seem to have been among the main reasons for inviting Molotov to Berlin. In the mind of the Germans, the aim of the Molotov conference was probably to ascertain whether Russia could be used provisionally to assist Germany before her own ultimate destruction; whether, in fact, she could be made to dig her own grave. Certainly the conference had no concrete result. Russia was prepared to join the Tripartite Pact only on certain conditions: if German troops evacuated Finland; if Bulgaria concluded a non-aggression pact with Russia and granted her bases within range of the Bosphorus; if the region south of the Caucasus in the direction of the Persian Gulf were recognised as the goal of Russian aspirations; and if Japan would renounce her rights to concessions for coal and oil in the northern part of the island of Sakhalin. The two first conditions would never have been accepted by Germany.

Bulgaria was in a delicate position, but the Germans in Roumania were nearer than the Russians, and there was also the possibility of action by Turkey. Eventually she signed a treaty of friendship and non-aggression with the Turks on February 17, and on March 1st she joined the Axis Tripartite Pact, allowing the Germans to march their troops through the country with a view to an attack on Greece.

On 5 December 1940 Hitler held a conference to co-ordinate strategy for the spring, at which Brauchitsch, Halder, Keitel and Jodl were present. It was agreed that the air war against Britain in the Eastern Mediterranean should start after December 15; the attack on Gibraltar was to begin early in February and would last four weeks, enabling the troops to be deployed elsewhere by the middle of May; the invasion of Greece would last no longer than three or four weeks, beginning early in March if weather was favourable. Any forces assigned to this operation but not required for it would be available as reinforcements for the Russian campaign. But this must start on time. Even if weather was normal, the date could not be earlier than the middle of May. Hitler estimated that 130 to 140 divisions should be sufficient. A fortnight later the directive for 'Barbarossa' was issued.

Admiral Raeder had throughout protested against such a dispersion of strength. The attack on Russia should be postponed, he said on November 14, until after victory over England. The end of the war was not yet in sight. He made his last protest on December 27, declaring the necessity of realising that the greatest task of the hour was to concentrate all Germany's strength against Britain. The Navy and the Luftwaffe must be given the weapons they needed. Hitler, by way of consolation, promised to speed up the construction of U-boats. But, considering Russia's inclination to interfere in the Balkans, it was necessary to eliminate the last remaining enemy on the Continent. For this purpose the Army must be given sufficient strength. After that, the needs of the other two Services should have priority.[1] The Army chiefs were less outspoken in their criticism, but at the end of January Brauchitsch and Halder expressed misgivings: the object of the Russian adventure was not clear; it would not strike at the English.

Complications in the general scheme and in the time-table were caused by Franco's unwillingness to co-operate and by Wavell's threat to eject the Italians from North Africa. But Hitler was determined to carry out 'Barbarossa', and plans of strategic deception were prepared. There would be two periods or phases. During the first, until the middle of April, it would be possible to maintain the existing uncertainty as to Germany's intentions; the impression of an impending invasion would be fostered by indications from new weapons and transportation equipment, and an exaggerated importance would be given to minor operations, namely those in the Balkans and North Africa. In the second period it would be too late to conceal the concentration in eastern Europe, but the troops themselves should be made to believe that they were really to be used against Britain; it was to be 'the greatest deceptive undertaking in the history of warfare'.[2]

On the surface there was little change in the relations between Russia and the two major belligerents during the early months of 1941. Sir Stafford Cripps was still cold-shouldered in Moscow, and in January a new Russo-German trade agreement was accompanied by a Pact of Friendship providing for the settlement of questions connected with the annexation of the Baltic countries and the frontier in Poland. But from the middle of March onwards the British Foreign Office began to receive an increasing number of reports pointing to the possibility of a German attack on Russia. For a long time to come, however, it was difficult to tell whether such reports indicated a real purpose or were part of a 'war of nerves' intended to frighten the Soviet Government into accepting full co-operation with Germany.

In March, when German troops were moving into Bulgaria, matters came to a head in the neighbouring country of Yugoslavia, which was rent by political dissensions. On the 5th the Prince Regent, visiting Hitler at Berchtesgaden, received a renewed demand that his country should line up with the Axis. The Belgrade Cabinet were

---

[1] *F.N.C.* pp. 153, 162.

[2] *F.D.* No. 23 of 6 Feb.; Naval Directive No. 1 for operation 'Barbarossa', 6 March; pp. 137, 156.

divided, but after three members had resigned the Prime Minister and Foreign Minister signed the Tripartite Pact at Vienna on the 25th.[1] The Simovitch Government, which came into power as the result of the consequent *coup d'état*, obtained a non-aggression pact from Moscow, but nothing more. Their reluctance to commit themselves openly with the British has been mentioned in chapter XIX, as has their failure, none the less, to escape Hitler's vengeance. This unexpected hitch in the development of his Balkan policy had, however, an important effect on the Führer's military plans.

The Germans were working to a time-table. In December 1940 Hitler had said that operations in Spain and Greece would have to be finished as soon as possible in order to release forces for 'Barbarossa'; in January 1941 Halder pointed out that the execution of 'Felix' would prevent essential items, especially motorised artillery and mobile units, from being available in the East; and as late as May 1 four of the twenty armoured divisions required for Russia had not been brought up to strength. Any further delay might therefore be serious, in view of Hitler's intention to start the Russian campaign with an overwhelming onslaught in which armour and aircraft would play the principal part. The earliest possible date mentioned for this offensive was May 15. The directive of December 18 merely ordered that those preparations which would take longer than eight weeks should be ready by that date. On January 24 a memorandum reviewing the oil situation mentioned June 1 as the prospective date.

As March proceeded it became evident that the British were building up a force in Greece, and at a German staff conference on March 17 it was decided that in view of the extended objectives of 'Marita' certain forces intended for 'Barbarossa' must be diverted from the latter. There is evidence too of German anxiety for the defence of the French and Norwegian coasts; the Lofoten raid had shown offensive spirit and offensive capacity.[2] Nevertheless, there is no mention in the German records of a postponement of 'Barbarossa' until the *coup d'état* of March 27 in Belgrade, which led Hitler to undertake 'Operation 25' against Yugoslavia. On that day the Russian adventure was put off for about four weeks, and on April 7 Brauchitsch issued an order stating that the development of the situation in Yugoslavia, with the necessary deployment of greater forces in the south-east, required changes in the course of preparations for 'Barbarossa'. The postponement would be from four to six weeks; all preliminary plans would be completed in such a way as to make it possible to start the offensive about June 22. This date was finally confirmed on April 30.

---

[1] M. Beloff, *The Foreign Policy of Soviet Russia* (Oxford 1949) II 364.
[2] Above, p. 486.

These details are of great significance; for the argument seems valid, that 'if as a result of the delaying influence of Operation 25 the High Command were already on 7 April contemplating launching "Barbarossa" on 22 June and confirmed this date on 30 April, then events occurring in the intervening period could scarcely have caused an additional postponement'.[1] On the other hand, even if the fighting in Greece, in Crete, and in North Africa after April 7 did not cause the postponement of the blow against Russia, it may to some extent have weakened it. Army units were transferred for the attack on Crete at the expense of 'Barbarossa' and, though there were sufficient forces for the execution of both 'Barbarossa' and 'Merkur', the heavy losses in Crete must have had their effect on Germany's later air efforts.

Sir Winston Churchill has told how he rightly appreciated the importance of information received in March concerning the movement of German armoured units by rail in eastern Europe.[2] Three out of five Panzer divisions moving from Bucharest to Cracow at the time when the Belgrade Government were compliant were redirected to Roumania after the *coup d'état*: this must surely mean that an intention to attack Russia had been checked by the need to dispose of Yugoslavia first, but would be carried out later. Sir Winston tells also how his attempt to give immediate warning of these facts by a personal message to Stalin was frustrated by the British Ambassador; not till April 23 was the British Government informed that the message had at last reached its destination.

Such an indication however was by no means precise. To advise on German intentions was the duty of the Joint Intelligence Committee. This body had set up in March an Axis Planning Section to present reports on probable action by the enemy; reports would be based on appreciations of the situation as he might be supposed to view it. On April 14 the Chiefs of Staff had before them one of these reports, which the J.I.C. had sponsored. Prefacing that two new factors had occurred recently—the unexpected turn of events in Yugoslavia and a number of reports that the Germans were planning to attack the U.S.S.R.—the paper took for granted that Germany's present aim was a successful peace in 1941 and that her main effort must be the elimination of Britain. One of several courses whereby Britain might be made ripe for peace negotiations or invasion was 'to advance into Russia to seize the economic riches of the Ukraine and Caucasus'. The writers thought that a clash between Germany and

---

[1] Quoted from Mr. E. M. Robertson's unpublished monograph.
[2] Churchill III 319.

Russia must come some time, unless Germany were defeated first, and agreed that Germany had considerable military forces available in the East, but they gave a series of reasons why it was not to her interest to force war now. They concluded that a direct attack on Russia was unlikely at present, but that preparations would 'continue for the double purpose of providing a threat which will keep Russia amenable and of being able to take immediate action when required'.

The Chiefs of Staff merely took note of this report. A week later, on April 22, they summoned the members of the Joint Intelligence Committee to discuss with them Germany's next move. At this meeting, whereas the War Office representative could see no advantage from the Germans' point of view in attacking Russia until they had attempted the invasion of Great Britain, and guessed that in any case an attack on Russia would not take place until after the harvest, the Foreign Office view was that the threat to Russia might well develop as soon as the Greek war was over. The weekly résumé of the military situation prepared for the Cabinet stated at the end of April that there were 'no reliable indications of imminent hostilities' between the two Powers. A week later, reliable reports were mentioned of Roumanian troops and civilians having been removed from the region of the Soviet frontier to make room for German troops, but an invasion of the United Kingdom was still spoken of as likely. In the middle of May, while it was suggested that preparations for operations against Russia would soon be complete and that a clash was regarded in many quarters as inevitable, the Service appreciation was that probably no decision had yet been taken whether Russia should be attacked or merely persuaded by threats to comply with German wishes.

No information of value concerning German intentions was obtained from Rudolph Hess after his mad flight to Scotland on the night of May 10. He declared that Germany had certain demands to make of Russia which would have to be satisfied, but denied rumours that an attack on Russia was being planned.[1]

On 31 May the Chiefs of Staff endorsed a report by the Joint Intelligence Committee to the effect that 'although many good reasons could be adduced why Hitler should decide, after the capture of Crete, to exploit his success by action towards Egypt, all the evidence points to Germany's next move being an attempt to enforce her demands on the Soviet by means of a threat of force which can immediately be turned into action'. The preparations of the Luftwaffe, said the report, were of so thorough a nature and so similar to those which had preceded campaigns in other theatres that it seemed

---

[1] See Churchill III 43–49.

that they could only portend such drastic demands on Russia that Hitler was doubtful of their acceptance and was therefore prepared to follow up his threats by actual operations. On June 12 it could be said that evidence of German preparations for military action against Russia was steadily accumulating and over one-third of the German army was now disposed on the Russian frontier. Indeed, on that day the Joint Intelligence Committee were persuaded that Hitler had made up his mind to have done with the Soviet obstruction and to attack. It was premature to fix a date, but they thought matters were likely to come to a head in the second half of June.

On June 14 the Joint Intelligence Committee produced a report on the possible effect of a German-Soviet war. The Soviet forces available were large, it said, but much of their equipment was obsolescent, and they suffered from certain inherent failings, such as lack of initiative, fear of accepting responsibility, and bad maintenance. Thus their value for war was low, but Russians were at their best in defence, and they had vast territories to fall back on. Any estimate of the phases of the campaign, they admitted, must be largely a matter of speculation. The first phase, assumed to involve the occupation of the Ukraine and of Moscow, might take as little as three to four weeks, or as long as six weeks (or longer). The principal military effects would be that any attempt to invade the United Kingdom would be postponed until the air forces and essential army formations could be withdrawn and regrouped; there would be a large dispersal of Ge man forces, thus still further straining the German military machine; the air effort would entail a reduction in the forces available for the Atlantic or for bombing Britain and dangerously reduce Germany's fighter defences in the West; major operations elsewhere would have to be temporarily abandoned; and the threat to our position in the Middle East would be diminished, at any rate for the time being. But a successful campaign would finally eliminate for Germany the threat of war on two fronts and leave her free, in the long run, to concentrate on the West. The economic gains and short-term disadvantages that would accrue to Germany were then pointed out.

We had not withheld our information from the Soviet authorities; but indeed they were very conscious of the piling up of German forces against their frontier. They would not however recognise the imminence of war, hoping to stave it off by complaisance—which implied continued ungraciousness to any British approach. It was thought in London that they might go very far in meeting German demands.

At the end of May a threat to the Caucasian oil-field had been thought of as a means of putting pressure on the Russians to refuse concessions to Germany; the Chiefs of Staff decided on June 12 that arrangements should be made to enable heavy and medium bombers to operate from Mosul against the Baku oil refineries without delay.

On June 13 Mr. Eden informed the Soviet Ambassador that in the event of a German attack on Russia we should be prepared to send a military mission and to give urgent consideration to her economic needs. But there was as usual no response. The Turks, moreover, contrary to our wishes, signed a treaty of friendship, in fact of reinsurance, with Germany on June 18 'within the limits of' their present commitments.[1] This might well point to a desire on the Germans' part to stabilise their southern flank in a war with Russia. Evidence that invasion was imminent was indeed mounting up, though 'to the moment of the German attack, there was no definite and conclusive evidence [in diplomatic quarters] that Germany intended to attack Russia and not merely to use diplomatic and military threats to intimidate the Soviet Government'.

On the morning of June 22 the attack was launched without even the pretence of an ultimatum such as Mussolini had offered to the Greeks, and that evening Mr. Churchill made his momentous broadcast.

> 'We shall proceed upon the principle that any nation of Europe that starts up with a determination to oppose a power which, whether professing insidious peace or declaring open war, is the common enemy of all nations, whatever may be the existing political relations of that nation with Great Britain, becomes instantly our essential ally.'

So spoke George Canning in June 1808.[2] Mr. Churchill, offering all the assistance in our power to the Soviet Government and armies, was true to that tradition, and the Government of the United States followed the same course.[3]

It cannot be said that the impending extension of the war influenced British strategy. Alike its outbreak and its outcome were too uncertain. Up to the last we could not be sure that Moscow would not feel obliged to yield to superior force and grant Hitler's demands, however humiliating. Should on the other hand Moscow resist, most of the British experts, like the German, believed that the campaign in European Russia would be over in a few months or even weeks,

---

[1] See Sir H. Knatchbull-Hugessen, *Diplomat in Peace and War* (1949), p. 170.

[2] House of Commons, 15 June 1808: quoted by Temperley and Penson, *Foundations of British Foreign Policy* p. 23.

[3] See *The Undeclared War* pp. 537–541.

after which Germany would be free to carry out her other designs. She could bring powerful forces to bear in the Western, or in the Eastern Mediterranean, or could restage 'Sea Lion'. It was true that from October 1940 onwards the preparations for invasion which were noted in England were part of the German deception plan, but it was a deception which could easily be converted into reality. The British staff report of June 14 on the possible effect of a German-Soviet war calculated that the regrouping of air and land formations for an invasion would take from four to eight weeks according to the duration of the campaign in the east. On the assumption, therefore, that an attempt at invasion was something to be taken seriously—an assumption which a British Government in 1941 could hardly avoid —it is not easy to see how the probability of a German invasion of Russia could have affected our dispositions.

The actual strength of the garrison in the United Kingdom was thus stated in an appreciation considered by the Chiefs of Staff on May 16.

> 'Apart from units on guard duties, the land forces available in this country after the despatch of 50th division [to the Middle East] are, *on paper*
>> 5 armoured divisions
>> 3 army tank brigades
>> 22 divisions
>> 10 "County" divisions (holding beach defences)
>> 9 infantry brigades.
>
> The infantry available is in our opinion the bare minimum, but the weakness is in armoured forces. By June we shall have only the equivalent of 3 *fully trained and equipped armoured* divisions. Normal maintenance for the Middle East will necessitate the despatch overseas of about 50 tanks each month, and it will be March 1942 before we have 6 armoured divisions and 4 army tank brigades fully trained and equipped, which are the minimum requirement for the security of the United Kingdom.'

As regards the air, 'after air forces now under orders have been despatched to the Middle East, the number of squadrons in Fighter Command will be the absolute minimum considered necessary for security. We cannot despatch additional bomber forces during the next few months without reducing our security against invasion. All bomber forces in the United Kingdom have an important anti-invasion role in addition to their offensive operations. In view, however, of the grave weakness in the Middle East and the improbability of invasion in the next few weeks, a temporary reduction in the aircraft and crew strength of our medium bomber force might be accepted.'

The relevant part of this appreciation was eventually compressed into three short paragraphs in a telegram sent to the Dominion Prime Ministers on May 31:

> 'Invasion is not imminent since it would take Germany up to eight weeks to bring back necessary air forces from the Middle East. Scale of invasion is estimated at 6 armoured, 4 air-borne and 26 infantry divisions. Five to seven days would elapse before concentration of naval forces against enemy sea communications could be completed.
>
> We are confident of maintaining air superiority so long as our aerodromes are adequately defended against all forms of attack. Our chief weakness is in armoured forces which are now less than half the strength considered necessary for security. Equipment is short and many formations only newly constituted. Infantry is widely dispersed owing to length of vulnerable coastline and demands for defence of aerodromes and vital points.
>
> We have had to take risks with our land strength at home, particularly in tanks, to meet the needs of the Middle East. Nothing sent overseas can be brought back within the limited period of warning. Land strength at home cannot be sensibly reduced this summer.'

Strategically we were on the outer lines and, even had the Government been prepared to release land and air forces from the United Kingdom and had the necessary shipping been available, it would have been a long business to transport them to any theatre where offensive action was possible. In any case previous consultation with the Russians was ruled out by the attitude of their Government. In the circumstances of the time the country in which we were interested as a prospective co-belligerent was not the Soviet Union but the United States.

CHAPTER XXIV

REVIEW OF STRATEGY AND ORGANISATION, JUNE 1941

THE GERMAN invasion of Russia opened a new phase in the war; though its full importance was not obvious at first, it was a real turning-point. From 22 June 1941 Germany was inextricably involved in an eastern war from which she knew no respite until the Russian hordes overran the ruins of the Wilhelmstrasse. To Britain the breach between the two eastern despotisms brought no such assurance of ultimate victory as did the entry of the United States into the war six months later; but it meant at least a momentary slackening of pressure at a time of heavy strain, with the further hope that our military isolation was over for good and all, as turned out to be the case. For twelve months the British Commonwealth had resisted the triumphant Axis without a major ally, though sustained by increasing material help from across the Atlantic. For twelve months London had been the acknowledged capital of all who fought for freedom, her scars a visible proof of what the enemy could, and of what he could not do. For twelve months, and this touches the plan of the present history, the strategic decisions had been taken by Britain alone. The close of the volume covering this unique period seems therefore a fitting place for an interim review of the British conduct of the war up to the point we have reached.

Neither the grand strategy, nor the machinery, nor the method of working of the high command had changed in essential respects in these last twelve months. Before looking back, however, on the strategic decisions of the period, we should take note of the elaborate Review of Future Strategy produced at this time (June 14) by the Future Operations Section of the Joint Planning Staff in response to a request made by the Minister of Defence three months earlier. This document was never officially adopted as a statement of British policy, and indeed the German invasion of Russia and the Russian resistance soon rendered much of it out of date. Nevertheless it has interest as a summary of the economic position as seen in June 1941 and an exposition of how the future course of the war was viewed by an able group of strategists enjoying access to all official sources of

547

information. Moreover, it formed the basis for an appreciation by the Chiefs of Staff which was later discussed with the Americans.

To a considerable extent its estimates of the present position and our capacity for further effort, as regards manpower, imports, shipping and Service programmes, deal with matters covered in previous chapters (especially chapter XX), and in parts it has been quoted. A few conclusions may be recalled.

> 'Apart from Imperial resources, man-power considerations in Great Britain and Northern Ireland make it impossible to expand the present Service Programmes, except for redistribution between and within the Services . . .
>
> The total import figure for the calendar year 1941 may not exceed 28½ million tons (excluding oil). To avoid reduction of present home production and civilian standards of living, a total import figure of 36 million tons (excluding oil) is required. Our oil stocks, which are already low, will drop still further during 1941 . . .
>
> For the next twelve months or so, apart from assistance from the U.S.A., we cannot hope to do more than maintain our present rate of imports of about 28 million tons per year. If Sir Arthur Salter's negotiations are successfully concluded, we may, perhaps, receive American tonnage sufficient to import an additional 6 or 7 million tons during the third year of war.[1] There is no real margin of safety to be achieved without a reduction in the present rate of losses. To this end, every effort should be made to bring the U.S.A. into the war since this is the most effective way of reducing our shipping losses quickly . . . Our shipping resources are so limited at present that, even if America enters the war, we shall not, until the position has actually improved, have shipping available to undertake any new large-scale military commitment involving an ocean passage . . .'

The forecast of the effects of our blockade of Germany was cautious:

> 'Our general conclusion as to the future of German economy is that, largely owing to the more serious leaks in the blockade than were expected last autumn, her deficiencies are not such as necessarily to limit her strategic plans in 1941, although a temporary shortage of oil might prevent full-scale operations in the west during the critical period of the autumn. On the other hand, should Germany go all out in 1941, without achieving decisive success, her capacity for prolonged resistance might be seriously affected . . .'

Nor was there anything very new in the forecast of Germany's

---

[1] Sir Arthur Salter had been in Washington since April pressing on the Americans our requests for shipping.

probable action. Although she would seize any favourable opportunity for the invasion of the United Kingdom, her present main objectives lay in the East. 'Failing an attack on Russia early this summer, Germany's main objective will be Egypt.'

The novelty of the appreciation lay in the attempt to envisage more realistically than hitherto the way in which the war might be ended and won. The planners did not conceal their belief that 'the active belligerency of the United States has become essential for a successful prosecution and conclusion of the war'. But, for practical reasons, this did not imply the despatch of large American armies overseas. 'The effort involved in shipping modern armies with the ground staff of Air Forces is so great that even with American help we can never hope to build up a very large force on the Continent.'

The acceptance of the present shipping restrictions as more or less permanent was one major miscalculation of the report; another was to ignore the factor of Russian resistance to Germany as likely to have any decisive significance. They led to the conclusion that in view of Germany's immense superiority on land—250 divisions with a powerful Air Force—and her possession of interior lines, it was vain to think of defeating the existing German army in the field. Some day, in order to impose our will on the enemy, it would be necessary to occupy and control portions of his territory, and this would involve land operations; but the German war machine must first be worn down by a process of attrition. Only indeed by a similar process could Germany hope to defeat Great Britain, unless she could strike us down once for all by invasion.

As for our other enemies, Italy had passed completely under Nazi domination and could hardly be regarded as an independent Power. Japan was for the present engaged on peaceful penetration southwards, but 'she would always be prepared to resort to war with us, if her peaceful penetration was definitely checked, if we were in extreme difficulties elsewhere, or if she were convinced of U.S.A. indifference to her action. . . . Owing to British and American economic pressure, which is being increased, her economic capacity for war will progressively deteriorate. If, therefore, Japan should decide to run the risk of war with us, it would be to her advantage to take that risk sooner than later.'

They concluded that the effect of Japan's entry into the war would depend upon the fate of Singapore. The strategic consequences of its loss would be disastrous. If we held it, Japan's intervention, though adding greatly to our difficulties, 'should have no decisive effect on the war in the west'.

In considering the methods of conducting the war of attrition against Germany, the report of course emphasised the recognised procedures of blockade and control at source, and also an increasing bombing attack; but it also laid more stress than was customary on subversive activity within the occupied countries and on propaganda, and on the co-ordination of these with 'our other forms of offensive'. Taking into account the probable development of all these weapons, as well as what might be expected of the enemy, the report concluded that we ought not to wait indefinitely to launch the final offensive. 'As Germany's strength wanes, rather will there be an optimum moment to strike with all that we have then got.' That time, in their opinion, would be the autumn of 1942.

The last Section of the report, on The Distant Future, suggested, as the Joint Planners commented, a line of action for which so far very little provision had been made. This was the organising of armed patriots within the occupied countries to supplement our own modest force—some ten or more divisions, mostly armoured, were suggested—and the 'free' Allied contingents outside the enemy's territories, in order to conduct campaigns of liberation.

This appreciation was never vouched for in its entirety by the Chiefs of Staff, or indeed by the Joint Planning Staff. The latter remarked that the proposals of the last section were attractive, but could not be recommended for unqualified approval until their implications had been further examined. Subject to this proviso they gave the Review their general approval, regarding it as a 'document of high importance'. If its conclusions were accepted, it would provide a valuable background for the whole planning and conduct of the war including the direction of the American war effort. The Chiefs of Staff likewise expressed general agreement with the paper —the immediate entry of the United States into the war was essential —and asked that the Defence Committee should give it their blessing and authorise its communication to the Dominion Prime Ministers and Commanders-in-Chief abroad. But the invasion of Russia had now begun and the Prime Minister was doubtful of the value of such a distribution of papers which rapidly became out-of-date. The Defence Committee gave it merely a preliminary discussion and the Prime Minister minuted later that it had been superseded by the results of his Atlantic meeting with the President. He regarded it in any case as somewhat academic.

The Prime Minister's attitude to this Review of Future Strategy recalls his reservations with regard to the elaborate appreciation of the previous summer, which he had commended as 'a valuable staff study'.[1] He was reluctant to approve as accepted policy proposals based on assumptions which could be only speculative. The future action of the United States, of Russia and Japan was still uncertain in the early summer of 1941, and throughout the period covered by

---

[1] Above, p. 343.

the present volume the initiative, by and large, rested with Germany. The Allies could plan to mine the Norwegian Leads or to drive the Italians out of North Africa, but the Germans could wreck their plans by occupying Norway and Greece or hamper them by threats to descend on Syria or Gibraltar. We were greatly restricted too by the refusal of neutral Governments to allow us to take measures on their behalf which might bring down German vengeance upon them. We have seen the vain attempts of the Allies to win the active support of the Scandinavian countries, the Low Countries, Yugoslavia and Turkey; on various occasions also British action was influenced by the desire not to offend opinion in the United States. This indeed was one of the fixed points of Mr. Churchill's policy, and there were of course others. America must be brought into the war, France must be restored, Russia must be supported, Germany must be bombed on an ever-increasing scale; the active war in the Middle East must not be prejudiced by the possibility of war in the Far East, nor must the security of the United Kingdom as the centre of the free world's resistance and base of its operations be jeopardised for any reason whatever. So far as grand strategy was more precisely formulated, it was in the particular appreciations of the Chiefs of Staff which received the approval of the Cabinet or Defence Committee and in the occasional directives of the Prime Minister and Minister of Defence which had received or assumed like approval.

It is worth while to look back on the major decisions of grand strategy in the period of this volume and note in what circumstances, and by whom, they were taken. Strategy during the war was naturally to a great extent determined by decisions taken in the months and years before it. Reference need not be made to the negative or delayed decisions in the matter of rearmament to be recounted in Volume I, but credit may be given for the positive decisions which just in time provided fighter aircraft of the highest quality and made possible the saving grace of radar. There were more recent decisions, however, which directly affected our strategy at the outset of war, such as those of the British and French Governments to offer guarantees to Poland and to Greece, and those of the British to send an expeditionary force to France and not, for the time being, to send capital ships to the Far East. Another was the decision that Italy's neutrality was to our advantage, that her equivocal position of non-belligerency should be accepted, and that nothing should be done which might provoke her.

At the beginning of September 1939 the Allied Governments agreed not to initiate a bombing offensive. Conscious of their inferiority in the air, both were unwilling to precipitate the German blitz which they expected to descend on their cities at any moment. They announced that they would strike only at military targets defined in the narrowest terms. The decision was in accordance with both expediency and humanity. These self-imposed restrictions were maintained by the Allies until the violation of the Low Countries by the Germans, and the air offensive which then began, never to cease until May 1945, still for some time respected previous conventions. The successive removals of the restrictions were authorised by the Cabinet.

With regard to Chemical Warfare, as it came to be known, namely the use of poison gas and other noxious substances, no decision was needed. Such methods were forbidden by international law, and there was never any question on the British side of resorting to them except in retaliation. The use of them, however, by Germany, as in 1915, needed to be provided against, and throughout the war Chemical Warfare played a prominent part in our preparations.

In the maritime war the sinking of the *Athenia* on September 3 convinced the Allies, wrongly, that Germany had from the outset resolved to flout accepted international law; we now know that, while Hitler had never intended to observe legal restrictions at sea for long, he did not actually give *OKM* a free hand for some months. But illegal and inhumane acts soon occurred, and in November 1939 the British Government announced their intention to stop German exports as a measure of reprisal.[1] It was on similar, though more specific, grounds that they first justified the breach of Norwegian neutrality involved in mining the Leads.

It would be unfair to attribute to the Chamberlain Government responsibility for the failure to afford relief to Poland by attacking the Siegfried line. In almost desperate circumstances they had given her a guarantee as a warning to Hitler and as a gesture of solidarity, but there was nothing they could do to make it immediately effective. The British staffs made it clear that Poland's salvation would not depend on our ability to relieve pressure on her at the outset of a war.[2] Polish resistance had in fact collapsed before any British army units had arrived, or could have arrived, in France, and it was out of the question for London to press a French Commander-in-Chief to attack with French troops contrary to his set purpose. The important decision which the London Cabinet took at this time was to plan for a three years war and authorise the expansion of the Services; the passing of the National Service Act on September 1 spared them much of the trouble which had beset their predecessors in the earlier war.

---

[1] Above, p. 78.
[2] See above, p. 12.

Strategy for south-east Europe was complicated by anxiety not to provoke Italy, but the principle of building up a defensive Balkan front, with Turkey as its keystone, was agreed on by the Allies in December 1939. Parliament had approved in the spring the creation of a strategic reserve in the Middle East, and precision was given to this policy at the end of the year.

Earlier chapters have shown how intervention in Scandinavia, first urged in the autumn by Mr. Churchill as a measure of economic blockade, and later by the French in the hope of diverting German strength from their own front, was finally approved by both Governments as a means of breaking the deadlock and gaining the initiative; we have seen how it was delayed by various scruples long after all hope of surprise had vanished, and then suffered in execution from the lack of consistent direction and unified control, as well as from more tangible deficiencies. The decision to abandon north Norway after the capture of Narvik was taken under the pressure of events in France.

For the disaster in France the responsibility cannot fairly be laid on the British Government. Plan D was Gamelin's decision; no objection to it was raised by Lord Gort, who was Gamelin's subordinate, and the British Cabinet saw no reason to interfere; they can hardly be blamed for not making it a condition of their approval that Gamelin should modify his dispositions for the defence of the Meuse and the placing of his reserves. Reasons have been suggested above for their rejection of the functions of criticism and even of informing themselves fully of the French dispositions. The decision to evacuate the British Expeditionary Force was unavoidable; the credit for its being taken in time is primarily due to Lord Gort, and for its being possible at all to the efficiency of all three Services, and not least the Navy. But Mr. Churchill's Cabinet had agonising decisions to take when besought by our ally to dissipate our fighter strength by sending more units to shore up the lost battle in France. A point was reached when the Cabinet, for the eventual good of both countries, resisted further appeals, while they provided for the near future by giving a free hand to Lord Beaverbrook as Minister of Aircraft Production.

In retaining a minimum fighter strength at home the Cabinet acted on the urgent advice of Sir Hugh Dowding and the Air Staff; in a no less painful decision concerning the balance of naval strength, in the ultimatum at Mers-el-Kebir, they acted with the final acquiescence, but against the first advice, of the Naval Staff. We have seen, too, how later on Mr. Churchill disagreed with the Naval Staff as to the dangers of antagonising what remained of the French Fleet. A yet more vital naval decision had been taken in June 1940. We were now at war with Italy, without the French naval assistance on which we had counted in all our plans, and it is not surprising that the question should have been raised in the Admiralty whether it was wise to retain our own fleet in the Eastern Mediterranean. Mr. Churchill, however, like Admiral Cunningham, had no doubts, and the suggestion to withdraw the fleet does not seem to have been even discussed at the highest level. One can only speculate on how the course of the war would have been changed had the control of those waters been surrendered to the Italians. Even bolder were the decisions to defend Malta and, when everything pointed to an attempt at invasion at home, to send a substantial part of our exiguous armoured force to Egypt; in the latter case the decision was made by the Prime Minister and the War Office, the Cabinet merely taking note afterwards.[1]

The Prime Minister was heart and soul in the war in the Middle East. It was the only theatre where we could strike at the enemy, and his eagerness to lose no opportunity of doing so made him impatient with the Commanders-in-Chief; they were in no way lacking in the offensive spirit, but they possessed a closer understanding of the administrative necessities of modern warfare. Wavell's decision to attack the Italians before they reached Matruh was his own; its success helped our efforts in East Africa, where the timing of events depended rather on local resources and on progress on other fronts than on instructions from London.

When Wavell's victories gained us the initiative at the beginning of 1941, it was the Defence Committee which decided on partly political, partly military grounds to halt his advance at Benghazi, and to build up in Egypt a mobile reserve available for Europe. But, when the imminence of a German southward advance in the Balkans disposed the Greeks to welcome such help as we could give, it was the Cabinet which, on broad grounds of policy, took the difficult decisions of February 24 and March 7 to open a new theatre of operations in Greece. They were advised by the absent Foreign Secretary and Chief of the Imperial General Staff, who were in touch with our Ambassadors as well as the Commanders-in-Chief in the Middle East and were able to consult General Smuts in person in Cairo. So far were the Cabinet from pressing intervention on the local commanders that on March 5 they were inclined to drop the whole scheme, in the now more hazardous conditions, and only decided finally to approve it after learning from their various representatives in the Middle East how serious would be the effect of cancelling it now that it had gone so far.[2]

---

[1] See above, p. 308.

[2] See above, p. 446. Similarly in the final stage of the Dakar expedition the reluctance of the authorities at home was overborne by the enthusiasm of the men on the spot. See above, p. 318.

The need of obtaining the Australian and New Zealand Governments' consent to the proposed use of their troops in the expedition illustrated the difficulties incident to a division of authority when time is urgent; in this case they were modified by the presence of Mr. Menzies at all the critical meetings in London. In one matter trouble was narrowly avoided. Mr. Eden had been instructed by his Cabinet to act on his own authority if time did not allow reference home, and he and Sir John Dill did in fact on March 4 agree to a joint plan with the Greeks. But the Cabinet admitted Mr. Menzies' protest that the Dominion Governments would resent a claim that such an agreement bound themselves, and their sanction was belatedly obtained.[1]

The reverses of April and May put a heavy strain on those concerned, in England and the Middle East. The misgivings felt by many as to the military justification for the Greek expedition were proved well founded. The unexpected set-back in Cyrenaica reflected on Wavell's judgement and at the end of April it appeared to the Prime Minister—though not to the Chiefs of Staff—that sufficiently vigorous steps were not being taken by any of the three Services to strike the Germans before they became stronger and to prevent the arrival of reinforcements and stores. Then came the demands on the hard-pressed Wavell to undertake fresh commitments in Iraq and Syria. In both cases his opinion was overruled, and in the former he had to admit later that he had been wrong; in the latter the Defence Committee let him know that they were willing to accept his resignation. By now his credit with them was severely shaken, and the loss of Crete was a further blow to it. Consciousness that his judgement had been at fault in the Habbaniya episode sapped his self-confidence and he was the less able to resist pressure from the Prime Minister to join battle, prematurely as he thought, with Rommel in the desert.

As to the urgent importance of strengthening the Middle East, there was no difference between the Prime Minister and his Service advisers. This was not so with regard to the Far East. In September 1940 he overruled the Chiefs of Staff's advice as to the destination of an Australian division and spoke scornfully of the decision to employ two Indian brigades in the Malayan jungles against a possible war with Japan and a still more unlikely siege of Singapore.[2] Again, in the spring of 1941 Sir John Dill thought it necessary to remind him that it had been an accepted principle of our strategy that in the last resort the security of Singapore ranked before that of Egypt, adding that quite a small increase of force in Malaya would make all the difference between running a serious risk and achieving full security.

---

[1] See above, pp. 447–448.

[2] See above, p. 337.

But the Prime Minister was prepared to run the risk and assumed for the Government the responsibility of giving the Service Departments warning in good time—which meant, they pointed out to him, not less than three months.[1]

Our resources were, as always, too small to meet all the many calls on them. Mr. Churchill acted evidently on the principle that sufficient unto the day is the evil thereof: one should not starve an active front for the sake of one which might never become active. If it should, he relied on the deterrent effect, or in the extreme case on the practical assistance, of the United States Navy, and to some extent on the strength of the 'fortress of Singapore'.

But even the presence of an American fleet in a certain area was as nothing compared with the securing of America as an ally. This dominant feature of Mr. Churchill's policy, so often referred to, is illustrated by his welcoming of the American decision, in April 1941, to transfer part of the Pacific Fleet to the Atlantic.[2] Similarly at the end of June, referring to the offer of United States escort vessels on the North-Western Approaches, he insisted that no question of naval strategy in the Atlantic was comparable with the importance of drawing the Americans to this side. This must be accepted as a decision of policy.

In spite of these differences over the strength to be maintained in the Far East, there was, at least in the period covered by this volume, no such deep cleavage of opinion on any issue as had existed in the earlier war between Westerners and Easterners. The controversy which may perhaps be best compared with it is the controversy between the Navy and the Royal Air Force over the right use of our long-range aircraft. The Army indeed, like the Navy, cherished a grievance over the failure to satisfy its peculiar needs in the air, but never asserted it as forcibly. The Navy believed that a more generous allocation of long-range aircraft to the destruction of U-boats, both in port and more especially at sea, would have brought earlier victory in the Battle of the Atlantic; they considered that the concentration on the strategic air offensive against Germany was at this period wasteful and futile in comparison. But it was only at the end of our period that long-range aircraft were arriving in any numbers; thus it is over their employment in the later phases of the Battle of the Atlantic that controversy raged fiercest. Not that there was ever any doubt in the minds of the Government that the strategic air offensive was to be developed to the utmost. This strategy was a legacy from the years before the war; it remained an article of faith to the Air Staff; and we have seen how in the autumn of 1940 Mr.

---

[1] See above, p. 506.
[2] See above, p. 502.

Churchill accepted it as the only hope of victory. The war-winning capacity, however, of strategic bombing was still unproven. What had already, by June 1941, been demonstrated beyond dispute was the necessity of powerful air support for the successful execution of any major military enterprise by sea or land.

The machinery of government at the highest level underwent no important change during Mr. Churchill's first year of power. Replying to Mr. Lloyd George in the Commons debate of 7 May 1941 the Prime Minister said:

'. . . My right hon. Friend the Member for Carnarvon Boroughs made his usual criticisms about the composition and character of the Government, of the war control and of the War Cabinet, and the House is entitled to know, has a right to know, who are responsible for the conduct of the war. The War Cabinet consists of eight members, five of whom have no regular Departments, and three of whom represent the main organisms of the State, to wit, Foreign Affairs, Finance and Labour, which in their different ways come into every great question that has to be settled. That is the body which gives its broad sanction to the main policy and conduct of the war. Under their authority, the Chiefs of Staff of the three Services sit each day together, and I, as Prime Minister and Minister of Defence, convene with them and preside over them when I think it necessary, inviting, when business requires it, the three Service Ministers. All large issues of military policy are brought before the Defence Committee, which has for several months consisted of the three Chiefs of Staff, the three Service Ministers and four members of the War Cabinet, namely, myself, the Lord Privy Seal, who has no Department, the Foreign Secretary and Lord Beaverbrook. This is the body, this is the machine; it works easily and flexibly at the present time, and I do not propose to make any changes in it until further advised . . .'[1]

With regard to civil organisation it is only necessary to mention the amalgamation in May 1941 of the two departments of Shipping and Transport into the Ministry of War Transport, whose first chief was Mr. F. J. Leathers; it had become plain that a single authority was needed to control ships, ports and railways. At the same time Colonel J. C. T. Moore-Brabazon became Minister of Aircraft Production in place of Lord Beaverbrook, whose new function, as Minister of State in the War Cabinet, was to perform 'supervisory and referee functions in regard to priorities'. At the end of June Lord Beaverbrook was to succeed Sir Andrew Duncan as Minister of Supply, with a

---

[1] *House of Commons Debates* vol. 371, cols. 936–937.

special mission to galvanise the production of tanks as in the previous year he had galvanised the production of aircraft.[1]

The war had not created any formal machinery for consultation, leading to common action, between the political leaders of the nations of the Commonwealth. There was never any question of securing the permanent presence of a Dominion statesman as a member of the War Cabinet, as in the later months of the earlier war. The Prime Ministers were wanted at home, and in any case, on both constitutional and practical grounds, Mr. Churchill denied the possibility of the Dominions being represented at every meeting: the numbers of the War Cabinet were large enough already—some thought too large. Mr. Menzies, however, and Mr. Fraser were welcomed to sit as members when visiting England in the spring and summer of 1941, while General Smuts had flown north early in March to confer with Mr. Eden in Cairo, and ideas were constantly exchanged by correspondence between him and his old friend Mr. Churchill.

In April 1940 the United Kingdom Government suggested the meeting of an Imperial Conference, but it was found impracticable to arrange one: neither Mr. Mackenzie King nor General Smuts could have attended, nor did they favour a meeting at that time. Later on, suggestions that a conference of Prime Ministers would be useful were made both in the United Kingdom and in Australia and New Zealand. Such a conference might have been expected to deal either with matters immediately affecting the conduct of the war or, in a preliminary survey, with the post-war situation. But for the latter purpose the time seemed premature, and for the former, though a meeting would have been welcome in London, in Canberra and in Wellington, there seemed no sufficient case to outweigh the objections of the Prime Ministers of Canada and the Union of South Africa. The same difficulties were found to obtain in June 1941. In Mr. Mackenzie King's opinion the present method was working well, and there were no complaints of it in Canada.

In strictly military matters, arrangements concerning the strategic use of Dominion troops did not always work smoothly. The instructions issued by the Australian Government to General Blamey in April 1940 stated that questions of policy regarding the employment of the force were to be decided by the United Kingdom and Commonwealth Governments in consultation; except that in an emergency the commander of the force might take a decision on such a question at his discretion, informing his Government that he was so

---

[1] See Appendix VII for a diagram of the War Cabinet organisation in March 1941.

doing.[1] This principle, whether explicitly stated or not, was no doubt generally acceptable, but there were occasions when certain Governments felt that London, however unintentionally, had taken action which did not accord with it. For instance, in April 1940 the Canadian Government considered that they, as well as General McNaughton, the Canadian commander in England, should have been consulted before their troops were assigned to the proposed direct attack on Trondheim.[2] We have seen how, in a more important matter, the Australian and New Zealand Governments felt that they had not been consulted fully and promptly enough with regard to the despatch of their divisions to Greece, and how misunderstandings occurred as to what consents had been given.[3] In both cases it may be assumed that there was no intention to evade Dominion approval, and in both cases time pressed. Nevertheless it might have been better if more formal steps had been taken to obtain the Dominion Governments' consent.

The South African Government had decided in May 1940 that only volunteers might be employed outside the frontiers of the Union, and they, for the present, not outside the African continent; after serving first in East Africa troops of the Union were later made available for Egypt.[4]

The Dominion Governments also desired more voice in the determination of strategy, especially where their special interests were concerned. In any question of naval strategy in the Pacific Australia and New Zealand were involved of necessity, not, as in the Middle East, because their troops happened to be there. We have seen how jealously they watched any proposals tending to weaken our strength in Far Eastern waters, and how Mr. Menzies successfully asserted their right to be consulted with regard to the American proposal of April 1941.[5] But it is not clear what change of system could have ensured a joint direction of the war without loss of efficiency. Later volumes of the present series will describe the elaborate machine constructed at Washington to secure a fair sharing of control between the British and American high commands; but it is obvious that such parity of control is not likely to be conceded unless there is something like parity of strength, and that every addition to the number of participating States must tend against speed of decision and preservation of secrecy.

Discussions with representatives of the United States still had to be discreetly veiled, but they were becoming frequent and important,

---

[1] G. Long, *To Benghazi* (Canberra 1952) p. 101.

[2] *See* above p. 136; C. P. Stacey, *Six Years of War*, I 258–263.

[3] See above, pp. 447–448.

[4] See above, p. 43.

[5] *See* above, p. 502.

and assumed a more and more practical nature. American officers attended strategical conferences at Singapore in October 1940 and February and April 1941; the staff conversations held at Washington in February and March 1941 had led to the formation in London of the nucleus of a distinguished military mission, the 'United States Special Observer Group', while the British Cabinet had agreed to set up, also under an innocuous title, a permanent Joint Staff Mission at Washington. And all this time the correspondence between the President and the Former Naval Person continued to supplement and transcend official negotiations.

There had never been the same intimate correspondence with the French, nor had the meetings of the Supreme War Council, or the occasional visits of Ministers and Service chiefs, established complete harmony of thought and action. The Permanent Military Representatives in London, whose meetings had been intended to create such unity, did not enjoy the necessary authority, nor were they in sufficiently close touch with their principals. More generally, there had not been time for the separate interests and sentiments of the two countries to be fused in a single policy. Perhaps the failure of the still-born Declaration of Union was symbolical. After the armistice, though the importance of co-operation between the British and the Free French was accepted by both sides, the British, for reasons which need not be repeated, often found its practical application difficult.

In June 1941 Mr. Churchill was in favour of arranging a 'rally' of all the Allied Powers represented in London, and sending out invitations for an 'inter-Allied Council'. But the event did not go beyond a meeting of Allied Representatives at St. James's Palace on June 12. The presence of so many Allied Governments, besides the leaders of Free France, had given London a unique position as an international capital, but it was not possible to share with them the direction of the war. The whole responsibility for the formulation of strategy and, so far as the enemy allowed, for its execution now rested on the British.

What this implied in practice has been told in Mr. Churchill's account to the House of Commons; essentially it meant the teamwork of the Minister of Defence and Chiefs of Staff, the Defence Committee being invoked when matters of special importance called for decision, and the Cabinet when large political issues were involved or the highest sanction required.

Figures show how in the course of the period under review the meetings of the Cabinet became fewer, falling to two or three a week, while the Chiefs of Staff or their deputies continued to meet normally at least once every day. The meetings of the Defence Committee were few or many according to the state of affairs.

	1939 (*Sept.–* (*Dec.*)	*1940* (*to 10* *May*)	*1940* (*from 10* *May*)	*1941* (*Jan.–* *June*)
War Cabinet	123	119	196	64
Military Co-ordination Committee	16	38	—	—
Defence Committee (Operations) .	—	—	52	44
Chiefs of Staff	118	119	322	229

The Minister of Defence is recorded as having attended and presided at twenty of the Chiefs of Staff's meetings in 1940 and seventeen in the first six months of 1941. The Chiefs of Staff regularly attended Cabinet meetings when military questions were discussed, and Mr. Churchill was of course in constant touch with them individually. His personal contribution to the processes of executive government was the presentation of short minutes directed to Ministers, officials, and Service chiefs. Sometimes these minutes asked for information, sometimes they initiated action, sometimes they demanded further consideration, often they protested against alleged inertia or incompetence; they were by no means confined to questions of policy, but expressed opinions on strategy and tactics. Many of them have been published in Mr. Churchill's book; it must not be supposed that they were left unanswered or unchallenged; but it must not be supposed either that he was in the habit of issuing orders on military matters without the concurrence of his responsible advisers.

There is no need to repeat what has been said in previous chapters of his and their method of work, the strain under which they all laboured, their occasional mutual irritation, their fundamental mutual trust, and the loyal mediation of General Ismay. The Chiefs of Staff had behind them the resources of their Departments and the collective wisdom of the Joint Planning Staff and Joint Intelligence Committee—and it may be remarked in passing that our Intelligence was now far more effective than in the early months. Mr. Churchill held all the strings of the war effort in his fingers, and his considerable military knowledge, though his advisers might think it in some respects out of date, could not be ignored; apart from his political position his main strength lay in his towering personality. Great, however, as was his authority and formidable his powers of argument, Mr. Churchill was reluctant to override the Chiefs of Staff in a technical matter; it was different when 'a political decision' was called for. But even on technical points he pressed them hard and it was not easy to resist his impact. We find him telling his colleagues that he is trying to persuade the Chiefs of Staff to change their views as to the sending of mechanical transport ships through the Mediterranean in August 1940, and he acquiesced most unwillingly in their refusal to sanction an attempt on the island of Pantelleria. On minor points they may sometimes have thought it prudent to yield to him, even against their better judgement, in order to safeguard essential matters on which they were not prepared to compromise. Undoubtedly some signals went out from the Admiralty which the First Sea Lord strongly disliked. But even those who resented Mr. Churchill's methods and distrusted his interventions in purely military matters welcomed his forceful leadership; they knew that his whole mind and strength were devoted to the winning of the war, and that he possessed, without a rival or alternative, the confidence of the country. The *union sacrée*, forged in May 1940, remained unbroken, and even in the disgruntled debate of 10 June a year later no desire was expressed for a change of command.

If a contemporary historian, who is also a civilian, may offer an opinion, it would be that, while in large issues Mr. Churchill's instincts were sound, he did not in this early period of the war show greatness as a strategist in the narrower sense. The main characteristic of his cherished projects was audacity, and in his impatience he was apt to mistake criticism by professional knowledge and experience for timidity and inertia. He seemed not always to remember that, as one of the commanders in Norway put it, what is operationally desirable may not be administratively possible. Nor was he in this period always successful in his selection and handling of men. He was too much inclined to consider boldness a sufficient qualification for high command, too intolerant of men with temperaments unlike his own. His greatness lay elsewhere, as a national leader in critical times, and it was his glory that, the more formidable the crisis, the clearer and steadier shone his genius. There had been no one like him since Chatham—Lloyd George, for all his vigour and resource, had not the same understanding of either the technique of war or the Service mind—and Mr. Churchill possessed the human quality which Chatham lacked. He showed greatness as a statesman in his foresight and in his concentration on the essential points. Above all he was great as an energiser, keying the whole people—Ministers, commanders, officials, fighting men, factory workers and sufferers in the devastated cities—up to the highest pitch of effort and endurance. It is not too fanciful to see in the Britain of those days an embodiment of Milton's vision of 'a noble and puissant nation rousing herself like a strong man after sleep and shaking her invincible locks'. This upsurge of the national spirit was in part a response to the challenge of instant danger; but Mr. Churchill did much to evoke, to foster, and to maintain it. He possessed in a supreme degree the qualities needed by the hour: vigilance, drive, joy of battle, love of responsibility, resounding eloquence, and above all courage and faith. He had taken up his task, he told the House of Commons, with buoyancy and hope; he felt sure that our cause would not be suffered to fail among men.

Appendices

Appendices

APPENDIX I

Bombing Policy

(a) ALLIED POLICY, SEPTEMBER 1939–MAY 1940

The Anglo-French Declaration of 2 September 1939, of which the text is given below, was issued in answer to President Roosevelt's appeal of the previous day to every belligerent Government 'publicly to affirm its determination that its armed forces shall in no event and under no circumstances undertake bombardment from the air of civilian populations or unfortified cities, upon the understanding that the same rules of warfare will be scrupulously observed by all their opponents'.

Speaking in the House of Commons on 21 June 1938 Mr. Chamberlain, the Prime Minister, after prefacing that there was in fact at present 'no international code of law with respect to aerial warfare which is the subject of general agreement', had stated that none the less there were three rules or principles of international law which were as applicable to warfare from the air as to war at sea or on land. First, it was against international law to bomb civilians as such and to make deliberate attacks upon civilian populations. Secondly, targets aimed at from the air must be legitimate military objectives and must be capable of identification. Thirdly, reasonable care must be taken in attacking such military objectives not to bomb a civilian population in the neighbourhood.[1]

These principles, which had been unanimously approved by the Assembly of the League of Nations, were quoted in Air Ministry Instructions of 22 August 1939.

Hitler replied to President Roosevelt in the same sense as the Allies, stating that the German Air Force had received the command to confine itself to military objectives.[2]

During the Polish campaign the British War Cabinet considered on several occasions whether in view of the activities of the German Air Force they should change their own policy. The question was decided in the negative on grounds of expediency, but the Chiefs of Staff reported also on the question of fact. Up to September 12 it did not appear to them, on the available evidence, that the Germans had adopted a policy of disregarding the accepted principles; but soon afterwards reliable evidence was received of the indiscriminate bombing of open towns, and the bombing of Warsaw on September 24 and 25 was by no means confined to military objectives.[3] On October 16, after a meeting of the Cabinet on the 14th, the Chief of the Air Staff informed Air Marshal Barratt, Head of No. 1 Air Mission in France, as follows: 'Owing to German action in

---

[1] *House of Commons Debates* vol. 337 cols. 936 ff.

[2] J. M. Spaight, *Air Power and War Rights* (3rd ed. 1947) pp. 258–260.

[3] Cf. the evidence of Mr. Biddle, the American Ambassador to Poland, reporting on Sept. 14, *The Memoirs of Cordell Hull* I 677.

Poland we are no longer bound by restrictions under the instructions . . . of 22 August, nor by our acceptance of Roosevelt's appeal. Our action is now governed entirely by expediency, i.e., what it suits us to do having regard to (a) the need to conserve our resources, (b) probable enemy retaliatory action, and (c) our need still to take into account to some extent influential neutral opinion.' In fact our policy remained unchanged until 15 May 1940.[1]

Anglo-French Declaration on the Conduct of Warfare. (2 September 1939)

'The Governments of the United Kingdom and France solemnly and publicly affirm their intention, should a war be forced upon them, to conduct hostilities with a firm desire to spare the civilian population and to preserve in every way possible those monuments of human achievement which are treasured in all civilised countries.

'In this spirit they have welcomed with deep satisfaction President Roosevelt's appeal on the subject of bombing from the air. Fully sympathising with the humanitarian sentiments by which that appeal was inspired they have replied to it in similar terms.

'They had indeed some time ago sent explicit instructions to the commanders of their armed forces prohibiting the bombardment, whether from the air or the sea, or by artillery on land, of any except strictly military objectives in the narrowest sense of the word.

'Bombardment by artillery on land will exclude objectives which have no strictly defined military importance, in particular large urban areas situated outside the battle zone. They will furthermore make every effort to avoid the destruction of localities or buildings which are of value to civilisation.

'As regards the use of naval forces, including submarines, the two Governments will abide strictly by the rules laid down in the Submarine Protocol of 1936, which have been accepted by nearly all civilised nations. Further, they will only employ their aircraft against merchant shipping at sea in conformity with the recognised rules applicable to the exercise of belligerent rights by warships.

'Finally the two Allied Governments re-affirm their intention to abide by the terms of the Geneva Protocol of 1925, prohibiting the use in war of asphyxiating or poisonous or other gases or of bacteriological methods of warfare. An enquiry will be addressed to the German Government as to whether they are prepared to give an assurance to the same effect.

'It will of course be understood that in the event of the enemy not observing any of the restrictions which the Governments of the United Kingdom and France have imposed on the operations of their armed forces these Governments reserve the right to take all such action as they may consider appropriate.'

---

[1] For the Cabinet decision of October 14 and Allied differences as to the action to be taken in specific hypothetical cases, see above, pp. 167 ff.

(b) THE GERMAN BOMBING OF ROTTERDAM

(*This paper has been produced by the Air Ministry Historical Branch*)

The bombing of Rotterdam on 14 May 1940 presents a problem of some complexity. There are two aspects to be considered. Firstly, the legitimate tactical use of air bombardment in support of the ground operations. Secondly, the more questionable use of air power to hasten the surrender of the town.

On the first point, the German attitude, as revealed by contemporary Army documents, was that Rotterdam could no longer be regarded as an 'open city' as areas of the town had been fortified and troops were defending them against the Germans, who were, in fact, being hard pressed to hold their positions. The G.O.C. XXXIX Corps (General Schmidt) accordingly prepared an assault to be launched on 14 May, preceded by a bombing attack from 13.30 to 14.00 hours,[1] for which one Stuka Geschwader (about 100 aircraft) of Fliegerkorps Putzier was allotted. Göring and Kesselring (who was commanding Luftflotte 2 at the time), in their post-war statements, have claimed that the actual attack was carried out solely as a tactical operation, but an examination of all the available evidence clearly shows that there were other considerations.

This leads us to the second point—the significance of the raid in relation to the surrender of the city. To appreciate this fully, it will be useful to give some account of the actual events.

On the evening of 13 May, Eighteenth Army sent the following order to General Schmidt: 'Resistance in Rotterdam will be broken with every means; if necessary destruction of the town will be threatened and carried out.' At 10.30 the following morning, therefore, the Dutch authorities received an ultimatum which threatened the 'complete destruction' of the city unless resistance ceased forthwith. The Dutch were given two hours in which to reply. At 12.10, although there was still no official answer from the Dutch, General Schmidt learnt that surrender was likely and he immediately took steps to postpone the bombing, scheduled for 13.30. The War Diary of XXXIX Corps records that 'Fliegerkorps Putzier received at 12.10 hours, through 7th Parachute Division, the following order: "bombing attack Rotterdam postponed owing to surrender negotiations".'

The Dutch reply was received at about 12.30 but it merely asked for the signature and rank of the officer sending the ultimatum—which had, by some chance, been omitted. The Germans interpreted this, probably correctly, as an attempt to play for time. Accordingly, Schmidt drew up the terms of surrender, which demanded that all negotiations must be completed in time for the German occupation to take place before dark. A new time-limit of 3 hours (up to 16.30) was fixed, but no threats were made. This communication was handed over to the Dutch representative, who left the meeting-place at 13.20. A few minutes later, a formation of bombers was seen approaching and General Schmidt gave the order to fire red flares as a signal to the aircraft to refrain from bombing. Nevertheless, at 13.30 the bombing started, causing large fires and considerable

---

[1] Local time has been used throughout this paper.

damage.[1] Two hours later, Rotterdam formally surrendered and the German troops took possession of the city. The capitulation of the whole Dutch Army followed the next morning (15 May). It is clear, from the above evidence, that General Schmidt did his best to call off the air attack. Why, then, was it carried out when surrender negotiations were in progress? In his memoirs, Kesselring declares that he had no knowledge of these negotiations but this is hard to believe, particularly as Göring admitted at Nuremberg that there was radio communication between Rotterdam and Luftflotte 2 via his (Göring's) headquarters. It seems reasonable to assume, therefore, that the message from General Schmidt to the Air Corps, postponing the attack, must have been known to Kesselring and probably also to Göring. There is, unfortunately, no record of what was said during the telephone conversation between Göring and Kesselring which, according to the latter, went on throughout the morning on the question of the air attack. However, it is unlikely that Göring would ignore the psychological effect of the attack and, with Warsaw in mind, he must have realised that a display of air power would probably hasten the Dutch surrender. He may, therefore, have decided to over-ride the Schmidt request on the grounds that the surrender was not yet an accomplished fact. When the bomber force arrived over Rotterdam, about one-half saw the red flares and did not drop their bombs on the city. The other half either did not see the flares or failed to appreciate their significance, and bombed according to plan.[2]

To sum up, it can fairly be said that, even if the attack was not completely indiscriminate, it was quite unnecessary, and cannot be excused, as Göring and Kesselring have suggested, on the grounds of inadequate means of communication between ground and air. We have clear evidence that the Germans were prepared to be ruthless and had threatened the destruction of the city if it did not surrender. Although complete evidence is lacking, it would appear probable that Göring decided to hasten the surrender by intimidating the defenders with a display of air power, not unmindful of the probable repercussions on the Dutch Army as a whole. In fact, as the German air attaché, Wenninger, told Kesselring, in consequence of the attack, the whole of the Dutch Army capitulated.

It is not, perhaps, without significance that, after the bombing, General Schmidt expressed his regret to the Dutch Commander in Rotterdam that the attack had been carried out.

---

[1] Contemporary estimates of casualties were greatly exaggerated. The figure given at the time was about 30,000, but it is now known that the total civilian death-roll was about 980.

[2] It has been generally believed that the attack was carried out by Stukas, and the *OKW* communiqué of 14 May referred to 'attacks by German dive-bombers'. It is now established, however, that the unit concerned was Kampfgeschwader 54, which was equipped with Heinkel 111's. A total of 94 tons of bombs was dropped, suggesting that some 45 to 50 aircraft, or half the Geschwader, dropped their load on the city. The use of the Heinkel, which could carry a much greater bomb-load than the Ju. 87, may be an indication of Göring's desire to demonstrate the destructive powers of the Luftwaffe. It will be remembered that in the orders for the *tactical* use of the air arm, a Stuka Geschwader was allotted to the support of the ground forces.

APPENDIX II

TABLE I

British, Allied and Neutral Merchant Ship Losses and Causes

(from S. W. Roskill, *The War at Sea*, Vol. I)

1939

Month	Submarines	Aircraft	Mine	Warship raider	Merchant raider	E-boat	Unknown and other causes	Total
September	153,879 (41)	—	29,537 (8)	5,051 (1)	—	—	6,378 (3)	194,845 (53)
October	134,807 (27)	—	29,490 (11)	32,058 (8)	—	—	—	196,355 (46)
November	51,589 (21)	—	120,958 (27)	1,722 (2)	—	—	—	174,269 (50)
December	80,881 (25)	2,949 (10)	82,712 (33)	22,506 (4)	—	—	875 (1)	189,923 (72)
Total	421,156 (114)	2,949 (10)	262,697 (79)	61,337 (15)	—	—	7,253 (4)	755,392 (222)

1940

Month	Submarines	Aircraft	Mine	Warship raider	Merchant raider	E-boat	Unknown and other causes	Total
January	111,263 (40)	23,693 (11)	77,116 (21)	—	—	—	2,434 (1)	214,506 (73)
February	169,566 (45)	853 (2)	54,740 (15)	1,761 (1)	—	—	—	226,920 (63)
March	62,781 (23)	8,694 (7)	35,501 (14)	—	—	—	33 (1)	107,009 (45)
April	32,467 (7)	13,409 (7)	19,799 (11)	—	5,207 (1)	151 (1)	87,185 (31)	158,218 (58)
May	55,580 (13)	158,348 (48)	47,716 (20)	—	6,199 (1)	694 (1)	19,924 (18)	288,461 (101)
June	284,113 (58)	105,193 (22)	86,076 (22)	25,506 (2)	29,225 (4)	6,856 (3)	48,527 (29)	585,496 (140)
July	195,825 (38)	70,193 (33)	35,598 (14)	—	67,494 (11)	13,302 (6)	4,501 (3)	386,913 (105)
August	267,618 (56)	53,283 (15)	11,433 (5)	—	61,767 (11)	1,583 (2)	1,545 (3)	397,229 (92)
September	295,335 (59)	56,328 (15)	8,269 (7)	—	65,386 (8)	14,951 (7)	8,352 (4)	448,621 (100)
October	352,407 (63)	8,752 (6)	32,548 (24)	—	30,539 (4)	1,595 (1)	17,144 (5)	442,985 (103)
November	146,613 (32)	66,438 (18)	46,762 (24)	48,748 (11)	74,923 (9)	—	2,231 (3)	385,715 (97)
December	212,590 (37)	14,890 (8)	54,331 (24)	20,971 (3)	25,904 (5)	8,853 (2)	12,029 (3)	349,568 (82)
Total	2,186,158 (471)	580,074 (192)	509,889 (201)	96,986 (17)	366,644 (54)	47,985 (23)	203,905 (101)	3,991,641 (1,059)

1941

Month	Submarines	Aircraft	Mine	Warship raider	Merchant raider	E-boat	Unknown and other causes	Total
January	126,782 (21)	78,597 (20)	17,107 (10)	18,738 (3)	78,484 (20)	—	532 (2)	320,240 (76)
February	196,783 (39)	89,305 (27)	16,507 (10)	79,086 (17)	7,031 (1)	2,979 (3)	11,702 (5)	403,393 (102)
March	243,020 (41)	113,314 (41)	23,585 (19)	89,838 (17)	28,707 (4)	20,361 (9)	10,881 (8)	529,706 (139)
April	249,375 (43)	323,454 (116)	24,888 (6)	—	43,640 (6)	4,299 (3)	42,245 (21)	687,901 (195)
May	325,492 (58)	146,302 (65)	23,194 (9)	—	15,002 (3)	—	1,052 (4)	511,042 (139)
June	310,143 (61)	61,414 (25)	15,326 (10)	—	17,759 (4)	—	27,383 (9)	432,025 (109)
July	94,209 (22)	9,275 (11)	8,583 (7)	—	5,792 (1)	—	3,116 (2)	120,975 (43)
August	80,310 (23)	23,862 (9)	1,400 (3)	—	21,378 (3)	3,519 (2)	230 (1)	130,699 (41)
September	202,820 (53)	40,812 (12)	14,948 (9)	7,500 (1)	8,734 (2)	6,676 (3)	4,452 (4)	285,942 (84)
October	156,554 (32)	35,222 (10)	19,737 (4)	—	—	3,305 (2)	3,471 (3)	218,289 (51)
November	62,196 (13)	23,015 (10)	1,714 (5)	—	—	17,715 (7)	—	104,640 (35)
December	124,070 (26)	72,850 (25)	63,853 (19)	6,661 (2)	—	—	316,272 (213)	583,706 (285)
Total	2,171,754 (432)	1,017,422 (371)	230,842 (111)	201,823 (40)	226,527 (44)	58,854 (29)	421,336 (272)	4,328,558 (1,299)

TABLE II

British, Allied and Neutral Merchant Ship Losses according to theatres

1939

Month	North Atlantic	United Kingdom	South Atlantic	Mediterranean	Indian Ocean	Pacific	Total
September	104,829 (19)	84,965 (33)	5,051 (1)	—	—	—	194,845 (53)
October	110,619 (18)	63,368 (24)	22,368 (4)	—	—	—	196,355 (46)
November	17,895 (6)	155,668 (43)	—	—	706 (1)	—	174,269 (50)
December	15,852 (4)	152,107 (66)	21,964 (3)	—	—	—	189,923 (73)
Total	249,195 (47)	456,108 (166)	49,383 (8)	—	706 (1)	—	755,392 (222)

1940

Month	North Atlantic	United Kingdom	South Atlantic	Mediterranean	Indian Ocean	Pacific	Total
January	35,970 (9)	178,536 (64)	—	—	—	—	214,506 (73)
February	74,759 (17)	152,161 (46)	—	—	—	—	226,920 (63)
March	11,215 (2)	95,794 (43)	—	—	—	—	107,009 (45)
April	24,570 (4)	133,648 (54)	—	—	—	—	158,218 (58)
May	49,087 (9)	230,607 (90)	6,199 (1)	2,568 (1)	—	—	288,461 (101)
June	296,529 (53)	208,924 (77)	—	45,402 (6)	15,445 (2)	19,196 (2)	585,496 (140)
July	141,474 (28)	192,331 (67)	31,269 (6)	6,564 (2)	15,275 (5)	—	386,913 (105)
August	190,048 (39)	162,956 (45)	—	1,044 (1)	31,001 (5)	12,180 (2)	397,229 (92)
September	254,553 (52)	131,150 (39)	17,801 (1)	5,708 (2)	39,409 (6)	—	448,621 (100)
October	286,644 (56)	131,620 (43)	—	2,897 (1)	14,621 (2)	7,203 (1)	442,985 (103)
November	201,341 (38)	92,713 (48)	—	—	57,665 (7)	33,996 (4)	385,715 (97)
December	239,304 (42)	83,308 (34)	—	—	—	26,956 (6)	349,568 (82)
Total	1,805,494 (349)	1,793,748 (650)	55,269 (8)	64,183 (13)	173,416 (24)	99,531 (15)	3,991,641 (1,059)

1941

Month	North Atlantic	United Kingdom	South Atlantic	Mediterranean	Indian Ocean	Pacific	Total
January	214,382 (42)	36,975 (15)	58,585 (17)	—	10,298 (2)	—	320,240 (76)
February	317,378 (69)	51,381 (26)	—	8,343 (2)	26,291 (5)	—	403,393 (102)
March	364,689 (63)	152,862 (73)	—	11,868 (4)	—	287 (1)	529,706 (139)
April	260,451 (45)	99,031 (40)	21,807 (3)	292,518 (105)	14,094 (2)	—	687,901 (195)
May	324,550 (58)	100,655 (99)	11,339 (2)	70,835 (19)	3,663 (1)	—	511,042 (139)
June	318,740 (68)	86,381 (34)	10,134 (2)	9,145 (3)	7,625 (2)	—	432,025 (109)
July	97,813 (23)	15,265 (18)	—	7,897 (2)	—	—	120,975 (43)
August	83,661 (25)	19,791 (11)	—	5,869 (2)	—	21,378 (3)	130,699 (41)
September	184,546 (51)	54,779 (13)	15,526 (2)	15,951 (4)	10,347 (3)	4,793 (1)	285,942 (84)
October	154,593 (32)	35,996 (12)	5,297 (1)	22,403 (6)	—	—	218,269 (51)
November	50,215 (10)	30,332 (20)	4,953 (1)	19,140 (1)	—	—	104,640 (35)
December	50,682 (10)	56,845 (19)	6,275 (1)	37,394 (9)	837 (5)	431,673 (241)	583,706 (285)
Total	2,421,700 (496)	740,293 (350)	133,916 (29)	501,363 (158)	73,155 (20)	458,131 (246)	4,328,558 (1,299)

P P

APPENDIX III

Note for the Foreign Secretary, February 1941 [1]

12 February, 1941

1. During his visit to the Mediterranean theatre the Foreign Secretary will represent His Majesty's Government in all matters diplomatic and military. He will report whenever necessary to the War Cabinet through the Prime Minister.

2. His principal object will be the sending of speedy succour to Greece. For this purpose he will initiate any action he may think necessary with the Commander-in-Chief of the Middle East, with the Egyptian Government, and with the Governments of Greece, Yugoslavia, and Turkey. He will of course keep the Foreign Office informed, and he will himself be informed by the Foreign Office or the Prime Minister of all changes of plan or view occurring at home.

3. The C.I.G.S. will advise on the military aspect, and the Foreign Secretary will make sure that in case of any difference his views are also placed before His Majesty's Government.

4. The following points require particular attention:

(a) What is the minimum garrison that can hold the western frontier of Libya and Benghazi, and what measures should be taken to make Benghazi a principal naval and air base? The extreme importance is emphasised of dropping the overland communications at the earliest moment.

(b) The regime and policy to be enforced in Cyrenaica, having regard to our desire to separate the Italian nation from the Mussolini system.

(c) The execution of the operation 'Mandibles' [Rhodes] at the earliest moment, including, if necessary, repacking of the Commandos at Capetown [for an opposed landing], having regard however to its not becoming an impediment to the main issue.

(d) The formation in the Delta of the strongest and best-equipped force in divisional or brigade organisations which can be dispatched to Greece at the earliest moment.

(e) The drain to be made upon our resources for the purpose of finishing up in Eritrea and breaking down the Italian positions in Abyssinia. The former is urgent; the latter, though desirable, must not conflict with major issues. It may be necessary to leave it to rot by itself.

(f) The great mass of troops, over 70,000, now engaged in the Kenya theatre must be severely scrutinised in order particularly to liberate the South African divisions for service in Egypt. Any communication with General Smuts had better pass through the Prime

---

[1] Printed with a few verbal alterations in Churchill III 60-62.

Minister. A further conference between the Foreign Secretary and General Smuts might well be convenient.

(g) The Foreign Secretary, when visiting Athens with the C.I.G.S., General Wavell, and any other officers, is fully empowered to formulate with the Greek Government the best arrangements possible in the circumstances. He will at the same time try to keep H.M.G. informed, or seek their aid as far as possible. In an emergency he must act as he thinks best.

(h) He will communicate direct with the Governments of Yugoslavia and Turkey, duplicating his messages to the Foreign Office. The object will be to make them both fight at the same time or do the best they can. For this purpose he should summon the Minister at Belgrade or the Ambassador in Turkey to meet him as may be convenient. He will bear in mind that while it is our duty to fight, and, if need be, suffer with Greece, the interests of Turkey in the second stage are no less important to us than those of Greece. It should be possible to reconcile the Greek and Turkish claims for air and munitions support.

(i) The Foreign Secretary will address himself to the problem of securing the highest form of war economy in the armies and air forces of the Middle East for all the above purposes, and to making sure that the many valuable military units in that theatre all fit into a coherent scheme and are immediately pulling their weight.

(j) He should advise H.M.G. through the Prime Minister upon the selection of commanders for all the different purposes in view. In this he will no doubt consult with General Wavell, who enjoys so large a measure of the confidence of H.M.G. The selection of the general who commands in Greece is of the highest consequence, and it is hoped that an agreed recommendation may be made on this point.

(k) Air Chief Marshal Longmore will be required to give effect to the wishes and decisions of the Foreign Secretary in accordance with the general scope of the policy here set out. But here again in the event of any difference the Foreign Secretary will transmit the Air Chief Marshal's views to the War Cabinet through the Prime Minister. The duty of the Air Force in the Middle East is to provide the maximum air effort in Greece and Turkey agreeable with the nourishing of operations in the Soudan and Abyssinia and the maintenance of Benghazi.

(l) The Foreign Secretary will consult with Admiral Cunningham upon naval operations necessary for all the above purposes, and will ask H.M.G. for any further support, either by transports or warships, which may seem necessary.

(m) He will propose to H.M.G. any policy concerning Iraq, Palestine, or Arabia which will harmonise with the above purposes. He may communicate direct with these countries and with the Government of India, though not in a mandatory sense. The India Office must be kept informed.

(n) He will report upon the whole position at Gibraltar, Malta, and, if possible, on return, at Takoradi.

(o) In short, he is to gather together all the threads, and propose continuously the best solutions for our difficulties, and not be deterred from acting upon his own authority if the urgency is too great to allow reference home.

APPENDIX IV

Exchange of views between the Prime Minister and the Chiefs of Staff, April–May 1941

(a)

The Prime Minister's Directive of 28 April 1941

MOST SECRET

War Cabinet

Directive by the Prime Minister and Minister of Defence

Japan is unlikely to enter the war unless the Germans make a successful invasion of Great Britain, and even a major disaster like the loss of the Middle East would not necessarily make her come in, because the liberation of the British Mediterranean Fleet which might be expected and also any troops evacuated from the Middle East to Singapore would not weaken the British war-making strength in Malaya. It is very unlikely, moreover, that Japan will enter the war either if the United States have come in, or if Japan thinks that they would come in consequent upon a Japanese declaration of war. Finally, it may be taken as almost certain that the entry of Japan into the war would be followed by the immediate entry of the United States on our side.

These conditions are to be accepted by the Service Departments as a guide for all plans and actions. Should they cease to hold good, it will be the responsibility of Ministers to notify the Service Staffs in good time.

2. The loss of Egypt and the Middle East would be a disaster of the first magnitude to Great Britain, second only to successful invasion and final conquest. Every effort is to be made to reinforce General Wavell with military and Air forces, and if Admiral Cunningham requires more ships, the Admiralty will make proposals for supplying them. It is to be impressed upon all ranks, especially the highest, that the life and honour of Great Britain depends upon the successful defence of Egypt. It is not to be expected that the British forces of the land, sea and Air in the Mediterranean would wish to survive so vast and shameful a defeat as would be entailed by our expulsion from Egypt, having regard to the difficulties of the enemy and his comparatively small numbers. Not only must Egypt be defended, but the Germans have to be beaten and thrown out of Cyrenaica. This offensive objective must be set before the troops.

3. All plans for evacuation of Egypt or for closing or destroying the Suez Canal are to be called in and kept under the strict personal control of Headquarters. No whisper of such plans is to be allowed. No surrenders by officers and men will be considered tolerable unless at least 50 per cent casualties are sustained by the Unit or force in question. According to Napoleon's maxim, 'when a man is caught alone and unarmed, a surrender may be made'. But Generals and Staff Officers surprised by the

enemy are to use their pistols in self-defence. The honour of a wounded man is safe . . .[1]

4. The Army of the Nile is to fight with no thought of retreat or with-drawal. This task is enforced upon it by physical facts, for it will be utterly impossible to find the shipping for moving a tithe of the immense masses of men and stores which have been gathered in the Nile Valley.

5. In considering reinforcements for the Middle East, the question of the defence of Great Britain against invasion does not arise, as the avail-able shipping would be far less than the ships which would contain the number of troops who could be safely sent.

6. Should 'Tiger' succeed, the empty ships would be returned by the short cut, keeping their deck armaments for this purpose. It must be remembered that General Wavell has, with the troops returned from Greece, a trained personnel of 8 or 9 Tank Regiments, for which the Tanks now sent or in his possession are barely sufficient. Moreover, the personnel of the Tank Corps now going round the Cape will require other Tanks besides those already provided to await them on their arrival. Therefore we must contemplate a repetition of 'Tiger' at the earliest moment. The situation, however, must be judged when and if the M.T. ships return.

7. 'Double Winch'[2] having succeeded again, should be repeated with the utmost speed, all preparations being made to the aircraft in the meanwhile.

8. There is no need at the present time to make any further dispositions for the defence of Malaya and Singapore, beyond those modest arrange-ments which are in progress, until or unless conditions set out in para-graph 1 are modified.

(Inltd.) w. s. c.

April 28, 1941

(b)

Minute by the Chiefs of Staff, 7 May 1941

MOST SECRET

Prime Minister

We have considered your Directive of the 28th April, and we feel that we should be failing in our duty if we did not submit a frank expression of our opinion before it is regarded as final.

2. As we see it, the main purpose of the Directive is to ensure that there is no uncertainty in the minds of either the High Command in the Middle East or of the troops under their command as to the general conduct of the campaign. As to this, we entirely agree that 'the loss of Egypt and the Middle East would be a disaster of the first magnitude', and we would welcome an exhortation to the Army of the Nile that they are 'to fight with no thought of retreat or withdrawal'.

3. There are, however, certain points which in our opinion call for amplification or amendment.

---

[1] One sentence has been omitted.

[2] The air reinforcement of Malta.

4. We note that 'it will be the responsibility of Ministers to notify the Service Staffs in good time' of any change in the political hypothesis laid down in paragraph 1 of the Directive. We wish to emphasise that, when dealing with the Far East, 'good time' means at least three months, since that is the minimum period within which reinforcements and equipment could reach Malaya.

5. With reference to paragraph 2, we submit that it is an overstatement to say that 'the life . . . of Great Britain depends upon the successful defence of Egypt'. Surely our life continues so long as we are not successfully invaded, and do not lose the Battle of the Atlantic.

6. With reference to paragraph 3, we share your view that the very existence of any plan for evacuation should be known only to a most secret circle, and we can assure you that the outline plans which were prepared by General Wavell to meet the 'worst possible case', have been seen and discussed by only very few officers in London or the Middle East. At the same time, we think it necessary that these plans should be continually revised and kept up to date. However confident we may be of victory, it would be tempting providence to disregard the possibility of a reverse. In particular, should we be forced to abandon the Canal, it is essential that it should be blocked.

This cannot be done effectively unless the necessary preparations are made in advance, and in particular the provision and preparation of blockships, which it is estimated will take some weeks.

It is therefore essential to prepare the necessary blockships at once. This can be done under the pretext that they are required for blocking enemy ports.

7. If the Royal Navy and the Royal Air Force should be unable to interfere sufficiently with the enemy's sea communications, it is possible that the Germans may be able to build up a superior force in the Western Desert. They may develop a serious threat from the Islands and from Asia Minor as well. Should their preponderance of strength in the Middle East become overwhelming, we could not, it is true, ever hope to evacuate the great mass of stores and base installations in Egypt. They would all be required to sustain our forces in the fierce fighting which would take place.

8. But, if the worst came to the worst, we should certainly hope to withdraw in good order a large proportion of our personnel and their fighting equipment to areas further south and east. We have room to give ground and would still have behind us Ports on which to base an offensive later on, when the enemy's strength became diminished by his extension.

9. We feel that paragraph 5 of the Directive requires some qualification. It is true that at the moment shipping is a limiting factor, but the accession of American naval forces and shipping might enable us to despatch reinforcements to the Middle East to an extent which would jeopardise the safety of the United Kingdom.

10. For the Germans a successful invasion is the only quick way of ending the war. As American aid increases, up to the point of actual participation, our naval and mercantile fleets will be augmented and the weight of our bombing attack on Germany will increase. At the same time Germany's military and economic commitments grow with every conquest.

Hitler must realise that time is fighting against him, and he will be more and more tempted to make the desperate gamble of invasion in the hope of gaining a knock-out before American help destroys his last hope of success.

11. The enemy on interior lines can change front over the land from East to West far more quickly than we can by sea. It is therefore essential that sufficient forces be kept in the United Kingdom to provide adequate defence against invasion.

(signed): DUDLEY POUND
J. G. DILL
C. PORTAL

7th May, 1941

(c)

*Reply by the C.I.G.S. to the Prime Minister's minute of May 13
(of which the greater part is printed in Churchill III 376–7)*

War Office,
Whitehall, London, S.W.1

SECRET AND PERSONAL

Prime Minister

I am very much obliged to you for your Minute of 13th May. There are some points in it on which I feel I should make my position quite clear to you.

Your paragraph 1. I can say from my own personal knowledge that a number of British soldiers did regard Gamelin's plan for the advance into Belgium with considerable misgivings. Some of their criticisms reached Gamelin himself, and I understand that he remarked that it was his plan, that it was a very good plan, and that he meant to carry it out.

I am sure that you, better than anyone else, must realise how difficult it is for a soldier to advise against a bold offensive plan. One lays oneself open to charges of defeatism, of inertia, or even of 'cold feet'. Human nature being what it is, there is a natural tendency to acquiesce in an offensive plan of doubtful merit rather than to face such charges. It takes a lot of moral courage not to be afraid of being thought afraid. Be this as it may, the responsible military advisers, both in this country and in France, under-rated the Germans. I agree that expert military opinion often errs amid the many uncertainties of war. But it is less likely to err as time goes on if it takes account of past mistakes. My only concern in this particular problem is that we should not repeat our previous mistake of under-rating the enemy.

Your paragraph 2. The idea which I intended to convey in my paragraph 9 is the same as you yourself expressed in a memorandum on the naval defence of Australia, which you prepared on November 17th, 1939. In paragraph 4 of this paper you say:

> 'But we wish to make it plain that we regard the defence of Australia, and of Singapore as a stepping-stone to Australia, as ranking next to the mastering of the principal fleet to which we are opposed, and that if the choice were presented of defending

Australia against a serious attack, or sacrificing British interests in the Mediterranean, our duty to Australia would take precedence.'

I quite agree with you that the alternative of losing Egypt or losing Singapore is not likely to present itself. I have great hopes that the tide of the German advance may already have reached its high-water mark in the Middle East and that we shall stem it there. But it is possible that it may not prove to be so. In this unlikely event of our having to withdraw from Egypt, I do not think we should be faced with the surrender or ruin of an army of half a million. A great proportion of the half million in the Middle East are not in the Nile Valley. I hope that we should be able to withdraw in good order a large proportion of the fighting personnel and equipment to hold the Germans on the next line of resistance, and to advance again when the enemy in his turn was forced to fall back, as he certainly would be in the end.

I agree with you that the defence of Singapore requires only a fraction of the troops required for the defence of Egypt. That is the very reason why I am so anxious not to starve Malaya at the expense of Egypt. Quite a small addition at Singapore will make all the difference between running a serious risk and achieving full security. The same resources put into Egypt would add comparatively little to the strength of its defences. But since three months must be allowed for shipments to reach Malaya, it is necessary to look well ahead. If we wait till emergency arises in the Far East, we shall be too late.

A somewhat similar situation arose over the Middle East earlier in the war. You may recall that the Chiefs of Staff recommended in December 1939 that administrative preparations should be put in hand for the building up of a strategic reserve in the Middle East. At the time all eyes were on France and Italy was not in the war. War in the Middle East was still below the horizon. Yet if we had concentrated all our efforts on France to the exclusion of preparations in the Middle East, we should have been in a very difficult situation when Italy declared war in the summer.

Your paragraph 3. The formidable difficulties to which I referred in the Balkans were those of terrain and administration, rather than of armed opposition. The way in which the Germans pushed their mechanised forces through mountainous country, often on tracks which were thought to be passable only to mules and foot soldiers, was a remarkable achievement.

Your paragraph 4. I certainly intended to imply that if we reach a point when the maintenance of our position in Egypt would endanger either the United Kingdom or Singapore, we should hold fast to the two latter, even if this meant the loss of Egypt. That is my considered opinion, and it is, I think, in line with your own ideas as expressed in your memorandum of November 17th, 1939. Nevertheless, I feel most strongly that any plans for a possible withdrawal must be kept as deadly secrets. To think and plan too much for a withdrawal is to be half way towards carrying it out.

. . . .

(signed)   J. G. DILL
C.I.G.S.

15th May, 1941

APPENDIX V

A List of the Holders of Certain Appointments

The names of members of the War Cabinets are underlined; broken lines denote Ministers who became members of the War Cabinet after the date on which they assumed the office shown.

(I) MINISTERS

	In Mr. Chamberlain's Administration	In Mr. Churchill's Administration
Prime Minister	Mr. Chamberlain	Mr. Churchill
Minister of Defence		Mr. Churchill
Lord President of the Council	Earl Stanhope	Mr. Chamberlain (till 3.10.40) Sir John Anderson (from 3.10.40)
Lord Privy Seal	Sir Samuel Hoare (till 3.4.40) Sir Kingsley Wood (from 3.4.40)	Mr. Attlee
Chancellor of the Exchequer	Sir John Simon	Sir Kingsley Wood (Cabinet from 3.10.40)
Secretary of State for Foreign Affairs	Viscount Halifax	Viscount Halifax (till 22.12.40) Mr. Eden (from 22.12.40)
First Lord of Admiralty	Mr. Churchill	Mr. A. V. Alexander
Secretary of State for War	Mr. Hore-Belisha (till 5.1.40) Colonel O. Stanley (from 5.1.40)	Mr. Eden (till 22.12.40) Captain Margesson (from 22.12.40)

Secretary of State for Air	Sir Kingsley Wood (till 3.4.40) Sir Samuel Hoare (from 3.4.40)	Sir A. Sinclair

Minister without Portfolio	Lord Hankey	Mr. Greenwood
Minister for Co-ordination of Defence	Lord Chatfield (till 3.4.40)	
Secretary of State for Home Affairs and Minister for Home Security	Sir John Anderson	Sir John Anderson (till 3.10.40) Mr. H. Morrison (from 3.10.40)
Secretary of State for Dominions	Mr. Eden	Viscount Caldecote (till 3.10.40) Viscount Cranborne (from 3.10.40)
Secretary of State for Colonies	Mr. M. Macdonald	Lord Lloyd (till 8.2.41) Lord Moyne (from 8.2.41)
Secretary of State for India and Burma	Marquess of Zetland	Mr. Amery
Chancellor of Duchy of Lancaster	Mr. W. S. Morrison (till 3.4.40) Major G. C. Tryon (from 3.4.40)	Lord Hankey
President of the Board of Trade	Colonel O. Stanley (till 5.1.40) Sir Andrew Duncan (from 5.1.40)	Sir A. Duncan (till 3.10.40) Mr. O. Lyttelton (from 3.10.40)
Minister of Labour and National Service	Mr. E. Brown	Mr. E. Bevin (Cabinet from 3.10.40)
Minister of Aircraft Production		Lord Beaverbrook (till 1.5.41) (Cabinet from 2.8.40) Colonel Moore-Brabazon (from 1.5.41)
Minister of Economic Warfare	Mr. R. S. Hudson (till 3.4.40) Mr. W. S. Morrison (from 3.4.40)	Mr. Dalton
Minister of Food	Mr. W. S. Morrison (till 3.4.40) Lord Woolton (from 3.4.40)	Lord Woolton

	In Mr. Chamberlain's Administration	*In Mr. Churchill's Administration*
Minister of Supply	Mr. Burgin	Mr. H. Morrison (till 3.10.40) Sir A. Duncan (from 3.10.40)
Minister of Information	Lord Macmillan (till 5.1.40) Sir John Reith (from 5.1.40)	Mr. A. Duff Cooper
Minister of Transport	Captain E. Wallace	Sir John Reith (till 3.10.40) Colonel Moore-Brabazon (from 3.10.40 till 1.5.41)
Minister of Shipping (est. 13.10.39)	Sir John Gilmour (till 3.4.40) Mr. Hudson (from 3.4.40)	Mr. Cross (till 1.5.41)
Minister of War Transport (est. 1.5.41)		Lord Leathers
Minister of State		Lord Beaverbrook (from 1.5.41)

(2) THE CHIEFS OF STAFF

	In Mr. Chamberlain's Administration	*In Mr. Churchill's Administration*
Chief of Naval Staff	Admiral of the Fleet Sir Dudley Pound	
Chief of the Imperial General Staff	General Sir Edmund Ironside General Sir John Dill	till 27 May 1940 from 27 May 1940
Chief of Air Staff	Air Chief Marshal Sir Cyril Newall Air Chief Marshal Sir Charles Portal	till 25 October 1940 from 25 October 1940

Major-General H. L. Ismay became a member of the Chiefs of Staff Committee on 2 May 1940

(3) THE VICE-CHIEFS OF STAFF (APRIL 1940)

	In Mr. Chamberlain's Administration	*In Mr. Churchill's Administration*
Vice-Chief of Naval Staff	Vice-Admiral T. S. V. Phillips	
Vice-Chief of the Imperial General Staff	General Sir John Dill Lieut.-General Sir R. H. Haining Lieut.-General Sir Henry Pownall	till May 1940 from May 1940 till May 1941 from May 1941
Vice-Chief of Air Staff	Air Marshal R. E. C. Peirse Air Chief Marshal Sir Wilfred Freeman	till November 1940 from November 1940

(4) THE JOINT PLANNING STAFF

Director of Plans, Admiralty	Captain V. H. Danckwerts	till March 1940
	Captain C. S. Daniel	from March 1940
Director of Plans, War Office	Brigadier J. N. Kennedy	till December 1939
	Brigadier I. S. O. Playfair	December 1939 to May 1941
	Brigadier V. Dykes	from May 1941
Director of Plans, Air Ministry	Air Commodore J. C. Slessor	till October 1940
	Air Commodore C. E. H. Medhurst	October 1940 to April 1941
	Air Commodore W. F. Dickson	from April 1941

(5) THE JOINT INTELLIGENCE STAFF

Foreign Office Representative	Mr. R. C. Skrine Stevenson	till December 1939
	Mr. V. F. W. Cavendish-Bentinck	from December 1939
Director of Naval Intelligence	Rear-Admiral J. H. Godfrey	
Director of Military Intelligence	Major-General F. G. Beaumont-Nesbitt	till December 1940
	Major-General F. H. M. Davidson	from December 1940
Director of Intelligence Air Ministry	Air Commodore A. R. Boyle	till April 1941
Assistant Chief of Air Staff (Intelligence)	Air Vice-Marshal C. E. H. Medhurst	from April 1941

APPENDIX VI

Code-names

Avonmouth	Narvik expedition, as first planned
Battle-axe	Operation in Western Desert, June 1941
Brevity	Operation in Western Desert, May 1941
Brisk	Proposed occupation of Azores
Catapult	Naval operation against French Fleet, July 1940
Catherine	Proposed operation by surface ships in Baltic, winter 1939–40
Claymore	Raid on Lofoten Islands, March 1941
Compass	Operation in Western Desert, December 1940
Cromwell	Alarm word for imminent invasion of Great Britain
Demon	Evacuation from Greece, April 1941
Dynamo	Evacuation from Dunkirk, May–June 1940
Exporter	Operation in Syria, June 1941
Habforce	Expedition to Iraq, May 1941
Hammer	Proposed direct attack on Trondheim, April 1940
Hats	Reinforcement of Malta and Egypt, August–September 1940
Hurry	Reinforcement of Malta, July 1940
Jaguar	Air reinforcement of Malta, 1941
Lustre	Expedition to Greece, March 1941
Mandibles	Proposed occupation of Dodecanese
Marie	Proposed Free French operation to recover Jibuti
Maurice	Operation against Trondheim based on Namsos
Menace	Dakar expedition
Puma	Proposed occupation of Canary Islands, 1941
R 4	Army project for landing in Norway, 1940
Rupert	Narvik expedition as finally conceived
Scipio	Dakar expedition, first plan
Sickle	Operation against Trondheim based on Aandelsnes
Stratford	Proposed southern landings in Norway
Tiger	Reinforcement of Egypt, April 1941
Wilfred	Naval plan for mining Norwegian Leads, 1940
Winch	Reinforcement of Malta, Winter 1940–1941
Workshop	Proposed capture of Pantelleria, Winter 1940–1941

Alpenveilchen (Cyclamen)	Proposed operation in Albania, January 1941
Attila	Proposed invasion of 'Unoccupied' France, Winter 1940–1941

Barbarossa	Invasion of Russia
Felix	Proposed capture of Gibraltar
Gelb	See 'Yellow'
Isabella	Proposed operation to expel British from Spain, 1941
Marita	Occupation of Greece
Merkur	Occupation of Crete
Mittelmeer	Air operations in Mediterranean, December 1940– January 1941
Sea Lion (Seeloewe)	Proposed invasion of Great Britain
Sonnenblume (Sunflower)	Reinforcement of North Africa with German troops, February 1941
Unternehmen (operation) 25	Invasion of Yugoslavia, April 1941
Weiss	See 'White'
Weserübung, (Weser Exercise)	Occupation of Denmark and Norway
White	Invasion of Poland
Yellow	Invasion of Low Countries and France

Index

INDEX

Ps. 508375. Wt. 2764. 1/57. B.&T. Ltd. Gp. 1272/1   S.O. Code No. 63-111-22-5*

EUROPE AND THE MEDITERRANEAN

3rd September 1940

MILES 100 0 100 200 300 400 MILES

Legend

	Area under Allied control.
	Area under Enemy control.
	Area brought under Enemy control between 3rd September 1940 and 1st June 1941.
	Area under control of Vichy.
	U.S.S.R.

Arctic

Iceland

Norway

Sweden

North Sea

Denmark

Eire

United Kingdom

Holland

Belgium

Germany

Czechoslov

Atlantic Ocean

France

Switzerland

Austria

H

Jugos

Portugal

Spain

Corsica

Italy

Gibraltar

Sardinia

Sp

Mediterran

Sicily

French Morocco

Malta

Tunisia

Rio de Oro (Sp)

Algeria

Libya